Contexts for
COMPOSITION

Edited by

STANLEY A. CLAYES

and

DAVID G. SPENCER

Both of Loyola University

Contexts for
COMPOSITION

Second Edition

Appleton-Century-Crofts

Educational Division

Meredith Corporation *New York*

to Jeff

Preface

In revising *Contexts for Composition* our main concern has been to take out those essays that colleagues in various parts of the country found, after classroom use, to be less than successful and to add pieces, some as old as those by Swift and Thoreau, others as recent as those from the last two years (Gibson, Clark, Keniston, Harding, Simon, Jencks, and Hutchins) that are of more current interest to students. These recent selections, though they have the value of freshness and novelty, are not typical of the anthology's content over all. The majority of pieces included here are not strangers to freshman readers; indeed, they appear once again because their usefulness has long been proven. Students who have difficulty in seeing how the methods of long essays by master stylists can be adapted to freshman themes, should grasp the lessons of organization and style more readily in shorter, less formal pieces. For them we have added other selections new to freshman readers: those by Eric Berne, John Updike, Eleanor Clark, and all the articles in the section on education.

Like the first, this edition, while containing nothing that precludes the use of a separate rhetoric text, is designed as an anthology that does not require one. Not only do the selections themselves exemplify aspects of rhetoric, but many of them also examine principles of rhetoric deliberately and in detail: for example, the essays by Hayakawa, Altick, Davis, Orwell, Barzun, Booth, and Ciardi. Introductions precede chapters that require essential distinctions any reader and writer should master at the very outset. The organization of this edition is the same as the first. Part One is still selected and arranged according to the most common methods of exposition, but three selections have been added to illustrate the use of personal experience to make an expository point. Part Two offers a variety of pieces of writing to teach various aspects of style. Essays on style are followed by a small section of poems and two stories for teaching precise diction. The principles that may be taught with these essays, poems, and stories are then shown at work in modern English prose writing of a high order, which ranges from the personal voices of Baldwin and Kazin to the public voices of C.S. Lewis and John F. Kennedy, from the plain styles of Orwell, Lewis, and Leighton to the ornate styles of Baldwin and Kennedy. Part Three presents essays largely persuasive and argumentative under four topical headings that still seem to us the most successful in freshman classrooms and freshman writing. But essays under three of the headings have been substituted by new ones to bring these topics closer to current interests of students. In making the new selections, we have been at some pains to echo thematic relations of the various parts of the book.

Questions follow many selections; initially each set focuses on language and rhetorical principles and toward the end shifts to the selection's subject matter and the student's own experience and outlook. One or more topics, which suggest themes for writing from the selection's discourse and are within the student's grasp, conclude most reading assignments. At times we have refrained from punctuating a selection with questions and theme topics on the ground that individual instructors—and indeed students themselves—may occasionally wish to provide, without interference, their own editorial direction.

To many friends and associates in various parts of the country we again owe debts of gratitude for repeated discussions on the teachability of the works chosen (and discarded) for this book. To Fran Spencer and Renée Wolfe Johnson for their generous help with the manuscript, and to Jeff Spencer for sharing her intelligence and taste, we are both especially indebted.

S.A.C.
D.G.S.

Contents

PART ONE

Methods of Exposition

Defining

Techniques for definition

Definition is a method of analysis, as logical as possible, in which the subject is located in a general class and then distinguished from all other members of that class. If a definition is effective, the reader will understand the word *in much the same way* that the author intended.

Such an understanding is made difficult by the connotative meanings most words convey (for a definition of connotation see the second essay of this section), and it is these meanings that must be reduced and controlled in the language of reports. In the case of abstract terms, connotative meanings are especially difficult to control as well as difficult to define. Our understanding of a word is obviously limited by our experience and our opinions, and no two sets of experiences and opinions are identical. A word like "liberal" or "conservative" has widely varied meanings for different people. Hence one must try to define the sense in which he uses such terms; one must say how they are to be understood or run the risk of alienating a large portion of his audience, those who respond only emotionally to words as signs of everything they approve or disapprove.

A number of techniques or methods of definition are useful to the writer and at times indispensable. In reading the essays of this section, try to observe as many instances of their use as possible.

1. *Assigning the Term to a Genus or Class.* To say "a dog is an animal," "my Fritz is a schnauzer" is to assign a species to a genus, an individual to a class; the same is true with statements such as "a table is a piece of furniture," "that is a Louis Quinze taboret." But if we go on to say "love is an emotion," the genus is not so precise since a psychological dimension in which we all exist has not yet been neatly charted. Again, communism may be defined by classifying it, along with socialism and fascism, as a type of statist society. But now the burden becomes one of describing clearly and definitely the essential characteristics of statist society and its varied and recognizable forms.

2. *Comparing and Contrasting.* Or the term communism may be defined by pointing out its similarities to and differences from the term socialism. Or again a term may be compared and contrasted as laconically as Samuel Johnson is reported to have defined the word "surprise" in the apocryphal story. His wife, entering the room unexpectedly, found him with the maid on his lap and said: "Dr. Johnson, I am surprised!" "No, madam," he replied, "I am surprised. You are astonished."

3. *Using Analogy.* The term may be defined by referring it to more easily understood concepts. An eloquent example is the definition of drama Hamlet sketches for the troupe of itinerant actors: "the purpose of playing, whose end, both at the first and now, was and is, to hold as 'twere the mirror up to nature, to show virtue her own feature, scorn her own image, and the very age and body of the time his form and pressure." An analogy, originally fresh, may become so imbedded in the language that it sinks to the class of clichés, for example, "the ship of state," "a house divided against itself must fall."

4. *Using Familiar Examples.* "Prejudice" may be defined extensively by listing examples familiar to all of us, terms that most of us accept as connoting a prejudiced point of view: "wop," "frog," "kraut," "spic."

5. *Using Historical Meanings.* It provides some insight into the present meaning of the term to know that among the earlier meanings of "technique," for example, are those of "art" and "trick."

6. *Defining Negatively.* "Courtesy" and "manners" are often considered as equivalents, yet one can define courtesy negatively by pointing out that someone may show good manners but lack entirely a sense of common courtesy.

7. *Enumerating Essential Characteristics.* Rather than define "democracy" by pointing to governments or to acts that are or are not democratic, one may list some of the attributes or essential characteristics of democracy; for example, "everyone is to count for one and no one for more than one," "freedom and justice for all," "governments derive their just powers from the consent of the governed."

8. *Isolating One Essential Characteristic.* Notice how St. Paul isolates an essential quality of the Christian. "Brethren: if I should speak with the tongues of men and of angels, but do not have charity, I have become as sounding brass or a tinkling cymbal, and if I have prophecy and know all mysteries and all knowledge, and if I have all faith so as to remove mountains, yet do not have charity, I am nothing—and if I distribute all my goods to feed the poor, and if I deliver my body to be burned, yet do not have charity, it profits me nothing."

1 S. I. HAYAKAWA

Reports, Inferences, Judgments

To put it briefly, in human speech, different sounds have different meanings. To study this co-ordination of certain sounds with certain meanings is to study language. This co-ordination makes it possible for man to interact with great precision. When we tell someone, for instance, the address of a house he has never seen, we are doing something which no animal can do.

—LEONARD BLOOMFIELD

Vague and insignificant forms of speech, and abuse of language, have so long passed for mysteries of science; and hard or misapplied words with little or no meaning have, by prescription, such a right to be mistaken for deep learning and height of speculation, that it will not be easy to persuade either those who speak or those who hear them, that they are but the covers of ignorance and hindrance of true knowledge.

—JOHN LOCKE

1   For the purposes of the interchange of information, the basic symbolic act is the *report* of what we have seen, heard, or felt: "There is a ditch on each side of the road." "You can get those at Smith's hardware store for $2.75." "There aren't any fish on that side of the lake, but there are on this side." Then there are reports of reports: "The longest waterfall in the world is Victoria Falls in Rhodesia." "The Battle of Hastings took place in 1066." "The papers say that there was a smash-up on Highway 41 near Evansville." Reports adhere to the following rules: first, they are *capable of verification;* second, they *exclude,* as far as possible, *inferences* and *judgments.* (These terms will be defined later.)

2   Reports are verifiable. We may not always be able to verify them ourselves, since we cannot track down the evidence for every piece of history we know, nor can we all go to Evansville to see the remains of the smash-up before they are cleared away. But if we are roughly agreed on the names of things, on what constitutes a "foot," "yard," "bushel," and so on, and on how to measure time, there is relatively little danger of our misunderstanding each other. Even in a world such as we have today, in which everybody seems to be quarreling with everybody else, *we still to a surprising degree trust each other's reports.* We ask directions of total strangers when we are traveling. We follow directions on road signs without being suspicious of the people who put them up. We read books of

information about science, mathematics, automotive engineering, travel, geography, the history of costume, and other such factual matters, and we usually assume that the author is doing his best to tell us as truly as he can what he knows. And we are safe in so assuming most of the time. With the interest given today to the discussion of biased newspapers, propagandists, and the general untrustworthiness of many of the communications we receive, we are likely to forget that we still have an enormous amount of reliable information available and that deliberate misinformation, except in warfare, is still more the exception than the rule. The desire for self-preservation that compelled men to evolve means for the exchange of information also compels them to regard the giving of false information as profoundly reprehensible.

3   At its highest development, the language of reports is the language of science. By "highest development" we mean greatest general usefulness. Presbyterian and Catholic, workingman and capitalist, East German and West German, *agree* on the meanings of such symbols as *2 × 2 = 4, 100° C., HNO₃, 3:35* A.M., *1940* A.D., *1000 kilowatts, Quercus agrifolia,* and so on. But how, it may be asked, can there be agreement about even this much among people who disagree about political philosophies, ethical ideas, religious beliefs, and the survival of my business *versus* the survival of yours? The answer is that circumstances *compel men to agree,* whether they wish to or not. If, for example, there were a dozen different religious sects in the United States, each insisting on its own way of naming the time of the day and the days of the year, the mere necessity of having a dozen different calendars, a dozen different kinds of watches, and a dozen sets of schedules for business hours, trains, and television programs, to say nothing of the effort that would be required for translating terms from one nomenclature to another, would make life as we know it impossible.[1]

4   The language of reports, then, including the more accurate reports of science, is "map" language, and because it gives us reasonably accurate representations of the "territory," it enables us to get work done. Such language may often be dull or uninteresting reading: one does not usually read logarithmic tables or telephone directories for entertainment. But we

---

[1] According to information supplied by the Association of American Railroads, "Before 1883 there were nearly 100 different time zones in the United States. It wasn't until November 18 of that year that . . . a system of standard time was adopted here and in Canada. Before then there was nothing but local or 'solar' time. . . . The Pennsylvania Railroad in the East used Philadelphia time, which was five minutes slower than New York time and five minutes faster than Baltimore time. The Baltimore & Ohio used Baltimore time for trains running out of Baltimore, Columbus time for Ohio, Vincennes (Indiana) time for those going out of Cincinnati. . . . When it was noon in Chicago, it was 12:31 in Pittsburgh; 12:24 in Cleveland; 12:17 in Toledo; 12:13 in Cincinnati; 12:09 in Louisville; 12:07 in Indianapolis; 11:50 in St. Louis; 11:48 in Dubuque; 11:39 in St. Paul, and 11:27 in Omaha. There were 27 local time zones in Michigan alone. . . . A person traveling from Eastport, Maine, to San Francisco, if he wanted always to have the right railroad time and get off at the right place, had to twist the hands of his watch 20 times en route." Chicago *Daily News* (September 29, 1948).

could not get along without it. There are numberless occasions in the talking and writing we do in everyday life that *require that we state things in such a way that everybody will be able to understand and agree with our formulation.*

Inferences

5   The reader will find that practice in writing reports is a quick means of increasing his linguistic awareness. It is an exercise which will constantly provide him with his own examples of the principles of language and interpretation under discussion. The reports should be about first-hand experience—scenes the reader has witnessed himself, meetings and social events he has taken part in, people he knows well. They should be of such a nature that they can be verified and agreed upon. For the purpose of this exercise, inferences will be excluded.

6   Not that inferences are not important—we rely in everyday life and in science as much on *inferences* as on reports—in some areas of thought, for example, geology, paleontology, and nuclear physics, reports are the foundations, but inferences (and inferences upon inferences) are the main body of the science. An inference, as we shall use the term, is *a statement about the unknown made on the basis of the known.* We may *infer* from the material and cut of a woman's clothes her wealth or social position; we may *infer* from the character of the ruins the origin of the fire that destroyed the building; we may *infer* from a man's calloused hands the nature of his occupation; we may infer from a senator's vote on an armaments bill his attitude toward Russia; we may *infer* from the structure of the land the path of a prehistoric glacier; we may *infer* from a halo on an unexposed photographic plate that it has been in the vicinity of radioactive materials; we may *infer* from the sound of an engine the condition of its connecting rods. Inferences may be carelessly or carefully made. They may be made on the basis of a broad background of previous experience with the subject matter, or no experience at all. For example, the inferences a good mechanic can make about the internal condition of a motor by listening to it are often startlingly accurate, while the inferences made by an amateur (if he tries to make any) may be entirely wrong. But the common characteristic of inferences is that they are statements about matters which are not directly known, statements made on the basis of what has been observed.

7   The avoidance of inferences in our suggested practice in report-writing requires that we make no guesses as to what is going on in other people's minds. When we say, "He was angry," we are not reporting; we are making an inference from such observable facts as the following: "He pounded his fist on the table; he swore; he threw the telephone directory at his stenographer." In this particular example, the inference appears to

be fairly safe; nevertheless, it is important to remember, especially for the purposes of training oneself, that it is an inference. Such expressions as "He thought a lot of himself," "He was scared of girls," "He has an inferiority complex," made on the basis of casual social observation, and "What Russia really wants to do is to establish a world communist dictatorship," made on the basis of casual newspaper reading, are highly inferential. We should keep in mind their inferential character and, in our suggested exercises, should substitute for them such statements as "He rarely spoke to subordinates in the plant," "I saw him at a party, and he never danced except when one of the girls asked him to," "He wouldn't apply for the scholarship although I believe he could have won it easily," and "The Russian delegation to the United Nations has asked for *A, B,* and *C.* Last year they voted against *M* and *N,* and voted for *X* and *Y.* On the basis of facts such as these, the newspaper I read makes the inference that what Russia really wants is to establish a world communist dictatorship. I agree."

8   In spite of the exercise of every caution in avoiding inferences and reporting only what is seen and experienced, we all remain prone to error, since the making of inferences is a quick, almost automatic process. We may watch a car weaving as it goes down the road and say, "Look at that *drunken driver,*" although what we *see* is only *the irregular motion of the car.* The writer once saw a man leave a one-dollar tip at a lunch counter and hurry out. Just as the writer was wondering why anyone should leave so generous a tip in so modest an establishment, the waitress came, picked up the dollar, put it in the cash register as she punched up ninety cents, and put a dime in her pocket. In other words, the writer's description to himself of the event, "a one-dollar tip," turned out to be not a report but an inference.

9   All this is not to say that we should never make inferences. The inability to make inferences is itself a sign of mental disorder. For example, the speech therapist Laura L. Lee writes, "The aphasic [brain-damaged] adult with whom I worked had great difficulty in making inferences about a picture I showed her. She could tell me what was happening at the moment in the picture, but could not tell me what might have happened just before the picture or just afterward." [2] Hence the question is not whether or not we make inferences; the question is whether or not we are aware of the inferences we make.

Judgments

10   In our suggested writing exercise, judgments are also to be excluded. By judgments, we shall mean *all expressions of the writer's ap-*

[2] "Brain Damage and the Process of Abstracting: A Problem in Language Learning," *ETC.: A Review of General Semantics,* XVI (1959), 154–62.

proval or disapproval of the occurrences, persons, or objects he is describing. For example, a report cannot say, "It was a wonderful car," but must say something like this: "It has been driven 50,000 miles and has never required any repairs." Again statements such as "Jack lied to us" must be suppressed in favor of the more verifiable statement, "Jack told us he didn't have the keys to his car with him. However, when he pulled a handkerchief out of his pocket a few minutes later, a bunch of car keys fell out." Also a report may not say, "The senator was stubborn, defiant, and uncooperative," or "The senator courageously stood by his principles"; it must say instead, "The senator's vote was the only one against the bill."

11   Many people regard statements such as the following as statements of "fact": "Jack *lied* to us," "Jerry is a *thief*," "Tommy is *clever*." As ordinarily employed, however, the word "lied" involves first an inference (that Jack knew otherwise and deliberately misstated the facts) and second a judgment (that the speaker disapproves of what he has inferred that Jack did). In the other two instances, we may substitute such expressions as, "Jerry was convicted of theft and served two years at Waupun," and "Tommy plays the violin, leads his class in school, and is captain of the debating team." After all, to say of a man that he is a "thief" is to say in effect, "He has stolen *and will steal again*"—which is more of a prediction than a report. Even to say, "He has stolen," is to make an inference (and simultaneously to pass a judgment) on an act about which there may be difference of opinion among those who have examined the evidence upon which the conviction was obtained. But to say that he was "convicted of theft" is to make a statement capable of being agreed upon through verification in court and prison records.

12   Scientific verifiability rests upon the external observation of facts, not upon the heaping up of judgments. If one person says, "Peter is a deadbeat," and another says, "I think so too," the statement has not been verified. In court cases, considerable trouble is sometimes caused by witnesses who cannot distinguish their judgments from the facts upon which those judgments are based. Cross-examinations under these circumstances go something like this:

WITNESS: That dirty double-crosser Jacobs ratted on me.
DEFENSE ATTORNEY: Your honor, I object.
JUDGE: Objection sustained. (Witness's remark is stricken from the record.) Now, try to tell the court exactly what happened.
WITNESS: He double-crossed me, the dirty, lying rat!
DEFENSE ATTORNEY: Your honor, I object!
JUDGE: Objection sustained. (Witness's remark is again stricken from the record.) Will the witness try to stick to the facts.
WITNESS: But I'm telling you the facts, your honor. He did double-cross me.

This can continue indefinitely unless the cross-examiner exercises some ingenuity in order to get at the facts behind the judgment. To the witness it is a "fact" that he was "double-crossed." Often patient questioning is required before the factual bases of the judgment are revealed.

13   Many words, of course, simultaneously convey a report and a judgment on the fact reported, as will be discussed more fully in a later chapter. For the purposes of a report as here defined, these should be avoided. Instead of "sneaked in," one might say "entered quietly"; instead of "politicians," "congressmen" or "aldermen" or "candidates for office"; instead of "bureaucrat," "public official"; instead of "tramp," "homeless unemployed"; instead of "dictatorial set-up," "centralized authority"; instead of "crackpots," "holders of nonconformist views." A newspaper reporter, for example, is not permitted to write, "A crowd of suckers came to listen to Senator Smith last evening in that rickety firetrap and ex-dive that disfigures the south edge of town." Instead he says, "Between seventy-five and a hundred people heard an address last evening by Senator Smith at the Evergreen Gardens near the South Side city limits."

Snarl-words and purr-words

14   Throughout this book, it is important to remember that we are not considering language as an isolated phenomenon. Our concern, instead, is with language in action—language in the full context of the nonlinguistic events which are its setting. The making of noises with the vocal organs is a muscular activity and, like other muscular activities, often involuntary. Our responses to powerful stimuli, such as to things that make us very angry, are a complex of muscular and physiological events: the contracting of fighting muscles, the increase of blood pressure, a change in body chemistry, clutching of our hair, *and* the making of noises, such as growls and snarls. We are a little too dignified, perhaps, to growl like dogs, but we do the next best thing and substitute series of words, such as "You dirty double-crosser!" "The filthy scum!" Similarly, if we are pleasurably agitated, we may, instead of purring or wagging the tail, say things like "She's the sweetest girl in all the world!"

15   Speeches such as these are, as direct expressions of approval or disapproval, judgments in their simplest form. They may be said to be human equivalents of snarling and purring. "She's the sweetest girl in all the world" is not a statement about the girl; it is a purr. This seems to be a fairly obvious fact; nevertheless, it is surprising how often, when such a statement is made, both the speaker and the hearer feel that something has been said about the girl. This error is especially common in the interpretation of utterances of orators and editorialists in some of their more excited denunciations of "Reds," "greedy monopolists," "Wall Street," "radicals," "foreign ideologies," and in their more fulsome dithyrambs

about "our way of life." Constantly, because of the impressive sound of the words, the elaborate structure of the sentences, and the appearance of intellectual progression, we get the feeling that something is being said about something. On closer examination, however, we discover that these utterances merely say, "What I hate ('Reds,' 'Wall Street,' or whatever) I hate very, very much," and "What I like ('our way of life') I like very, very much." We may call such utterances "snarl-words" and "purr-words." They are not reports describing conditions in the extensional world in any way.

16   To call these judgments "snarl-words" and "purr-words" does not mean that we should simply shrug them off. It means that we should be careful to *allocate the meaning correctly*—placing such a statement as "She's the sweetest girl in the world" as a revelation of the speaker's state of mind, and not as a revelation of facts about the girl. If the "snarl-words" about "Reds" or "greedy monopolists" are accompanied by verifiable reports (which would also mean that we have previously agreed as to who, specifically, is meant by the terms "Reds" or "greedy monopolists"), we might find reason to be just as disturbed as the speaker. If the "purr-words" about the sweetest girl in the world are accompanied by verifiable reports about her appearance, manners, character, and so on, we might find reason to admire her too. But "snarl-words" and "purr-words" as such, unaccompanied by reports, offer nothing further to discuss, except possibly the question, "Why do you feel as you do?"

17   It is usually fruitless to debate such questions as "Is President Kennedy a great statesman or merely a skillful politician?" "Is the music of Wagner the greatest music of all time, or is it merely hysterical screeching?" "Which is the finer sport, tennis or baseball?" "Could Joe Louis in his prime have licked Bob Fitzsimmons in his prime?" To take sides on such issues of conflicting judgments is to reduce oneself to the same level of stubborn imbecility as one's opponents. But to ask questions of the form, "Why do you like (or dislike) Kennedy (or Wagner, or tennis, or Joe Louis)?" is to learn something about one's friends and neighbors. After listening to their opinions and their reasons for them, we may leave the discussion slightly wiser, slightly better informed, and perhaps slightly less one-sided than we were before the discussion began.

How judgments stop thought

18   A judgment ("He is a fine boy," "It was a beautiful service," "Baseball is a healthful sport," "She is an awful bore") is a conclusion, summing up a large number of previously observed facts. The reader is probably familar with the fact that students almost always have difficulty in

writing themes of the required length because their ideas give out after a paragraph or two. The reason for this is that those early paragraphs contain so many judgments that there is little left to be said. When the conclusions are carefully excluded, however, and observed facts are given instead, there is never any trouble about the length of papers; in fact, they tend to become too long, since inexperienced writers, when told to give facts, often give far more than are necessary, because they lack discrimination between the important and the trivial.

19   Still another consequence of judgments early in the course of a written exercise—and this applies also to hasty judgments in everyday thought —is the temporary blindness they induce. When, for example, a description starts with the words, "He was a real Madison Avenue executive," or "She was a typical sorority girl," if we continue writing at all, we must make all our later statements consistent with those judgments. The result is that all the individual characteristics of this particular "executive" or this particular "sorority girl" are lost sight of; and the rest of the account is likely to deal not with observed facts but with the writer's private notion (based on previously read stories, movies, pictures, and so forth) of what "Madison Avenue executives" or "typical sorority girls" are like. The premature judgment, that is, often prevents us from seeing what is directly in front of us, so that clichés take the place of fresh description. Therefore, even if the writer feels sure at the beginning of a written account that the man he is describing is a "real leatherneck" or that the scene he is describing is a "beautiful residential suburb," he will conscientiously keep such notions out of his head, lest his vision be obstructed. He is specifically warned against describing *anybody* as a "beatnik"—a term (originally applied to literary and artistic Bohemians) which was blown up by sensational journalism and movies into an almost completely fictional and misleading stereotype. If a writer applies the term to any actual living human being, he will have to spend so much energy thereafter explaining what he does *not* mean by it that he will save himself trouble by not bringing it up at all.

Slanting

20   In the course of writing reports of personal experiences, it will be found that in spite of all endeavors to keep judgments out, some will creep in. An account of a man, for example, may go like this: "He had apparently not shaved for several days, and his face and hands were covered with grime. His shoes were torn, and his coat, which was several sizes too small for him, was spotted with dried clay." Now, in spite of the fact that no judgment has been stated, a very obvious one is implied. Let us

contrast this with another description of the same man. "Although his face was bearded and neglected, his eyes were clear, and he looked straight ahead as he walked rapidly down the road. He seemed very tall; perhaps the fact that his coat was too small for him emphasized that impression. He was carrying a book under his left arm, and a small terrier ran at his heels." In this example, the impression about the same man is considerably changed, simply by the inclusion of new details and the subordination of unfavorable ones. Even if explicit judgments are kept out of one's writing, implied judgments will get in.

21　　How, then, can we ever give an impartial report? The answer is, of course, that we cannot attain complete impartiality while we use the language of everyday life. Even with the very impersonal language of science, the task is sometimes difficult. Nevertheless, we can, by being aware of the favorable or unfavorable feelings that certain words and facts can arouse, attain enough impartiality for practical purposes. Such awareness enables us to balance the implied favorable and unfavorable judgments against each other. To learn to do this, it is a good idea to write two accounts of the same subject, both strict reports, to be read side by side: the first to contain facts and details likely to prejudice the reader in favor of the subject, the second to contain those likely to prejudice the reader against it. For example:

For	*Against*
He had white teeth.	His teeth were uneven.
His eyes were blue, his hair blond and abundant.	He rarely looked people straight in the eye.
He had on a clean white shirt.	His shirt was frayed at the cuffs.
His speech was courteous.	He had a high-pitched voice.
His employer spoke highly of him.	His landlord said he was slow in paying his rent.
He liked dogs.	He disliked children.

22　　This process of selecting details favorable or unfavorable to the subject being described may be termed *slanting*. Slanting gives no explicit judgments, but it differs from reporting in that it deliberately makes certain judgments inescapable. Let us assume for a moment the truth of the statement "When Clyde was in New York last November he was seen having dinner with a show girl. . . ." The inferences that can be drawn from this statement are changed considerably when the following words are added: ". . . and her husband and their two children." Yet, if Clyde is a married man, his enemies could conceivably do him a great deal of harm by talking about his "dinner-date with a New York show girl." One-sided or biased slanting of this kind, not uncommon in private gossip and backbiting, and all too common in the "interpretative reporting" of newspapers and news magazines, can be described as a technique of lying without actually telling any lies.

Discovering one's bias

23   Here, however, a caution is necessary. When, for example, a newspaper tells a story in a way that we dislike, leaving out facts we think important and playing up important facts in ways that we think unfair, we are tempted to say, "Look how unfairly they've slanted the story!" In making such a statement we are, of course, making an inference about the newspaper's editors. We are assuming that what seems important or unimportant to us seems equally important or unimportant to them, and on the basis of that assumption we infer that the editors "deliberately" gave the story a misleading emphasis. Is this necessarily the case? Can the reader, as an outsider, say whether a story assumes a given form because the editors "deliberately slanted it that way" or because that was the way the events appeared to them?

24   The point is that, by the process of selection and abstraction imposed on us by our own interests and background, experience comes to all of us (including newspaper editors) already "slanted." If you happen to be pro-labor, pro-Catholic, and a stock-car racing fan, your ideas of what is important or unimportant will of necessity be different from those of a man who happens to be indifferent to all three of your favorite interests. If, then, some newspapers often seem to side with the big businessman on public issues, the reason is less a matter of "deliberate" slanting than the fact that publishers are often, in enterprises as large as modern urban newspapers, big businessmen themselves, accustomed both in work and in social life to associating with other big businessmen. Nevertheless, the best newspapers, whether owned by "big businessmen" or not, do try to tell us as accurately as possible what is going on in the world, because they are run by newspapermen who conceive it to be part of their professional responsibility to present fairly the conflicting points of view in controversial issues. Such newspapermen are *reporters* indeed.

25   The writer who is neither an advocate nor an opponent avoids slanting, except when he is seeking special literary effects. The avoidance of slanting is not only a matter of being fair and impartial; it is even more importantly a matter of making good maps of the territory of experience. The profoundly biased individual cannot make good maps because he can see an enemy *only* as an enemy and a friend *only* as a friend. The individual with genuine skill in writing—one who has imagination and insight—can look at the same subject from many points of view. The following examples may illustrate the fullness and solidity of descriptions thus written:

Adam turned to look at him. It was, in a way, as though this were the first time he had laid eyes on him. He saw the strong, black shoulders under the red-check calico, the long arms lying loose, forward over the knees, the strong hands, seamed and calloused, holding the reins. He looked at the face. The thrust of the jawbone was strong, but the lips were heavy and low, with a piece of chewed straw hanging out one side of the mouth. The eyelids were pendulous, slightly swollen-looking, and the eyes bloodshot. Those eyes, Adam knew, could sharpen to a quick, penetrating, assessing glance. But now, looking at that slack, somnolent face, he could scarcely believe that.

—ROBERT PENN WARREN, *Wilderness*

Soon after the little princess, there walked in a massively built, stout young man in spectacles, with a cropped head, light breeches in the mode of the day, with a high lace ruffle and a ginger-coloured coat. This stout young man [Pierre] was the illegitimate son of a celebrated dandy of the days of Catherine, Count Bezuhov, who was now dying in Moscow. He had not yet entered any branch of the service; he had only just returned from abroad, where he had been educated, and this was his first appearance in society. Anna Pavlovna greeted him with a nod reserved for persons of the very lowest hierarchy in her drawing-room. . . .

Pierre was clumsy, stout and uncommonly tall, with huge, red hands; he did not, as they say, know how to come into a drawing-room and still less how to get out of one, that is, how to say something particularly agreeable on going away. Moreover, he was dreamy. He stood up, and picking up a three-cornered hat with the plume of a general in it instead of his own, he kept hold of it, pulling the feathers until the general asked him to restore it. But all his dreaminess and his inability to enter a drawing-room or talk properly in it were atoned for by his expression of good-nature, simplicity and modesty.

—COUNT LEO TOLSTOY, *War and Peace*
(Translated by Constance Garnett)

Applications

I. Here are a number of statements which the reader may attempt to classify as judgments, inferences, or reports. Since the distinctions are not always clear-cut, a one-word answer will not ordinarily be adequate. Note that we are concerned here with the nature of the statements, not the truth or falsity of them; for example, the statement, "Water freezes at 10° centigrade," is, although inaccurate, a report.

1. She goes to church only in order to show off her clothes.

   SAMPLE ANALYSIS: In usual circumstances under which such a statement would be made, this would be an *inference,* since people ordinarily do not admit that they go to church for that reason. A *judgment* is also strongly implied, since it is assumed that one ought to have better reasons.

2. There is something essentially unclean about eating meat and fish.

3. Cary Grant has lots of personality.

4. Rough-grained Split Leather Brief Case; artificial leather gussets. 3 position lock with key. 16 × 11 in. Color: black or brown. Shpg. wt. 2 lbs. Price, $4.86.   —Sears, Roebuck and Company Catalog

5. Commuter—one who spends his life
   In riding to and from his wife;
   A man who shaves and takes a train
   And then rides back to shave again.
                              —E. B. WHITE

6. To commit murder is wrong under all circumstances.

7. The Russian people do not want war.

8. He is a typical bureaucrat.

9. An intelligent man makes his own opportunities.

10. The senator's support of the bill was a move to catch the veteran vote.

11. That time of year thou may'st in me behold
    When yellow leaves, or few, or none do hang
    Upon those boughs that shake against the cold,
    Bare ruined choirs where late the sweet birds sang.
                              —WILLIAM SHAKESPEARE

12. And Adam lived an hundred and thirty years, and begat a son in his like-
    ness, after his image; and called his name Seth: And the days of Adam after
    he had begotten Seth were eight hundred years: and he begat sons and
    daughters: And all the days that Adam lived were nine hundred and thirty
    years: and he died.   —GENESIS 5:3–5

13. Crisp as Jack Frost, crunchy and crackle-happy . . . redder than a fire sale
    of long-handle flannels. Your big delicious beauties arrive so fresh we don't
    guarantee they won't talk back to folks . . . in a flavor-full language all
    their own. Shipping weight about 9 pounds.
                              —Advertising material accompanying
                              a Fruit-of-the-Month Club delivery

14. William Jameson is a skinny, crippled, tuberculosis-ridden little man, weigh-
    ing only 95 pounds and standing only 5 feet tall. And every ounce and inch
    of him is criminal—incorrigible, remorseless and vicious.
                              —New York *World-Telegram & Sun*

15. Research scientists proved that regular after-meal brushing with new Ipana
    reduced bacteria in the mouth—including decay and bad-breath bacteria—
    by an average of 84%.   —Advertisement for Ipana toothpaste

16. *C'est Magnifique! Une maison Ranch très originale avec 8 rooms, 2½ baths
    . . . 2-Cadillac garage . . . $21,990 . . . No cash for veterans.*
                              —Advertisement for a Long Island development

17. Our shameful Justice of the Peace system allows many legal ignoramuses—
    more intent on picking our pockets than on guarding our rights—to mis-
    handle the law in rural areas.   —*Reader's Digest*

18. But the delegates [at the U.S. Chamber of Commerce convention] remained
    wary. "He [President Kennedy] gave a nice speech," said one of them after-

ward, "but actions speak louder than words. Nothing he said here this morning erased his actions taken against the steel industry." The business
community had cause for concern. Kennedy is not ideologically against
business; he probably thinks he is all for it. But the fact is that as a millionaire's son with no experience in any calling but politics, the President has
led an economically sheltered life—and he does not seem to understand
business or businessmen too well.   *—Time*

II. In addition to trying such exercises in report-writing and the exclusion of judgments and inferences as are suggested in this chapter, the
reader might try writing (a) reports heavily slanted *against* persons or organizations he *likes,* and (b) reports heavily slanted *in favor of* persons or
organizations he *dislikes.* For example, imagine that your luncheon club
or fraternity or lodge is a subversive organization and report the facts
about its activities and members upon which unfavorable inferences could
be made; or imagine that one of your most disagreeable neighbors has
been offered a job two thousand miles away and write a factual letter of
recommendation to help him get the job.

It is also amusing and instructive to write parodies of biased writing,
i.e., to write with so strong a bias that you ridicule the bias. A strongly
biased account consists, of course, of slanted reports and unqualified judgments. The following is a quotation from *Mad* magazine's attempt to see
the Boy Scouts through *Pravda's* eyes:

After three years of servitude in the Cub Scouts, the boys, now hooligan adolescents, are forced to join the older, more corrupt Boy Scouts. Here, they are
snatched away from their families and taken to primitive forests where they
must live in unheated tents.

The most deceitful ritual is the shameful "Court of Honor," where the
young warmongers are decorated with so-called "Merit Badges." It is here that
they receive awards for their work in such insidious fields as "Swimming" (Un-
derwater Demolition and Sabotage), "Chemistry" (Germ and Poison Gas Warfare), "Pathfinding" (Counter-espionage), and "Pioneering" (Exploitation of
Undeveloped Nations).

III. "A youth and a man were killed and three teenagers seriously injured early today in two auto accidents." Write:

1. A *report* of these accidents, inventing names and places.

2. A *slanted report* for a newspaper campaigning for stricter laws against juvenile delinquency. (Be sure to use factual statements only, letting your reader
make his own inferences and judgments.)

6. A *slanted report* for a newspaper highly critical of the local city administration. (Again, use factual statements only.)

IV. Discuss the use of inference in the following passage from Sir
Arthur Conan Doyle. Are the inferences made by Sherlock Holmes the

kind that are described in this chapter? Comment on the validity and verifiability of Holmes's inferences.

With a resigned air and a somewhat weary smile, Holmes begged the beautiful intruder to take a seat, and to inform us what it was that was troubling
her.

"At least it cannot be your health," said he, as his keen eyes darted over
her; "so ardent a bicyclist must be full of energy."

She glanced down in surprise at her own feet, and I observed the slight
roughening of the side of the sole caused by the friction of the edge of the
pedal.

"Yes, I bicycle a good deal, Mr. Holmes. . . ."

My friend took the lady's ungloved hand, and examined it with as close
an attention and as little sentiment as a scientist would show to a specimen.

"You will excuse me, I am sure. It is my business," said he, as he dropped
it. "I nearly fell into the error of supposing you were typewriting. Of course,
it is obvious that it is music. You observe the spatulate finger-ends, Watson,
which is common to both professions? There is a spirituality about the face,
however"—she gently turned it towards the light—"which the typewriter does
not generate. This lady is a musician."

"Yes, Mr. Holmes, I teach music."

"In the country, I presume, from your complexion."

"Yes, sir, near Farnham, on the borders of Surrey."

v. "Harry Thompson visited Russia in 1958"; "Rex Davis is a millionaire"; "Betty Armstrong does not believe in God"; "Dr. Baxter is in
disagreement with the policies of the American Medical Association."
Accepting these statements as true, write several hundred words of unfounded inferences, and inferences upon inferences about these people. Of
course, you don't know who they are, but don't let that stop you. Just go
ahead and make inferences.

This exercise is also amusing and instructive for discussion groups,
the members taking turns in adding inferences.

vi. Select a topic about which you have little information but many
prejudices, such as "Whither Modern Youth?" "The Menace of Federal
Encroachments on American Freedom," "The National Association of
Manufacturers: A Threat to Democracy," "Big Unions: A Threat to Free
Enterprise," "What's Wrong with Modern Women," "Let's Cut the Fads
and Frills from Education," or "The South: Yesterday and Today," and
write a one-thousand-word essay consisting solely of sweeping generalizations, broad judgments, and unfounded inferences. Use plenty of "loaded"
words. Knock off five points (out of a possible 100) for each verifiable
fact used. If you can consistently score 95 or better on all these and other
such topics, and your grammar and spelling are plausible, leave your
present job. Or quit school. Fame and fortune are within your grasp.

Questions

1. In paragraph 1, why does Hayakawa exclude inferences and judgments in reports? Why does he qualify this statement with "as far as possible"?

2. Why, in paragraph 3, does he italicize an entire clause? Show how this clause is a key assumption.

3. If report language is "map" language, how does Hayakawa justify inferences? Would he consider news editorials largely inferential? Why?

4. Distinguish between inference and judgment.

5. Illustrate how his article on the language of reports is written in the language of reports.

6. What technique of definition is Hayakawa using in paragraph 2? Show how he develops this technique.

7. In paragraph 5, he makes a series of statements about inference. What technique does he use here consistently? Assess its effectiveness or special appropriateness to his subject?

8. In paragraphs 20 and 21, what technique does Hayakawa make use of to define "slanting"?

2   RICHARD D. ALTICK

Denotation and Connotation

1   Incidents like this are happening every day. A teacher in a college English course has returned a student's theme on the subject of a poem. One sentence in the theme reads, "Like all of Keats's best work, the 'Ode to Autumn' has a sensual quality that makes it especially appealing to me." The instructor's red pencil has underscored the word *sensual,* and in the margin he has written "Accurate?" or whatever his customary comment is in such cases. The student has checked the dictionary and comes back puzzled. "I don't see what you mean," he says. "The dictionary says *sensual* means 'of or pertaining to the senses or physical sensation.' And that's what I wanted to say. Keats's poem is filled with words and images that suggest physical sensation."

2   "Yes," replies the instructor, "that's what the word *means*—according to the dictionary." And then he takes his copy of the *American College*

Dictionary, which contains the definition the student quoted, and turns to the word *sensual.* "Look here," he says, pointing to a passage in small type just after the various definitions of the word:

Sensual, sensuous, voluptuous refer to experience through the senses. Sensual refers, usually unfavorably, to the enjoyments derived from the senses, generally implying grossness or lewdness: *a sensual delight in eating, sensual excesses.* Sensuous refers, favorably or literally, to what is experienced through the senses: *sensuous impressions, sensuous poetry.* Voluptuous implies the luxurious gratification of sensuous or sensual desires: *voluptuous joys, voluptuous beauty.*[1]

3   The student reads the passage carefully and begins to see light. The word *sensual* carries with it a shade of meaning, an unfavorable implication, which he did not intend; the word he wanted was *sensuous.* He has had a useful lesson in the dangers of taking dictionary definitions uncritically, as well as in the vital difference between denotation and connotation.

4   The difference between the two is succinctly phrased in another of those small-type paragraphs of explanation, taken this time from *Webster's New Collegiate Dictionary:* "Denote implies all that strictly belongs to the definition of the word, *connote* all of the ideas that are suggested by the term; thus, 'home' *denotes* the place where one lives with one's family, but it usually *connotes* comfort, intimacy, and privacy. The same implications distinguish *denotation* and *connotation.*"[2] The denotation of a word is its dictionary definition, which is what the word "stands for." According to the dictionary, *sensuous* and *sensual* have the same general denotation: they agree in meaning "experience through the senses." Yet they *suggest* different things. And that difference in suggestion constitutes a difference in connotation.

5   Nothing is more essential to intelligent, profitable reading than sensitivity to connotation. Only when we possess such sensitivity can we understand both what the author *means,* which may be pretty plain, and what he wants to *suggest,* which may actually be far more important than the superficial meaning. The difference between reading a book or story or essay or poem for surface meaning and reading it for implication is the difference between listening to the New York Philharmonic Symphony Orchestra on a battered old radio and listening to it on a high-fidelity stereophonic record player. Only the latter brings out the nuances that are often more significant than the obvious, and therefore easily comprehended, meaning.

6   An unfailing awareness of the connotative power of words is just as vital, of course, to the writer. His eternal task is to select the word which will convey, not approximately but exactly, what he wants to say. He must

[1] Reprinted by courtesy of the publishers from *The American College Dictionary.* Copyright 1947 by Random House, Inc.

[2] By permission. From *Webster's New Collegiate Dictionary,* copyright, 1949, 1951, 1953, by G. & C. Merriam Co.

remember that two words may be "synonymous" in respect to denotation; that is, they *mean* the same thing. But to the practiced writer, as to the practiced reader, few if any words are exactly synonymous in connotation; in a given context one particular word will convey the precise implication the writer desires to communicate to his reader. The inexperienced writer, forgetting this, often has recourse to Roget's *Thesaurus,* where he finds, conveniently marshaled, whole regiments of synonyms; not knowing which to choose, he either closes his eyes and picks a word at random or else chooses the one that "sounds" best. In either case he is neglecting the delicate shadings of implication which differentiate each word in a category from its neighbors. To be certain that the word he has selected conveys exactly the sense he has in mind, he should check it in those invaluable little paragraphs in the dictionary.[3] For further help, he can look up the fuller discussions in *Webster's Dictionary of Synonyms.*

Exercise 1

Explain why the italicized words in the following sentences reflect the writer's insensitivity to connotation, and in each case supply a more appropriate word.

1. Although she was really twenty-one, there was a certain *childishness* in her voice and manner which set her apart from the other girls and delighted everyone who met her.
2. Handle this Ming vase with extreme care. It's very *brittle.*
3. What especially interests newcomers is the absolute *smoothness* of the countryside.
4. When she got out of the hospital she was pretty *lean,* but a good wholesome diet of home cooking soon remedied that.
5. Attractive though it was in terms of pay and prospects for advancement, Clem decided finally to *spurn* the offer and look for some other job.
6. I've been taking aspirins by the carload, but they haven't *healed* my headache.
7. I knew she had studied the lesson thoroughly, so after asking my question I waited a little. Finally the *retort* came, in her usual quiet, almost hesitant manner.
8. One of the best things the Scouts and Hi-Y did for him was to develop genuinely *mannish* qualities. He's a fine, upstanding youth.
9. I was glad to see by his *agile* gait as he strode down the street that he was fully recovered.

[3] If the definition of the word in question is not followed by a paragraph discriminating between its "synonyms," there is a cross-reference to the place where this paragraph occurs.

10. What I *pined* for above all was a thick, juicy hamburger, with plenty of relish and a side order of French fries and onions.

Exercise 2

   Explain the differences in connotation among the members of each of the following groups of words. Make up sentences that illustrate the accurate use of as many words as your instructor directs. (It is also useful, as well as entertaining, to compose sentences in which the words are conspicuously misused, as in the preceding exercise.)

1. dash, hurry, race, gallop, speed, hurtle, run
2. corpulent, plump, obese, heavy-set, fleshy, fat, paunchy, burly, overweight, rolypoly, bulky
3. mansion, dwelling, domicile, residence, house, home
4. racket, uproar, hubbub, clatter, noise, commotion
5. titter, giggle, chuckle, guffaw, laugh, roar
6. dress, frock, costume, outfit, gown, ensemble, get-up, apparel, clothes
7. dilapidated, ramshackle, ruined, neglected, deteriorated, tumbledown
8. shrewd, cunning, calculating, sly, adroit, knowing, clever, astute
9. cheat, phony, quack, crook, impostor, charlatan
10. admire, love, relish, like, approve, idolize, respect, revere, esteem
11. snooty, arrogant, conceited, cocky, egotistical, proud, high-and-mighty, overbearing, high-hat
12. common, ordinary, vulgar, run-of-the-mill, average, everyday
13. frighten, alarm, terrify, scare, intimidate, startle
14. impertinent, impudent, saucy, cheeky, insolent, fresh
15. confess, acknowledge, concede, grant, admit, come clean

Exercise 3

   The difference between denotation and connotation is often illustrated by the fact that of two words which roughly "mean" the same, one has a complimentary, the other an unflattering, connotation. Thus while you may like to think of yourself as an idealist, people who do not sympathize with your attitudes might call you prudish. Taking as many of the following pairs as your instructor designates, write paragraphs explaining why you would like to be described by one of the terms but not by the other.

a middle-of-the-roader/a fence sitter	trusting/gullible
enthusiastic/fanatical	original/screwball
cautious/cowardly	stolid/even-tempered
touchy/sensitive	thrifty/penny-pinching
fluent/gabby	practical/unimaginative
coy/modest	hypocritical/tactful

7   Not all words possess connotative powers. Articles, conjunctions, prepositions, and many common adverbs lack connotative qualities because they are words used to connect ideas and to show relationships between them; these parts of speech do not themselves stand for ideas. But most words which stand for ideas have connotations, even though they are often scarcely perceptible. That is because ideas themselves have connotations: they produce some sort of intellectual or emotional reaction inside us.

Connotations: personal and general

8   There are two types of connotation: personal and general. Personal connotations are the result of the experience of the individual man or woman. The way we react to ideas and objects, and thus to the words that stand for those "referents," is determined by the precise nature of our earlier experience with the referents. Taken all together, the connotations that surround most of the words in our vocabulary are a complex and intimate record of our life to date. Our present reaction to a word may be the cumulative result of all our experiences with the word and its referent. In the case of another word, our reaction may have been determined once and for all by an early or a particularly memorable experience with it. A student's reaction to the word *teacher,* for instance, may be determined by all his experience with teachers, which has been subtly synthesized, in the course of time, into a single image or emotional response. In it are mingled memories of Miss Smith, the first-grade teacher who dried his tears when he lost a fight in the schoolyard at recess; of Miss Jones, the sixth-grade teacher who bored her pupils with thrice-told tales of her trip to Mexico ten years earlier; of Mr. Johnson, the high-school gym teacher who merely laughed when he saw the brush burns a boy sustained when he inexpertly slid down a rope; of Mr. Miller, the college professor who somehow packed a tremendous amount of information into lectures that seemed too entertaining to be instructive. Or, on the other hand, when the student thinks of *teacher* he may think of a particular teacher who for one reason or another has made an especially deep impression upon him—the chemistry teacher in high school, for instance, who encouraged him, by example and advice, to make chemistry his life work.

9   A moment's thought will show the relationship between personal and general connotations as well as the fact that there is no line of demarcation between the two types. Since "the mass mind" is the sum total of the individual minds that comprise it, general connotations result when the reaction of the majority of people to a specific word is substantially the same. The reasons why one word should possess a certain connotation, while an-

other word has a quite different connotation, are complex. We shall spend a little time on the subject later. Here it need only be said that differences in general connotation derive from at least two major sources. For one thing, the exact shade of meaning a word possesses in our language is often due to the use to which it was put by a writer who had especially great influence over the language because he was, and is, so widely read. The King James version of the Bible, for instance, is responsible for the crystallizing of many connotations. People came to know a given word from its occurrence in certain passages in the Bible, and thus the word came to connote to them on *all* occasions what it connoted in those familiar passages; it was permanently colored by particular associations. Such words include *trespass, money-changers, manger, Samaritan* (originally the name of a person living in a certain region of Asia Minor), *salvation, vanity, righteous, anoint,* and *charity.* The same is true of many words used in other books which, being widely read and studied, influenced the vocabularies of following generations—Malory's *Morte d'Arthur,* for example, or Shakespeare's plays, or the essays of Addison and Steele.

10   But general connotation is not always a matter of literary development. It can result also from the experience that men as a social group have had with the ideas which words represent. Before 1938, the word *appease* had an inoffensive connotation. In the edition of *Webster's Collegiate Dictionary* current in that year it was defined simply as "to pacify, often by satisfying; quiet; calm; soothe; allay." But then the word became associated with the ill-fated attempts of Neville Chamberlain to stave off war with Hitler by giving in to his demands, and that association has now strongly colored its meaning. The latest edition of the same dictionary adds to the meaning quoted above this newer one: "to conciliate by political, economic, or other considerations;—now usually signifying a sacrifice of moral principle in order to avert aggression." Laden as the word is with its suggestions of the disaster of Munich, no British or American official ever uses it in referring to a conciliating move in foreign policy for which he wants to win public acceptance. On the other hand, opponents of that move use the word freely to arouse sentiment against it, even though the situation in question may have little or no resemblance to that of Munich. In other words, events have conditioned us to react in a particular way to the verb *appease* and the noun *appeasement.* If our support is desired for a policy of *give and take, live and let live,* or *peaceful coexistence* in international relations, its advocates will use the terms just italicized, as well as *negotiation* and *compromise,* which convey the idea of mutual concessions without sacrifice of principle; or *horse-trading,* which has a homely American flavor, suggesting shrewd bargaining with the additional implication that a good profit can be made on the deal.

11   All general connotations thus have their origin in private connotations—in personal, individual, but generally shared reactions to words and

the ideas for which they stand. But later, after general connotations have been established, the process works the other way: the individual, who may have had no personal experience with the idea represented by a given word, may acquire a personal attitude toward it by observing how society in general reacts to the word. In the future, men and women who were children when Klaus Fuchs and other men stole American and British atomic secrets and relayed them to Russia may react negatively to mention of such names. If they do, it will be because they have acquired the feelings of revulsion that people associate with the names of traitors—just as Americans almost two centuries later still react to the mention of Benedict Arnold.

12   Every writer must cultivate his awareness of the differentiation between general connotations and personal ones. It is the general ones—those which he can be reasonably sure his readers share with him—which he must rely on to convey the accurate spirit of his message. If he uses words which have additional connotations to him alone, he runs the risk of writing in a private shorthand to which only he holds the key. Since there is no clear dividing line between general and personal connotations, it would, of course, be unrealistic to require that a writer absolutely confine himself to the former. Moreover, some of the subtle richness of poetry, and to some degree that of imaginative prose, is derived (assuming that the reader discovers the secret) from the author's use of words in private sense. But in most forms of practical communication, the writer does well to confine himself to words whose connotations are approximately the same to his readers as they are to him.

The uses of connotations

13   What forms do our reactions to words take? By no means all words evoke any distinguishable emotional response; *delusion* and *illusion,* for instance, probably do not do so for most people. Here the response is largely an intellectual one, a recognition that the two words are customarily used in different contexts, that they "imply" slightly different things.

14   But for our purposes the most important words are the ones which touch the emotions of those who hear or see them. They are words that arouse people to a positive or negative judgment—words that often stir them to action. *Atheist* arouses deep-seated prejudices for or against the ideas that the word is said to represent, for or against people who are said to be atheists. *Streamlined* connotes modern design, clean lines, efficiency, and thus has a generally pleasant suggestion. (On the other hand, like many words that become too fashionable and thus are overused and even abused, *streamlined* has come to have a negative connotation to many fas-

tidious readers. Too often it has been loosely used as a means of glossing over, skimping and corner-cutting—as in *streamlined* education.) Mention of *McCarthy* evokes fervent sentiments, of very diverse quality, from both those who admired him and those who did not. *Subdeb* eases the selling of clothing to adolescent girls, of whom not one in a hundred thousand will ever have a debut. *Nigger* connotes very different things to a champion of white supremacy in Mississippi and a member of the National Association for the Advancement of Colored People. *Draft* and *selective service* mean the same thing, but one term has a more unpleasant connotation than the other. And so on, *ad infinitum*.

15   Intimately associated with emotional response, and often directly responsible for it, are the images that many words inspire in our minds. The commonest type of image is the visual: that is, a given word habitually calls forth a certain picture on the screen of our inner consciousness. Mention of places we have seen and people we have known produces a visual recollection of them. Of course the precise content of these pictures is determined by the sort of experience one has had with their originals. *Mary* may not recall the picture of one's childhood sweetheart, but it may evoke instead a picture of a pink hair-ribbon which Mary must once have worn. *Boston* may recall only the picture of a street accident, which was the most vivid memory one carried away from that city. And so on! It is a fascinating game to examine in this fashion the mental images thus spontaneously conjured up by words; equally rewarding is the effort to explain why many words evoke images which on first thought seem so completely irrelevant to their denotations.

16   It is not only words referring to concrete objects which have this power of evoking a visual response in the imagination. Our picture-making faculty also enables us to visualize abstractions in concrete terms—and, as we shall see, it gets us into a great deal of trouble on that account. *Capitalist* is an abstract noun; it denotes a person who has a certain function in a certain kind of economic system. But to many people it connotes a definite picture, obviously derived from the old-time cartoonist's stock figure, of a bloated banker in striped pants, cutaway coat, top hat, and spats; he is smoking a Corona-Corona cigar, on his fingers are rings with huge stones, and across his middle reposes a gold watch chain with links as thick as frankfurters. To many, in a similar way, the noun *radical* conjures up a picture of an intellectual-looking man with thick glasses, bushy hair, wrinkled clothes, and a wild expression on his face. Thus abstractions are made concrete, and our reactions to the words that represent those abstractions are patterned in terms of that visual image. What visual images do the words *statesman* and *politician* suggest to you?

17   In addition to visual responses in the imagination, words evoke responses associated with the other senses. Many words have connotations that appeal to our inward ear: *tick-tock, harmony, squeak, trumpet, dirge,*

shrill, thunder, croon, lisp. Others appeal to our sense of touch—*gritty, needle, ice-cold, lather, soft, kiss, baby's cheek, woolen underwear.* Another class invites palatal responses—*buttermilk, spicy, mellow, roast beef, castor oil, menthol, bitter.* And a final group invites olfactory responses—*burning dump, incense, new-mown hay, sweaty, coffee roaster, fragrance, Diesel fumes.* Many words, like some already mentioned, appeal to two or more senses at once: for instance, *dry, bubbly, satin, wine, wrinkle, mossy, sea breeze, snowy, cigarette, sugar.*

18   Since our sensory experience may be either pleasant or unpleasant, the words that evoke their imaginative equivalents have the power to sway us to accept or reject an idea. "So soft, yet manageable . . . so sweetly clean! Come-hither loveliness—that's what your hair has after a luxurious Prell shampoo! It's caressably soft, yet *so obedient!* Yes, angel-soft, smooth as satin, glowing with that 'Radiantly Alive' look *he'll* love!" Thus exclaims the advertising man who wants millions of women to buy a certain solution for washing their hair. Or: "It's a foul, evil-smelling mess!" Thus speaks a minority-party congressman who is dissatisfied with something the administration has done.

19   In some of the pages that follow, we shall concentrate upon this persuasive power of words, especially as found in advertising and political discussion. There is perhaps no simpler or better way of showing how connotation works. But this preliminary emphasis on the ways in which language may be manipulated for selfish purposes must not lead you to assume that all, or even most, writers have wicked designs upon you. On the contrary, the greater part of what people read has the sole purpose of informing or entertaining them—of giving them new knowledge, or fresh food for the imagination and the emotions. And here language is used simply to heighten the effectiveness, the accuracy, and the vividness of the writer's communication.

20   Take the best of today's journalism—not run-of-the-mill newspaper reporting, but, say, feature stories and magazine articles. Really good descriptive journalism requires a high degree of skill in the use of words; and the more skillfully and attentively we read what the author has set down, the greater will be our pleasure. Examine the sure sense of connotative values employed in this description of a Pennsylvania industrial town:

> Donora is twenty-eight miles south of Pittsburgh and covers the tip of a lumpy point formed by the most convulsive of the Monongahela's many horseshoe bends. Though accessible by road, rail, and river, it is an extraordinarily secluded place. The river and the bluffs that lift abruptly from the water's edge to a height of four hundred and fifty feet enclose it on the north and east and south, and just above it to the west is a range of rolling but even higher hills. On its outskirts are acres of sidings and rusting gondolas, abandoned mines, smoldering slag piles, and gulches filled with rubbish. Its limits are marked by sooty signs that read, "Donora. Next to Yours the Best Town in the U.S.A." It

is a harsh, gritty town, founded in 1901 and old for its age, with a gaudy main street and a thousand identical gaunt gray houses. Some of its streets are paved with concrete and some are cobbled, but many are of dirt and crushed coal. At least half of them are as steep as roofs, and several have steps instead of sidewalks. It is treeless and all but grassless, and much of it is slowly sliding downhill. After a rain, it is a smear of mud. Its vacant lots and many of its yards are mortally gullied, and one of its three cemeteries is an eroded ruin of gravelly clay and toppled tombstones. Its population is 12,300.[4]

Here, in familiar but carefully chosen words, the reporter has produced a graphic impression of a dismal community. He was obviously depressed by what he saw—a feeling he means us to have, too. And, were we to read on past the passage quoted, we would discover that even the seemingly casual reference to the population and the cemeteries is part of his plan; for the article as a whole is about the poison-laden smog that descended on Donora some years ago and killed at least a score of its inhabitants. The whole passage, with its single-minded stress on language suggestive of griminess, ugliness, deterioration, prepares us for the disaster to come.

21   In the same way, but on a less ephemeral plane of interest, with more exalted purpose and greater intensity of feeling, poets too utilize the connotative potentialities of language. They employ words lovingly, unschemingly, wishing to delight and move the reader through an imparting of their own vivid experience:

> Season of mists and mellow fruitfulness,
>   Close bosom-friend of the maturing sun;
> Conspiring with him how to load and bless
>   With fruit the vines that round the thatch-eaves run;
> To bend with apples the mossed cottage-trees,
>   And fill all fruit with ripeness to the core;
>   To swell the gourd, and plump the hazel shells
>   With a sweet kernel; to set budding more,
> And still more, later flowers for the bees,
> Until they think warm days will never cease,
>   For Summer has o'er-brimmed their clammy cells.

Or:

> It is a beauteous evening, calm and free,
> The holy time is quiet as a Nun
> Breathless with adoration; the broad sun
> Is sinking down in its tranquillity;
> The gentleness of heaven broods o'er the Sea:
> Listen! the mighty Being is awake,
> And doth with his eternal motion make
> A sound like thunder—everlastingly.

[4] Berton Roueché, "The Fog," *The New Yorker,* Sept. 30, 1950. Reprinted with the permission of *The New Yorker.*

Exercise 4

A scholarly study has shown that the following nouns and adjectives are among those most frequently used by English poets in the past five hundred years. They are part of the basic vocabulary of poetry. How many of them possess particularly strong emotional appeal today? Why are these so filled with suggestion?

good, great, day, God, heart, king, life, lord, love, man, thing, time, soul, youth, long, light, spirit, cruel, dear, fair, high, old, poor, sweet, true, beauty, death, eye, fortune, gold, hand, heaven, lady, night, pain, woe, word, world, earth, bright, dark, happy, new, rich, blood, face, fire, grace, name, nature, power, sin, son, sun, tear, year, soft, air, friend, joy, divine, nature, proud, tender, vain, art, breast, fate, flower, head, hour, land, maid, sky, song, virtue, deep, dim, holy, child, dream, father, hope, mother, prayer, sea, star, white, black, green, bird, leaf, moon, nothing, stone, tree, water, wind

Exercise 5

What are the present connotations of the following words? To what extent do your answers agree with those of others in the class?

Winston Churchill, sputnik, brainwashing, censorship, security, United Nations, socialized medicine, minority group, Hitler, concentration camp, thermonuclear warfare, imperialism, witch hunt, welfare state, inflation

Exercise 6

1. What reaction, if any, do you have when you hear the name "Gwendolyn"? Do you see any specific picture in your mind? How can you account for it? Try the same experiment with "Elmer."
2. What personal connotations does each of the following names have to you? Do your reactions match those of others in the class? Explain why they do—or don't.

   Bill, Will, Willy, William, Billy
   Meg, Margie, Margaret, Peg, Peggy, Marge

Exercise 7

What do the following words or phrases connote to you personally?

1. serenade, examination, sandpaper, romantic, wryly, skunk, Inquisition, mangled, primitive, kiss, trample, messily, slither, mother, doleful, crackle, sunrise, ostentatiously, cooperate, refresh, bleak, celestial,

chocolate, orchid, gurgle, midnight oil, crimson, soggy, space man, cathedral
2. an old biddy, an old fuddy-duddy, a smooth operator, a campus queen, a junior executive
3. Madison Avenue, Wall Street, the Pentagon, Shangri-La, the Kremlin, Main Street, Bali, Sun Valley, San Francisco, Siberia, the Nile

Devote paragraphs to several of these words, describing, as accurately and in as concrete detail as possible, the pictures and reactions that are evoked in your mind when you happen to encounter each term. Search your memory for the personal associations and experiences that have resulted in the word's present cluster of connotations.

Exercise 8

According to chronological age, you probably are one of those persons who can be described as a teen-ager, an adolescent, a youth, a juvenile, a guy, or a gal. Write a short theme analyzing your personal responses to these words as they apply to you. Do you like them or dislike them? Why? What does each connote? Are there any other words that you prefer as self-description?

Exercise 9

To most people the following words have more or less pronounced connotations. Select two or three words that arouse particularly strong reactions in you and devote a paragraph to each, explaining why the word affects you as it does.

socialism	working class
puritanical	plagiarism
liberal	chastity
Jew	intolerance
capitalism	racial integration
atheism	conformity

Exercise 10

How sensitive to connotative values are you in your own writing? Take one of the subjects listed below and write about it, at whatever length is appropriate. Your sole purpose is to portray it, as precisely and vividly as you can: to make the reader share the sensations (sight, sound, touch, odor) that you have, or had. The best way to perform this exercise is to write it as soon as you can, in as good a form as possible. Then put it out of sight for at least twenty-four hours. At the end of that time, look at it again, with fresh eyes. Test for connotation every word (noun, adjective, verb, adverb) that has descriptive force. Check the dictionary for every word about which you have the slightest doubt. Try to find better—that is, more accurate—words. Then rewrite the paper. The final test is: Have I succeeded in communicating to my reader the true nature and flavor of my observation and experience?

The inside of a good restaurant (or of a restaurant I'd rather die than go
    into again)
The scene of a bad accident
A room decorated in the modern manner (or a "period" room)
A barber shop (or a beauty parlor)
An empty auditorium
The city room in a newspaper office
A small shop where a product is made by hand
One set in a television studio
A hen house (or a horse barn)
A florist's shop or greenhouse
The latest thing in motels (or a run-down tourist court)
An old-fashioned kitchen
A jet airliner (or a helicopter) takes off—with me inside
Kickoff!
Landing a big one
Stuck!
Getting awake (or coming out of anesthesia)
Sunrise (or sunset) in ————
Then the lights went out
A sudden storm
Pursuit!
The time I *knew* one's heart could be in one's mouth (or butterflies can
    flutter in one's stomach)
A piece of antique furniture
A modern fire truck
A prize-winning animal (dog, shoat, bull, or whatnot)
The contents of a baker's shop window
The cover of the current issue of a magazine
A coin machine in a campus hangout
A girl behind the counter in the five-and-ten
A super-sandwich (or a super-sundae)
A much-used telephone booth
A man in a white coat
An example of "calendar art"

3　C. S. LEWIS

What Christians Believe

1　　I have been asked to tell you what Christians believe, and I am going to begin by telling you one thing that Christians don't need to believe. If you are a Christian you don't have to believe that all the other religions are simply wrong all through. If you are an atheist you do have to believe that the main point in all the religions of the whole world is simply one huge mistake. If you are a Christian, you are free to think that all these religions, even the queerest ones, contain at least some hint of the truth. When I was an atheist I had to try to persuade myself that the whole human race were pretty good fools until about one hundred years ago; when I became a Christian I was able to take a more liberal view. But, of course, being a Christian does mean thinking that where Christianity differs from other religions, Christianity is right and they are wrong. Like in arithmetic—there's only one right answer to a sum, and all other answers are wrong: but some of the wrong answers are much nearer being right than others.

2　　The first big division of humanity is into the majority, who believe in some kind of God or gods, and the minority who don't. On this point, Christianity lines up with the majority—lines up with ancient Greeks and Romans, modern savages, Stoics, Platonists, Hindoos, Mohammedans, etc., against the modern Western European materialist. There are all sorts of different reasons for believing in God, and here I'll mention only one. It is this. Supposing there was no intelligence behind the universe, no creative mind. In that case nobody designed my brain for the purpose of thinking. It is merely that when the atoms inside my skull happen for physical or chemical reasons to arrange themselves in a certain way, this gives me, as a by-product, the sensation I call thought. But if so, how can I trust my own thinking to be true? It's like upsetting a milk-jug and hoping that the way the splash arranges itself will give you a map of London. But if I can't trust my own thinking, of course I can't trust the arguments leading to atheism, and therefore have no reason to be an atheist, or anything else. Unless I believe in God, I can't believe in thought: so I can never use thought to disbelieve in God.

3　　Now I go on to the next big division. People who all believe in God can be divided according to the sort of God they believe in. There are two very different ideas on this subject. One of them is the idea that He is beyond good and evil. *We* call one thing good and another thing bad. But according to some people that's merely our human point of view. These people would say that the wiser you become the less you'd want to call anything good or bad, and the more clearly you'd see that everything is good in one way and bad in another, and that nothing could have been different. Consequently, these people think that long before you got anywhere near the divine point of view the distinction would have disappeared altogether. We call a cancer bad, they'd say, because it kills a man; but you might just as well call a successful surgeon bad because he kills a cancer. It all depends on the point of view. The other and opposite idea is that God is quite definitely "good" or "righteous," a God who takes sides, who loves love and hates hatred, who wants us to behave in one way and not in another. The first of these views—the one that thinks God beyond good and evil—is called Pantheism. It was held by the great Prussian philosopher Hegel and, as far as I can understand them, by the Hindoos. The other view is held by Jews, Mohammedans, and Christians.

4   And with this big difference between Pantheism and the Christian idea of God, there usually goes another. Pantheists usually believe that God, so to speak, animates the universe as you animate your body: that the universe almost *is* God, so that if it didn't exist He wouldn't exist either, and anything you find in the universe is a part of God. The Christian idea is quite different. They think God *made* the universe—like a man making a picture or composing a tune. A painter isn't a picture, and he doesn't die if his picture is destroyed. You may say, "He's put a lot of himself into it," but that only means that all its beauty and interest have come out of his head. His skill isn't in the picture in the same way that it's in his head, or even in his hands. I expect you see how this difference between Pantheists and Christians hangs together with the other one. If you don't take the distinction between good and bad very seriously, then it's easy to say that anything you find in this world is a part of God. But, of course, if you think some things really bad, and God really good, then you can't talk like that. You must believe that God is separate from the world and that some of the things we see in it are contrary to His will. Confronted with a cancer or a slum the Pantheist can say, "If you could only see it from the divine point of view, you would realise that this also is God." The Christian replies, "Don't talk damned nonsense." [1] For Christianity is a fighting religion. It thinks God made the world—that space and time, heat and cold, and all the colours and tastes, and all the animals and vegetables, are things that God "made up out of His head" as a man makes up a story. But it also thinks that a great many things have gone

---

[1] One listener complained of the word *damned* as frivolous swearing. But I mean exactly what I say—nonsense that is *damned* is under God's curse, and will (apart from God's grace) lead those who believe it to eternal death.

wrong with the world that God made and that God insists, and insists very loudly, on our putting them right again.

5　　And, of course, that raises a very big question. If a good God made the world why has it gone wrong? And for many years I simply wouldn't listen to the Christian answers to this question, because I kept on feeling "whatever you say, and however clever your arguments are, isn't it much simpler and easier to say that the world was *not* made by any intelligent power? Aren't all your arguments simply a complicated attempt to avoid the obvious?" But then that threw me back into those difficulties about atheism which I spoke of a moment ago. And soon I saw another difficulty.

6　　My argument against God was that the universe seemed so cruel and unjust. But how had I got this idea of *just* and *unjust?* A man doesn't call a line crooked unless he has some idea of a straight line. What was I comparing this universe with when I called it unjust? If the whole show was bad and senseless from A to Z, so to speak, why did I, who was supposed to be part of the show, find myself in such violent reaction against it? A man feels wet when he falls into water, because man isn't a water animal: a fish wouldn't feel wet. Of course I could have given up my idea of justice by saying it was nothing but a private idea of my own. But if I did that then my argument against God collapsed too—for the argument depended on saying that the world was really unjust, not that it just didn't happen to please my private fancies. Thus in the very act of trying to prove that God didn't exist—in other words, that the whole of reality was senseless—I found I was forced to assume that one part of reality—namely my idea of justice—was full of sense. Consequently atheism turns out to be too simple. If the whole universe has no meaning, we should never have found out that it has no meaning: just as if there were no light in the universe and therefore no creatures with eyes we should never know it was dark. *Dark* would be a word without meaning.

II

7　　Very well then, atheism is too simple. And I'll tell you another view that is also too simple. It's the view I call Christianity-and-water, the view that just says there's a good God in Heaven and everything is all right—leaving out all the difficult and terrible doctrines about sin and hell and the devil, and the redemption. Both these are boys' philosophies.

8　　It is no good asking for a simple religion. After all, real things *aren't* simple. They *look* simple, but they're not. The table I'm sitting at looks simple: but ask a scientist to tell you what it's really made of—all about the atoms and how the light waves rebound from them and hit my eye and what they do to the optic nerve and what it does to my brain—and, of course, you find that what we call "seeing a table" lands you in mysteries and complications which you can hardly get to the end of. A child, saying a child's prayer, looks simple. And if you're content to stop here, well and good. But if you're not—and the modern world usually isn't—if you want to go on and ask what's really happening—then you must be prepared for something difficult. If we ask for something more than simplicity, it's silly then to complain that the something more isn't simple. Another thing I've noticed about reality is that, besides being difficult, it's odd: it isn't neat, it isn't what you expect. I mean, when you've grasped that the earth and the other planets all go round the sun, you'd naturally expect that all the planets were made to match—all at equal distances from each other, say, or distances that regularly increased, or all the same size, or else getting bigger or smaller as you go further from the sun. In fact, you find no rhyme or reason (that we can see) about either the sizes or the distances; and some of them have one moon, one has four, one has two, some have none, and one has a ring.

9   Reality, in fact, is always something you couldn't have guessed. That's *one* of the reasons I believe Christianity. It's a religion you couldn't have guessed. If it offered us just the kind of universe we'd always expected, I'd feel we were making it up. But, in fact, it's not the sort of thing anyone would have made up. It has just that queer twist about it that real things have. So let's leave behind all these boys' philosophies—these over-simple answers. The problem isn't simple and the answer isn't going to be simple either.

10   What is the problem? A universe that contains much that is obviously bad and apparently meaningless, but containing creatures like ourselves who know that it is bad and meaningless. There are only two views that face all the facts. One is the Christian view that this is a good world that has gone wrong, but still retains the memory of what it ought to have been. The other is the view called Dualism. Dualism means the belief that there are two equal and independent powers at the back of everything, one of them good and the other bad, and that this universe is the battlefield in which they fight out an endless war. I personally think that next to Christianity Dualism is the manliest and most sensible creed on the market. But it has a catch in it.

11   The two powers, or spirits, or gods—the good one and the bad one—are supposed to be quite independent. They both existed from all eternity. Neither of them made the other, neither of them has any more right than the other to call itself God. Each presumably thinks it is good and thinks the other bad. One of them likes hatred and cruelty, the other likes love and mercy, and each backs its own view. Now what do we mean when we call one of them the Good Power and the other the Bad Power?

Either we're merely saying that we happen to prefer the one to the other —like preferring beer to cider—or else we're saying that, whatever *they* say about it, and whichever *we* happen to like, one of them is actually wrong, actually mistaken, in regarding itself as good. Now if we mean merely that we happen to prefer the first, then we must give up talking about good and evil at all. For good means what you ought to prefer quite regardless of what you happen to like at any given moment. If "being good" meant simply joining the side you happened to fancy, for no real reason, then good wouldn't *be* good. So we must mean that one of the two powers is actually wrong and the other actually right.

12   But the moment you say that, you are putting into the universe a third thing in addition to the two Powers: some law or standard or rule of good which one of the powers conforms to and the other fails to conform to. But since the two powers are judged by this standard, then this standard, or the being who made this standard, is farther back and higher up than either of them, and He will be the real God. In fact, what we meant by calling them good and bad turns out to be that one of them is in a right relation to the real ultimate God and the other in a wrong relation to Him.

13   The same point can be made in a different way. If Dualism is true, then the Bad Power must be a being who likes badness for its own sake. But in reality we have no experience of anyone liking badness just because it is bad. The nearest we can get to it is in cruelty. But in real life people are cruel for one of two reasons—either because they are sadists, that is, because they have a sexual perversion which makes cruelty a cause of sensual pleasure to them, or else for the sake of something they are going to get out of it—money, or power, or safety. But pleasure, money, power, and safety are all, as far as they go, good things. The badness consists in pursuing them by the wrong method, or in the wrong way, or too much. I don't mean, of course, that the people who do this aren't desperately wicked. I do mean that wickedness, when you examine it, turns out to be the pursuit of some good in the wrong way. You can be good for the mere sake of goodness: you can't be bad for the mere sake of badness. You can do a kind action when you're not feeling kind and when it gives you no pleasure, simply because kindness is right; but no one ever did a cruel action simply because cruelty is wrong—only because cruelty was pleasant or useful to him. In other words, badness can't succeed even in being bad *in the same way* in which goodness is good. Goodness is, so to speak, itself: badness is only spoiled goodness. And there must be something good first before it can be spoiled. We called Sadism a sexual perversion; but you must first have the idea of a normal sexuality before you can talk of it being perverted; and you can see which is the perversion, because you can explain the perverted from the normal, and can't explain the normal from

the perverted. It follows that the Bad Power, who is supposed to be on an equal footing with the Good Power, and to love badness in the same way as the good one loves goodness, is a mere bogey. In order to be bad he must have good things to want and then to pursue in the wrong way: he must have impulses which were originally good in order to be able to pervert them. But if he is bad he can't supply himself either with good things to desire or with good impulses to pervert. He must be getting both from the Good Power. And if so, then he is not independent. He is part of the Good Power's world: he was made either by the Good Power or by some power above them both.

14   Put it more simply still. To be bad, he must exist and have intelligence and will. But existence, intelligence, and will are in themselves good. Therefore he must be getting them from the Good Power: even to be bad he must borrow or steal from his opponent. And do you now begin to see why Christianity has always said that the devil is a fallen angel? That isn't a mere story for the children. It's a real recognition of the fact that evil is a parasite, not an original thing. The powers which enable evil to carry on are powers given it by goodness. All the things which enable a bad man to be effectively bad are in themselves good things—resolution, cleverness, good looks, existence itself. That's why Dualism, in a strict sense, won't work.

15   But I want to say that real Christianity (as distinct from Christianity-and-water) goes much nearer to Dualism than people think. One of the things that surprised me when I first read the New Testament seriously was that it was always talking about a Dark Power in the universe—a mighty evil spirit who was held to be the Power behind death and disease, and sin. The difference is that Christianity thinks this Dark Power was created by God, and was good when he was created, and went wrong. Christianity agrees with Dualism that this universe is at war. But it doesn't think this is a war between independent powers. It thinks it's a civil war, a rebellion, and that we are living in a part of the universe occupied by the rebel.

16   Enemy-occupied territory—that's what this world is. Christianity is the story of how the rightful king has landed, you might say landed in disguise, and is calling us all to take part in a great campaign of sabotage. When you go to church you're really listening in to the secret wireless from our friends: that's why the enemy is so anxious to prevent us going. He does it by playing on our conceit and laziness and intellectual snobbery. I know someone will ask me, "Do you really mean, at this time of day, to re-introduce our old friend the devil—hoofs and horns and all?" Well, what the time of day has to do with it I don't know. And I'm not particular about the hoofs and horns. But in other respects my answer is, "Yes, I do." I don't claim to know anything about his personal appearance.

If anybody really wants to know him better I'd say to that person, "Don't worry. If you really want to, you will. Whether you'll like it when you do is another question."

III

17   Christians, then, believe that an evil power has made himself for the present the Prince of this World. And, of course, that raises problems. Is this state of affairs in accordance with God's will or not? If it is, He's a strange God, you'll say: and if it isn't, how *can* anything happen contrary to the will of a being with absolute power?

18   But anyone who has been in authority knows how a thing can be in accordance with your will in one way and not in another. It may be quite sensible for a mother to say to the children, "I'm not going to go and make you tidy the school-room every night. You've got to learn to keep it tidy on your own." Then she goes up one night and finds the Teddy bear and the ink and the French Grammar all lying in the grate. That's against her will. She would prefer the children to be tidy. But on the other hand, it is her will which has left the children free to be untidy. The same thing arises in any regiment, or trades union, or school. You make a thing voluntary and then half the people don't do it. That isn't what you willed, but your will has made it possible.

19   It's probably the same in the universe. God created things which had free will. That means creatures which can go wrong *or* right. Some people think they can imagine a creature which was free but had no possibility of going wrong, but I can't. If a thing is free to be good it's also free to be bad. And free will is what has made evil possible. Why, then, did God give them free will? Because free will, though it makes evil possible, is also the only thing that makes possible any love or goodness or joy worth having. A world of automata—of creatures that worked like machines—would hardly be worth creating. The happiness which God designs for His higher creatures is the happiness of being freely, voluntarily united to Him and to each other in an ecstasy of love and delight compared with which the most rapturous love between a man and a woman on this earth is *mere milk and water*. And for that they've got to be free.

20   Of course God knew that would happen if they used their freedom the wrong way: apparently He thought it worth the risk. Perhaps we feel inclined to disagree with Him. But there's a difficulty about disagreeing with God. He is the source from which all your reasoning power comes: you couldn't be right and He wrong any more than a stream can rise higher than its own source. When you are arguing against Him you're

arguing against the very power that makes you able to argue at all: it's like cutting off the branch you're sitting on. If God thinks this state of war in the universe a price worth paying for free will—that is, for making a *real* world in which creatures can do real good or harm and something of real importance can happen, instead of a toy world which only moves when He pulls the strings—then we may take it it *is* worth paying.

21   When we've understood about free will, we shall see how silly it is to ask, as somebody once asked me: "Why did God make a creature of such rotten stuff that it went wrong?" The better stuff a creature is made of—the cleverer and stronger and freer it is—then the better it will be if it goes right, but also the worse it will be if it goes wrong. A cow can't be very good or very bad; a dog can be both better and worse; a child better and worse still; an ordinary man, still more so; a man of genius, still more so; a superhuman spirit best—or worst—of all.

22   How did the Dark Power go wrong? Well, the moment you have a self at all, there is a possibility of putting yourself first—wanting to be the centre—wanting to *be* God, in fact. That was the sin of Satan: and that was the sin he taught the human race. Some people think the fall of man had something to do with sex, but that's a mistake. What Satan put into the heads of our remote ancestors was the idea that they could "be like gods"—could set up on their own as if they had created themselves—be their own masters—invent some sort of happiness for themselves outside God, apart from God. And out of that hopeless attempt has come nearly all that we call human history—money, poverty, ambition, war, prostitution, classes, empires, slavery—the long terrible story of man trying to find something other than God which will make him happy.

23   The reason why it can never succeed is this. God made us: invented us as a man invents an engine. A car is made to run on petrol, and it won't run properly on anything else. Now God designed the human machine to run on Himself. He Himself is the fuel our spirits were designed to burn, or the food our spirits were designed to feed on. There isn't any other. That's why it's just no good asking God to make us happy in our own way without bothering about religion. God can't give us a happiness and peace apart from Himself, because it isn't there. There's no such thing.

24   That is the key to history. Terrific energy is expended—civilisations are built up—excellent institutions devised; but each time something goes wrong. Some fatal flaw always brings the selfish and cruel people to the top and it all slides back into misery and ruin. In fact, the machine konks. It seems to start up all right and runs a few yards, and then it breaks down. They're trying to run it on the wrong juice. That's what Satan has done to us humans.

25   And what did God do? First of all He left us conscience, the sense of right and wrong: and all through history there have been people trying (some of them very hard) to obey it. None of them ever quite succeeded.

Secondly, He sent the human race what I call good dreams: I mean those queer stories scattered all through the heathen religions about a god who dies and comes to life again and, by his death, has somehow given new life to men. Thirdly, He selected one particular people and spent several centuries hammering into their heads the sort of God He was—that there was only one of Him and that He cared about right conduct. Those people were the Jews, and the Old Testament gives an account of the hammering process.

26   Then comes the real shock. Among these Jews there suddenly turns up a man who goes about talking as if He was God. He claims to forgive sins. He says He has always existed. He says He is coming to judge the world at the end of time. Now let us get this clear. Among Pantheists, like the Indians, anyone might say that he was a part of God, or one with God: there'd be nothing very odd about it. But this man, since He was a Jew, couldn't mean that kind of God. God, in their language, meant the Being outside the world Who had made it and was infinitely different from anything else. And when you've grasped that, you will see that what this man said was, quite simply, the most shocking thing that has ever been uttered by human lips.

27   I'm trying here to prevent anyone from saying the really silly thing that people often say about Him: "I'm ready to accept Jesus as a great moral teacher, but I don't accept His claim to be God." That's the one thing we mustn't say. A man who was merely a man and said the sort of things Jesus said wouldn't be a great moral teacher. He'd either be a lunatic—on a level with the man who says he's a poached egg—or else he'd be the Devil of Hell. You must make your choice. Either this man was, and is, the Son of God; or else a madman or something worse. You can shut Him up for a fool; you can spit at Him and kill Him as a demon; or you can fall at His feet and call Him Lord and God. But don't let us come with any patronising nonsense about His being a great human teacher. He hasn't left that open to us. He didn't intend to.

Questions

1. Lewis' essay is a very tightly organized argument that utilizes several techniques of definition. What are these techniques?

2. Examine the first six paragraphs. Comment on Lewis' use of classification.

3. What linking devices does Lewis use and how appropriate are they to the classification technique?

4. In what sense does Lewis' definition of Christianity depend on his distinction between "the universe almost *is* God" and "God *made* the universe"?

5. After considering Lewis' initial distinctions, trace the development of his argument. Consider the last three sentences. What effect has the decreasing sentence length?

6. In Lewis' essay we have reached the opposite pole from Hayakawa's. Here we find connotation used heavily, and in such a fashion that the words seem almost paradoxical in the context in which they appear: for example, in paragraph 1 what meanings does Lewis attach to "liberal"? In what way does he use this word to point up a paradoxical difference between Christianity and atheism?

7. In paragraph 2, what justification is there for saying that "materialist" is a loaded word?

8. List the terms used by Lewis with a heavy burden of connotation and state what the connotations are in each case.

9. In paragraph 4, what functions does the word "damned" perform?

10. Although Lewis deals with very complex matters in his essay, he achieves deceptive simplicity in style and thought. Examine the entire essay in the light of this statement; point out the devices used by Lewis to produce simple assent to most complex propositions.

Theme topics

1. Using Lewis' techniques, write an essay in which you explain a belief or feeling of your own: for example, you might explain to those who condemn teenagers the real feelings of this group, or you might attempt to define your own religious feeling, or lack of it, or your political beliefs.

2. Write an essay on Lewis' article in which you analyze the slanting techniques, observe the lack of evidence, and attempt to justify these qualities.

4   JEAN-PAUL SARTRE

Existentialism

1   I should like on this occasion to defend existentialism against some charges which have been brought against it.

2   First, it has been charged with inviting people to remain in a kind of desperate quietism because, since no solutions are possible, we should have to consider action in this world as quite impossible. We should then end

From "The Humanism of Existentialism," *The Philosophy of Existentialism* (New York: Philosophical Library, 1965), pp. 31–50, 62. Reprinted by permission of Philosophical Library.

up in a philosophy of contemplation; and since contemplation is a luxury, we come in the end to a bourgeois philosophy. The communists in particular have made these charges.

3   On the other hand, we have been charged with dwelling on human degradation, with pointing up everywhere the sordid, shady, and slimy, and neglecting the gracious and beautiful, the bright side of human nature; for example, according to Mlle. Mercier, a Catholic critic, with forgetting the smile of the child. Both sides charge us with having ignored human solidarity, with considering man as an isolated being. The communists say that the main reason for this is that we take pure subjectivity, the Cartesian *I think,* as our starting point; in other words, the moment in which man becomes fully aware of what it means to him to be an isolated being; as a result, we are unable to return to a state of solidarity with the men who are not ourselves, a state which we can never reach in the *cogito.*

4   From the Christian standpoint, we are charged with denying the reality and seriousness of human undertakings, since, if we reject God's commandments and the eternal verities, there no longer remains anything but pure caprice, with everyone permitted to do as he pleases and incapable, from his own point of view, of condemning the points of view and acts of others.

5   I shall try today to answer these different charges. Many people are going to be surprised at what is said here about humanism. We shall try to see in what sense it is to be understood. In any case, what can be said from the very beginning is that by existentialism we mean a doctrine which makes human life possible and, in addition, declares that every truth and every action implies a human setting and a human subjectivity.

6   As is generally known, the basic charge against us is that we put the emphasis on the dark side of human life. Someone recently told me of a lady who, when she let slip a vulgar word in a moment of irritation, excused herself by saying, "I guess I'm becoming an existentialist." Consequently, existentialism is regarded as something ugly; that is why we are said to be naturalists; and if we are, it is rather surprising that in this day and age we cause so much more alarm and scandal than does naturalism, properly so called. The kind of person who can take in his stride such a novel as Zola's *The Earth* is disgusted as soon as he starts reading an existentialist novel; the kind of person who is resigned to the wisdom of the ages—which is pretty sad—finds us even sadder. Yet, what can be more disillusioning than saying "true charity begins at home" or "a scoundrel will always return evil for good"?

7   We know the commonplace remarks made when this subject comes up, remarks which always add up to the same thing: we shouldn't struggle against the powers-that-be; we shouldn't resist authority; we shouldn't try to rise above our station; any action which doesn't conform to authority is romantic; any effort not based on past experience is doomed to failure;

experience shows that man's bent is always toward trouble, that there must be a strong hand to hold him in check, if not, there will be anarchy. There are still people who go on mumbling these melancholy old saws, the people who say, "It's only human!" whenever a more or less repugnant act is pointed out to them, the people who glut themselves on *chansons réalistes;* these are the people who accuse existentialism of being too gloomy, and to such an extent that I wonder whether they are complaining about it, not for its pessimism, but much rather its optimism. Can it be that what really scares them in the doctrine I shall try to present here is that it leaves to man a possibility of choice? To answer this question, we must re-examine it on a strictly philosophical plane. What is meant by the term *existentialism?*

8   Most people who use the word would be rather embarrassed if they had to explain it, since, now that the word is all the rage, even the work of a musician or painter is being called existentialist. A gossip columnist in *Clartés* signs himself *The Existentialist,* so that by this time the word has been so stretched and has taken on so broad a meaning, that it no longer means anything at all. It seems that for want of an advance-guard doctrine analogous to surrealism, the kind of people who are eager for scandal and flurry turn to this philosophy which in other respects does not at all serve their purposes in this sphere.

9   Actually, it is the least scandalous, the most austere of doctrines. It is intended strictly for specialists and philosophers. Yet it can be defined easily. What complicates matters is that there are two kinds of existentialist; first, those who are Christian, among whom I would include Jaspers and Gabriel Marcel, both Catholic; and on the other hand the atheistic existentialists, among whom I class Heidegger, and then the French existentialists and myself. What they have in common is that they think that existence precedes essence, or, if you prefer, that subjectivity must be the starting point.

10   Just what does that mean? Let us consider some object that is manufactured, for example, a book or a paper-cutter: here is an object which has been made by an artisan whose inspiration came from a concept. He referred to the concept of what a papercutter is and likewise to a known method of production, which is part of the concept, something which is, by and large, a routine. Thus, the paper-cutter is at once an object produced in a certain way and, on the other hand, one having a specific use; and one can not postulate a man who produces a paper-cutter but does not know what it is used for. Therefore, let us say that, for the paper-cutter, essence—that is, the ensemble of both the production routines and the properties which enable it to be both produced and defined—precedes existence. Thus, the presence of the paper-cutter or book in front of me is determined. Therefore, we have here a technical view of the world whereby it can be said that production precedes existence.

11   When we conceive God as the Creator, He is generally thought of as a superior sort of artisan. Whatever doctrine we may be considering, whether one like that of Descartes or that of Leibnitz, we always grant that will more or less follows understanding or, at the very least, accompanies it, and that when God creates He knows exactly what He is creating. Thus, the concept of man in the mind of God is comparable to the concept of paper-cutter in the mind of the manufacturer, and, following certain techniques and a conception, God produces man, just as the artisan, following a definition and a technique, makes a paper-cutter. Thus, the individual man is the realisation of a certain concept in the divine intelligence.

12   In the eighteenth century, the atheism of the philosophers discarded the idea of God, but not so much for the notion that essence precedes existence. To a certain extent, this idea is found everywhere; we find it in Diderot, in Voltaire, and even in Kant. Man has a human nature; this human nature, which is the concept of the human, is found in all men, which means that each man is a particular example of a universal concept, man. In Kant, the result of this universality is that the wild-man, the natural man, as well as the bourgeois, are circumscribed by the same definition and have the same basic qualities. Thus, here too the essence of man precedes the historical existence that we find in nature.

13   Atheistic existentialism, which I represent, is more coherent. It states that if God does not exist, there is at least one being in whom existence precedes essence, a being who exists before he can be defined by any concept, and that this being is man, or, as Heidegger says, human reality. What is meant here by saying that existence precedes essence? It means that, first of all, man exists, turns up, appears on the scene, and, only afterwards, defines himself. If man, as the existentialist conceives him, is indefinable, it is because at first he is nothing. Only afterward will he be something, and he himself will have made what he will be. Thus, there is no human nature, since there is no God to conceive it. Not only is man what he conceives himself to be, but he is also only what he wills himself to be after this thrust toward existence.

14   Man is nothing else but what he makes of himself. Such is the first principle of existentialism. It is also what is called subjectivity, the name we are labeled with when charges are brought against us. But what do we mean by this, if not that man has a greater dignity than a stone or table? For we mean that man first exists, that is, that man first of all is the being who hurls himself toward a future and who is conscious of imagining himself as being in the future. Man is at the start a plan which is aware of itself, rather than a patch of moss, a piece of garbage, or a cauliflower; nothing exists prior to this plan; there is nothing in heaven; man will be what he will have planned to be. Not what he will want to be. Because by the word "will" we generally mean a conscious decision, which is subse-

quent to what we have already made of ourselves. I may want to belong to a political party, write a book, get married; but all that is only a manifestation of an earlier, more spontaneous choice that is called "will." But if existence really does precede essence, man is responsible for what he is. Thus, existentialism's first move is to make every man aware of what he is and to make the full responsibility of his existence rest on him. And when we say that a man is responsible for himself, we do not only mean that he is responsible for his own individuality, but that he is responsible for all men.

15   The word subjectivism has two meanings, and our opponents play on the two. Subjectivism means, on the one hand, that an individual chooses and makes himself; and, on the other, that it is impossible for man to transcend human subjectivity. The second of these is the essential meaning of existentialism. When we say that man chooses his own self, we mean that every one of us does likewise; but we also mean by that that in making this choice he also chooses all men. In fact, in creating the man that we want to be, there is not a single one of our acts which does not at the same time create an image of man as we think he ought to be. To choose to be this or that is to affirm at the same time the value of what we choose, because we can never choose evil. We always choose the good, and nothing can be good for us without being good for all.

16   If, on the other hand, existence precedes essence, and if we grant that we exist and fashion our image at one and the same time, the image is valid for everybody and for our whole age. Thus, our responsibility is much greater than we might have supposed, because it involves all mankind. If I am a workingman and choose to join a Christian trade-union rather than be a communist, and if by being a member I want to show that the best thing for man is resignation, that the kingdom of man is not of this world, I am not only involving my own case—I want to be resigned for everyone. As a result, my action has involved all humanity. To take a more individual matter, if I want to marry, to have children; even if this marriage depends solely on my own circumstances or passion or wish, I am involving all humanity in monogamy and not merely myself. Therefore, I am responsible for myself and for everyone else. I am creating a certain image of man of my own choosing. In choosing myself, I choose man.

17   This helps us understand what the actual content is of such rather grandiloquent words as anguish, forlornness, despair. As you will see, it's all quite simple.

18   First, what is meant by anguish? The existentialists say at once that man is anguish. What that means is this: the man who involves himself and who realizes that he is not only the person he chooses to be, but also a lawmaker who is, at the same time, choosing all mankind as well as himself, can not help escape the feeling of his total and deep responsibility. Of course, there are many people who are not anxious; but we claim that they

are hiding their anxiety, that they are fleeing from it. Certainly, many people believe that when they do something, they themselves are the only ones involved, and when someone says to them, "What if everyone acted that way?" they shrug their shoulders and answer, "Everyone doesn't act that way." But really, one should always ask himself, "What would happen if everybody looked at things that way?" There is no escaping this disturbing thought except by a kind of double-dealing. A man who lies and makes excuses for himself by saying "not everybody does that," is someone with an uneasy conscience, because the act of lying implies that a universal value is conferred upon the lie.

19   Anguish is evident even when it conceals itself. This is the anguish that Kierkegaard called the anguish of Abraham. You know the story: an angel has ordered Abraham to sacrifice his son; if it really were an angel who has come and said, "You are Abraham, you shall sacrifice your son," everything would be all right. But everyone might first wonder, "Is it really an angel, and am I really Abraham? What proof do I have?"

20   There was a madwoman who had hallucinations; someone used to speak to her on the telephone and give her orders. Her doctor asked her, "Who is it who talks to you?" She answered, "He says it's God." What proof did she really have that it was God? If an angel comes to me, what proof is there that it's an angel? And if I hear voices, what proof is there that they come from heaven and not from hell, or from the subconscious, or a pathological condition? What proves that they are addressed to me? What proof is there that I have been appointed to impose my choice and my conception of man on humanity? I'll never find any proof or sign to convince me of that. If a voice addresses me, it is always for me to decide that this is the angel's voice; if I consider that such an act is a good one, it is I who will choose to say that it is good rather than bad.

21   Now, I'm not being singled out as an Abraham, and yet at every moment I'm obliged to perform exemplary acts. For every man, everything happens as if all mankind had its eyes fixed on him and were guiding itself by what he does. And every man ought to say to himself, "Am I really the kind of man who has the right to act in such a way that humanity might guide itself by my actions?" And if he does not say that to himself, he is masking his anguish.

22   There is no question here of the kind of anguish which would lead to quietism, to inaction. It is a matter of a simple sort of anguish that anybody who has had responsibilities is familiar with. For example, when a military officer takes the responsibility for an attack and sends a certain number of men to death, he chooses to do so, and in the main he alone makes the choice. Doubtless, orders come from above, but they are too broad; he interprets them, and on this interpretation depend the lives of ten or fourteen or twenty men. In making a decision he can not help having a certain anguish. All leaders know this anguish. That doesn't keep them

from acting; on the contrary, it is the very condition of their action. For it implies that they envisage a number of possibilities, and when they choose one, they realize that it has value only because it is chosen. We shall see that this kind of anguish, which is the kind that existentialism describes, is explained, in addition, by a direct responsibility to the other men whom it involves. It is not a curtain separating us from action, but is part of action itself.

23   When we speak of forlornness, a term Heidegger was fond of, we mean only that God does not exist and that we have to face all the consequences of this. The existentialist is strongly opposed to a certain kind of secular ethics which would like to abolish God with the least possible expense. About 1880, some French teachers tried to set up a secular ethics which went something like this: God is a useless and costly hypothesis; we are discarding it; but, meanwhile, in order for there to be an ethics, a society, a civilization, it is essential that certain values be taken seriously and that they be considered as having an *a priori* existence. It must be obligatory, *a priori,* to be honest, not to lie, not to beat your wife, to have children, etc., etc. So we're going to try a little device which will make it possible to show that values exist all the same, inscribed in a heaven of ideas, though otherwise God does not exist. In other words—and this, I believe, is the tendency of everything called reformism in France—nothing will be changed if God does not exist. We shall find ourselves with the same norms of honesty, progress, and humanism, and we shall have made of God an outdated hypothesis which will peacefully die off by itself.

24   The existentialist, on the contrary, thinks it very distressing that God does not exist, because all possibility of finding values in a heaven of ideas disappears along with Him; there can no longer be an *a priori* Good, since there is no infinite and perfect consciousness to think it. Nowhere is it written that the Good exists, that we must be honest, that we must not lie; because the fact is we are on a plane where there are only men. Dostoevsky said, "If God didn't exist, everything would be possible." That is the very starting point of existentialism. Indeed, everything is permissible if God does not exist, and as a result man is forlorn, because neither within him nor without does he find anything to cling to. He can't start making excuses for himself.

25   If existence really does precede essence, there is no explaining things away by reference to a fixed and given human nature. In other words, there is no determinism, man is free, man is freedom. On the other hand, if God does not exist, we find no values or commands to turn to which legitimize our conduct. So, in the bright realm of values, we have no excuse behind us, nor justification before us. We are alone, with no excuses.

26   That is the idea I shall try to convey when I say that man is condemned to be free. Condemned, because he did not create himself, yet, in other respects is free; because, once thrown into the world, he is respon-

sible for everything he does. The existentialist does not believe in the power of passion. He will never agree that a sweeping passion is a ravaging torrent which fatally leads a man to certain acts and is therefore an excuse. He thinks that man is responsible for his passion.

27   The existentialist does not think that man is going to help himself by finding in the world some omen by which to orient himself. Because he thinks that man will interpret the omen to suit himself. Therefore, he thinks that man, with no support and no aid, is condemned every moment to invent man. Ponge, in a very fine article, has said, "Man is the future of man." That's exactly it. But if it is taken to mean that this future is recorded in heaven, that God sees it, then it is false, because it would really no longer be a future. If it is taken to mean that, whatever a man may be, there is a future to be forged, a virgin future before him, then this remark is sound. But then we are forlorn.

28   To give you an example which will enable you to understand forlorn-ness better, I shall cite the case of one of my students who came to see me under the following circumstances: his father was on bad terms with his mother, and, moreover, was inclined to be a collaborationist; his older brother had been killed in the German offensive of 1940, and the young man, with somewhat immature but generous feelings, wanted to avenge him. His mother lived alone with him, very much upset by the half-treason of her husband and the death of her older son; the boy was her only consolation.

29   The boy was faced with the choice of leaving for England and joining the Free French Forces—that is, leaving his mother behind—or remaining with his mother and helping her to carry on. He was fully aware that the woman lived only for him and that his going-off—and perhaps his death—would plunge her into despair. He was also aware that every act that he did for his mother's sake was a sure thing, in the sense that it was helping her to carry on, whereas every effort he made toward going off and fighting was an uncertain move which might run aground and prove completely useless; for example, on his way to England he might, while passing through Spain, be detained indefinitely in a Spanish camp; he might reach England or Algiers and be stuck in an office at a desk job. As a result, he was faced with two very different kinds of action: one, concrete, imme-diate, but concerning only one individual; the other concerned an incom-parably vaster group, a national collectivity, but for that very reason was dubious, and might be interrupted en route. And, at the same time, he was wavering between two kinds of ethics. On the one hand, an ethics of sym-pathy, of personal devotion; on the other, a broader ethics, but one whose efficacy was more dubious. He had to choose between the two.

30   Who could help him choose? Christian doctrine? No. Christian doc-trine says, "Be charitable, love your neighbor, take the more rugged path, etc., etc." But which is the more rugged path? Whom should he love as a

brother? The fighting man or his mother? Which does the greater good, the vague act of fighting in a group, or the concrete one of helping a particular human being to go on living? Who can decide *a priori?* Nobody. No book of ethics can tell him. The Kantian ethics says, "Never treat any person as a means, but as an end." Very well, if I stay with my mother, I'll treat her as an end and not as a means; but by virtue of this very fact, I'm running the risk of treating the people around me who are fighting, as means; and, conversely, if I go to join those who are fighting, I'll be treating them as an end, and, by doing that, I run the risk of treating my mother as a means.

31   If values are vague, and if they are always too broad for the concrete and specific case that we are considering, the only thing left for us is to trust our instincts. That's what this young man tried to do; and when I saw him, he said, "In the end, feeling is what counts. I ought to choose whichever pushes me in one direction. If I feel that I love my mother enough to sacrifice everything else for her—my desire for vengeance, for action, for adventure—then I'll stay with her. If, on the contrary, I feel that my love for my mother isn't enough, I'll leave."

32   But how is the value of a feeling determined? What gives his feeling for his mother value? Precisely the fact that he remained with her. I may say that I like so-and-so well enough to sacrifice a certain amount of money for him, but I may say so only if I've done it. I may say "I love my mother well enough to remain with her" if I have remained with her. The only way to determine the value of this affection is, precisely, to perform an act which confirms and defines it. But, since I require this affection to justify my act, I find myself caught in a vicious circle.

33   On the other hand, Gide has well said that a mock feeling and a true feeling are almost indistinguishable; to decide that I love my mother and will remain with her, or to remain with her by putting on an act, amount somewhat to the same thing. In other words, the feeling is formed by the acts one performs; so, I can not refer to it in order to act upon it. Which means that I can neither seek within myself the true condition which will impel me to act, nor apply to a system of ethics for concepts which will permit me to act. You will say, "At least, he did go to a teacher for advice." But if you seek advice from a priest, for example, you have chosen this priest; you already knew, more or less, just about what advice he was going to give you. In other words, choosing your adviser is involving yourself. The proof of this is that if you are a Christian, you will say, "Consult a priest." But some priests are collaborating, some are just marking time, some are resisting. Which to choose? If the young man chooses a priest who is resisting or collaborating, he has already decided on the kind of advice he's going to get. Therefore, in coming to see me he knew the answer I was going to give him, and I had only one answer to give: "You're free, choose, that is, invent." No general ethics can show you

what is to be done; there are no omens in the world. The Catholics will reply, "But there are." Granted—but, in any case, I myself choose the meaning they have.

34   When I was a prisoner, I knew a rather remarkable young man who was a Jesuit. He had entered the Jesuit order in the following way: he had had a number of very bad breaks; in childhood, his father died, leaving him in poverty, and he was a scholarship student at a religious institution where he was constantly made to feel that he was being kept out of charity; then, he failed to get any of the honors and distinctions that children like; later on, at about eighteen, he bungled a love affair; finally, at twenty-two, he failed in military training, a childish enough matter, but it was the last straw.

35   This young fellow might well have felt that he had botched everything. It was a sign of something, but of what? He might have taken refuge in bitterness or despair. But he very wisely looked upon all this as a sign that he was not made for secular triumphs, and that only the triumphs of religion, holiness, and faith were open to him. He saw the hand of God in all this, and so he entered the order. Who can help seeing that he alone decided what the sign meant?

36   Some other interpretation might have been drawn from this series of setbacks; for example, that he might have done better to turn carpenter or revolutionist. Therefore, he is fully responsible for the interpretation. Forlornness implies that we ourselves choose our being. Forlornness and anguish go together.

37   As for despair, the term has a very simple meaning. It means that we shall confine ourselves to reckoning only with what depends upon our will, or on the ensemble of probabilities which make our action possible. When we want something, we always have to reckon with probabilities. I may be counting on the arrival of a friend. The friend is coming by rail or streetcar; this supposes that the train will arrive on schedule, or that the streetcar will not jump the track. I am left in the realm of possibility; but possibilities are to be reckoned with only to the point where my action comports with the ensemble of these possibilities, and no further. The moment the possibilities I am considering are not rigorously involved by my action, I ought to disengage myself from them, because no God, no scheme, can adapt the world and its possibilities to my will. When Descartes said, "Conquer yourself rather than the world," he meant essentially the same thing.

38   The Marxists to whom I have spoken reply, "You can rely on the support of others in your action, which obviously has certain limits because you're not going to live forever. That means: rely on both what others are doing elsewhere to help you, in China, in Russia, and what they will do later on, after your death, to carry on the action and lead it to its fulfillment, which will be the revolution. You even *have* to rely upon that, otherwise you're immoral." I reply at once that I will always rely on

fellow-fighters insofar as these comrades are involved with me in a common struggle, in the unity of a party or a group in which I can more or less make my weight felt; that is, one whose ranks I am in as a fighter and whose movements I am aware of at every moment. In such a situation, relying on the unity and will of the party is exactly like counting on the fact that the train will arrive on time or that the car won't jump the track. But, given that man is free and that there is no human nature for me to depend on, I can not count on men whom I do not know by relying on human goodness or man's concern for the good of society. I don't know what will become of the Russian revolution; I may make an example of it to the extent that at the present time it is apparent that the proletariat plays a part in Russia that it plays in no other nation. But I can't swear that this will inevitably lead to a triumph of the proletariat. I've got to limit myself to what I see.

39 Given that men are free and that tomorrow they will freely decide what man will be, I can not be sure that, after my death, fellow-fighters will carry on my work to bring it to its maximum perfection. Tomorrow, after my death, some men may decide to set up Fascism, and the others may be cowardly and muddled enough to let them do it. Fascism will then be the human reality, so much the worse for us.

40 Actually, things will be as man will have decided they are to be. Does that mean that I should abandon myself to quietism? No. First, I should involve myself; then, act on the old saw, "Nothing ventured, nothing gained." Nor does it mean that I shouldn't belong to a party, but rather that I shall have no illusions and shall do what I can. For example, suppose I ask myself, "Will socialization, as such, ever come about?" I know nothing about it. All I know is that I'm going to do everything in my power to bring it about. Beyond that, I can't count on anything. Quietism is the attitude of people who say, "Let others do what I can't do." The doctrine I am presenting is the very opposite of quietism, since it declares, "There is no reality except in action." Moreover, it goes further, since it adds, "Man is nothing else than his plan; he exists only to the extent that he fulfills himself; he is therefore nothing else than the ensemble of his acts, nothing else than his life."

41 According to this, we can understand why our doctrine horrifies certain people. Because often the only way they can bear their wretchedness is to think, "Circumstances have been against me. What I've been and done doesn't show my true worth. To be sure, I've had no great love, no great friendship, but that's because I haven't met a man or woman who was worthy. The books I've written haven't been very good because I haven't had the proper leisure. I haven't had children to devote myself to because I didn't find a man with whom I could have spent my life. So there remains within me, unused and quite viable, a host of propensities, inclinations, possibilities, that one wouldn't guess from the mere series of things I've done."

42   Now, for the existentialist there is really no love other than one which manifests itself in a person's being in love. There is no genius other than one which is expressed in works of art; the genius of Proust is the sum of Proust's works; the genius of Racine is his series of tragedies. Outside of that, there is nothing. Why say that Racine could have written another tragedy, when he didn't write it? A man is involved in life, leaves his impress on it, and outside of that there is nothing. To be sure, this may seem a harsh thought to someone whose life hasn't been a success. But, on the other hand, it prompts people to understand that reality alone is what counts, that dreams, expectations, and hopes warrant no more than to define a man as a disappointed dream, as miscarried hopes, as vain expectations. In other words, to define him negatively and not positively. However, when we say, "You are nothing else than your life," that does not imply that the artist will be judged solely on the basis of his works of art; a thousand other things will contribute toward summing him up. What we mean is that a man is nothing else than a series of undertakings, that he is the sum, the organization, the ensemble of the relationships which make up these undertakings.

43   When all is said and done, what we are accused of, at bottom, is not our pessimism, but an optimistic toughness. If people throw up to us our works of fiction in which we write about people who are soft, weak, cowardly, and sometimes even downright bad, it's not because these people are soft, weak, cowardly, or bad; because if we were to say, as Zola did, that they are that way because of heredity, the workings of environment, society, because of biological or psychological determinism, people would be reassured. They would say, "Well, that's what we're like, no one can do anything about it." But when the existentialist writes about a coward, he says that this coward is responsible for his cowardice. He's not like that because he has a cowardly heart or lung or brain; he's not like that on account of his physiological make-up; but he's like that because he has made himself a coward by his acts. There's no such thing as a cowardly constitution; there are nervous constitutions; there is poor blood, as the common people say, or strong constitutions. But the man whose blood is poor is not a coward on that account, for what makes cowardice is the act of renouncing or yielding. A constitution is not an act; the coward is defined on the basis of the acts he performs. People feel, in a vague sort of way, that this coward we're talking about is guilty of being a coward, and the thought frightens them. What people would like is that a coward or a hero be born that way.

44   One of the complaints most frequently made about *The Ways of Freedom* [1] can be summed up as follows: "After all, these people are so

---

[1] *Les Chemins de la Liberté,* M. Sartre's projected trilogy of novels, two of which, *L'Age de Raison* (*The Age of Reason*) and *Le Sursis* (*The Reprieve*) have already appeared.—Translator's note.

spineless, how are you going to make heroes out of them?" This objection almost makes me laugh, for it assumes that people are born heroes. That's what people really want to think. If you're born cowardly, you may set your mind perfectly at rest; there's nothing you can do about it; you'll be cowardly all your life, whatever you may do. If you're born a hero, you may set your mind just as much at rest; you'll be a hero all your life; you'll drink like a hero and eat like a hero. What the existentialist says is that the coward makes himself cowardly, that the hero makes himself heroic. There's always a possibility for the coward not to be cowardly any more and for the hero to stop being heroic. What counts is total involvement; some one particular action or set of circumstances is not total involvement. . . .

45   From these few reflections it is evident that nothing is more unjust than the objections that have been raised against us. Existentialism is nothing else than an attempt to draw all the consequences of a coherent atheistic position. It isn't trying to plunge man into despair at all. But if one calls every attitude of unbelief despair, like the Christians, then the word is not being used in its original sense. Existentialism isn't so atheistic that it wears itself out showing that God doesn't exist. Rather, it declares that even if God did exist, that would change nothing. There you've got our point of view. Not that we believe that God exists, but we think that the problem of His existence is not the issue. In this sense existentialism is optimistic, a doctrine of action, and it is plain dishonesty for Christians to make no distinction between their own despair and ours and then to call us despairing.

Questions

1. What evidence is there that Sartre's purpose is not merely to define but also to defend existentialism? Against what charges?
2. By what method of definition does Sartre begin in the opening paragraphs?
3. Paragraphs 6 and 7 suggest an attitude that Sartre discounts as pessimistic. Why is it pessimistic? Why is the alternative of the existential attitude optimistic?
4. By what method of definition is paragraph 9 developed? Paragraphs 10 and 11?
5. What technique of definition does Sartre begin to develop from paragraph 17 on?
6. What essential differences can you locate from paragraph 13 on between existentialism as defined by Sartre and Christianity as defined by C. S. Lewis? See particularly paragraphs 24 and 45 of Sartre's essay.
7. In paragraph 31 Sartre says that since values are vague the only thing left is to trust our instincts, and many people oppose existentialism on the basis

that it provides too much freedom for man's instinct. How does Sartre's development partially answer the objection? To what extent are our instincts themselves partly determined by traditional values?

Theme topics

1. Write a theme in which you develop the difference between the belief of Christians as defined by C. S. Lewis and that of Sartre as defined here. What is the critical point of difference and what effect does it have?
2. Write an essay developing a critical or defensive definition of some such term as atheist, liberal, conservative, radical, socialist, reactionary.
3. Just as Sartre begins by isolating and dismissing misconceptions, write a definition in which you begin by eliminating misconceptions. You might define a word like "love" or a term like "the intellectual" or "the artist"; you might define defensively or critically any one of the sub-cultures of American youth; or you might characterize a national group like the Irish, the Italians, Puerto Ricans, German-Americans, etc.

5   DONALD B. GIBSON

The Negro: An Essay on Definition

1   When Robert Penn Warren interviews James Baldwin in *Who Speaks for the Negro?* Warren asks a question about the responsibility of the Negro. Baldwin replies initially that he isn't sure what a Negro is. Warren characterizes Baldwin's response as a "tendency to undercut a specific issue and plunge into the shadowy depth." Baldwin's reply, as Warren saw it, could quickly become an academic or even metaphysical problem and therefore of limited relevance to his book. At the same time, however, Warren, as he admits, was wrong. Too few, black and white, liberal and conservative, have asked the question—what is a Negro?—from any perspective whatever; and those who have asked it have not usually questioned the assumption underlying the question itself, the assumption that there exists in reality (rather than metaphorically) a concrete entity described by the term "Negro."

2   Now, I do not wish to argue that there is no such thing as a Negro. Rather, I wish to argue that the assumption of the existence of a clearly

From *The Yale Review,* 57 (March, 1968) 337–345. Copyright Yale University 1968. Reprinted by permission of Yale University.

definable "Negro" group, as necessary and useful as it may be to the sociologist, has traditionally been and remains one of the major hindrances to understanding of and communication about the problem of race. It is a mistake to assume that there exists a group of people called "Negro" who possess those characteristics of a cultural nature which all other non-native minority groups have had. The implications of this proposition explain a great deal about the people called "Negro" in America and point to the un-realized complexity of the racial problem.

3   The present cultural circumstances of the Negro have their roots in the very beginning of his unsought association with America. From the start the groups of Africans transported to America were treated in such a way as to discourage either the continuation of old cultural habits or the establishment of new ones strong enough to replace the old. Though prac-tically all slaves were from West Africa, they came from different areas tribal groups, spoke different languages, and observed different customs and mores. Those who spoke a common language, possessed a common religion or body of mythology, and honored a common system of institu-tions were separated in order better to assure compliance in the new en-vironment. Those cultural elements responsible for the internal cohesion of any ethnic group were consciously eliminated by slave traders and slave masters.

4   In point of culture it is clear that the African group differed from all other non-native groups whose native cultures have been more continuous in the American environment. Even if we take into account elements of the African cultural past which have been retained, the fact remains that there does not exist a discrete Negro culture separable in any meaningful degree from the larger American culture. Among Negroes there does not exist, nor has there ever existed, a common language, religion, or mythology, nor a common habit of social interaction. This is to say that though the black man has been enough a part of the American environment to absorb the basic elements of the dominant culture, he has not been separate enough to develop a discrete culture.

5   The fact of the cultural situation of the Negro has many practical ramifications. For example, confusion and lack of communication occurs when people try to think or talk about race and at the same time assume that a Negro-American stands in the same relation to an ethnic group as does an Irish-American or Italian-American individual. Clearly he doesn't.

6   Lacking his own institutions, lacking those basic elements of a culture which allow other groups a firm sense of group identity, the Negro forms a far more diverse element of the population than any other group. Negroes are Negroes primarily because of the definitions applied by the society; therefore, any cohesiveness which the group has or can have is the result of defense against the white aggressor. Other ethnic groups possessing a common language, religion, or mythology, and common habits of social

interaction feel an inner cohesiveness stemming from an internalized system of values. Negroes, on the other hand, only feel a defensive, externally motivated sense of group identity.

7   This explains why Negroes have not been able to emulate the Jewish population, for example, who traditionally have united in order to defend themselves against a hostile majority. Certainly the Jewish people throughout history have had to unite defensively against aggression, but the difference is that the Jews over the centuries developed strong internal links, especially of a religious character, which served to give the group cohesiveness beyond the necessities imposed by external conditions.

8   Jews were never separated from their past in the way Negroes were. The history of the Negro was cut off when he was loaded on ships and brought to America and his past was erased from his memory. At best the Negro can salvage a knowledge of his recent past in America; Jews have records of a past extending far back into antiquity, a past which has been kept alive and an integral part of the Jewish cultural heritage. There is no mode of religious thought and experience among Negroes comparable to Judaism, no mythology comparable to the mythologies which exist in any discrete culture.

9   And finally, language was an important factor which allowed greater cohesion among Jews in America. Though Yiddish was technically not a language, for all practical purposes it was, because in the American environment it differed significantly from the language of the majority. Of course there was never a time when all American Jews spoke Yiddish, yet it was a greater source of internal cohesiveness than Negro dialect, which was never far removed from Southern dialect and from the American language of the majority.

10   The fact that the Negro group is not culturally monolithic also bears on the relation between the middle-class and lower-class Negroes. Recent attention has been focused on the tendency of the Negro middle class to desert the lower classes once middle-class status has been gained, a phenomenon long ago recognized by Negroes themselves. The Negro middle class has been taken to task for not recognizing its responsibility to the less fortunate Negro. Traditionally, even civil rights groups have been concerned with enlisting middle-class Negroes into their ranks while neglecting and even disparaging alliances with the lower classes. The reasons for the existence of this relationship become obvious when the matter is viewed from the perspective outlined here.

11   In actuality, the attitude of the middle-class Negro does not differ greatly from the attitude of the majority of the middle class toward the lower class. Those who would expect him to act otherwise are simply not aware that the cultural ties which would allow him to reach back and help those he left behind do not exist. He has no cultural basis for feeling united to the lower class. Indeed, the only basis for his feeling identification

with the lower class is that stemming from the mutual need for defense against a threatening white society.

12   For this reason, the militant civil rights groups attempt to appeal to the middle-class Negro by reminding him of the forces arrayed against him and of the resulting need for mutual defense. If there were internal cohesiveness within the group, there would be a basis for appeal in terms other than defensive ones. As things presently are, the Negro middle class will continue to be a group unto itself as long as the need for defense grows no greater. It is therefore meaningless to berate the Negro middle class for failure to exercise a responsibility which it has no cultural basis for recognizing.

13   Given the diverse character of the Negro group, it is no wonder that for years Negroes have bemoaned the lack of unity within, even among those in the same or similar economic circumstances. Today, despite the greater appearance of unity than ever before, the cultural makeup of the group legislates against the type of unified thought and action which could take adequate steps toward alleviating the plight of the group in any but the most long-range terms. Unity to the degree achieved by the National Association for the Advancement of Colored People and the Student Nonviolent Coordinating Committee is at best difficult to achieve. Powerful and effective as these groups are, they involve a very small percentage of the Negro population.

14   To be convinced of the diversity of thought and feeling among the Negro group, one need only assess attitudes among Negroes toward the notion of black power. First of all, there is no more agreement about its meaning among Negroes than there seems to be among whites. And further, there is as much fear, among Negroes, of the term and of its possible implications as there apparently is among the majority of the population. This is evidenced by the large numbers of Negroes of all classes who have publicly repudiated the concept. If the Negro group were monolithic, as it is assumed to be by the majority, and if Negroes interpreted black power as most whites seem to feel it should be interpreted, there might be more justifiable cause for fear of violence than there presently is. The only ground for fear lies in the strength of the white backlash and the withdrawal of sympathy for the Negro's cause by white "liberals." If these actions force Negroes to assume a more defensive posture—thereby uniting the group—then there could be cause for offensive action beyond throwing Coke bottles through the windows of shoeshine parlors.

15   The cultural situation of the Negro has resulted in severe problems of social identity. Though many in the society feel problems of identity, the problem of the Negro is more acute, for his difficulty with identity exists on a more basic plane. There are ways which the most disenchanted white, by virtue of his color alone, can identify with the majority culture which are not available to Negroes.

16   However, larger and larger numbers of Negroes are trying in various ways to solve the problem of social identity by relating to ideals and values different from those embodied in the rejecting culture. The attempt, which is also an effort on the part of many to bring about internal cohesion within the group, has taken many forms. The most full-scale attempt exists among the Black Muslims, who have managed to create internal cohesion within their group primarily by means of religion. The group has its own mythology and instills new habits of life and thought, of custom and manners into its converts. Such a movement could never have existed had there been a culture in the sense that I have defined it with which Negroes could identify.

17   The white majority has only itself to blame for the existence of such a group. It came about entirely as a result of a need for defense in a hostile environment and a need for social identity in a society that withholds it.

18   It is of significance that the Muslims have chosen alien cultural symbols as their basis for union, and that these alien ideas of thought and conduct could come to exist in viable form. The reasons that the group looked to the Middle East for its basis of union underscores the point I am making here: symbols indicating the existence of a monolithic Negro culture do not exist presently in the American environment.

19   Others have looked to Africa for the solution of the problem of social and cultural identity. Not too long ago a Negro might insult another by likening him to an African. Now the reverse is frequently true. Many Negroes look proudly toward Africa, studying its history and culture, buying African art objects. Some groups have gone so far as to adopt certain African native dress in an attempt to identify with an old, established culture.

20   Others have taken elements they feel to be characteristic of the Negro group and attempted to create a culture from these. Many feel positively toward blackness of skin and no longer attach the stigma to it which Negroes previously have done in emulating the ideals of the majority. Fewer Negro men use hair straighteners and some Negro women have begun to wear their hair unstraightened. Some Negroes, even educated ones, prefer to use Negro slang and dialect because they feel it is more theirs than standard American English.

21   The study of Negro literature and history is probably wider in scope and greater in depth than ever before within the Negro group. Many who do not usually read are beginning to read books by and about Negroes in the present and in the past. Some school libraries, often at the insistence of Negro parents, have begun to shelve books having to do with Negroes. All this has come about in an attempt to foster a viable culture.

22   The assumption of a monolithic Negro culture and the consequent lack of awareness of the heterogeneity of the group have been responsible

for the existence of what I call the "myth of the race leader." Since the nineteenth century, whites have assumed that if they wanted to know anything about Negroes or to communicate with Negroes, they need only contact a "leader." For years during the late nineteenth and well into the twentieth century, Booker T. Washington was considered *the* Negro leader. Anyone who wanted to know what the Negro thought about anything needed only to ask Booker T. He had the ear of presidents and millionaire philanthropists and was considered by the majority of whites as one who spoke for the Negro. Even he felt so, despite the fact that he could hardly have done so given his own personal interests, limitations, and philosophy.

23   Since that time there has grown up a myth of the Negro leader, of a Negro who may not only speak to the country of affairs concerning the Negro, but is at the same time one who wields power and authority over a homogeneous following. Presidents have frequently met with "leaders" (successful middle-class Negroes) for talks about the Negro question in the same way that they might meet with leaders of foreign countries. The myth of the Negro leader is so deeply embedded in the thinking of the majority that any Negro who leads any organization of Negroes will be referred to by the press as a Negro leader.

24   If the Negro population is as diverse as I have said, it stands to reason that there cannot be any person who will unite even a simple majority into one group. Hence the absurdity of the notion that there are Negro leaders who may speak for the Negro in the same sense that leaders of countries, communities, or religious sects may speak for their citizens or congregations. Only one of the people whom the newspapers designate "leader" (Roy Wilkins of the NAACP) leads as many as a half million people—a small percentage of the twenty-two millions who, according to census figures, live in the United States.

25   The myth of the Negro leader was responsible for Mayor Wagner's calling Martin Luther King during the Harlem riot of 1964. The mayor assumed that since King is indeed a leader of Negroes and the problem at hand involved Negroes, the man could aid in the solution of his problem. Had Wagner recognized the cultural diversity existing among Negroes, he would have known that Dr. King's influence and prestige would not necessarily be effective in that particular slum environment at that particular time. He was probably shocked and puzzled by the hostile reception which Harlemites gave Dr. King.

26   The same faulty thinking which prompted Mayor Wagner to call in Dr. King also prompted President Johnson last summer to urge Negroes to stop rioting in the streets. The President might have saved his breath, for the people rioting were not listening to the speech and could not have cared less about his admonition. But the President was not talking to the microscopically small minority who were throwing rocks and Molotov cocktails. Mr. Johnson was talking to *the* Negro and assuming that *the*

Negro is an entity which can be addressed and influenced as such. If he assumed that the "responsible" Negro community was listening and would exert influence on the violent few, then he was simply being naive, for the relationship between the "responsible" and "irresponsible" is more complex than he might think. But Mr. Johnson was being no more naive than those mayors and governors of places where riots have occurred who have immediately appealed to the "responsible Negro community," the "leaders," in order to control rioting.

27   These are some of the implications of the fact that there exists no discrete, monolithic Negro culture. The major problem emerging from this consideration is that the racial problem is far more complex than most know or are willing publicly to admit. Perhaps, however, I underestimate the thinking behind, for example, the poverty program, which could well be based upon some of the observations made here. That is, is it an accident that one effect of the poverty program is to give jobs to Negroes who are middle class in background or orientation? Is it an accident that giving jobs to these people brings them enough into the mainstream so as to reduce their need for defensive cohesiveness and thus assure that Negroes of the middle and lower classes will not form a single bloc? I do not know the answer to this question.

28   What I've said so far should also reveal the relevance of Baldwin's statement that he isn't sure what a Negro is. What indeed is a Negro? Seen from the perspective I suggest here, the question is not merely an academic one; it has extremely practical ramifications. Most people believe they know what "Negro" means, but I do not know, and I speak from inside. As long as most of us assume that "Negro" implies some kind of discrete identity, understanding is impossible. At the same time, the possibility of the majority of people's recognizing the diversity of the Negro group is dim. At best some may be able to realize and accept the limited reality of the general conception of "Negro," and understand the extent to which it is a kind of metaphor, a poetic expression. Until, however, those talking and thinking about the problem recognize the facts, any kind of meaningful progress toward full solution is unlikely.

Comparing and Contrasting

Comparison, contrast, and analogy

In everyday writing or conversation, nothing is more common than such statements as "How like his father Charlie is," "Utopia State Teachers is certainly no Harvard," "She's really an all-American girl." These statements exemplify the techniques of comparing and contrasting. Their purpose is to make a vivid comment or to clarify a position by drawing our attention to similarities or dissimilarities that exist between an object presently under scrutiny and others with which we are already familiar. All three of the examples here presuppose a knowledge of the referent—Charlie's father, Harvard, the all-American girl. Neither of these two comparisons nor the single contrast is fully elucidated. Indeed, a given act of comparison or contrast is seldom complete and may frequently be indirect. The writer generally presupposes some knowledge on the part of his reader. For the same reason one rarely thinks or talks in perfect syllogisms. Something is generally implied or omitted.

Comparing and contrasting are almost always concerned either with arguing or illustrating a point of view, a position, a subject. The important thing is the core of the illustration; the peripheral implications are brushed aside. Suppose we want to show the differences between two students; both are "A" caliber, but one is plodding, uninspired and methodical, while the other is brilliant and intuitive but erratic. Here our interest lies in the differences. The fact that both are "A" students, both twenty, both male, both juniors (all facts dear to the hearts of pollsters)—all this is, for the moment, irrelevant. On the other hand, suppose we should wish to compare society in the United States with that of the Roman Empire during its decline and fall. Our purpose would be to stress the supposed decadence of the United States, the point of comparison being that it too is now moving toward dissolution. For this purpose we would ignore the many differences: that our economy is not based on slavery, that our senators have not assassinated a head of state, that our agricultural problems arise not from scarcity but abundance, that a millennium and a half lies between ourselves and ancient Rome. A person searching for similarities would have either to ignore such differences or to declare them irrelevant.

Comparing our condition with that of the citizens of imperial Rome may lead, if one is ready to dismiss substantive differences between the two, to false analogy. A dazzling inventory of likenesses and complete silence about dissimilarities or firm declarations of their insignificance, will not alter the case. Here the differences between the two societies are so substantive that they create a difference in kind rather than in degree. And the process of comparing and contrasting, if its end is not simply that of the mind at play for its own sake, must be between entities that exhibit real kinship, between things of the same class (A:B::A':B'). Analogy emphasizes resemblances between things of different classes (A:B::C:D) and, when true, does not insist upon resemblances at the expense of dismissing or hiding unlikenesses.

Unlike the prose writer, whose aim is unequivocal meaning, the poet uses concrete terms analogically in the form of similes ("His folks/Pursue their lives like toy trains on a track") and metaphors, explicit or implicit ("My vegetable Love should grow"). In the hands of a good poet words and their values, denotative as well as connotative, can achieve immediacy and evocation, precision and ambiguity, simultaneously. The vision of a nation and its government as "a ship of state," for example, may possess immediacy and precision in its first poetic appearance and serve as a point of departure for generations of cartoonists. To the prose writer, however, the implied identifications in this or in other poetic figures of speech may be wearisome and unfortunate, certainly in his own struggle for immediacy and precision. Who or what is the rudder? The foremast? The anchor? Or even the atomic pile?

The above considerations lead to certain conclusions about the effective use of the principle of comparison and contrast. You should:

1. Compare things of the same class.
2. Be clear and distinct in your own mind about the purpose for which the comparing is being done.
3. Deal with meaningful details of contrast, not with obvious but irrelevant ones.
4. Establish the basis upon which two things are comparable before proceeding to make your point, whether your point is that one is preferable or that what happened in one case may occur in the other.
5. Work for details that are accurate, ones that you can endow with meaning and, if possible, ones that also have a force and a color of their own.

In the essays that follow various techniques of comparison and contrast are illustrated, each conditioned by the author's purpose. Sartre uses implied contrast in distinguishing New York from European cities, and

2. Write an essay in which you show how the physical conditions and the history of a place have conditioned the habits and beliefs of the people living there.

7 ALISTAIR COOKE

New York, New York

1 An English novelist came through New York a little time ago and, as all travellers must, brooded awhile about our ways. When he got home he did a radio talk about it. Nothing more would have been heard about it if the script of this talk had not been reprinted in the *New York Times*. It was no sooner out than the ambulances were summoned to handle a rush of high-blood-pressure cases, and the mail-trucks dumped bags of protests on the *New York Times*. From these outcries you would never have guessed that Mr. Priestley had just been a delegate to the United Nations Educational, Scientific and Cultural Organization, and that he was a man chosen to spread light and understanding among us.

2 Too bad, said Mr. Priestley, that New York's skyscrapers are not dedicated 'to God or to some noble aspect of communal life' but only to 'buying and selling dividends.' 'Is that so?' asked one correspondent. 'Then let me tell him that the American Bible Society, the American Association of Social Workers, the American Cancer Society, the Medical Society of New York and the British Information Services, to name only a few,' don't buy or sell dividends. Mr. Rockefeller of course might plead guilty, but his conviction would carry the reminder that his skill in these things helped to cure a lot of dysentery and scurvy in tropical places and helped a lot of Englishmen to come to the United States and have the leisure, after their work with microscopes, to share some of Mr. Priestley's feelings about New York. Mr. Priestley conceded that this was 'just a passing thought.'

3 'It hardly seems worth while holding on to,' snapped this New Yorker.

4 As for the dismal state of the drama in these parts our man referred Mr. Priestley to the theatre pages of the newspapers, 'where he will note many plays he may later see in London.'

5 New York is overcrowded, complained Mr. Priestley. Granted, said the New Yorker, but New York takes to people and likes to crowd them in.

6   I creep into the argument at this point only because I possess a rather dog-eared but still unexpired credential. It is that I have lived in New York steadily—continuously, anyway—for nearly fifteen years; that I came here first as a transatlantic visitor, on money dished out from one of Mr. Harkness's skyscrapers; and that in those days I saw New York much as Mr. Priestley sees it now. I think we were both wrong. And I hope it will throw light on more places than New York if I try to say why.

7   Neither a native nor a traveller can ever be objective about any place on the map. And all we can sensibly discuss is how true for each of them are their feelings about the place. There is a special flow of moods in a traveller. And I think Mr. Priestley now, and I nineteen years ago, were talking more about ourselves than about New York. Because travellers are never the same at home and abroad. They always think they are, but the people you travel among notice pretty soon that you have thrown off your responsibilities to your own country and don't have to take on any of theirs. This is the state of natural anarchy and for some grown-ups is the only time they know again the huge relief of kids when school's out. Travellers, however, once they are no longer young and scampy, feel embarrassed, not to say guilty, about their freedom. They can express it in one of two ways. They can be secretly frightened by the alien life around them and retreat more tenaciously than ever into habits that belong to their country and nowhere else. Hence the cricket clubs in Brazil and Hollywood, which, I have noticed, manage to recruit some Britons who would not be playing cricket at home. I have known Englishmen who in England can take their tea or leave it but who get to insist on it in the United States, precisely because afternoon tea is not a custom of the country.

8   The other reflex looks like the opposite, but deep in the springs of our childish fear it may be only another reaction to the same threat. It is to go out and do with much bravery all the things you do not do at home. Thus the Englishman who becomes a baseball fan or learns to shudder at Brussels sprouts. This is a plucky show that he is no longer bound by nostalgia or habit to the old life he left behind him.

9   I believe there is a peculiar mythical appeal to Englishmen in the distant prospect of America. It may go as far back as the Elizabethans, the travellers' tales of fat turkeys, gigantic oysters and succulent fruits, the news of an Eldorado begging for settlement. 'Oh My America, my new founde land!' cried Donne, though at that particular moment he wasn't thinking of leaving home. This myth has been modified down the years, until there are at least two or three generations of Britons conditioned by a whole childhood literature about the West, and now by the glittering stereotypes of the movies, and more regrettably by the solid tradition of reporting back to England only what is corrupt or eccentric or scandalous. From this there emerges a modern myth about America, some of which is poetic and true, some of which is a punching-bag for stay-at-homes. The

city of New York has come to crystallize the nightmare aspect of this
dream country. It becomes a hard and hideous place, with frightening
canyons of skyscrapers. Its life is, in Mr. Priestley's words, 'restless . . .
in its nightly pursuit of diminishing pleasures. Not a flower,' he moans,
'can blossom on these concrete cliffs.' Well, I am told that in the granite
veins of this city, on Manhattan alone, they have found a hundred and
seventy varieties of semi-precious stones. Slit into the grey hunk of rock
we inhabit there are garnets and amethysts and opals and beryls and tour-
malines, and other jewels even less pronounceable. There are still about
half as many trees as human beings. And the commonest backyard tree is
the ailanthus, which—I hate to tell Mr. Priestley—the Chinese call the tree
of heaven.

10   But this doesn't fit in with anything Europeans have been told, and
the heck with it. To more Europeans than would admit it, there is always
at the back of the mind this neon-lit image of New York as Babylon, where
innocence is banished, where anything goes, where everything has its
price, where—in the vivacious version current among my schoolmates in
England—you rode a perpetual shoot-the-chutes and bounded the waves
of pleasure, to the music of Duke Ellington, while at your side snuggled a
beautiful girl, beautiful and up to no good.

11   If you think I am romancing about this, let me remind you that the
symbol of an island of pleasure, presided over by a beckoning female, is
almost a constant of the human imagination. It was Circe in Greece, Iza-
nami in Japan, Semiramis who built Babylon. These, you may say, are only
legends. But what is more real and indispensable than the ideas that burst
into life from men's imaginations precisely because they do not exist?
They express the permanent dissatisfactions of man with his lot, and this
particular one relieves the secret fear that, like Marley's ghost, we may be
wasting our days on earth weaving chains of bankbooks, files, ledgers, insurance policies.

12   When Mr. Priestley calls New York 'Babylon piled on Imperial
Rome,' I think he is the victim of this myth. Once you stay and live in this
city, you have to admit that it is nothing of the sort. The intelligentsia will
claim that New York tries to be the city they would like to despise. But
the intelligentsia is the same everywhere and is a poor guide to the real
life of cities. And to the people who live this life, the overpowering number of middle-class New Yorkers, who have as much town pride as Leeds
or Manchester, there was one sentence of old Jeremiah Priestley's that
really hurt: 'The lonely heart of man cannot come home here.'

13   No? On Manhattan Island alone (and Mr. Priestley was talking about
only one of the five boroughs) there are two million people who won't
live anywhere else and wouldn't want to, even after three drinks. New
York is their home town. It is not Babylon. It is the place where we rise in
the mornings to the clicking of the radiator or the bawling of the down-

stairs brat. We take in the milk. We descend on the schools with a rush of kisses and a greeting of neighbors. We head for the subway. We hear a great bass reverberate over the island. It is not, as Mr. Priestley might suspect, the trump of doom. It is only the *basso profundo* of the *Queen Elizabeth* going downriver. We spend the day at work, restlessly perhaps to the extent of leaving home for a distant workshop and then at the end of the day reversing the process and leaving the workshop to go home again. Maybe, if it is not slushy or damp, we decide to walk home and watch a copper sun sinking into an El Greco sky over against the Jersey shore. If the skies of New York often lift us, miserable ants that we are, into delusions of grandeur, we will often spot on the corner, as we turn to go in our building, something casual or scurrilous that restores us to the affectionate human scale. On the wall of a bricked-up lot a tiny New Yorker scribbled a typical sentence. 'Nuts,' it said. 'Nuts to all the boys on Second Avenue'—a long struggling pause, then the concession, 'except between 68th and 69th Streets.'

14   We come in and we play with the children or bawl them out. We enjoy, if we have any sense, the variety of the people of our town, and there is often some crazy thing to tell. I have daily dealings with a score of Americans whom I shall only identify here as an Italian shoeshine man, a garrulous German elevator man, a warm, wise-cracking Jewish newsagent, and a range of shopkeepers who span the gamut of New York names from Mr. O'Byrne De Witt to Circumstance H. Smith, a Negro with fine manners.

15   The thermometer dips overnight and we look forward to tomorrow, when the red ball goes up over Central Park—no signal for revolution this, Mr. Priestley, or even retribution, but the City's cue to tell us there's going to be skating. Whenever we go to the Park and find, say, there's not enough sand in the sand box the children play in, we telephone the office of Mr. Moses, the Park Commissioner. Next morning two attendants come along with replenishing boxes of sand. The city works pretty hard on the organizing of the citizen's play, and in summer there are handball courts to be repaired, there are city band concerts, city outdoor opera, city fish to be fed into the surrounding streams, and swimming for thousands who leap the trains for the vast, city-sponsored lay-out of Jones Beach.

16   In the evening, what do we do? Well, I see from a city survey that only one in fifteen of us has ever been in a night-club. We sit and read, or have friends in, listen to the radio or go to lectures, or a movie, play pinochle or checkers or poker, putter with this and that. And ninety-two in a hundred of us begin to go to bed about ten-thirty.

17   Our days and months are bound by work, and fun, and quarrels, and taxes, and movies and savings, and children and death and friendship. When we are far from home we think of New York, and it is not Circe with a henna rinse bawling into a night-club microphone. We see in imag-

ination the white steam hissing through the pavements. We smell the fishy smell of the Fulton market, or the whiff of chicory over Foley Square, or the malty brew that hangs around the East Nineties. We recall the Bronx Zoo, and Mercury standing on his muscular thighs over the traffic lights on Fifth Avenue. We see in the mind's eye the magic dioramas of Africa and Hawaii in the Museum of Natural History, or the pink front page of the morning tabloids. We hear of a girl who was loaded with furs and automobiles by a sharpie using absconded funds. Over the transatlantic wires they flash her confession: 'I never knew he was in an illegal business. He told me he was a gambler.' Glory be! We know her for our own.

18   Or some dank day in Britanny or Paris, we recall the one day in three or four that is blindingly clear, brilliant as a knight in armour, the sun slashing down the avenues like a sword. On such a day, my cab-driver stopped for a red light at St. Patrick's. And so did a herd of young teenagers before they turned in to say their prayers. Most of them, I should say, were in sweaters of every colour. He leered at their faces and caught their twinkling shapes in the shafts of sunlight. He hit the steering-wheel with his open hand. And said to me, or perhaps to God: 'They come in all shapes and sizes. Yes, sir. Great stuff. Whaddya say, Mac?' He laughed himself silly.

19   Restless we *are,* and very small, threading through our canyons. But are we, as Mr. Priestley assures us we are, 'full of unease, disquiet, bewilderment'? Last summer Dr. Gallup found that over ninety percent of us thought we were happy. Suppose we allow ten per cent for pride or bravado and another ten per cent for Mr. Priestley's transatlantic insight. That still leaves seventy per cent who believe, maybe wrongly, that they are happy. Better let 'em wallow in their ignorance, Mr. Priestley, these placid dopes who don't even know when they're 'deeply bewildered and frustrated.' Whaddya say, Mac?

Questions

1. What details in paragraph 1 give you the impression that Mr. Cooke does not regard Priestley's view of New York too seriously?
2. Why does Cooke quote the correspondent in paragraph 2?
3. Mr. Priestley's first name is John. Why then does Cooke refer to him in paragraph 12 as "old Jeremiah Priestley"?
4. What is the function of the "No?" at the beginning of paragraph 13 and how effective is it?
5. In view of the essay's point, what is the function of the shifts in the level of diction and the kind of detail he uses? How does this detail differ from Sartre's?

6. How in the following details has Cooke confined himself to meaningful ones —rising to the clicking of the radiator, taking in milk, skating in Central Park, coming home with some crazy story to tell, and the girl loaded with furs who thought her boy friend was just a gambler?

7. How does the last sentence of paragraph 13 restore us to the "affectionate human scale"?

8. What is the function of the contrast between two kinds of travelers in paragraphs 7 and 8? If neither is going to form an accurate picture of what he sees and one is Cooke, isn't Cooke admitting some distortion for his own view here? Why does he do this?

9. Why does Cooke conclude a literate essay with the highly colloquial "Whaddya say, Mac?"

Theme topics

1. Alistair Cooke's essay is an excellent refutation of the distorted view of reality that results from a moralizing mind. Write an essay refuting another distorted view, perhaps of teenagers, or drinking, or a novel, a movie or a play.

2. Write an essay with the thesis that we see everything with either the distortion of our own prejudices or the limitations of our own insights.

8   DAVID DAICHES

Education in a Democratic Society

1   The other day I heard a professor of education at an important Midwestern university give a talk to a group of his colleagues on his experiences in Thailand, where he had been for over a year advising on education. In shocked tones he told his audience that in Thai schools the pupils have to pass an examination before they can be moved up from one grade into the next. He added that the American team out there were trying to remove this dangerously undemocratic practice, and so enable a much higher percentage of pupils to move up each year and complete their schooling. Thus everybody would be educated, not only a tiny few, with the happy consequence that the people would be fortified against the seductions of Communism. At another point in his talk he said that Thai

From *Commentary* (April, 1957). Copyright by the American Jewish Committee. Reprinted by permission of the author and *Commentary*.

education was too "intellectual" and not sufficiently practical and vocational: no garage mechanic in Thailand was really competent to do automobile repairs. (Whether the kind of technical education which the
professor advocated, a kind of education in which Soviet Russia, if the
statistics published in the Western press are accurate, leads the world,
was also a defense against Communism, he did not say.) In general, he
seemed to regard education as either (a) the moving up a ladder to the
top, regardless of what was done or learned in the process of moving, or
(b) training to do a particular job of work, which will be the pupil's means
of livelihood in afterlife.

2   Educators in Britain and America would agree that education must
be democratic and it must be useful. Of course these are sensible ideals;
few would claim that education ought to be undemocratic and useless.
The difference between the British and the American approach lies in their
respective definitions, or at least implicit definitions, of democracy and
usefulness as applied to education. A democracy, in British eyes, has the
duty of providing free education to every child according to his "age,
ability, and aptitude" (in the words of the Education Act of 1944). The
more democratic the educational system, the more the schools will strive
to give to each pupil, whatever his class or economic background, that
education which encourages and makes full use of whatever abilities he
possesses.

3   As for the *usefulness* of education, there is still much general feeling
in England that the function of education is to teach the pupil how to
spend money, not how to make it. That is one reason why the British are
having such difficulty in persuading youngsters to go in for the sciences
rather than the humanities; the latter are concerned with the art of living,
with books and music and good conversation, with the training of "a gentleman or noble person in virtuous and gentle discipline" (as Spenser put
it in explaining the object of his *Faerie Queene*). A surprising number of
British middle-class parents still consider that kind of education the "best,"
and they want their children to have it. So if—to oversimplify—the
American definition of the democratic and the useful in education leads to
the contradictory ideals of equality of curriculum and of promotion on the
one hand, and vocational training according to a future job on the other, the
British definition of the same terms leads to the equally contradictory
ideals of training according to individual abilities and aptitude on the one
hand, and on the other to a general preference for the "arts side" over the
"science side."

4   This, of course, applies to secondary education rather than to the colleges and universities, and each attitude is rooted in history in a complex
manner. (The Harvard report on *General Education in a Free Society*
discusses the historical background of the American situation with considerable insight.) I begin with a reference to secondary education deliber-

ately, because the whole pattern of differences between the British and American academic scenes derives from basic differences in their attitudes to secondary education. The British have always put far more emphasis on secondary education; the large majority of the educational reforms of the last hundred years in England have been concerned with the elementary or secondary education, and in the last quarter-century and more all concern about the curriculum, about "general education in a free society," about distinguishing between pupils of different abilities within the same age group, about language teaching, aptitude testing, teaching methods, and so on, has been concentrated on education at the secondary level.

5   The schools, not the colleges and universities, have been the main objects of controversy between humanists and scientists and between all other opposed or professedly opposed schools of thought about education. On the whole, the universities have gone quietly on training the relatively few people sent up to them from the top forms of the secondary schools. My impression is that in America many more of these problems have been discussed with reference to the colleges (e.g., the question of "freshman English" and of basic literature courses) and there has been more excitement among serious and responsible educators about the college curriculum than about earlier educational levels (e.g., the Hutchins experiment in Chicago, the Harvard report, the continuous experimentation in so many liberal arts colleges).

6   The reason for this appears to me to be that while in America the ideal is that everybody should move right up to the top of the educational ladder—that is, right up to the university—the British ideal is that it is the object of secondary education, going ideally up to the age of seventeen or eighteen, to train the complete man, or as much of him as is available in any given individual, and that education beyond that level is for a minority with special gifts or special purposes. American secondary education is in some respects committed by its interpretation of the democratic doctrine to going at the pace of the slowest, and thus the high school curriculum is watered, leaving much basic knowledge to be acquired at college. British secondary education, which has chosen the other horn of the dilemma and tends to go at the pace of the quickest, being geared really to the needs of the brightest pupils and giving them every kind of special treatment and "forcing," puts the main burden of education onto the secondary level. The British schoolboy who is at all bright will work harder between the ages of, say, thirteen and eighteen than he will ever need to work at the university.

7   I remember myself with what immense relief I left school at Edinburgh to proceed to the university. Now at last I was free to do only the subjects that really interested me, and no longer hard hours of homework every evening on a great variety of subjects. I had had five years each of mathematics, physics and chemistry, and Greek; and six years each of

English, history, and Latin, together with three years of French and two of German. (In recent years there has been an increasing tendency to specialize in the last two years of school, and concentrate on two or three subjects in preparation for university scholarship examinations.) And these subjects were all learned cumulatively, building each year on what was learned the year before, not taken in isolated units as is so often done in American high schools. I am not saying that my education was ideal—it was fiercely competitive, and it did very little for the large number of pupils who could not keep up with the competitive pace set by the bright pupils at the top, and it also was sometimes too formal and mechanical—but it was *solid*. It told me nothing about how to be a good citizen, but it taught me some basic skills, including several languages and more mathematics and sciences than is generally taught in the first and sometimes the second year of American colleges. It also taught me how to write essays, one of the most stressed features of British secondary education.

8   There is a good case against this kind of secondary education. American educators would say that it penalized heavily the non-academic type of pupil, and that the whole curriculum was conceived in too narrowly academic terms. The first charge is certainly justified; the second can be debated. The Education Act of 1944 tried to meet the first charge by distinguishing between different types of schools, or of curricula within a single "comprehensive" school, at which a child was entitled to a free education. There was the academic "grammar school" for those who showed an aptitude for it, and "modern" schools or technical schools for the others. The sifting is done by the now famous—or notorious—"eleven plus" examination.[1] Thus the non-academic students are taken care of in a much more general and flexible kind of education, but not at the expense of the progress of the traditional "bright boy." The trouble is that the "grammar school" (which alone leads to the university) still enjoys the highest social prestige, and middle-class parents want to send their children there whether they qualify for a free place or not. The Education Act promised "parity of esteem" between the different types of school and of teacher; but it has not worked out that way. The British know very well that the grammar school type of education is for the brightest pupils—in the traditional sense of that term—and it is they who are being trained as an elite to do the most responsible of the nation's jobs. And, naturally, they want their children to be among the elite.

9   All this is by way of explanation of the often noted fact that the British student generally knows more when he comes up to the university than the American college freshman does. If going to college is a democratic right, then education must be spread out in order to leave something for the college to do for those who have no aptitude for higher learning. At

[1] An examination (in English and arithmetic, together with intelligence and aptitude tests) taken as a rule when the child is eleven years old or a little over.

Indiana University, where I am at the moment, the freshman and even sophomore courses in language and literature represent, in both content and level of teaching, what is taught in Britain two or even three years before the end of secondary education. And yet this is not altogether true. For the American freshman and sophomore has often a kind of curiosity, a provocative, uninformed but insistent "show me" attitude, an insistence on pitting his own limited experience against his teacher's knowledge, that makes the American college classroom at these levels very different indeed from the classroom of either the British grammar school or the British university.

10   "Why did Ulysses spend all that time in getting home to his wife after he left Troy?" a freshman asked one of my colleagues here the other day, during a lesson on the Odyssey. "If he'd really wanted to get home quickly, he would have managed it. I think he was kidding himself when he said he was so anxious to get back." This is naïve, but it is not stupid, and it is not the kind of thing an English schoolboy would ask. The bright English schoolboy would mug up the standard works on the Homeric world and turn out a sophisticated essay on "Homer and the Heroic Age" based on a conflation of half a dozen books he had read in the school library; but it would never occur to him to ask whether Ulysses was kidding himself when he expressed his anxiety to return home quickly. The English schoolboy tends to relate knowledge to other knowledge, in order to form an elegant pattern (the bright essay being always the standard of achievement in the humanities); the American freshman wants to relate everything he reads or is told to his own experience. The latter as a rule has no sense of history or of form or of the *otherness* of different times and places; the former often lacks a sense of personal implication in what he studies.

11   To British—and indeed European—eyes, American education seems to waste some of the best learning years, at least for the brighter pupils, and to postpone until an unnecessarily late stage the essential core of education. But there is another side to the picture. The better American students are less blasé and work harder than their British opposite numbers, and by the end of their four undergraduate years have often achieved a kind of sophistication in terms of their subject which is at the opposite pole from the attitude revealed by the freshman's question about Ulysses. That kind of sophistication, which is particularly noticeable among the brighter students of literature, is consciously won by hard effort; it is (and I am talking of the best students) often the prelude to the use of specialized techniques in graduate work. The English student, building on his school training, will develop his accustomed skill with a kind of leisurely elegance and often, by the time he gets his degree, is not fundamentally any better educated than when he left school. He is likely to be less ambitious, more skeptical, less fundamentally serious than the American.

12   In such fields as literature, philosophy, and history, at least, the bright British student will most appreciate the lecturer who plays with ideas cleverly and suggestively, but the bright American student resents that: he wants the truth, or the right methods, and no nonsense. "Do you believe in that view of literature you were developing in your lecture this morning?" a Cornell student once asked me. I said that I did not, but I thought it was interesting to play with the idea a little and see where it led us. He replied, almost angrily, that if I did not believe the theory to be true I should not waste my own and the class's time discussing it at such length; it was sheer verbal gymnastics, and the students were there to *learn*, not to be played with. "Is C. S. Lewis's book on sixteenth-century literature a book to be read?" a graduate student asked me the other day at Indiana. I replied that it was a fresh and sometimes brilliant reading of the texts of the period, and though I quarreled sharply with some of the views expressed in it, I thought it a most stimulating book, well worth reading. "But will it give me a proper view of the period?" she persisted. "I don't know," I replied. "I'm not sure what the 'proper' view of the period is. Read it and make up your own mind about it." This answer was not regarded as satisfactory.

13   I often have the feeling that the American student, who works hard and learns fast, never has time to enjoy his work. I am thinking especially of those who go on to graduate study. They have learned an immense amount by the time they enter graduate school and have often surpassed in knowledge and in methodological skill their British counterparts, but they have the air of never having lived long enough with their subject. A graduate student in English literature will rush on to do research on Marvell's imagery before he is really at home in English literature and really inward with its traditions and achievements. And there will be even less likelihood of his having any true sense of European culture as a whole. The reason for this is partly, of course, that he is American and not English or European, and to this extent it is unfair to take a European literature as an example. But there is another reason, too: his whole education —his *real* education, that is, which began with college—has been too rushed. No one, I might suggest in passing, ought ever to take a course in such a subject as "Masterpieces of World Literature," for one can only become acquainted with the great tradition in world literature by leisurely reading over a long period of time. It is true, as modern educational psychologists so often point out, that adults learn faster than children and that there is no point in pushing youngsters to learn over a long period of time what concentrated effort can teach them later in life. But I think there is something to be said for spreading things out,[2] for slow and cumulative

---

[2] This may appear to contradict what I said earlier about the excessive spreading in American high school teaching, but that spreading is not the result of steady cumulative study but of scattered and fragmented study.

learning. The hard-working, conscientious, somewhat puritanical American graduate student often outstrips his British opposite number at surprising speed; but in the process he grows old faster, too, and he also learns to regard his subject as a field to be covered rather than as a body of knowledge to be explored and relished.

14   The dangers on the British side are, however, just as great, though different. They differ not only from the American dangers I have described but also among different British universities. For there are three main types of British universities, as distinct from each other in methods, organization, and traditions as British universities as a whole are from American universities. The three groups are: Oxford and Cambridge; the four Scottish universities; and the English universities other than Oxford and Cambridge—the so-called "provincial" universities. Oxford and Cambridge are unique in that the tutorial system rather than lecture courses provides the essential teaching, and although, at least in Cambridge, the complex relationship between the colleges and the university is showing signs of strain in some quarters, the main business of these universities remains the cultivation of the student's mind through regular discussion with a tutor or supervisor. This of course leaves the student at the mercy of the particular tutor he is landed with, and the student often has no contact at all with the most distinguished teachers of his subject in the university. The dangers of the Oxford and Cambridge system are dilettantism, a tendency, at least in arts subjects, to value a superficial "brilliance" above knowledge and deep understanding, and a disparity in tutorial possibilities. But the advantages are enormous, and my own conviction—having studied and taught at Edinburgh and Oxford, and taught at Chicago, Cornell, and Cambridge—is that it is still the best system that has been worked out.

15   It should be realized that the large majority of present-day students at Oxford and Cambridge as well as at other British universities have their fees and maintenance paid for by grants or scholarships of one kind of another. No one who can enter a university is now prevented by lack of means from going there. But no one who has not had the grammar school type of education can qualify for university entrance, and a pupil who has just missed qualifying for a free grammar school education at eleven plus, and whose parents are too poor to send him to a fee-paying grammar school or boarding school, may in this way be deprived of a university education. But, apart from this problem (and it is a serious one), it is true to say that the economic factor in sending one's children to a university is today less of a worry to British parents than it is to Americans.

16   The shifting social patterns at Oxford and Cambridge have had some interesting results. Before the war it was the regular thing for the good student to do the bulk of his reading in the vacations, and to spend his terms discussing what he had read or amusing himself. But now more and more students take jobs during vacations (not during term time,

which would be unthinkable, for the whole concept of university education demands that during term the student remain free to respond to all the currents flowing in a university community, of which formal teaching is only one). This means that they have not the time to do vast amounts of reading between terms, and this is shifting the whole pattern of teaching. The tendency to get by on a minimum of reading, often that done at school, and to compensate by wit and elegance for lack of knowledge, presents a real danger. To avoid that, tutors and supervisors (they are "tutors" at Oxford and "supervisors" at Cambridge) are growing more inclined to give out weekly reading assignments in the American manner.

17   The Scottish universities are in general organized more like the American. Teaching is done in formal lecture courses, and there is an air of serious professionalism about it. The student who takes an honors degree in English at a Scottish university is expected to plough through the whole of English literature. There is a great deal of reading of factual lectures to large classes, and a general conservatism in the form and content of the teaching. A degree in English literature at Cambridge is intended to produce a cultivated young man who has read and thought enough about a selected number of literary works to have an understanding and an appreciation of the values and varieties of literature. In Edinburgh, the objective is to train a future teacher of English, and a thorough, solid training is provided. The Cambridge degree in an arts subject is not designed primarily as a professional qualification, but at a Scottish university it is so designed.

18   Too much teaching at Scottish universities is plain dull. And even if the professor himself (there is only one person with the title of professor in each subject at British universities, and in Scotland and the provincial universities he runs the department) gives the large survey course to first-year students, the advantages of contact with the great man are often nullified by the routine way in which he fulfills his task. Here the liveliness and informality of American college teaching would be a welcome innovation.

19   The English provincial universities suffer from the fact that the best students still tend to be siphoned off to Oxford or Cambridge, and also from certain confusions about the nature and function of the teaching they provide. They fall sometimes between the two stools of Scottish professionalism and Oxford amateurism. But they have some of the best men in the country—particularly the younger men—on their staffs and, in spite of the large formal lecture course which carries much of the burden of teaching, there is often liveliness and experiment as well as a very high level of academic competence, notably in certain scientific subjects. But the shadow of Oxford and Cambridge still hangs over these universities, making both staff and students uncertain of themselves and sometimes restless and discontented. Kingsley Amis's novel *Lucky Jim* is set in a provincial

university, and the masochistic clowning through which Amis reveals that the graces of the older universities are not for him betrays an almost spiteful withdrawal from "culture" that is a disturbing symptom.

20   Finally, a word about administration. Britain has always resisted the notion that university administrators should form a separate class from scholars and teachers, and has almost always drawn its heads of universities from the world of scholarship. In Oxford and Cambridge, the vice-chancellor, who is the administrative head of the university, is drawn from the heads of colleges, each one serving only for a few years. The real work of administration on the academic policy level is done by committees of members of the faculty. Details of financial administration and the execution of policy as it affects the daily routine of university life are alone in the hands of permanent administrators. No single person in any British university has the power that a college dean has in America: such power is vested in the hands of faculty boards. There is no such thing as a board of trustees. Government money comes to the universities through the University Grants Committee, which consists of vice chancellors of the various universities, and whose function is to get government money without government control. The device works well, and the British universities, which are extremely jealous of their independence, are proud of the machinery they have set up for getting money from the Treasury without strings. No questions about universities can be asked in Parliament because no minister is responsible for them (the Minister of Education has no responsibility for or control over the universities).

21   But administration by committees has some serious drawbacks. It is a heart-breaking job to carry an organizational reform through, especially in Oxford or Cambridge, because the agreement of so many diverse persons must first be secured. A few older members of committees can successfully postpone any innovation almost indefinitely. No one in Britain could possibly do the sort of thing that, say, Hutchins did at the University of Chicago. The result is that traditions are maintained and continuity preserved, but often at the price of the indefinite postponement of needed reforms and the minimizing of profitable experimentation.

22   The American tendency to put non-academic administrators at the head of universities seems to me dangerous, though the sheer size of many of the American universities makes some aspects at least of administration a highly technical problem. And then there is the fund-raising aspect. But most of all it seems to me that the vitality and flexibility of American universities, which are their greatest assets, are seriously threatened by the I.B.M. machine. I am astonished at the degree to which procedures are *gleichgeschaltet* in a large state university and the human element ignored in order that the machines may be kept rolling.

23   The chief glory of the American university lies in the fact that it is not really a university in the British sense at all, but a vast collection of

educational machinery, good and bad, elementary and advanced, in which the most exciting and fruitful educational activities can go on, as well as the silliest and most useless. To it come students of every degree of ability and with all kinds of interests, and amidst all the proliferating courses and degrees each, if he is lucky, can find something to help him in one way or another. A British university, on the other hand, is an institution of higher learning intended for the minority of citizens who are interested in and can profit by higher learning. That, at least, is the ideal. Now the American system, which results from the belief that ideally every citizen should go to a university and that the university should therefore have something to offer in every sphere and at every level, needs a rigid administrative machinery to hold it together. If in the British system the high objectives of the universities are often found to be in contradiction with professional needs on the one hand, and with ideals of urbane gentlemanly culture on the other, in the American system the freedom and variety which its very lack of discrimination makes possible are threatened by growing administrative rigidity.

24   Underlying the many differences between the educational systems of the two countries are some significant differences in social philosophy. The British believe that the function of higher education is to train an elite who will perform the most responsible and demanding tasks of the nation. The more democratic you are the more you will strive to make sure that you will choose this elite on the basis of innate ability and aptitude alone, regardless of any other consideration, economic, social, or personal. Equalitarianism is preached by a large section of the British Labor party, and it is in fact being rapidly achieved. But it is *economic* equalitarianism: Britain today is probably the country with the most economic equality in the world. You train the best people to do the most important jobs—but you mustn't pay them any more than you pay people with a less academic education doing more routine jobs.

25   In spite of the well-meant efforts of left-wing politicians and educators, some kind of social snobbery is bound to continue in England, for it is bound up with the whole concept of different education for different abilities. But this snobbery will be a matter of kind of job, kind of accent (which in England largely depends on where you are educated), and level of intellectual interest, rather than of birth, ancestry, or income. How far an elite of this kind can mainain its dominance without economic superiority or stability of social background remains to be seen.

26   In America, where the paradox of equality and individualism has long existed (equality demands that everybody get the same education, which is anti-individualistic, but it also demands that each person get ahead in a free enterprise economy, which produces extreme economic individualism), the relation between education and prestige is much more complicated. Suspicion of the intellectual in politics, which strikes a European

as such a characteristic feature of the American scene, is bound up with the traditional national refusal to regard differences in quality of education as necessary or desirable. But as America becomes more and more the leader of the democratic world, the problem of training informed and responsible citizens to fill the crucial jobs in domestic and international affairs may well force American educators into accepting in both theory and practice greater differences in education than have hitherto been regarded as desirable.

27   Suspicion of the intellectual in politics is a feature of a self-contained and more or less isolated country; it may well be that America's role in world affairs today will have a greater long-term effect on the pattern of American education than any of the democratic theorists have had. It was Britain's need for an elite to run a vast empire in the nineteenth century that produced the basic pattern of modern British education, and America, which has taken over so many international responsibilities from the older powers, may have to modify its own educational system in order to fulfill them adequately.

Questions

1. What use of irony does Daiches make in paragraph 1? How does this irony prepare you for his own views?
2. Does Daiches accept either the (a) or (b) in paragraph 1?
3. Daiches points out that both English and American educators would agree that education must be "democratic" and "useful." How does Daiches then contrast American and English views of "democratic" or "useful"?
4. Does Daiches appear to agree with either view of "democratic" or "useful" education?
5. What reason does Daiches give for beginning with secondary education rather than going directly to college or university education?
6. Daiches seems to say in paragraph 5 that there is a controversy between scientists and humanists. Is the controversy central to his argument? Does he adopt one or the other side?
7. In paragraph 6 Daiches contrasts the two ideals of education. What is the essential difference?
8. What function does paragraph 7 serve in relation to the distinctions made in paragraph 6?
9. Is Daiches' secondary education at Edinburgh implicitly contrasted to American high school education? On what grounds? Does Daiches believe his training was superior?
10. If he had a superior training, why in paragraph 8 does he appear to argue against it?

11. Why, in paragraph 10, does Daiches use the rather peculiar word "conflation" in speaking of the "bright English schoolboy"? Why is the American student's naive question preferable to the English schoolboy's sophisticated essay?

12. In paragraphs 13 and 14 Daiches suggests the dangers inherent in each system. What are they? Which are more acute?

13. Daiches presents details on three methods of university instruction in Great Britain in paragraphs 14 through 19. What contrasting elements does he stress? Why? Which system does he appear to favor?

14. Why in paragraph 22 does Daiches say that it is dangerous to put non-academic administrators at the head of universities? How can an I.B.M. machine threaten a university?

15. What sequence of topics relevant to education in the United States and Great Britain does Daiches follow in his essay? How would you justify or challenge each transition in the sequence? What topics, if any, ought to have been explored but were not?

16. What is the chief glory of the American university? How does its system stem from American social philosophy? Do you agree with Daiches? Disagree? Why?

Theme topics

1. Compare and contrast methods of education you have observed in high school and college.

2. Write an essay in which you compare and contrast two ways of doing something, noting certain advantages of each: for example, two methods of quitting smoking, two modes of travel, two attitudes toward life, two teaching techniques, two ways of raising children.

Dividing and Classifying

Division and classification

When we try to understand an idea or an event, either we think of it as it relates to other, larger ideas or events; or we try to understand it by examining its component parts. We *divide* a group of things and we *classify* a single object. For example, a student might be classified as of A, B, C, D, or F quality. A group of students might be divided into these categories.

We understand politics better by dividing problems into foreign and domestic; we classify a given problem under one or the other category. Dividing a complex operation makes it easier for us to understand. Doctors recognize and classify the symptoms of ailments under categories too complex for the layman to understand, but meaningful to them in diagnosis and treatment.

Three general rules have proved valuable in dividing and classifying.

1. The basis for the division must be clear and consistent. We might divide paintings by technique into oils, gouaches, and water colors (though this division is hardly exhaustive). It would be incorrect, however, to divide paintings into oils, gouaches, water colors, and portraits. The basis for the division would no longer be consistent.

2. The classifications must be mutually exclusive. Overlapping classifications such as cars divided into U.S., foreign, and expensive create not clarity but confusion. The category "expensive" does not exclude the other two nor do they in turn exclude it.

3. The classification must exhaust the possibilities of the principle without becoming tedious. The approximate accuracy necessary to make a point clear is all that is required. The classification, long part of our Navy's folklore, of people who whistle into two groups—boatswain's mates and damned fools—makes its point unambiguously. But division of automobiles, say, into those of American and European manufacture does not exhaust the existing universe of automobiles, even though for some pur-

poses these two groupings might be adequate. A third category of "Other" would exhaust the possibilities; a listing of every country producing automobiles as distinguished from those that only manufacture parts and from those that only assemble parts manufactured exclusively abroad, would be unnecessarily tedious.

The same topic can be divided and classified in any number of ways. For purposes, let us say, of understanding the problem of high school dropouts, we might divide and classify them according to their reasons for leaving school. Some leave willingly, some against their will. Each category might then be subdivided one or more times: namely, those who leave willingly (a) because of feelings of social failure, (b) because of personal distress over their academic program, (c) because of greater attractions outside, for example, marriage, a lucrative job, or both. Those who leave unwillingly do so as a result of pressures from either outside or inside the school; they are expelled, must support someone financially, or become gravely ill. But this division might seem too complex. A different division of the same subject on the same basis—reasons for leaving—is then possible. A simple three-part division might be preferable: (1) deficiency in intelligence and ability, (2) psychological pressures, (3) practical and economic pressures. Notice that these three reasons, though the categories are themselves mutually exclusive, might all apply in any particular case; a single student might drop out of high school for all three reasons, but the classification is not thereby invalidated. It still serves its function in enabling us to analyze any particular case.

The principle of simple enumeration, employed by Robert Gorham Davis to present kinds of logical fallacies, is enormously useful in organizing categories whose interrelations are not always clear. The principle itself, however, carries little logical force since a listing of categories, to say nothing of citing examples, seldom exhausts all possibilities of classes and subclasses—and certainly not of individual instances—in a given subject. On the other hand, a set of exhaustive classes, which Eric Berne describes with some minor reservations is well illustrated in his division of all men on the basis of their physical appearance. This division is more simple and clear-cut than most because it is based on simple physiological facts. The attempt to divide personality types in corporate structures would be far more complex, requiring ingenuity and insight for which Berne's division would merely provide one possible basis. Finally, repeated use of the principles of division and classification, when applied to analysis and definition with the skill of Philip Wheelwright, makes intricate subjects easier for the writer to explain and for the reader to understand.

9 ROBERT GORHAM DAVIS
Logic and Logical Fallacies

Undefined terms

1   The first requirement for logical discourse is knowing what the words you use actually mean. Words are not like paper money or counters in a game. Except for technical terms in some of the sciences, they do not have a fixed face value. Their meanings are fluid and changing, influenced by many considerations of context and reference, circumstance and association. This is just as true of common words such as *fast* as it is of literary terms such as *romantic*. Moreover, if there is to be communication, words must have approximately the same meaning for the reader that they have for the writer. A speech in an unknown language means nothing to the hearer. When an adult speaks to a small child or an expert to a layman, communication may be seriously limited by lack of a mature vocabulary or ignorance of technical terms. Many arguments are meaningless because the speakers are using important words in quite different senses.

2   Because we learn most words—or guess at them—from the contexts in which we first encounter them, our sense of them is often incomplete or wrong. Readers sometimes visualize the Assyrian who comes down like the wolf on the fold as an enormous man dressed in cohorts (some kind of fancy armor, possibly) gleaming in purple and gold. "A rift in the lute" suggests vaguely a cracked mandolin. Failure to ascertain the literal meaning of figurative language is a frequent reason for mixed metaphors. We are surprised to find that the "devil" in "the devil to pay" and "the devil and the deep blue sea" is not Old Nick, but part of a ship. Unless terms mean the same thing to both writer and reader, proper understanding is impossible.

Abstractions

3   The most serious logical difficulties occur with abstract terms. An abstraction is a word which stands for a quality found in a number of different objects or events from which it has been "abstracted" or taken away. We may, for instance, talk of the "whiteness" of paper or cotton or snow without considering qualities of cold or inflammability or usefulness

which these materials happen also to possess. Usually, however, our minds carry over other qualities by association. See, for instance, the chapter called "The Whiteness of the Whale" in *Moby-Dick.*

4   In much theoretic discussion the process of abstraction is carried so far that although vague associations and connotations persist, the original objects or events from which the qualities have been abstracted are lost sight of completely. Instead of thinking of words like *sincerity* and *Americanism* as symbols standing for qualities that have to be abstracted with great care from examples and test cases, we come to think of them as real things in themselves. We assume that Americanism is Americanism just as a bicycle is a bicycle, and that everyone knows what it means. We forget that before the question, "Is Arthur Godfrey sincere?" can mean anything, we have to agree on the criteria of sincerity.

5   When we try to define such words and find examples, we discover that almost no one agrees on their meaning. The word *church* may refer to anything from a building on the corner of Spring Street to the whole tradition of institutionalized Christianity. *Germany* may mean a geographical section of Europe, a people, a governing group, a cultural tradition, or a military power. Abstractions such as *freedom, courage, race, beauty, truth, justice, nature, honor, humanism, democracy,* should never be used in a theme unless their meaning is defined or indicated clearly by the context. Freedom for whom? To do what? Under what circumstances? Abstract terms have merely emotional value unless they are strictly defined by asking questions of this kind. The study of a word such as *nature* in a good unabridged dictionary will show that even the dictionary, indispensable though it is, cannot determine for us the sense in which a word is being used in any given instance. Once the student understands the importance of definition, he will no longer be betrayed into fruitless arguments over such questions as whether free verse is "poetry" or whether you can change "human nature."

Name-calling

6   It is a common unfairness in controversy to place what the writer dislikes or opposes in a generally odious category. The humanist dismisses what he dislikes by calling it *romantic;* the liberal, by calling it *fascist;* the conservative, by calling it communistic. These terms tell the reader nothing. What is *piety* to some will be *bigotry* to others. *Non-Catholics* would rather be called *Protestants* than *heretics.* What is *right-thinking* except a designation for those who agree with the writer? Social security measures become *creeping socialism;* industrial organizations, *forces of reaction;* investigation into communism, *witch hunts;* prison reform, *coddling;* progressive education, *fads and frills.* Such terms are in-

tended to block thought by an appeal to prejudice and associative habits. Three steps are necessary before such epithets have real meaning. First, they must be defined; second, it must be shown that the object to which they are applied actually possesses these qualities; third, it must be shown that the possession of such qualities in this particular situation is necessarily undesirable. Unless a person is alert and critical both in choosing and in interpreting words, he may be alienated from ideas with which he would be in sympathy if he had not been frightened by a mere name.

Generalization

7   Similar to the abuse of abstract terms and epithets is the habit of presenting personal opinions in the guise of universal laws. The student often seems to feel that the broader the terms in which he states an opinion, the more effective he will be. Ordinarily the reverse is true. An enthusiasm for Thomas Wolfe should lead to a specific critical analysis of Wolfe's novels that will enable the writer to explain his enthusiasm to others; it should not be turned into the argument that Wolfe is "the greatest American novelist," particularly if the writer's knowledge of American novelists is somewhat limited. The same questions of *who* and *when* and *why* and under what *circumstances* which are used to check abstract terms should be applied to generalizations. Consider how contradictory proverbial wisdom is when detached from particular circumstances. "Look before you leap," but "he who hesitates is lost."

8   Superlatives and the words *right* and *wrong, true* and *untrue, never* and *always* must be used with caution in matters of opinion. When a student says flatly that X is true, he often is really saying that he or his family or the author of a book he has just been reading, persons of certain tastes and background and experience, *think* that X is true. If his statement is based not on logic and examination of evidence, but merely reproduces other people's opinions, it can have little value or relevance unless these people are identified and their reasons for thinking so explained. Because many freshmen are taking survey courses in which they read a single work by an author or see an historical event through the eyes of a single historian whose bias they may not be able to measure, they must guard against this error.

Sampling

9   Assertions of a general nature are frequently open to question because they are based on insufficient evidence. Some persons are quite

ready, after meeting one Armenian or reading one medieval romance, to generalize about Armenians and medieval romances. One ought, of course, to examine objectively as many examples as possible before making a generalization, but the number is less important than the representativeness of the example chosen. The Literary Digest Presidential Poll, sent to hundreds of thousands of people selected from telephone directories, was far less accurate than the Gallup Poll which questioned far fewer voters, but selected them carefully and proportionately from all different social groups. The "typical" college student, as portrayed by moving pictures and cartoons, is very different from the "average" college student as determined statistically. We cannot let uncontrolled experience do our sampling for us; instances and examples which impress themselves upon our minds do so usually because they are exceptional. In propaganda and arguments extreme cases are customarily treated as if they were characteristic.

10   If one is permitted arbitrarily to select some examples and ignore others, it is possible to find convincing evidence for almost any theory, no matter how fantastic. The fact that the mind tends naturally to remember those instances which confirm its opinions imposes a duty upon the writer, unless he wishes to encourage prejudice and superstition, to look carefully for exceptions to all generalizations which he is tempted to make. We forget the premonitions which are not followed by disaster and the times when our hunches failed to select the winner in a race. Patent medicine advertisements print the letters of those who survived their cure, and not of those who died during it. All Americans did not gamble on the stock exchange in the twenties, or become Marxists in the thirties, and all Vermonters are not thin-lipped and shrewd. Of course the search for negative examples can be carried too far. Outside of mathematics or the laboratory, few generalizations can be made airtight, and most are not intended to be. But quibbling is so easy that resort to it is very common, and the knowledge that people can and will quibble over generalizations is another reason for making assertions as limited and explicitly conditional as possible.

False analogy

11   Illustration, comparison, analogy are most valuable in making an essay clear and interesting. It must not be supposed, however, that they prove anything or have much argumentative weight. The rule that what is true of one thing in one set of circumstances is not necessarily true of another thing in another set of circumstances seems almost too obvious to need stating. Yet constantly nations and businesses are discussed as if they were human beings with human habits and feelings; human bodies are

discussed as if they were machines; the universe, as if it were a clock. It is assumed that what held true for seventeenth century New England or the thirteen Atlantic colonies also holds true for an industrial nation of 150,000,000 people. Carlyle dismissed the arguments for representative democracy by saying that if a captain had to take a vote among his crew every time he wanted to do something, he would never get around Cape Horn. This analogy calmly ignores the distinction between the lawmaking and the executive branches of constitutional democracies. Moreover, voters may be considered much more like the stockholders of a merchant line than its hired sailors. Such arguments introduce assumptions in a metaphorical guise in which they are not readily detected or easily criticized. In place of analysis they attempt to identify their position with some familiar symbol which will evoke a predictable, emotional response in the reader. The revival during the 1932 presidential campaign of Lincoln's remark, "Don't swap horses in the middle of the stream," was not merely a picturesque way of saying keep Hoover in the White House. It made a number of assumptions about the nature of depressions and the function of government. This propagandist technique can be seen most clearly in political cartoons.

Degree

12   Often differences in degree are more important than differences in kind. By legal and social standards there is more difference between an habitual drunkard and a man who drinks temperately, than between a temperate drinker and a total abstainer. In fact differences of degree produce what are regarded as differences of kind. At known temperatures ice turns to water and water boils. At an indeterminate point affection becomes love and a man who needs a shave becomes a man with a beard. The fact that no men or systems are perfect makes rejoinders and counter-accusations very easy if differences in degree are ignored. Newspapers in totalitarian states, answering American accusations of brutality and suppression, refer to lynchings and gangsterism here. Before a disinterested judge could evaluate these mutual accusations, he would have to settle the question of the degree to which violent suppression and lynching are respectively prevalent in the countries under consideration. On the other hand, differences in degree may be merely apparent. Lincoln Steffens pointed out that newspapers can create a "crime wave" any time they wish, simply by emphasizing all the minor assaults and thefts commonly ignored or given an inch or two on a back page. The great reported increases in insanity may be due to the fact that in a more urban and institutionalized society cases of insanity more frequently come to the attention of authorities and hence are recorded in statistics.

Causation

13   The most common way of deciding that one thing causes another thing is the simple principle: *post hoc, ergo propter hoc,* "After this,
therefore because of this." Rome fell after the introduction of Christianity;
therefore Christianity was responsible for the fall of Rome. Such reasoning
illustrates another kind of faulty generalization. But even if one could find
ten cases in which a nation "fell" after the introduction of Christianity, it
still would not be at all certain that Christianity caused the fall. Day, it
has frequently been pointed out, follows night in every observable instance, and yet night cannot be called the cause of day. Usually a combination of causes produces a result. Sitting in a draught may cause a cold,
but only given a certain physical condition in the person sitting there. In
such instances one may distinguish between necessary and sufficient conditions. Air is a necessary condition for the maintenance of plant life, but
air alone is not sufficient to produce plant life. And often different causes
at different times may produce the same result. This relation is known as
plurality of causes. If, after sitting in a stuffy theatre on Monday, and then
again after eating in a stuffy restaurant on Thursday, a man suffered from
headaches, he might say, generalizing, that bad air gave him headaches.
But actually the headache on Monday may have been caused by eyestrain
and on Thursday by indigestion. To isolate the causative factor it is necessary that all other conditions be precisely the same. Such isolation is
possible, except in very simple instances, only in the laboratory or with
scientific methods. If a picture falls from the wall every time a truck passes,
we can quite certainly say that the truck's passing is the proximate or immediate cause. But with anything as complex and conditional as a nation's
economy or human character, the determination of cause is not easy or
certain. A psychiatrist often sees a patient for an hour daily for a year or
more before he feels that he understands his neurosis.

14   Ordinarily when we speak of cause we mean the proximate or immediate cause. The plants were killed by frost; we had indigestion from
eating lobster salad. But any single cause is one in an unbroken series.
When a man is murdered, is his death caused by the loss of blood from
the wound, or by the firing of the pistol, or by the malice aforethought of
the murderer? Was the World War "caused" by the assassination at Sara-
jevo? Were the Navigation Acts or the ideas of John Locke more important in "causing" the American Revolution? A complete statement of
cause would comprise the sum total of the conditions which preceded an
event, conditions stretching back indefinitely into the past. Historical
events are so interrelated that the isolation of a causative sequence is dependent chiefly on the particular preoccupations of the historian. An

economic determinist can "explain" history entirely in terms of economic developments; an idealist, entirely in terms of the development of ideas.

Syllogistic reasoning

15   The formal syllogism of the type,

> All men are mortal
> John is a man
> Therefore John is mortal,

is not so highly regarded today as in some earlier periods. It merely fixes an individual as a member of a class, and then assumes that the individual has the given characteristics of the class. Once we have decided who John is, and what "man" and "mortal" mean, and have canvassed all men, including John, to make sure that they are mortal, the conclusion naturally follows. It can be seen that the chief difficulties arise in trying to establish acceptable premises. Faults in the premises are known as "material" fallacies, and are usually more serious than the "formal" fallacies, which are logical defects in drawing a conclusion from the premises. But although directly syllogistic reasoning is not much practiced, buried syllogism can be found in all argument, and it is often a useful clarification to outline your own or another writer's essay in syllogistic form. The two most frequent defects in the syllogism itself are the undistributed and the ambiguous middle. The middle term is the one that appears in each of the premises and not in the conclusion. In the syllogism,

> All good citizens vote
> John votes
> Therefore John is a good citizen,

the middle term is not "good citizens," but "votes." Even though it were true that all good citizens vote, nothing prevents bad citizens from voting also, and John may be one of the bad citizens. To distribute the middle term "votes" one might say (but only if that is what one meant),

> All voters are good citizens
> John is a voter
> Therefore John is a good citizen.

16   The ambiguous middle term is even more common. It represents a problem in definition, while the undistributed middle is a problem in generalization. All acts which benefit others are virtuous, losing money at poker benefits others, therefore losing at poker is a virtuous act. Here the middle term "act which benefits others" is obviously used very loosely and ambiguously.

Non-sequitur

17   This phrase, meaning "it does not follow," is used to characterize the kind of humor found in pictures in which the Marx Brothers perform. It is an amusing illogicality because it usually expresses, beneath its apparent incongruity, an imaginative, associative, or personal truth. "My ancestors came over on the Mayflower; therefore I am naturally opposed to labor unions." It is not logically necessary that those whose ancestors came over on the Mayflower should be opposed to unions; but it may happen to be true as a personal fact in a given case. It is usually a strong personal conviction which keeps people from realizing that their arguments are non-sequiturs, that they do not follow the given premises with logical necessity. Contemporary psychologists have effectively shown us that there is often such a wide difference between the true and the purported reasons for an attitude that, in rationalizing our behavior, we are often quite unconscious of the motives that actually influence us. A fanatical antivivisectionist, for instance, may have temperamental impulses toward cruelty which he is suppressing and compensating for by a reasoned opposition to any kind of permitted suffering. We may expect, then, to come upon many conclusions which are psychologically interesting in themselves, but have nothing to do with the given premises.

Ignoratio elenchi

18   This means, in idiomatic English, "arguing off the point," or ignoring the question at issue. A man trying to show that monarchy is the best form of government for the British Empire may devote most of his attention to the charm of Elizabeth II and the affection her people feel for her. In ordinary conversational argument it is almost impossible for disputants to keep to the point. Constantly turning up are tempting side-issues through which one can discomfit an opponent or force him to irrelevant admissions that seem to weaken his case.

Begging the question; arguing in a circle

19   The first of these terms means to assume in the premises what you are pretending to prove in the course of your argument. The function of logic is to demonstrate that because one thing or group of things is true, another must be true as a consequence. But in begging the question you

simply say in varying language that what is assumed to be true is assumed to be true. An argument which asserts that we shall enjoy immortality because we have souls which are immaterial and indestructible establishes nothing, because the idea of immortality is already contained in the assumption about the soul. It is the premise which needs to be demonstrated, not the conclusion. Arguing in a circle is another form of this fallacy. It proves the premise by the conclusion and the conclusion by the premise. The conscience forbids an act because it is wrong; the act is wrong because the conscience forbids it.

Arguments ad hominem and ad populum

20   It is very difficult for men to be persuaded by reason when their interest or prestige is at stake. If one wishes to preach the significance of physiognomy, it is well to choose a hearer with a high forehead and a determined jaw. The arguments in favor of repealing the protective tariff on corn or wheat in England were more readily entertained by manufacturers than by landowners. The cotton manufacturers in New England who were doing a profitable trade with the South were the last to be moved by descriptions of the evils of slavery. Because interest and desire are so deeply seated in human nature, arguments are frequently mingled with attempts to appeal to emotion, arouse fear, play upon pride, attack the characters of proponents of an opposite view, show that their practice is inconsistent with their principles; all matters which have, strictly speaking, nothing to do with the truth or falsity, the general desirability or undesirability, of some particular measure. If men are desperate enough they will listen to arguments proper only to an insane asylum but which seem to promise them relief.

21   After reading these suggestions, which are largely negative, the student may feel that any original assertion he can make will probably contain one or several logical faults. This assumption is not true. Even if it were, we know from reading newspapers and magazines that worldly fame is not dimmed by the constant and, one suspects, conscious practice of illogicality. But generalizations are not made only by charlatans and sophists. Intelligent and scrupulous writers also have a great many fresh and provocative observations and conclusions to express and are expressing them influentially. What is intelligence but the ability to see the connection between things, to discern causes, to relate the particular to the general, to define and discriminate and compare? Any man who thinks and feels and observes closely will not want for something to express.

22   And in his expression a proponent will find that a due regard for logic does not limit but rather increases the force of his argument. When

statements are not trite, they are usually controversial. Men arrive at truth dialectically; error is weeded out in the course of discussion, argument, attack, and counterattack. Not only can a writer who understands logic show the weaknesses of arguments he disagrees with, but also, by antici-pating the kind of attack likely to be made on his own ideas, he can so arrange them, properly modified with qualifications and exceptions, that the anticipated attack is made much less effective. Thus, fortunately, we do not have to depend on the spirit of fairness and love of truth to lead men to logic; it has the strong support of argumentative necessity and of the universal desire to make ideas prevail.

Questions

Identify logical fallacies in the statements that follow. Some may contain more than one fallacy as described by Davis.

1. Give me liberty or give me death!
2. Either you agree with me or your position is un-American.
3. Because all urban areas in the United States have a higher incidence of violent crimes than suburban ones, people who live in U.S. cities are more criminally inclined than those who live in its suburbs.
4. No one with such unattractive features could possibly make a good district attorney.
5. Anyone who does not love animals should not be elected to the Presidency of the United States.
6. Of course he is guilty! He is on trial, isn't he?
7. Unless we have effective ordinances to control air pollution in urban areas, it will eventually be impossible for anyone to live in them.
8. A tough and unbending attitude is all we need to solve this crisis. Remem-ber how our ancestors defied the British?
9. Man's tranquility began to be threatened seriously because illuminating gas began to give way to the electric light.
10. The latest figures show that the price of rum in Jamaica rises with the sala-ries of Presbyterian ministers in Vermont. The WCTU ought to investigate.
11. To the extent a culture devotes its resources to funerary processions and memorials it makes death less real.
12. Why study for my mathematics test? I studied for English and flunked it.
13. I guess my dog is a tiger. After all, he has four feet, a tail, and whiskers.
14. Cigarettes cannot be bad for you. Don't baseball players smoke them?
15. You can not vote for Adams for Senator. He never met a payroll, did he?
16. Franklin D. Roosevelt, who was President when World War II began, must have been responsible for the war.

10 ERIC BERNE

Can People Be Judged
by Their Appearance?

1   Everyone knows that a human being, like a chicken, comes from an egg. At a very early stage, the human embryo forms a three-layered tube, the inside layer of which grows into the stomach and lungs, the middle layer into bones, muscles, joints, and blood vessels, and the outside layer into the skin and nervous system.

2   Usually these three grow about equally, so that the average human being is a fair mixture of brains, muscles, and inward organs. In some eggs, however, one layer grows more than the others, and when the angels have finished putting the child together, he may have more gut than brain, or more brain than muscle. When this happens, the individual's activities will often be mostly with the overgrown layer.

3   We can thus say that while the average human being is a mixture, some people are mainly "digestion-minded," some "muscle-minded," and some "brain-minded," and correspondingly digestion-bodied, muscle-bodied, or brain-bodied. The digestion-bodied people look thick; the muscle-bodied people look wide; and the brain-bodied people look long. This does not mean the taller a man is the brainier he will be. It means that if a man, even a short man, looks long rather than wide or thick, he will often be more concerned about what goes on in his mind than about what he does or what he eats; but the key factor is slenderness and not height. On the other hand, a man who gives the impression of being thick rather than long or wide will usually be more interested in a good steak than in a good idea or a good long walk.

4   Medical men use Greek words to describe these types of body-build. For the man whose body shape mostly depends on the inside layer of the egg, they use the word *endomorph*. If it depends mostly upon the middle layer, they call him a *mesomorph*. If it depends upon the outside layer, they call him an *ectomorph*. We can see the same roots in our English words "enter," "medium," and "exit," which might just as easily have been spelled "ender," "mesium," and "ectit."

5   Since the inside skin of the human egg, or endoderm, forms the inner organs of the belly, the viscera, the endomorph is usually belly-minded;

From *A Layman's Guide to Psychiatry and Psychoanalysis* (New York: Grove Press, 1962) pp. 3–5. Copyright © 1949, 1957, by Eric Berne. Reprinted by permission of Simon & Schuster, Inc.

since the middle skin forms the body tissues, or soma, the mesomorph is usually muscle-minded; and since the outside skin forms the brain, or cerebrum, the ectomorph is usually brain-minded. Translating this into Greek, we have the viscerotonic endomorph, the somatatonic mesomorph, and the cerebrotonic ectomorph.

6   Words are beautiful things to a cerebrotonic, but a viscerotonic knows you cannot eat a menu no matter what language it is printed in, and a somatotonic knows you cannot increase your chest expansion by reading a dictionary. So it is advisable to leave these words and see what kinds of people they actually apply to, remembering again that most individuals are fairly equal mixtures and that what we have to say concerns only the extremes. Up to the present, these types have been thoroughly studied only in the male sex.

7   *Viscerotonic endomorph.* If a man is definitely a thick type rather than a broad or long type, he is likely to be round and soft, with a big chest but a bigger belly. He would rather eat than breathe comfortably. He is likely to have a wide face, short, thick neck, big thighs and upper arms, and small hands and feet. He has overdeveloped breasts and looks as though he were blown up a little like a balloon. His skin is soft and smooth, and when he gets bald, as he does usually quite early, he loses the hair in the middle of his head first.

8   The short, jolly, thickset, red-faced politician with a cigar in his mouth, who always looks as though he were about to have a stroke, is the best example of this type. The reason he often makes a good politician is that he likes people, banquets, baths, and sleep; he is easygoing, soothing, and his feelings are easy to understand.

9   His abdomen is big because he has lots of intestines. He likes to take in things. He likes to take in food, and affection and approval as well. Going to a banquet with people who like him is his idea of a fine time. It is important for a psychiatrist to understand the natures of such men when they come to him for advice.

10   *Somatotonic mesomorph.* If a man is definitely a broad type rather than a thick or long type, he is likely to be rugged and have lots of muscle. He is apt to have big forearms and legs, and his chest and belly are well formed and firm, with the chest bigger than the belly. He would rather breathe than eat. He has a bony head, big shoulders, and a square jaw. His skin is thick, coarse, and elastic, and tans easily. If he gets bald, it usually starts on the front of the head.

11   Dick Tracy, Li'l Abner, and other men of action belong to this type. Such people make good lifeguards and construction workers. They like to put out energy. They have lots of muscles and they like to use them. They go in for adventure, exercise, fighting, and getting the upper hand. They are bold and unrestrained, and love to master the people and things around them. If the psychiatrist knows the things which give such people satisfac-

tion, he is able to understand why they may be unhappy in certain situations.

12   *Cerebrotonic ectomorph.* The man who is definitely a long type is likely to have thin bones and muscles. His shoulders are apt to sag and he has a flat belly with a dropped stomach, and long, weak legs. His neck and fingers are long, and his face is shaped like a long egg. His skin is thin, dry, and pale, and he rarely gets bald. He looks like an absent-minded professor and often is one.

13   Though such people are jumpy, they like to keep their energy and don't fancy moving around much. They would rather sit quietly by themselves and keep out of difficulties. Trouble upsets them, and they run away from it. Their friends don't understand them very well. They move jerkily and feel jerkily. The psychiatrist who understands how easily they become anxious is often able to help them get along better in the sociable and aggressive world of endomorphs and mesomorphs.

14   In the special cases where people definitely belong to one type or another, then, one can tell a good deal about their personalities from their appearance. When the human mind is engaged in one of its struggles with itself or with the world outside, the individual's way of handling the struggle will be partly determined by his type. If he is a viscerotonic he will often want to go to a party where he can eat and drink and be in good company at a time when he might be better off attending to business; the somatotonic will want to go out and do something about it, master the situation, even if what he does is foolish and not properly figured out, while the cerebrotonic will go off by himself and think it over, when perhaps he would be better off doing something about it or seeking good company to try to forget it.

15   Since these personality characteristics depend on the growth of the layers of the little egg from which the person developed, they are very difficult to change. Nevertheless, it is important for the individual to know about these types, so that he can have at least an inkling of what to expect from those around him, and can make allowances for the different kinds of human nature, and so that he can become aware of and learn to control his own natural tendencies, which may sometimes guide him into making the same mistakes over and over again in handling his difficulties.

11   PHILIP WHEELWRIGHT

The Meaning of Ethics

For you see, Callicles, our discussion is concerned with a matter in which even a man of slight intelligence must take the profoundest interest—namely, what course of life is best.   —SOCRATES, in Plato's *Gorgias*

1   Man is the animal who can reflect. Like other animals, no doubt, he spends much of his time in merely reacting to the pressures and urgencies of his environment. But being a man he has moments also of conscious stock-taking, when he becomes aware not only of his world but of himself confronting his world, evaluating it, and making choices with regard to it. It is this ability to know himself and on the basis of self-knowledge to make evaluations and reflective choices that differentiates man from his subhuman cousins.

2   There are, as Aristotle has pointed out, two main ways in which man's power of reflection becomes active. They are called, in Aristotle's language, *theoretikos* and *praktikos* respectively; which is to say, thinking about what is actually the case and thinking about what had better be done. In English translation the words *contemplative* and *operative* probably come closest to Aristotle's intent. To think contemplatively is to ask oneself what *is;* to think operatively is to ask oneself what to *do.* These are the two modes of serious, one might even say of genuine thought—as distinguished from daydreams, emotional vaporizings, laryngeal chatter, and the repetition of clichés. To think seriously is to think either for the sake of knowing things as they are or for the sake of acting upon, and producing or helping to produce, things as they might be.

3   Although in practice the two types of thinking are much interrelated, it is operative thinking with which our present study is primarily concerned. Ethics, although it must be guided, limited, and qualified constantly by considerations of what is actually the case, is focused upon questions of what should be done. The converse, however, does not follow. Not all questions about what should be done are ethical questions. Much of our operative thinking is given to more immediate needs—to means whereby some given end can be achieved. A person who deliberates as to the most effective way of making money, or of passing a course, or of winning a battle, or of achieving popularity, is thinking operatively, but

Philip Wheelright, *A Critical Introduction to Ethics,* Third Edition (New York: Odyssey Press, 1959), pp. 3–20. Copyright © by The Odyssey Press, Inc. Reprinted by permission of the copyright holder.

if that is as far as his planning goes it cannot be called ethical. Such deliberations about adapting means to an end would acquire an ethical character only if some thought were given to the nature and value of the end itself. Ethics cannot dispense with questions of means, but neither can it stop there.

4   Accordingly, ethics may be defined as that branch of philosophy which is the systematic study of reflective choice, of the standards of right and wrong by which it is to be guided, and of the goods toward which it may ultimately be directed. The relation between the parts of this definition, particularly between standards of right and wrong on the one hand and ultimately desirable goods on the other, will be an important part of the forthcoming study.

The nature of moral deliberation

5   The soundest approach to ethical method is through reflection on our experience of moral situations which from time to time we have had occasion to face, or through an imagined confrontation of situations which others have faced and which we can thus make sympathetically real to ourselves. For instance:

Arthur Ames is a rising young district attorney engaged on his most important case. A prominent political boss has been murdered. Suspicion points at a certain ex-convict, known to have borne the politician a grudge. Aided by the newspapers, which have reported the murder in such a way as to persuade the public of the suspect's guilt, Ames feels certain that he can secure a conviction on the circumstantial evidence in his possession. If he succeeds in sending the man to the chair he will become a strong candidate for governor at the next election.

During the course of the trial, however, he accidentally stumbles on some fresh evidence, known only to himself and capable of being destroyed if he chooses, which appears to establish the ex-convict's innocence. If this new evidence were to be introduced at the trial an acquittal would be practically certain. What ought the District Attorney to do? Surrender the evidence to the defence, in order that, as a matter of fair play, the accused might be given every legitimate chance of establishing his innocence? But to do that will mean the loss of a case that has received enormous publicity; the District Attorney will lose the backing of the press; he will appear to have failed, and his political career may be blocked. In that event not only will he himself suffer disappointment, but his ample plans for bestowing comforts on his family and for giving his children the benefits of a superior education may have to be curtailed. On the other hand, ought he to be instrumental in sending a man to the chair for a crime that in all probability he did not commit? And yet the ex-convict is a bad lot; even if innocent in the present case he has doubtless committed many other crimes in which he has escaped detection. Is a fellow like that worth the sacrifice of one's career? Still, there is no proof that he has ever committed a crime punishable by death. Until a man has been proved guilty he must be regarded, by a sound principle of American legal theory, as innocent. To conceal and destroy the new evidence, then, is not that tantamount to railroading an innocent man to the chair?

So District Attorney Ames reasons back and forth. He knows that it is a widespread custom for a district attorney to conceal evidence prejudicial to his side of a case. But is the custom, particularly when a human life is at stake, morally right? A district attorney is an agent of the government, and his chief aim in that capacity should be to present his accusations in such a way as to ensure for the accused not condemnation but justice. The question, then, cannot be answered by appealing simply to law or to legal practice. It is a moral one: *What is Arthur Ames' duty? What ought he to do?*

Benjamin Bates has a friend who lies in a hospital, slowly dying of a painful and incurable disease. Although there is no hope of recovery, the disease sometimes permits its victim to linger on for many months, in ever greater torment and with threatened loss of sanity. The dying man, apprised of the outcome and knowing that the hospital expenses are a severe drain on his family's limited financial resources, decides that death had better come at once. His physician, he knows, will not run the risk of providing him with the necessary drug. There is only his friend Bates to appeal to.

How shall Bates decide? Dare he be instrumental in hastening another's death? Has he a moral right to be accessory to the taking of a human life? Besides, suspicion would point his way, and his honorable motives would not avert a charge of murder. On the other hand, can he morally refuse to alleviate a friend's suffering and the financial distress of a family when the means of doing so are in his hands? And has he not an obligation to respect a friend's declared will in the matter? To acquiesce and to refuse seem both somehow in different ways wrong, yet one course or the other must be chosen. *What ought Bates to do? Which way does his duty lie?*

In the city occupied by Crampton College a strike is declared by the employees of all the public-transit lines. Their wages have not been increased to meet the rising cost of living, and the justice of their grievance is rather widely admitted by neutral observers. The strike ties up business and causes much general inconvenience; except for the people who have cars of their own or can afford taxi fare, there is no way of getting from one part of the city to another. Labor being at this period scarce, an appeal is made by the mayor to college students to serve the community by acting in their spare time as motormen and drivers. The appeal is backed by a promise of lucrative wages and by the college administration's agreement to coöperate by permitting necessary absences from classes.

What ought the students of Crampton College to do? If they act as strikebreakers they aid in forcing the employees back to work on the corporation's own terms. Have they any right to interfere so drastically and one-sidedly in the lives and happiness of others? On the other hand, if they turn down the mayor's request the community will continue to suffer grave inconveniences until the fight is somehow settled. *What is the students' duty in the matter? What is the right course for them to follow?*

6   These three situations, although perhaps unusual in the severity of their challenge, offer examples of problems distinctively moral. When the act of moral deliberation implicit in each of them is fully carried out, certain characteristic phases can be discerned.

7   (i) *Examination and clarification of the alternatives.* What are the relevant possibilities of action in the situation confronting me? Am I clear about the nature of each? Have I clearly distinguished them from one another? And are they mutually exhaustive, or would a more attentive search reveal others? In the case of District Attorney Ames, for example, a third alternative might have been to make a private deal with the ex-convict by which, in exchange for his acquittal, the District Attorney would receive the profits from some lucrative racket of which the ex-convict had control. No doubt to a reputable public servant this line of conduct would be too repugnant for consideration; it exemplifies, nevertheless, the ever-present logical possibility of going "between the horns" [1] of the original dilemma.

8   (ii) *Rational elaboration of consequences.* The next step is to think out the probable consequences of each of the alternatives in question. As this step involves predictions about a hypothetical future, the conclusions can have, at most, a high degree of probability, never certainty. The degree of probability is heightened according as there is found some precedent in past experience for each of the proposed choices. Even if the present situation seems wholly new, analysis will always reveal *some* particulars for which analogies in past experience can be found or to which known laws of causal sequence are applicable. Such particulars will be dealt with partly by analogy (an act similar to the one now being deliberated about had on a previous occasion such and such consequences) and partly by the inductive-deductive method: appealing to general laws (deduction) which in turn have been built up as generalizations from observed particulars (induction). Mr. Ames, we may suppose, found the materials for this step in his professional knowledge of law and legal precedent, as well as in his more general knowledge of the policies of the press, the gullibility of its readers, and the high cost of domestic luxuries.

9   (iii) *Imaginative projection of the self into the predicted situation.* It is not enough to reason out the probable consequences of a choice. In a moral deliberation the chief interests involved are not scientific but human and practical. The only way to judge the comparative desirability of two possible futures is to live through them both in imagination. The third step, then, is to project oneself imaginatively into the future; i.e., establish a dramatic identification of the present self with that future

[1] I.e., finding a third alternative.

self to which the now merely imagined experiences may become real. Few persons, unfortunately, are capable of an imaginative identification forceful enough to give the claims of the future self an even break. Present goods loom larger than future goods, and goods in the immediate future than goods that are remote. The trained ethical thinker must have a sound *temporal perspective,* the acquisition of which is to be sought by a frequent, orderly, and detailed exercise of the imagination with respect to not yet actual situations.

10   (iv) *Imaginative identification of the self with the points of view of those persons whom the proposed act will most seriously affect.* Whatever decision I make here and now, if of any importance, is likely to have consequences, in varying degrees, for persons other than myself. An important part of a moral inquiry is to envisage the results of a proposed act as they will appear to those other persons affected by them. I must undertake, then, a dramatic identification of my own self with the selves of other persons. The possibility of doing this is evident from a consideration of how anyone's dramatic imagination works in the reading of a novel or the witnessing of a play. If the persons in the novel or play are dramatically convincing it is not because their characters and actions have been established by logical proof, but because they are presented so as to provoke in the reader an impulse to project himself into the world of the novel or play, to identify himself with this and that character in it, to share their feelings and moods, to get their slant on things.

11   In most persons, even very benevolent ones, the social consciousness works by fits and starts. To examine fairly the needs and claims of other selves is no less hard and is often harder than to perform a similar task with regard to one's own future self. Accordingly the ethical thinker must develop *social perspective*—that balanced appreciation of others' needs and claims which is the basis of justice.

12   In this fourth, as in the third step, the imaginative projection is to be carried out for each of the alternatives, according as their consequences shall have been predicted by Step ii.

13   (v) *Estimation and comparison of the values involved.* Implicit in the third and fourth steps is a recognition that certain values both positive and negative are latent in each of the hypothetical situations to which moral choice may lead. The values must be made explicit in order that they may be justly compared, for it is as a result of their comparison that a choice is to be made. To make values explicit is to give them a relatively abstract formulation; they still, however, derive concrete significance from their imagined exemplifications. District Attorney Ames, for example, might have envisaged his dilemma as a choice between family happiness and worldly success on the one hand as against professional honor on the other. Each of these is undoubtedly good, that is to say a value, but the values cannot be reduced to a common denominator. Family happiness enters as

a factor into Benjamin Bates' dilemma no less than into that of Arthur Ames, but it stands to be affected in a different way and therefore, in spite of the identical words by which our linguistic poverty forces us to describe it, it does not mean the same thing. Family happiness may mean any number of things; so may success, and honor—although these different meanings have, of course, an intelligible bond of unity. Arthur Ames' task is to compare not just any family happiness with any professional honor but the particular exemplifications of each that enter into his problem. The comparison is not a simple calculation but an imaginative deliberation, in which the abstract values that serve as the logical ground of the comparison are continuous with, and interactive with, the concrete particulars that serve as its starting-point.

14   (vi) *Decision.* Comparison of the alternative future situations and the values embodied in each must terminate in a decision. Which of the possible situations do I deem it better to bring into existence? There are no rules for the making of this decision. I must simply decide as wisely and as fairly and as relevantly to the total comparison as I can. Every moral decision is a risk, for the way in which a person decides is a factor in determining the kind of self he is going to become.

15   (vii) *Action.* The probable means of carrying out the decision have been established by Step ii. The wished-for object or situation is an end, certain specific means toward the fulfillment of which lie here and now within my power. These conditions supply the premises for an ethical syllogism. When a certain end, x, is recognized as the best of the available alternatives, and when the achievement of it is seen to be possible through a set of means a, b, c . . . which lie within my power, then whichever of the means a, b, c . . . is an action that can here and now be performed becomes at just this point my duty. If the deliberative process has been carried out forcefully and wisely it will have supplied a categorical answer to the question, What ought I to do?—even though the answer in some cases may be, Do nothing.

16   Naturally, not all experiences of moral deliberation and choice reveal these seven phases in a distinct, clear-cut way. Nor is the order here given always the actual order. Sometimes we may begin by deliberating about the relative merits of two ends, seeking the means simultaneously with this abstract inquiry, or after its completion. The foregoing analysis does, however, throw some light on the nature of a moral problem, and may be tested by applying it to the three cases described at the beginning of the chapter.

Logical analysis of a moral situation

17   The usual sign of a moral question is the auxiliary verb, *ought.* Not every "ought," however, is a moral ought. There must be distin-

guished: (1) the logical "ought," as in "The balance ought to be $34 but I make it $29," "From the appearance of the sky I should say we ought to have snow tonight," "The story ought never to have had a happy ending"; (2) the prudential "ought," as in "If you want to avoid colds you ought to try Hydrolux Vapo-lite." These two uses of the word "ought" express, like the moral ought, propriety with respect to a certain end or standard. But unlike the moral ought, the ought in (1) does not refer directly to human conduct, and while the ought in (2) does have this reference, the imperative that it expresses is conditional on a wish. The imperative expressed by the moral ought is, on the contrary, unconditional: You ought to be honorable—not *if* you wish men to respect you; men's respect is a desirable adjunct of being honorable, but you ought to be honorable in any case. The moral ought is what Kant has called a categorical imperative. In being categorical it is distinguished from the prudential ought; in being an imperative, i.e., a call to action, it is distinguished also from the logical ought. It is the moral ought that is the subject-matter of ethics, and it is in this ethical sense, therefore, that the word "ought" will be used in the present volume. We may now consider the principal factors which the moral ought involves.

Value and possibility

18   The first factor to be noted in a moral situation is the *presence of value*. Whenever an inclination is felt, that toward which the inclination points is felt to have value. What is felt to have value need not on reflection be *judged* to have value. Judgment can correct our immediate feelings of value, just as in an act of sense-perception judgment corrects and interprets the immediate sense-data. Inclination is thus not identical with value; but it is the psycho-physical basis of its presence.

19   To say that a value is present in an object is to declare that the object is *in some sense* good. We may therefore restate the first requirement of a moral situation by saying that some things must be recognized as good; or, since good is a relative term, that *some things are recognized as better than others*. But if *a* is better than *b*, *b* is worse than *a*. It follows, then, that some things are *worse* than others, and the first requirement may therefore be restated as an ability to distinguish what is comparatively good from what is comparatively bad. What particular things are good, and what bad, is of course another question. The principle here laid down is simply that to a person who did not set a higher value on some things than on others there could be no moral problem. (Indeed, it is a little hard to see how such a person could have any *problems* at all.) A moral situation presupposes, then, as the first condition of its existence, the recognition of some values or other.

20   This primary characteristic of a moral situation defines ethics as a normative science. Ethics is not a science at all in the same way that the

empirical sciences are so designated, and its methods are fundamentally distinct. It shares, nevertheless, the larger meaning of science, for its subject-matter can be arranged systematically and certain guiding principles be found. But while such sciences as physics, psychology, economics, etc. are primarily concerned with the recording, predicting, and structuralizing of facts, ethics is concerned with facts only secondarily, only so far as they are morally evaluated or judged to be in some way relevant to the application of moral values. That skies are sunny in New Mexico is a fact; that many people are without lucrative employment is also a fact. Both are equally facts, but our valuations of them differ. It is such differences in valuation, such *normative* differences, that establish the basis of a moral situation.

21   A second element in any moral situation is *the presence of possible alternatives*. To evaluate anything as good is equivalent to declaring that it ought to be, or ought to persist. Ethics does not stop with the good, with what merely ought to *be;* it accepts this as but one element in the question, What ought to *be done?* To say that a person ought to do a thing implies a power on his part *to do or refrain from doing it*. We do not say that the President of the United States ought to put an immediate stop to all human suffering, for the President, however much he might desire such a consummation, has not the power of achieving it; the most we can say is that the President ought to take such steps as may lie within his power to move toward the goal. Nor, on the other hand, do we say, speaking accurately, that a man ought to obey the law of gravitation, for this is something that he must do willy-nilly. Neither "must" nor "cannot" is in the strict sense compatible with "ought."

22   These two elements, the presence of value and the presence of possible alternatives in a moral situation, are intimately related, for in order that the alternatives may have moral significance some kind of value must be attached to each of them. In some cases the value of each alternative is assigned rationally. In other cases, the most familiar of which are those described as "battling with temptation," our rational judgment assigns value to only one of the alternatives; the other is merely *felt* to have value, as a result of our experiencing a strong inclination toward it. But in either type of situation there must be some value, whether deliberately judged or spontaneously felt, attached to both alternatives, in order that there may be a moral problem.

23   For example, there exist for me the possible alternatives of plucking a blade of grass or of not doing so, but the situation is not a moral one, for neither alternative has (on any likely occasion) any value. Or again, it lies in my power to go without my dinner. In this instance one of the alternatives (eating dinner) has value, the other (going without it) has probably none, so that again there is no moral problem. If, however, I judged that abstention from dinner would be a stoic discipline good

for my character, or if by abstaining I could afford to attend a play that I wanted to see, or could devote the dinner hour to some work that needed to be done, the situation would be to this extent a moral one, for a value would be set on each of the alternatives. Indeed, the great difficulty of moral problems and the indecisiveness of much moral deliberation are due principally to this fact, that both of the alternatives with which our deliberation is concerned are in some manner valued and their values are often incommensurate.

Moral insight

24   A moral situation, furthermore, must have a consequential character. Even where value and possibility are both present a situation may still be amoral—which is to say, it may be a situation to which ethical considerations do not properly apply. Choosing between different dishes on a restaurant menu provides a familiar example. If pot roast and sweetbreads are offered as alternative choices at the same price, the only thing that a diner would ordinarily have to consider is which one of them he would prefer. If his decision is not automatic, if he spends any time in deliberating over the choice, then he must evidently have set some value upon each of the two dishes, between which he regards himself as free to choose. Thus the first two conditions of a moral situation are met: there is a conflict between values, and a choice between them is possible. Nevertheless, the situation as it stands is not a moral one. The alternatives are considered simply as ends in themselves; the values involved in the diner's choice will terminate in the enjoyment of what he has chosen, and the duration of that enjoyment will be short. Nothing of any significance will be entailed by his ordering one meat rather than the other. The situation is pretty much isolated from the main lines of his experience and his choices.

25   Even where no social relationships are immediately involved, a choice may have moral character, to the degree that it is significantly consequential. If a certain action promises a greater intensity of pleasure at the moment but appears likely to entail later pains or inconveniences of an important kind, moral insight into these future consequences is called for, and the situation is thus a moral one, although not in a social way. Whether consideration must be taken of the claims of other selves or only of one's own future self, in either case the choice is related to, and partly concerned with, something beyond the immediate result. Mechanical computation is not possible here as it is in the case of physical measurements, for there are no sets of physical units that can be compared. In a moral situation the difference between the competing values is at least partly one of kind, not merely of degree, and human interests and valuations are not manifold, so subject to continual growth and reconsideration, that the

insights themselves have only a tenuous stability. What is required is an insight into the remoter values involved, and the probable embodiments they would take in relation to those affected. It is in the deepening and maturing of men's moral insights that the best index of human development is to be found.

26   The third requirement of a moral situation, then, has a double aspect. The choice must be consequential, and this may be seen from two sides. The alternatives are not simple ends-in-themselves terminating here and now; they involve values over and beyond the values of immediate enjoyment. And the agent by whom the choice is to be made must therefore have an imaginative grasp of the consequences, an imaginative insight into the nature of the values that are only hinted at in the immediate situation.

27   But is insight enough? Even when I fully comprehend that a certain course of action is both possible and the best one for me to undertake, is it guaranteed that I will therefore undertake it? We all know that it is not. The experience of temptation is familiar to everybody—the inward tension and struggle in which I perceive that one way of acting is the right way but am powerfully drawn towards some enticing but more limited good. Let us look at the nature of this kind of experience more closely.

The good and the right

28   What I want to do is frequently opposed to what I know I ought to do: i.e., the present good is often incompatible with what seems to be right. As previously stated, there must be some inclination toward both of the alternatives with which any moral deliberation is concerned. This is the same thing as to say that both alternatives are felt or thought to be somehow good. But the qualities of the competing goods may be radically different. Say that I am tempted to sit drinking beer with friends when I know that I ought to be devoting the evening to my studies. There is an inclination to linger on; there is also an inclination, of another kind, to say good night and leave. The former inclination is strong and attractive but without rational sanction; whereas—

Quite other is the prompting of the "ought." It is not so much a drive as an inner exhortation. It is not impulsive, but imperative. And what we experience is not ourselves impelled, but ourselves impelling, ourselves impelling ourselves, indeed ourselves impelling ourselves against impulse.[2]

The situation is a sufficiently familiar one. The strongest actual propensity at a given moment is toward a course of action contrary to the one toward which duty beckons. An effort is required to break away from the fascination of the immediate. The sense that such an effort is required, that it

[2] Horace G. Wyatt, *The Art of Feeling,* pp. 169–170.

can be made, and that it would be better to make it because the result would be an eventually greater good, are conditions of a feeling of "ought."

29   The good and the right, though often specifically opposed, are related at bottom. Their actual conflicts are explained by a distinction within the meaning of "good"—between intrinsic and extrinsic goods. A good is called *intrinsic* when it is judged worthy of being sought for its own sake, i.e., when it is an end in itself; *extrinsic* or *instrumental* when it is sought as a means to some other good. The relation is a shifting one, for it is not always possible to distinguish sharply between the end and the means: what is an end from one point of view may be regarded as a means from another. Nevertheless we can say in general that the good of a surgical operation is extrinsic: it must be referred to the greater health that is to come. The enjoyment of a glass of wine is an intrinsic good, a "good in itself": the wine is not enjoyed for the sake of anything distinct from the enjoyment. Still other goods are at once intrinsic and extrinsic; an enjoyable *and* nourishing dinner, a refreshing *and* cleansing bath, and the like. Often the right course of action will consist in choosing some extrinsic good (say, diligent study) which is the only available means to the attainment of some important intrinsic good (say, a professional career). On such occasions the rightness of the action is founded on the good to which it leads, but to the agent it may not appear to partake of any of the character of that remote good. Thus it happens that if the agent is tempted by some more immediate good (such as the pleasures of a lazy life) the conflict, which would be more rationally conceived as a conflict between two goods (present leisure vs. future career) acquires the appearance of a conflict between the present good (leisure) and the present right course of action (diligent study).

The paradox of volition

30   Situations in which there is a genuine moral struggle, in which a temptation must be conquered by a putting forth of moral effort, are crucial for morality. The ultimate justification of a moral principle (and, indirectly, for any ethical theory) is the possibility that it can be made an effective force in moral struggles. William James describes the moral struggle as a situation in which "a rarer and more ideal impulse is called upon to neutralize others of a more instinctive and habitual kind"; in which "strongly explosive tendencies are checked, or strongly obstructive conditions overcome." He continues:

We *feel,* in all hard cases of volition, as if the line taken, when the rarer and more ideal motives prevail, were the line of greater resistance, as if the line of coarser motivation were the more previous and easy one, even at the very moment when we refuse to follow it. He who under the surgeon's knife represses cries of pain, or he who exposes himself to social obloquy for duty's sake, feels as if he were following the line of greatest temporary resistance. . . .

The ideal impulse appears . . . a still small voice which must be artificially reinforced to prevail. Effort is what reinforces it, making things seem as if, while the force of propensity were essentially a fixed quantity, the ideal force might be of various amount. But what determines the amount of the effort when, by its aid, an ideal motive becomes victorious over a great sensual resistance? The very greatness of the resistance itself. If the sensual propensity is small, the effort is small. The latter is *made great* by the presence of a great antagonist to overcome. And if a brief definition of ideal or moral action were required, none could be given which would better fit the appearances than this: *It is action in the line of greatest resistance.*[3]

31   In order to understand James' profoundly valid paradox we must avoid the popular tendency to explain a moral situation wholly by analogies drawn from the physical world. In those aspects of nature studied by physics and chemistry it is always the line of least, never of greater resistance that is followed. The universality of the physical law of least physical resistance, however, is due to the fact that it is not directly applicable to concrete experience, for in *concrete* experience no laws are applicable with unremitting exactitude. Physicists may be allowed to formulate their own laws by the methodology which their technical interests require. But scientific laws tell us nothing directly about moral experience. In this province everyone must be, to a large extent, his own observer. And what is a more assured fact of introspective observation than that in cases of moral struggle *we often can and sometimes do follow the path of greatest resistance?*

32   What we ought to do, however unappealing originally, can be made, by a concentration of purpose, what we want to do. Intelligence (or, as it has previously been called, insight) is the mediator. The reason why it may be *right for my present self* to forego the pleasure of a drinking party is that the sacrifice may promote *a good for my future self:* time for study, or a clear head for tomorrow morning, or money saved, or all three. What I choose is distinct from the greatest immediate satisfaction but not separate from all satisfaction whatever. I have put myself imaginatively in the place of my future self and am thus able to consider the good or the pleasure or the emotional satisfaction apart from, *abstracted* from (i.e., separated by the imagination from) the present experience. This abstractive ability of man is what marks him as rational, and, so far as it becomes effective in directing his conduct, as moral.

33   There is another way, too, in which man's abstractive ability shows itself: in the altruistic "ought." A person can recognize duties not only toward his own future self but toward other persons also.

Here again intelligence is the mediator. Man is able to consider the good or the pleasure or the emotional satisfaction apart from the individual to be satisfied, apart not only from [the particular experience] but from the experi-

[3] William James, *The Principles of Psychology,* Vol. II, pp. 548–549.

encer. If emotional satisfaction is the thing desired, it is so for B, C, D and others as well as for A. The happiness of others is just as much an end as my happiness and just as much to be sought after. The "ought" is the peculiar emotion which now enters to convert this intellectual achievement into conduct.[4]

By this abstractive process the Golden Rule of Jesus, "Do unto others as you would have them do unto you," and the less positive form of the same command, given half a millennium earlier by Confucius, "Refrain from doing to others what you would not have them do to yourself," can be realized as expressions of a binding obligation.

34   Right and wrong, then, are not hollow sounds nor is discussion about them an idle game. If we mean what we say in designating an action right or wrong, if we are doing more than mouthing a conventional formula, our judgment will in some manner affect our subsequent conduct. Ethics is not a pastime for the understanding alone. Ethical theory calls for moral practice, and the full meaning of ethics becomes intelligible only as we translate theories into moral principles that can be made effective forces in the struggle toward ideal ends.

The search for a standard

35   But how, it will be asked, is the particular character of right and wrong on any given occasion to be determined? How can one be sure that the development of moral insight (even if such an accomplishment were not in any case formidably difficult) will necessarily lead to a "right" judgment of where one's duties lie? Or, to shift the perspective, how can one be sure that one's moral insight is sufficiently developed? Superior intelligence is not always enough; it may be put at the service of evil ends. Satan, whatever his delinquencies, was no fool. What clear test, then, (so the popular quandary runs) can be applied to human conduct so as to determine on each occasion whether it is right or wrong; or (from a somewhat more mature point of view) so as to distinguish the higher of two contending values from the lower? Various criteria are proposed, such as the following.

36   (i) *Natural inclinations.* "Follow your impulses; do whatever gives you the most enjoyment": people sometimes talk as if in these trite maxims they had discovered a significant moral truth. Actually they have done the contrary: they have denied that moral truth exists. If inclinations are the only standard of conduct, then there is no standard by which to choose between one inclination and another. Whatever inclination is strongest at any moment becomes for that reason right. Temptation becomes honorable by the sheer fact of being tempting. Evidently there is no moral standard offered here; there is merely a negation of moral standard.

[4] Wyatt, *op. cit.,* p. 168.

37   Sometimes the claims of irrational impulse are bolstered by philosophical arguments based on the alleged facts of human nature. Such arguments will be examined more fully in Chapter 3; here it need only be remarked that human nature is too complex and mysterious to be reduced to any single set or type of facts. If it is a fact that men yield to impulse it is no less a fact that they can and sometimes do rationally redirect or halt their initial impulses. To overcome and remake one's nature is itself an expression of one's nature. That a man faced with alternatives can choose the harder course as against the easier is a supremely important fact, without which moral action would be powerless and moral judgment empty. But it is just this kind of *ideal fact* which the champions of impulse, instinct, and inclination as sufficient guides of life habitually overlook.

38   (ii) *Statute law.* The law of the land is a standard of right and wrong from which no individual is wholly exempt. At the same time it is safe to say that no one obeys all the laws. In the first place, there are numerous laws on the statute books that have long ago become obsolete without ever having been annulled. To obey all the laws an individual would have to employ legal aid to find out what laws there are and exactly what they require in terms of conduct. Secondly, even among the laws that are known, some are held in higher respect than others. During the period when the eighteenth amendment to the Constitution was in force there were many so-called "law-abiding citizens" who had no scruples about buying a drink. Besides, it is a recognized right of an American citizen (by voting and in related ways) to seek to change the existing laws. There must, therefore, be some standard by which the goodness or badness of actual laws, as well as of proposed laws, can be judged.

39   (iii) *Public opinion* is in the long run more authoritative than statute law, for a law that lacks public support will not be obeyed and in the end will either be repealed or, as in the case of many "blue laws," ignored by common consent. Nevertheless, public opinion is often wrong. Its fallibility in particular cases is recognized even by those who accept it as a generally reliable guide. The vast majority of men think emotionally and gregariously. One of the chief tasks of education is admittedly to raise the standard of public opinion. There must be some higher standard, then, by which we can judge the state of public opinion at any time to be bad or good.

40   (iv) There are those who hold that the higher standard is furnished by *religious authority.* Such a view presupposes: (1) a belief in God, (2) a belief that God communicates His will either directly or indirectly to men, and (3) more particularly, a belief that one's own Church or sect or Holy Book is the channel through which God's will is revealed, as a check on the vagaries of one's individual conscience. Even if these beliefs can all be accepted without difficulty, questions of interpretation frequently arise.

The Ten Commandments, for example, forbid stealing. Does this prohibition apply to the practice of ruining your business competitor by price-cutting, and so eventually pocketing his expected receipts? Does it apply to the practice of certain oil, mining, and lumber companies of wasting the country's (i.e., the American people's) natural resources for private gain? Since no clear definition of stealing receives universal consent, the divine command, though indubitably just and important, is subject to numerous ambiguities. Again, Christ's law of love is pretty clearly the key-note of his teaching. But Christians disagree widely on the method of applying that law to such socially urgent problems as war and labor relations.

41   (v) *Conscience* is a part of everyone's standard. Regardless of how we may explain it the existence of a "still small voice" that sometimes on crucial occasions says "Do!" or "Refrain!" is an inescapable phenomenon. The voice of conscience often opposes itself to the inclinations of the moment, sometimes to public opinion; and in fundamental matters it may be, for the dedicated man, a higher court of appeal than any outer law, secular or religious. Still, conscience is far from infallible. It can and ought to be educated, and when a man relies on it uncritically it may turn out to be but the prompting of self-interest satanically masquerading in holy dress.

42   (vi) Conscience then must be controlled, and revelation must be interpreted, by *reason*. Very true. But that is not to say that reason is *the* standard. Immanuel Kant is the outstanding example of a philosopher who tried to make it so, and as might have been expected, his *applications* of his rationally established principles are quite as debatable as those of any other moralist. If generosity is better than selfishness that is not because it is more rational: some philosophers, in fact, have held it to be less so. Rationality is a necessary aspect of ethics but not its sufficient criterion. Ethics, in short, must be logical, but ethics is not logic.

43   Evidently no isolated standard of right and wrong is proof against attack. The function of ethics is not to provide a simple and sure rule by which moral problems can be "solved." An active intelligence revolts against whatever doctrine claims to utter the last word on any matter. Especially is this true in ethics, where the conclusions sought are of such intimate importance to each serious inquirer. Immediate decisions will often have to be reached by appealing to some convenient rule of thumb or to some already developed habit or preference. But it is an advantage of theories that they can be inquired into at leisure. The task of theoretical ethics is not to lay down static norms by which each new moral problem that arises can be decisively answered. Its task is rather to develop a method suitable for the evaluation and criticism of existing norms and for the exploration of new value possibilities, in order that when moral decisions have henceforth to be made their grounds may be more adequate and more worthy.

Assigning Causes

Causal relations

As Erich Fromm's essay illustrates, the process of assigning causes to effect is often, as we can observe without disagreement, a matter of individual interpretation. When the existence of the effect itself may be questioned—for example, Fromm's view that we *are* a society of repressed conformists—the situation becomes even more complex. The mind of an educated man continues, though baffled, to assign causes to effects it perceives, that is, to recognize similarities and differences in the sequence of two discernible things or events. What event invariably and immediately precedes another event? What event invariably and immediately succeeds another?

When almost everyone at the scene of an accident or a fire wants to know how the catastrophe happened, many people remain without curiosity about the proximate and remote causes of political behavior, civil disobedience, or economic hardship in other societies, and even in their own. Indeed, they are equally incurious and unreflective about their own behavior in arguing, drinking, fighting, divorcing; they lead unexamined lives. The enlightened man, however, is engaged in trying to understand himself, his acquaintances, and the problems of his business or profession and those of society at large. Instead of simply accepting effects, he hypothesizes causes with a temper of mind that is always open to fresh observations and ready for new evaluations. For his reasoning mind, the perceivable world is not held together entirely by chance (or freedom) but also by causality (or necessity). If he is to avoid painful consequences and discover those that are pleasureful, he must know, from his own experiences and from scrutiny of reports by others, how events associate themselves.

Establishing probable causes for observed effects and predicting likely effects from known causes may be largely matters of opinion, but it is often in exchanging opinion that men arrive at truth. Why an automobile accident occurred is not often in dispute (though drivers may lie and spectators render various accounts), but why a national election was won or a war lost, why sales fell or a temperature rose, why love ended or death came so soon are questions men have pondered and debated as long as there have been love, death, war, and sales charts. Simple minds accept more easily acts of chance, fate, and God. Educated men attempt to understand and control effects as far as human nature, chance, and God will allow.

Developing the ability to analyze cause and effect with accuracy and insight is a matter of practice. The college freshman should not assume he knows nothing of the causes of certain phenomena in our society. He is at least informed on aspects of his own generation. He may write with the authority of an eyewitness on the causes of juvenile delinquency, the rise of high school dropouts, the causes of conformity, the popularity of teenage entertainment idols, the reasons that youth today seeks minimal success with security rather than dubious success but a venturesome life, the pressures of an organized society in a nuclear age—all subjects on which an older generation needs the opinions of a younger if it is to do more than flounder into our future.

Frequently a bewildering number of causes, which may be classified in various ways, exist in a given situation. An act by officials in our State Department may result in a foreign power's responding in a certain way. We would call this act the *immediate* cause of that government's response. The *ultimate* cause, however, must be sought in factors that shaped the differences in the political and social structures of the two nations. One may also distinguish, and most easily among repeatable and controllable events, between a *necessary* and a *sufficient* condition to cause a given effect. In saying *"x is a cause of y"* we may mean that whenever x exists y follows and that y will also follow when conditions other than x occur. For example, "The Dutch elm disease is fatal to any American elms it infects"; but other factors—the runoff of salts used to melt snow and ice, or bulldozers from the state highway department—may also be fatal to elms, especially near highways. The Dutch elm disease is then a sufficient cause for the death of an elm, even though it does not follow that because an elm died it must have had the disease. On the other hand, a necessary cause is *a* condition that must have been present for the effect, even though the particular effect is not guaranteed by the presence of that condition. We may mean when we say *"x is a cause of y"* that y will not follow unless x occurs. That is, whenever y occurs, x is a necessary and prior condition; but, given $x,$ we have no assurance y does in fact follow. For example, "Water makes plants grow," but the mere adding of water to soil surrounding plants will not guarantee their growth. A "broken home" may be an ultimate cause and sufficient condition for delinquency but not, except in certain cases, the immediate cause. It is quite unlikely to be a necessary condition since some persons who come from homes that are classifiable legally and sociologically as "broken" escape delinquency, and some delinquents come from compatible, unbroken homes.

Events may appear to observers to be so coexistent, so numerous, or so entwined that any causal relation, whether immediate, ultimate, sufficient, or necessary, is difficult if not impossible to establish. As Orwell points out, "an effect can become a cause, reinforcing the original cause and producing the same effect in an intensified form and so on indefinitely. A man may take to drink because he feels himself to be a failure, and then fail all the more completely because he drinks." In such cases, however, one can often take practical steps that will slow, if not completely halt, such spirals even though he may not be able to reduce the complex interplay of cause-and-effect to a set of causal statements.

12   ERICH FROMM
The Illusion of Individuality

1   It is important to consider how our culture fosters this tendency to conform, even though there is space for only a few outstanding examples. The suppression of spontaneous feelings, and thereby of the development of genuine individuality, starts very early, as a matter of fact with the earliest training of a child. This is not to say that training must inevitably lead to suppression of spontaneity if the real aim of education is to further the inner independence and individuality of the child, its growth and integrity. The restrictions which such a kind of education may have to impose upon the growing child are only transitory measures that really support the process of growth and expansion. In our culture, however, education too often results in the elimination of spontaneity and in the substitution of original psychic acts by superimposed feelings, thoughts, and wishes. (By original I do not mean, let me repeat, that an idea has not been thought before by someone else, but that it originates in the individual, that it is the result of his own activity and in this sense is *his* thought.) To choose one illustration somewhat arbitrarily, one of the earliest suppressions of *feelings* concerns hostility and dislike. To start with, most children have a certain measure of hostility and rebelliousness as a result of their conflicts with a surrounding world that tends to block their expansiveness and to which, as the weaker opponent, they usually have to yield. It is one of the essential aims of the educational process to eliminate this antagonistic reaction. The methods are different; they vary

from threats and punishments, which frighten the child, to the subtler methods of bribery or "explanations," which confuse the child and make him give up his hostility. The child starts with giving up the expression of his feeling and eventually gives up the very feeling itself. Together with that, he is taught to suppress the awareness of hostility and insincerity in others; sometimes this is not entirely easy, since children have a capacity for noticing such negative qualities in others without being so easily deceived by words as adults usually are. They still dislike somebody "for no good reason"—except the very good one that they feel the hostility, or insincerity, radiating from that person. This reaction is soon discouraged; it does not take long for the child to reach the "maturity" of the average adult and to lose the sense of discrimination between a decent person and a scoundrel, as long as the latter has not committed some flagrant act.

2   On the other hand, early in his education, the child is taught to have feelings that are not at all "his"; particularly is he taught to like people, to be uncritically friendly to them, and to smile. What education may not have accomplished is usually done by social pressure in later life. If you do not smile you are judged lacking in a "pleasing personality"—and you need to have a pleasing personality if you want to sell your services, whether as a waitress, a salesman, or a physician. Only those at the bottom of the social pyramid, who sell nothing but their physical labor, and those at the very top do not need to be particularly "pleasant." Friendliness, cheerfulness, and everything that a smile is supposed to express, become automatic responses which one turns on and off like an electric switch.[1]

3   To be sure, in many instances the person is aware of merely making a gesture; in most cases, however, he loses that awareness and thereby the ability to discriminate between the pseudo feeling and spontaneous friendliness.

4   It is not only hostility that is directly suppressed and friendliness that is killed by superimposing its counterfeit. A wide range of spontaneous emotions are suppressed and replaced by pseudo feelings. Freud has taken one such suppression and put it in the center of his whole system, namely the suppression of sex. Although I believe that the discouragement of sexual joy is not the only important suppression of spontaneous reactions but one of many, certainly its importance is not to be underrated. Its results are obvious in cases of sexual inhibitions and also in those where sex assumes a compulsive quality and is consumed like liquor or a

---

[1] As one telling illustration of the commercialization of friendliness I should like to cite *Fortune's* report on "The Howard Johnson Restaurants." (*Fortune,* September, 1940, p. 96.) Johnson employs a force of "shoppers" who go from restaurant to restaurant to watch for lapses. "Since everything is cooked on the premises according to standard recipes and measurements issued by the home office, the inspector knows how large a portion of steak he should receive and how the vegetable should taste. He also knows how long it should take for the dinner to be served and he knows the exact degree of friendliness that should be shown by the hostess and the waitress."

drug, which has no particular taste but makes you forget yourself. Regardless of the one or the other effect, their suppression, because of the intensity of sexual desires, not only affects the sexual sphere but also weakens the person's courage for spontaneous expression in all other spheres.

5   In our society emotions in general are discouraged. While there can be no doubt that any creative thinking—as well as any other creative activity—is inseparably linked with emotion, it has become an ideal to think and to live without emotions. To be "emotional" has become synonymous with being unsound or unbalanced. By the acceptance of this standard the individual has become greatly weakened; his thinking is impoverished and flattened. On the other hand, since emotions cannot be completely killed, they must have their existence totally apart from the intellectual side of the personality; the result is the cheap and insincere sentimentality with which movies and popular songs feed millions of emotion-starved customers.

6   There is one tabooed emotion that I want to mention in particular, because its suppression touches deeply on the roots of personality: the sense of tragedy. As we saw in an earlier chapter, the awareness of death and of the tragic aspect of life, whether dim or clear, is one of the basic characteristics of man. Each culture has its own way of coping with the problem of death. For those societies in which the process of individuation has progressed but little, the end of individual existence is less of a problem since the experience of individual existence itself is less developed. Death is not yet conceived as being basically different from life. Cultures in which we find a higher development of individuation have treated death according to their social and psychological structure. The Greeks put all emphasis on life and pictured death as nothing but a shadowy and dreary continuation of life. The Egyptians based their hopes on a belief in the indestructibility of the human body, at least of those whose power during life was indestructible. The Jews admitted the fact of death realistically and were able to reconcile themselves with the idea of the destruction of individual life by the vision of a state of happiness and justice ultimately to be reached by mankind in this world. Christianity has made death unreal and tried to comfort the unhappy individual by promises of a life after death. Our own era simply denies death and with it one fundamental aspect of life. Instead of allowing the awareness of death and suffering to become one of the strongest incentives for life, the basis for human solidarity, and an experience without which joy and enthusiasm lack intensity and depth, the individual is forced to repress it. But, as is always the case with repression, by being removed from sight the repressed elements do not cease to exist. Thus the fear of death lives an illegitimate existence among us. It remains alive in spite of the attempt to deny it, but being repressed it remains sterile. It is one source of the flatness of other

experiences, of the restlessness pervading life, and it explains, I would venture to say, the exorbitant amount of money this nation pays for its funerals.

7   In the process of tabooing emotions modern psychiatry plays an ambiguous role. On the one hand its greatest representative, Freud, has broken through the fiction of the rational, purposeful character of the human mind and opened a path which allows a view into the abyss of human passions. On the other hand psychiatry, enriched by these very achievements of Freud, has made itself an instrument of the general trends in the manipulation of personality. Many psychiatrists, including psychoanalysts, have painted the picture of a "normal" personality which is never too sad, too angry, or too excited. They use words like "infantile" or "neurotic" to denounce traits or types of personalities that do not conform with the conventional pattern of a "normal" individual. This kind of influence is in a way more dangerous than the older and franker forms of name-calling. Then the individual knew at least that there was some person or some doctrine which criticized him and he could fight back. But who can fight back at "science"?

8   The same distortion happens to original *thinking* as happens to feeling and emotions. From the very start of education original thinking is discouraged and ready-made thoughts are put into people's heads. How this is done with young children is easy enough to see. They are filled with curiosity about the world, they want to grasp it physically as well as intellectually. They want to know the truth, since that is the safest way to orient themselves in a strange and powerful world. Instead, they are not taken seriously, and it does not matter whether this attitude takes the form of open disrespect or of the subtle condescension which is usual towards all who have no power (such as children, aged or sick people). Although this treatment by itself offers strong discouragement to independent thinking, there is a worse handicap: the insincerity—often unintentional—which is typical of the average adult's behavior toward a child. This insincerity consists partly in the fictitious picture of the world which the child is given. It is about as useful as instructions concerning life in the Arctic would be to someone who has asked how to prepare for an expedition to the Sahara Desert. Besides this general misrepresentation of the world there are the many specific lies that tend to conceal facts which, for various personal reasons, adults do not want children to know. From a bad temper, which is rationalized as justified dissatisfaction with the child's behavior, to concealment of the parents' sexual activities and their quarrels, the child is "not supposed to know" and his inquiries meet with hostile or polite discouragement.

9   The child thus prepared enters school and perhaps college. I want to mention briefly some of the educational methods used today which in effect further discourage original thinking. One is the emphasis on knowledge

of facts, or I should rather say on information. The pathetic superstition prevails that by knowing more and more facts one arrives at knowledge of reality. Hundreds of scattered and unrelated facts are dumped into the heads of students; their time and energy are taken up by learning more and more facts so that there is little left for thinking. To be sure, thinking without a knowledge of facts remains empty and fictitious; but "information" alone can be just as much of an obstacle to thinking as the lack of it.

10   Another closely related way of discouraging original thinking is to regard all truth as relative. Truth is made out to be a metaphysical concept, and if anyone speaks about wanting to discover the truth he is thought backward by the "progressive" thinkers of our age. Truth is declared to be an entirely subjective matter, almost a matter of taste. Scientific endeavor must be detached from subjective factors, and its aim is to look at the world without passion and interest. The scientist has to approach facts with sterilized hands as a surgeon approaches his patient. The result of this relativism, which often presents itself by the name of empiricism or positivism or which recommends itself by its concern for the correct usage of words, is that thinking loses its essential stimulus—the wishes and interests of the person who thinks; instead it becomes a machine to register "facts." Actually, just as thinking in general has developed out of the need for mastery of material life, so the quest for truth is rooted in the interests and needs of individuals and social groups. Without such interest the stimulus for seeking the truth would be lacking. There are always groups whose interest is furthered by truth, and their representatives have been the pioneers of human thought; there are other groups whose interests are furthered by concealing truth. Only in the latter case does interest prove harmful to the cause of truth. The problem, therefore, is not that there is *an* interest at stake, but *which kind* of interest is at stake. I might say that inasmuch as there is some longing for the truth in every human being, it is because every human being has some need for it.

11   This holds true in the first place with regard to a person's orientation in the outer world, and it holds especially true for the child. As a child, every human being passes through a state of powerlessness, and truth is one of the strongest weapons of those who have no power. But the truth is in the individual's interest not only with regard to his orientation in the outer world; his own strength depends to a great extent on his knowing the truth about himself. Illusions about oneself can become crutches useful to those who are not able to walk alone; but they increase a person's weakness. The individual's greatest strength is based on the maximum of integration of his personality, and that means also on the maximum of transparence to himself. "Know thyself" is one of the fundamental commands that aim at human strength and happiness.

12   In addition to the factors just mentioned there are others which actively tend to confuse whatever is left of the capacity for original thinking

in the average adult. With regard to all basic questions of individual and social life, with regard to psychological, economic, political, and moral problems, a great sector of our culture has just one function—to befog the issues. One kind of smokescreen is the assertion that the problems are too complicated for the average individual to grasp. On the contrary it would seem that many of the basic issues of individual and social life are very simple, so simple, in fact, that everyone should be expected to understand them. To let them appear to be so enormously complicated that only a "specialist" can understand them, and he only in his limited field, actually—and often intentionally—tends to discourage people from trusting their own capacity to think about those problems that really matter. The individual feels helplessly caught in the chaotic mass of data and with pathetic patience waits until the specialists have found out what to do and where to go.

13   The result of this kind of influence is a twofold one: one is a scepticism and cynicism towards everything which is said or printed, while the other is a childish belief in anything that a person is told with authority. This combination of cynicism and naïveté is very typical of the modern individual. Its essential result is to discourage him from doing his own thinking and deciding.

Questions

1. Fromm presents his case establishing the causes of conformity by making other generalizations about the nature of our society for which he then cites examples. List these generalizations.

2. Is training a necessary or a sufficient condition leading to suppression of spontaneous feeling? See paragraph 1.

3. Would you agree with Fromm that Christianity by promising an afterlife has made death unreal? Is it not a characteristic of most religions to promise an afterlife?

4. What observations of life in America as you see it seem to support Fromm's assertion that our era simply denies death? What evidence to the contrary can you see? Do his observations have an inner consistency? Are there any which might have proved inconsistent and are glaring by the fact of their omission?

5. Would you agree that modern problems—psychological, economic, political, and moral—are so complex that they discourage individuals from attempting to understand them? Granted their complexity to the point of insolvability, does it necessarily follow that the individual, feeling helplessly caught in a chaotic mass of data and controlled by decisions of specialists, becomes increasingly conformist?

6. State Fromm's point in paragraphs 10 and 11 in your own words. Have there not always been individuals whose interests were furthered by con-

cealing truth? Is his point in paragraph 10, therefore, merely that there are more such persons with more power in our age?

7. By what logic does Fromm move from his point in paragraph 10 to the "Know Thyself" point in paragraph 11?

8. Why is it more difficult to know oneself in our age?

9. Do you agree or disagree that there are absolute truths in economic, political, and moral realms that ought neither to be denied nor concealed, that individuals have a natural desire to know and accept them, and that denial of them will have harmful effects upon the individual and the society? Name some. (See C. S. Lewis, "The Law of Right and Wrong.")

10. Assuming Fromm's view of the causes of our conformity and insecurity to be accurate, what corrective action might we take as individuals and as a society?

Theme topics

1. Write your own account of the causes of conformity in your own personality.

2. Write your understanding of the causes of teen-age delinquency.

3. If we begin in America to educate in separate vocational schools students on the lower levels of intelligence and ability, describe the probable effects of this separation upon the attitudes and personalities of students in vocational as well as academic high schools.

4. After doing some reading on a current event in national or international politics, write a paper discussing its causes.

5. Discuss the reasons for the popularity with your generation of a certain book, movie, or play.

13   BRUNO BETTELHEIM
Adjustment for Survival

Old and new prisoners

1   Perhaps the changes forced upon most survivors in the concentration camp may best be illustrated by comparing "new" prisoners, in whom the process of enforced self reeducation had barely started, with

Reprinted with permission of the publisher from *The Informed Heart* by Bruno Bettelheim. Copyright © 1960 by The Free Press, a Corporation.

Bruno Bettelheim, born in Vienna in 1903, studied psychoanalysis there, and in 1938–39 was sent by the Nazis to the concentration camps at Dachau and Buchenwald.

"old" prisoners, in whom it was nearly finished. The term "new" prisoner is used for those who had spent no more than one year in the camp; "old" prisoners are those who had been there at least three years. As far as old prisoners are concerned, I can offer only observations but no findings based on introspection.

2   There was, of course, considerable variation in the time it took prisoners to make their peace with the possibility of having to spend the rest of their lives in the camp. Some became part of camp life rather soon, some probably never, though they may have spent more than ten years in the camps. When a new prisoner arrived he was told, "if you survive the first three weeks, you have a good chance of surviving a year; if you survive three months you will survive the next three years." [1]

3   During the first month in camp (including casualties of the transport) the monthly death rate for newcomers actually was at least 10% and probably close to 15%. In the following month—if there were no special mass persecutions—this figure was usually cut in half; that is, the death rate among new prisoners during the second month might be somewhere around 7%. During the third month it might again be halved to about 3%. And from then on (again barring mass executions) the monthly death rate for the surviving 75% may have dropped to 1% or less, where it remained, by and large.

4   This reduction in the death rate was due largely to the fact that by that time all those who could not survive the rigors of camp life had been weeded out. Those with physical disabilities, such as heart conditions, were already dead. So were most of those with personalities too rigid to develop the necessary defenses and adjustments; they, too, succumbed in the first few weeks. The lowered death rate was thus a measure of both the survival of the fittest, and of the heightened chances for survival as one learned to adjust. By the same token the halt in deaths was a compelling reason for prisoners to change, to do it on their own steam, and do it fast, if they meant to survive. [2]

5   The chief concerns of new prisoners were to remain physically intact and return to the outer world the same person who had left it. Therefore

[1] At the time this comment was made, the yearly death rate, in my estimation, was about 30%. The yearly death rate of 50% . . . pertains to a later period of the camps.

[2] What I have explained here by statistics has been described by an "old" prisoner as an inner experience.

Kupfer, after two years at Dachau, reflected on what went on in him as he adjusted to life in the camp: "Now I am a 'Dachauer,' prisoner no. 24814. I think and feel as is fitting for a prisoner at Dachau. Slowly a process of acclimatization has taken place in me. I did not realize it then, but for life in the camp this is great progress, because whoever becomes a concentration camp prisoner through and through does not perish so soon, compared to the prisoner who remains a newcomer inside, and therefore one who externally and internally tries to remain outside of it all. I began in the very center of my inner life, but also in all externals, to act and feel like a true 'Dachauer,' ["old prisoner"—B. B.] though I did not realize this at all at the time."

all efforts were directed toward these goals, and they tried to combat as much as possible any weakening of their maturity or self sufficiency. Old prisoners seemed mainly concerned with the problem of how to live as well as possible inside the camp. Therefore they tried to reorganize their personalities as well as they could to become more acceptable to the SS. Once they had embraced this attitude, everything that happened to them, even the worst atrocity, was "real." No longer was there a split between a figure to whom things happened and the prisoner who observed in detachment. The split in personality had disappeared, but at the price of the prisoner's personality no longer being integrated. It dropped to a different, lower level: one of resignation, dependency, submission, and passivity.

6   Old prisoners could accept this because they could scarcely believe they would ever return to the outer world which had grown strange to them. But once they had changed, there was every indication that they were afraid of returning. They did not admit it directly, but from their talk it was clear that in their own minds, only a cataclysmic event—a world war or world revolution—could free them. They seemed aware of what had happened to them as they aged in the camp. They realized they had adapted to camp life and that this process had brought a basic change in their personalities.

7   The realization was given dramatic expression by those few prisoners who became convinced that no one could live in the camps longer than a certain number of years without changing his attitudes so radically that he could no longer be considered, or again become, the person he once was. Therefore they set a time limit for themselves beyond which, in their opinion, there was no point in staying alive since from then on life would simply consist of being prisoners in a concentration camp. These were men who could not endure acquiring those attitudes and behaviors they saw developing in most old prisoners. They therefore set a fixed date for committing suicide. One of them set the sixth anniversary of his arrival in the camp because he felt that nobody there was worth saving after five years. His friends tried to watch him carefully on that day, but nevertheless he succeeded.[3]

8   One characteristic difference between old and new prisoners was that old prisoners could no longer evaluate correctly the outside, non-Gestapo controlled world. Whereas new prisoners tried to retain their attitude toward the world of the camp as being nonreal, to old prisoners it was the only reality. How long it took a prisoner to stop considering life outside the camp as real depended to a great extent on the strength of his emotional ties to his family and friends, the strength and richness of his personality and the degree to which he was able to preserve important aspects of his old interests and attitudes. The greater the area of his interests, and the

---

[3] I witnessed this suicide. A very similar suicide is described by Kautsky, p. 283.

more he contrived to take advantage of them in the camp situation, the better able he was to protect his personality against too early impoverishment.

9   Some indications of changes in attitude were: the tendency toward scheming to find a better place of work in the camp rather than trying to contact the outer world. New prisoners, for instance, would spend all their money on efforts to smuggle letters out of the camp or to get letters without having them censored. Old prisoners used their money to get "soft" jobs such as clerical work in the camp offices, or labor in the shops where they at least had protection from the weather. This change also found expression in their dominant thoughts and topics of conversation: new prisoners were most concerned with life outside of camp; old prisoners were interested only in camp life.

10   It so happened, for instance, that on one and the same day, news was received of a speech by President Roosevelt denouncing Hitler and Germany, and rumors spread that one SS officer was going to be replaced by another. New prisoners discussed the President's speech excitedly and paid scant attention to the rumors; old prisoners were indifferent to the speech, but devoted their conversation to the rumored change in camp officers.

11   When old prisoners were asked why they spoke so little about their futures outside the camp, they often admitted they could no longer visualize themselves living in a free world, making decisions, taking care of themselves and their families.

12   The attitude of the old prisoner toward his family had undergone a significant change. One reason for this was the total reversal of his status within the family. In line with the paternalistic structure of most German households, the family had been wholly dependent on the man for decisions, much more so than would be true in an American family. Now he was not only unable to influence his wife's or his children's decisions, but was utterly dependent upon them for taking steps to secure his release and to send him the money that was so important to him in the camp.

13   As a matter of fact, although many families behaved decently toward prisoners, serious problems were created. During the first months they spent a great deal of energy, time, and money in their efforts to free the prisoners, quite often more than they could afford. Later on they ran out of money, while new demands were being made on their time and energy. To have lost the wage earner meant great hardship for the family. Also, it should not be overlooked that the wife had often objected to the husband's political activities as being too dangerous or too time consuming. Now as she pleaded with the Gestapo, an unpleasant task at best, they told her repeatedly that it was the prisoner's own fault that he was imprisoned. Wives had a hard time finding employment because a family member was suspect; they were excluded from public relief; their children

had difficulties at school, etc. So it was natural that many came to resent having a family member in the camp.

14   Their friends showed them little compassion, because the German population at large developed its own defenses against the concentration camp, most important of which was denial. As discussed in the last chapter, they refused to believe that prisoners in the camps had not committed outrageous crimes to warrant such punishment.

15   Another subtle, but most effective device the SS used to alienate the family from the prisoners, was to tell the wife or other relatives (usually only closest relatives were permitted to plead the prisoner's case), that not only was it the prisoner's own fault that he was in the camp, but that he would have been released long ago had he behaved there as he should. This led to recriminations in letters; relatives pleaded with the prisoner to behave better, which often outraged him, considering the conditions of his camp existence.[4] He, of course, could not answer such accusations. At the same time he was resentful because what probably enraged him most was the family's own ability to act and move about freely when he was so helplessly unable to act for himself. In any case it was one more experience separating the prisoner from his few remaining ties to the non-camp world.

16   These and similar attitudes were reflected in letters to and from home, but often mail for prisoners came irregularly or not at all. Naturally, letters contained hopes and promises of reunion, sometimes because the Gestapo had made promises to the family, sometimes because relatives were trying to cheer the prisoners up. But when promises did not materialize, they led to still greater disappointment, and added resentment toward home.

17   In another effort to cut prisoners off from all connection with the outer world, the SS forbade them to have pictures of their relatives; if they got hold of any pictures, they were taken away and the prisoners were punished for keeping them. So actually a slow alienation took place between the men and their families. But for the new prisoners, this process was only beginning. As recollections of the family grew dimmer, this strongest bond linking prisoners to the outside world grew weaker. The resentment of those who, rightly or wrongly, felt deserted by their families

---

[4] The Gestapo had numerous devices to make pleading for the prisoner seem senseless, and make it easy for the family in self-preservation to separate itself from the prisoner. They would set a date for the prisoner's release, only to inform the relatives on that date that some new misdeed made freedom impossible. Often not even that much reason was given for misinformation. My mother was several times given a date for my release, each one untrue. Once she was told I was probably home already, waiting for her, and to hurry home. Another time she was encouraged to travel from Vienna to Weimar, the town closest to Buchenwald, either to receive me on my release, or at least have a visit with me. She presented herself in Weimar, where she was given a run-around for several days until in desperation she returned to Vienna.

only reinforced it. The less emotional support they got from the outside, the more they were forced to adjust to life in the camp.

18   Therefore, old prisoners did not like to be reminded of their families and former friends. When they spoke about them, it was in a very detached way. They still liked to get letters, but it was not very important to them because they had lost touch with the events related in them. Also, they had come to hate all those living outside the camp, who "enjoyed life as if we were not rotting away." This outside world which continued to live as if nothing had happened was represented, in the minds of the prisoners, by those whom they used to know best, namely their relatives and friends. But even this hatred was very subdued in old prisoners. Just as they had forgotten how to love their kin, they seemed to have lost the ability to hate them. Showing little emotion either way, they seemed unable to feel strongly about anybody.

19   New prisoners, after an initial delay, were usually the ones who received more letters, money, and other signs of attention. But even newcomers consistently accused their families of not doing enough, of betraying them. At the same time they loved to speak of their families and friends even when they were complaining about them. Despite open ambivalence, they never doubted they were going to resume living with them just where they had left off.

20   Similarly they hoped to continue their professional lives just as before. Unlike old prisoners, they loved to talk about their positions in the outside world and of their hopes for the future. They spoke boastfully, and seemed to be trying to keep their pride alive by letting others know how important they had been, the implication being that they were still important people. Old prisoners seemed to have accepted their state of dejection; to compare it with their former splendor (and anything was magnificent compared to their present existence) was probably too depressing.

21   For such reasons it made a difference to prisoners, psychologically, whether the camp was enclosed by just a wire fence (which let them see the surrounding world) or whether a solid wall blocked their view. The wire fence was usually preferred by new prisoners who tried to deny their exclusion from the world, while those who preferred the additional wall sought protection from nostalgia. On labor assignments outside the camp, prisoners were always in contact with some segments of the outside world, but were also exposed to the sometimes curious but often hostile stare of the passerby. Here again, old prisoners detested the experience while newcomers enjoyed seeing civilians, particularly women and children.

22   Probably as a result of malnutrition, mental anguish, and ambivalence toward the outside world, prisoners tended to forget names, places and events of their past lives. Often they could not recall the names of their closest relatives, even while remembering insignificant details. It was

as if their emotional ties to the past were breaking, as if the ordinary order of importance, of the connections of experiences, was no longer valid. Prisoners were quite upset about this loss of memory for things past, which added to their sense of frustration and incompetence. This too was a process which had only begun for new prisoners, and was nearly completed in most old prisoners.

23   All prisoners engaged in a great deal of daydreaming. Both individual and group daydreams were wildly wishfulfilling and a favorite pastime if the general emotional climate was not too depressed. Nevertheless, there was a marked difference between the daydreams of new and old prisoners. In general, the longer the time a prisoner had spent in camp, the less specific, concrete and true to reality were his daydreams. This was in line with the expectation that only such an event as the end of the existing world order would liberate them.

24   They would vaguely daydream of some coming cataclysm. Out of this earth shaking event they felt sure of emerging as the new leaders of Germany, if not the world. This was the least to which their sufferings entitled them. Alongside of these grandiose expectations went a great vagueness about the nature of their leadership, or what ends it would serve; they were even more nebulous about how they were going to arrange their future private lives. In their daydreams they were certain to emerge as prominent leaders of the future, but they were less certain they would continue to live with their wives and children, or be able to resume their roles as husbands and fathers. Partly these fantasies were an effort to deny their utter dejection, and partly a confession of the feeling that only high public office could help them to regain standing within their families, or win back their own good opinion of themselves.

25   In the process of forcing prisoners to relinquish maturity, the group exercised a strong influence. The group did not interfere with a prisoner's private daydreams or his ambivalence toward his family, but it asserted its power over those who objected to childlike deviations from normal adult behavior. Those who objected to an absolute obedience to the guards were accused of risking the security of the group, an accusation that was not without foundation, since the SS punished the group for the individual misdeed. Therefore, regression into childlike behavior was more inescapable than other types of behavior imposed on the individual because it was triply enforced: by the SS, by the prisoner's inner psychological defenses, and by his fellow prisoners.

26   The result was that most prisoners developed types of behavior more usually characteristic of infancy or early youth. Some of these behaviors developed slowly, others were immediately imposed on the prisoners and increased only in intensity as time went on.

27   The prisoners, like children, sought their satisfactions in empty daydreams, or worse, in contradictory ones. If real satisfactions were available,

they were the most primitive kind: eating, sleeping, resting. Like children, they lived only in the immediate present; they lost their feeling for the sequence of time, they became unable to plan for the future or to give up tiny immediate satisfactions to gain greater ones in the near future. They were unable to establish durable relations. Friendships developed as quickly as they broke up. Prisoners would, like children, fight one another tooth and nail, declare they would never look at one another or speak to one another, only to become fast friends within minutes. They were boastful, telling tales of what they had achieved in their former lives, or how they had contrived to cheat foremen or guards. Like children, they felt not at all set back or ashamed when it became known that they had lied about their prowess.

Final adjustment

28   The result of all these changes, by no means fully produced in all old prisoners, was a personality structure willing and able to accept SS values and behavior as its own. Of these, German nationalism and the Nazi race ideology seemed easiest to accept. It was notable how far even well-educated political prisoners went in this identification. At one time, for instance, American and English newspapers were full of stories about cruelties committed in the camps. The SS punished prisoners for the appearance of these stories, true to its policy of group punishment—for the stories must have originated in reports by former prisoners. In discussing this event old prisoners insisted that foreign newspapers had no business bothering with internal German institutions and expressed their hatred of the journalists who tried to help them.

29   When in 1938 I asked more than one hundred old political prisoners if they thought the story of the camp should be reported in foreign newspapers, many hesitated to agree that it was desirable. When asked if they would join a foreign power in a war to defeat National Socialism, only two made the unqualified statement that everyone escaping Germany ought to fight the Nazis to the best of his ability.

30   Nearly all non-Jewish prisoners believed in the superiority of the German race. Nearly all of them took great pride in the so-called achievements of the National Socialist state, particularly its policy of expansion through annexation. In line with their acceptance of the new ideology, most old prisoners took over Gestapo attitudes toward the so-called unfit prisoner. Even before an extermination policy went into effect, the Gestapo had been liquidating unfit persons. Prisoners, for reasons of their own, followed their example. They considered their actions justifiable; some even thought them to be correct.

31   Newcomers to the camp presented old prisoners with difficult problems. Their complaints about the misery of the camp situation added new strain to life in the barracks; so did their inability to adjust to it. Bad behavior in the labor gang or in the barrack endangered the whole group. To become conspicuous was always dangerous, and usually the group to which the conspicuous person belonged at the moment would also be singled out by the SS for special attention. So newcomers who did not stand up well under the strain tended to be a liability to others.

32   Moreover, weaklings were those most apt to turn traitor. Weaklings, it was reasoned, usually died in the first weeks anyway, so it seemed as well to get rid of them sooner. Therefore, old prisoners were sometimes instrumental in getting rid of so-called unfit new prisoners, thus patterning their own behavior after Gestapo ideology. They did it by giving newcomers dangerous assignments, or by denying them help that could have been given.

33   This was one of many situations in which old prisoners showed toughness, that modeled their way of treating fellow prisoners on examples set by the SS. That it was really a taking over of SS attitudes could be seen from their handling of traitors. Self protection asked for the elimination of traitors, but the way in which they were tortured for days and slowly killed was taken over from the Gestapo. Here the excuse was that it might deter others. Yet the rationalization did not apply when prisoners turned their hostility against one another, as they did continuously. New prisoners did it much as they would have done in the world outside the camp. But slowly most prisoners accepted terms of verbal aggression that definitely did not originate in their previous vocabulary, but were taken over from the very different vocabulary of the SS. Only attempts to emulate the SS can explain such behavior.

34   From copying SS verbal aggressions to copying their form of bodily aggression was one more step, but it took several years to reach that. It was not unusual, when prisoners were in charge of others, to find old prisoners (and not only former criminals) behaving worse than the SS. Sometimes they were trying to find favor with the guards, but more often it was because they considered it the best way to treat prisoners in the camp.

35   Old prisoners tended to identify with the SS not only in their goals and values, but even in appearance. They tried to arrogate to themselves old pieces of SS uniforms, and when that was not possible they tried to sew and mend their prison garb until it resembled the uniforms. The lengths prisoners would go to was sometimes hard to believe, particularly since they were sometimes punished for trying to look like the SS. When asked why they did it, they said it was because they wanted to look smart. To them looking smart meant to look like their enemies.

36 Old prisoners felt great satisfaction if, during the twice daily counting of prisoners, they really had stood well at attention or given a snappy salute. They prided themselves on being as tough, or tougher, than the SS. In their identification they went so far as to copy SS leisure time activities. One of the games played by the guards was to find out who could stand being hit the longest without uttering a complaint. The game was copied by old prisoners, as if they were not hit often enough without repeating the experience as a game.

37 Often an SS man would for a while enforce some nonsensical rule, originating in a whim of the moment. Usually it was quickly forgotten, but there were always some old prisoners who continued to observe it and tried to enforce it on others long after the SS had lost interest. Once, for example, an SS man was inspecting the prisoners' apparel and found that some of their shoes were dirty on the inside. He ordered all prisoners to wash their shoes inside and out with soap and water. Treated this way, the heavy shoes became hard as stone. The order was never repeated, and many prisoners did not even carry it out the first time, since the SS, as was often the case, gave the order, stood around for a few minutes, and then left. Until he was gone, every prisoner busied himself with carrying out the order, after which they promptly quit. Nevertheless there were some old prisoners who not only continued to wash the insides of their shoes every day but cursed all who failed to do so as being negligent and dirty. These prisoners believed firmly that all rules set down by the SS were desirable standards of behavior, at least in the camp.

38 Since old prisoners had accepted, or been forced to accept, a childlike dependency on the SS, many of them seemed to want to feel that at least some of the people they were accepting as all-powerful father images were just and kind. Therefore, strange as it may seem, they also had positive feelings toward the SS. They divided their positive and negative feelings in such a way that all positive emotions were concentrated on a few officers relatively far up in the hierarchy of the camp, but hardly ever on the commander himself. They insisted that behind a rough exterior these officers hid feelings of justice and propriety. They were alleged to be genuinely interested in the prisoners and even trying, in a small way, to help them. Since not much of these assumed feelings became apparent, it was explained that they had to be well hidden or there would be no way for them to help.

39 The eagerness of some prisoners to find reasons for such claims was sometimes pitiful. A whole legend was woven around the fact that of two SS inspecting a barrack, one had cleaned the mud off his shoes before entering. He probably did it automatically, but it was interpreted as a rebuff to the other, and a clear demonstration of how he felt about the concentration camp.

40   These examples, to which many could be added, suggest how, and to what degree, old prisoners came to identify with the enemy, and tried to justify it somehow in their own eyes. But was the SS really just an enemy any more? If so, the identification would be hard to understand. The SS was in fact the callous, unpredictable enemy, and remained so. But the longer prisoners survived in the camp—that is, the more they became old prisoners who had lost hope of any other life and tried to make a go of the camps—the more prisoners and SS found areas in common where cooperation was better for both of them than being at cross purposes. Having to live together, if one can call it that, led with necessity to such areas of common interest.

41   For example, one or several barracks were usually supervised by a noncommissioned SS officer, called a blockleader. Each blockleader wanted his barracks to be beyond reproach. It should not only be inconspicuous, but the one found in best order; this would keep him out of trouble with his superiors or even gain him a promotion. But the prisoners who lived there had the same interest: namely, that he should find it beyond reproach, and thus avoid severe penalty for themselves. In this sense they shared a common interest.

42   This was even more true of the workshops. The N.C.O. in charge of a production unit was vitally interested that everything in his workshop be in top shape when it was inspected by his superiors, that the output should be great, etc. The prisoners, for their own reasons, had identical interests. And the longer a prisoner had been in the camp, the more skilled his labor, or the more a particular SS came to rely on it for making his command show up well with his superiors, the greater the area of common interest.[5]

43   The fate of a Jewish command of bricklayers at Buchenwald is a telling example. While tens of thousands of Jewish prisoners were killed in the camp this group of some forty Jews survived with only a few losses of life. The group, made up of Jewish political prisoners, decided at the beginning of the war that with the shortage of steel, concrete, etc., the camp command would soon return to using bricks for its buildings. They managed to be assigned to the bricklayers' command, and since skilled bricklayers were scarce, they were considered unexpendable throughout the war. While nearly all other Jews were destroyed, most of this command was alive on the day of liberation. Had they served the SS poorly, they would have served themselves not at all. But had they taken professional pride in their bricklaying skill, without continuing to hate having to work for the SS, their inner resistance might have died, and they with it.

---

[5] A parallel to this development may be found in the situation of the anti-Nazi German outside the camp. He could not help himself from taking advantage of certain features of the Nazi regime, such as acquiring a better home or livelihood from the expropriation of Jewish property, the exploitation of Polish slave labor, etc.

44   In closing this summary of the adjustments made by old prisoners,
I wish to emphasize again that all these changes worked only within
limitations, that there were great individual variations, that in reality the
categories of old and new prisoners were always overlapping. Despite
what I have said about the psychological reasons forcing old prisoners to
conform and identify with the SS, it must be stressed that this was only
part of the picture; there were also strong defenses within them that
worked in the opposite direction. All prisoners, including those old prisoners who identified with the SS on many levels, at other times defined its
rules. In doing so, a few occasionally showed extraordinary courage, and
many more retained some of their decency and integrity all during their
stay in the camps.

14   JAMES THURBER
Sex ex Machina

1   With the disappearance of the gas mantle and the advent of the
short circuit, man's tranquility began to be threatened by everything he
put his hand on. Many people believe that it was a sad day indeed when
Benjamin Franklin tied that key to a kite string and flew the kite in a
thunderstorm; other people believed that if it hadn't been Franklin, it
would have been someone else. As, of course, it was in the case of the
harnessing of steam and the invention of the gas engine. At any rate, it
has come about that so-called civilized man finds himself today surrounded by the myriad mechanical devices of a technological world.
Writers of books on how to control your nerves, how to conquer fear, how
to cultivate calm, how to be happy in spite of everything, are of several
minds as regards the relation of man and the machine. Some of them are
prone to believe that the mind and body, if properly disciplined, can get
the upper hand of this mechanized existence. Others merely ignore the
situation and go on to the profitable writing of more facile chapters of
inspiration. Still others attribute the whole menace of the machine to sex,
and so confuse the average reader that he cannot always be certain
whether he has been knocked down by an automobile or is merely in love.

2   Dr. Bisch, the Be-Glad-You're-Neurotic man, has a remarkable
chapter which deals, in part, with man, sex, and the machine. He ex-

amines the case of three hypothetical men who start across a street on a red light and get in the way of an oncoming automobile. A dodges successfully; B stands still, "accepting the situation which calm and resignation," thus becoming one of my favorite heroes in modern belles-lettres; and C hesitates, wavers, jumps backward and forward, and finally runs head on into the car. To lead you through Dr. Bisch's complete analysis of what was wrong with B and C would occupy your whole day. He mentions what the McDougallians would say ("Instinct!"), what the Freudians would retort ("Complexes!"), and what the behaviorists would shout ("Conditioned reflexes!"). He also brings in what the physiologists would say—deficient thyroid, hypoadrenal functioning, and so on. The average sedentary man of our time who is at all suggestible must emerge from this chapter believing that his chances of surviving a combination of instinct, complexes, reflexes, glands, sex, and present-day traffic conditions are about equal to those of a one-legged blind man trying to get out of a labyrinth.

3   Let us single out what Dr. Bisch thinks the Freudians would say about poor Mr. C, who ran right into the car. He writes, " 'Sex hunger,' the Freudians would declare. 'Always keyed up and irritable because of it. Undoubtedly suffers from insomnia and when he does sleep his dream life must be productive, distorted, and possibly frightening. Automobile unquestionably has sex significance for him . . . to C the car is both enticing and menacing at one and the same time. . . . A thorough analysis is indicated. . . . It might take months. But then, the man needs an analysis as much as food. He is heading for a complete nervous collapse.' " It is my studied opinion, not to put too fine a point on it, that Mr. C is heading for a good mangling, and that if he gets away with only a nervous collapse, it will be a miracle.

4   I have not always, I am sorry to say, been able to go the whole way with the Freudians, or even a very considerable distance. Even though, as Dr. Bisch says, "One must admit that the Freudians have had the best of it thus far. At least they have received the most publicity." It is in matters like their analysis of men and machines, of Mr. C and the automobile, that the Freudians and I part company. Of course, the analysis above is simply Dr. Bisch's idea of what the Freudians would say, but I think he has got it down pretty well. Dr. Bisch himself leans toward the Freudian analysis of Mr. C, for he says in this same chapter, "An automobile bearing down upon you may be a sex symbol at that, you know, especially if you dream it." It is my contention, of course, that even if you dream it, it is probably not a sex symbol, but merely an automobile bearing down upon you. And if it bears down upon you in real life, I am sure it is an automobile. I have seen the same behavior that characterized Mr. C displayed by a squirrel (Mr. S) that lives in the grounds of my house in the country. He is a fairly tame squirrel, happily mated and not sex-

hungry, if I am any judge, but nevertheless he frequently runs out toward my automobile when I start down the driveway, and then hesitates, wavers, jumps forward and backward, and occasionally would run right into the car except that he is awfully fast on his feet and that I always hurriedly put on the brakes of the 1935 V-8 Sex Symbol that I drive.

5   I have seen this same behavior in the case of rabbits (notoriously uninfluenced by any sex symbols save those of other rabbits), dogs, pigeons, a doe, a young hawk (which flew at my car), a blue heron that I encountered on a country road in Vermont, and once, near Paul Smith's in the Adirondacks, a fox. They all acted exactly like Mr. C. The hawk, unhappily, was killed. All the others escaped with nothing worse, I suppose, than a complete nervous collapse. Although I cannot claim to have been conversant with the private life and the secret compulsions, the psychoneuroses and the glandular activities of all these animals, it is nevertheless my confident and unswervable belief that there was nothing at all the matter with any one of them. Like Mr. C, they suddenly saw a car swiftly bearing down upon them, got excited, and lost their heads. I do not believe, you see, there was anything the matter with Mr. C, either. But I do believe that, after a thorough analysis lasting months, with a lot of harping on the incident of the automobile, something might very well come to be the matter with him. He might even actually get to suffering from the delusion that he believes automobiles are sex symbols.

6   It seems to me worthy of note that Dr. Bisch, in reciting the reactions of three persons in the face of an oncoming car, selected three men. What would have happened had they been Mrs. A, Mrs. B, and Mrs. C? You know as well as I do: all three of them would have hesitated, wavered, jumped forward and backward, and finally run head on into the car if some man hadn't grabbed them. (I used to know a motorist who, every time he approached a woman standing on a curb preparing to cross the street, shouted, "Hold it, stupid!") It is not too much to say that, with a car bearing down upon them, ninety-five women out of a hundred would act like Mr. C—or Mr. S, the squirrel, or Mr. F, the fox. But it is certainly too much to say that ninety-five out of every hundred women look upon an automobile as a sex symbol. For one thing, Dr. Bisch points out that the automobile serves as a sex symbol because of the "mechanical principle involved." But only one woman in a thousand really knows anything about the mechanical principle involved in an automobile. And yet, as I have said, ninety-five out of a hundred would hesitate, waver, and jump, just as Mr. C did. I think we have the Freudians here. If we haven't proved our case with rabbits and a blue heron, we have certainly proved it with women.

7   To my notion, the effect of the automobile and of other mechanical contrivances on the state of our nerves, minds, and spirits is a problem which the popular psychologists whom I have dealt with know very little

about. The sexual explanation of the relationship of man and the machine is not good enough. To arrive at the real explanation, we have to begin very far back, as far back as Franklin and the kite, or at least as far back as a certain man and woman who appear in a book of stories written more than sixty years ago by Max Adeler. One story in this book tells about a housewife who bought a combination ironing board and card table, which some New England genius had thought up in his spare time. The husband, coming home to find the devilish contraption in the parlor, was appalled. "What is that thing?" he demanded. His wife explained that it was a card table, but that if you pressed a button underneath, it would become an ironing board. Whereupon she pushed the button and the table leaped a foot into the air, extended itself, and became an ironing board. The story goes on to tell how the thing finally became so finely sensitized that it would change back and forth if you merely touched it— you didn't have to push the button. The husband stuck it in the attic (after it had leaped up and struck him a couple of times while he was playing euchre), and on windy nights it could be heard flopping and banging around, changing from a card table to an ironing board and back. The story serves as one example of our dread heritage of annoyance, shock, and terror arising out of the nature of mechanical contrivances *per se*. The mechanical principle involved in this damnable invention had, I believe, no relationship to sex whatsoever. There are certain analysts who see sex in anything, even a leaping ironing board, but I think we can ignore these scientists.

8   No man (to go on) who has wrestled with a self-adjusting card table can ever be quite the man he once was. If he arrives at the state where he hesitates, wavers, and jumps at every mechanical device he encounters, it is not, I submit, because he recognizes the enticements of sex in the device, but only because he recognizes the menace of the machine as such. There might very well be, in every descendant of the man we have been discussing, an inherited desire to jump at, and conquer, mechanical devices before they have a chance to turn into something twice as big and twice as menacing. It is not reasonable to expect that his children and their children will have entirely escaped the stigma of such traumata. I myself will never be the man I once was, nor will my descendants prob- ably ever amount to much, because of a certain experience I had with an automobile.

9   I had gone out to the barn of my country place, a barn which was used both as a garage and a kennel, to quiet some large black poodles. It was 1 A.M. of a pitch-dark night in winter and the poodles had apparently been terrified by some kind of a prowler, a tramp, a turtle, or perhaps a fiend of some sort. Both my poodles and I myself believed, at the time, in fiends, and still do. Fiends who materialize out of nothing and nowhere, like winged pigweed or Russian thistle. I had quite a time quieting the

dogs, because their panic spread to me and mine spread back to them again, in a kind of vicious circle. Finally, a hush as ominous as their uproar fell upon them, but they kept looking over their shoulders, in a kind of apprehensive way. "There's nothing to be afraid of," I told them as firmly as I could, and just at that moment the klaxon of my car, which was just behind me, began to shriek. Everybody has heard a klaxon on a car suddenly begin to sound; I understand it is a short circuit that causes it. But very few people have heard one scream behind them while they were quieting six or eight alarmed poodles in the middle of the night in an old barn. I jump now whenever I hear a klaxon, even the klaxon on my own car when I push the button intentionally. The experience has left its mark. Everybody, from the day of the jumping card table to the day of the screaming klaxon, has had similar shocks. You can see the result, entirely unsuperinduced by sex, in the strained faces and muttering lips of people who pass you on the streets of great, highly mechanized cities. There goes a man who picked up one of those trick matchboxes that whir in your hands; there goes a woman who tried to change a fuse without turning off the current; and yonder toddles an ancient who cranked an old Reo with the spark advanced. Every person carries in his consciousness the old scar, or the fresh wound, of some harrowing misadventure with a contraption of some sort. I know people who would not deposit a nickel and a dime in a cigarette-vending machine and push the lever even if a diamond necklace came out. I know dozens who would not climb into an airplane even if it didn't move off the ground. In none of these people have I discerned what I would call a neurosis, an "exaggerated" fear; I have discerned only a natural caution in a world made up of gadgets that whir and whine and whiz and shriek and sometimes explode.

10   I should like to end with the case history of a friend of mine in Ohio named Harvey Lake. When he was only nineteen, the steering bar of an old electric runabout broke off in his hand, causing the machine to carry him through a fence and into the grounds of the Columbus School for Girls. He developed a fear of automobiles, trains, and every other kind of vehicle that was not pulled by a horse. Now, the psychologists would call this a complex and represent the fear as abnormal, but I see it as a purely reasonable apprehension. If Harvey Lake had, because he was catapulted into the grounds of the Columbus School for Girls, developed a fear of girls, I would call that a complex; but I don't call his normal fear of machines a complex. Harvey Lake never in his life got into a plane (he died in a fall from a porch), but I do not regard that as neurotic, either, but only sensible.

11   I have, to be sure, encountered men with complexes. There was, for example, Marvon Belt. He had a complex about airplanes that was quite interesting. He was not afraid of machinery, or of high places, or of crashes. He was simply afraid that the pilot of any plane he got into

might lose his mind. "I imagine myself high over Montana," he once said to me, "in a huge, perfectly safe tri-motored plane. Several of the passengers are dozing, others are reading, but I am keeping my eyes glued on the door to the cockpit. Suddenly the pilot steps out of it, a wild light in his eyes, and in a falsetto like that of a little girl he says to me, 'Conductor, will you please let me off at One-Hundred-and-Twenty-fifth Street?' " "But," I said to Belt, "even if the pilot does go crazy, there is still the co-pilot." "No, there isn't," said Belt. "The pilot has hit the co-pilot over the head with something and killed him." Yes, the psychoanalysts can have Marvin Belt. But they can't have Harvey Lake, or Mr. C, or Mr. S, or Mr. F, or, while I have my strength, me.

Using Personal Experience

Writing from personal experience

Using personal experience as a source for writing requires, like all writing, disciplines of diction, tone, and purpose. Since there is very little inherent in any personal experience that will make it of interest to others, the interest must come from the attitudes, the passion and the intelligence of the teller, from the writing itself. "Nothing ever happens to me," complains the freshman who misses the point that the important thing for writing about experience is not the color of the experience itself but the awareness he must bring to it. Selecting the right experience for writing is not a matter of finding the most important (embarrassing, horrible, amusing) incident of a lifetime but of finding an incident that awareness can do most to shape. The matter of awareness is double. We have one attitude in living an experience and another looking back. In the difference there will be irony of some sort. Looking back we are amused, detached, regretful, but the important thing for style is an aware and critical eye, an eye that need not be cold, but one that must search out what is essential, ironical, human and meaningful.

The idea that a report of experience must teach a lesson or have a didactic meaning is the source of much bad student writing as is the idea that the experience reported must be true. The incident chosen must be self-contained, but its purpose should be conceived as much broader than teaching a lesson. The "meaning" may be merely a demonstration of how the gap operates between humans of differing groups—generations, races, sexes, nationalities, neighborhoods. The incident may illustrate a particular kind of experience such as James Baldwin's report of his boyhood as a Negro in Harlem (see Part II). It may work ironically as John Updike's piece in this section does with an implied contract between his boyhood attitudes and his present mature ones towards members of his family. Or it may progress from simple experience to highly informed reflection as does the piece that follows by Loren Eiseley. The important thing is that the tone, a matter of choosing words to control the reader's response, communicate the attitudes of the narrator, and that those attitudes be made interesting through having been accurately observed, passionately felt or intelligently examined. The reader will find his own lessons if only in seeing how experience works on the personality of a highly perceptive individual who possesses the style to report it as it was for him. The truth to be aimed at is a larger one than that of the literal facts; for the important thing is not those facts but how the author responds to them, how his passions and mind are engaged.

15   JOHN UPDIKE

The Lucid Eye in Silver Town

The first time I visited New York City, I was thirteen and went with my father. I went to meet my Uncle Quin and to buy a book about Vermeer. The Vermeer book was my idea, and my mother's; meeting Uncle Quin was my father's. A generation ago, my uncle had vanished in the direction of Chicago and become, apparently, rich; in the last week he had come east on business and I had graduated from the eighth grade with high marks. My father claimed that I and his brother were the smartest people he had ever met—"go-getters," he called us, with perhaps more irony than at the time I gave him credit for—and in his visionary way he suddenly, irresistibly felt that now was the time for us to meet. New York   10 in those days was seven dollars away; we measured everything, distance and time, in money then. World War II was over but we were still living in the Depression. My father and I set off with the return tickets and a five-dollar bill in his pocket. The five dollars was for the book.

My mother, on the railway platform, suddenly exclaimed, "I *hate the Augusts.*" This surprised me, because we were all Augusts—I was an August, my father was an August, Uncle Quincy was an August, and she, I had thought, was an August.

My father gazed serenely over her head and said, "You have every reason to. I wouldn't blame you if you took a gun and shot us all. Except   20 for Quin and your son. They're the only ones of us ever had any get up and git." Nothing was more infuriating about my father than his way of agreeing.

Uncle Quin didn't meet us at Pennsylvania Station. If my father was disappointed, he didn't reveal it to me. It was after one o'clock and all we had for lunch were two candy bars. By walking what seemed to me a very long way on pavements only a little broader than those of my home town, and not so clean, we reached the hotel, which sprouted somehow from the caramel-colored tunnels under Grand Central Station. The lobby smelled of perfume. After the clerk had phoned Quincy August that a man who said he was his brother was at the desk, an elevator took us to the twentieth floor. Inside the room sat three men, each in a gray or blue suit with freshly pressed pants and garters peeping from under the cuffs when they crossed their legs. The men were not quite interchangeable. One had a caterpillar-shaped mustache, one had tangled blond eyebrows like my 10 father's, and the third had a drink in his hand—the others had drinks, too, but were not gripping them so tightly.

"Gentlemen, I'd like you to meet my brother Marty and his young son," Uncle Quin said.

"The kid's name is Jay," my father added, shaking hands with each of the two men, staring them in the eye. I imitated my father, and the mustached man, not expecting my firm handshake and stare, said, "Why hello there, Jay!"

"Marty, would you and the boy like to freshen up? The facilities are through the door and to the left." 20

"Thank you, Quin. I believe we will. Excuse me, gentlemen."

"Certainly."

"Certainly."

My father and I went into the bedroom of the suite. The furniture was square and new and all the same shade of maroon. On the bed was an opened suitcase, also new. The clean, expensive smells of leather and lotion were beautiful to me. Uncle Quin's underwear looked silk and was full of fleurs-de-lis. When I was through in the lavatory, I made for the living room, to rejoin Uncle Quin and his friends.

"Hold it," my father said. "Let's wait in here." 30

"Won't that look rude?"

"No. It's what Quin wants."

"Now, Daddy, don't be ridiculous. He'll think we've died in here."

"No he won't, not my brother. He's working some deal. He doesn't want to be bothered. I know how my brother works; he got us in here so we'd stay in here."

"*Really,* Pop. You're such a schemer." But I did not want to go in there without him. I looked around the room for something to read. There was nothing, not even a newspaper, except a shiny little phamphlet about the hotel itself. I wondered when we would get a chance to look for the 40 Vermeer book, and what the men in the next room were talking about. I wondered why Uncle Quin was so short, when my father was so tall. By leaning out of the window, I could see taxicabs maneuvering like wind-up toys.

My father came and stood beside me. "Don't lean out too far."

I edged out inches farther and took a big bite of the high cold air spiced by the distant street noises. "Look at the green cab cut in front of the yellow," I said. "Should they be making U-turns on that street?"

"In New York it's O.K. Survival of the fittest is the only law here."

"Isn't that the Chrysler Building?"

"Yes, isn't it graceful though? It always reminds me of the queen of the chessboard."

"What's the one beside it?"

"I don't know. Some big gravestone. The one deep in back, from this window, is the Woolworth Building. For years it was the tallest building in the world."

As, side by side at the window, we talked, I was surprised that my father could answer so many of my questions. As a young man, before I was born, he had travelled, looking for work; this was not *his* first trip to New York. Excited by my new respect, I longed to say something to remold that calm, beaten face.

"Do you really think he meant for us to stay out here?" I asked.

"Quin is a go-getter," he said, gazing over my head. "I admire him. Anything he wanted, from little on up, he went after it. Slam. Bang. His thinking is miles ahead of mine—just like your mother's. You can feel them pull out ahead of you." He moved his hands, palms down, like two taxis, the left quickly pulling ahead of the right. "You're the same way."

"Sure, sure." My impatience was not merely embarrassment at being praised; I was irritated that he considered Uncle Quin as smart as myself. At that point in my life I was sure that only stupid people took an interest in money.

When Uncle Quin finally entered the bedroom, he said, "Martin, I hoped you and the boy would come out and join us."

"Hell, I didn't want to butt in. You and those men were talking business."

"Lucas and Roebuck and I? Now, Marty, it was nothing that my own brother couldn't hear. Just a minor matter of adjustment. Both those men are fine men. Very important in their own fields. I'm disappointed that you couldn't see more of them. Believe me, I hadn't meant for you to hide in here. Now what kind of drink would you like?"

"I don't care. I drink very little any more."

"Scotch-and-water, Marty?"

"Swell."

"And the boy? What about some ginger ale, young man? Or would you like milk?"

"The ginger ale," I said.

"There was a day, you know, when your father could drink any two men under the table."

As I remember it, a waiter brought the drinks to the room, and while we were drinking them I asked if we were going to spend all afternoon in this room. Uncle Quin didn't seem to hear, but five minutes later he suggested that the boy might like to take a look around the city—Gotham, he called it, Bagdad-on-the-Subway. My father said that that would be a once-in-a-lifetime treat for the kid. He always called me "the kid" when I was sick or had lost at something or was angry—when he felt sorry for me, in short. The three of us went down in the elevator and took a taxi ride down Broadway, or up Broadway—I wasn't sure. "This is what they call the Great White Way," Uncle Quin said several times. Once he apologized, "In daytime it's just another street." The trip didn't seem so much designed for sight-seeing as for getting Uncle Quin to the Pickernut Club, a little restaurant set in a block of similar canopied places. I remember we stepped down into it and it was dark inside. A piano was playing "There's a Small Hotel."

"He shouldn't do that," Uncle Quin said. Then he waved to the man behind the piano. "How are you, Freddie? How are the kids?"

"Fine, Mr. August, fine," Freddie said, bobbing his head and smiling and not missing a note.

"That's Quin's song," my father said to me as we wriggled our way into a slippery curved seat at a round table.

I didn't say anything, but Uncle Quin, overhearing some disapproval in my silence, said, "Freddie's a first-rate man. He has a boy going to Colgate this autumn."

I asked, "Is that really your song?"

Uncle Quin grinned and put his warm broad hand on my shoulder; I hated, at that age, being touched. "I let them think it is," he said, oddly purring. "To me, songs are like young girls. They're all pretty."

A waiter in a red coat scurried up. "Mr. August! Back from the West? How are you, Mr. August?"

"Getting by, Jerome, getting by. Jerome, I'd like you to meet my kid brother, Martin."

"How do you do, Mr. Martin. Are you paying New York a visit? Or do you live here?"

My father quickly shook hands with Jerome, somewhat to Jerome's surprise. "I'm just up for the afternoon, thank you. I live in a hick town in Pennsylvania you never heard of."

"I see, sir. A quick visit."

"This is the first time in six years that I've had a chance to see my brother."

"Yes, we've seen very little of him these past years. He's a man we can never see too much of, isn't that right?"

Uncle Quin interrupted. "This is my nephew Jay."

"How do you like the big city, Jay?"

"Fine." I didn't duplicate my father's mistake of offering to shake hands.

"Why, Jerome," Uncle Quin said, "my brother and I would like to have a Scotch-on-the-rocks. The boy would like a ginger ale."

"No, wait," I said. "What kinds of ice cream do you have?"

"Vanilla and chocolate, sir."

I hesitated. I could scarcely believe it, when the cheap drugstore at home had fifteen flavors.

"I'm afraid it's not a very big selection," Jerome said.

"I guess vanilla."   10

"Yes, sir. One plate of vanilla."

When my ice cream came it was a golf ball in a flat silver dish; it kept spinning away as I dug at it with my spoon. Uncle Quin watched me and asked, "Is there anything especially you'd like to do?"

"The kid'd like to get into a bookstore," my father said.

"A bookstore. What sort of book, Jay?"

I said, "I'd like to look for a good book of Vermeer."

"Vermeer," Uncle Quin pronounced slowly, relishing the r's, pretending to give the matter thought. "Dutch school."

"He's Dutch, yes."   20

"For my own money, Jay, the French are the people to beat. We have four Degas ballet dancers in our living room in Chicago, and I could sit and look at one of them for hours. I think it's wonderful, the feeling for balance the man had."

"Yeah, but don't Degas' paintings always remind you of colored drawings? For actually *looking* at things in terms of paint, for the lucid eye, I think Vermeer makes Degas look sick."

Uncle Quin said nothing, and my father, after an anxious glance across the table, said, "That's the way he and his mother talk all the time. It's all beyond me. I can't understand a thing they say."   30

"Your mother is encouraging you to be a painter, is she, Jay?" Uncle Quin's smile was very wide and his cheeks were pushed out as if each held a candy.

"Sure, I suppose she is."

"Your mother is a very wonderful woman, Jay," Uncle Quin said.

It was such an embarrassing remark, and so much depended upon your definition of "wonderful," that I dug at my ice cream, and my father asked Uncle Quin about his own wife, Tessie. When we left, Uncle Quin signed the check with his name and the name of some company. It was close to five o'clock.   40

My uncle didn't know much about the location of bookstores in New York—his last twenty years had been spent in Chicago—but he thought that if we went to Forty-second Street and Sixth Avenue we should find something. The cab driver let us out beside a park that acted as kind of a backyard for the Public Library. It looked so inviting, so agreeably dusty, with the pigeons and the men nodding on the benches and the office girls in their taut summer dresses, that, without thinking, I led the two men into it. Shimmering buildings arrowed upward and glinted through the treetops. This was New York, I told myself: the silver town. Towers of ambition rose, crystalline, within me. "If you stand here," my father said, "you can see the Empire State." I went and stood beneath my father's arm and followed with my eyes the direction of it. Something sharp and hard fell into my right eye. I ducked my head and blinked; it was painful.

"What's the trouble?" Uncle Quin's voice asked.

My father said, "The poor kid's got something into his eye. He has the worst luck that way of anybody I ever knew."

The thing seemed to have life. It bit. "Ow," I said, angry enough to cry.

"If we can get him out of the wind," my father's voice said, "maybe I can see it."

"No, now, Marty, use your head. Never fool with the eyes or ears. The hotel is within two blocks. Can you walk two blocks, Jay?"

"I'm blind, not lame," I snapped.

"He has a ready wit," Uncle Quin said.

Between the two men, shielding my eye with a hand, I walked to the hotel. From time to time, one of them would take my other hand, or put one of theirs on my shoulder, but I would walk faster, and the hands would drop away. I hoped our entrance into the hotel lobby would not be too conspicuous; I took my hand from my eye and walked erect, defying the impulse to stoop. Except for the one lid being shut and possibly my face being red, I imagined I looked passably suave. However, my guardians lost no time betraying me. Not only did they walk at my heels, as if I might topple any instant, but my father told one old bum sitting in the lobby, "Poor kid got something in his eye," and Uncle Quin, passing the desk, called, "Send up a doctor to Twenty-eleven."

"You shouldn't have done that, Quin," my father said in the elevator. "I can get it out, now that he's out of the wind. This is happening all the time. The kid's eyes are too far front."

"Never fool with the eyes, Martin. They are your most precious tool in life."

"It'll work out," I said, though I didn't believe it would. It felt like a steel chip, deeply embedded.

Up in the room, Uncle Quin made me lie down on the bed. My father, a handkerchief wadded in his hand so that one corner stuck out, approached me, but it hurt so much to open the eye that I repulsed him. "Don't torment me," I said, twisting my face away. "What good does it do? The doctor'll be up."

Regretfully my father put the handkerchief back into his pocket.

The doctor was a soft-handed man with little to say to anybody; he wasn't pretending to be the family doctor. He rolled my lower eyelid on a thin stick, jabbed with a Q-tip, and showed me, on the end of the Q-tip, an eyelash. He dropped three drops of yellow fluid into the eye to remove any chance of infection. The fluid stung, and I shut my eyes, leaning back into the pillow, glad it was over. When I opened them, my father was passing a bill into the doctor's hand. The doctor thanked him, winked at me, and left. Uncle Quin came out of the bathroom.

"Well, young man, how are you feeling now?" he asked.   10

"Fine."

"It was just an eyelash," my father said.

"*Just* an eyelash! Well I know how an eyelash can feel like a razor blade in there. But, now that the young invalid is recovered, we can think of dinner."

"No, I really appreciate your kindness, Quin, but we must be getting back to the sticks. I have an eight-o'clock meeting I should be at."

"I'm extremely sorry to hear that. What sort of meeting, Marty?"

"A church council."

"So you're still doing church work. Well, God bless you for it."   20

"Grace wanted me to ask you if you couldn't possibly come over some day. We'll put you up overnight. It would be a real treat for her to see you again."

Uncle Quin reached up and put his arm around his younger brother's shoulders. "Martin, I'd like that better than anything in the world. But I am solid with appointments, and I must head west this Thursday. They don't let me have a minute's repose. Nothing would please my heart better than to share a quiet day with you and Grace in your home. Please give her my love, and tell her what a wonderful boy she is raising. The two of you are raising."   30

My father promised, "I'll do that." And, after a little more fuss, we left.

"The child better?" the old man in the lobby called to us on the way out.

"It was just an eyelash, thank you, sir," my father said.

When we got outside, I wondered if there were any bookstores still open.

"We have no money."

"None at all?"

"The doctor charged five dollars. That's how much it costs in New   40 York to get something in your eye."

"I didn't do it on purpose. Do you think I pulled out the eyelash and stuck it in there myself? I didn't tell you to call the doctor."

"I know that."

"Couldn't we just go into a bookstore and look a minute?"

"We haven't time, Jay."

But when we reached Pennsylvania Station, it was over thirty minutes until the next train left. As we sat on a bench, my father smiled reminiscently. "Boy, he's smart, isn't he? His thinking is sixty light-years ahead of mine."

"Whose?"

"My brother. Notice the way he hid in the bathroom until the doctor was gone? That's how to make money. The rich man collects dollar bills like the stamp collector collects stamps. I knew he'd do it. I knew it when he told the clerk to send up a doctor that I'd have to pay for it." 10

"Well, why *should* he pay for it? *You* were the person to pay for it."

"That's right. Why should he?" My father settled back, his eyes forward, his hands crossed and limp in his lap. The skin beneath his chin was loose; his temples seemed concave. The liquor was probably disagreeing with him. "That's why he's where he is now, and that's why I am where I am."

The seed of my anger seemed to be a desire to recall him to himself, to scold him out of being old and tired. "Well, why'd you bring along only five dollars? You might have known something would happen."

"You're right, Jay. I should have brought more." 20

"Look. Right over there is an open bookstore. Now if you had brought *ten* dollars—"

"Is it open? I don't think so. They just left the lights in the window on."

"What if it isn't? What does it matter to us? Anyway, what kind of art book can you get for five dollars? Color plates cost money. How much do you think a decent book of Vermeer costs? It'd be cheap at fifteen dollars, even second-hand, with the pages all crummy and full of spilled coffee." I kept on, shrilly flailing the passive and infuriating figure of my father, until we left the city. Once we were on the homeward train, my 30 tantrum ended; it had been a kind of ritual, for both of us, and he had endured my screams complacently, nodding assent, like a midwife assisting at the birth of family pride. Years passed before I needed to go to New York again.

Questions

1. In what ways are John Updike's attitudes toward his father different at the time of writing from what they were in his youth? What details communicate the different attitudes?

2. What does Updike achieve by having the book be about Vermeer? What different effects would be created by books on each of the following: airplanes, something difficult in mathematics, farming, the cinema?

3. How is the title justified in the narrative. What are the various applications of the words "lucid eye" and "silver?"

4. What does Updike achieve by having the cinder in his eye turn out to be only an eyelash?

5. Show where Updike's emotion during the various phases of the trip is illustrated in the action rather than merely stated.

6. Explain how the critical view of the father and uncle (who in reality probably had more redeeming features than Updike allows here) contributes to the design of the episode.

7. What details of the hotel room and the restaurant create our attitude toward them? What is the function of that attitude?

Theme topics

1. Write a narrative incident, based on your experience, to illustrate the difference between the narrator's present and past attitudes toward a person of another generation, sex, race or nationality. Use dialogue to get just right the tone of the speakers—their age, nationality, race; their attitudes, opinions, anxieties and intelligence. Avoid stock characters, stock responses and stereotyped dialectal phrases.

2. Write an essay in which you explain the significance of the concluding phrase "the birth of family pride" in terms of Updike's development of the entire episode.

16   ELEANOR CLARK

The Great Divide

1   Most of us have a strong tendency, most often frustrated, to try to do, or wish we could decently do, what we are told; and what we literary and other "humanist" characters are most often being told to do nowadays is to get together with the world of science. Understand it; make it understand us; something like that. It sounds fine, and what I want to jot down for posterity is not any objection—heavens no!—but merely some personal difficulties in the matter, as exemplified in this very sentence. I am embarrassed already.

From *The New York Times Book Review* (March 20, 1966), p. 2, 20. © 1966 by The New York Times Company. Reprinted by permission of The New York Times Company and Eleanor Clark.

2   That word "heavens" slipped out before I could stop it; it is just engrained in my "culture." (I am scared of all these words suddenly.) But what does it mean? What shape in space? What distance in light-years? In an effort to take up my share of the great challenge I recently visited the Kitt Peak National Observatory in Arizona, and I tremble to think what anybody there would make of such irresponsibility. Honestly, look at this problem at any little single point like that and you're in trouble right away. It's only on the propaganda level that it all sounds so simple.

3   I know of a foundation or a branch of one that has to do with relating art and churches, and where the girl at the switchboard answers all phone calls with a seraphic "Art and Worship!" I'll bet there's one somewhere by now answering in the same beautiful tones, "Science and Humanities!" You'd think we would be all set, and I suppose there do exist a few supermen as well as a number of freaks who really manage to think both ways, whether at the same time or on alternate days I don't know. There is also a rapidly growing race of middlemen who trot back and forth between the two camps with briefcases full of samples and communiqués. The expositor, the commentator, the nonoriginal thinker has never had so splendid a role.

4   For the mass of us drones of the creative life, the heavenly concord ends where it starts, at the switchboard, if there is one. Beyond that the words are all awry, the frequencies mismatched. We and the "disciplines" (science) are glumly huddled at opposite walls, or more politely, exchanging data on the skiing conditions or platitudes on the plight of education—great levelers, those two subjects. I use the word "disciplines" not because I like it or even think it particularly appropriate in that sentence, but because of a grudge I have to confess.

5   We self-employed humanist types (hereinafter to be referred to as S.E.H.'s; with all the grand verbiage now current in these areas, such words as poet, painter, novelist have come to sound old-fashioned and trivial)—anyway, we, as I was saying, used to think discipline was something you had to have a lot of to be any good at your business, but it would have been indecent to mention it, still less flaunt it. Still, now that the world has been snitched from us altogether I feel deprived and peevish, especially as a discipline in science these days, as I understand it, is apt to melt into some other from one day to the next, whereas in our usage the meaning was plain and the habit, barring alcoholism or other such misfortune, usually permanent.

6   But back to communication and the Great Divide—and I must insist that I am speaking purely as an S.E.H., with no reference to education or anything else outside my business—if a top-flight physicist and a true poet have ever, in the period covered by Nobel Prizes, had a really illuminating conversation I will forfeit my ski boots, one to each. Not that a writer or other S.E.H. can't have a scientist friend. I have had one myself for

years—a biochemist, at least originally; I suppose he must be a geomathematician or astroneurologist too by now. We are skiing companions.

7   Aside from that, the relation is based on such common factors as financial probity, similar world view (mournful) and drinking habits (reasonable) etc.; also mutual respect, because we are both intellectual snobs and have heard well of one another's work from reputable third parties. We certainly couldn't judge for ourselves, though we establish contact with one another's "field" to this extent: He asks me what I think of John O'Hara, and I ask him what I should think of, say, milk. If we have been intercommunicating some higher sense of order all these years, or doing anything else the seminars are now calling for, it must have been by osmosis, since neither of us would be caught dead talking like that.

8   It might be that behind this reticence there lies a mutual awareness of the possibility of doing each other great damage, though I should imagine the risk was more on my side. Whatever the likeness in our procedures, and Wordsworth to the contrary notwithstanding, my friend's world is and must be anti-poetry. Of course an occasional image from it can strike a spark over where I live; science has undone the rearing horse in my line of work; obviously we have to keep our senses open to whatever is happening. I once visited, with this same friend, a lab full of sick canaries that he had been methodically (how else?) inoculating, and found the experience quite fruitful. I mean it set my imagination off. But if I had tried to follow my friend's basic thinking on the canary problem I would have lost a very good and gruesome thing.

9   When it comes to *content* on the professional side, he frankly states that nothing is as boring to him as trying to explain his work to a layman, and I suspect that what he means is not so much boring as degrading, by association with the horrid spectacle that present tendencies in the news world are making more and more common. That is of second-raters, in any line of work, building up public reputation or personal self-esteem, or both, by impressing the ignorant or rather the pseudo-informed. (Practically everybody knows a little about practically everything now.) My friend is above that. He would rather have no reputation than that kind. Consequently I haven't the faintest idea what goes on in his lab.

10   Of course literature is not so obviously inaccessible, and free fireside chats about it are easy enough to come by, but not from its best practitioners—except in very special circumstances and then not about their own work. That could be only among intimates, and rare at that. The *pudeur* (delicacy, restraint: we have no true equivalent) in the two cases is identical, and in both is as essential to the work as legs to running or water to tea. Without that area of privacy, or secrecy if you will, the creative imagination quickly dries up. The scientist is then a mere technician, however brainy, and the S.E.H. a mere commentator on art, or more pitifully a worker-over of somebody else's big idea.

11   It seems that to try to understand each other in true Science-and-Humanities fashion, not through our own natural human rapport, my friend and I would have to start blabbing and prying just where it is least healthy, and the only certain result would be the rupture of an old and valuable friendship. True, that is a small sacrifice to make for country and mankind, but what I wish I could see is just what the contribution would stack up to.

12   If I go around saying "O.K. Science, here I come," and "Listen to me, you scientists, and I'll give you the real lowdown on what we're doing over here," is it really going to improve my next novel or stop nuclear war? Suppose a few scientists do, with heroic effort, find time to read a few extra novels or poems a year, since when has this vague beast called Humanities stopped any public disaster, viz.: pre-Nazi Germany? What you need for this is political sense, in scientists and everybody else, and by and large the S.E.H.'s aren't going to help much about that.

13   As for the supposed guilt of so many scientists, for all the terrible things they are now smart enough to do, of course we have to sympathize with anybody who is worried and unhappy, but the direct alleviation of suffering has never been the function of the arts either. Maybe a priest or a psychiatrist could help. I scarcely see how an occasional tussle of semantics could, although they are now as fashionable, or even how an original mind could stand the tedium of many such dialogues, whatever their public value. So it must be for our benefit, somehow to be siphoned over to the public through our works, that we're supposed to get tuned in on science.

14   Well, I'm all for anybody who wants to do me a good turn, but now I come to the painful part of this confession. I've tried. Kitt Peak wasn't half of it, and I don't mean just on the ski slopes either. Incidentally, I should have mentioned that my skiing scientist friend is of European origin and grew up in the kind of natural respect for and acquaintance with nonscientific culture that many American-born scientists seem not to have had around them very closely in childhood. But now that people have to start specializing at the age of 9 or 10, perhaps that general humanist base is becoming more rare in Europe too.

15   I was recently driving with a group including a much younger European scientist—going skiing, of course—and at a certain beautiful turn of the road, at which I am used to people saying "Oh what a lovely view!" or something to that effect, he asked sternly, "What made the hills?" Shaken out of daydream I said, "Why, God," smiling, and have been feeling like an intellectual toad ever since. "Something glacial, I suppose," I quickly amended, but the damage had been done. No rapport there; the young man considers me an idiot.

16   He's not the only one who does, in his bailiwick, and I'm not the only one in mine they think it of. I have, I had, a literary friend, a woman of

some repute for her unique genre in prose, which reviewers used to compare to both Mallarmé and Mark Twain. At any rate it did involve a high order of imaginative creation, outside of both fiction and criticism, and I admired it very much myself.

17   Suddenly in middle life, not long ago, the poor lady got bitten by the science bug, and moving in her feelings from inadequacy to guilt, she decided, quite mistakenly, that she had been "basking in the mystery of it all" and leaving out one of the most crucial facets of any subject. I say mistakenly, because she had never been in the least sentimental and there was nothing to be gained by her floundering around among mathematical formulae. That is what happened.

18   The subject that had struck her fancy that year had to do with the sea, and happening to be in Paris, she got hold of a scientific volume on waves, in the supposedly popular French pamphlet series with the overall title *"Que Sais-je?"* She showed it to me later. *Que sais-je?* indeed. It was formula after formula, with scarcely a sentence she could read, though she had actually taken a couple of math courses in college. It all seemed to her more bitter, too, when she reflected that the author of that little book could have gotten some sort of experience from "the melancholy, long, withdrawing roar" or "the mermaids singing each to each," whereas for her his work, even so popularized, was a total blank.

19   To tell only the end of this sad affair, for months she haunted the oceanographic labs and zoology, paleontology and other such departments of some of our great universities. The professors were very kind, but since they were not aware of her kinship with Mallarmé or anybody else, and furthermore most of them had only a nominal acquaintance with Arnold or Eliot either, they had no way of grasping the nature of her purpose. Oddly enough, several of them were rather accomplished musicians, but that is a common peculiarity of scientists and rarely carries over into anything else. They all assumed that she was doing another "vulgarization," which as a matter of fact was true enough in their terms but insulting and inaccurate in hers.

20   In my opinion she shouldn't have minded; she should have gotten what she could from them and gone on about her business. But she was too proud to be a beggar and too honest to be a thief, and the falsity and condescension of those interviews finished her off. At last report she had moved into a sea-shell museum in the basement of a certain oceanographic building, presided over by a gentle guardian with vast knowledge of shells but no academic degrees. There she wanders, happy at last and loony as a hoot-owl, her imagination feeding on drawer upon drawer of fossil mollusks and rare conches, from which she expects some day to create the long-awaited epithalamium of Science and Humanities.

21   I have told her story in order to by-pass my own, which involved physics, a subject I used to get A in at school. This was really too horrible

to relate; it was only the thought of my children that got me out in time. From one conversation in that line, it is true, I have retained a marvelous image, usable by my humanist mind as the sick canaries were, but that took place years before.

22   I sat at dinner once with Victor Hess, winner of the Nobel Prize in physics for his work long ago in the discovery of cosmic rays. To test his theories he had taken long flights over Europe alone in a balloon, several of them at night, and although that had been early in the century, when he spoke of those flights his face still glowed with the old elation. "It was so beautiful up there," he said. "So peaceful!" Many times since I have felt myself drifting up there with him in his adventure, his dangerous joy, and have thought, "Oh but I know this, I understand!"—imagining that science and I were on speaking terms after all. Insane illusion. He was a very old man, from another world, another time, and at that moment he had been speaking as a poet, as scientists still sometimes might in his era, 50 years ago.

23   Nevertheless, I swear I will persist, at least in the biological sciences, though I should end up with that other lady among the sea-shells as a result. With physics, I'm afraid the rupture is definite. But I will never again refer to, for instance, moss, without finding out when it appeared on earth, where it stands in the scale of life and so on. That is the least a writer can do for his Golden Age. It will be hard sometimes, but I'm sure there will be that new golden voice at the switchboard, and I put my faith in that. Any time I am in despair, unwanted, useless, the Mesozoic gone adrift and the sky frivolous with intimations of immortality, I will be able to dial that number and be restored by the angelic syllables, "Science and Humanities!" Just so I don't get the answering service, and hear instead the sepulchral query, *"Que sais-je?"*

Questions

1. The idea that the humanist must understand science and technology, that the divide must be crossed—both ways, is usually treated in accents of high seriousness. Examine any four successive paragraphs word-by-word and show what phrases and strategies characterize the tone of each.
2. What do we learn of Eleanor Clark, her personality and interests, in reading her description of the problem of "the great divide?"
3. List the persons, events and objects Miss Clark returns to, unexpectedly and in a fresh context, to unify her essay and to make it more persuasive.
4. Show how Miss Clark uses elements of comparison and contrast.
5. What logical progression, if any, can you discern in the sequence of anecdotes and images from Kitt Peak National Observatory to *"Que sais-je?"* ("What do I know?")?

17 LOREN EISELEY
The Flow of the River

1   If there is magic on this planet, it is contained in water. Its least stir even, as now in a rain pond on a flat roof opposite my office, is enough to bring me searching to the window. A wind ripple may be translating itself into life. I have a constant feeling that some time I may witness that momentous miracle on a city roof, see life veritably and suddenly boiling out of a heap of rusted pipes and old television aerials. I marvel at how suddenly a water beetle has come and is submarining there is a spatter of green algae. Thin vapors, rust, wet tar and sun are an alembic remarkably like the mind; they throw off odorous shadows that threaten to take real shape when no one is looking.

2   Once in a lifetime, perhaps, one escapes the actual confines of the flesh. Once in a lifetime, if one is lucky, one so merges with sunlight and air and running water that whole eons, the eons that mountains and deserts know, might pass in a single afternoon without discomfort. The mind has sunk away into its beginnings among old roots and the obscure tricklings and movings that stir inanimate things. Like the charmed fairy circle into which a man once stepped, and upon emergence learned that a whole century had passed in a single night, one can never quite define this secret; but it has something to do, I am sure, with common water. Its substance reaches everywhere; it touches the past and prepares the future; it moves under the poles and wanders thinly in the heights of air. It can assume forms of exquisite perfection in a snowflake, or strip the living to a single shining bone cast up by the sea.

3   Many years ago, in the course of some scientific investigations in a remote western county, I experienced, by chance, precisely the sort of curious absorption by water—the extension of shape by osmosis—at which I have been hinting. You have probably never experienced in yourself the meandering roots of a whole watershed or felt your outstretched fingers touching, by some kind of clairvoyant extension, the brooks of snow-line glaciers at the same time that you were flowing toward the Gulf over the eroded debris of worn-down mountains. A poet, MacKnight Black, has spoken of being "limbed . . . with waters gripping pole and pole." He had the idea, all right, and it is obvious that these sensations are not

unique, but they are hard to come by; and the sort of extension of the senses that people will accept when they put their ear against a sea shell, they will smile at in the confessions of a bookish professor. What makes it worse is the fact that because of a traumatic experience in childhood, I am not a swimmer, and am inclined to be timid before any large body of water. Perhaps it was just this, in a way, that contributed to my experience.

4   As it leaves the Rockies and moves downward over the high plains towards the Missouri, the Platte River is a curious stream. In the spring floods, on occasion, it can be a mile-wide roaring torrent of destruction, gulping farms and bridges. Normally, however, it is a rambling, dispersed series of streamlets flowing erratically over great sand and gravel fans that are, in part, the remnants of a mightier Ice Age stream bed. Quicksand and shifting islands haunt its waters. Over it the prairie suns beat mercilessly throughout the summer. The Platte, "a mile wide and an inch deep," is a refuge for any heat-weary pilgrim along its shores. This is particularly true on the high plains before its long march by the cities begins.

5   The reason that I came upon it when I did, breaking through a willow thicket and stumbling out through ankle-deep water to a dune in the shade, is of no concern to this narrative. On various purposes of science I have ranged over a good bit of that country on foot, and I know the kinds of bones that come gurgling up through the gravel pumps, and the arrowheads of shining chalcedony that occasionally spill out of water-loosened sand. On that day, however, the sight of sky and willows and the weaving net of water murmuring a little in the shallows on its way to the Gulf stirred me, parched as I was with miles of walking, with a new idea: I was going to float. I was going to undergo a tremendous adventure.

6   The notion came to me, I suppose, by degrees. I had shed my clothes and was floundering pleasantly in a hole among some reeds when a great desire to stretch out and go with this gently insistent water began to pluck at me. Now to this bronzed, bold, modern generation, the struggle I waged with timidity while standing there in knee-deep water can only seem farcical; yet actually for me it was not so. A near-drowning accident in childhood had scarred my reactions; in addition to the fact that I was a nonswimmer, this "inch-deep river" was treacherous with holes and quicksands. Death was not precisely infrequent along its wandering and illusory channels. Like all broad wastes of this kind, where neither water nor land quite prevails, its thickets were lonely and untraversed. A man in trouble would cry out in vain.

7   I thought of all this, standing quietly in the water, feeling the sand shifting away under my toes. Then I lay back in the floating position that left my face to the sky, and shoved off. The sky wheeled over me. For an instant, as I bobbed into the main channel, I had the sensation of sliding down the vast tilted face of the continent. It was then that I felt the cold

needles of the alpine springs at my fingertips, and the warmth of the Gulf pulling me southward. Moving with me, leaving its taste upon my mouth and spouting under me in dancing springs of sand, was the immense body of the continent itself, flowing like the river was flowing, grain by grain, mountain by mountain, down to the sea. I was streaming over ancient sea beds thrust aloft where giant reptiles had once sported; I was wearing down the face of time and trundling cloud-wreathed ranges into oblivion. I touched my margins with the delicacy of a crayfish's antennae, and felt great fishes glide about their work.

8   I drifted by stranded timber cut by beaver in mountain fastnesses; I slid over shallows that had buried the broken axles of prairie schooners and the mired bones of mammoth. I was streaming alive through the hot and working ferment of the sun, or oozing secretively through shady thickets. I *was* water and the unspeakable alchemies that gestate and take shape in water, the slimy jellies that under the enormous magnification of the sun writhe and whip upward as great barbeled fish mouths, or sink indistinctly back into the murk out of which they arose. Turtle and fish and the pinpoint chirpings of individual frogs are all watery projections, concentrations—as man himself is a concentration—of that indescribable and liquid brew which is compounded in varying proportions of salt and sun and time. It has appearances, but at its heart lies water, and as I was finally edged gently against a sand bar and dropped like any log, I tottered as I rose. I knew once more the body's revolt against emergence into the harsh and unsupporting air, its reluctance to break contact with that mother element which still, at this late point in time, shelters and brings into being nine tenths of everything alive.

9   As for men, those myriad little detached ponds with their own swarming corpuscular life, what were they but a way that water has of going about beyond the reach of rivers? I, too, was a microcosm of pouring rivulets and floating driftwood gnawed by the mysterious animalcules of my own creation. I was three fourths water, rising and subsiding according to the hollow knocking in my veins: a minute pulse like the eternal pulse that lifts Himalayas and which, in the following systole, will carry them away.

10   Thoreau, peering at the emerald pickerel in Walden Pond, called them "animalized water" in one of his moments of strange insight. If he had been possessed of the geological knowledge so laboriously accumulated since his time, he might have gone further and amusedly detected in the planetary rumblings and eructations which so delighted him in the gross habits of certain frogs, signs of that dark interior stress which has reared sea bottoms up to mountainous heights. He might have developed an acute inner ear for the sound of the surf on Cretaceous beaches where now the wheat of Kansas rolls. In any case, he would have seen, as the long trail of life was unfolded by the fossil hunters, that his animalized water had

changed its shapes eon by eon to the beating of the earth's dark millennial heart. In the swamps of the low continents, the amphibians had flourished and had their day; and as the long skyward swing—the isostatic response of the crust—had come about, the era of the cooling grasslands and mammalian life had come into being.

11 A few winters ago, clothed heavily against the weather, I wandered several miles along one of the tributaries of that same Platte I had floated down years before. The land was stark and ice-locked. The rivulets were frozen, and over the marshlands the willow thickets made such an array of vertical lines against the snow that tramping through them produced strange optical illusions and dizziness. On the edge of a frozen backwater, I stopped and rubbed my eyes. At my feet a raw prairie wind had swept the ice clean of snow. A peculiar green object caught my eye; there was no mistaking it.

12 Staring up at me with all his barbels spread pathetically, frozen solidly in the wind-ruffled ice, was a huge familiar face. It was one of those catfish of the twisting channels, those dwellers in the yellow murk, who had been about me and beneath me on the day of my great voyage. Whatever sunny dream had kept him paddling there while the mercury plummeted downward and that Cheshire smile froze slowly, it would be hard to say. Or perhaps he was trapped in a blocked channel and had simply kept swimming until the ice contracted around him. At any rate, there he would lie till the spring thaw.

13 At that moment I started to turn away, but something in the bleak, whiskered face reproached me, or perhaps it was the river calling to her children. I termed it science, however—a convenient rational phrase I reserve for such occasions—and decided that I would cut the fish out of the ice and take him home. I had no intention of eating him. I was merely struck by a sudden impulse to test the survival qualities of high-plains fishes, particularly fishes of this type who get themselves immured in oxygenless ponds or in cut-off oxbows buried in winter drifts. I blocked him out as gently as possible and dropped him, ice and all, into a collecting can in the car. Then we set out for home.

14 Unfortunately, the first stages of what was to prove a remarkable resurrection escaped me. Cold and tired after a long drive, I deposited the can with its melting water and ice in the basement. The accompanying corpse I anticipated I would either dispose of or dissect on the following day. A hurried glance had revealed no signs of life.

15 To my astonishment, however, upon descending into the basement several hours later, I heard stirrings in the receptacle and peered in. The ice had melted. A vast pouting mouth ringed with sensitive feelers confronted me, and the creature's gills labored slowly. A thin stream of silver bubbles rose to the surface and popped. A fishy eye gazed up at me protestingly.

16   "A tank," it said. This was no Walden pickerel. This was a yellow-green, mud-grubbing, evil-tempered inhabitant of floods and droughts and cyclones. It was the selective product of the high continent and the waters that pour across it. It had outlasted prairie blizzards that left cattle standing frozen upright in the drifts.

17   "I'll get the tank," I said respectfully.

18   He lived with me all that winter, and his departure was totally in keeping with his sturdy, independent character. In the spring a migratory impulse or perhaps sheer boredom struck him. Maybe, in some little lost corner of his brain, he felt, far off, the pouring of the mountain waters through the sandy coverts of the Platte. Anyhow, something called to him, and he went. One night when no one was about, he simply jumped out of his tank. I found him dead on the floor next morning. He had made his gamble like a man—or, I should say, a fish. In the proper place it would not have been a fool's gamble. Fishes in the drying shallows of intermittent prairie streams who feel their confinement and have the impulse to leap while there is yet time may regain the main channel and survive. A million ancestral years had gone into that jump, I thought as I looked at him, a million years of climbing through prairie sunflowers and twining in and out through the pillared legs of drinking mammoth.

19   "Some of your close relatives have been experimenting with air breathing," I remarked, apropos of nothing, as I gathered him up. "Suppose we meet again up there in the cottonwoods in a million years or so."

20   I missed him a little as I said it. He had for me the kind of lost archaic glory that comes from the water brotherhood. We were both projections out of that timeless ferment and locked as well in some greater unity that lay incalculably beyond us. In many a fin and reptile foot I have seen myself passing by—some part of myself, that is, some part that lies unrealized in the momentary shape I inhabit. People have occasionally written me harsh letters and castigated me for a lack of faith in man when I have ventured to speak of this matter in print. They distrust, it would seem, all shapes and thoughts but their own. They would bring God into the compass of a shopkeeper's understanding and confine Him to those limits, lest He proceed to some unimaginable and shocking act—create perhaps, as a casual afterthought, a being more beautiful than man. As for me, I believe nature capable of this, and having been part of the flow of the river, I feel no envy—any more than the frog envies the reptile or an ancestral ape should envy man.

21   Every spring in the wet meadows and ditches I hear a little shrilling chorus which sounds for all the world like an endlessly reiterated "We're here, we're here, we're here." And so they are, as frogs, of course. Confident little fellows. I suspect that to some greater ear than ours, man's optimistic pronouncements about his role and destiny may make a similar little ringing sound that travels a small way out into the night. It is only its

nearness that is offensive. From the heights of a mountain, or a marsh at evening, it blends, not too badly, with all the other sleepy voices that, in croaks or chirrups, are saying the same thing.

22　　After a while the skilled listener can distinguish man's noise from the katydid's rhythmic assertion, allow for the offbeat of a rabbit's thumping, pick up the autumnal monotone of crickets, and find in all of them a grave pleasure without admitting any to a place of preëminence in his thoughts. It is when all these voices cease and the waters are still, when along the frozen river nothing cries, screams or howls, that the enormous mindlessness of space settles down upon the soul. Somewhere out in that waste of crushed ice and reflected stars, the black waters may be running, but they appear to be running without life toward a destiny in which the whole of space may be locked in some silvery winter of dispersed radiation.

23　　It is then, when the wind comes straitly across the barren marshes and the snow rises and beats in endless waves against the traveler, that I remember best, by some trick of the imagination, my summer voyage on the river. I remember my green extensions, my catfish nuzzlings and minnow wrigglings, my gelatinous materializations out of the mother ooze. And as I walk on through the white smother, it is the magic of water that leaves me a final sign.

24　　Men talk much of matter and energy, of the struggle for existence that molds the shape of life. These things exist, it is true; but more delicate, elusive, quicker than the fins in water, is that mysterious principle known as "organization," which leaves all other mysteries concerned with life stale and insignificant by comparison. For that without organization life does not persist is obvious. Yet this organization itself is not strictly the product of life, nor of selection. Like some dark and passing shadow within matter, it cups out the eyes' small windows or spaces the notes of a meadow lark's song in the interior of a mottled egg. That principle—I am beginning to suspect—was there before the living in the deeps of water.

25　　The temperature has risen. The little stinging needles have given way to huge flakes floating in like white leaves blown from some great tree in open space. In the car, switching on the lights, I examine one intricate crystal on my sleeve before it melts. No utilitarian philosophy explains a snow crystal, no doctrine of use or disuse. Water has merely leapt out of vapor and thin nothingness in the night sky to array itself in form. There is no logical reason for the existence of a snowflake any more than there is for evolution. It is an apparition from that mysterious shadow world beyond nature, that final world which contains—if anything contains —the explanation of men and catfish and green leaves.

PART TWO
Style

Words and Tone

18 GEORGE ORWELL
Politics and the English Language

1   Most people who bother with the matter at all would admit that the English language is in a bad way, but it is generally assumed that we cannot by conscious action do anything about it. Our civilization is decadent, and our language—so the argument runs—must inevitably share in the general collapse. It follows that any struggle against the abuse of language is a sentimental archaism, like preferring candles to electric light or hansom cabs to aeroplanes. Underneath this lies the half-conscious belief that language is a natural growth and not an instrument which we shape for our own purposes.

2   Now, it is clear that the decline of a language must ultimately have political and economic causes: it is not due simply to the bad influence of this or that individual writer. But an effect can become a cause, reinforcing the original cause and producing the same effect in an intensified form, and so on indefinitely. A man may take to drink because he feels himself to be a failure, and then fail all the more completely because he drinks. It is rather the same thing that is happening to the English language. It becomes ugly and inaccurate because our thoughts are foolish, but the slovenliness of our language makes it easier for us to have foolish thoughts. The point is that the process is reversible. Modern English, especially written English, is full of bad habits which spread by imitation and which can be avoided if one is willing to take the necessary trouble. If one gets rid of these habits one can think more clearly, and to think clearly is a necessary first step towards political regeneration: so that the fight against bad English is not frivolous and is not the exclusive concern

of professional writers. I will come back to this presently, and I hope that by that time the meaning of what I have said here will have become clearer. Meanwhile, here are five specimens of the English language as it is now habitually written.

3   These five passages have not been picked out because they are especially bad—I could have quoted far worse if I had chosen—but because they illustrate various of the mental vices from which we now suffer. They are a little below the average, but are fairly representative samples. I number them so that I can refer back to them when necessary:

(1) I am not, indeed, sure whether it is not true to say that the Milton who once seemed not unlike a seventeenth-century Shelley had not become, out of an experience ever more bitter in each year, more alien (*sic*) to the founder of that Jesuit sect which nothing could induce him to tolerate.
    —PROFESSOR HAROLD LASKI (Essay in *Freedom of Expression*)

(2) Above all, we cannot play ducks and drakes with a native battery of idioms which prescribes such egregious collocations of vocables as the Basic *put up with* for *tolerate* or *put at a loss* for *bewilder*.
    —PROFESSOR LANCELOT HOGBEN (*Interglossa*)

(3) On the one side we have the free personality; by definition it is not neurotic, for it has neither conflict nor dream. Its desires, such as they are, are transparent, for they are just what institutional approval keeps in the forefront of consciousness; another institutional pattern would alter their number and intensity; there is little in them that is natural, irreducible, or culturally dangerous. But *on the other side,* the social bond itself is nothing but the mutual reflection of these self-secure integrities. Recall the definition of love. Is not this the very picture of a small academic? Where is there a place in this hall of mirrors for either personality or fraternity?
    —ESSAY ON PSYCHOLOGY in *Politics* (New York)

(4) All the "best people" from the gentlemen's clubs, and all the frantic fascist captains, united in common hatred of Socialism and bestial horror of the rising tide of the mass revolutionary movement, have turned to acts of provocation, to foul incendiarism, to medieval legends of poisoned wells, to legalize their own destruction of proletarian organizations, and rouse the agitated petty-bourgeoisie to chauvinistic fervor on behalf of the fight against the revolutionary way out of the crisis.   —COMMUNIST PAMPHLET

(5) If a new spirit *is* to be infused into this old country, there is one thorny and contentious reform which must be tackled, and that is the humanization and galvanization of the B.B.C. Timidity here will bespeak canker and atrophy of the soul. The heart of Britain may be sound and of strong beat, for instance, but the British lion's roar at present is like that of Bottom in Shakespeare's *Midsummer Night's Dream*—as gentle as any sucking dove. A virile new Britain cannot continue indefinitely to be traduced in the eyes, or rather ears, of the world by the effete languors of Langham Place, brazenly masquerading as "standard English." When the Voice of Britain is heard at nine o'clock, better

far and infinitely less ludicrous to hear aitches honestly dropped than the present priggish, inflated, inhibited, school-ma'am-ish arch braying of blameless bashful mewing maidens.   —LETTER in *Tribune*

4   Each of these passages has faults of its own, but quite apart from avoidable ugliness, two qualities are common to all of them. The first is staleness of imagery; the other is lack of precision. The writer either has a meaning and cannot express it, or he inadvertently says something else, or he is almost indifferent as to whether his words mean anything or not. This mixture of vagueness and sheer incompetence is the most marked characteristic of modern English prose, and especially of any kind of political writing. As soon as certain topics are raised, the concrete melts into the abstract and no one seems able to think of turns of speech that are not hackneyed: prose consists less and less of *words* chosen for the sake of their meaning, and more and more of *phrases* tacked together like the sections of a prefabricated hen-house. I list below, with notes and examples, various of the tricks by means of which the work of prose-construction is habitually dodged:

Dying metaphors. A newly-invented metaphor assists thought by evoking a visual image, while on the other hand a metaphor which is technically "dead" (e.g., *iron resolution*) has in effect reverted to being an ordinary word and can generally be used without loss of vividness. But in between these two classes there is a huge dump of worn-out metaphors which have lost all evocative power and are merely used because they save people the trouble of inventing phrases for themselves. Examples are: *Ring the changes on, take up the cudgels for, toe the line, ride roughshod over, stand shoulder to shoulder with, play into the hands of, an axe to grind, grist to the mill, fishing in troubled waters, on the order of the day, Achilles' heel, swan song, hotbed.* Many of these are used without knowledge of their meaning (what is a "rift," for instance?), and incompatible metaphors are frequently mixed, a sure sign that the writer is not interested in what he is saying. Some metaphors now current have been twisted out of their original meaning without those who use them even being aware of the fact. For example, *toe the line* is sometimes written *tow the line.* Another example is *the hammer and the anvil,* now always used with the implication that the anvil gets the worst of it. In real life it is always the anvil that breaks the hammer, never the other way about: a writer who stopped to think what he was saying would be aware of this, and would avoid perverting the original phrase.

Operators, or *verbal false limbs.* These save the trouble of picking out appropriate verbs and nouns, and at the same time pad each sentence with extra syllables which give it an appearance of symmetry. Characteristic phrases are: *render inoperative, militate against, prove unacceptable, make contact with, be subjected to, give rise to, give grounds for, having the effect of, play a leading part (role) in, make itself felt, take effect, exhibit a tendency to, serve the purpose of, etc., etc.* The keynote is the elimination of simple verbs. Instead of being a single word, such as *break, stop, spoil, mend, kill,* a verb becomes a phrase, made up of a noun or adjective tacked on to some general-purposes verb as *prove, serve form, play, render.* In addition, the passive voice is wherever possible used in preference to the active, and noun constructions are used instead of gerunds (*by examination of* instead of *by examining*). The range of verbs is further cut down by means of the *-ize* and *de-* formations, and banal statements are given an appearance of profundity by means of the *not un-* formation. Simple conjunctions and prepositions are replaced by such phrases as *with respect to, having regard to, the fact that, by dint of, in view of, in the interests of, on the hypothesis that;* and the ends of sentences are saved from anti-climax by such resounding commonplaces as *greatly to be desired, cannot be left out of account, a development to be expected in the near future, deserving of serious consideration, brought to a satisfactory conclusion,* and so on and so forth.

Pretentious diction. Words like *phenomenon, element, individual* (as noun), *objective, categorical, effective, virtual, basis, primary, promote, constitute, exhibit, exploit, utilize, eliminate, liquidate,* are used to dress up simple statements and give an air of scientific impartiality to biased judgments. Adjectives like *epoch-making, epic, historic, unforgettable, triumphant, age-old, inevitable, inexorable, veritable,* are used to dignify the sordid processes of international politics, while writing that aims at glorifying war usually takes on an archaic color, its characteristic words being: *realm, throne, chariot, mailed fist, trident, sword, shield, buckler, banner, jackboot, clarion.* Foreign words and expressions such as *cul de sac, ancien régime, deus ex machina, mutatis mutandis, status quo, gleichschaltung, weltanschauung,* are used to give an air of culture and elegance. Except for the useful abbreviations *i.e., e.g.,* and *etc.,* there is no real need for any of the hundreds of foreign phrases now current in English. Bad writers, and especially scientific, political and sociological writers, are nearly always haunted by the notion that Latin or Greek words are grander than Saxon ones, and unnecessary words like *expedite, ameliorate, predict, extraneous, deracinated, clandestine, subaqueous* and hundreds of others constantly gain ground from their Anglo-Saxon opposite numbers.[1] The jargon peculiar to Marxist writing (*hyena, hangman, cannibal, petty bourgeois, these gentry, lackey, flunky, mad dog, White Guard, etc.*) consists largely of words and phrases translated from Russian, German or French;

[1] An interesting illustration of this is the way in which the English flower names which were in use till very recently are being ousted by Greek ones, *snap-dragon* becoming *antirrhinum, forget-me-not* becoming *myosotis,* etc. It is hard to see any practical reason for this change of fashion: it is probably due to an instinctive turning-away from the more homely word and a vague feeling that the Greek word is scientific.

but the normal way of coining a new word is to use a Latin or Greek root with the appropriate affix and, where necessary, the -*ize* formation. It is often easier to make up words of this kind (*deregionalize, impermissible, extramarital, non-fragmentary* and so forth) than to think up the English words that will cover one's meaning. The result, in general, is an increase in slovenliness and vagueness.

Meaningless words. In certain kinds of writing, particularly in art criticism and literary criticism, it is normal to come across long passages which are almost completely lacking in meaning.[2] Words like *romantic, plastic, values, human, dead, sentimental, natural, vitality,* as used in are criticism, are strictly meaningless, in the sense that they not only do not point to any discoverable object, but are hardly even expected to do so by the reader. When one critic writes, "The outstanding feature of Mr. X's work is its living quality," while another writes, "The immediately striking thing about Mr. X's work is its peculiar deadness," the reader accepts this as a simple difference of opinion. If words like *black* and *white* were involved, instead of the jargon words *dead* and *living,* he would see at once that language was being used in an improper way. Many political words are similarly abused. The word *Fascism* has now no meaning except in so far as it signifies "something not desirable." The words *democracy, socialism, freedom, patriotic, realistic, justice,* have each of them several different meanings which cannot be reconciled with one another. In the case of a word like *democracy,* not only is there no agreed definition, but the attempt to make one is resisted from all sides. It is almost universally felt that when we call a country democratic we are praising it: consequently the defenders of every kind of régime claim that it is a democracy, and fear that they might have to stop using the word if it were tied down to any one meaning. Words of this kind are often used in a consciously dishonest way. That is, the person who uses them has his own private definition, but allows his hearer to think he means something quite different. Statements like *Marshal Pétain was a true patriot, The Soviet Press is the freest in the world, The Catholic Church is opposed to persecution,* are almost always made with intent to deceive. Other words used in variable meanings, in most cases more or less dishonestly, are: *class, totalitarian, science, progressive, reactionary, bourgeois, equality.*

5   Now that I have made this catalogue of swindles and perversions, let me give another example of the kind of writing that they lead to. This time it must of its nature be an imaginary one. I am going to translate a

---

[2] Example: "Comfort's catholicity of perception and image, strangely Whitmanesque in range, almost the exact opposite in aesthetic compulsion, continues to evoke that trembling atmospheric accumulative hinting at a cruel, an inexorably serene timelessness . . . Wrey Gardiner scores by aiming at simple bullseyes with precision. Only they are not so simple, and through this contented sadness runs more than the surface bittersweet of resignation." (*Poetry Quarterly.*)

passage of good English into modern English of the worst sort. Here is a well-known verse from *Ecclesiastes:*

I returned, and saw under the sun, that the race is not to the swift, nor the battle to the strong, neither yet bread to the wise, nor yet riches to men of understanding, nor yet favor to men of skill; but time and chance happeneth to them all.

Here it is in modern English:

Objective consideration of contemporary phenomena compels the conclusion that success or failure in competitive activities exhibits no tendency to be commensurate with innate capacity, but that a considerable element of the unpredictable must invariably be taken into account.

6   This is a parody, but not a very gross one. Exhibit (3), above, for instance, contains several patches of the same kind of English. It will be seen that I have not made a full translation. The beginning and ending of the sentence follow the original meaning fairly closely, but in the middle the concrete illustrations—race, battle, bread—dissolve into the vague phrase "success or failure in competitive activities." This had to be so, because no modern writer of the kind I am discussing—no one capable of using phrases like "objective consideration of contemporary phenomena" —would ever tabulate his thoughts in that precise and detailed way. The whole tendency of modern prose is away from concreteness. Now analyze these two sentences a little more closely. The first contains 49 words but only 60 syllables, and all its words are those of everyday life. The second contains 38 words of 90 syllables: 18 of its words are from Latin roots, and one from Greek. The first sentence contains six vivid images, and only one phrase ("time and chance") that could be called vague. The second contains not a single fresh, arresting phrase, and in spite of its 90 syllables it gives only a shortened version of the meaning contained in the first. Yet without a doubt it is the second kind of sentence that is gaining ground in modern English. I do not want to exaggerate. This kind of writing is not yet universal, and outcrops of simplicity will occur here and there in the worst-written page. Still, if you or I were told to write a few lines on the uncertainty of human fortunes, we should probably come much nearer to my imaginary sentence than to the one from *Ecclesiastes.*

7   As I have tried to show, modern writing at its worst does not consist in picking out words for the sake of their meaning and inventing images in order to make the meaning clearer. It consists in gumming together long strips of words which have already been set in order by someone else, and making the results presentable by sheer humbug. The attraction of this way of writing is that it is easy. It is easier—even quicker, once you have the habit—to say *In my opinion it is a not unjustifiable assumption that* than to say I *think.* If you use ready-made phrases, you not only don't have to hunt about for words; you also don't have to bother with the rhythms of your sentences, since these phrases are generally so arranged as to be

more or less euphonious. When you are composing in a hurry—when you are dictating to a stenographer, for instance, or making a public speech—it is natural to fall into a pretentious, Latinized style. Tags like *a consideration which we should do well to bear in mind* or *a conclusion to which all of us would readily assent* will save many a sentence from coming down with a bump. By using stale metaphors, similes and idioms, you save much mental effort at the cost of leaving your meaning vague, not only for your reader but for yourself. This is the significance of mixed metaphors. The sole aim of a metaphor is to call up a visual image. When these images clash—as in *The Fascist octopus has sung its swan song, the jackboot is thrown into the melting pot*—it can be taken as certain that the writer is not seeing a mental image of the objects he is naming; in other words he is not really thinking. Look again at the examples I gave at the beginning of this essay. Professor Laski (1) uses five negatives in 53 words. One of these is superfluous, making nonsense of the whole passage, and in addition there is the slip *alien* for akin, making further nonsense, and several avoidable pieces of clumsiness which increase the general vagueness. Professor Hogben (2) plays ducks and drakes with a battery which is able to write prescriptions, and, while disapproving of the everyday phrase *put up with,* is unwilling to look *egregious* up in the dictionary and see what it means. (3), if one takes an uncharitable attitude towards it, is simply meaningless: probably one could work out its intended meaning by reading the whole of the article in which it occurs. In (4), the writer knows more or less what he wants to say, but an accumulation of stale phrases chokes him like tea leaves blocking a sink. In (5), words and meaning have almost parted company. People who write in this manner usually have a general emotional meaning—they dislike one thing and want to express solidarity with another—but they are not interested in the detail of what they are saying. A scrupulous writer, in every sentence that he writes, will ask himself at least four questions, thus: What am I trying to say? What words will express it? What image or idiom will make it clearer? Is this image fresh enough to have an effect? And he will probably ask himself two more: Could I put it more shortly? Have I said anything that is avoidably ugly? But you are not obliged to go to all this trouble. You can shirk it by simply throwing your mind open and letting the ready-made phrases come crowding in. They will construct your sentences for you—even think your thoughts for you, to a certain extent—and at need they will perform the important service of partially concealing your meaning even from yourself. It is at this point that the special connection between politics and the debasement of language becomes clear.

8   In our time it is broadly true that political writing is bad writing. Where it is not true, it will generally be found that the writer is some kind of rebel, expressing his private opinions and not a "party line." Orthodoxy, of whatever color, seems to demand a lifeless, imitative style.

The political dialects to be found in pamphlets, leading articles, manifestoes, White Papers and the speeches of under-secretaries do, of course, vary from party to party, but they are all alike in that one almost never finds in them a fresh, vivid, home-made turn of speech. When one watches some tired hack on the platform mechanically repeating the familiar phrases—*bestial atrocities, iron heel, bloodstained tyranny, free peoples of the world, stand shoulder to shoulder*—one often has a curious feeling that one is not watching a live human being but some kind of dummy: a feeling which suddenly becomes stronger at moments when the light catches the speaker's spectacles and turns them into blank discs which seem to have no eyes behind them. And this is not altogether fanciful. A speaker who uses that kind of phraseology has gone some distance towards turning himself into a machine. The appropriate noises are coming out of his larynx, but his brain is not involved as it would be if he were choosing his words for himself. If the speech he is making is one that he is accustomed to make over and over again, he may be almost unconscious of what he is saying, as one is when one utters the responses in church. And this reduced state of consciousness, if not indispensable, is at any rate favorable to political conformity.

9   In our time, political speech and writing are largely the defense of the indefensible. Things like the continuance of British rule in India, the Russian purges and deportations, the dropping of the atom bombs on Japan, can indeed be defended, but only by arguments which are too brutal for most people to face, and which do not square with the professed aims of political parties. Thus political language has to consist largely of euphemism, question-begging and sheer cloudy vagueness. Defenseless villages are bombarded from the air, the inhabitants driven out into the countryside, the cattle machine-gunned, the huts set on fire with incendiary bullets: this is called *pacification*. Millions of peasants are robbed of their farms and sent trudging along the roads with no more than they can carry: this is called *transfer of population* or *rectification of frontiers*. People are imprisoned for years without trial, or shot in the back of the neck or sent to die of scurvy in Arctic lumber camps: this is called *elimination of unreliable elements*. Such phraseology is needed if one wants to name things without calling up mental pictures of them. Consider for instance some comfortable English professor defending Russian totalitarianism. He cannot say outright, "I believe in killing off your opponents when you can get good results by doing so." Probably, therefore, he will say something like this:

While freely conceding that the Soviet régime exhibits certain features which the humanitarian may be inclined to deplore, we must, I think, agree that a certain curtailment of the right to political opposition is an unavoidable concomitant of transitional periods, and that the rigors which the Russian people have been called upon to undergo have been amply justified in the sphere of concrete achievement.

10   The inflated style is itself a kind of euphemism. A mass of Latin words falls upon the facts like soft snow, blurring the outlines and covering up all the details. The great enemy of clear language is insincerity. When there is a gap between one's real and one's declared aims, one turns, as it were instinctively, to long words and exhausted idioms, like a cuttlefish squirting out ink. In our age there is no such thing as "keeping out of politics." All issues are political issues, and politics itself is a mass of lies, evasions, folly, hatred and schizophrenia. When the general atmosphere is bad, language must suffer. I should expect to find—this is a guess which I have not sufficient knowledge to verify—that the German, Russian and Italian languages have all deteriorated in the last ten or fifteen years as a result of dictatorship.

11   But if thought corrupts language, language can also corrupt thought. A bad usage can spread by tradition and imitation, even among people who should and do know better. The debased language that I have been discussing is in some ways very convenient. Phrases like *a not unjustifiable assumption, leaves much to be desired, would serve no good purpose, a consideration which we should do well to bear in mind,* are a continuous temptation, a packet of aspirins always at one's elbow. Look back through this essay, and for certain you will find that I have again and again committed the very faults I am protesting against. By this morning's post I have received a pamphlet dealing with conditions in Germany. The author tells me that he "felt impelled" to write it. I open it at random, and here is almost the first sentence that I see: "[The Allies] have an opportunity not only of achieving a radical transformation of Germany's social and political structure in such a way as to avoid a nationalistic reaction in Germany itself, but at the same time of laying the foundations of a cooperative and unified Europe." You see, he "feels impelled" to write— feels, presumably, that he has something new to say—and yet his words, like cavalry horses answering the bugle, group themselves automatically into the familiar dreary pattern. This invasion of one's mind by ready-made phrases (*lay the foundations, achieve a radical transformation*) can only be prevented if one is constantly on guard against them, and every such phrase anesthetizes a portion of one's brain.

12   I said earlier that the decadence of our language is probably curable. Those who deny this would argue, if they produced an argument at all, that language merely reflects existing social conditions, and that we cannot influence its development by any direct tinkering with words and constructions. So far as the general tone or spirit of a language goes, this may be true, but it is not true in detail. Silly words and expressions have often disappeared, not through any evolutionary process but owing to the con-

scious action of a minority. Two recent examples were *explore every avenue* and *leave no stone unturned,* which were killed by the jeers of a few journalists. These is a long list of fly-blown metaphors which could similarly be got rid of if enough people would interest themselves in the job; and it should also be possible to laugh the *not un-* formation out of existence,[3] to reduce the amount of Latin and Greek in the average sentence, to drive out foreign phrases and strayed scientific words, and, in general, to make pretentiousness unfashionable. But all these are minor points. The defense of the English language implies more than this, and perhaps it is best to start by saying what it does *not* imply.

To begin with, it has nothing to do with archaism, with the salvaging of obsolete words and turns of speech, or with the setting-up of a "standard-English" which must never be departed from. On the contrary, it is especially concerned with the scrapping of every word or idiom which has outworn its usefulness. It has nothing to do with correct grammar and syntax, which are of no importance so long as one makes one's meaning clear, or with the avoidance of Americanisms, or with having what is called a "good prose style." On the other hand it is not concerned with fake simplicity and the attempt to make written English colloquial. Nor does it even imply in every case preferring the Saxon word to the Latin one, though it does imply using the fewest and shortest words that will cover one's meaning. What is above all needed is to let the meaning choose the word, and not the other way about. In prose, the worst thing one can do with words is to surrender them. When you think of a concrete object, you think wordlessly, and then, if you want to describe the thing you have been visualizing, you probably hunt about till you find the exact words that seem to fit it. When you think of something abstract you are more inclined to use words from the start, and unless you make a conscious effort to prevent it, the existing dialect will come rushing in and do the job for you, at the expense of blurring or even changing your meaning. Probably it is better to put off using words as long as possible and get one's meaning as clear as one can through pictures or sensations. Afterwards one can choose—not simply *accept*—the phrases that will best cover the meaning, and then switch round and decide what impressions one's words are likely to make on another person. This last effort of the mind cuts out all stale or mixed images, all prefabricated phrases, needless repetitions, and humbug and vagueness generally. But one can often be in doubt about the effect of a word or a phrase, and one needs rules that one can rely on when instinct fails. I think the following rules will cover most cases:

(i) Never use a metaphor, simile or other figure of speech which you are used to seeing in print.
(ii) Never use a long word where a short one will do.

[3] One can cure oneself of the *non un-* formation by memorizing this sentence: *A not unblack dog was chasing a not unsmall rabbit across a not ungreen field.*

(iii) If it is possible to cut a word out, always cut it out.

(iv) Never use the passive where you can use the active.

(v) Never use a foreign phrase, a scientific word or a jargon word if you can think of an everyday English equivalent.

(vi) Break any of these rules sooner than say anything barbarous.

These rules sound elementary, and so they are, but they demand a deep change of attitude in anyone who has grown used to writing in the style now fashionable. One could keep all of them and still write bad English, but one could not write the kind of stuff that I quoted in these five specimens at the beginning of this article.

14   I have not here been considering the literary use of language, but merely language as an instrument for expressing and not for concealing or preventing thought. Stuart Chase and others have come near to claiming that all abstract words are meaningless, and have used this as a pretext for advocating a kind of political quietism. Since you don't know what Fascism is, how can you struggle against Fascism? One need not swallow such absurdities as this, but one ought to recognize that the present political chaos is connected with the decay of language, and that one can probably bring about some improvement by starting at the verbal end. If you simplify your English, you are freed from the worst follies of orthodoxy. You cannot speak any of the necessary dialects, and when you make a stupid remark its stupidity will be obvious, even to yourself. Political language—and with variations this is true of all political parties, from Conservatives to Anarchists—is designed to make lies sound truthful and murder respectable, and to give an appearance of solidity to pure wind. One cannot change this all in a moment, but one can at least change one's own habits, and from time to time one can even, if one jeers loudly enough, send some worn-out and useless phrase—some *jackboot, Achilles' heel, hotbed, melting pot, acid test, veritable inferno* or other lump of verbal refuse—into the dustbin where it belongs.

19   SAMUEL T. WILLIAMSON

How to Write Like a Social Scientist

1   During my years as an editor, I have seen probably hundreds of job applicants who were either just out of College or in their senior year. All wanted "to write." Many brought letters from their teachers. But I do

From *The Saturday Review of Literature* (October 4, 1947). Reprinted by permission of *The Saturday Review* and Mrs. Cora Chase Williamson.

not recall one letter announcing that its bearer could write what he wished to say with clarity and directness, with economy of words, and with pleasing variety of sentence structure.

2   Most of these young men and women could not write plain English. Apparently their noses had not been rubbed in the drudgery of putting one simple well-chosen word behind the other. If this was true of teachers' pets, what about the rest? What about those going into business and industry? Or those going into professions? What about those who remain at college —first for a Master of Arts degree, then an instructorship combined with work for a Ph.D., then perhaps an assistant professorship, next a full professorship and finally, as an academic crown of laurel, appointment as head of a department or as dean of a faculty?

3   Certainly, faculty members of a front-rank university should be better able to express themselves than those they teach. Assume that those in the English department have this ability. Can the same be said of the social scientists—economists, sociologists, and authorities on government? We need today as we never needed so urgently before all the understanding they can give us of problems of earning a living, caring for our fellows, and governing ourselves. Too many of them, I find, can't write as well as their students.

4   I am still convalescing from overexposure some time ago to products of the academic mind. One of the foundations engaged me to edit manuscripts of a socio-economic research report designed for the thoughtful citizen as well as for the specialist. My expectations were not high—no deathless prose, merely a sturdy, no-nonsense report of explorers into the wilderness of statistics and half-known facts. I knew from experience that economic necessity compels many a professional writer to be a cream-skimmer and a gatherer of easily obtainable material; for unless his publishers will stand the extra cost, he cannot afford the exhaustive investigation which endowed research makes possible. Although I did not expect fine writing from a trained, professional researcher, I did assume that a careful fact-finder would write carefully.

5   And so, anticipating no literary treat, I plunged into the forest of words of my first manuscript. My weapons were a sturdy eraser and several batteries of sharpened pencils. My armor was a thesaurus. And if I should become lost, a near-by public library was a landmark, and the Encyclopedia of Social Sciences on its reference shelves was an ever-ready guide.

6   Instead of big trees, I found underbrush. Cutting through involved, lumbering sentences was bad enough, but the real chore was removal of the burdocks of excess verbiage which clung to the manuscript. Nothing was big or large; in my author's lexicon, it was "substantial." When he meant "much," he wrote "to a substantially high degree." If some event took place in the early 1920's, he put it "in the early part of the decade of

the twenties." And instead of "that depends," my author wrote, "any answer to this question must bear in mind certain peculiar characteristics of the industry."

7   So it went for 30,000 words. The pile of verbal burdocks grew—sometimes twelve words from a twenty-word sentence. The shortened version of 20,000 words was perhaps no more thrilling than the original report; but it was terser and crisper. It took less time to read and it could be understood quicker. That was all I could do. As S. S. McClure once said to me, "An editor can improve a manuscript, but he cannot put in what isn't there."

8   I did not know the author I was editing; after what I did to his copy it may be just as well that we have not met. Aside from his cat-chasing-its-own-tail verbosity, he was a competent enough workman. Apparently he is well thought of. He has his doctorate, he is a trained researcher and a pupil of an eminent professor. He has held a number of fellowships and he has performed competently several jobs of economic research. But, after this long academic preparation for what was to be a life work, it is a mystery why so little attention was given to acquiring use of simple English.

9   Later, when I encountered other manuscripts, I found I had been too hard on this promising Ph.D. Tone-deaf as he was to words, his report was a lighthouse of clarity among the chapters turned in by his so-called academic betters. These brethren—and sister'n—who contributed the remainder of the foundation's study were professors and assistant professors in our foremost colleges and universities. The names of one or two are occasionally in newspaper headlines. All of them had, as the professorial term has it, "published."

10   Anyone who edits copy, regardless of whether it is good or bad, discovers in a manuscript certain pet phrases, little quirks of style and other individual traits of its author. But in the series I edited, all twenty reports read alike. Their words would be found in any English dictionary, grammar was beyond criticism, but long passages in these reports demanded not editing but actual translation. For hours at a time, I floundered in brier patches like this: "In eliminating wage changes due to purely transitory conditions, collective bargaining has eliminated one of the important causes of industrial conflict, for changes under such conditions are almost always followed by a reaction when normal conditions appear."

11   I am not picking on my little group of social scientists. They are merely members of a caste; they are so used to taking in each other's literary washing that it has become a habit for them to clothe their thoughts in the same smothering verbal garments. Nor are they any worse than most of their colleagues, for example:

In the long run, developments in transportation, housing, optimum size of plant, etc., might tend to induce an industrial and demographic pattern similar to the one that consciousness of vulnerability would dictate. Such a tendency might be advanced by public persuasion and governmental inducement, and advanced more effectively if the causes of urbanization had been carefully studied.

12   Such pedantic Choctaw may be all right as a sort of code language or shorthand of social science to circulate among initiates, but its perpetrators have no right to impose it on others. The tragedy is that its users appear to be under the impression that it is good English usage.

13   Father, forgive them; for they know not what they do! There once was a time when everyday folk spoke one language, and learned men wrote another. It was called the Dark Ages. The world is in such a state that we may return to the Dark Ages if we do not acquire wisdom. If social scientists have answers to our problems yet feel under no obligation to make themselves understood, then we laymen must learn their language. This may take some practice, but practice should become perfect by following six simple rules of the guild of social science writers. Examples which I give are sound and well tested; they come from manuscripts I edited.

14   *Rule 1. Never use a short word when you can think of a long one.* Never say "now," but "currently." It is not "soon" but "presently." You did not have "enough" but a "sufficiency." Never do you come to the "end" but to the "termination." This rule is basic.

15   *Rule 2. Never use one word when you can use two or more.* Eschew "probably." Write, "it is improbable," and raise this to "it is not improbable." Then you'll be able to parlay "probably" into "available evidence would tend to indicate that it is not unreasonable to suppose."

16   *Rule 3. Put one-syllable thought into polysyllabic terms.* Instead of observing that a work force might be bigger and better, write, "In addition to quantitative enlargement, it is not improbable that there is need also for qualitative improvement in the personnel of the service." If you have discovered that musicians out of practice can't hold jobs, report that "the fact of rapid deterioration of musical skill when not in use soon converts the employed into the unemployable." Resist the impulse to say that much men's clothing is machine made. Put it thus: "Nearly all operations in the industry lend themselves to performance by machine, and all grades of men's clothing sold in significant quantity involve a very substantial amount of machine work."

17   *Rule 4. Put the obvious in terms of the unintelligible.* When you write that "the product of the activity of janitors is expended in the identical locality in which that activity takes place," your lay reader is in for a time of it. After an hour's puzzlement, he may conclude that janitors' sweepings are thrown on the town dump. See what you can do with this: "Each article sent to the cleaner is handled separately." You become a member of the guild in good standing if you put it like this. "Within the cleaning plant proper the business of the industry involves several well-defined processes, which, from the economic point of view, may be char-

acterized simply by saying that most of them require separate handling of each individual garment or piece of material to be cleaned."

18   *Rule 5. Announce what you are going to say before you say it.* This pitcher's wind-up technique before hurling towards—not at—home plate has two varieties. First in the quick wind-up: "In the following section the policies of the administration will be considered." Then you become strong enough for the contortionist wind-up: "Perhaps more important, therefore, than the question of what standards are in a particular case, there are the questions of the extent of observance of these standards and the methods of their enforcement." Also you can play with reversing Rule 5 and *say what you have said after you have said it.*

19   *Rule 6. Defend your style as "scientific."* Look down on—not up to —clear simple English. Sneer at it as "popular." Scorn it as "journalistic." Explain your failure to put more mental sweat into your writing on the ground that "the social scientists who want to be scientific believe that we can have scientific description of human behavior and trustworthy predictions in the scientific sense only as we build adequate taxonomic systems for observable phenomena and symbolic systems for the manipulation of ideal and abstract entities."

20   For this explanation I am indebted to Lyman Bryson in the *Saturday Review of Literature* article (Oct. 13, 1945) "Writers: Enemies of Social Science." Standing on ground considerably of his own choosing, Mr. Bryson argued against judging social science writing by literary standards.

21   Social scientists are not criticized because they are not literary artists. The trouble with social science does not lie in its special vocabulary. Those words are doubtless chosen with great care. The trouble is that too few social scientists take enough care with words outside their special vocabularies.

22   It is not much to expect that teachers should be more competent in the art of explanation than those they teach. Teachers of social sciences diligently try to acquire knowledge; too few exert themselves enough to impart it intelligently.

23   Too long has this been excused as "the academic mind." It should be called by what it is: intellectual laziness and grubbymindedness.

20 WILLIAM H. WHYTE, JR.

You, Too, Can Write the Casual Style

1   A revolution has taken place in American prose. No longer the short huffs and puffs, the unqualified word, the crude gusto of the declarative sentence. Today the fashion is to write casually.

2   The Casual Style is not exactly new. Originated in the early Twenties, it has been refined and improved and refined again by a relatively small band of writers, principally for the *New Yorker,* until now their mannerisms have become standards of sophistication. Everybody is trying to join the club. Newspaper columnists have forsaken the beloved metaphors of the sports page for the Casual Style, and one of the quickest ways for an ad man to snag an award from other ad men is to give his copy the low-key, casual pitch; the copy shouldn't sing these days—it should whisper. Even Dr. Rudolf Flesch, who has been doing so much to teach people how to write like other people, is counseling his followers to use the Casual Style. Everywhere the ideal seems the same: be casual.

3   But how? There is very little down-to-earth advice. We hear about the rapier-like handling of the bromide, the keen eye for sham and pretension, the exquisite sense of nuance, the unerring ear for the vulgate. But not much about actual technique. The layman, as a consequence, is apt to look on the Casual Style as a mandarin dialect which he fears he may never master.

4   Nonsense. The Casual Style is within everyone's grasp. It has now become so perfected by constant polishing that its devices may readily be identified, and they change so little that their use need be no more difficult for the novice than for the expert. (That's not quite all there is to it, of course. Some apparently casual writers, Thurber and E. B. White, among others, rarely use the devices.)

5   The subject matter, in the first place, is not to be ignored. Generally speaking, the more uneventful it is, or the more pallid the writer's reaction to it, the better do form and content marry. Take, for example, the cocktail party at which the writer can show how bored everyone is with everyone else, and how utterly fatuous they all are anyhow. Since a non-casual statement—*e.g.,* "The party was a bore"—would destroy the reason for writing about it at all, the Casual Style here is not only desirable but mandatory.

From *Harper's Magazine* (October, 1953). Reprinted by permission of *Harper's Magazine* and William H. Whyte, Jr.

6   Whatever the subject, however, twelve devices are the rock on which all else is built. I will present them one by one, illustrating them with examples from such leading casual stylists as Wolcott Gibbs, John Crosby, John McCarten, and (on occasion) this magazine's "Mr. Harper." If the reader will digest what follows, he should be able to dash off a paragraph indistinguishable from the best casual writing being done today.

7   (1) *Heightened Understatement.* Where the old-style writer would say, "I don't like it," "It is not good," or something equally banal, the casual writer says it is *"something less than* good." He avoids direct statement and strong words—except, as we will note, where he is setting them up to have something to knock down. In any event, he qualifies. "Somewhat" and "rather," the bread-and-butter words of the casual writer, should become habitual with you; similarly with such phrases as "I suppose," "it seems to me," "I guess," or "I'm afraid." "Elusive" or "elude" are good, too, and if you see the word "charm" in a casual sentence you can be pretty sure that "eludes me," or "I find elusive," will not be far behind.

8   (2) *The Multiple Hedge.* Set up an ostensibly strong statement, and then, with your qualifiers, shoot a series of alternately negative and positive charges into the sentence until finally you neutralize the whole thing. Let's take, for example, the clause, "certain names have a guaranteed nostalgic magic." Challenge enough here; the names not only have magic, they have guaranteed magic. A double hedge reverses the charge. "Names which have, *I suppose* [hedge 1], a guaranteed nostalgic magic, *though there are times that I doubt it* [hedge 2]. . . ."

9   We didn't have to say they were guaranteed in the first place, of course, but without such straw phrases we wouldn't have anything to construct a hedge on and, frequently, nothing to write at all. The virtue of the hedge is that by its very negating effect it makes any sentence infinitely expansible. Even if you have so torn down your original statement with one or two hedges that you seem to have come to the end of the line, you have only to slip in an anti-hedge, a strengthening word (*e.g.,* "definitely," "unqualified," etc.), and begin the process all over again. Witness the following quadruple hedge: "I found Mr. Home entertaining *from time to time* [hedge 1] on the ground, *I guess* [hedge 2,] that the singular idiom and unearthly detachment of the British upper classes have *always* [anti-hedge] seemed *reasonably* [hedge 3] droll to me, *at least in moderation* [hedge 4]." The art of plain talk, as has been pointed out, does not entail undue brevity.

10   If you've pulled hedge on hedge and the effect still remains too vigorous, simply wipe the slate clean with a cancellation clause at the end. "It was all exactly as foolish as it sounds," says Wolcott Gibbs, winding up some 570 casual words on a subject, "and I wouldn't give it another thought."

11   (3) *Narcissizing Your Prose.* The casual style is nothing if not personal; indeed, you will usually find in it as many references to the writer as to what he's supposed to be talking about. For you do not talk about the subject; you talk about its impact on you. With the reader peering over your shoulder, you look into the mirror and observe your own responses as you run the entire range of the casual writer's emotions. You may reveal yourself as, in turn, listless ("the audience seemed not to share my boredom"); insouciant ("I was really quite happy with it"); irritated ("The whole thing left me tired and cross"); comparatively gracious ("Being in a comparatively gracious mood, I won't go into the details I didn't like"); or hesitant ("I wish I could say that I could accept his hypothesis").

12   (4) *Preparation for the Witticism.* When the casual writer hits upon a clever turn of phrase or a nice conceit, he uses this device to insure that his conceit will not pass unnoticed. Suppose, for example, you have thought of something to say that is pretty damn good if you say so yourself. The device, in effect, is to say so yourself. If you want to devastate a certain work as "a study of vulgarity in high places," don't say this flat out. Earlier in the sentence prepare the reader for the drollery ahead with something like "what I am tempted to call" or "what could best be described as" or "If it had to be defined in a sentence, it might well be called. . . ."

13   Every writer his own claque.

14   (5) *Deciphered Notes Device; or Cute-Things-I-Have-Said.* In this one you are your own stooge as well. You feed yourself lines. By means of the slender fiction that you have written something on the back of an envelope or the margin of a program, you catch yourself good-humoredly trying to decipher these shrewd, if cryptic, little jottings. *Viz.:* "Their diagnoses are not nearly as crisp as those I find in my notes"; ". . . sounds like an inadequate description, but it's all I have in my notes, and it may conceivably be a very high compliment."

15   (6) *The Kicker.* An echo effect. "My reactions [included] an irritable feeling that eleven o'clock was past Miss Keim's bedtime,"—and now the Kicker—*"not to mention my own."* This type of thing practically writes itself. "She returns home. She should never have left home in the first place. —— ———— ——— ——." [1]

16   (7) *Wit of Omission.* By calling attention to the fact that you are not going to say it, you suggest that there is something very funny you could say if only you wanted to. "A thought occurred to me at this point," you may say, when otherwise stymied, "but I think we had better not go into *that.*"

17   (8) *The Planned Colloquialism.* The casual writer savors colloquialisms. This is not ordinary colloquial talk—nobody is more quickly provoked than the casual writer by ordinary usage. It is, rather, a playful

[1] "And neither should I."

descent into the vulgate. Phrases like "darn," "awfully," "as all getout," "mighty," and other folksy idioms are ideal. The less you would be likely to use the word normally yourself the more pointed the effect. Contrast is what you are after, for it is the facetious interplay of language levels— a blending, as it were, of the East Fifties and the Sticks—that gives the Casual Style its off-hand charm.

18   (9) *Feigned Forgetfulness.* Conversation gropes; it is full of "what I really meant was" and "maybe I should have added," backings and fillings and second thoughts of one kind or another. Writing is different; theoretically, ironing out second thoughts beforehand is one of the things writers are paid to do. In the Casual Style, however, it is exactly this exposure of the writer composing in public that makes it so casual. For the professional touch, then, ramble, rebuke yourself in print ("what I really meant, I guess"), and if you have something you feel you should have said earlier, don't say it earlier, but say later that you guess you should have said it earlier.

19   (10) *The Subject-Apologizer, or Pardon-Me-for-Living.* The Casual Stylist must always allow for the possibility that his subject is just as boring to the reader as it is to him. He may forestall this by seeming to have stumbled on it by accident, or by using phrases like: "If this is as much news to you as it is to me," or "This, in case you've been living in a cave lately, is. . . ."

20   (11) *The Omitted Word.* This all began modestly enough the day a *New Yorker* writer dropped the articles "the" and "a" from the initial sentence of an anecdote (*e.g.,* "Man we know told us"; "Fellow name of Brown"). Now even such resolutely lowbrow writers as Robert Ruark affect it, and they are applying it to any part of speech anywhere in the sentence. You can drop a pronoun ("Says they're shaped like pyramids"); verb ("You been away from soap opera the last couple of weeks?"); or preposition ("Far as glamour goes . . .").

21   (12) *The Right Word.* In the lexicon of the casual writer there are a dozen or so adjectives which in any context have, to borrow a phrase, a guaranteed charm. Attrition is high—"brittle," "febrile," "confected," for example, are at the end of the run. Ten, however, defy obsolescence: *antic, arch, blurred, chaste, chill, crisp, churlish, disheveled, dim, disembodied.*

22   They are good singly, but they are even better when used in tandem; *c.f.,* "In an arch, antic sort of way"; "In an arch, blurred sort of way"; "In an arch, crisp sort of way." And so on.

23   Finally, the most multi-purpose word of them all: "altogether." Frequently it is the companion of "charming" and "delightful," and in this coupling is indispensable to any kind of drama criticism. It can also modify the writer himself (*e.g.,* "Altogether, I think . . ."). Used best, however, it just floats, unbeholden to any other part of the sentence.

24   Once you have mastered these twelve devices, you too should be able to write as casually as all getout. At least it seems to me, though I may be wrong, that they convey an elusive archness which the crisp literary craftsman, in his own dim sort of way, should altogether cultivate these days. Come to think of it, the charm of the Casual Style is something less than clear to me, but we needn't go into *that*. Fellow I know from another magazine says this point of view best described as churlish. Not, of course, that it matters.

21   JACQUES BARZUN

How to Write and Be Read

1   Writing comes before reading, in logic and also in the public mind. No one cares whether you read fast or slow, well or ill, but as soon as you put pen to paper, somebody may be puzzled, angry, bored, or ecstatic; and if the occasion permits, your reader is almost sure to exclaim about the schools not doing their duty. This is the oldest literary tradition, of which here is a modern instance:—

What kind of teaching in the primary schools?

BY 'DISGUSTED'

Recently a letter came into my office from a boy who described himself as a first-year high school student. He wanted *infirmation* about *Africia,* because for his project in the social studies class he had *chozen Africia.* If we could not help him, *were* could he write? In closing, he was ours *sinceerly.* His handwriting was comparable to that of my 6-year-old nephew.

2   Too bad, but I am not alarmed. This student of 'Africia' may or may not learn to spell: it is not nearly so important as his diction and his sentence structure, which the plaintiff withheld, though they would have better enabled us to judge what the schools were really doing. What I fear about this boy is that when grown-up and provided with a secretary who can spell, he will write something like this:—

From *Teacher in America* by Jacques Barzun, by permission of Little, Brown and Co.—Atlantic Monthly Press. Copyright 1944, 1945, by Jacques Barzun.

Dear Sir:—

As you know, security prices have been advancing rapidly in the recent past *in belated recognition of the favorable fundamentals that exist.* [Italics mine]

3   What is decadent about this I shall shortly explain. Meantime, the fact should be faced squarely that good writing is and has always been extremely rare. I do not mean fine writing, but the simple, clear kind that everyone always demands—from others. The truth is that Simple English is no one's mother tongue. It has to be worked for. As an historian, I have plowed through state papers, memoirs, diaries, and letters, and I know that the ability to write has only a remote connection with either intelligence, or greatness, or schooling. Lincoln had no schooling yet became one of the great prose writers of the world. Cromwell went to Cambridge and was hardly ever able to frame an intelligible sentence. Another man of thought and action, Admiral Lord Howe, generally refrained from writing out his plan of battle, so as to save his captains from inevitable misunderstanding. Yet Howe managed to win the famous First of June by tactics that revolutionized the art, and led directly to Nelson's Trafalgar plan— itself a rather muddled piece of prose. Let us then start with no illusion of an imaginary golden age of writing.

4   Which leaves the problem of doing the best with what nature gives us. And here I have some convictions born of long struggle, with myself and with others. First, I pass by all considerations of penmanship and elementary spelling to remark only that I think it a mistake to start children writing on typewriters, and worse yet to let them grow up unable to do anything but print capitals.

5   Above the beginner's level, the important fact is that writing cannot be taught exclusively in a course called English Composition. Writing can only be taught by the united efforts of the entire teaching staff. This holds good of any school, college, or university. Joint effort is needed, not merely to 'enforce the rules'; it is needed to insure accuracy in every subject. How can an answer in physics or a translation from the French or an historical statement be called correct if the phrasing is loose or the key word wrong? Students argue that the reader of the paper knows perfectly well what is meant. Probably so, but a written exercise is designed to be read; it is not supposed to be a challenge to clairvoyance. My Italian-born tailor periodically sends me a postcard which runs: 'Your clothes is ready and should come down for a fitting.' I understand him, but the art I honor him for is cutting cloth, not precision of utterance. Now a student in college must be inspired to achieve in all subjects the utmost accuracy of perception combined with the utmost artistry of expression. The two merge and develop the sense of good workmanship, of preference for quality and truth, which is the chief mark of the genuinely educated man.

6   This is obviously a collective task, in which every department and every faculty has a common stake. But it is not enough to give notice that

these are the faculty's sentiments. Even supposing that all teachers were willing and able to exert vigilance over written work, there would still be many practical problems of detail. And first, what motive for writing well can the student be made to feel? There is only one valid motive: the desire to be read. You will say that most students have no urge either to write or to be read. True, but (*a*) they know that they have to write and (*b*) most of them want to be well thought of. They should accordingly be made to see that reading the ordinary student paper can be a nuisance and a bore to the teacher, and that the proper aim of writing should be to make it a pleasure. This is another way of saying that most school writing is bad because student and teacher play at writing and reading instead of taking it seriously. The teacher expects second-rate hokum and the student supplies it. Let the teacher assert his rights just as the students do: in many college classes the men protest—quite rightly—when they are asked to read a dull or ill-organized book. Similarly, the instructor may warn the students that when they turn in filler and padding, jargon and lingo, stuff and nonsense, he will mark them down, not only in his grade book, but in his violated soul.

7   Naturally, this conscious brutality must go with a helping hand; in fact a revision of all usual practices is in order. The embargo on hokum will already work a healthy elimination of bad prose. Then the long Term Paper must be discarded and replaced with the short essay, not more than five typewritten pages in length. Students always ask how long a final paper should be and they are absolutely right in believing that most instructors are impressed by mere bulk. But when one knows how difficult it is to articulate even three measly thoughts around a single point, it is folly to ask eighteen-year-olds to produce thirty- or forty-page monographs that shall be readable. What they produce is an uncarded mattress of quotations, paraphrase, 'however's,' and 'Thus we see's.' Size being aimed at, there is not time for rewriting or reordering the material culled from half a dozen books, and the main effort goes into the irrelevant virtues of neat typing, plentiful footnotes, and the mannerisms of scholarship.

8   The short paper—and I speak from a large pile accumulted over twelve years—aims and arrives at different ends. It answers the reader's eternal question: Just what are you trying to tell me? It is in that spirit that student writing must be read, corrected, and if need be rewritten. When first presented, it must already be a second or third draft. The only reason I can think of for the somewhat higher average of good writing in France is that the *brouillon* is a national institution. The *brouillon* (literally: scrambled mess) is the first draft, and even the concierge writing to the police about anarchists on the third floor begins with a *brouillon,* later found by his heirs.

9   Of course it is no use telling an American boy or girl that the essay must be written, laid aside, and rewritten at least once before handing in:

the innocents do not know what to do after their first painful delivery. So the simplest thing is to ask early in the term for a good five-page essay, which turns out to be pretty bad. This is fully annotated by the reader and turned back before the next one is called for. But the corrections on it are not merely the conventional *sp., ref., punc.,* and *awk.* which the writers have seen in their margins from the seventh grade on. The comments are intensely and painfully personal, being the responses that an alert reader would feel if he were encountering the essay in print. The result is that even the best students feel abashed, if not actually resentful. To which one can only say that they should resent the neglect in which all their previous teachers have left them.

10   This neglect has not damaged their grammar so much as their vocabulary. Since the last thing any writer learns is the uses of words, it is no wonder if untutored youths of ability write like the stockbroker whom I quoted about 'favorable fundamentals that exist'—spineless, vague, and incoherent prose. Indeed, the exact parallel comes this moment under my hand, taken from a very able student's report on Newman's *University Sketches:* 'A University that rests on a firm financial foundation has the greater ability to unleash the minds of its students.' Despite the difference in names, the stockbroker is that boy's putative father. Their failure comes from a like inattention to meaning—their own and that of the words they use.

11   This means that words and tone are the main things to be taught. Spelling, grammar, and punctuation do not precede but follow in the order of importance. They follow also quite naturally in the order of facility. Accordingly, the teacher-critic must slowly and carefully explain to the student what each word conveys in its particular context. I find that in the essay just cited I have written such comments as: 'I can't follow—This repeats in disguise—"avocational fruit" suggests alligator pears: why?— We now have about eight "problems" on hand: Begin!—What! more issues and problems?—Commercial lingo—Who is "we"?—Why "cradle": the metaphor is lost—Who says this?—"Patina" is not "clothing"—Don't scold and then trail off in this way—This is your point at last.' In addition, images are changed, synonyms proposed, and bad sentences recast, sometimes in alternative ways, in order to show precisely how the original misleads and how clarity is to be reached.

12   Tone grows naturally out of diction, but the choice of words betrays feelings of which the young writer is usually unaware. 'Are you pleading, denouncing, coaxing, or laughing? Do you back up this exaggeration? Why suddenly talk down, or turn pedant? If you want to change the mood inside the piece, you must modulate, otherwise your reader will stumble and you will lose him.' The student who learns to quiz himself in this fashion over his first draft is learning not only something about English, about writing, and about thinking, but about the human heart as well.

13   At the risk of tediousness I repeat that what has to be done is to dramatize the relation between writer and reader. The blunt comments are just a device to break the spell of routine, and though they administer an unpleasant shock at first, they are also flattering. 'Somebody cares about what I want to say.' The teacher is no longer a paid detective hunting stray commas.

14   To point these lessons up in minute detail to a student of average powers is of course time-consuming—but what else is the teacher there for? Time spent on reading and writing, in any subject, is never a waste, and the reward almost always comes, often astonishingly great. The excitement aroused by the discovery that words live is like finding that you can balance on skates. A new world of motion and of feeling is opened out to the student, a source of some anguish balanced by lifelong delight. George Gissing writes somewhere that he saw an excursion steamer advertised as being 'Replete with Ladies' Lavatories' and he comments on how many people could pass by the sign without a smile. My own favorite recollection is of a guarantee pasted on a modest shop window: 'Hats fitted to the head exclusively'—fun in every ad and at the company's expense.

15   The pleasure to be taken in words is as innocent and satisfying as the moral effect is clear: unless words are used deftly to set the imagination on its travels, language, literature, conversation, and friendship are full of snares. Much of our modern anxiety about the tyranny of words and of our desire for foolproof Basic comes from the uneasy suspicion that we have lost the art of diction and with it the control over our own minds. This is more serious than it seems, for there is no doubt that the world outside the school largely checks what present instruction attempts, as we shall see. But having spoken of the imagination, let me first meet a likely objection to the advice here proposed. I can fancy some reader for whom school compositions were torture shaking a skeptical head and saying: 'Most young children have very little to say and school assignments blot out even that little.' I agree and the second great practical problem is, What to ask boys and girls to write about?

16   The don'ts are easy. Don't ask them for 'A vacation experience,' or 'My most embarrassing moment,' or 'I am the Mississippi River.' Such topics will only elicit the driest kind of hokum, though to be fair I must say that they are an improvement on the older practice of expecting infant moralizing and 'What the flag means to me.' Although as a child I enjoyed writing—history chiefly—I can remember the blankness of mind that overtook me when we had to do a *dissertation morale*. I still have a school text with some of those themes checked as having been done—for example: '*The Faithful Dog*.—A poor man has resolved to drown his dog. Thrown into the river, the dog tries to scramble up the bank, but his master lunges out to kill him with a stick. In so doing, he slips and falls. The dog saves him. Remorse of the owner.'

17   I regret to say that French school life is stuffed with such thorns as these, but I am not sure that the opposite 'progressive' extreme of turning children into researchers on their own is desirable either. The eleven-year-old son of a friend of mine once told me that he was writing a 'project' on Papyrus. Why papyrus? Well, the class had been 'doing' Egypt and each child was assigned one aspect of Egyptian civilization. Where was the information to come from? From encyclopedias, museums, friends, and paper manufacturers—hence such letters to strangers as the one about 'Africia' quoted earlier. As I see it, two things are wrong with this scheme. One is that it gives a false freedom; the other is that it hardly trains in the art of composing. Did this boy care at all about Egypt, let alone about the technicalities of papyrology? A child should select a topic that truly engages his interest. To eliminate pretense he must be helped to do this by means of questions and suggestions. At any age, it is very reassuring to be told that you don't really want to write about the Tariff. After two or three casts a real subject emerges, satisfactory to both parties.

18   Next should come into play the single good feature of the French dissertation, namely its furnishing a plan or program. Depending on the child's age a briefer or longer table of contents should be set out for each theme, either in logically organized form, or pell-mell for the student himself to disentangle. After all, what is wanted is prose, not a riot of fancy. In my experience, even examination questions are answered better when they consist of five or six sentences outlining a topic for discussion. This means further that brevity should never be accounted a fault in itself. After thirty, we can all spin tall tales, mostly secondhand,[1] but students, even of college age, have had very little conscious experience of life or books and it is no wonder their minds are bone dry. One should moreover keep in view the possibility that in some of them brevity may come from genius. American schoolmarms who relate the anecdote of Lincoln's 'failure' with the Gettysburg Address are just as likely to say at one glance, 'Jane, this is too short.' How do they know? Perhaps they unwittingly agree with the Gettysburg crowd that Everett's speech, being longer, was better.

19   Some secondary schools, particularly the private ones, require the writing of verse as well as of prose. If the students are really shown how to go about versifying and are not expected to be 'poetic,' there is no harm in it. Verse writing is excellent practice for the prose writer and the striving for correct rhythm and rhyme gives the student of literature a feeling for words that may not otherwise be obtained. What can be done in this way before college by a gifted teacher has been shown by the experience of my friend, the poet Dudley Fitts, formerly at Choate and now at

---

[1] No course, therefore, should ever be called Creative Writing. Let us have at least a collective modesty and leave to charlatans the advertising of 'How to Write Powerful Plays.'

Andover. In collegiate circles, it is now well known that a freshman prepared under him is a literate, sometimes a polished writer, who can be safely allowed to skip into advanced work. No doubt Fitts has had his failures like all of us, but it is the successes we are looking for and that count in leavening the mass.

20   I am not so foolish as to think that carrying out my few suggestions would get rid of illiterate A.B.'s. I am too conscious of my initial point about 'Education,' which is that the school does not work in a vacuum but rather in a vortex of destructive forces. As regards writing, we in the twentieth century must offset not only the constant influence of careless speech and the indifference of parents, but the tremendous output of jargon issuing from the new mechanical means at man's disposal. Worst of all, circumstances have conspired to put the most corrupting force at the very heart of the school system. It is not newspapers, radio scripts, and movies that spoil our tongue so much as textbooks, official documents, commencement speeches, and learned works.[2]

21   The rise, at the turn of the century, of what James called 'the softer pedagogy' is responsible for a debasement of language beyond all bounds of forgiveness. The desire to be kind, to sound new, to foster useful attitudes, to appear 'scientific,' and chiefly also the need to produce rapidly, account for this hitherto unheard-of deliquescence. In the victims, the softness goes to the very roots of the mind and turns it into mush. And among the 'new' educators thus afflicted, the Progressive vanguard has naturally outstripped the rest. I shall not multiply examples from catalogues, reports, and speeches, though over the years I have gathered a blush-making collection. I want only to identify the evil because it spreads like the plague.

22   It consists mainly of what our forefathers called 'cant phrases,' strung together without continuity, like wash on a line. At a faculty meeting, a teacher asks the Director of Admissions why there seem to be more music students applying than before. The Director replies, 'Well, I should say that the forces undergirding the process are societal.' Or a committee chairman wants to know what we do next. 'I think,' says the secretary, 'that we should go on to institute actual implementation.'

23   Teachers steeped in this medium are bound to ooze it out themselves, particularly if weekly and daily they receive official instructions like these: 'Specify the kinds of change or permanence the student seems to crave, reject, or fear; the reasons given for liking-disliking, giving up-persistence; complaining-boasting . . . It cannot be too strongly emphasized that

[2] See Mr. Maury Maverick's excellent denunciation of what he calls Gobbledygook in the *New York Times* for May 21, 1944. The rebuttals attempting to show that round-about expressions spare shocks to the sick are hardly to the point. The healthy ought to be able to stand directness and even mention of 'death and taxes.' 'Loss of life' and 'fiscal levies' cost just as much in the end.

the observations of characteristics associated with age and background are not being made in the general area of adolescent behavior but under specific and limited conditions—those set by the aims, emphases, and assumptions of one particular faculty.[3] Moreover, the observations of what appear to be the interests of freshmen conceal a possible ambiguity. The term "interests" may refer to fairly superficial interests in the sense of surprise, pleasure, enjoyment, which are comparatively temporary; or "interests" may involve an awakening curiosity which leads to consistent inquiry along the lines of some project.' The reader must imagine not merely a paragraph taken at random, but pages and pages of similar woolly abstractions, mimeographed at the rate of nine and one-half pounds per person per semester. If the words 'specific' and 'objective' were blotted out of the English language, Progressive Education would have to shut up . . . shop.

24   As for students in teachers' colleges, the long climb up the ladder of learning comes to mean the mastering of this ghoulish *Desperanto,* so that with the attainment of the M.A. degree, we get the following utterance:—

> In the proposed study I wish to describe and evaluate representative programs in these fields as a means of documenting what seems to me a trend of increasing concern with the role of higher education in the improvement of interpersonal and intergroup relations and of calling attention in this way to outstanding contributions in practice.

25   Some readers might think this quotation very learned and highbrow indeed. But in fact it says nothing definite. It only embodies the disinclination to think. This is a general truth, and nothing is more symptomatic of the whole jargon than the fantastic use and abuse it makes of the phrase 'in terms of.' The fact is worth a moment's attention. 'In terms of' used to refer to things that had terms, like algebra. 'Put the problem in terms of *a* and *b*.' This makes sense. But in educational circles today 'in terms of' means any connection between any two things. 'We should grade students in terms of their effort'—that is, *for* or *according to* their effort. The *New York Public Library Bulletin* prints: 'The first few months of employment would be easier . . . and more efficient in terms of service . . .'—that is, would yield more efficient service. But no one seems to care how or when or why his own two ideas are related. The gap in thought is plugged with 'in terms of.' I have been asked, 'Will you have dinner with me, not tonight or tomorrow, but *in terms of* next week?' A modern Caesar would write: 'All Gaul is to be considered in terms of three parts.' [4]

26   From this Educator's patois, easily the worst English now spoken, we ought to pass to the idiom of textbooks, since they are written either

---

[3] I regret to say that 'faculty' here means 'faculty member'—a usage so far confined to the progressive schools.

[4] The objectionable phrase is now to be found in newspapers, business reports, and private correspondence. It is a menace *in terms of* the whole nation.

by educators or by teachers. Happily, there is a standard set by other books—trade books—and it is not true that all textbooks are as badly written as those on education. On the contrary, it is very encouraging that the leading ones in every field are usually well planned *and* well written. The success of Morison and Commager's *Growth of the American Republic* is only the most recent case in point. Students, nevertheless, are asked to read many ill-written books. There is no excuse for this, though it is by no means the only source of error. We must remember that students do not read only books; they read what every man reads, and this would do no harm—it does no harm—when the mind is trained to resilience by the kind of writing practice I have advocated.

27   Unfortunately, with the vast increase in public schooling since 1870, an entirely new notion of what is good English has come to prevail. Awakened by free schooling, the people have shown worthy intentions. They want to be right and even elegant, and so become at once suspicious of plainness and pedantic. They purchase all sorts of handbooks that make a fetish of spelling, of avoiding split infinitives, of saying 'it is I' (with the common result of 'between you and I')—in short, dwell on trivialities or vulgarisms which do not affect style or thought in the slightest. But with this intolerance towards crude and plain error goes a remarkable insensitivity to inflated nonsense. Most bad journalism is only highbrow verbosity, yet the popular mind continues to believe that the pedantry which it likes is simple and the simplicity which it finds hard is complex. Here is the opening of a serial thriller in a Boston paper:—

     Strange things happen in Chinatown. But even that exotic and perverse district seldom presented drama as fantastic as the secret that hid among the silk and jade and porcelain splendors of the famous House of the Mandarin on Mulberry Lane.

28   There is a certain art in this, and I take note of 'porcelain splendors' as the *mot juste* for bathtubs on exhibit. But the passage as a whole contains nothing but arty and highfalutin words, joined by the good will of the reader rather than the mind of the writer. Still, every newspaper reader feels he understands it. Take now a well-known sentence composed of common words, all but two of them single syllables: 'If there are more trees in the world than there are leaves on any one tree, then there must be at least two trees with the same number of leaves.' Read this aloud and almost any listener will respond with 'Huh? Say that again.' For this sentence records a thought, and the Chinatown 'drama' did not.

29   The close logic in the truly 'simple' sentence makes the contrast sharper, but it would be just as sharp between a feeling clearly put and a feeble attempt to thrill. Thus there is a superstition that the novels of Henry James are written in a 'difficult style.' Yet if you examine them, you will find that the words and sentences—in *The Ambassadors,* for example

—are in themselves quite usual. But the feelings they convey are unusual and subtle, and require attention. At the same time they also compel it, which is all that an artist takes pains for in writing.

30   Conversely, the only thing that can be asked of a writer is that he should know his own meaning and present it as forcibly as he can. The rule has not changed since Byron affirmed that 'easy writing makes damned hard reading.' Hence there is great value, as I think, in having college graduates recognize good prose when they see it, know that a tolerable paragraph must have gone through six or seven versions, and be ready to follow athletically on the trail of articulate thoughts, rather than look for the soapy incline to muddled meaning.

31   One does not have to go very far for the enjoyment of precise, sinewy writing. The same newspaper that furnishes tripe for the morning meal also brings such rarer tidbits as these: 'They [the robot bombs] are of much the same shape and size as a small fighter plane, with stubby wings. They come over with tails aglow from the propelling rocket force, like little meteors moving at a nightmare pace by dark, and by day like little black planes with tails afire.' This is perfection; and here is poetry: 'Mr. McCaffrey, himself the father of two children, *and therefore schooled in apprehension,* ran across the street . . . shouting a warning.'

32   When the daily reporter, harried by falling bombs or hustled by a city editor, can write like this, it is depressing to return to agencies closer to the school and find verbal laziness encouraged and imbecility taken for granted. One publisher of reference works sends out a circular stressing the fact that his books give the pronunciation of 'all difficult—"hard-to-say"—words.' Is this where we are after fifty years of quasi-universal literacy? Is the word 'difficult' so difficult that it has to be translated in its own sentence? The question is one for readers, and it is to the subject of readers that I now turn.

Theme topics

1. Compare and contrast the rules for good writing (Orwell) and the rules for writing like a social scientist (Williamson).

2. Draw up a list of twenty-five examples, none of which is listed by any of the four writers here, of dying metaphors, operators (or verbal false limbs), pretentious diction, meaningless words. Quote and cite, if possible, a source in which you have found each used.

3. Orwell asserts, "In our time it is broadly true that political writing is bad writing." Choose from the files of *The New York Times* or elsewhere, the text of two or more political speeches delivered by candidates for high political office in a state or national election. Analyze them from the point of view of the categories established by Orwell.

4. Take any issue of the *New Yorker* and analyze the sections entitled "The Talk of the Town" and "The Current Cinema" as well as that issue's short story from the point of view of the twelve devices of casual stylists listed by Whyte.

5. On the basis of inferences from evidence you find only in the four essays themselves, discuss the probable backgrounds of each of the authors, the audiences to which they seem to be speaking and the effectiveness with which each uses evidence and direct quotation to support his criticisms. Which one (or ones), in discussing the prevalence of stale imagery, imprecision and pretentiousness in contemporary writing, is the most vivid, precise, direct? Document your choice.

22   WAYNE C. BOOTH
The Rhetorical Stance

1   Last fall I had an advanced graduate student, bright, energetic, well-informed, whose papers were almost unreadable. He managed to be pretentious, dull, and disorganized in his paper on *Emma,* and pretentious, dull, and disorganized on *Madame Bovary.* On *The Golden Bowl* he was all these and obscure as well. Then one day, toward the end of term, he cornered me after class and said, "You know, I think you were all wrong about Robbe-Grillet's *Jealousy* today." We didn't have time to discuss it, so I suggested that he write me a note about it. Five hours later I found in my faculty box a four-page polemic, unpretentious, stimulating, organized, convincing. Here was a man who had taught freshman composition for several years and who was incapable of committing any of the more obvious errors that we think of as characteristic of bad writing. Yet he could not write a decent sentence, paragraph, or paper until his rhetorical problem was solved—until, that is, he had found a definition of his audience, his argument, and his own proper tone of voice.

2   The word "rhetoric" is one of those catch-all terms that can easily raise trouble when our backs are turned. As it regains a popularity that it once seemed permanently to have lost, its meanings seem to range all the way from something like "the whole art of writing on any subject," as in Kenneth Burke's *The Rhetoric of Religion,* through "the special arts of persuasion," on down to fairly narrow notions about rhetorical figures and devices. And of course we still have with us the meaning of "empty bombast," as in the phrase "merely rhetorical."

From *College Composition and Communication,* 14 (October, 1963). Reprinted with the permission of the National Council of Teachers of English and Wayne C. Booth.

3   I suppose that the question of the role of rhetoric in the English course is meaningless if we think of rhetoric in either its broadest or its narrowest meanings. No English course could avoid dealing with rhetoric in Burke's sense, under whatever name, and on the other hand nobody would ever advocate anything so questionable as teaching "mere rhetoric." But if we settle on the following, traditional, definition, some real questions are raised: "Rhetoric is the art of finding and employing the most effective means of persuasion on any subject, considered independently of intellectual mastery of that subject." As the students say, "Prof. X knows his stuff but he doesn't know how to put it across." If rhetoric is thought of as the art of "putting it across," considered as quite distinct from mastering an "it" in the first place, we are immediately landed in a bramble bush of controversy. Is there such an art? If so, what does it consist of? Does it have a content of its own? Can it be taught? Should it be taught? If it should, how do we go about it, head on or obliquely?

4   Obviously it would be foolish to try to deal with many of these issues in twenty minutes. But I wish that there were more signs of our taking all of them seriously. I wish that along with our new passion for structural linguistics, for example, we could point to the development of a rhetorical theory that would show just how knowledge of structural linguistics can be useful to anyone interested in the art of persuasion. I wish there were more freshman texts that related every principle and every rule to functional principles of rhetoric, or, where this proves impossible, I wish one found more systematic discussion of why it is impossible. But for today, I must content myself with a brief look at the charge that there is nothing distinctive and teachable about the art of rhetoric.

5   The case against the isolability and teachability of rhetoric may look at first like a good one. Nobody writes rhetoric, just as nobody ever writes writing. What we write and speak is always *this* discussion of the decline of railroading and *that* discussion of Pope's couplets and the other argument for abolishing the poll-tax or for getting rhetoric back into English studies.

6   We can also admit that like all the arts, the art of rhetoric is at best very chancy, only partly amenable to systematic teaching; as we are all painfully aware when our 1:00 section goes miserably and our 2:00 section of the same course is a delight, our own rhetoric is not entirely under control. Successful rhetoricians are to some extent like poets, born, not made. They are also dependent on years of practice and experience. And we can finally admit that even the firmest of principles about writing cannot be taught in the same sense that elementary logic or arithmetic or French can be taught. In my first year of teaching, I had a student who started his first two essays with a swear word. When I suggested that perhaps the third paper ought to start with something else, he protested that his high school teacher had taught him always to catch to catch the reader's atten-

tion. Now the teacher was right, but the application of even such a firm principle requires reserves of tact that were somewhat beyond my freshman.

7   But with all of the reservations made, surely the charge that the art of persuasion cannot in any sense be taught is baseless. I cannot think that anyone who has ever read Aristotle's *Rhetoric* or, say, Whateley's *Elements of Rhetoric* could seriously make the charge. There is more than enough in these and the other traditional rhetorics to provide structure and content for a year-long course. I believe that such a course, when planned and carried through with intelligence and flexibility, can be one of the most important of all educational experiences. But it seems obvious that the arts of persuasion cannot be learned in one year, that a good teacher will continue to teach them regardless of his subject matter, and that we as English teachers have a special responsibility at all levels to get certain basic rhetorical principles into all of our writing assignments. When I think back over the experiences which have had any actual effect on my writing, I find the great good fortune of a splendid freshman course, taught by a man who believed in what he was doing, but I also find a collection of other experiences quite unconnected with a specific writing course. I remember the instructor in psychology who penciled one word after a peculiarly pretentious paper of mine: *bull*. I remember the day when P. A. Christensen talked with me about my Chaucer paper, and made me understand that my failure to use effective transitions was not simply a technical fault but a fundamental block in my effort to get him to see my meaning. His off-the-cuff pronouncement that I should never let myself write a sentence that was not in some way explicitly attached to preceding and following sentences meant far more to me at that moment, when I had something I wanted to say, than it could have meant as part of a pattern of such rules offered in a writing course. Similarly, I can remember the devastating lessons about my bad writing that Ronald Crane could teach with a simple question mark on a graduate seminar paper, or a penciled "Evidence for this?" or "Why this section here?" or "Everybody says so. Is it true?"

8   Such experiences are not, I like to think, simply the result of my being a late bloomer. At least I find my colleagues saying such things as "I didn't learn to write until I became a newspaper reporter," or "The most important training in writing I had was doing a dissertation under old *Blank*." Sometimes they go on to say that the freshman course was useless; sometimes they say that it was an indispensable preparation for the later experience. The diversity of such replies is so great as to suggest that before we try to reorganize the freshman course, with or without explicit confrontations with rhetorical categories, we ought to look for whatever there is in common among our experiences, both of good writing and of good writing instruction. Whatever we discover in such an enterprise

ought to be useful to us at any level of our teaching. It will not, presumably, decide once and for all what should be the content of the freshman course, if there should be such a course. But it might serve as a guideline for the development of widely different programs in the widely differing institutional circumstances in which we must work.

9   The common ingredient that I find in all of the writing I admire—excluding for now novels, plays and poems—is something that I shall reluctantly call the rhetorical stance, a stance which depends on discovering and maintaining in any writing situation a proper balance among the three elements that are at work in any communicative effort: the available arguments about the subject itself, the interests and peculiarities of the audience and the voice, the implied character, of the speaker. I should like to suggest that it is this balance, this rhetorical stance, difficult as it is to describe, that is our main goal as teachers of rhetoric. Our ideal graduate will strike this balance automatically in any writing that he considers finished. Though he may never come to the point of finding the balance easily, he will know that it is what makes the difference between effective communication and mere wasted effort.

10   What I mean by the true rhetorician's stance can perhaps best be seen by contrasting it with two or three corruptions, unbalanced stances often assumed by people who think they are practicing the arts of persuasion.

11   The first I'll call the pedant's stance; it consists of ignoring or underplaying the personal relationship of speaker and audience and depending entirely on statements about a subject—that is, the notion of a job to be done for a particular audience is left out. It is a virtue, of course, to respect the bare truth of one's subject, and there may even be some subjects which in their very nature define an audience and a rhetorical purpose so that adequacy to the subject can be the whole art of presentation. For example, an article on "The relation of the ontological and teleological proofs," in a recent *Journal of Religion,* requires a minimum of adaptation of argument to audience. But most subjects do not in themselves imply in any necessary way a purpose and an audience and hence a speaker's tone. The writer who assumes that it is enough merely to write an exposition of what he happens to know on the subject will produce the kind of essay that soils our scholarly journals, written not for readers but for bibliographies.

12   In my first year of teaching I taught a whole unit on "exposition" without ever suggesting, so far as I can remember, that the students ask themselves what their expositions were *for.* So they wrote expositions like this one—I've saved it, to teach me toleration of my colleagues: the title is "Family relations in More's *Utopia.*" "In this theme I would like to discuss some of the relationships with the family which Thomas More elaborates and sets forth in his book, *Utopia.* The first thing that I would like to discuss about family relations is that overpopulation, according to More, is a

just cause of war." And so on. Can you hear that student sneering at me, in this opening? What he is saying is something like "you ask for a meaningless paper, I give you a meaningless paper." He knows that he has no audience except me. He knows that I don't want to read his summary of family relations in *Utopia,* and he knows that I know that he therefore has no rhetorical purpose. Because he has not been led to see a question which he considers worth answering, or an audience that could possibly care one way or the other, the paper is worse than no paper at all, even though it has no grammatical or spelling errors and is organized right down the line, one, two, three.

13 An extreme case, you may say. Most of us would never allow ourselves that kind of empty fencing? Perhaps. But if some carefree foundation is willing to finance a statistical study, I'm willing to wager a month's salary that we'd find at least half of the suggested topics in our freshman texts as pointless as mine was. And we'd find a good deal more than half of the discussions of grammar, punctuation, spelling, and style totally divorced from any notion that rhetorical purpose to some degree controls all such matters. We can offer objective descriptions of levels of usage from now until graduation, but unless the student discovers a desire to say something to somebody and learns to control his diction for a purpose, we've gained very little. I once gave an assignment asking students to describe the same classroom in three different statements, one for each level of usage. They were obedient, but the only ones who got anything from the assignment were those who intuitively imported the rhetorical instructions I had overlooked—such purposes as "Make fun of your scholarly surroundings by describing this classroom in extremely elevated style," or "Imagine a kid from the slums accidentally trapped in these surroundings and forced to write a description of this room." A little thought might have shown me how to give the whole assignment some human point, and therefore some educative value.

14 Just how confused we can allow ourselves to be about such matters is shown in a recent publication of the Educational Testing Service, called "Factors in Judgments of Writing Ability." In order to isolate those factors which affect differences in grading standards, ETS set six groups of readers—business men, writers and editors, lawyers, and teachers of English, social science and natural science—to reading the same batch of papers. Then ETS did a hundred-page "factor analysis" of the amount of agreement and disagreement, and of the elements which different kinds of graders emphasized. The authors of the report express a certain amount of shock at the discovery that the median correlation was only .31 and that 94% of the papers received either 7, 8, or 9 of the 9 possible grades.

15 But what *could* they have expected? In the first place, the students were given no purpose and no audience when the essays were assigned. And then all these editors and business men and academics were asked to

judge the papers in a complete vacuum, using only whatever intuitive standards they cared to use. I'm surprised that there was any correlation at all. Lacking instructions, some of the students undoubtedly wrote polemical essays, suitable for the popular press; others no doubt imagined an audience, say, of *Reader's Digest* readers, and others wrote with the English teachers as implied audience; an occasional student with real philosophical bent would no doubt do a careful analysis of the pros and cons of the case. This would be graded low, of course, by the magazine editors, even though they would have graded it high if asked to judge it as a speculative contribution to the analysis of the problem. Similarly, a creative student who has been getting A's for his personal essays will write an amusing colorful piece, failed by all the social scientists present, though they would have graded it high if asked to judge it for what it was. I find it shocking that tens of thousands of dollars and endless hours should have been spent by students, graders, and professional testers analyzing essays and grading results totally abstracted from any notion of purposeful human communication. Did nobody protest? One might as well assemble a group of citizens to judge students' capacity to throw balls, say, without telling the students or the graders whether altitude, speed, accuracy or form was to be judged. The judges would be drawn from football coaches, hai-lai experts, lawyers, and English teachers, and asked to apply whatever standards they intuitively apply to ball throwing. Then we could express astonishment that the judgments did not correlate very well, and we could do a factor analysis to discover, lo and behold, that some readers concentrated on altitude, some on speed, some on accuracy, some on form—and the English teachers were simply confused.

16   One effective way to combat the pedantic stance is to arrange for weekly confrontations of groups of students over their own papers. We have done far too little experimenting with arrangements for providing a genuine audience in this way. Short of such developments, it remains true that a good teacher can convince his students that he is a true audience, if his comments on the papers show that some sort of dialogue is taking place. As Jacques Barzun says in *Teacher in America,* students should be made to feel that unless they have said something to someone, they have failed; to bore the teacher is a worse form of failure than to anger him. From this point of view we can see that the charts of grading symbols that mar even the best freshman texts are not the innocent time savers that we pretend. Plausible as it may seem to arrange for more corrections with less time, they inevitably reduce the student's sense of purpose in writing. When he sees innumerable W13's and P19's in the margin, he cannot possibly feel that the art of persuasion is as important to his instructor as when he reads personal comments, however few.

17   This first perversion, then, springs from ignoring the audience or over-reliance on the pure subject. The second which might be called the ad-

vertiser's stance, comes from *under*valuing the subject and overvaluing pure effect: how to win friends and influence people.

18   Some of our best freshman texts—Sheridan Baker's *The Practical Stylist,* for example—allow themselves on occasion to suggest that to be controversial or argumentative, to stir up an audience is an end in itself. Sharpen the controversial edge, one of them says, and the clear implication is that one should do so even if the truth of the subject is honed off in the process. This perversion is probably in the long run a more serious threat in our society than the danger of ignoring the audience. In the time of audience-reaction meters and pre-tested plays and novels, it is not easy to convince students of the old Platonic truth that good persuasion is honest persuasion, or even of the old Aristotelian truth that the good rhetorician must be master of his subject, no matter how dishonest he may decide ultimately to be. Having told them that good writers always to some degree accommodate their arguments to the audience, it is hard to explain the difference between justified accommodation—say changing *point one* to the final position—and the kind of accommodation that fills our popular magazines, in which the very substance of what is said is accommodated to some preconception of what will sell. "The publication of *Eros* [magazine] represents a major breakthrough in the battle for the liberation of the human spirit."

19   At a dinner about a month ago I sat between the wife of a famous civil rights lawyer and an advertising consultant. "I saw the article on your book yesterday in the Daily News," she said, "but I didn't even finish it. The title of your book scared me off. Why did you ever choose such a terrible title? Nobody would buy a book with a title like that." The man on my right, whom I'll call Mr. Kinches, overhearing my feeble reply, plunged into a conversation with her, over my torn and bleeding corpse. "Now with my *last* book," he said, "I listed 20 possible titles and then tested them out on 400 business men. The one I chose was voted for by 90 percent of the businessmen." "That's what I was just saying to Mr. Booth," she said. "A book title ought to grab you, and *rhetoric* is not going to grab anybody." "Right," he said. "My *last* book sold 50,000 copies already; I don't know how this one will do, but I polled 200 businessmen on the table of contents, and . . ."

20   At one point I did manage to ask him whether the title he chose really fit the book. "Not quite as well as one or two of the others," he admitted, "but that doesn't matter, you know. If the book is designed right, so that the first chapter pulls them in, and you *keep* 'em in, who's going to gripe about a little inaccuracy in the title?"

21   Well, rhetoric is the art of persuading, not the art of seeming to persuade by giving everything away at the start. It presupposes that one has a purpose concerning a subject which itself cannot be fundamentally modified by the desire to persuade. If Edmund Burke had decided that he could win more votes in Parliament by choosing the other side—as he most

certainly could have done—we would hardly hail this party-switch as a master stroke of rhetoric. If Churchill had offered the British "peace in our time," with some laughs thrown in, because opinion polls had shown that more Britishers were "grabbed" by these than by blood, sweat, and tears, we could hardly call his decision a sign of rhetorical skill.

22   One could easily discover other perversions of the rhetorician's balance—most obviously what might be called the entertainer's stance—the willingness to sacrifice substance to personality and charm. I admire Walker Gibson's efforts to startle us out of dry pedantry, but I know from experience that his exhortations to find and develop the speaker's voice can lead to empty colorfulness. A student once said to me, complaining about a colleague, "I soon learned that all I had to do to get an A was imitate Thurber."

23   But perhaps this is more than enough about the perversions of the rhetorical stance. Balance itself is always harder to describe than the clumsy poses that result when it is destroyed. But we all experience the balance whenever we find an author who succeeds in changing our minds. He can do so only if he knows more about the subject than we do, and if he then engages us in the process of thinking—and feeling—it through. What makes the rhetoric of Milton and Burke and Churchill great is that each presents us with the spectacle of a man passionately involved in thinking an important question through, in the company of an audience Though each of them did everything in his power to make his point persuasive, including a pervasive use of the many emotional appeals that have been falsely scorned by many a freshman composition text, none would have allowed himself the advertiser's stance; none would have polled the audience in advance to discover which position would get the votes. Nor is the highly individual personality that springs out at us from their speeches and essays present for the sake of selling itself. The rhetorical balance among speakers, audience, and argument is with all three men habitual, as we see if we look at their non-political writings. Burke's work on the Sublime and Beautiful is a relatively unimpassioned philosophical treatise, but one finds there again a delicate balance: though the implied author of this is a far different person, far less obtrusive, far more objective, than the man who later cried *sursum corda* to the British Parliament, he permeates with his philosophical personality his philosophical work. And though the signs of his awareness of his audience are far more subdued, they are still here: every effort is made to involve the *proper* audience, the audience of philosophical minds, in a fundamentally interesting inquiry, and to lead them through to the end. In short, because he was a man engaged with men in the effort to solve a human problem, one could never call what he wrote dull, however difficult or abstruse.

24   Now obviously the habit of seeking this balance is not the only thing we have to teach under the heading of rhetoric. But I think that everything worth teaching under that heading finds its justification finally in that

balance. Much of what is now considered irrelevant or dull can, in fact, be brought to life when teachers and students know what they are seeking. Churchill reports that the most valuable training he ever received in rhetoric was in the diagramming of sentences. Think of it! Yet the diagramming of a sentence, regardless of the grammatical system, can be a live subject as soon as one asks not simply "How is this sentence put together," but rather "Why is it put together in this way?" or "Could the rhetorical balance and hence the desired persuasion be better achieved by writing it differently?"

25   As a nation we are reputed to write very badly. As a nation, I would say, we are more inclined to the perversions of rhetoric than to the rhetorical balance. Regardless of what we do about this or that course in the curriculum, our mandate would seem to be, then, to lead more of our students than we now do to care about and practice the true arts of persuasion.

The Triumph of Language

23   JOHN CIARDI
The Act of Language

1   At the beginning of *The Divine Comedy,* Dante finds himself in a Dark Wood, lost from the light of God. It was no single, specific evil act that led Dante into that darkness but, rather, the sin of omission. Its name is Acedia, the fourth of the Seven Deadly Sins, and by us generally translated "Sloth."

2   In American-English, however, Sloth may seem to imply mere physical laziness and untidiness. The torpor of Acedia, it must be understood, is spiritual rather than physical. It is to know the good, but to be lax in its pursuit.

3   Whether one thinks of it as a sin or as a behavioral failure, Acedia is also the one fault for which no artist can be forgiven. Time, as W. H. Auden wrote in his poem titled *In Memory of W. B. Yeats:*

> Worships language and forgives
> Everyone by whom it lives;
> Pardons cowardice, conceit,
> Lays its honors at their feet.

4   In place of cowardice and conceit, Auden might have cited any catalogue of pride, envy, wrath, avarice, gluttony or carnality, and he could still have said that time forgives. The poet may cheat anything else and still win honor from time, but he may not cheat the poem and live.

5   For a man is finally defined by what he does with his attention. It was Simone Weil who said, "Absolute attention is absolute prayer." I do not, of course, know what an absolute attention is, except as an absolutely unattainable goal. But certainly to seek that increasing purity and concentration of one's attention that will lead to more and more meaningful per-

ception, is not only possible but is the basic human exercise of any art. It must be added, however, that *in art it does not matter what one pays attention to; the quality of the attenion is what counts.*

6   I have just made a dangerous statement; one that will probably breed protest, that will be difficult to explain, and that will turn out in the end to be only partly true. It is still necessary to make the statement first, and then to go the long way round to explaining why it is necessary, and in what way it is true.

7   The need to go the long way round brings matters back to another parable of poetry that one may read in Dante's opening situation. The language of parables is always likely to be apt to the discussion of poetry.

8   As soon as Dante realizes that he is in darkness, he looks up and sees the first light of the dawn shawling the shoulders of a little hill. (In Dante, the Sun is always a symbol of God as Divine Illumination.) The allegory should be clear enough: The very realization that one is lost is the beginning of finding oneself.

9   What happens next is the heart of the matter. His goal in sight, Dante tries to race straight up the hill—to reach the light, as it were, by direct assault. Note that common sense would certainly be on Dante's side. There is the light and there is the hill: go to it. Nothing could be simpler. Nor, as Dante discovers, could anything be more false. Almost immediately his way is blocked by three beasts. These beasts—a Leopard, a Lion and a She-wolf—represent all the sins of the world. They represent, therefore, the world's total becloudment of any man's best attention, for all that has ever lured any man away from his own good is contained within them.

10   The three beasts drive Dante back into the darkness. There Dante comes on the soul of Virgil, who symbolizes Human Reason. In that role Virgil explains that a man may reach the light only by going the long way round. Dante must risk the dangerous descent into Hell—to the recognition of sin. And he must make the arduous ascent of Purgatory—to the renunciation of sin. Only then may he enter, bit by bit, the final presence of the light, which is to say, Heaven.

11   The point of the parable is that in art as in theology—as in all things that concern a man in his profoundest being—the long way round is the only way home. Short cuts are useful only in mechanics. The man who seeks mortal understanding must go the long, encompassing way of his deepest involvement.

12   Americans, susceptible as they are to the legend of mechanical know-how and get-it-done, may especially need to be told that there is no easy digest of understanding and no gift package of insight. May they learn, too, that "common sense," useful as it can be in its own sphere, cannot lead a man as deeply into himself as he must be led if he is to enter a meaningful experience of art or of life. Every man who looks long enough at the stars must come to feel their other-reality engulfing his mortal state,   and

nothing from the world's efficiencies and practicalities is specific to that awareness in him.

13   Poetry is written of that man under the stars in trouble and in joy, and the truth of poetry cannot be spoken meaningfully in simple common-sense assertions. In poetry, as in all our deepest emotions, many feelings and many thoughts and half-thoughts happen at once. Often these feelings and thoughts are in conflict:

14   We love and hate the same thing, desire it and dread it, need it and are destroyed by it. Always, too, there are more thoughts and feelings in a profound experience than we can put a finger on. What has common sense to say to such states of man? Common sense tends always to the easier assumption that only one thing is "really" happening in a man at one time, and that a simple, straightforward course of action will take care of it.

15   Such an assumption can only blind one to poetry. To read a poem with no thought in mind but to paraphrase it into a single, simple, and usually high-minded, prose statement is the destruction of poetry. Nor does it make much difference that one can quote poetry, and good poetry, in defense of such destruction. At the end of *Ode on a Grecian Urn,* John Keats wrote:

> "Beauty is truth, truth beauty,"—that is all
> Ye know on earth, and all ye need to know.

16   Heaven knows how many enthusiasts have used these lines as evidence that poetry is somehow an act of inspiration not to be measured by any criteria but an undefined devotion to "beauty," "truth" and "inspiring message."

17   But if beauty and truth are all that Grecian urns and men need know on earth, Keats makes evident by his own practice that a poet also needs to know a great deal about his trade, and that he must be passionately concerned for its basic elements.

18   Those basic elements are not beauty and truth but *rhythm, diction, image* and *form.* Certainly Keats cared about beauty and truth. Any sensitive man must care. No matter that one must forever fumble at the definition of such ideas; they are still matters of ultimate concern. But so was Dante's yearning for the light, and he discovered at once that it can be reached only by the long way round.

19   The poet's way round is by way of rhythm, diction, image and form. It is the right, the duty and the joy of his trade to be passionate about these things. To be passionate about them in the minutest and even the most frivolous detail. To be passionate about them, if need be, to the exclusion of what is generally understood by "sincerity" and "meaning." To be more passionate about them than he is about the cold war, the Gunpowder Plot, the next election, abolition, the H-bomb, the Inquisition, juvenile delinquency, the Spanish Armada, or his own survival.

20   The good poets have not generally sneered at the world of affairs. Some have, but many others have functioned well within that world. Yet the need and the right of all poets to detach themselves from the things of the world in order to pursue the things of the poetic trade have always been inseparable from their success as poets.

21   The poet must be passionate about the four elements of his trade for the most fundamental of reasons. He must be so because those passions are both a joy and an addiction within him. Because they are the life of the poem, without which nothing of value can happen either in the poem or to the reader. Because writing a poem is a more sentient way of living than not writing it, because no poem can be written well except as these passions inform it, and because only when the poem is so written can the beauty and truth of that more sentient way of living be brought to mortal consequence.

22   The act of poetry may seem to have very simple surfaces, but it is always compounded of many things at once. As Robert Frost wrote in *Two Tramps in Mud Time:*

> Only where love and need are one,
> And the work is play for mortal stakes,
> Is the deed ever really done
> For Heaven and the future's sakes.

23   The voice of common sense rises immediately in protest. "Mystification!" it cries. "A poem still has to *mean* something. What does it *mean?*" And the poet must answer, "Never what you think. Not when you ask the question in that way."

24   But how shall the question be asked? Let the questioner listen first to a kind of statement he has probably passed over without enough attention. He can find one such in Walter Pater's essay on Winckelman. "Let us understand by poetry," wrote Pater, "all literary production which attains the power of giving pleasure by its form as distinct from its matter."

25   He can find another in a book titled *The Fire and the Fountain* by the English poet and critic John Press. "The essence of the poet," wrote Press, "is to be found less in his opinions than in his idiom." He may even find one in a textbook titled *Reading Poems,* in which Prof. Wright Thomas says, "The *subject* is a very poor indication of what the *poem* is" —to which I should add only that it is no indication whatever.

26   But if the meaning is not in the subject, what then does a poem mean? It means always and above all else the poet's deep involvement in the four basic elements of his trade. It means not the subject but the way the poetic involvement transfigures the subject. It means, that is to say, the very act of language by which it comes into existence. The poem may purport to be about anything from pussy willows to battleships, but the meaning of any good poem is its act of language.

27   Because it is an act of language, a good poem is deeply connected with everything men are and do. For language is certainly one of the most fundamental activities in which human beings engage. Take away a man's language, and you take most of his ability to think and to experience. Enrich his language, and you cannot fail to enrich his experience. Any man who has let great language into his head is the richer for it.

28   He is not made richer by what is being said. It is the language itself that brings his enrichment. Could poetry be meaningful aside from its act of language, it would have no reason for being, and the whole history of poetry could be reduced to a series of simple paraphrases.

29   Consider as simple a passage as the beginning of Herrick's *Upon Julia's Clothes:*

> Whenas in silks my Julia goes,
> Then, then, methinks, how sweetly flows
> The liquefaction of her clothes.

30   Who can read those lines without a thrill of pleasure? But now consider the paraphrase: "I like the rustle of Julia's silks when she walks." The poetry and the paraphrase are certainly about equal in subject matter. The difference is that the poetry is a full and rich act of language, whereas the paraphrase, though faultless, lacks, among other things, measure, pause, stress, rhyme and the pleasure of lingering over the word "liquefaction."

31   "But what is Julia doing there?" cries that voice of common sense, "She must have something to do with the poem or she wouldn't be in it!"

32   The owner of that voice would do well to ponder the relation between a good portrait and its subject. The subject is there, to be sure—at least in most cases. But the instant the painter puts one brush stroke on the canvas and then another, the two brush strokes take on a relation to each other and to the space around them. The two then take on a relation to the third, and it to them. And so forth. The painting immediately begins to exert its own demands upon the painter, its own way of going. Immediately the subject begins to disappear.

33   All too soon, for that matter, the subject will have changed with age or will have died. After a while no living person will have any recollection of what the subject looked like. All that will remain then is a portrait head which must be either self-validating or worthless. Because the subject cannot validate the painting, he or she will have become irrelevant. All that can finally validate the portrait is the way in which the painter engaged the act of painting.

34   And one more thing—the good artist always thinks in long terms. He knows, even at the moment of the painting, that both he and the subject will disappear. Any good painter will be painting for the painting—for the time when the subject will have blown away into time.

35   So with poetry. The one final and enduring meaning of any poem lies not in what it seems to have set out to say, but in its act of language.

36   The only test of that act of language is the memory of the race. Bad poetry is by nature forgettable; it is, therefore, soon forgotten. But good poetry, like any good act of language, hooks onto human memory and stays there. Write well, and there will always be someone somewhere who carries in his mind what you have written. It will stay in memory because man is the language animal, and because his need of language is from the roots of his consciousness. That need in him is not a need for meaning. Rather, good language in him takes possession of meaning; it fills him with a resonance that the best of men understand only dimly, but without which no man is entirely alive. Poetry is that presence and that resonance. As Archibald MacLeish put it in his much-discussed *Ars Poetica:*

> A poem should not mean
> But be.

37   If the reader truly wishes to engage poetry, let him forget meaning. Let him think rather: "I shall summon great language to mind. I shall summon language so fully, so resonantly and so precisely used that it will bring all my meanings to me." Then let him turn to poetry, and let him listen to the passions of the poet's trade.

38   Listen to great rhythms. Here is the opening stanza of John Donne's *The Anniversarie:*

> All Kings, and all their favorites,
> All glory of honours, beauties, wits,
> The Sun it selfe, which makes times as they passe,
> Is elder by a yeare, now, than it was
> When thou and I first one another saw:
> All other things, to their destruction draw,
> Only our love hath no decay;
> This, no to morrow hath, nor yesterday.
> Running, it never runs from us away,
> But truly keeps his first, last, everlasting day.

39   Worldly things pass away, but true love is constant, says the subject matter. All true enough and tried enough. But listen to the rhythm enforce itself upon the saying, especially in the last four lines. For present purposes, let the voice ignore the lesser accents. Let it stress only those syllables printed in capital letters below, while observing the pauses as indicated by the slash marks. And forget the meaning. Read for the voice emphasis and the voice pauses:

> Only OUR LOVE hath no deCAY //
> THIS // no to MOrrow hath // nor YESterday //

RUNning // it never runs from us aWAY //
But truly keeps his FIRST // LAST // EVerlasting DAY

40   Not all rhythms are so percussive, so measured out by pauses, and so metrically irregular. Listen to this smoother rhythm from Poe's *Israfel:*

> If I could dwell
> Where Israfel
>   Hath dwelt, and he where I,
> He might not sing so wildly well
>   A mortal melody,
> While a bolder note than his might swell
> From my lyre within the sky.

41   Or the rhythm may be percussive, but without substantial pauses, as in the last line of this passage from the end of Gerard Manley Hopkins' *Felix Randal,* an elegy for a blacksmith:

> How far from then forethought of, all thy more boisterous years,
> When thou at the random grim forge, powerful amidst peers,
> Didst fettle for the great gray drayhorse his bright and battering sandal.

42   Listen to the hammerfall of that last line: "Didst FEttle for the GREAT GRAY DRAYhorse his BRIGHT and BAttering SANdal."

43   Or listen to the spacing of the "ah" sounds as a rhythmic emphasis in the last line of this final passage from Meredith's *Lucifer in Starlight:*

> Around the ancient track marched, rank on rank,
> The ARmy of unALterable LAW.

44   Percussive, smooth, flowing or studded with pauses—there is no end to the variety and delight of great language rhythms. For the poet, his rhythms are forever more than a matter of making a "meaningful" statement; they are a joy in their own right. No poet hates meaning. But the poet's passion is for the triumph of language. No reader can come to real contact with a poem until he comes to it through the joy of that rhythmic act of language.

45   As for rhythm, so for diction. The poet goes to language—or it comes to him and he receives it—for his joy in the precision of great word choices. Give him such a line as Whitman's "I witness the corpse with the dabbled hair," and he will register the corpse, to be sure, but it will be "dabbled" he seizes upon with the joy of a botanist coming on a rare specimen. So when Keats speaks of Ruth amid "the alien corn" or when Theodore Roethke speaks of sheep "strewn" on a field, the good reader will certainly care about the dramatic situation of the poem, but he cannot fail to answer with a special joy to "alien" and to "strewn."

46   What, after all, is the subject as compared to his joy in such rich precision? Thousands of English poems have described the passing of win-

ter and the coming of spring. Certainly there is little in that subject as a subject to attract him. But listen to the pure flutefall of the word choices I have italicized in the following passage from Stanley Kunitz's *Deciduous Bough,* and note how the self-delight in language makes everything immediate and new again:

> Winter that *coils* in the thicket now
> Will *glide* from the field, the *swinging* rain
> Be *knotted* with flowers, on every bough
> A bird will *meditate* again.

47   "Poetry," said Coleridge, "is the best words in the best order." How can anyone reading the Kunitz passage escape a sense that the language is being ultimately and unimprovably selected? The delight one feels in coming on such language is not only in the experience of perfection but also in the fact that perfection has been made to seem not only effortless but inevitable.

48   And let this much more be added to the idea of poetic meaning: Nothing in a good poem happens by accident; every word, every comma, every variant spelling must enter as an act of the poet's choice. A poem is a machine for making choices. The mark of the good poet is his refusal to make easy or cheap choices. The better the poet, the greater the demands he makes upon himself; and the higher he sets his level of choice. Thus, a good poem is not only an act of mind but an act of devotion to mind. The poet who chooses cheaply or lazily is guilty of aesthetic acedia, and he is lost thereby. The poet who spares himself nothing in his search for the most demanding choices is shaping a human attention that offers itself as a high and joyful example to all men of mind and devotion. Every act of great language, whatever its subject matter, illustrates an idea of order and a resonance of human possibility without which no man's mind can sense its own fullest dimensions.

49   As for rhythm and diction, so for imagery. To be sure, every word is at root an image, and poetic images must be made of words. Yet certainly there is in a well-constructed image an effect that cannot be said to rise from any one word choice, but from the total phrasing.

50   So for the sensory shiver of Keats' "The silver snarling trumpets 'gan to chide." So for the wonderfully woozy effect of John Frederick Nims' "The drunk clambering on his undulant floor." So for the grand hyperbole of Howard Nemerov saying that the way a young girl looks at him "sets his knees to splashing like two waves."

51   We learn both imagination and precision from the poet's eye. And we learn correspondences. Consider the following image from *Aereopagus* by Louis MacNeice, a poem as playful as it is serious, in which MacNeice describes Athens as a cradle of the western mind. Cradles, he makes clear, generally contain children, and all those boy-gods and girl-goddesses had their childish side:

> . . . you still may glimpse
> The child-eyed Fury tossing her shock of snakes,
> Careering over the Parthenon's ruined playpen.

52   It is a bit shocking to have the Parthenon spoken of as a playpen, but once the shock has passed, what a triumph there is in the figure: everything corresponds! Think how much would have been lost had the Parthenon a surviving roof, or had its general proportions or the placement of the pillars—slats—resisted the comparison. The joy of it is that, despite the first shock, nothing resists the comparison; and we find that the surprise turns out to be a true correspondence.

53   One of the poet's happiest—and most mortal—games is in seeking such correspondences. But what flows from them is more than a game. Every discovery of a true correspondence is an act of reason and an instruction to the mind. For intelligence does not consist of masses of factual detail. It consists of seeing essential likenesses and essential differences and of relating them, allowing for differences with the likenesses and for likenesses within the differences. Mentality is born of analogy.

54   Note, too, that the image-idea of "ruined playpen" does not simply happen, but is prepared for in "child-eyed." And note, further, the nice double meaning of "careering" as both "a wild rush" and "to make a career of."

55   A good extended image, that is to say, is made of various elements and is marked by both sequence and structure. Thus we have already touched upon the essence of the fourth element of the poet's trade: form.

56   There are many kinds of poetic form, but since all are based on pattern and sequence, let a tightly patterned poem illustrate. Here is Emily Dickinson's *The Soul Selects:*

> The soul selects her own society,
> Then shuts the door;
> On her divine majority
> Obtrude no more.
>
> Unmoved, she notes the chariot's pausing
> At her low gate;
> Unmoved, an emperor is kneeling
> Upon her mat.
>
> I've known her from an ample nation
> Choose one;
> Then close the valves of her attention
> Like stone.

57   Whatever the hunters of beauty and truth find for their pleasure in such a poem, the poet's joy will be in its form and management. He responds to the passion of the language for its own sparseness, to the pattern

of rhyme and half-rhyme, to the flavor of the images (connotation), and to the way those flavors relate to one another. He responds to the interplay of the four-foot feminine lines (feminine lines end on an unaccented sylla-ble) and the two-foot masculine lines (which end on an accented syllable).

58   And he responds, above all, to the way those two-foot lines develop in the last stanza into two boldly stroked syllables apiece (monosyllabic feet) so that the emotion held down throughout the poem by the sparse-ness of the language is hammered into sensation by the beat of those last two words: "Like stone"—thud! thud!

59   Beauty and truth are no irrelevancies, but they are abstractions that must remain meaningless to poetry until they are brought to being in the management of a specific form. It is that management the poet must love: the joy of sensing the poem fall into inescapable form, and therefore into inescapable experience. For the poet's trade is not to talk about expe-rience, but to make it happen. His act of making is all he knows of beauty and truth. It is, in fact, his way of knowing them. His only way of know-ing them.

60   As I. A. Richards, poet and scholar of the language, put it in a recent poem titled *The Ruins:*

> Sometimes a word is wiser much than men:
> "Faithful" e.g., "responsible" and "true."
> And words it is, not poets, make up poems.
> Our words, we say, but we are theirs, too,
> For words made men and may unmake again.

61   And now, at last, it is time to repeat the statement from which this long way round began. "In art," I said, "it does not matter what one pays attention to; the quality of the attention is what counts." It is time to amend that necessary false statement.

62   For it does matter where the poet fixes his attention. Attention must be to *something*. That something, however, is so casually connected with the subject of the poem that any reader will do well to dismiss the subject as no more than a point of departure. Any impassioning point of depar-ture will do. The poet, being a man, must believe something, but what that something is does not matter so long as he believes it strongly enough to be passionate about it. What he believes, moreover, may be touched off by an image, a rhythm, or the quality of a word *in pursuit of which the subject is invented.*

63   The poem, in any case, is not in its point of departure, but in its journey to itself. That journey, the act of the poem, is its act of language. That act is the true final subject and meaning of any poem. It is to that act of language the poet shapes his most devoted attention—to the fullness of rhythm, diction, image and form. Only in that devotion can he seize the world and make it evident.

Questions

1. What are the four elements of a poet's trade? To which of them, if any, does Ciardi seem to devote most of his discussion?

2. In talking about the poet and his acts of language, what word, in various forms, does Ciardi use most frequently? How is the meaning of this word related on the one hand to the element of a poet's trade and on the other to Ciardi's general assertion (later amended) about art?

3. List at least four striking images that Ciardi, who is also a practicing poet, uses in his own discussion of the act of language.

4. "Mentality," says Ciardi, "is born of analogy." What extensive analogy from a past writer does he cite? Name the point of correspondence Ciardi achieves throughout his entire piece between this analogy and his own special analogic use of it.

5. How many quotations—acts of language other than his own—does Ciardi use? How many are from poems, how many from prose works? Does he quote the same poem or poet twice? Examine the *occasion* for each quotation: that is, does it illustrate a generalization he has just made, formulate succinctly a point of view he endorses? Examine the *sequel* to each quotation. In which cases does he (1) explain the quotation's fuller import for his discourse, (2) anticipate the reader's reaction and attempt to discount it, (3) make no comment at all?

6. What function does "the voice of common sense" play in Ciardi's article? What is its relation to your answers to question 2 above?

24   W. H. AUDEN

The Unknown Citizen

(To JS/07/M/378 This Marble Monument Is Erected by the State)

He was found by the Bureau of Statistics to be
One against whom there was no official complaint,
And all the reports on his conduct agree
That, in the modern sense of an old-fashioned word, he was a saint,
For in everything he did he served the Greater Community.

Except for the War till the day he retired
He worked in a factory and never got fired,
But satisfied his employers, Fudge Motors Inc.
Yet he wasn't a scab or odd in his views,
For his Union reports that he paid his dues,   10
(Our report on his Union shows it was sound)
And our Social Psychology workers found
That he was popular with his mates and liked a drink.
The Press are convinced that he bought a paper every day
And that his reactions to advertisements were normal in every way.
Policies taken out in his name prove that he was fully insured,
And his Health-card shows he was once in hospital but left it cured.
Both Producers Research and High-Grade Living declare
He was fully sensible to the advantages of the Installment Plan
And had everything necessary to the Modern Man,   20
A phonograph, a radio, a care and a frigidaire.
Our researchers into Public Opinion are content
That he held the proper opinions for the time of year;
When there was peace, he was for peace; when there was war, he went.
He was married and added five children to the population,
Which our Eugenist says was the right number for a parent of his generation,
And our teachers report that he never interfered with their education.
Was he free? Was he happy? The question is absurd:
Had anything been wrong, we should certainly have heard.

25   WILLIAM BLAKE

London

I wander thro' each charter'd street,
Near where the charter'd Thames does flow,
And mark in every face I meet
Marks of weakness, marks of woe.

In every cry of every Man,
In every Infant's cry of fear,
In every voice, in every ban,
The mind-forg'd manacles I hear.

How the Chimney-sweeper's cry
Every black'ning Church appalls;   10
And the hapless Soldier's sigh
Runs in blood down Palace walls.

But most thro' midnight streets I hear
How the youthful Harlot's curse
Blasts the new born Infant's tear,
And blights with plagues the Marriage hearse.

26   ROBERT HUFF

Rainbow

After the shot the driven feathers rock
In the air and are by sunlight trapped.
Their moment of descent is eloquent.
It is the rainbow echo of a bird
Whose thunder, stopped, puts in my daughter's eyes
A question mark. She does not see the rainbow,
And the folding bird-fall was for her too quick.
It is about the stillness of the bird
Her eyes are asking. She is three years old;
Has cut her fingers; found blood tastes of salt;   10
But she has never witnessed quiet blood,
Nor ever seen before the peace of death.
I say: "The feathers—Look!" but she is torn
And wretched and draws back. And I am glad
That I have wounded her, have winged her heart,
And that she goes beyond my fathering.

From *Colonel Johnson's Ride* by Robert Huff. Copyright 1959, by Wayne State University Press. Reprinted by permission of the author.

27   W. D. SNODGRASS

Ten Days Leave

He steps down from the dark train, blinking; stares
At trees like miracles. He will play games
With boys or sit up all night touching chairs.
Talking with friends, he can recall their names.

Noon burns against his eyelids, but he lies
Hunched in his blankets; he is half awake
But still lacks nerve to open up his eyes;
Supposing it were just his old mistake?

But no; it seems just like it seemed. His folks
Pursue their lives like toy trains on a track.   10
He can foresee each of his father's jokes
Like words in some old movie that's come back.

He is like days when you've gone some place new
To deal with certain strangers, though you never
Escape the sense in everything you do,
"We've done this all once. Have I been here, ever?"

But no; he thinks it must recall some old film, lit
By lives you want to touch; as if he's slept
And must have dreamed this setting, peopled it,
And wakened out of it. But someone's kept   20

His dream asleep here like a small homestead
Preserved long past its time in memory
Of some great man who lived here and is dead.
They have restored his landscape faithfully:

The hills, the little houses, the costumes:
How real it seems! But he comes, wide awake,
A tourist whispering through the priceless rooms
Who must not touch things or his hand might break

Their sleep and black them out. He wonders when
He'll grow into his sleep so sound again.   30

28　WILLIAM SHAKESPEARE

Since Brass, nor Stone . . .

Since brass, nor stone, nor earth, nor boundless sea,
But sad mortality o'er-sways their power,
How with this rage shall beauty hold a plea,
Whose action is no stronger than a flower?
O, how shall summer's honey breath hold out
Against the wrackful siege of battering days,
When rocks impregnable are not so stout,
Nor gates of steel so strong, but Time decays?
O fearful meditation! where, alack,
Shall Time's best jewel from Time's chest lie hid?　　　10
Or what strong hand can hold his swift foot back?
Or who his spoil of beauty can forbid?
　　O, none, unless this miracle have might,
　　That in black ink my love may still shine bright.

29　GERARD MANLEY HOPKINS

Spring and Fall: To a Young Child

Márgarét, are you gríeving
Old Goldengrove unleaving?
Leáves, like the things of man, you
With your fresh thoughts care for, can you?
Áh! ás the heart grows older
It will come to such sights colder
By and by, nor spare a sigh
Though worlds of wanwood leafmeal lie;
And yet you wíll weep and know why.
Now no matter, child, the name:　　　10

From *The Poems of Gerard Manley Hopkins,* Third ed. 1948. Reprinted by permission of Oxford University Press, Inc.

Sórrow's springs áre the same.
Nor mouth had, no nor mind, expressed
What heart heard of, ghost guessed:
It ís the blight man was born for,
It is Margaret you mourn for.

30   ANDREW MARVELL

To His Coy Mistress

Had we but World enough, and Time,
This coyness Lady were no crime.
We would sit down, and think which way
To walk, and pass our long Loves Day.
Thou by the *Indian Ganges* side
Should'st Rubies find: I by the Tide
Of *Humber* would complain. I would
Love you ten years before the Flood:
And you should if you please refuse
Till the Conversion of the *Jews*.   10
My vegetable Love should grow
Vaster than Empires, and more slow.
And hundred years should go to praise
Thine Eyes, and on thy Forehead Gaze.
Two hundred to adore each Breast:
But thirty thousand to the rest.
An Age at least to every part,
And the last Age should show your Heart.
For Lady you deserve this State;
Nor would I love at lower rate.   20
     But at my back I alwaies hear
Times winged Charriot hurrying near:
And yonder all before us lye
Desarts of vast Eternity.
Thy Beauty shall no more be found;
Nor, in thy marble Vault, shall sound
My ecchoing Song: then Worms shall try
That long preserv'd Virginity:
And your quaint Honour turn to dust;

And into ashes all my Lust.   30
The Grave's a fine and private place,
But none I think do there embrace.
    Now therefore, while the youthful hew
Sits on thy skin like morning lew,[1]
And while thy willing Soul transpires
At every pore with instant Fires,
Now let us sport us while we may;
And now, like am'rous birds of prey,
Rather at once our Time devour,
Than languish in his slow chapt pow'r.   40
Let us roll all our Strength, and all
Our sweetness, up into one Ball:
And tear our Pleasures with rough strife,
Thorough the Iron gates of Life.
Thus, though we cannot make our Sun
Stand still, yet we will make him run.

31   PHILIP LARKIN

Poetry of Departures

Sometimes you hear, fifth-hand,
As epitaph:
He chucked up everything
And just cleared off,
And always the voice will sound
Certain you approve
This audacious, purifying,
Elemental move.

And they are right, I think.
We all hate home   10
And having to be there:
I detest my room,
Its specially-chosen junk,

[1] warmth

"Poetry of Departures" by Philip Larkin is reprinted from *The Less Deceived,* © The Marvell Press 1955, 1969, by permission of The Marvell Press, Hessle, Yorkshire, England.

The good books, the good bed,
And my life, in perfect order:
So to hear it said

He walked out on the whole crowd
Leaves me flushed and stirred,
Like *Then she undid her dress*
Or *Take that you bastard;*   20
Surely I can, if he did?
And that helps me stay
Sober and industrious.
But I'd go today,

Yes, swagger the nut-strewn roads,
Crouch in the fo'c'sle
Stubbly with goodness, if
It weren't so artificial,
Such a deliberate step backwards
To create an object: 30
Books; china; a life
Reprehensibly perfect.

32   SYLVIA PLATH

Daddy

You do not do, you do not do
Any more, black shoe
In which I have lived like a foot
For thirty years, poor and white,
Barely daring to breathe or Achoo.

Daddy, I have had to kill you.
You died before I had time—
Marble-heavy, a bag full of God,
Ghastly statue with one grey toe
Big as a Frisco seal   10

And a head in the freakish Atlantic
Where it pours bean green over blue
In the waters off beautiful Nauset.
I used to pray to recover you.
Ach, du.

In the German tongue, in the Polish town
Scraped flat by the roller
Of wars, wars, wars.
But the name of the town is common.
My Polack friend   20

Says there are a dozen or two.
So I never could tell where you
Put your foot, your root,
I never could talk to you.
The tongue stuck in my jaw.

It stuck in a barb wire snare.
Ich, ich, ich, ich,
I could hardly speak.
I thought every German was you.
And the language obscene   30

An engine, an engine
Chuffing me off like a Jew.
A Jew to Dachau, Auschwitz, Belsen.
I began to talk like a Jew.
I think I may well be a Jew.

The snows of the Tyrol, the clear beer of Vienna
Are not very pure or true.
With my gypsy ancestress and my weird luck
And my Taroc pack and my Taroc pack
I may be a bit of a Jew.   40

I have always been scared of you,
With your Luftwaffe, your gobbledygoo.
And your neat moustache
And your Aryan eye, bright blue.
Panzer-man, panzer-man, O You—

Not God but a swastika
So black no sky could squeak through.
Every woman adores a Fascist,
The boot in the face, the brute
Brute heart of a brute like you.   50

You stand at the blackboard, daddy,
In the picture I have of you,
A cleft in your chin instead of your foot
But no less a devil for that, no not
Any less the black man who

Bit my pretty red heart in two.
I was ten when they buried you.
At twenty I tried to die
And get back, back, back to you.
I thought even the bones would do.   60

But they pulled me out of the sack,
And they stuck me together with glue.
And then I knew what to do.
I made a model of you,
A man in black with a Meinkampf look

And a love of the rack and the screw.
And I said I do, I do.
So daddy, I'm finally through.
The black telephone's off at the root,
The voices just can't worm through.   70

If I've killed one man, I've killed two—
The vampire who said he was you
And drank my blood for a year,
Seven years, if you want to know.
Daddy, you can lie back now.

There's a stake in your fat black heart
And the villagers never liked you.
They are dancing and stamping on you.
They always *knew* it was you.
Daddy, daddy, you bastard, I'm through.   80

33   EUDORA WELTY

Death of a Travelling Salesman

R. J. Bowman, who for fourteen years had travelled for a shoe company through Mississippi, drove his Ford along a rutted dirt path. It was a long day! The time did not seem to clear the noon hurdle and settle into soft afternoon. The sun, keeping its strength here even in winter, stayed at the top of the sky, and every time Bowman stuck his head out of the dusty car to stare up the road, it seemed to reach a long arm down and push against the top of his head, right through his hat—like the practical joke of an old drummer, long on the road. It made him feel all the more angry and helpless. He was feverish, and he was not quite sure of the way.

This was his first day back on the road after a long siege of influenza. He had had very high fever, and dreams, and had become weakened and pale, enough to tell the difference in the mirror, and he could not think clearly. . . . All afternoon, in the midst of his anger, and for no reason, he had thought of his dead grandmother. She had been a comfortable soul. Once more Bowman wished he could fall into the big feather bed that had been in her room. . . . Then he forgot her again.

This desolate hill country! And he seemed to be going the wrong way— it was as if he were going back, far back. There was not a house in sight. . . . There was no use wishing he were back in bed, though. By paying the hotel doctor his bill he had proved his recovery. He had not even been sorry when the pretty trained nurse said good-bye. He did not like illness, he distrusted it, as he distrusted the road without signposts. It angered him. He had given the nurse a really expensive bracelet, just because she was packing up her bag and leaving.

But now—what if in fourteen years on the road he had never been ill before and never had an accident? His record was broken, and he had even begun almost to question it. . . . He had gradually put up at better hotels, in the bigger towns, but weren't they all, eternally, stuffy in summer and draughty in winter? Women? He could only remember little rooms within little rooms, like a nest of Chinese paper boxes, and if he thought of one woman he saw the worn loneliness that the furniture of that room seemed built of. And he himself—he was a man who always wore rather wide-brimmed black hats, and in the wavy hotel mirrors had looked something like a bull-fighter, as he paused for that inevitable instant on the land-ing, walking downstairs to supper. . . . He leaned out of the car again, and once more the sun pushed at his head.

Bowman had wanted to reach Beulah by dark, to go to bed and sleep off his fatigue. As he remembered, Beulah was fifty miles away from the last town, on a gravelled road. This was only a cow trail. How had he ever come to such a place? One hand wiped the sweat from his face, and he drove on.

He had made the Beulah trip before. But he had never seen this hill or this petering-out path before—or that cloud, he thought shyly, looking up and then down quickly—any more than he had seen this day before. Why did he not admit he was simply lost and had been for miles? . . . He was not in the habit of asking the way of strangers, and these people never knew where the very roads they lived on went to; but then he had not even been close enough to anyone to call out. People standing in the fields now and then, or on top of the haystacks, had been too far away, looking like leaning sticks or weeds, turning a little at the solitary rattle of his car across their countryside, watching the pale sobered winter dust where it chunked out behind like big squashes down the road. The stares of these distant people had followed him solidly like a wall, impenetrable, behind which they turned back after he had passed.

The cloud floated there to one side like the bolster on his grandmother's bed. It went over a cabin on the edge of a hill, where two bare chinaberry trees clutched at the sky. He drove through a heap of dead oak leaves, his wheels stirring their weightless sides to make a silvery melancholy whistle as the car passed through their bed. No car had been along this way ahead of him. Then he saw that he was on the edge of a ravine that fell away, a red erosion, and that this was indeed the road's end.

He pulled the brake. But it did not hold, though he put all his strength into it. The car, tipped toward the edge, rolled a little. Without doubt, it was going over the bank.

He got out quietly, as though some mischief had been done him and he had his dignity to remember. He lifted his bag and sample case out, set them down, and stood back and watched the car roll over the edge. He heard something—not the crash he was listening for, but a slow un-uproarious crackle. Rather distastefully he went to look over, and he saw that his car had fallen into a tangle of immense grape vines as thick as his arm, which caught it and held it, rocked it like a grotesque child in a dark cradle, and then, as he watched, concerned somehow that he was not still inside it, re-leased it gently to the ground.

He sighed.

Where am I? he wondered with a shock. Why didn't I do something? All his anger seemed to have drifted away from him. There was the house, back on the hill. He took a bag in each hand and with almost childlike willingness went toward it. But his breathing came with difficulty, and he had to stop to rest.

It was a shotgun house, two rooms and an open passage between, perched on the hill. The whole cabin slanted a little under the heavy heaped-up vine that covered the roof, light and green, as though forgotten from summer. A woman stood in the passage.

He stopped still. Then all of a sudden his heart began to behave strangely. Like a rocket set off, it began to leap and expand into uneven patterns of beats which showered into his brain, and he could not think. But in scattering and falling it made no noise. It shot up with great power, almost elation, and fell gently, like acrobats into nets. It began to pound profoundly, then waited irresponsibly, hitting in some sort of inward mockery first at his ribs, then against his eyes, then under his shoulder blades, and against the roof of his mouth when he tried to say, "Good afternoon, madam." But he could not hear his heart—it was as quiet as ashes falling. This was rather comforting; still, it was shocking to Bowman to feel his heart beating at all.

Stockstill in his confusion, he dropped his bags, which seemed to drift in slow bulks gracefully through the air and to cushion themselves on the grey prostrate grass near the doorstep.

As for the woman standing there, he saw at once that she was old. Since she could not possibly hear his heart, he ignored the pounding and now looked at her carefully, and yet in his distraction dreamily, with his mouth open.

She had been cleaning the lamp, and held it, half blackened, half clear, in front of her. He saw her with the dark passage behind her. She was a big woman with a weather-beaten but unwrinkled face; her lips were held tightly together, and her eyes looked with a curious dulled brightness into his. He looked at her shoes, which were like bundles. If it were summer she would be barefoot. . . . Bowman, who automatically judged a woman's age on sight, set her age at fifty. She wore a formless garment of some grey coarse material, rough-dried from a washing, from which her arms appeared pink and unexpectedly round. When she never said a word, and sustained her quiet pose of holding the lamp, he was convinced of the strength in her body.

"Good afternoon, madam," he said.

She stared on, whether at him or at the air around him he could not tell, but after a moment she lowered her eyes to show that she would listen to whatever he had to say.

"I wonder if you would be interested—" He tried once more. "An accident—my car . . ."

Her voice emerged low and remote, like a sound across a lake. "Sonny he ain't here."

"Sonny?"

"Sonny ain't here now."

Her son—a fellow able to bring my car up, he decided in blurred relief. He pointed down the hill. "My car's in the bottom of the ditch. I'll need help."

"Sonny ain't here, but he'll be here."

She was becoming clearer to him and her voice stronger, and Bowman saw that she was stupid.

He was hardly surprised at the deepening postponement and tedium of his journey. He took a breath, and heard his voice speaking over the silent   10 blows of his heart. "I was sick. I am not strong yet. . . . May I come in?"

He stooped and laid his big black hat over the handle on his bag. It was a humble motion, almost a bow, that instantly struck him as absurd and betraying of all his weakness. He looked up at the woman, the wind blowing his hair. He might have continued for a long time in this unfamiliar attitude; he had never been a patient man, but when he was sick he had learned to sink submissively into the pillows, to wait for his medicine. He waited on the woman.

Then she, looking at him with blue eyes, turned and held open the door, and after a moment Bowman, as if convinced in his action, stood erect   20 and followed her in.

Inside, the darkness of the house touched him like a professional hand, the doctor's. The woman set the half-cleaned lamp on a table in the centre of the room and pointed, also like a professional person, a guide, to a chair with a yellow cowhide seat. She herself crouched on the hearth, drawing her knees up under the shapeless dress.

At first he felt hopefully secure. His heart was quieter. The room was enclosed in the gloom of yellow pine boards. He could see the other room, with the foot of an iron bed showing, across the passage. The bed had been   30 made up with a red-and-yellow pieced quilt that looked like a map or a picture, a little like his grandmother's girlhood painting of Rome burning.

He had ached for coolness, but in this room it was cold. He stared at the hearth with dead coals lying on it and iron pots in the corners. The hearth and smoked chimney were of the stone he had seen ribbing the hills, mostly slate. Why is there no fire? he wondered.

And it was so still. The silence of the fields seemed to enter and move familiarly through the house. The wind used the open hall. He felt that he was in a mysterious, quiet, cool danger. It was necessary to do what? . . . To talk.   40

"I have a nice line of women's low-priced shoes . . ." he said.

But the woman answered, "Sonny'll be here. He's strong. Sonny'll move your car."

"Where is he now?"

"Farms for Mr. Redmond."

Mr. Redmond. Mr. Redmond. That was someone he would never have to encounter, and he was glad. Somehow the name did not appeal to him. . . . In a flare of touchiness and anxiety, Bowman wished to avoid even mention of unknown men and their unknown farms.

"Do you two live here alone?" He was surprised to hear his old voice, chatty, confidential, inflected for selling shoes, asking a question like that—a thing he did not even want to know.

"Yes. We are alone."

He was surprised at the way she answered. She had taken a long time to say that. She had nodded her head in a deep way too. Had she wished to affect him with some sort of premonition? he wondered unhappily. Or was it only that she would not help him, after all, by talking with him? For he was not strong enough to receive the impact of unfamiliar things without a little talk to break their fall. He had lived a month in which nothing had happened except in his head and his body—an almost inaudible life of heartbeats and dreams that came back, a life of fever and privacy, a delicate life which had left him weak to the point of—what? Of begging. The pulse in his palm leapt like a trout in a brook.

He wondered over and over why the woman did not go ahead with cleaning the lamp. What prompted her to stay there across the room, silently bestowing her presence upon him? He saw that with her it was not a time for doing little tasks. Her face was grave; she was feeling how right she was. Perhaps it was only politeness. In docility he held his eyes stiffly wide; they fixed themselves on the woman's clasped hands as though she held the cord they were strung on.

Then, "Sonny's coming," she said.

He himself had not heard anything, but there came a man passing the window and then plunging in at the door, with two hounds beside him. Sonny was a big enough man, with his belt slung low about his hips. He looked at least thirty. He had a hot, red face that was yet full of silence. He wore muddy blue pants and an old military coat stained and patched. World War? Bowman wondered. Great God, it was a Confederate coat. On the back of his light hair he had a wide filthy black hat which seemed to insult Bowman's own. He pushed down the dogs from his chest. He was strong with dignity and heaviness in his way of moving. . . . There was the resemblance to his mother.

They stood side by side. . . . He must account again for his presence here.

"Sonny, this man, he had his car to run off over the prec'pice an' wants to know if you will git it out for him," the woman said after a few minutes.

Bowman could not even state his case.

Sonny's eyes lay upon him.

He knew he should offer explanations and show money—at least appear either penitent or authoritative. But all he could do was to shrug slightly.

Sonny brushed by him going to the window, followed by the eager dogs, and looked out. There was effort even in the way he was looking, as if he could throw his sight out like a rope. Without turning Bowman felt that his own eyes could have seen nothing: it was too far.

"Got me a mule out there an' got me a block an' tackle," said Sonny meaningfully. "I *could* catch me my mule an' git me my ropes, an' before long I'd git your car out the ravine."

He looked completely round the room, as if in meditation, his eyes   10
roving in their own distance. Then he pressed his lips firmly and yet shyly together, and with the dogs ahead of him this time, he lowered his head and strode out. The hard earth sounded, cupping to his powerful way of walking —almost a stagger.

Mischievously, at the suggestion of those sounds, Bowman's heart leapt again. It seemed to walk about inside him.

"Sonny's goin' to do it," the woman said. She said it again, singing it almost, like a song. She was sitting in her place by the hearth.

Without looking out, he heard some shouts and the dogs barking and the pounding of hoofs in short runs on the hill. In a few minutes Sonny   20
passed under the window with a rope, and there was a brown mule with quivering, shining, purple-looking ears. The mule actually looked in the window. Under its eyelashes it turned target-like eyes into his. Bowman averted his head and saw the woman looking serenely back at the mule, with only satisfaction in her face.

She sang a little more, under her breath. It occurred to him, and it seemed quite marvellous, that she was not really talking to him, but rather following the thing that came about with words that were unconscious and part of her looking.

So he said nothing, and this time when he did not reply he felt a curi-   30
ous and strong emotion, not fear, rise up in him.

This time, when his heart leapt, something—his soul—seemed to leap too, like a little colt invited out of a pen. He stared at the woman while the frantic nimbleness of his feeling made his head sway. He could not move; there was nothing he could do, unless perhaps he might embrace this woman who sat there growing old and shapeless before him.

But he wanted to leap up, to say to her, I have been sick and I found out then, only then, how lonely I am. Is it too late? My heart puts up a struggle inside me, and you may have heard it, protesting against empti-ness. . . . It should be full, he would rush on to tell her, thinking of his   40
heart now as a deep lake, it should be holding love like other hearts. It should be flooded with love. There would be a warm spring day . . . Come and stand in my heart, whoever you are, and a whole river would cover your feet and rise higher and take your knees in whirlpools, and draw you down to itself, your whole body, your heart too.

But he moved a trembling hand across his eyes, and looked at the placid crouching woman across the room. She was still as a statue. He felt ashamed and exhausted by the thought that he might, in one more moment, have tried by simple words and embraces to communicate some strange thing—something which seemed always to have just escaped him . . .

Sunlight touched the farthest pot on the hearth. It was late afternoon. This time to-morrow he would be somewhere on a good gravelled road, driving his car past things that happened to people, quicker than their happening. Seeing ahead to the next day, he was glad, and knew that this was no time to embrace an old woman. He could feel in his pounding temples   10
the readying of his blood for motion and for hurrying away.

"Sonny's hitched up your car by now," said the woman. "He'll git it out the ravine right shortly."

"Fine!" he cried with his customary enthusiasm.

Yet it seemed a long time that they waited. It began to get dark. Bowman was cramped in his chair. Any man should know enough to get up and walk around while he waited. There was something like guilt in such stillness and silence.

But instead of getting up, he listened. . . . His breathing restrained,   20
his eyes powerless in the growing dark, he listened uneasily for a warning sound, forgetting in wariness what it would be. Before long he heard something—soft, continuous, insinuating.

"What's the noise?" he asked, his voice jumping into the dark. Then wildly he was afraid it would be his heart beating so plainly in the quiet room, and she would tell him so.

"You might hear the stream," she said grudgingly.

Her voice was closer. She was standing by the table. He wondered why she did not light the lamp. She stood there in the dark and did not light it.

Bowman would never speak to her now, for the time was past. I'll   30
sleep in the dark, he thought, in his bewilderment pitying himself.

Heavily she moved on to the window. Her arm, vaguely white, rose straight from her full side and she pointed out into the darkness.

"That white speck's Sonny," she said, talking to herself.

He turned unwillingly and peered over her shoulder; he hesitated to rise and stand beside her. His eyes searched the dusky air. The white speck floated smoothly toward her finger, like a leaf on a river, growing whiter in the dark. It was as if she had shown him something secret, part of her life, but had offered no explanation. He looked away. He was moved almost to tears, feeling for no reason that she had made a silent declaration equivalent   40
to his own. His hand waited upon his chest.

Then a step shook the house, and Sonny was in the room. Bowman felt how the woman left him there and went to the other man's side.

"I done got your car out, mister," said Sonny's voice in the dark. "She's settin' a-waitin' in the road, turned to go back where she come from."

"Fine!" said Bowman, projecting his own voice to loudness. "I'm surely much obliged—I could never have done it myself—I was sick. . . ."

"I could do it easy," said Sonny.

Bowman could feel them both waiting in the dark, and he could hear the dogs panting out in the yard, waiting to bark when he should go. He felt strangely helpless and resentful. Now that he could go, he longed to stay. From what was he being deprived? His chest was rudely shaken by the violence of his heart. These people cherished something here that he could not see, they withheld some ancient promise of food and warmth and light. Between them they had a conspiracy. He thought of the way she had   10 moved away from him and gone to Sonny, she had flowed toward him. He was shaking with cold, he was tired, and it was not fair. Humbly and yet angrily he stuck his hand into his pocket.

"Of course I'm going to pay you for everything—"

"We don't take money for such," said Sonny's voice belligerently.

"I want to pay. But do something more . . . Let me stay—to-night. . . ." He took another step toward them. If only they could see him, they would know his sincerity, his real need! His voice went on, "I'm not very strong yet, I'm not able to walk far, even back to my car, maybe, I don't know—I don't know exactly where I am—"   20

He stopped. He felt as if he might burst into tears. What would they think of him!

Sonny came over and put his hands on him. Bowman felt them pass (they were professional too) across his chest, over his hips. He could feel Sonny's eyes upon him in the dark.

"You ain't no revenuer come sneakin' here, mister, ain't got no gun?"

To this end of nowhere! And yet *he* had come. He made a grave answer. "No."

"You can stay."

30

"Sonny," said the woman, "you'll have to borry some fire."

"I'll go git it from Redmond's," said Sonny.

"What?" Bowman strained to hear their words to each other.

"Our fire, it's out, and Sonny's got to borry some, because it's dark an' cold," she said.

"But matches—I have matches—"

"We don't have no need for 'em," she said proudly. "Sonny's goin' after his own fire."

"I'm goin' to Redmond's," said Sonny with an air of importance, and he went out.   40

After they had waited a while, Bowman looked out the window and saw a light moving over the hill. It spread itself out like a little fan. It zigzagged along the field, darting and swift, not like Sonny at all. . . . Soon enough, Sonny staggered in, holding a burning stick behind him in tongs, fire flowing in his wake, blazing light into the corners of the room.

"We'll make a fire now," the woman said, taking the brand.

When that was done she lit the lamp. It showed its dark and light. The whole room turned golden-yellow like some sort of flower, and the walls smelled of it and seemed to tremble with the quiet rushing of the fire and the waving of the burning lampwick in its funnel of light.

The woman moved among the iron pots. With the tongs she dropped hot coals on top of the iron lids. They made a set of soft vibrations, like the sound of a bell far away.

She looked up and over at Bowman, but he could not answer. He was trembling. . . .   10

"Have a drink, mister?" Sonny asked. He had brought in a chair from the other room and sat astride it with his folded arms across the back. Now we are all visible, to one another, Bowman thought, and cried, "Yes sir, you bet, thanks!"

"Come after me and do just what I do," said Sonny.

It was another excursion into the dark. They went through the hall, out to the back of the house, past a shed and a hooded well. They came to a wilderness of thicket.

"Down on your knees," said Sonny.

"What?" Sweat broke out on his forehead.   20

He understood when Sonny began to crawl through a sort of tunnel that the bushes made over the ground. He followed, startled in spite of himself when a twig or a thorn touched him gently without making a sound, clinging to him and finally letting him go.

Sonny stopped crawling and, crouched on his knees, began to dig with both his hands into the dirt. Bowman shyly struck matches and made a light. In a few minutes Sonny pulled up a jug. He poured out some of the whisky into a bottle from his coat pocket, and buried the jug again. "You never know who's liable to knock at your door," he said, and laughed. "Start back," he said, almost formally. "Ain't no need for us to drink out-   30
doors, like hogs."

At the table by the fire, sitting opposite each other in their chairs, Sonny and Bowman took drinks out of the bottle, passing it across. The dogs slept; one of them was having a dream.

"This is good," said Bowman. "That is what I needed." It was just as though he were drinking the fire off the hearth.

"He makes it," said the woman with quiet pride.

She was pushing the coals off the pots, and the smells of corn bread and coffee circled the room. She set everything on the table before the men, with a bone-handled knife stuck into one of the potatoes, splitting out   40
its golden fiber. Then she stood for a minute looking at them, tall and full above them where they sat. She leaned a little toward them.

"You-all can eat now," she said, and suddenly smiled.

Bowman had just happened to be looking at her. He set his cup back

on the table in unbelieving protest. A pain pressed at his eyes. He saw that
she was not an old woman. She was young, still young. He could think of no
number of years for her. She was the same age as Sonny, and she belonged
to him. She stood with the deep dark corner of the room behind her, the
shifting yellow light scattering over her head and her grey formless dress,
trembling over her tall body when it bent over them in its sudden communication. She was young. Her teeth were shining and her eyes glowed.
She turned and walked slowly and heavily out of the room, and he heard
her sit down on the cot and then lie down. The pattern on the quilt moved.

"She goin' to have a baby," said Sonny, popping a bite into his mouth.   10

Bowman could not speak. He was shocked with knowing what was
really in this house. A marriage, a fruitful marriage. That simple thing. Anyone could have had that.

Somehow he felt unable to be indignant or protest, although some sort
of joke had certainly been played upon him. There was nothing remote or
mysterious here—only something private. The only secret was the ancient
communication between two people. But the memory of the woman's waiting silently by the cold hearth, of the man's stubborn journey a mile away to
get fire, and how they finally brought out their food and drink and filled the
room proudly with all they had to show, was suddenly too clear and too   20
enormous within him for response. . . .

"You ain't as hungry as you look," said Sonny.

The woman came out of the bedroom as soon as the men had finished,
and ate her supper while her husband stared peacefully into the fire.

Then they put the dogs out, with the food that was left.

"I think I'd better sleep here by the fire, on the floor," said Bowman.

He felt that he had been cheated, and that he could afford now to be
generous. Ill though he was, he was not going to ask them for their bed. He
was through with asking favours in this house, now that he understood what
was there.   30

"Sure, mister."

But he had not known yet how slowly he understood. They had not
meant to give him their bed. After a little interval they both rose and looking at him gravely went into the other room.

He lay stretched by the fire until it grew low and dying. He watched
every tongue of blaze lick out and vanish. "There will be special reduced
prices on all footwear during the month of January," he found himself repeating quietly, and then he lay with his lips tight shut.

How many noises the night had! He heard the stream running, the fire
dying, and he was sure now that he heard his heart beating, too, the sound it   40
made under his ribs. He heard breathing, round and deep, of the man and
his wife in the room across the passage. And that was all. But emotion
swelled patiently within him, and he wished that the child were his.

He must get back to where he had been before. He stood weakly before the red coals, and put on his overcoat. It felt too heavy on his shoulders. As he started out he looked and saw that the woman had never got through with cleaning the lamp. On some impulse he put all the money from his billfold under its fluted glass base, almost ostentatiously.

Ashamed, shrugging a little, and then shivering, he took his bags and went out. The cold of the air seemed to lift him bodily. The moon was in the sky.

On the slope he began to run, he could not help it. Just as he reached the road, where his car seemed to sit in the moonlight like a boat, his heart began to give off tremendous explosions like a rifle, bang bang bang.   10

He sank in fright on to the road, his bags falling about him. He felt as if all this had happened before. He covered his heart with both hands to keep anyone from hearing the noise it made.

But nobody heard it.

Questions

1. What images in the first four paragraphs seem particularly vivid to you? Which is established more clearly by means of these images and the paragraphs as a whole, Bowman's character or his environment?
2. What additional dimension does Miss Welty use to reveal Bowman that she does not use to reveal Sonny and his wife? How did this difference shape your own psychological responses toward the characters as the story progressed?
3. How does the author, without fatiguing the reader or appearing uncertain herself, gradually convey a sense of fatigue and uncertainty in Bowman which culminates in panic and death?
4. At what points in the story does the author emphasize the difference between the way Bowman feels and thinks and the way he speaks and acts?
5. What are the apparent dignities of Bowman's life and the apparent indignities in the lives of Sonny and his wife? How, by diction, event and tone, are both sets of appearances extinguished and new sets of realities established?

Theme topics

1. Write a study of the diction and style of "Death of a Travelling Salesman" as they relate to its meaning.
2. Discuss the salesman of this story as he was conditioned by his environment and as he is representative of conditioning forces in America.

34 FLANNERY O'CONNOR
Everything That Rises Must Converge

Her doctor had told Julian's mother that she must lose twenty pounds on account of her blood pressure, so on Wednesday nights Julian had to take her downtown on the bus for a reducing class at the Y. The reducing class was designed for working girls over fifty, who weighed from 165 to 200 pounds. His mother was one of the slimmer ones, but she said ladies did not tell their age or weight. She would not ride the buses by herself at night since they had been integrated, and because the reducing class was one of her few pleasures, necessary for her health, and *free,* she said Julian could at least put himself out to take her, considering all she did for him. Julian did not like to consider all she did for him, but every Wednesday night he braced himself and took her.

She was almost ready to go, standing before the hall mirror, putting on her hat, while he, his hands behind him, appeared pinned to the door frame, waiting like Saint Sebastian for the arrows to begin piercing him. The hat was new and had cost her seven dollars and a half. She kept saying, "Maybe I shouldn't have paid that for it. No, I shouldn't have. I'll take it off and return it tomorrow. I shouldn't have bought it."

Julian raised his eyes to heaven. "Yes, you should have bought it," he said. "Put it on and let's go." It was a hideous hat. A purple velvet flap came down on one side of it and stood up on the other; the rest of it was green and looked like a cushion with the stuffing out. He decided it was less comical than jaunty and pathetic. Everything that gave her pleasure was small and depressed him.

She lifted the hat one more time and set it down slowly on top of her head. Two wings of gray hair protruded on either side of her florid face, but her eyes, sky-blue, were as innocent and untouched by experience as they must have been when she was ten. Were it not that she was a widow who had struggled fiercely to feed and clothe and put him through school and who was supporting him still, "until he got on his feet," she might have been a little girl that he had to take to town.

"It's all right, it's all right," he said. "Let's go." He opened the door himself and started down the walk to get her going. The sky was a dying violet and the houses stood out darkly against it, bulbous liver-colored monstrosities of a uniform ugliness though no two were alike. Since this had been a fashionable neighborhood forty years ago, his mother persisted in thinking they did well to have an apartment in it. Each house had a narrow collar of dirt around it in which sat, usually, a grubby child. Julian walked with his hands in his pockets, his head down and thrust forward and his eyes glazed with the determination to make himself completely numb during the time he would be sacrificed to her pleasure.

The door closed and he turned to find the dumpy figure, surmounted by the atrocious hat, coming toward him. "Well," she said, "you only live once and paying a little more for it, I at least won't meet myself coming and going."

"Some day I'll start making money," Julian said gloomily—he knew he never would—"and you can have one of those jokes whenever you take the fit." But first they would move. He visualized a place where the nearest neighbors would be three miles away on either side.

"I think you're doing fine," she said, drawing on her gloves. "You've only been out of school a year. Rome wasn't built in a day."

She was one of the few members of the Y reducing class who arrived in hat and gloves and who had a son who had been to college. "It takes time," she said, "and the world is in such a mess. This hat looked better on me than any of the others, though when she brought it out I said, 'Take that thing back. I wouldn't have it on my head,' and she said, 'Now wait till you see it on,' and when she put it on me, I said, 'We-ull,' and she said, 'If you ask me, that hat does something for you and you do something for the hat, and besides,' she said, 'with that hat, you won't meet yourself coming and going.'"

Julian thought he could have stood his lot better if she had been selfish, if she had been an old hag who drank and screamed at him. He walked along, saturated in depression, as if in the midst of his martyrdom he had lost his faith. Catching sight of his long, hopeless, irritated face, she stopped suddenly with a grief-stricken look, and pulled back on his arm. "Wait on me," she said. "I'm going back to the house and take this thing off and tomorrow I'm going to return it. I was out of my head. I can pay the gas bill with that seven-fifty."

He caught her arm in a vicious grip. "You are not going to take it back," he said. "I like it."

"Well," she said, "I don't think I ought . . ."

"Shut up and enjoy it," he muttered, more depressed than ever.

"With the world in the mess it's in," she said, "it's a wonder we can enjoy anything. I tell you, the bottom rail is on the top."

Julian sighed.

"Of course," she said, "if you know who you are, you can go anywhere." She said this every time he took her to the reducing class. "Most of them in it are not our kind of people," she said, "but I can be gracious to anybody. I know who I am."

"They don't give a damn for your graciousness," Julian said savagely. "Knowing who you are is good for one generation only. You haven't the foggiest idea where you stand now or who you are."

She stopped and allowed her eyes to flash at him. "I most certainly do know who I am," she said, "and if you don't know who you are, I'm ashamed of you."

"Oh hell," Julian said.   10

"Your great-grandfather was a former governor of this state," she said. "Your grandfather was a prosperous landowner. Your grandmother was a Godhigh."

"Will you look around you," he said tensely, "and see where you are now?" and he swept his arm jerkily out to indicate the neighborhood, which the growing darkness at least made less dingy.

"You remain what you are," she said. "Your great-grandfather had a plantation and two hundred slaves."

"There are no more slaves," he said irritably.

"They were better off when they were," she said. He groaned to see   20 that she was off on that topic. She rolled onto it every few days like a train on an open track. He knew every stop, every junction, every swamp along the way, and knew the exact point at which her conclusion would roll majestically into the station: "It's ridiculous. It's simply not realistic. They should rise, yes, but on their own side of the fence."

"Let's skip it," Julian said.

"The ones I feel sorry for," she said, "are the ones that are half white. They're tragic."

"Will you skip it?"

"Suppose we were half white. We would certainly have mixed feelings."   30

"I have mixed feelings now," he groaned.

"Well let's talk about something pleasant," she said. "I remember going to Grandpa's when I was a little girl. Then the house had double stairways that went up to what was really the second floor—all the cooking was done on the first. I used to like to stay down in the kitchen on account of the way the walls smelled. I would sit with my nose pressed against the plaster and take deep breaths. Actually the place belonged to the Godhighs but your grandfather Chestny paid the mortgage and saved it for them. They were in reduced circumstances," she said, "but reduced or not, they never forgot who they were."   40

"Doubtless that decayed mansion reminded them," Julian muttered. He never spoke of it without contempt or thought of it without longing. He had seen it once when he was a child before it had been sold. The double stairways had rotted and been torn down. Negroes were living in it. But it remained in his mind as his mother had known it. It appeared in his dreams regularly. He would stand on the wide porch, listening to the rustle of oak leaves, then wander through the high-ceilinged hall into the parlor that opened onto it and gaze at the worn rugs and faded draperies. It occurred to him that it was he, not she, who could have appreciated it. He preferred its threadbare elegance to anything he could name and it was because of it that all the neighborhoods they had lived in had been a torment to him—whereas she had hardly known the difference. She called her insensitivity "being adjustable."

"And I remember the old darky who was my nurse, Caroline. There   10
was no better person in the world. I've always had a great respect for my colored friends," she said. "I'd do anything in the world for them and they'd . . ."

"Will you for God's sake get off that subject?" Julian said. When he got on a bus by himself, he made it a point to sit down beside a Negro, in reparation as it were for his mother's sins.

"You're mighty touchy tonight," she said. "Do you feel all right?"

"Yes I feel all right," he said. "Now lay off."

She pursed her lips. "Well, you certainly are in a vile humor," she observed. "I just won't speak to you at all."   20

They had reached the bus stop. There was no bus in sight and Julian, his hands still jammed in his pockets and his head thrust forward, scowled down the empty street. The frustration of having to wait on the bus as well as ride on it began to creep up his neck like a hot hand. The presence of his mother was borne in upon him as she gave a pained sigh. He looked at her bleakly. She was holding herself very erect under the preposterous hat, wearing it like a banner of her imaginary dignity. There was in him an evil urge to break her spirit. He suddenly unloosened his tie and pulled it off and put it in his pocket.

She stiffened. "Why must you look like *that* when you take me to   30
town?" she said. "Why must you deliberately embarrass me?"

"If you'll never learn where you are," he said, "you can at least learn where I am."

"You look like a—thug," she said.

"Then I must be one," he murmured.

"I'll just go home," she said. "I will not bother you. If you can't do a little thing like that for me . . ."

Rolling his eyes upward, he put his tie back on. "Restored to my class," he muttered. He thrust his face toward her and hissed, "True culture is in the mind, the *mind*," he said, and tapped his head, "the mind."   40

"It's in the heart," she said, "and in how you do things and how you do things is because of who you *are.*"

"Nobody in the damn bus cares who you are."

"I care who I am," she said icily.

The lighted bus appeared on top of the next hill and as it approached, they moved out into the street to meet it. He put his hand under her elbow and hoisted her up on the creaking step. She entered with a little smile, as if she were going into a drawing room where everyone had been waiting for her. While he put in the tokens, she sat down on one of the broad front seats for three which faced the aisle. A thin woman with protruding teeth and long yellow hair was sitting on the end of it. His mother moved up beside her and left room for Julian beside herself. He sat down and looked at the floor across the aisle where a pair of thin feet in red and white canvas sandals were planted.   10

His mother immediately began a general conversation meant to attract anyone who felt like talking. "Can it get any hotter?" she said and removed from her purse a folding fan, black with a Japanese scene on it, which she began to flutter before her.

"I reckon it might could," the woman with the protruding teeth said, "but I know for a fact my apartment couldn't get no hotter."

"It must get the afternoon sun," his mother said. She sat forward and looked up and down the bus. It was half filled. Everybody was white. "I see we have the bus to ourselves," she said. Julian cringed.

"For a change," said the woman across the aisle, the owner of the red   20
and white canvas sandals. "I come on one the other day and they were thick as fleas—up front and all through."

"The world is in a mess everywhere," his mother said. "I don't know how we've let it get in this fix."

"What gets my goat is all those boys from good families stealing automobile tires," the woman with the protruding teeth said. "I told my boy, I said you may not be rich but you been raised right and if I ever catch you in any such mess, they can send you on to the reformatory. Be exactly where you belong."

"Training tells," his mother said. "Is your boy in high school?"   30

"Ninth grade," the woman said.

"My son just finished college last year. He wants to write but he's selling typewriters until he gets started," his mother said.

The woman leaned forward and peered at Julian. He threw her such a malevolent look that she subsided against the seat. On the floor across the aisle there was an abandoned newspaper. He got up and got it and opened it out in front of him. His mother discreetly continued the conversation in a lower tone but the woman across the aisle said in a loud voice, "Well that's nice. Selling typewriters is close to writing. He can go right from one to the other."   40

"I tell him," his mother said, "that Rome wasn't built in a day."

Behind the newspaper Julian was withdrawing into the inner compartment of his mind where he spent most of his time. This was a kind of mental bubble in which he established himself when he could not bear to be a part of what was going on around him. From it he could see out and judge but in it he was safe from any kind of penetration from without. It was the only place where he felt free of the general idiocy of his fellows. His mother had never entered it but from it he could see her with absolute clarity.

The old lady was clever enough and he thought that if she had started from any of the right premises, more might have been expected of her. She lived according to the laws of her own fantasy world, outside of which he had never seen her set foot. The law of it was to sacrifice herself for him after she had first created the necessity to do so by making a mess of things. If he had permitted her sacrifices, it was only because her lack of foresight had made them necessary. All of her life had been a struggle to act like a Chestny without the Chestny goods, and to give him everything she thought a Chestny ought to have; but since, said she, it was fun to struggle, why complain? And when you had won, as she had won, what fun to look back on the hard times! He could not forgive her that she had enjoyed the struggle and that she thought *she* had won.

What she meant when she said she had won was that she had brought him up successfully and had sent him to college and that he had turned out so well—good looking (her teeth had gone unfilled so that his could be straightened), intelligent (he realized he was too intelligent to be a success), and with a future ahead of him (there was of course no future ahead of him). She excused his gloominess on the grounds that he was still growing up and his radical ideas on his lack of practical experience. She said he didn't yet know a thing about "life," that he hadn't even entered the real world—when already he was as disenchanted with it as a man of fifty.

The further irony of all this was that in spite of her, he had turned out so well. In spite of going to only a third-rate college, he had, on his own initiative, come out with a first-rate education; in spite of growing up dominated by a small mind, he had ended up with a large one; in spite of all her foolish views, he was free of prejudice and unafraid to face facts. Most miraculous of all, instead of being blinded by love for her as she was for him, he had cut himself emotionally free of her and could see her with complete objectivity. He was not dominated by his mother.

The bus stopped with a sudden jerk and shook him from his meditation. A woman from the back lurched forward with little steps and barely escaped falling in his newspaper as she righted herself. She got off and a large Negro got on. Julian kept his paper lowered to watch. It gave him a certain satisfaction to see injustice in daily operation. It confirmed his view that with a few exceptions there was no one worth knowing within a radius of three hundred miles. The Negro was well dressed and carried a briefcase. He looked around and then sat down on the other end of the seat where the woman with the red and white canvas sandals was sitting. He immediately unfolded a newspaper and obscured himself behind it. Julian's mother's elbow at once prodded insistently into his ribs. "Now you see why I won't ride on these buses by myself," she whispered.

The woman with the red and white canvas sandals had risen at the same time the Negro sat down and had gone further back in the bus and taken the seat of the woman who had got off. His mother leaned forward and cast her an approving look.

Julian rose, crossed the aisle, and sat down in the place of the woman with the canvas sandals. From this position, he looked serenely across at his mother. Her face had turned an angry red. He stared at her, making his eyes the eyes of a stranger. He felt his tension suddenly lift as if he had openly declared war on her.

He would have liked to get in conversation with the Negro and to talk with him about art or politics or any subject that would be above the comprehension of those around them, but the man remained entrenched behind his paper. He was either ignoring the change of seating or had never noticed it. There was no way for Julian to convey his sympathy.

His mother kept her eyes fixed reproachfully on his face. The woman with the protruding teeth was looking at him avidly as if he were a type of monster new to her.

"Do you have a light?" he asked the Negro.

Without looking away from his paper, the man reached in his pocket and handed him a packet of matches.

"Thanks," Julian said. For a moment he held the matches foolishly. A NO SMOKING sign looked down upon him from over the door. This alone would not have deterred him; he had no cigarettes. He had quit smoking some months before because he could not afford it. "Sorry," he muttered and handed back the matches. The Negro lowered the paper and gave him an annoyed look. He took the matches and raised the paper again.

His mother continued to gaze at him but she did not take advantage of his momentary discomfort. Her eyes retained their battered look. Her face seemed to be unnaturally red, as if her blood pressure had risen. Julian allowed no glimmer of sympathy to show on his face. Having got the advantage, he wanted desperately to keep it and carry it through. He would have liked to teach her a lesson that would last her a while, but there seemed no way to continue the point. The Negro refused to come out from behind his paper.

Julian folded his arms and looked stolidly before him, facing her but as if he did not see her, as if he had ceased to recognize her existence. He visualized a scene in which, the bus having reached their stop, he would remain in his seat and when she said, "Aren't you going to get off?" he would look at her as at a stranger who had rashly addressed him. The corner they got off on was usually deserted, but it was well lighted and it would not hurt her to walk by herself the four blocks to the Y. He decided to wait until the time came and then decide whether or not he would let her get off by herself. He would have to be at the Y at ten to bring her back, but he could leave her wondering if he was going to show up. There was no reason for her to think she could always depend on him.

He retired again into the high-ceilinged room sparsely settled with large pieces of antique furniture. His soul expanded momentarily but then he became aware of his mother across from him and the vision shriveled. He studied her coldly. Her feet in little pumps dangled like a child's and did not quite reach the floor. She was training on him an exaggerated look of reproach. He felt completely detached from her. At that moment he could with pleasure have slapped her as he would have slapped a particularly obnoxious child in his charge.

He began to imagine various unlikely ways by which he could teach her a lesson. He might make friends with some distinguished Negro professor or lawyer and bring him home to spend the evening. He would be entirely justified but her blood pressure would rise to 300. He could not push her to the extent of making her have a stroke, and moreover, he had never been successful at making any Negro friends. He had tried to strike up an acquaintance on the bus with some of the better types, with ones that looked like professors or ministers or lawyers. One morning he had sat down next to a distinguished-looking dark brown man who had answered his questions with a sonorous solemnity but who had turned out to be an undertaker. Another day he had sat down beside a cigar-smoking Negro with a diamond ring on his finger, but after a few stilted pleasantries, the Negro had rung the buzzer and risen, slipping two lottery tickets into Julian's hand as he climbed over him to leave.

He imagined his mother lying desperately ill and his being able to secure only a Negro doctor for her. He toyed with that idea for a few minutes and then dropped it for a momentary vision of himself participating as a sympathizer in a sit-in demonstration. This was possible but he did not linger with it. Instead, he approached the ultimate horror. He brought home a beautiful suspiciously Negroid woman. Prepare yourself, he said. There is nothing you can do about it. This is the woman I've chosen. She's intelligent, dignified, even good, and she's suffered and she hasn't thought it *fun*. Now persecute us, go ahead and persecute us. Drive her out of here, but remember, you're driving me too. His eyes were narrowed and through the indignation he had generated, he saw his mother across the aisle, purple-faced, shrunken to the dwarf-like proportions of her moral nature, sitting like a mummy beneath the ridiculous banner of her hat.

He was tilted out of his fantasy again as the bus stopped. The door opened with a sucking hiss and out of the dark a large, gaily dressed, sullen-looking colored woman got on with a little boy. The child, who might have been four, had on a short plaid suit and a Tyrolean hat with a blue feather in it. Julian hoped that he would sit down beside him and that the woman would push in beside his mother. He could think of no better arrangement.

As she waited for her tokens, the woman was surveying the seating possibilities—he hoped with the idea of sitting where she was least wanted. There was something familiar-looking about her but Julian could not place what it was. She was a giant of a woman. Her face was set not only to meet opposition but to seek it out. The downward tilt of her large lower lip was like a warning sign: DON'T TAMPER WITH ME. Her bulging figure was encased in a green crepe dress and her feet overflowed in red shoes. She had on a hideous hat. A purple velvet flap came down on one side of it and stood up on the other; the rest of it was green and looked like a cushion   10
with the stuffing out. She carried a mammoth red pocketbook that bulged throughout as if it were stuffed with rocks.

To Julian's disappointment, the little boy climbed up on the empty seat beside his mother. His mother lumped all children, black and white, into the common category, "cute," and she thought little Negroes were on the whole cuter than little white children. She smiled at the little boy as he climbed on the seat.

Meanwhile the woman was bearing down upon the empty seat beside Julian. To his annoyance, she squeezed herself into it. He saw his mother's face change as the woman settled herself next to him and he realized with   20
satisfaction that this was more objectionable to her than it was to him. Her face seemed almost gray and there was a look of dull recognition in her eyes, as if suddenly she had sickened at some awful confrontation. Julian saw that it was because she and the woman had, in a sense, swapped sons. Though his mother would not realize the symbolic significance of this, she would feel it. His amusement showed plainly on his face.

The woman next to him muttered something unintelligible to herself. He was conscious of a kind of bristling next to him, a muted growling like that of an angry cat. He could not see anything but the red pocketbook upright on the bulging green thighs. He visualized the woman as she had stood   30
waiting for her tokens—the ponderous figure, rising from the red shoes upward over the solid hips, the mammoth bosom, the haughty face, to the green and purple hat.

His eyes widened.

The vision of the two hats, identical, broke upon him with the radiance of a brilliant sunrise. His face was suddenly lit with joy. He could not believe that Fate had thrust upon his mother such a lesson. He gave a loud chuckle so that she would look at him and see that he saw. She turned her eyes on him slowly. The blue in them seemed to have turned a bruised purple. For a moment he had an uncomfortable sense of her innocence, but it   40
lasted only a second before principle rescued him. Justice entitled him to laugh. His grin hardened until it said to her as plainly as if he were saying aloud: Your punishment exactly fits your pettiness. This should teach you a permanent lesson.

Her eyes shifted to the woman. She seemed unable to bear looking at him and to find the woman preferable. He became conscious again of the bristling presence at his side. The woman was rumbling like a volcano about to become active. His mother's mouth began to twitch slightly at one corner. With a sinking heart, he saw incipient signs of recovery on her face and realized that this was going to strike her suddenly as funny and was going to be no lesson at all. She kept her eyes on the woman and an amused smile came over her face as if the woman were a monkey that had stolen her hat. The little Negro was looking up at her with large fascinated eyes. He had been trying to attract her attention for some time.

"Carver!" the woman said suddenly. "Come heah!"

When he saw that the spotlight was on him at last, Carver drew his feet up and turned himself toward Julian's mother and giggled.

"Carver!" the woman said. "You heah me? Come heah!"

Carver slid down from the seat but remained squatting with his back against the base of it, his head turned slyly around toward Julian's mother, who was smiling at him. The woman reached a hand across the aisle and snatched him to her. He righted himself and hung backwards on her knees, grinning at Julian's mother. "Isn't he cute?" Julian's mother said to the woman with the protruding teeth.

"I reckon he is," the woman said without conviction.

The Negress yanked him upright but he eased out of her grip and shot across the aisle and scrambled, giggling wildly, onto the seat beside his love.

"I think he likes me," Julian's mother said, and smiled at the woman. It was the smile she used when she was being particularly gracious to an inferior. Julian saw everything lost. The lesson had rolled off her like rain on a roof.

The woman stood up and yanked the little boy off the seat as if she were snatching him from contagion. Julian could feel the rage in her at having no weapon like his mother's smile. She gave the child a sharp slap across his leg. He howled once and then thrust his head into her stomach and kicked his feet against her shins. "Be-have," she said vehemently.

The bus stopped and the Negro who had been reading the newspaper got off. The woman moved over and set the little boy down with a thump between herself and Julian. She held him firmly by the knee. In a moment he put his hands in front of his face and peeped at Julian's mother through his fingers.

"I see yoooooooo!" she said and put her hand in front of her face and peeped at him.

The woman slapped his hand down. "Quit yo' foolishness," she said, "before I knock the living Jesus out of you!"

Julian was thankful that the next stop was theirs. He reached up and pulled the cord. The woman reached up and pulled it at the same time. Oh my God, he thought. He had the terrible intuition that when they got off the

bus together, his mother would open her purse and give the little boy a
nickel. The gesture would be as natural to her as breathing. The bus stopped
and the woman got up and lunged to the front, dragging the child, who
wished to stay on, after her. Julian and his mother got up and followed. As
they neared the door, Julian tried to relieve her of her pocketbook.

"No," she murmured, "I want to give the little boy a nickel."

"No!" Julian hissed. "No!"

She smiled down at the child and opened her bag. The bus door
opened and the woman picked him up by the arm and descended with him,
hanging at her hip. Once in the street she set him down and shook him.   10

Julian's mother had to close her purse while she got down the bus step
but as soon as her feet were on the ground, she opened it again and began
to rummage inside. "I can't find but a penny," she whispered, "but it looks
like a new one."

"Don't do it!" Julian said fiercely between his teeth. There was a
streetlight on the corner and she hurried to get under it so that she could
better see into her pocketbook. The woman was heading off rapidly down
the street with the child still hanging backward on her hand.

"Oh little boy!" Julian's mother called and took a few quick steps and
caught up with them just beyond the lamppost. "Here's a bright new penny   20
for you," and she held out the coin, which shone bronze in the dim light.

The huge woman turned and for a moment stood, her shoulders lifted
and her face frozen with frustrated rage, and stared at Julian's mother. Then
all at once she seemed to explode like a piece of machinery that had been
given one ounce of pressure too much. Julian saw the black fist swing out
with the red pocketbook. He shut his eyes and cringed as he heard the
woman shout, "He don't take nobody's pennies!" When he opened his eyes,
the woman was disappearing down the street with the little boy staring wide-
eyed over her shoulder. Julian's mother was sitting on the sidewalk.

"I told you not to do that," Julian said angrily. "I told you not to do   30
that!"

He stood over her for a minute, gritting his teeth. Her legs were
stretched out in front of her and her hat was on her lap. He squatted down
and looked her in the face. It was totally expressionless. "You got exactly
what you deserved," he said. "Now get up."

He picked up her pocketbook and put what had fallen out back in it.
He picked the hat up off her lap. The penny caught his eye on the sidewalk
and he picked that up and let it drop before her eyes into the purse. Then
he stood up and leaned over and held his hands out to pull her up. She remained immobile. He sighed. Rising above them on either side were black   40
apartment buildings, marked with irregular rectangles of light. At the end of
the block a man came out of a door and walked off in the opposite direction. "All right," he said, "suppose somebody happens by and wants to
know why you're sitting on the sidewalk?"

She took the hand and, breathing hard, pulled heavily up on it and then stood for a moment, swaying slightly as if the spots of light in the darkness were circling around her. Her eyes, shadowed and confused, finally settled on his face. He did not try to conceal his irritation. "I hope this teaches you a lesson," he said. She leaned forward and her eyes raked his face. She seemed trying to determine his identity. Then, as if she found nothing familiar about him, she started off with a headlong movement in the wrong direction.

"Aren't you going on to the Y?" he asked.

"Home," she muttered.

"Well, are we walking?"

For answer she kept going. Julian followed along, his hands behind him. He saw no reason to let the lesson she had had go without backing it up with an explanation of its meaning. She might as well be made to understand what had happened to her. "Don't think that was just an uppity Negro woman," he said. "That was the whole colored race which will no longer take your condescending pennies. That was your black double. She can wear the same hat as you, and to be sure," he added gratuitously (because he thought it was funny), "it looked better on her than it did on you. What all this means," he said, "is that the old world is gone. The old manners are obsolete and your graciousness is not worth a damn." He thought bitterly of the house that had been lost for him. "You aren't who you think you are," he said.

She continued to plow ahead, paying no attention to him. Her hair had come undone on one side. She dropped her pocketbook and took no notice. He stooped and picked it up and handed it to her but she did not take it.

"You needn't act as if the world had come to an end," he said, "because it hasn't. From now on you've got to live in a new world and face a few realities for a change. Buck up," he said, "it won't kill you."

She was breathing fast.

"Let's wait on the bus," he said.

"Home," she said thickly.

"I hate to see you behave like this," he said. "Just like a child. I should be able to expect more of you." He decided to stop where he was and make her stop and wait for a bus. "I'm not going any farther," he said, stopping. "We're going on the bus."

She continued to go on as if she had not heard him. He took a few steps and caught her arm and stopped her. He looked into her face and caught his breath. He was looking into a face he had never seen before. "Tell Grandpa to come get me," she said.

He stared, stricken.

"Tell Caroline to come get me," she said.

Stunned, he let her go and she lurched forward again, walking as if one leg were shorter than the other. A tide of darkness seemed to be sweeping her from him. "Mother!" he cried. "Darling, sweetheart, wait!" Crumpling she fell to the pavement. He dashed forward and fell at her side, crying, "Mamma, Mamma!" He turned her over. Her face was fiercely distorted. One eye, large and staring, moved slightly to the left as if it had become unmoored. The other remained fixed on him, raked his face again, found nothing and closed.

"Wait here, wait here!" he cried and jumped up and began to run for help toward a cluster of lights he saw in the distance ahead of him. "Help, help!" he shouted, but his voice was thin, scarcely a thread of sound. The lights drifted farther away the faster he ran and his feet moved numbly as if 10 they carried him nowhere. The tide of darkness seemed to sweep him back to her, postponing from moment to moment his entry into the world of guilt and sorrow.

Parallelism, Repetition, Metaphor

35 JAMES BALDWIN
Notes of a Native Son

1   On the 29th of July, in 1943, my father died. On the same day, a few hours later, his last child was born. Over a month before this, while all our energies were concentrated in waiting for these events, there had been, in Detroit, one of the bloodiest race riots of the century. A few hours after my father's funeral, while he lay in state in the undertaker's chapel, a race riot broke out in Harlem. On the morning of the 3rd of August, we drove my father to the graveyard through a wilderness of smashed plate glass.

2   The day of my father's funeral had also been my nineteenth birthday. As we drove him to the graveyard, the spoils of injustice, anarchy, discontent, and hatred were all around us. It seemed to me that God himself had devised, to mark my father's end, the most sustained and brutally dissonant of codas. And it seemed to me, too, that the violence which rose all about us as my father left the world had been devised as a corrective for the pride of his eldest son. I had declined to believe in that apocalypse which had been central to my father's vision; very well, life seemed to be saying, here is something that will certainly pass for an apocalypse until the real thing comes along. I had inclined to be contemptuous of my father for the conditions of his life, for the conditions of our lives. When his life had ended I began to wonder about that life and also, in a new way, to be apprehensive about my own.

3   I had not known my father very well. We had got on badly, partly because we shared, in our different fashions, the vice of stubborn pride. When he was dead I realized that I had hardly ever spoken to him. When he had been dead a long time I began to wish I had. It seems to be typical

of life in America, where opportunities, real and fancied, are thicker than anywhere else on the globe, that the second generation has no time to talk to the first. No one, including my father, seems to have known exactly how old he was, but his mother had been born during slavery. He was of the first generation of free men. He, along with thousands of other Negroes, came North after 1919 and I was part of that generation which had never seen the landscape of what Negroes sometimes call the Old Country.

4   He had been born in New Orleans and had been a quite young man there during the time that Louis Armstrong, a boy, was running errands for the dives and honky-tonks of what was always presented to me as one of the most wicked of cities—to this day, whenever I think of New Orleans, I also helplessly think of Sodom and Gomorrah. My father never mentioned Louis Armstrong, except to forbid us to play his records; but there was a picture of him on our wall for a long time. One of my father's strongwilled female relatives had placed it there and forbade my father to take it down. He never did, but he eventually maneuvered her out of the house and when, some years later, she was in trouble and near death, he refused to do anything to help her.

5   He was, I think, very handsome. I gather this from photographs and from my own memories of him, dressed in his Sunday best and on his way to preach a sermon somewhere, when I was little. Handsome, proud, and ingrown, "like a toe-nail," somebody said. But he looked to me, as I grew older, like pictures I had seen of African tribal chieftains: he really should have been naked, with war-paint on and barbaric mementos, standing among spears. He could be chilling in the pulpit and indescribably cruel in his personal life and he was certainly the most bitter man I have ever met; yet it must be said that there was something else in him, buried in him, which lent him his tremendous power and, even, a rather crushing charm. It had something to do with his blackness, I think—he was very black—with his blackness and his beauty, and with the fact that he knew that he was black but did not know that he was beautiful. He claimed to be proud of his blackness but it had also been the cause of much humiliation and it had fixed bleak boundaries to his life. He was not a young man when we were growing up and he had already suffered many kinds of ruin; in his outrageously demanding and protective way he loved his children, who were black like him and menaced, like him; and all these things sometimes showed in his face when he tried never to my knowledge with any success, to establish contact with any of us. When he took one of his children on his knee to play, the child always became fretful and began to cry; when he tried to help one of us with our homework the absolutely unabating tension which emanated from him caused our minds and our tongues to become paralyzed, so that he, scarcely knowing why, flew into a rage and the child, not knowing why, was punished. If it ever entered his head to bring a surprise home for his children, it was, almost

unfailingly, the wrong surprise and even the big watermelons he often brought home on his back in the summertime led to the most appalling scenes. I do not remember, in all those years, that one of his children was ever glad to see him come home. From what I was able to gather of his early life, it seemed that this inability to establish contact with other people had always marked him and had been one of the things which had driven him out of New Orleans. There was something in him, therefore, groping and tentative, which was never expressed and was buried with him. One saw it most clearly when he was facing new people and hoping to impress them. But he never did, not for long. We went from church to smaller and more improbable church, he found himself in less and less demand as a minister, and by the time he died none of his friends had come to see him for a long time. He had lived and died in an intolerable bitterness of spirit and it frightened me, as we drove him to the graveyard through those unquiet, ruined streets, to see how powerful and overflowing this bitterness could be and to realize that this bitterness now was mine.

6   When he died I had been away from home for a little over a year. In that year I had had time to become aware of the meaning of all my father's bitter warnings, had discovered the secret of his proudly pursed lips and rigid carriage: I had discovered the weight of white people in the world. I saw that this had been for my ancestors and now would be for me an awful thing to live with and that the bitterness which had helped to kill my father could also kill me.

7   He had been ill a long time—in the mind, as we now realized, reliving instances of his fantastic intransigence in the new light of his affliction and endeavoring to feel a sorrow for him which never, quite, came true. We had not known that he was being eaten up by paranoia, and the discovery that his cruelty, to our bodies and our minds, and been one of the symptoms of his illness was not, then, enough to enable us to forgive him. The younger children felt, quite simply, relief that he would not be coming home anymore. My mother's observation that it was he, after all, who had kept them alive all these years meant nothing because the problems of keeping children alive are not real for children. The older children felt, with my father gone, that they could invite their friends to the house without fear that their friends would be insulted or, as had sometimes happened with me, being told that their friends were in league with the devil and intended to rob our family of everything we owned. (I didn't fail to wonder, and it made me hate him, what on earth we owned that anybody else would want.)

8   His illness was beyond all hope of healing before anyone realized that he was ill. He had always been so strange and had lived, like a prophet, in such unimaginably close communion with the Lord that his long silences which were punctuated by moans and hallelujahs and snatches

of old songs while he sat at the living-room window never seemed odd to us. It was not until he refused to eat because, he said, his family was trying to poison him that my mother was forced to accept as a fact what had, until then, been only an unwilling suspicion. When he was committed, it was discovered that he had tuberculosis and, as it turned out, the disease of his mind allowed the disease of his body to destroy him. For the doctors could not force him to eat, either, and, though he was fed intravenously, it was clear from the beginning that there was no hope for him.

9   In my mind's eye I could see him, sitting at the window, locked up in his terrors; hating and fearing every living soul including his children who had betrayed him, too, by reaching towards the world which had despised him. There were nine of us. I began to wonder what it could have felt like for such a man to have had nine children whom he could barely feed. He used to make little jokes about our poverty, which never, of course, seemed very funny to us; they could not have seemed very funny to him, either, or else our all too feeble response to them would never have caused such rages. He spent great energy and achieved, to our chagrin, no small amount of success in keeping us away from the people who surrounded us, people who had all-night rent parties to which we listened when we should have been sleeping, people who cursed and drank and flashed razor blades on Lenox Avenue. He could not understand why, if they had so much energy to spare, they could not use it to make their lives better. He treated almost everybody on our block with a most uncharitable asperity and neither they, nor, of course, their children were slow to reciprocate.

10   The only white people who came to our house were welfare workers and bill collectors. It was almost always my mother who dealt with them, for my father's temper, which was at the mercy of his pride, was never to be trusted. It was clear that he felt their very presence in his home to be a violation: this was conveyed by his carriage, almost ludicrously stiff, and by his voice, harsh and vindictively polite. When I was around nine or ten I wrote a play which was directed by a young, white schoolteacher, a woman, who then took an interest in me, and gave me books to read and, in order to corroborate my theatrical bent, decided to take me to see what she somewhat tactlessly referred to as "real" plays. Theater-going was forbidden in our house, but, with the really cruel intuitiveness of a child, I suspected that the color of this woman's skin would carry the day for me. When, at school, she suggested taking me to the theater, I did not, as I might have done if she had been a Negro, find a way of discouraging her, but agreed that she should pick me up at my house one evening. I then, very cleverly, left all the rest to my mother, who suggested to my father, as I knew she would, that it would not be very nice to let such a kind woman make the trip for nothing. Also, since it was a schoolteacher, I

imagine that my mother countered the idea of sin with the idea of "education," which word, even with my father, carried a kind of bitter weight.

11 Before the teacher came my father took me aside to ask *why* she was coming, what *interest* she could possibly have in our house, in a boy like me. I said I didn't know but I, too, suggested that it had something to do with education. And I understood that my father was waiting for me to say something—I didn't quite know what; perhaps that I wanted his protection against this teacher and her "education." I said none of these things and the teacher came and we went out. It was clear, during the brief interview in our living room, that my father was agreeing very much against his will and that he would have refused permission if he had dared. The fact that he did not dare caused me to despise him: I had no way of knowing that he was facing in that living room a wholly unprecedented and frightening situation.

12 Later, when my father had been laid off from his job, this woman became very important to us. She was really a very sweet and generous woman and went to a great deal of trouble to be of help to us, particularly during one awful winter. My mother called her by the highest name she knew: she said she was a "christian." My father could scarcely disagree but during the four or five years of our relatively close association he never trusted her and was always trying to surprise in her open, Midwestern face the genuine, cunningly hidden, and hideous motivation. In later years, particularly when it began to be clear that this "education" of mine was going to lead me to perdition, he became more explicit and warned me that my white friends in high school were not really my friends and that I would see, when I was older, how white people would do anything to keep a Negro down. Some of them could be nice, he admitted, but none of them were to be trusted and most of them were not even nice. The best thing was to have as little to do with them as possible. I did not feel this way and I was certain, in my innocence, that I never would.

13 But the year which preceded my father's death had made a great change in my life. I had been living in New Jersey, working in defense plants, working and living among southerners, white and black. I knew about the south, of course, and about how southerners treated Negroes and how they expected them to behave, but it had never entered my mind that anyone would look at me and expect *me* to behave that way. I learned in New Jersey that to be a Negro meant, precisely, that one was never looked at but was simply at the mercy of the reflexes the color of one's skin caused in other people. I acted in New Jersey as I had always acted, that is as though I thought a great deal of myself—I had to *act* that way—with results that were, simply, unbelievable. I had scarcely arrived before I had earned the enmity, which was extraordinarily ingenious, of all my superiors and nearly all my co-workers. In the beginning, to make matters worse, I simply did not know what was happening. I did not know what

I had done, and I shortly began to wonder what *anyone* could possibly do, to bring about such unanimous, active, and unbearably vocal hostility. I knew about jim-crow but I had never experienced it. I went to the same self-service restaurant three times and stood with all the Princeton boys before the counter, waiting for a hamburger and coffee; it was always an extraordinarily long time before anything was set before me; but it was not until the fourth visit that I learned that, in fact, nothing had ever been set before me: I had simply picked something up. Negroes were not served there, I was told, and they had been waiting for me to realize that I was always the only Negro present. Once I was told this, I determined to go there all the time. But now they were ready for me and, though some dreadful scenes were subsequently enacted in that restaurant, I never ate there again.

14   It was the same story all over New Jersey, in bars, bowling alleys, diners, places to live. I was always being forced to leave, silently, or with mutual imprecations. I very shortly became notorious and children giggled behind me when I passed and their elders whispered or shouted—they really believed that I was mad. And it did begin to work on my mind, of course; I began to be afraid to go anywhere and to compensate for this I went places to which I really should not have gone and where, God knows, I had no desire to be. My reputation in town naturally enhanced my reputation at work and my working day became one long series of acrobatics designed to keep me out of trouble. I cannot say that these acrobatics succeeded. It began to seem that the machinery of the organization I worked for was turning over, day and night, with but one aim: to eject me. I was fired once, and contrived, with the aid of a friend from New York, to get back on the payroll; was fired again, and bounced back again. It took a while to fire me for the third time, but the third time took. There were no loopholes anywhere. There was not even any way of getting back inside the gates.

15   That year in New Jersey lives in my mind as though it were the year during which, having an unsuspected predilection for it, I first contracted some dread, chronic disease, the unfailing symptom of which is a kind of blind fever, a pounding in the skull and fire in the bowels. Once this disease is contracted, one can never be really carefree again, for the fever, without an instant's warning, can recur at any moment. It can wreck more important things than race relations. There is not a Negro alive who does not have this rage in his blood—one has the choice, merely, of living with it consciously or surrendering to it. As for me, this fever has recurred in me, and does, and will until the day I die.

16   My last night in New Jersey, a white friend from New York took me to the nearest big town, Trenton, to go to the movies and have a few drinks. As it turned out, he also saved me from, at the very least, a violent

whipping. Almost every detail of that night stands out very clearly in my memory. I even remember the name of the movie we saw because its title impressed me as being so patly ironical. It was a movie about the German occupation of France, starring Maureen O'Hara and Charles Laughton and called *This Land Is Mine*. I remember the name of the diner we walked into when the movie ended: it was the "American Diner." When we walked in the counterman asked what we wanted and I remember answering with the casual sharpness which had become my habit: "We want a hamburger and a cup of coffee, what do you think we want?" I do not know why, after a year of such rebuffs, I so completely failed to anticipate his answer, which was, of course, "We don't serve Negroes here." This reply failed to discompose me, at least for the moment. I made some sardonic comment about the name of the diner and we walked out into the streets.

17   This was the time of what was called the "brown-out," when the lights in all American cities were very dim. When we re-entered the streets something happened to me which had the force of an optical illusion, or a nightmare. The streets were very crowded and I was facing north. People were moving in every direction but it seemed to me, in that instant, that all of the people I could see, and many more than that, were moving toward me, against me, and that everyone was white. I remember how their faces gleamed. And I felt, like a physical sensation, a *click* at the nape of my neck as though some interior string connecting my head to my body had been cut. I began to walk. I heard my friend call after me, but I ignored him. Heaven only knows what was going on in his mind, but he had the good sense not to touch me—I don't know what would have happened if he had—and to keep me in sight. I don't know what was going on in my mind, either; I certainly had no conscious plan. I wanted to do something to crush these white faces, which were crushing me. I walked for perhaps a block or two until I came to an enormous, glittering, and fashionable restaurant in which I knew not even the intercession of the Virgin would cause me to be served. I pushed through the doors and took the first vacant seat I saw, at a table for two, and waited.

18   I do not know how long I waited and I rather wonder, until today, what I could possibly have looked like. Whatever I looked like, I frightened the waitress who shortly appeared, and the moment she appeared all of my fury flowed towards her. I hated her for her white face, and for her great, astounded, frightened eyes. I felt that if she found a black man so frightening I would make her fright worth-while.

19   She did not ask me what I wanted, but repeated, as though she had learned it somewhere, "We don't serve Negroes here." She did not say it with the blunt, derisive hostility to which I had grown so accustomed, but, rather, with a note of apology in her voice, and fear. This made me colder

and more murderous than ever. I felt I had to do something with my hands. I wanted her to come close enough for me to get her neck between my hands.

20   So I pretended not to have understood her, hoping to draw her closer. And she did step a very short step closer, with her pencil poised incongruously over her pad, and repeated the formula: ". . . don't serve Negroes here."

21   Somehow, with the repetition of that phrase, which was already ringing in my head like a thousand bells of a nightmare, I realized that she would never come any closer and that I would have to strike from a distance. There was nothing on the table but an ordinary watermug half full of water, and I picked this up and hurled it with all my strength at her. She ducked and it missed her and shattered against the mirror behind the bar. And, with that sound, my frozen blood abruptly thawed, I returned from wherever I had been, I *saw,* for the first time, the restaurant, the people with their mouths open, already, as it seemed to me, rising as one man, and I realized what I had done, and where I was, and I was frightened. I rose and began running for the door. A round, potbellied man grabbed me by the nape of the neck just as I reached the doors and began to beat me about the face. I kicked him and got loose and ran into the streets. My friend whispered, *"Run!"* and I ran.

22   My friend stayed outside the restaurant long enough to misdirect my pursuers and the police, who arrived, he told me, at once. I do not know what I said to him when he came to my room that night. I could not have said much. I felt, in the oldest, most awful way, that I had somehow betrayed him. I lived it over and over and over again, the way one relives an automobile accident after it has happened and one finds oneself alone and safe. I could not get over two facts, both equally difficult for the imagination to grasp, and one was that I could have been murdered. But the other was that I had been ready to commit murder. I saw nothing very clearly but I did see this: that my life, my *real* life, was in danger, and not from anything other people might do but from the hatred I carried in my own heart.

II

23   I had returned home around the second week in June—in great haste because it seemed that my father's death and my mother's confinement were both but a matter of hours. In the case of my mother, it soon became clear that she had simply made a miscalculation. This had always been her tendency and I don't believe that a single one of us arrived in the world, or has since arrived anywhere else, on time. But none of us dawdled

so intolerably about the business of being born as did my baby sister. We sometimes amused ourselves, during those endless, stifling weeks, by picturing the baby sitting within in the safe, warm dark, bitterly regretting the necessity of becoming a part of our chaos and stubbornly putting it off as long as possible. I understood her perfectly and congratulated her on showing such good sense so soon. Death, however, sat as purposefully at my father's bedside as life stirred within my mother's womb and it was harder to understand why he so lingered in that long shadow. It seemed that he had bent, and for a long time, too, all of his energies towards dying. Now death was ready for him but my father held back.

24   All of Harlem, indeed, seemed to be infected by waiting. I had never before known it to be so violently still. Racial tensions throughout this country were exacerbated during the early years of the war, partly because the labor market brought together hundreds of thousands of ill-prepared people and partly because Negro soldiers, regardless of where they were born, received their military training in the south. What happened in defense plants and army camps had repercussions, naturally, in every Negro ghetto. The situation in Harlem had grown bad enough for clergymen, policemen, educators, politicians, and social workers to assert in one breath that there was no "crime wave" and to offer, in the very next breath, suggestions as to how to combat it. These suggestions always seemed to involve playgrounds, despite the fact that racial skirmishes were occurring in the playgrounds, too. Playground or not, crime wave or not, the Harlem police force had been augmented in March, and the unrest grew—perhaps, in fact, partly as a result of the ghetto's instinctive hatred of policemen. Perhaps the most revealing news item, out of the steady parade of reports of muggings, stabbings, shootings, assaults, gang wars, and accusations of police brutality, is the item concerning six Negro girls who set upon a white girl in the subway because, as they all too accurately put it, she was stepping on their toes. Indeed she was, all over the nation.

25   I had never *before* been so aware of policemen, on foot, on horseback, on corners, everywhere, always two by two. Nor had I ever been so aware of small knots of people. They were on stoops and on corners and in doorways, and what was striking about them, I think, was that they did not seem to be talking. Never, when I passed these groups, did the usual sound of a curse or a laugh ring out and neither did there seem to be any hum of gossip. There was certainly, on the other hand, occurring between them communication extraordinarily intense. Another thing that was striking was the unexpected diversity of the people who made up these groups. Usually, for example, one would see a group of sharpies standing on the street corner, jiving the passing chicks; or a group of older men, usually, for some reason, in the vicinity of a barber shop, discussing baseball scores, or the numbers, or making rather chilling observations about women they had known. Women, in a general way, tended to be seen less

often together—unless they were church women, or very young girls, or prostitutes met together for an unprofessional instant. But that summer I saw the strangest combinations: large, respectable, churchly matrons standing on the stoops or the corners with their hair tied up, together with a girl in sleazy satin whose face bore the marks of gin and the razor, or heavy-set, abrupt, no-nonsense older men, in company with the most disreputable and fanatical "race" men, or these same "race" men with the sharpies, or these sharpies with the churchly women. Seventh Day Adventists and Methodists and Spiritualists seemed to be hobnobbing with Holyrollers and they were all, alike, entangled with the most flagrant disbelievers; something heavy in their stance seemed to indicate that they had all, incredibly, seen a common vision, and on each face there seemed to be the same strange, bitter shadow.

26   The churchly women and the matter-of-fact, no-nonsense men had children in the Army. The sleazy girls they talked to had lovers there, the sharpies and the "race" men had friends and brothers there. It would have demanded an unquestioning patriotism, happily as uncommon in this country as it is undesirable, for these people not to have been disturbed by the bitter letters they received, by the newspaper stories they read, not to have been enraged by the posters, then to be found all over New York, which described the Japanese as "yellow-bellied Japs." It was only the "race" men, to be sure, who spoke ceaselessly of being revenged—how this vengeance was to be exacted was not clear—for the indignities and dangers suffered by Negro boys in uniform; but everybody felt a directionless, hopeless bitterness, as well as that panic which can scarcely be suppressed when one knows that a human being one loves is beyond one's reach, and in danger. This helplessness and this gnawing uneasiness does something, at length, to even the toughest mind. Perhaps the best way to sum all this up is to say that the people I knew felt, mainly, a peculiar kind of relief when they knew that their boys were being shipped out of the south, to do battle overseas. It was, perhaps, like feeling that the most dangerous part of a dangerous journey had been passed and that now, even if death should come, it would come with honor and without the complicity of their countrymen. Such a death would be, in short, a fact with which one could hope to live.

27   It was on the 28th of July, which I believe was a Wednesday, that I visited my father for the first time during his illness and for the last time in his life. The moment I saw him I knew why I had put off this visit so long. I had told my mother that I did not want to see him because I hated him. But this was not true. It was only that I *had* hated him and I wanted to hold on to this hatred. I did not want to look on him as a ruin: it was not a ruin I had hated. I imagine that one of the reasons people cling to their hates so stubbornly is because they sense, once hate is gone, that they will be forced to deal with pain.

28   We traveled out to him, his older sister and myself, to what seemed to be the very end of a very Long Island. It was hot and dusty and we wrangled, my aunt and I, all the way out, over the fact that I had recently begun to smoke and, as she said, to give myself airs. But I knew that she wrangled with me because she could not bear to face the fact of her brother's dying. Neither could I endure the reality of her despair, her unstated bafflement as to what had happened to her brother's life, and her own. So we wrangled and I smoked and from time to time she fell into a heavy reverie. Covertly, I watched her face, which was the face of an old woman; it had fallen in, the eyes were sunken and lightless; soon she would be dying, too.

29   In my childhood—it had not been so long ago—I had thought her beautiful. She had been quick-witted and quick-moving and very generous with all the children and each of her visits had been an event. At one time one of my brothers and myself had thought of running away to live with her. Now she could no longer produce out of her handbag some unexpected and yet familiar delight. She made me feel pity and revulsion and fear. It was awful to realize that she no longer caused me to feel affection. The closer we came to the hospital the more querulous she became and at the same time, naturally, grew more dependent on me. Between pity and guilt and fear I began to feel that there was another me trapped in my skull like a jack-in-the-box who might escape my control at any moment and fill the air with screaming.

30   She began to cry the moment we entered the room and she saw him lying there, all shriveled and still, like a little black monkey. The great, gleaming apparatus which fed him and would have compelled him to be still even if he had been able to move brought to mind, not beneficence, but torture; the tubes entering his arm made me think of pictures I had seen when a child, of Gulliver, tied down by the pygmies on that island. My aunt wept and wept, there was a whistling sound in my father's throat; nothing was said; he could not speak. I wanted to take his hand, to say something. But I do not know what I could have said, even if he could have heard me. He was not really in that room with us, he had at last really embarked on his journey; and though my aunt told me that he said he was going to meet Jesus, I did not hear anything except that whistling in his throat. The doctor came back and we left, into that unbearable train again, and home. In the morning came the telegram saying that he was dead. Then the house was suddenly full of relatives, friends, hysteria, and confusion and I quickly left my mother and the children to the care of those impressive women, who, in Negro communities at least, automatically appear at times of bereavement armed with lotions, proverbs, and patience, and an ability to cook. I went downtown. By the time I returned, later the same day, my mother had been carried to the hospital and the baby had been born.

III

31   For my father's funeral I had nothing black to wear and this posed a nagging problem all day long. It was one of those problems, simple, or impossible of solution, to which the mind insanely clings in order to avoid the mind's real trouble. I spent most of that day at the downtown apartment of a girl I knew, celebrating my birthday with whiskey and wondering what to wear that night. When planning a birthday celebration one naturally does not expect that it will be up against competition from a funeral and this girl had anticipated taking me out that night, for a big dinner and a night club afterwards. Sometime during the course of that long day we decided that we would go out anyway, when my father's funeral service was over. I imagine I decided it, since, as the funeral hour approached, it became clearer and clearer to me that I would not know what to do with myself when it was over. The girl, stifling her very lively concern as to the possible effects of the whiskey on one of my father's chief mourners, concentrated on being conciliatory and practically helpful. She found a black shirt for me somewhere and ironed it and, dressed in the darkest pants and jacket I owned, and slightly drunk, I made my way to my father's funeral.

32   The chapel was full, but not packed, and very quiet. There were, mainly, my father's relatives, and his children, and here and there I saw faces I had not seen since childhood, the faces of my father's one-time friends. They were very dark and solemn now, seeming somehow to suggest that they had known all along that something like this would happen. Chief among the mourners was my aunt, who had quarreled with my father all his life; by which I do not mean to suggest that her mourning was insincere or that she had not loved him. I suppose that she was one of the few people in the world who had, and their incessant quarreling proved precisely the strength of the tie that bound them. The only other person in the world, as far as I knew, whose relationship to my father rivaled my aunt's in depth was my mother, who was not there.

33   It seemed to me, of course, that it was a very long funeral. But it was, if anything, a rather shorter funeral than most, nor, since there were no overwhelming, uncontrollable expressions of grief, could it be called—if I dare to use the word—successful. The minister who preached my father's funeral sermon was one of the few my father had still been seeing as he neared his end. He presented to us in his sermon a man whom none of us had ever seen—a man thoughtful, patient, and forbearing, a Christian inspiration to all who knew him, and a model for his children. And no doubt the children, in their disturbed and guilty state, were almost ready to believe this; he had been remote enough to be anything and, anyway, the shock of the incontrovertible, that it was really our father lying up

there in that casket, prepared the mind for anything. His sister moaned and this grief-stricken moaning was taken as corroboration. The other faces held a dark, non-committal thoughtfulness. This was not the man they had known, but they had scarcely expected to be confronted with *him;* this was, in a sense deeper than questions of fact, the man they had not known, and the man they had not known may have been the real one. The real man, whoever he had been, had suffered and now he was dead: this was all that was sure and all that mattered now. Every man in the chapel hoped that when his hour came he, too, would be eulogized, which is to say forgiven, and that all of his lapses, greeds, errors, and strayings from the truth would be invested with coherence and looked upon with charity. This was perhaps the last thing human beings could give each other and it was what they demanded, after all, of the Lord. Only the Lord saw the midnight tears, only He was present when one of His children, moaning and wringing hands, paced up and down the room. When one slapped one's child in anger the recoil in the heart reverberated through heaven and became part of the pain of the universe. And when the children were hungry and sullen and distrustful and one watched them, daily, growing wilder, and further away, and running headlong into danger, it was the Lord who knew what the charged heart endured as the strap was laid to the backside; the Lord alone who knew what one *would* have said if one had had, like the Lord, the gift of the living word. It was the Lord who knew of the impossibility every parent in that room faced: how to prepare the child for the day when the child would be despised and how to *create* in the child—by what means?—a stronger antidote to this poison than one had found for oneself. The avenues, side streets, bars, billiard halls, hospitals, police stations, and even the playgrounds of Harlem—not to mention the houses of correction, the jails, and the morgue—testified to the potency of the poison while remaining silent as to the efficacy of whatever antidote, irresistibly raising the question of whether or not such an antidote existed; raising, which was worse, the question of whether or not an antidote was desirable; perhaps poison should be fought with poison. With these several schisms in the mind and with more terrors in the heart than could be named, it was better not to judge the man who had gone down under an impossible burden. It was better to remember: *Thou knowest this man's fall; but thou knowest not his wrassling.*

34   While the preacher talked and I watched the children—years of changing their diapers, scrubbing them, slapping them, taking them to school, and scolding them had had the perhaps inevitable result of making me love them, though I am not sure I knew this then—my mind was busily breaking out with a rash of disconnected impressions. Snatches of popular songs, indecent jokes, bits of books I had read, movie sequences, faces, voices, political issues—I thought I was going mad; all these impressions suspended, as it were, in the solution of the faint nausea produced in

me by the heat and liquor. For a moment I had the impression that my alcoholic breath, inefficiently disguised with chewing gum, filled the entire chapel. Then someone began singing one of my father's favorite songs and, abruptly, I was with him, sitting on his knee, in the hot, enormous, crowded church which was the first church we attended. It was the Abyssinia Baptist Church on 138th Street. We had not gone there long. With this image, a host of others came. I had forgotten, in the rage of my growing up, how proud my father had been of me when I was little. Apparently, I had had a voice and my father had liked to show me off before the members of the church. I had forgotten what he had looked like when he was pleased but now I remembered that he had always been grinning with pleasure when my solos ended. I even remembered certain expressions on his face when he teased my mother—had he loved her? I would never know. And when had it all begun to change? For now it seemed that he had not always been cruel. I remembered being taken for a haircut and scraping my knee on the footrest of the barber's chair and I remembered my father's face as he soothed my crying and applied the stinging iodine. Then I remembered our fights, fights, which had been of the worst possible kind because my technique had been silence.

35   I remembered the one time in all our life together when we had really spoken to each other.

36   It was on a Sunday and it must have been shortly before I left home. We were walking, just the two of us, in our usual silence, to or from church. I was in high school and had been doing a lot of writing and I was, at about this time, the editor of the high school magazine. But I had also been a Young Minister and had been preaching from the pulpit. Lately, I had been taking fewer engagements and preached as rarely as possible. It was said in the church, quite truthfully, that I was "cooling off."

37   My father asked me abruptly, "You'd rather write than preach, wouldn't you?"

38   I was astonished at his question—because it was a real question. I answered "Yes."

39   That was all we said. It was awful to remember that that was all we had *ever* said.

40   The casket now was opened and the mourners were being led up the aisle to look for the last time on the deceased. The assumption was that the family was too overcome with grief to be allowed to make this journey alone and I watched while my aunt was led to the casket and, muffled in black, and shaking, led back to her seat. I disapproved of forcing the children to look on their dead father, considering that the shock of his death, or, more truthfully, the shock of death as a reality, was already a little more than a child could bear, but my judgment in this matter had been overruled and there they were, bewildered and frightened and very small,

being led, one by one, to the casket. But there is also something very gallant about children at such moments. It has something to do with their silence and gravity and with the fact that one cannot help them. Their legs, somehow, seem *exposed,* so that it is at once incredible and terribly clear that their legs are all they have to hold them up.

41   I had not wanted to go to the casket myself and I certainly had not wished to be led there, but there was no way of avoiding either of these forms. One of the deacons led me up and I looked on my father's face. I cannot say that it looked like him at all. His blackness had been equivocated by powder and there was no suggestion in that casket of what his power had or could have been. He was simply an old man dead, and it was hard to believe that he had ever given anyone either joy or pain. Yet, his life filled that room. Further up the avenue his wife was holding his newborn child. Life and death so close together, and love and hatred, and right and wrong, said something to me which I did not want to hear concerning man, concering the life of man.

42   After the funeral, while I was downtown desperately celebrating my birthday, a Negro soldier, in the lobby of the Hotel Braddock, got into a fight with a white policeman over a Negro girl. Negro girls, white policemen, in or out of uniform, and Negro males—in or out of uniform—were part of the furniture of the lobby of the Hotel Braddock and this was certainly not the first time such an incident had occurred. It was destined, however, to receive an unprecedented publicity, for the fight between the policeman and the soldier ended with the shooting of the soldier. Rumor, flowing immediately to the streets outside, stated that the soldier had been shot in the back, an instantaneous and revealing invention, and that the soldier had died protecting a Negro woman. The facts were somewhat different—for example, the soldier had not been shot in the back, and was not dead, and the girl seems to have been as dubious a symbol of womanhood as her white counterpart in Georgia usually is, but no one was interested in the facts. They preferred the invention because this invention expressed and corroborated their hates and fears so perfectly. It is just as well to remember that people are always doing this. Perhaps many of those legends, including Christianity, to which the world clings began their conquest of the world with just some such concerted surrender to distortion. The effect, in Harlem, of this particular legend was like the effect of a lit match in a tin of gasoline. The mob gathered before the doors of the Hotel Braddock simply began to swell and to spread in every direction, and Harlem exploded.

43   The mob did not cross the ghetto lines. It would have been easy, for example, to have gone over Morningside Park on the west side or to have crossed the Grand Central railroad tracks at 125th Street on the east side, to wreak havoc in white neighborhoods. The mob seems to have been

mainly interested in something more potent and real than the white face, that is, in white power, and the principal damage done during the riot of the summer of 1943 was to white business establishments in Harlem. It might have been a far bloodier story, of course, if, at the hour the riot began, these establishments had still been open. From the Hotel Braddock the mob fanned out, east and west along 125th Street, and for the entire length of Lenox, Seventh, and Eighth avenues. Along each of these avenues, and along each major side street—116th, 125th, 138th, and so on— bars, stores, pawnshops, restaurants, even little luncheonettes had been smashed open and entered and looted—looted, it might be added, with more haste than efficiency. The shelves really looked as though a bomb had struck them. Cans of beans and soup and dog food, along with toilet paper, corn flakes, sardines, and milk tumbled every which way, and abandoned cash registers and cases of beer leaned crazily out of the splintered windows and were strewn along the avenues. Sheets, blankets, and clothing of every description formed a kind of path, as though people had dropped them while running. I truly had not realized that Harlem *had* so many stores until I saw them all smashed open; the first time the word *wealth* ever entered my mind in relation to Harlem was when I saw it scattered in the streets. But one's first, incongruous impression of plenty was countered immediately by an impression of waste. None of this was doing anybody any good. It would have been better to have left the plate glass as it had been and the goods lying in the stores.

44   It would have been better, but it would also have been intolerable, for Harlem had needed something to smash. To smash something is the ghetto's chronic need. Most of the time it is the members of the ghetto who smash each other, and themselves. But as long as the ghetto walls are standing there will always come a moment when these outlets do not work. That summer, for example, it was not enough to get into a fight on Lenox Avenue, or curse out one's cronies in the barber shops. If ever, indeed, the violence which fills Harlem's churches, pool halls, and bars erupts outward in a more direct fashion, Harlem and its citizens are likely to vanish in an apocalyptic flood. That this is not likely to happen is due to a great many reasons, most hidden and powerful among them the Negro's real relation to the white American. This relation prohibits, simply, anything as uncomplicated and satisfactory as pure hatred. In order really to hate white people, one has to blot so much out of the mind—and the heart— that this hatred itself becomes an exhausting and self-destructive pose. But this does no mean, on the other hand, that love comes easily: the white world is too powerful, too complacent, too ready with gratuitous humiliation, and, above all, too ignorant and too innocent for that. One is absolutely forced to make perpetual qualifications and one's own reactions are always canceling each other out. It is this, really, which has driven so

many people mad, both white and black. One is always in the position of having to decide between amputation and gangrene. Amputation is swift but time may prove that the amputation was not necessary—or one may delay the amputation too long. Gangrene is slow, but it is impossible to be sure that one is reading one's symptoms right. The idea of going through life as a cripple is more than one can bear, and equally unbearable is the risk of swelling up slowly, in agony, with poison. And the trouble, finally, is that the risks are real even if the choices do not exist.

45 "But as for me and my house," my father had said, "we will serve the Lord." I wondered, as we drove him to his resting place, what this line had meant for him. I had heard him preach it many times. I had preached it once myself, proudly giving it an interpretation different from my father's. Now the whole thing came back to me, as though my father and I were on our way to Sunday school and I were memorizing the golden text: *And if it seem evil unto you to serve the Lord, choose you this day whom you will serve; whether the gods which your fathers served that were on the other side of the flood, or the gods of the Amorites, in whose land ye dwell: but as for me and my house, we will serve the Lord.* I suspected in these familiar lines a meaning which had never been there for me before. All of my father's texts and songs, which I had decided were meaningless, were arranged before me at his death like empty bottles, waiting to hold the meaning which life would give them for me. This was his legacy: nothing is ever escaped. That bleakly memorable morning I hated the unbelievable streets and the Negroes and whites who had, equally, made them that way. But I knew that it was folly, as my father would have said, this bitterness was folly. It was necessary to hold on to the things that mattered. The dead man mattered, the new life mattered; blackness and whiteness did not matter; to believe that they did was to acquiesce in one's own destruction. Hatred, which could destroy so much, never failed to destroy the man who hated and this was an immutable law.

46 It began to seem that one would have to hold in the mind forever two ideas which seemed to be in opposittion. The first idea was acceptance, the acceptance, totally without rancor, of life as it is, and men as they are: in the light of this idea, it goes without saying that injustice is a commonplace. But this did not mean that one could be complacent, for the second idea was of equal power: that one must never, in one's own life, accept these injustices as commonplace but must fight them with all one's strength. This fight begins, however, in the heart and it now had been laid to my charge to keep my own heart free of hatred and despair. This intimation made my heart heavy and, now that my father was irrecoverable, I wished that he had been beside me so that I could have searched his face for the answers which only the future would give me now.

Questions

1. How do the ideas of paragraph 5 relate to the thesis of the whole selection? What is that thesis? In paragraph 5, find the places where Baldwin has repeated the same sound, and describe the effects achieved by the linking. Find the repetition of grammatical units that builds through parallel structure the sentence rhythms of paragraph 5.

2. What is the function of the incident with the waitress in New Jersey? What part does it illustrate of the whole thesis?

3. Baldwin speaks of his attending a movie entitled *"This Land is Mine"* and of going subsequently to a café labeled "American Diner" as—in view of his feelings and what happened to him—"patly ironical." What less "patly ironical" use can you perceive in Baldwin's emphasis on " 'real' " (paragraph 10) and *"real"* (paragraph 22)?

4. Notice that the opening paragraph suggests a connection between the race riots and the death of the author's father. Later we see this idea developed. What images are used? What is the point of making this connection? What is its relationship to the whole thesis?

5. Study paragraph 44. What devices of transition can you identify? Where is the style most vivid and concrete? Can the associations of the phrase "apocalyptic flood" be justified? Is there any paradox in Baldwin's application of the terms "ignorant and innocent" to the white world? Is there paradox in the last sentence? What does that sentence mean?

6. In paragraph 44 Baldwin says, "One is always in the position of having to decide between amputation and gangrene." Explain what he means. Is the analogy appropriate?

7. Find the Old Testament allusions in the selection. Find word choices suggesting the patriarchal temper of Baldwin's father. Does Baldwin's outlook as expressed here also show the influence of the Old Testament? If so, where?

8. Is Baldwin in any way speaking here beyond the context of the Negro's unhappy life in America? What evidence can you find for a definitive answer one way or another?

9. How does Baldwin fit the description of "the poet's way round" given by Ciardi in paragraph 19 of his essay?

36 JOHN FITZGERALD KENNEDY
Inaugural Address: 1961

1   We observe today not a victory of party but a celebration of freedom—symbolizing an end as well as a beginning—signifying renewal as well as change. For I have sworn before you and Almighty God the same solemn oath our forebears prescribed nearly a century and three-quarters ago.

2   The world is very different now. For man holds in his mortal hands the power to abolish all forms of human poverty and all forms of human life. And yet the same revolutionary beliefs for which our forebears fought are still at issue around the globe—the belief that the rights of man come not from the generosity of the state but from the hand of God.

3   We dare not forget today that we are the heirs of that first revolution. Let the word go forth from this time and place, to friend and foe alike, that the torch has been passed to a new generation of Americans—born in this century, tempered by war, disciplined by a hard and bitter peace, proud of our ancient heritage—and unwilling to witness or permit the slow undoing of those human rights to which this nation has always been committed, and to which we are committed today at home and around the world.

4   Let every nation know, whether it wishes us well or ill, that we shall pay any price, bear any burden, meet any hardship, support any friend, oppose any foe to assure the survival and the success of liberty.

5   This much we pledge—and more.

6   To those old allies whose cultural and spiritual origins we share, we pledge the loyalty of faithful friends. United, there is little we cannot do in a host of new cooperative ventures. Divided, there is little we can do—for we dare not meet a powerful challenge at odds and split asunder.

7   To those new states whom we welcome to the ranks of the free, we pledge our word that one form of colonial control shall not have passed away merely to be replaced by a far more iron tyranny. We shall not always expect to find them supporting our view. But we shall always hope to find them strongly supporting their own freedom—and to remember that, in the past, those who foolishly sought power by riding the back of the tiger ended up inside.

8   To those peoples in the huts and villages of half the globe struggling to break the bonds of mass misery, we pledge our best efforts to help them

Delivered at the Capitol in Washington, D.C., January 20, 1961.

help themselves, for whatever period is required—not because the Communists may be doing it, not because we seek their votes, but because it is right. If a free society cannot help the many who are poor, it cannot save the few who are rich.

9   To our sister republics south of our border, we offer a special pledge—to convert our good words into good deeds—in a new alliance for progress—to assist free men and free governments in casting off the chains of poverty. But this peaceful revolution of hope cannot become the prey of hostile powers. Let all our neighbors know that we shall join with them to oppose aggression or subversion anywhere in the Americas. And let every other power know that this hemisphere intends to remain the master of its own house.

10   To that world assembly of sovereign states, the United Nations, our last best hope in an age where the instruments of war have far outpaced the instruments of peace, we renew our pledge of support—to prevent it from becoming merely a forum for invective—to strengthen its shield of the new and the weak—and to enlarge the area in which its writ may run.

11   Finally, to those nations who would make themselves our adversary, we offer not a pledge but a request: that both sides begin anew the quest for peace, before the dark powers of destruction unleashed by science engulf all humanity in planned or accidental self-destruction.

12   We dare not tempt them with weakness. For only when our arms are sufficient beyond doubt can we be certain beyond doubt that they will never be employed.

13   But neither can two great and powerful groups of nations take comfort from our present course—both sides overburdened by the cost of modern weapons, both rightly alarmed by the steady spread of the deadly atom, yet both racing to alter that uncertain balance of terror that stays the hand of mankind's final war.

14   So let us begin anew—remembering on both sides that civility is not a sign of weakness, and sincerity is always subject to proof. Let us never negotiate out of fear. But let us never fear to negotiate.

15   Let both sides explore what problems unite us instead of belaboring those problems which divide us.

16   Let both sides, for the first time, formulate serious and precise proposals for the inspection and control of arms—and bring the absolute power to destroy other nations under the absolute control of all nations.

17   Let both sides seek to invoke the wonders of science instead of its terrors. Together let us explore the stars, conquer the deserts, eradicate disease, tap the ocean depths and encourage the arts and commerce.

18   Let both sides unite to heed in all corners of the earth the command of Isaiah—to "undo the heavy burdens . . . [and] let the oppressed go free."

19   And if a beachhead of cooperation may push back the jungles of suspicion, let both sides join in creating a new endeavor—not a new balance of power, but a new world of law, where the strong are just and the weak secure and the peace preserved.

20   All this will not be finished in the first 100 days. Nor will it be finished in the first 1,000 days, nor in the life of this Administration, nor even perhaps in our lifetime on this planet. But let us begin.

21   In your hands, my fellow citizens, more than mine, will rest the final success or failure of our course. Since this country was founded, each generation of Americans has been summoned to give testimony to its national loyalty. The graves of young Americans who answered the call to service surround the globe.

22   Now the trumpet summons us again—not as a call to bear arms, though arms we need—not as a call to battle, though embattled we are— but a call to bear the burden of a long twilight struggle year in and year out, "rejoicing in hope, patient in tribulation"—a struggle against the common enemies of man: tyranny, poverty, disease and war itself.

23   Can we forge against these enemies a grand and global alliance, north and south, east and west, that can assure a more fruitful life for all mankind? Will you join in that historic effort?

24   In the long history of the world, only a few generations have been granted the role of defending freedom in its hour of maximum danger. I do not shrink from this responsibility—I welcome it. I do not believe that any of us would exchange places with any other people or any other generation. The energy, the faith, the devotion which we bring to this endeavor will light our country and all who serve it—and the glow from that fire can truly light the world.

25   And so, my fellow Americans: ask not what your country can do for you—ask what you can do for your country.

26   My fellow citizens of the world: ask not what America will do for you, but what together we can do for the freedom of man.

27   Finally, whether you are citizens of America or citizens of the world, ask of us here the same high standards of strength and sacrifice which we ask of you. With a good conscience our only sure reward, with history the final judge of our deeds, let us go forth to lead the land we love, asking His blessing and His help, but knowing that here on earth God's work must truly be our own.

Questions

1. Comment upon the transition between paragraphs 1 and 2.
2. Why is the first sentence of paragraph 3 both a transitional and a topic sentence?
3. What repetition connects paragraphs 3 through 9?
4. Is paragraph 4 a periodic sentence?
5. What is the stylistic effect of the dash in paragraph 5?
6. In the last sentence of paragraph 6 what two allusions can you identify?
7. What is the meaning of paragraph 7? Describe a situation to which it applies. How is the allusion to riding the tiger appropriate?
8. Describe the sentence structure of paragraph 8. What is the meaning and logic of the last sentence?
9. Comment in paragraphs 8 and 9 upon the parallelism and the repetition of sounds and structure and words.
10. Find the metaphors and other figures of speech in the following paragraphs: 11, 13, 19, 22, 24.
11. Find as many examples of triads as you can throughout the speech.

Concreteness and Symbol

37 ALEXANDER H. LEIGHTON
That Day at Hiroshima

1   We approached Hiroshima a little after daybreak on a winter day, driving in a jeep below a leaden sky and in the face of a cold, wet wind. On either side of the road, black flat fields were turning green under winter wheat. Here and there peasants worked, swinging spades or grubbing in mud and water with blue hands. Some in black split-toed shoes left tracks like cloven hoofs. To the north, looming close over the level land, mountains thrust heavy summits of pine darkly against the overcast. To the south and far away, the bay lay in dull brightness under fitful rain.

2   "Hiroshima," said the driver, a GI from a Kansas farm, who had been through the city many times, "don't look no different from any other bombed town. You soon get used to it. You'll see little old mud walls right in the middle of town that wasn't knocked down. They been exaggerating about that bomb."

3   Within a few miles the fields along the road were replaced by houses and shops that looked worn and dull yet intact. On the road itself people straggled to work, some on bicycles, most of them on foot—tattered and bandy-legged old men, girls with red cheeks and bright eyes, ancient women under towering bundles, middle-aged men looking stiff in Western business suits. In one place there were several Koreans together, the women easily distinguished from the Japanese by their white blouses and the full skirts that swung as they strode. At a bus stop a crowd stood waiting in a line long enough to fill a train. Half a mile farther on we passed the bus, small, battered, and gray, standing half obliterated by the cloud of

From *Atlantic Monthly*, 178 (October, 1946) 85–90. Revised in *Human Relations in a Changing World* by Alexander H. Leighton. Copyright © 1949 by Alexander H. Leighton. Reprinted by permission of Russell & Volkening, Inc.

smoke that came from the charcoal burner at the back while the driver stood working at its machinery.

4   Children of all ages waved, laughed, and shouted at us as had the children in other parts of Japan.

5   "Haro-goodabye! Haro-goodabye!"

6   "Jeepu! Jeeeepu!"

7   Like the children of Hamelin to the piper, they came rushing, at the sound of our approach, from doorways and alleyways and from behind houses, to line up by the road and cheer. One little fellow of about six threw himself into the air, his little body twisting and feet kicking in a fit of glee.

8   The adults gazed at us with solemn eyes or looked straight ahead. They were more subdued than those I had seen elsewhere in Japan. The children seemed different, possessed by some common animation denied their elders—an animation which impelled them toward the occupation forces, toward the strong and the new.

9   Presently a two-story trade school appeared, with boards instead of window glass, and then a factory in the same condition. Soon there were shops and houses all along the way with windows missing. A house came into view with its roof pressed down, tiles scattered, and walls bulging outward. A shop with no front, like an open mouth, showed its contents, public and private, clear to the rear window.

10   The road turned to the Ota River, where the tide was running out and boats lay heaved over on the beach. A bridge ended suddenly like a headless neck. Now every house and shop was damaged and lay with only one end or a corner standing.

11   Then all the buildings ceased and we came as if from a forest out on a plain, as if from tumult into silence. Imagine a city dump with its smells of wet ashes, mold, and things rotting, but one that runs from your feet almost to the limits of vision. As is often the case with level and desolate places on the earth, the sky seemed close above it. The predominant colors were red and yellow, crumbles of stone, bricks, red earth, and rust. Low walls made rectangles that marked where houses had stood, like sites of prehistoric villages. Here and there in the middle distance, a few large buildings stood about, buttes in the rubble of the plain.

12   "You see them?" said the driver, as if it were a triumph for his side. "The bomb didn't knock *them* down."

13   Running like ruler lines through the waste were black roads surprisingly dotted with people, some on foot and some in carts of all sizes drawn by man, woman, horse, or cow. Clothing was old and tattered and of every combination from full European to full Japanese. People looked as if they had grabbed what they could from a rummage sale.

14   Occasionally, blending like protective coloration with the rubble were shacks built out of fragments of boards and iron. Around them were vege-

table gardens, for the most part full of *daikon,* Japanese radish. A few more pretentious sheds were going up, shining bright yellow with new boards.

15   We slowed down to go around a piece of cornice that lay partly across the road like a glacial boulder, and from somewhere in a band of children who cheered and called to us came the gift of a tangerine that landed on the floor of the jeep. Wondering at them, I picked it up and put it in my pocket.

16   When crossing a bridge, we could see down through the swiftly running water to the stones and shells on the bottom. This clearness gave a feeling of odd contrast to the disorder of the land. We passed a number of trees burned black but still holding up some leafless branches as if in perpetual winter.

17   The drive ended at a large building that was still standing, a former bank, now a police headquarters, where I had an appointment with the chief to arrange for office space and guides. The driver said, as he got out, "This is it."

II

18   One hears it said that, after all, Japanese cities were really a collection of tinderboxes, while American urban centers are made of stronger stuff. In Hiroshima there were many buildings of types common in the United States and some, prepared against earthquakes, far stronger. The engineers of the U.S. Strategic Bombing Survey concluded from their examination that "the overwhelming bulk of buildings in American cities would not stand up against an atomic bomb bursting at a mile or a mile and a half from them." To this must be added the realization that the bomb dropped at Hiroshima will be considered primitive by future standards.

19   The bank building which housed the police headquarters was a well-made structure of stone, three stories high. Through an imposing entrance my interpreter and I went past tall and solid metal doors that were bent inward like cardboard and no longer usable. The lobby was large and high, but dark because it had no window glass and the openings were boarded to keep out the wind. Through poor light there loomed the white face of a clock up on one wall, its hands pointing to 8:10—the time it had stopped on August 6.

20   In the years when that clock had been going, Hiroshima had been a city, at first unknown to Europe and America, then a source of immigrants to the United States, and finally an enemy port. It lay on a delta between the seven mouths of the Ota and was traversed by canals and an ancient highway that connected Kyoto in the east with Shimonoseki in the west.

Close around the city stood mountains covered with red pine, while before it stretched the bay, indented with headlands and spread with islands, in places narrow and steep like a fjord. In shallows near the shore, rows of poles stood as if in a bean patch, set in the sea to anchor oysters and to catch edible seaweed passing in the tide. In deeper water, fishing boats with hawkish prows and planked with red pine were tending nets. A few fishermen used cormorants to make their catch.

21   Hiroshima had expanses of park, residences, gardens, orange and persimmon trees. Since there had been much traveling back and forth by relatives of immigrants to California, the influence of the United States was marked. On main streets there were movies and restaurants with façades that would have fitted into shopping districts of Bakersfield or San Diego.

22   But Hiroshima was also ancient. Its feudal castle raised a five-story keep that could be seen a long distance over the level land of the delta. There were three large temples and many smaller ones and the tombs of the Asano family and of the wife and son of the leader of the Forty-seven Ronin, Oishi-Yoshio. There were also Christian churches, whose bells mingled with the temple gongs and the honking of auto horns and the rattling of trolleys.

23   The people of the city had earned their living by buying and selling farm produce and fish, by making mountain pines into boats for the fishing fleet of the Inland Sea, by meat packing, rubber processing, and oil refining, by making textiles from the cocoons of wild silkworms, by brewing rice and grape wine, by manufacturing paper umbrellas, needles, *tabi* socks, small arms, metal castings, and by working in utilities and services such as electricity, transportation, schools, and hospitals.

24   During the war there was an increase of industrialization, and plants grew up, chiefly in the outskirts.

25   There was a famous gay district with little streets along which a person walking in the night could hear laughter, the twang of the *shamisen,* and geishas singing.

26   The university had been an active cultural center but also stressed athletics, particularly swimming. There were sometimes mass aquatic exercises when hundreds of students would swim for miles, strung out in the bay in a long line with boats attending.

27   Although not a fortified town, Hiroshima was a major military command station, supply depot, and staging area because of its protected position and because of Ujina Harbor with access to the Pacific, the Sea of Japan, and the East China Sea. More than a third of the city's land was taken up with military installations, and from the harbor troopships left for Korea, Manchuria, China, and the southern regions. However, toward the end of hostilities, most of the shipping had ceased because of sinkings in the Inland Sea.

28   The population of Hiroshima was given as well over 300,000 before the war, but this was reduced by evacuation, before the atomic bomb fell, probably to about 245,000. It is still not certain how many the bomb killed, but the best estimate is from 70,000 to 80,000.

III

29   About seven o'clock on the morning of August 6 there was an air-raid warning and three planes were reported in the vicinity. No one was much disturbed. For a long time B-29's flying over in small numbers had been a common sight. At some future date, Hiroshima might suffer an incendiary raid from masses of planes such as had devastated other Japanese cities. With this possibility in mind there had been evacuations, and firebreaks were being prepared. But on this particular morning there could be no disaster from just three planes.

30   By 7:30 the "all clear" had sounded and people were thinking again of the day's plans, looking forward to their affairs and engagements of the morning and afternoon. The castle keep stood in the sun. Children bathed in the river. Farmers labored in the fields and fishermen on the water. City stores and factories got under way with their businesses.

31   In the heart of the city near the buildings of the Prefectural Government and at the intersection of the business streets, everybody had stopped and stood in a crowd gazing up at three parachutes floating down through the blue air.

32   The bomb exploded several hundred feet above their heads.

33   The people for miles around Hiroshima, in the fields, in the mountains, and on the bay, saw a light that was brilliant even in the sun, and felt heat. A countrywoman was going out to her farm when suddenly, "I saw a light reflected on the mountain and then a streak just like lightning came."

34   A town official was crossing a bridge on his bicycle about ten miles from the heart of the city when he felt the right side of his face seared, and thinking that he had sunstroke, he jumped to the ground.

35   A woman who was washing dishes noticed that she felt "very warm on the side of my face next the wall. I looked out the window toward the city and saw something like a sun in bright color."

36   At a slower pace, after the flash, came the sound of the explosion, which some people have no recollection of hearing, while others described it as an earth-shaking roar, like thunder or a big wind. A black smoky mass, lit up with color, ascended into the sky and impressed beholders with its beauty. Red, gold, blue, orange, and many other shades mingled with the black.

37   Nearer to the city and at its edges, the explosion made a more direct and individual impact on people. Almost everyone thought that an ordinary bomb had landed very close to him, and only later realized the extent of the damage.

38   A man who was oiling the machinery in a factory saw the lights go out and thought that something must be wrong with the electricity. "But when the roof started crumbling down, I was in a daze, wondering what was happening. Then I noticed my hands and feet were bleeding. I don't know how I hurt myself."

39   Another, who was putting points on needles, was knocked unconscious, and when he came to, found "all my surroundings burned to the ground and flames raging here and there. I ran home for my family without knowing I was burned around my head. When I arrived home, our house was devastated and destroyed by flames. I ran to the neighbors and inquired about my family and learned that they had all been taken to safety across the river."

40   An invalid who was drinking tea said, "The tin roof sidings came swirling into my room and everything was black. Rubble and glass and everything you can think of was blasted into my house."

41   Said a woman, "I was in the back of the house doing the washing. All of a sudden, the bomb exploded. My clothes were burned off and I received burns on my legs, arms, and back. The skin was just hanging loose. The first thing I did was run in the air-raid shelter and lie there exhausted. Then I thought of my baby in the house and ran back to it. The whole house was knocked down and was burning. My mother and father came crawling out of the debris, their faces and arms just black. I heard the baby crying, and crawled in and dug it out from under the burning embers. It was pretty badly burned. My mother carried it to the shelter."

42   In the heart of the city death prevailed and few were left to tell us about it. That part of the picture has to be reconstructed, as in archeology, from the remains.

43   The crowd that stood gazing upward at the parachutes went down withered and black, like a burned-out patch of weeds. Flames shot out of the castle keep. Trolleys bulging with passengers stopped, and all died at once, leaving burned figures still standing supporting each other and fingers fused to the straps. The military at their barracks and officers were wiped out. So too were factories full of workers, including students from schools, volunteers from neighboring towns working on the firebreaks, children scavenging for wood, the Mayor's staff, and the units for air-raid precaution, fire, welfare, and relief. The larger war industries, since they were on the fringe of the city, were for the most part not seriously damaged. Most of the personnel in the Prefectural Government offices were killed, though the Governor himself happened to be in Tokyo. In hospitals

and clinics, patients, doctors, and nurses all died together, as did the priests and pastors of the temples and the churches. Of 1780 nurses, 1654 were killed, and 90 per cent of the doctors in Hiroshima were casualties.

44   People who were in buildings that sheltered them from the instantaneous effects that accompanied the flash were moments later decapitated or cut to ribbons by flying glass. Others were crushed as walls and floors gave way even in buildings that maintained their outer shells erect. In the thousands of houses that fell, people were pinned below the wreckage, not killed in many cases, but held there till the fire that swept the city caught up with them and put an end to their screams.

45   A police chief said that he was in his back yard when the bomb went off. He was knocked down and a concrete wall fell over him, but he was able to dig himself out and go at once toward the police station in the bank. "When I arrived at the office, I found ten policemen, some severely wounded. These were evacuated to a place of safety where they could get aid. We tried to clean up the glass from the windows, but fire was spreading and a hot southerly wind was blowing. We used a hose with water from a hydrant and also formed a bucket brigade. At noon the water in the hydrants gave out, but in this building we were lucky because we could pump water from a well. We carried buckets up from the basement to the roof and threw water down over the building. People on the road were fainting from the heat and we threw water on them too and carried them into the one room in the building that had not been affected by the bomb. We applied oil and ointment to those who had burns.

46   "About 1:00 P.M. we began to apply first aid to the people outside, since the fire seemed under control as far as this building was concerned. A doctor came to help. He himself was wounded in one leg. By night this place was covered by a mass of people. One doctor applied all the first aid."

47   A doctor who was at a military hospital outside Hiroshima said that about an hour after the bomb went off, "many, many people came rushing to my clinic. They were rushing in all directions of the compass from the city. Many were stretcher cases. Some had their hair burned off, were injured in the back, had broken legs, arms, and thighs. The majority of the cases were those injured from glass; many had glass imbedded in the body. Next to the glass injuries, the most frequent were those who had their faces and hands burned, and also the chest and back. Most of the people arrived barefooted; many had their clothes burned off. Women were wearing men's clothing and men were wearing women's. They had put on anything they could pick up along the way.

48   "On the first day about 250 came, who were so injured they had to stay in the hospital, and we also attended about 500 others. Of all of these about 100 died."

49   A talkative man in a newspaper office said that the most severely burned people looked like red shrimps. Some had "skin which still burned sagging from the face and body with a reddish-white skin underneath showing."

50   A reporter who was outside the city at the time of the explosion, but came in immediately afterward, noticed among the dead a mother with a baby held tightly in her arms. He saw several women running around nude, red from burns, and without hair. Many people climbed into water tanks kept for putting out fires and there died. "The most pathetic cases were the small children looking for their parents. There was one child of about eleven with a four-year-old on his back, looking, looking for his mother in vain."

51   Shortly after the bomb fell, there was a high wind, or "fire storm" engendered by the heat, that tore up trees and, whirling over the river, made waterspouts. In some areas rain fell.

52   The severely burned woman who had been washing when the bomb fell said that she went down to the river, where "there were many people just dripping from their burns. Many of them were so badly burned that you could see the meat. By this time it was raining pretty badly. I could not walk or lie down or do anything. Water poured into the shelter and I received water blisters as well as blisters from the burns. It rained a lot right after the bomb."

53   Although the fire burned for days, the major destruction did not take very long. A fisherman out on the bay said, "I saw suddenly a flash of light. I thought something burned my face. I hid in the boat face down. When I looked up later, Hiroshima was completely burned."

IV

54   Hiroshima, of course, never had been prepared for a disaster of the magnitude which overtook it, but in addition the organized sources of aid that did exist were decimated along with everything else. As a result, rescue had to come from surrounding areas, and soon trucks and trains were picking up the wounded, while hospitals, schools, temples, assembly halls, and tents were preparing to receive them. However, the suburbs and surrounding areas were overwhelmed by the rush of immediate survivors out of the bombed region and so, for about a day, help did not penetrate far into the city. This, together with the fact that survivors who were physically uninjured were stunned and bewildered, resulted in great numbers of the wounded dying from lack of aid.

55   The vice-mayor of a neighboring town that began receiving the wounded about 11:30 in the morning said, "Everybody looked alike. The

eyes appeared to be a mass of melted flesh. The lips were split up and also looked like a mass of molten flesh. Only the nose appeared the same as before. The death scene was awful. The patient would turn blue and when we touched the body the skin would stick to our hands."

56 Those who ventured into Hiroshima were greeted by sights they were reluctant to describe. A businessman reported: "The bodies of half-dead people lay on the roadside, on the bridges, in the water, in the gardens, and everywhere. It was a sight no one wants to see. Practically all of these people were nude. Their color was brownish blackish and some of their bodies were dripping. There was a fellow whose head was half burned so that I thought he was wearing a hat." Another man said, "The bodies of the dead were so burned that we could not distinguish men from women."

57 In the public parks great numbers of both wounded and dead were congregated. There were cries for aid and cries for water and there were places where unidentifiable shapes merely stirred.

58 In the late afternoon, aid began to come farther into the city from the outer edges. Rice balls and other food were brought. From their mission up the valley a number of Jesuits came, and one of them, Father Siemes, gave a vivid and careful description of what he had seen, when he was later interviewed by members of the Bombing Survey in Tokyo. He said, "Beneath the wreckage of the houses along the way many had been trapped and they screamed to be rescued from the oncoming flames. They had to be left to their fate."

59 On a bridge, he encountered a procession of soldiers "dragging themselves along with the help of staves or carried by their less severely injured comrades. Abandoned on the bridge there stood with sunken heads a number of horses with large burns on their flanks.

60 "Fukai, the secretary of the mission, was completely out of his mind. He did not want to leave the house when the fires were burning closer, and explained that he did not want to survive the destruction of his fatherland." He had to be carried away by force.

61 After dark, the priests helped pull from the river two children who suffered chills and then died. There was a sand-spit in the river, covered with wounded, who cried for help and who were afraid that the rising tide would drown them. After midnight, "only occasionally did we hear calls for help."

62 Many patients were brought to an open field right behind Hiroshima station, and tents were set up for them. Doctors came in from the neighboring prefectures and from near-by towns such as Yamaguchi, Okayama, and Shimane. The Army also took part in relief measures, and all available military facilities and units were mobilized to that end.

63 A fisherman who came to Hiroshima to see what had happened said, "I cannot describe the situation in words, it was so pitiful. To see so many people dead was a terrible sight. Their clothes were shredded and their

bodies puffed up, some with tongues hanging out. They were dead in all shapes."

64   As late as the second day the priests noted that among cadavers there were still many wounded alive. "Frightfully injured forms beckoned to us and then collapsed."

65   They carried some to the hospitals, but "we could not move everybody who lay exposed to the sun." It did not make much difference, anyway, for in the hospitals there was little that could be done. They just lay in the corridors, row on row, and died.

66   A businessman came into Hiroshima on the third day. "I went to my brother's house in the suburbs and found that all were wounded but none killed. They were stunned and could hardly speak. The next day, one of the four children died. She got black and blue in the face, just as if you had mashed your finger, and had died fifteen minutes after that. In another half hour, her sister did the same thing and she died also."

67   The wife of a soldier who had been with the Hiroshima troops said, "My husband was a soldier and so he was to die, but when it actually happened, I wondered why we did not all go with him. They called me and I went to see. I was to find him in the heap, but I decided against looking at the bodies. I want to remember him as he was—big and healthy, not some horribly charred body. If I saw that, it would remain forever in my eyes."

68   A police chief told how the dead were collected and burned. "Many could not be identified. In cases where it was possible, the corpses or the ashes were given to the immediate family. Mostly, the cremation was done by the police or the soldiers, and the identified ashes were given to the family. The ashes of those not identified were turned over to the City Hall. There still are boxes in the City Hall. Occasionally even now one is identified, or is supposed to be identified, and is claimed."

69   The destroyed heart of Hiroshima consisted of 4.7 square miles, and the best estimates indicate that the mortality rate was 15,000 to the square mile. For many days funeral processions moved along the roads and through the towns and villages all around Hiroshima. The winds were pervaded by the smell of death and cremation. At night the skies were lit with the flames of funeral pyres.

V

70   Very few of the people we interviewed at Hiroshima attempted to make a play for sympathy or to make us feel guilty. The general manner was one which might be interpreted as due either to lingering apathy and absence of feeling consequent on shock, or to reserve which masked hate. It was probably a mixture of both, in varying degrees in different

people. But on the surface everyone appeared willing to coöperate and oblige.

71   An official of a near-by small town thought that "if America had such a weapon, there was no use to go on. Many high school students in Hiroshima who were wounded in the raid spoke incoherently on their death-beds, saying, 'Please avenge that raid for us somehow.' However, most of the people felt that since it was war, it was just *shikata ga nai,* could not be helped. But we were unified in the idea that we had to win the war."

72   A newspaper reporter said that after the bomb fell, some felt that this was the end, while others wanted to go on regardless. "Those who had actually experienced the bomb were the ones who wanted to quit, while those who had not, wanted to go on."

73   The wife of a soldier killed in the blast said, "Though many are resentful against America, I feel no animosity. It was an understood war and the use of weapons was fair. I only wonder why they didn't let the people know about this bomb and give us a chance, before bombing us, to give up."

74   A police chief believed that the general reaction among the people was one of surprise and a feeling that "we have taken the worst beating, we have been the goats." He said, "They felt that America had done a terrible thing and were very bitter, but after the surrender they turned on the Japanese military. They felt they had been fooled, and wondered if the military knew that the bomb was coming and why they did not take steps. The bomb made no difference in the fighting spirit of the people: it drew them together and made them more coöperative. My eldest son was killed, but I felt that it was destiny that ruled. When I see people who got away without any injury, I feel a little pang of envy naturally, but I don't feel bitter toward them."

75   Poking in the ruins one day, I came on the stone figure of a dog, one of that grinning type derived from China which commonly guards the entrances to temples. It was tilted on its pedestal but undamaged, and the grin gleamed out as if it were hailing me. Its rakish air and its look of fiendish satisfaction with all that lay around drew me on to inspect it more closely. It was then apparent that the look was not directed at me, but out somewhere beyond. It was, of course, only a piece of stone, and it displayed no particular artistic merit; yet in looking at it I felt that I was a clod, while it had a higher, sentient wisdom locked up within.

76   The look and the feeling it inspired were familiar and I groped to remember where I had seen it before other than on temple dogs. The eyes were creased in a fashion that did not exactly connotate mirth, and the lips were drawn far back in a smile that seemed to blend bitterness, glee, and compassion. The word "sardonic" came to mind, and this led to recognition and a realization of terrible appropriateness.

77   All who have acquaintance with the dead know the curious smile

that may creep over the human face as *rigor mortis* sets in, a smile of special quality called by doctors *risus sardonicus*. The dog had this look, and it seemed to me probable that some ancient Oriental sculptor, in seeking an expression for temple guardians that would drive off evil spirits, had taken this death grin as his model, and thus it had come down through hundreds of years to this beast looking out on Hiroshima.

78   Many a soldier has seen this face looking up at him from the field of battle, before he himself was wearing it, and many a priest and doctor has found himself alone with it in a darkened room. As with the dog, at first the look seems at you, and then beyond you, as if there lay at last behind it knowledge of the huge joke of life which the rest of us feel vaguely but cannot comprehend. And there is that tinge of compassion that is as dreadful as it is unknowable.

79   As I continued to study this stone face, it began to appear that the grin was not directed at the waste and the destruction around, at the red and yellow and the smells, any more than it was at me. It was not so much a face looking at Hiroshima as it was the face of Hiroshima. The carved eyes gazed beyond the rubble, beyond the gardens of radishes and fields of winter wheat, beyond the toiling adults and the rippling children with their tangerines and shouts of "Haro-goodabye!" surging up with new life like flowers and weeds spreading over devastation, beyond the mountains with red pines in the blue sky, beyond all these, over the whole broad shoulder of the world to where, in cities and towns, watches on wrists and clocks on towers still ticked and moved. The face seemed to be smiling and waiting for the harvest of the wind that had been sown.

80   There was one woman in Hiroshima who said, "If there are such things as ghosts, why don't they haunt the Americans?"

81   Perhaps they do.

Questions

1. The mind, when overwhelmed in experience with sheer pain, horror or numbers, tends to shut itself off. How does Leighton use the principles of *selectivity* and *contrast* throughout his report in order to keep the horror of that day fresh in the reader's mind as he recounts it?

2. In spite of the factual form of this essay, what indications can you find that Leighton is trying to persuade the reader to a point of view or emotional attitude? List them and describe it.

3. Explain the reasons for the essay's division into five parts. What unity does each part have and how are they related to each other?

4. What function does the driver serve in Part I?

5. Explain why Leighton presents the kind of census and guidebook information he does in Part II. What general justification can be made for its inclusion, for each of the details?

6. Should paragraphs 30 and 31 perhaps have been omitted since Leighton was not there and could not have seen what he reports?

7. In the final section of Part V, the symbol of the smiling stone dog is clearly a means for Leighton to make a statement about his experience. What is that statement? List the elements that paragraph 79 echoes from the first section of the essay. How does the perspective from which they are now seen differ from that of the first section? Why does he refer to clocks and watches in paragraph 79? What does the dog's sardonic knowledge seem to be?

38   ALFRED KAZIN

From the Subway to the Synagogue

1   . . . All my early life lies open to my eye within five city blocks. When I passed the school, I went sick with all my old fear of it. With its standard New York public-school brown brick courtyard shut in on three sides of the square and the pretentious battlements overlooking that cockpit in which I can still smell the fiery sheen of the rubber ball, it looks like a factory over which has been imposed the facade of a castle. It gave me the shivers to stand up in the courtyard again; I felt as if I had been mustered back into the service of those Friday morning "tests" that were the terror of my childhood.

2   It was never learning I associated with that school: only the necessity to succeed, to get ahead of the others in the daily struggle to "make a good impression" on our teachers, who grimly, wearily, and often with ill-concealed distaste watched against our relapsing into the natural savagery they expected of Brownsville boys. The white, cool, thinly ruled record book sat over us from their desks all day long, and had remorselessly entered into it each day—in blue ink if we had passed, in red ink if we had not—our attendance, our conduct, our "effort," our merits and demerits; and to the last possible decimal point in calculation, our standing in an unending series of "tests"—surprise tests, daily tests, weekly tests, formal midterm tests, final tests. They never stopped trying to dig out of us whatever small morsel of fact we had managed to get down the night before. We had to prove that we were really alert, ready for anything,

always in the race. That white thinly ruled record book figured in my mind as the judgment seat; the very thinness and remote blue lightness of its lines instantly showed its cold authority over me; so much space had been left on each page, columns and columns in which to note down everything about us, implacably and forever. As it lay there on a teacher's desk, I stared at it all day long with such fear and anxious propriety that I had no trouble believing that God, too, did nothing but keep such record books, and that on the final day He would face me with an account in Hebrew letters whose phonetic dots and dashes looked strangely like decimal points counting up my every sinful thought on earth.

3   All teachers were to be respected like gods, and God Himself was the greatest of all school superintendents. Long after I had ceased to believe that our teachers could see with the back of their heads, it was still understood, by me, that they knew everything. They were the delegates of all visible and invisible power on earth—of the mothers who waited on the stoops every day after three for us to bring home tales of our daily triumphs; of the glacially remote Anglo-Saxon principal, whose very name was King; of the incalculably important Superintendent of Schools who would someday rubberstamp his name to the bottom of our diplomas in grim acknowledgment that we had, at last, given satisfaction to him, to the Board of Superintendents, and to our benefactor the City of New York —and so up and up, the government of the United States and to the great Lord Jehovah Himself. My belief in teachers' unlimited wisdom and power rested not so much on what I saw in them—how impatient most of them looked, how wary—but on our abysmal humility, at least in those of us who were "good" boys, who proved by our ready compliance and "manners" that we wanted to get on. The road to a professional future would be shown us only as we pleased *them. Make a good impression the first day of the term, and they'll help you out. Make a bad impression, and you might as well cut your throat.* This was the first article of school folklore, whispered around the classroom the opening day of each term. You made the "good impression" by sitting firmly at your wooden desk, hands clasped; by silence for the greatest part of the live-long day; by standing up obsequiously when it was so expected of you; by sitting down noiselessly when you had answered a question; by "speaking nicely," which meant reproducing their painfully exact enunciation; by "showing manners," or an ecstatic submissiveness in all things; by outrageous flattery; by bringing little gifts at Christmas, on their birthdays, and at the end of the term—the well-known significance of these gifts being that they come not from us, but from our parents, whose eagerness in this matter showed a high level of social consideration, and thus raised our standing in turn.

4   It was not just our quickness and memory that were always being tested. Above all, in that word I could never hear without automatically

seeing it raised before me in gold-plated letters, it was our *character*. I always felt anxious when I heard the word pronounced. Satisfactory as my "character" was, on the whole, except when I stayed too long in the playground reading; outrageously satisfactory, as I can see now, the very sound of the word as our teachers coldly gave it out from the end of their teeth, with a solemn weight on each dark syllable, immediately struck my heart cold with fear—they could not believe I really had it. Character was never something you had; it had to be trained in you, like a technique. I was never very clear about it. On our side *character* meant demonstrative obedience; but teachers already had it—how else could they have become teachers? They had it; the aloof Anglo-Saxon principal whom we remotely saw only on ceremonial occasions in the assembly was positively encased in it; it glittered off his bald head in spokes of triumphant light; the President of the United States had the greatest conceivable amount of it. Character belonged to great adults. Yet we were constantly being driven onto it; it was the great threshold we had to cross. *Alfred Kazin, having shown proficiency in his course of studies and having displayed satisfactory marks of character. . . .* Thus someday the hallowed diploma, passport to my further advancement in high school. But there—I could already feel it in my bones—they would put me through even more doubting tests of character; and after that, if I should be good enough and bright enough, there would be still more. *Character* was a bitter thing, racked with my endless striving to please. The school—from every last stone in the courtyard to the battlements frowning down at me from the walls—was only the stage for a trial. I felt that the very atmosphere of learning that surrounded us was fake—that every lesson, every book, every approving smile was only a pretext for the constant probing and watching of me, that there was not a secret in me that would not be decimally measured into that white record book. All week long I lived for the blessed sound of the dismissal gong at three o'clock on Friday afternoon.

5   I was awed by this system, I believed in it, I respected its force. The alternative was "going bad." The school was notoriously the toughest in our tough neighborhood, and the dangers of "going bad" were constantly impressed upon me at home and in school in dark whispers of the "reform school" and in examples of boys who had been picked up for petty thievery, rape, or flinging a heavy inkwell straight into a teacher's face. Behind any failure in school yawned the great abyss of a criminal career. Every refractory attitude doomed you with the sound "Sing Sing." Anything less than absolute perfection in school always suggested to my mind that I might fall out of the daily race, be kept back in the working class forever, or—dared I think of it?—fall into the criminal class itself.

6   I worked on a hairline between triumph and catastrophe. Why the odds should always have felt so narrow I understood only when I realized how little my parents thought of their own lives. It was not for myself

alone that I was expected to shine, but for them—to redeem the constant anxiety of their existence. I was the first American child, their offering to the strange new God; I was to be the monument of their liberation from the shame of being—what they were. And that there was shame in this was a fact that everyone seemed to believe as a matter of course. It was in the gleeful discounting of themselves—what do we know? with which our parents greeted every fresh victory in our savage competition for "high averages," for prizes, for a few condescending words of official praise from the principal at assembly. It was in the sickening invocation of "Americanism"—the word itself accusing us of everything we apparently were not. Our families and teachers seemed tacitly agreed that we were somehow to be a little ashamed of what we were. Yet it was always hard to say why this should be so. It was certainly not—in Brownsville!— because we were Jews, or simply because we spoke another language at home, or were absent on our holy days. It was rather that a "refined," "correct," "nice" English was required of us at school that we did not naturally speak, and that our teachers could never be quite sure we would keep. This English was peculiarly the ladder of advancement. Every future young lawyer was known by it. Even the Communists and Socialists on Pitkin Avenue spoke it. It was bright and clean and polished. We were expected to show it off like a new pair of shoes. When the teacher sharply called a question out, then your name, you were expected to leap up, face the class, and eject those new words fluently off the tongue.

7   There was my secret ordeal: I could never say anything except in the most roundabout way; I was a stammerer. Although I knew all those new words from my private reading—I read walking in the street, to and from the Children's Library on Stone Avenue; on the fire escape and the roof; at every meal when they would let me; read even when I dressed in the morning, propping my book up against the drawers of the bureau as I pulled· on my long black stockings—I could never seem to get the easiest words out with the right dispatch, and would often miserably signal from my desk that I did not know the answer rather than get up to stumble and fall and crash on every word. If, angry at always being put down as lazy or stupid, I did get up to speak, the black wooden floor would roll away under my feet, the teacher would frown at me in amazement, and in unbearable loneliness I would hear behind me the groans and laughter: *tuh-tuh-tuh-tuh.*

8   The word was my agony. The word that for others was so effortless and so neutral, so unburdened, so simple, so exact, I had first to meditate in advance, to see if I could make it, like a plumber fitting together odd lengths and shapes of pipe. I was always preparing words I could speak, storing them away, choosing between them. And often, when the word did come from my mouth in its great and terrible birth, quailing and bleeding as if forced through a thornbush, I would not be able to look the

others in the face, and would walk out in the silence, the infinitely echoing silence behind my back, to say it all cleanly back to myself as I walked in the streets. Only when I was alone in the open air, pacing the roof with pebbles in my mouth, as I had read Demosthenes had done to cure himself of stammering; or in the street, where all words seemed to flow from the length of my stride and the color of the houses as I remembered the perfect tranquillity of a phrase in *Beethoven's Romance in F* I could sing back to myself as I walked—only then was it possible for me to speak without the infinite premeditations and strangled silences I toiled through whenever I got up at school to respond with the expected, the exact answer.

9   It troubled me that I could speak in the fullness of my own voice only when I was alone on the streets, walking about. There was something unnatural about it; unbearably isolated. I was not like the others! At midday, every freshly shocking Monday noon, they sent me away to a speech clinic in a school in East New York, where I sat in a circle of lispers and cleft palates and foreign accents holding a mirror before my lips and rolling difficult sounds over and over. To be sent there in the full light of the opening week, when everyone else was at school or going about his business, made me feel as if I had been expelled from the great normal body of humanity. I would gobble down my lunch on my way to the speech clinic and rush back to the school in time to make up for the classes I had lost. One day, one unforgettable dread day, I stopped to catch my breath on a corner of Sutter Avenue, near the wholesale fruit markets, where an old drugstore rose up over a great flight of steps. In the window were dusty urns of colored water floating off iron chains; cardboard placards advertising hairnets, EX-LAX: a great illustrated medical chart headed THE HUMAN FACTORY, which showed the exact course a mouthful of food follows as it falls from chamber to chamber of the body. I hadn't meant to stop there at all, only to catch my breath; but I so hated the speech clinic that I thought I would delay my arrival for a few minutes by eating my lunch on the steps. When I took the sandwich out of my bag, two bitterly hard pieces of hard salami slipped out of my hand and fell through a grate onto a hill of dust below the steps. I remember how sickeningly vivid an odd thread of hair looked on the salami, as if my lunch were turning stiff with death. The factory whistles called their short, sharp blasts stark through the middle of noon, beating at me where I sat outside the city's magnetic circle. I had never known, I knew instantly I would never in my heart again submit to such wild passive despair as I felt at that moment, sitting on the steps before THE HUMAN FACTORY, where little robots gathered and shoveled the food from chamber to chamber of the body. They had put me out into the streets, I thought to myself; with their mirrors and their everlasting pulling at me to imitate their effortless bright speech and their stupefaction that a boy could stammer and stumble on

every other English word he carried in his head, they had put me out into the streets, had left me high and dry on the steps of that drugstore staring at the remains of my lunch turning black and grimy in the dust.

Questions

1. What images convey "the terror of my childhood" in the first paragraph?

2. What words and phrases in paragraph 2 amplify and make concrete the causes of young Kazin's fear? Explain the symbolism involved in the final sentence of this paragraph.

3. How does the cultural premise "God is terrible but just" explain the young Kazin's outlook and control author Kazin's account of his early schooling? How does the imagery of the final paragraph reflect a basic psychological change in the author as a young boy?

4. What does THE HUMAN FACTORY symbolize in the last paragraph?

5. In paragraph 5, defend the ordering of the details in series in the second and last sentences. Is the first sentence arranged in the order of climax?

6. In the last paragraph what function is served by the sentence, "I remember how sickeningly vivid an odd thread of hair looked on the salami, as if my lunch were turning stiff with death"? Why is the hair vivid? Why does the sentence end in death?

7. Discuss the tone of the last paragraph by considering the following: "I would gobble down my lunch," EX-LAX, "two bitterly hard pieces of hard salami," the "sharp blasts stark through the middle noon," the paradox of "wild passive despair," the lunch "turning black and grimy in the dust," and the rhythm of the sentence structures.

8. How do Kazin's responses to his early years at school compare and contrast with your own?

Illustration and Naturalness

39 GEORGE ORWELL
Shooting an Elephant

1   In Moulmein, in Lower Burma, I was hated by large numbers of people—the only time in my life that I have been important enough for this to happen to me. I was sub-divisional police officer of the town, and in an aimless, petty kind of way anti-European feeling was very bitter. No one had the guts to raise a riot, but if a European woman went through the bazaars alone somebody would probably spit betel juice over her dress. As a police officer I was an obvious target and was baited whenever it seemed safe to do so. When a nimble Burman tripped me up on the football field and the referee (another Burman) looked the other way, the crowd yelled with hideous laughter. This happened more than once. In the end the sneering yellow faces of young men that met me everywhere, the insults hooted after me when I was at a safe distance, got badly on my nerves. The young Buddhist priests were the worst of all. There were several thousands of them in the town and none of them seemed to have anything to do except stand on street corners and jeer at Europeans.

2   All this was perplexing and upsetting. For at that time I had already made up my mind that imperialism was an evil thing and the sooner I chucked up my job and got out of it the better. Theoretically—and secretly, of course—I was all for the Burmese and all against their oppressors, the British. As for the job I was doing, I hated it more bitterly than I can perhaps make clear. In a job like that you see the dirty work of Empire at close quarters. The wretched prisoners huddling in the stinking cages of the lock-ups, the grey, cowed faces of the long-term convicts, the scarred buttocks of the men who had been flogged with bamboos—all these oppressed me with an intolerable sense of guilt. But I could get nothing into

perspective. I was young and ill-educated and I had had to think out my problems in the utter silence that is imposed on every Englishman in the East. I did not even know that the British Empire is dying, still less did I know that it is a great deal better than the younger empires that are going to supplant it. All I knew was that I was stuck between my hatred of the empire I served and my rage against the evil-spirited little beasts who tried to make my job impossible. With one part of my mind I thought of the British Raj as an unbreakable tyranny, as something clamped down, in *saecula saeculorum,* upon the will of prostrate peoples; with another part I thought that the greatest joy in the world would be to drive a bayonet into a Buddhist priest's guts. Feelings like these are the normal by-products of imperialism; ask any Anglo-Indian official, if you can catch him off duty.

3   One day something happened which in a roundabout way was enlightening. It was a tiny incident in itself, but it gave me a better glimpse than I had had before of the real nature of imperialism—the real motives for which despotic governments act. Early one morning the subinspector at a police station the other end of the town rang me up on the 'phone and said that an elephant was ravaging the bazaar. Would I please come and do something about it? I did not know what I could do, but I wanted to see what was happening and I got on to a pony and started out. I took my rifle, an old .44 Winchester and much too small to kill an elephant, but I thought the noise might be useful *in terrorem.* Various Burmans stopped me on the way and told me about the elephant's doings. It was not, of course, a wild elephant, but a tame one which had gone "must." It had been chained up, as tame elephants always are when their attack of "must" is due, but on the previous night it had broken its chain and escaped. Its mahout, the only person who could manage it when it was in that state, had set out in pursuit, but had taken the wrong direction and was now twelve hours' journey away, and in the morning the elephant had suddenly reappeared in the town. The Burmese population had no weapons and were quite helpless against it. It had already destroyed somebody's bamboo hut, killed a cow and raided some fruit-stalls and devoured the stock; also it had met the municipal rubbish van and, when the driver jumped out and took to his heels, had turned the van over and inflicted violences upon it.

4   The Burmese sub-inspector and some Indian constables were waiting for me in the quarter where the elephant had been seen. It was a very poor quarter, a labyrinth of squalid bamboo huts, thatched with palm-leaf, winding all over a steep hillside. I remember that it was a cloudy, stuffy morning at the beginning of the rains. We began questioning the people as to where the elephant had gone and, as usual, failed to get any definite information. That is invariably the case in the East; a story always sounds clear enough at a distance, but the nearer you get to the scene of events the vaguer it becomes. Some of the people said that the elephant had gone in one direction, some said that he had gone in another, some

professed not even to have heard of any elephant. I had almost made up my mind that the whole story was a pack of lies, when we heard yells a little distance away. There was a loud, scandalized cry of "Go away, child! Go away this instant!" and an old woman with a switch in her hand came round the corner of a hut, violently shooing away a crowd of naked children. Some more women followed, clicking their tongues and exclaiming; evidently there was something that the children ought not to have seen. I rounded the hut and saw a man's dead body sprawling in the mud. He was an Indian, a black Dravidian coolie, almost naked, and he could not have been dead many minutes. The people said that the elephant had come suddenly upon him round the corner of the hut, caught him with its trunk, put its foot on his back and ground him into the earth. This was the rainy season and the ground was soft, and his face had scored a trench a foot deep and a couple of yards long. He was lying on his belly with arms crucified and head sharply twisted to one side. His face was coated with mud, the eyes wide open, the teeth bared and grinning with an expression of unendurable agony. (Never tell me, by the way, that the dead look peaceful. Most of the corpses I have seen looked devilish.) The friction of the great beast's foot had stripped the skin from his back as neatly as one skins a rabbit. As soon as I saw the dead man I sent an orderly to a friend's house nearby to borrow an elephant rifle. I had already sent back the pony, not wanting it to go mad with fright and throw me if it smelt the elephant.

5   The orderly came back in a few minutes with a rifle and five cartridges, and meanwhile some Burmans had arrived and told us that the elephant was in the paddy fields below, only a few hundred yards away. As I started forward practically the whole population of the quarter flocked out of the houses and followed me. They had seen the rifle and were all shouting excitedly that I was going to shoot the elephant. They had not shown much interest in the elephant when he was merely ravaging their homes, but it was different now that he was going to be shot. It was a bit of fun to them, as it would be to an English crowd; besides they wanted the meat. It made me vaguely uneasy. I had no intention of shooting the elephant—I had merely sent for the rifle to defend myself if necessary— and it is always unnerving to have a crowd following you. I marched down the hill, looking and feeling a fool, with the rifle over my shoulder and an ever-growing army of people jostling at my heels. At the bottom, when you got away from the huts, there was a metalled road and beyond that a miry waste of paddy fields a thousand yards across, not yet ploughed but soggy from the first rains and dotted with coarse grass. The elephant was standing eight yards from the road, his left side towards us. He took not the slightest notice of the crowd's approach. He was tearing up bunches of grass, beating them against his knees to clean them and stuffing them into his mouth.

6   I had halted on the road. As soon as I saw the elephant I knew with

perfect certainty that I ought not to shoot him. It is a serious matter to shoot a working elephant—it is comparable to destroying a huge and costly piece of machinery—and obviously one ought not to do it if it can possibly be avoided. And at that distance, peacefully eating, the elephant looked no more dangerous than a cow. I thought then and I think now that his attack of "must" was already passing off; in which case he would merely wander harmlessly about until the mahout came back and caught him. Moreover, I did not in the least want to shoot him. I decided that I would watch him for a little while to make sure that he did not turn savage again, and then go home.

7   But at that moment I glanced round at the crowd that had followed me. It was an immense crowd, two thousand at the least and growing every minute. It blocked the road for a long distance on either side. I looked at the sea of yellow faces above the garish clothes—faces all happy and excited over this bit of fun, all certain that the elephant was going to be shot. They were watching me as they would watch a conjurer about to perform a trick. They did not like me, but with the magical rifle in my hands I was momentarily worth watching. And suddenly I realized that I should have to shoot the elephant after all. The people expected it of me and I had got to do it; I could feel their two thousand wills pressing me forward, irresistibly. And it was at this moment, as I stood there with the rifle in my hands, that I first grasped the hollowness, the futility of the white man's dominion in the East. Here was I, the white man with his gun, standing in front of the unarmed native crowd—seemingly the leading actor of the piece; but in reality I was only an absurd puppet pushed to and fro by the will of those yellow faces behind. I perceived in this moment that when the white man turns tyrant it is his own freedom that he destroys. He becomes a sort of hollow, posing dummy, the conventionalized figure of a sahib. For it is the condition of his rule that he shall spend his life in trying to impress the "natives," and so in every crisis he has got to do what the "natives" expect of him. He wears a mask, and his face grows to fit it. I had got to shoot the elephant. I had committed myself to doing it when I sent for the rifle. A sahib has got to act like a sahib; he has got to appear resolute, to know his own mind and do definite things. To come all that way, rifle in hand, with two thousand people marching at my heels, and then to trail feebly away, having done nothing—no, that was impossible. The crowd would laugh at me. And my whole life, every white man's life in the East, was one long struggle not to be laughed at.

8   But I did not want to shoot the elephant. I watched him beating his bunch of grass against his knees, with that preoccupied grandmotherly air that elephants have. It seemed to me that it would be murder to shoot him. At that age I was not squeamish about killing animals, but I had never shot an elephant and never wanted to. (Somehow it always seems

worse to kill a *large* animal.) Besides, there was the beast's owner to be considered. Alive, the elephant was worth at least a hundred pounds; dead, he would only be worth the value of his tusks, five pounds, possibly. But I had got to act quickly. I turned to some experienced-looking Burmans who had been there when we arrived, and asked them how the elephant had been behaving. They all said the same thing: he took no notice of you if you left him alone, but he might charge if you went too close to him.

9   It was perfectly clear to me what I ought to do. I ought to walk up to within, say, twenty-five yards of the elephant and test his behavior. If he charged, I could shoot; if he took no notice of me, it would be safe to leave him until the mahout came back. But also I knew that I was going to do no such thing. I was a poor shot with a rifle and the ground was soft mud into which one would sink at every step. If the elephant charged and I missed him, I should have about as much chance as a toad under a steam-roller. But even then I was not thinking particularly of my own skin, only of the watchful yellow faces behind. For at that moment, with the crowd watching me, I was not afraid in the ordinary sense, as I would have been if I had been alone. A white man mustn't be frightened in front of "natives"; and so, in general, he isn't frightened. The sole thought in my mind was that if anything went wrong those two thousand Burmans would see me pursued, caught, trampled on and reduced to a grinning corpse like that Indian up the hill. And if that happened it was quite probable that some of them would laugh. That would never do. There was only one alternative. I shoved the cartridges into the magazine and lay down on the road to get a better aim.

10   The crowd grew very still, and a deep, low, happy sigh, as of people who see the theatre curtain go up at last, breathed from innumerable throats. They were going to have their bit of fun after all. The rifle was a beautiful German thing with cross-hair sights. I did not then know that in shooting an elephant one would shoot to cut an imaginary bar running from ear-hole to ear-hole. I ought, therefore, as the elephant was sideways on, to have aimed straight at his ear-hole; actually I aimed several inches in front of this, thinking the brain would be further forward.

11   When I pulled the trigger I did not hear the bang or feel the kick— one never does when a shot goes home—but I heard the devilish roar of glee that went up from the crowd. In that instant, in too short a time, one would have thought, even for the bullet to get there, a mysterious, terrible change had come over the elephant. He neither stirred nor fell, but every line of his body had altered. He looked suddenly stricken, skrunken, immensely old, as though the frightful impact of the bullet had paralysed him without knocking him down. At last, after what seemed a long time— it might have been five seconds, I dare say—he sagged flabbily to his knees. His mouth slobbered. An enormous senility seemed to have settled

upon him. One could have imagined him thousands of years old. I fired again into the same spot. At the second shot he did not collapse but climbed with desperate slowness to his feet and stood weakly upright, with legs sagging and head drooping. I fired a third time. That was the shot that did for him. You could see the agony of it jolt his whole body and knock the last remnant of strength from his legs. But in falling he seemed for a moment to rise, for as his hind legs collapsed beneath him he seemed to tower upward like a huge rock toppling, his trunk reaching skyward like a tree. He trumpeted, for the first and only time. And then down he came, his belly towards me, with a crash that seemed to shake the ground even where I lay.

12   I got up. The Burmans were already racing past me across the mud. It was obvious that the elephant would never rise again, but he was not dead. He was breathing very rhythmically with long rattling gasps, his great mound of a side painfully rising and falling. His mouth was wide open—I could see far down into caverns of pale pink throat. I waited a long time for him to die, but his breathing did not weaken. Finally I fired my two remaining shots into the spot where I thought his heart must be. The thick blood welled out of him like red velvet, but still he did not die. His body did not even jerk when the shots hit him, the tortured breathing continued without a pause. He was dying, very slowly and in great agony, but in some world remote from me where not even a bullet could damage him further. I felt that I had got to put an end to that dreadful noise. It seemed dreadful to see the great beast lying there, powerless to move and yet powerless to die, and not even to be able to finish him. I sent back for my small rifle and poured shot after shot into his heart and down his throat. They seemed to make no impression. The tortured gasps continued as steadily as the ticking of a clock.

13   In the end I could not stand it any longer and went away. I heard later that it took him half an hour to die. Burmans were bringing dahs and baskets even before I left, and I was told they had stripped his body almost to the bones by the afternoon.

14   Afterwards, of course, there were endless discussions about the shooting of the elephant. The owner was furious, but he was only an Indian and could do nothing. Besides, legally I had done the right thing, for a mad elephant has to be killed, like a mad dog, if its owner fails to control it. Among the Europeans opinion was divided. The older men said I was right, the younger men said it was a damn shame to shoot an elephant for killing a coolie, because an elephant was worth more than any damn Coringhee coolie. And afterwards I was very glad that the coolie had been killed; it put me legally in the right and it gave me a sufficient pretext for shooting the elephant. I often wondered whether any of the others grasped that I had done it solely to avoid looking a fool.

40 C. S. LEWIS
The Law of Right and Wrong

1   Every one has heard people quarrelling. Sometimes it sounds funny and sometimes it sounds merely unpleasant; but however it sounds, I believe we can learn something very important from listening to the kind of things they say. They say things like this: "That's my seat, I was there first"—"Leave him alone, he isn't doing you any harm"—"Why should you shove in first?"—"Give me a bit of your orange, I gave you a bit of mine"—"How'd you like it if anyone did the same to you?"—"Come on, you promised." People say things like that every day, educated people as well as uneducated, and children as well as grown-ups.

2   Now what interests me about all these remarks is that the man who makes them isn't just saying that the other man's behaviour doesn't happen to please him. He is appealing to some kind of standard of behaviour which he expects the other man to know about. And the other man very seldom replies, "To hell with your standard." Nearly always he tries to make out that what he has been doing doesn't really go against the standard, or that if it does, there is some special excuse. He pretends there is some special reason in this particular case why the person who took the seat first should not keep it, or that things were quite different when he was given the bit of orange, or that something has turned up which lets him off keeping his promise. It looks, in fact, very much as if both parties had in mind some kind of Law or Rule of fair play or decent behaviour or morality or whatever you like to call it, about which they really agreed. And they have. If they hadn't, they might, of course, fight like animals, but they couldn't *quarrel* in the human sense of the word. Quarrelling means trying to show that the other man is in the wrong. And there'd be no sense in trying to do that unless you and he had some part of agreement as to what Right and Wrong are; just as there'd be no sense in saying that a footballer had committed a foul unless there was some agreement about the rules of football.

3   Now this Law or Rule about Right and Wrong used to be called the Law of Nature. Nowadays, when we talk of the "laws of nature" we usually mean things like gravitation, or heredity, or the laws of chemistry. But when the older thinkers called the Law of Right and Wrong the Law of Nature, they really meant the Law of *Human* Nature. The idea was that,

just as falling stones are governed by the law of gravitation and chemicals by chemical laws, so the creature called man also had *his* law—with this great difference, that the stone couldn't choose whether it obeyed the law of gravitation or not, but a man could choose either to obey the Law of Human Nature or to disobey it. They called it Law of Nature because they thought that every one knew it by nature and didn't need to be taught it. They didn't mean, of course, that you mightn't find an odd individual here and there who didn't know it, just as you find a few people who are colour-blind or have no ear for a tune. But taking the race as a whole, they thought that the human idea of Decent Behaviour was obvious to every one. And I believe they were right. If they weren't, then all the things we say about this war are nonsense. What is the sense in saying the enemy are in the wrong unless Right is a real thing which the Germans at bottom know as well as we do and ought to practise? If they had no notion of what we mean by right, then, though we might still have to fight them, we could no more blame them for that than for the colour of their hair.

4   I know that some people say the idea of Law of Nature or decent behaviour known to all men is unsound, because different civilisations and different ages have had quite different moralities. But they haven't. They have only had *slightly* different moralities. Just think what a *quite* different morality would mean. Think of a country where people were *admired* for running away in battle, or where a man felt *proud* for double-crossing all the people who had been kindest to him. You might just as well to try to imagine a country where two and two made five. Men have differed as regards what people you ought to be unselfish to—whether it was only your own family, or your fellow countrymen, or every one. But they have always agreed that you oughtn't to put yourself first. Selfishness has never been admired. Men have differed as to whether you should have one wife or four. But they have always agreed that you mustn't simply have any woman you liked.

5   But the most remarkable thing is this. Whenever you find a man who says he doesn't believe in a real Right and Wrong, you will find the same man going back on this a moment later. He may break his promise to you, but if you try breaking one to him he'll be complaining "It's not fair" before you can say Jack Robinson. A nation may say treaties don't matter; but then, next minute, they spoil their case by saying that the particular treaty they want to break was an unfair one. But if treaties don't matter, and if there's no such things as Right and Wrong—in other words, if there is no Law of Nature—what is the difference between a fair treaty and an unfair one? Haven't they given away the fact that, whatever they say, they really know the Law of Nature just like anyone else?

6   It seems, then, we are forced to believe in a real Right and Wrong. People may be sometimes mistaken about them, just as people sometimes get their sums wrong; but they are not a matter of mere taste and opinion any more than the multiplication table. Now if we're agreed about that,

I go on to my next point, which is this. None of us are really keeping the Law of Nature. If there are any exceptions among you, I apologise to them. They'd better switch on to another station, for nothing I'm going to say concerns them. And now, turning to the ordinary human beings who are left:

7   I hope you won't misunderstand what I'm going to say. I'm not preaching, and Heaven knows I'm not pretending that I'm better than anyone else. I'm only trying to call attention to a fact; the fact that this year, or this month, or, more likely, this very day, we have failed to practise ourselves the kind of behaviour we expect from other people. There may be all sorts of excuses for us. That time you were so unfair to the children was when you were very tired. That slightly shady business about the money—the one you've almost forgotten—came when you were very hard up. And what you promised to do for old So-and-so and have never done— well, you never would have promised if you'd known how frightfully busy you were going to be. And as for your behaviour to your wife (or husband), if I knew how irritating they could be, I wouldn't wonder at it— and who the dickens am I, anyway? I am just the same. That is to say, I don't succeed in keeping the Law of Nature very well, and the moment anyone tells me I'm not keeping it, there starts up in my mind a string of excuses as long as your arm. The question at the moment is not whether they are good excuses. The point is that they are one more proof of how deeply, whether we like it or not, we believe in the Law of Nature. If we didn't believe in decent behaviour, why should we be so anxious to make excuses for not having behaved decently? The truth is, we believe in decency so much—we feel the Rule or Law pressing on us so—that we can't bear to face the fact that we're breaking it, and consequently we try to shift the responsibility. For you notice that it's only for our bad behaviour that we find all these explanations. We put our *bad* temper down to being tired or worried or hungry; we put our good temper down to ourselves.

8   Well, those are the two points I wanted to make tonight. First, that human beings, all over the earth, have this curious idea that they *ought* to behave in a certain way, and can't really get rid of it. Secondly, that they don't in fact behave in that way. They know the Law of Nature; they break it. These two facts are the foundation of all clear thinking about ourselves and the universe we live in.

II

9   If they are the foundation, I had better stop to make that foundation firm before I go on. Some of the letters I have had from listeners show that a good many people find it difficult to understand just what this Law of Human Nature, or Moral Law, or Rule of Decent Behaviour is.

10   For example, some people write to me saying, "Isn't what you call the Moral Law simply our herd instinct and hasn't it been developed just like all our other instincts?" Now I don't deny that we may have a herd instinct: but that isn't what I mean by the Moral Law. We all know what it feels like to be prompted by instinct—by mother love, or sexual instinct, or the instinct for food. It means you feel a strong want or desire to act in a certain way. And, of course, we sometimes do feel just that sort of desire to help another person: and no doubt that desire is due to the herd instinct. But feeling a desire to help is quite different from feeling that you ought to help whether you want to or not. Supposing you hear a cry for help from a man in danger. You will probably feel two desires—one a desire to give help (due to your herd instinct), the other a desire to keep out of danger (due to the instinct for self-preservation). But you will find inside you, in addition to these two impulses, a third thing which tells you that you ought to follow the impulse to help, and suppress the impulse to run away. Now this thing that judges between two instincts, that decides which should be encouraged, can't itself be either of them. You might as well say that the sheet of music which tells you, at a given moment, to play one note on the piano and not another, is itself one of the notes on the keyboard. The Moral Law is, so to speak, the tune we've got to play: our instincts are merely the keys.

11   Another way of seeing that the Moral Law is not simply one of our instincts is this. If two instincts are in conflict, and there is nothing in a creature's mind except those two instincts, obviously the stronger of the two must win. But at those moments when we are most conscious of the Moral Law, it usually seems to be telling us to side with the weaker of the two impulses. You probably *want* to be safe much more than you want to help the man who is drowning: but the Moral Law tells you to help him all the same. And doesn't it often tell us to try to make the right impulse stronger than it naturally is? I mean, we often feel it our duty to stimulate the herd instinct, by waking up our imaginations and arousing our pity and so on, so as to get up enough steam for doing the right thing. But surely we are not acting *from* instinct when we set about making an instinct stronger than it is? The thing that says to you, "Your herd instinct is asleep. Wake it up," can't itself *be* the herd instinct. The thing that tells you which note on the piano needs to be played louder can't itself be that note!

12   Here is a third way of seeing it. If the Moral Law was one of our instincts, we ought to be able to point to some one impulse inside us which was always what we call "good," always in agreement with the rule of right behaviour. But you can't. There is none of our impulses which the Moral Law won't sometimes tell us to suppress, and none which it won't sometimes tell us to encourage. It is a mistake to think that some of our impulses—say, mother love or patriotism—are good, and others, like sex

or the fighting instinct, are bad. All we mean is that the occasions on which the fighting instinct or the sexual desire need to be restrained are rather more frequent than those for restraining mother love or patriotism. But there are situations in which it is the duty of a married man to encourage his sexual impulse and of a soldier to encourage the fighting instinct. There are also occasions on which a mother's love for her own children or a man's love for his own country have to be suppressed or they'll lead to unfairness towards other people's children or countries. Strictly speaking, there aren't such things as good and bad impulses. Think once again of a piano. It hasn't got two kinds of notes on it, the "right" notes and the "wrong" ones. Every single note is right at one time and wrong at another. The Moral Law isn't any one instinct or any set of instincts: it is something which makes a kind of tune (the tune we call goodness or right conduct) by directing the instincts.

13   By the way, this point is of great practical consequence. The most dangerous thing you can do is to take any one impulse of your own nature and set it up as the thing you ought to follow at all costs. There's not one of them which won't make us into devils if we set it up as an absolute guide. You might think love of humanity in general was safe, but it isn't. If you leave out justice you'll find yourself breaking agreements and faking evidence in trials "for the sake of humanity," and become in the end a cruel and treacherous man.

14   Other people write to me saying, "Isn't what you call the Moral Law just a social convention, something that is put into us by education?" I think there is a misunderstanding here. The people who ask that question are usually taking it for granted that if we have learned a thing from parents and teachers, then that thing must be merely a human invention. But, of course, that isn't so. We all learned the multiplication table at school. A child who grew up alone on a desert island wouldn't know it. But surely it doesn't follow that the multiplication table is simply a human convention, something human beings have made up for themselves and might have made different if they had liked? *Of course* we learn the Rule of Decent Behaviour from parents and teachers, as we learn everything else. But some of the things we learn are mere convention which might have been different—we learn to keep to the left of the road, but it might just as well have been the rule to keep to the right—and others of them, like mathematics, are real truths. The question is which class the Law of Human Nature belongs to.

15   There are two reasons for saying it belongs to the same class as mathematics. The first is, as I said last time, that though there are differences between the moral ideas of one time or country and those of another, the differences aren't really very big—you can recognise the same Law running through them all: whereas mere conventions—like the rule of the road or the kind of clothes people wear—differ completely. The other

reason is this. When you think about these differences between the morality of one people and another, do you think that the morality of one people is ever better or worse than that of another? Have any of the changes been improvements? If not, then of course there could never be any moral progress. Progress means not just changing, but changing for the better. If no set of moral ideas were truer or better than any other there would be no sense in preferring civilised morality to savage morality, or Christian morality to Nazi morality. In fact, of course, we all do believe that some moralities *are* better than others. We do believe that some of the people who tried to change the moral ideas of their own age were what we'd call Reformers or Pioneers—people who understood morality better than their neighbours did. Very well then. The moment you say that one set of moral ideas can be better than another, you are, in fact, measuring them both by a standard, saying that one of them conforms to that standard more nearly than the other. But the standard that measures two things is something different from either. You are, in fact, comparing them both with some Real Morality, admitting that there is *really* such a thing as Right, independent of what people think, and that some people's ideas get nearer to that real Right than others. Or put it this way. If your moral ideas can be truer, and those of the Nazis less true, there must be something—some Real Morality—for them to be true *about*. The reason why your idea of New York can be truer or less true than mine is that New York is a real place, existing quite apart from what either of us thinks. If when each of us said "New York" each meant merely "The town I am imagining in my own head," how could one of us have truer ideas than the other? There'd be no question of truth or falsehood at all. In the same way, if the Rule of Decent Behaviour meant simply, "whatever each nation happens to approve," there'd be no sense in saying that any one nation had ever been more correct in its approval than any other; no sense in saying that the world could ever grow better or worse.

16   So you see that though the differences between people's ideas of Decent Behaviour often make you suspect that there is no real natural Law of Behaviour at all, yet the things we are bound to think about these differences really prove just the opposite. But one word before I end. I think that some listeners have been exaggerating the differences, because they have not distinguished between differences of morality and differences of belief about facts. For example, one listener wrote and said, "Three hundred years ago people in England were putting witches to death. Was that what you call the Rule of Human Nature or Right Conduct?" But surely the reason we don't execute witches is that we don't believe there are such things. If we did—if we really thought that there were people going about who had sold themselves to the devil and received supernatural powers from him in return and were using these powers to kill their neighbours or drive them mad or bring bad weather, surely we'd all agree that if

anyone deserved the death penalty, then these filthy quislings did? There's no difference of moral principle here: the difference is simply about matter of fact. It may be a great advance in *knowledge* not to believe in witches: there's no moral advance in not executing them when you don't think they are there! You wouldn't call a man humane for ceasing to set mouse-traps if he did so because he believed there were no mice in the house.

Theme topics

1. Write a description of an event (an accident, a fire, a lost child) or a place (a mountain or sea in storm, a desert, a city street, an airport, bus or train station) first with the disciplined reporting of concrete details of Leighton's style then employing some of the more elaborate devices and personal response of Baldwin's style.

2. Describe a place or a person, first making the person or place attractive, then, using many of the same details, making it unattractive.

3. Write a description of a street in which you employ details from all five senses and discipline them to create a single dominant impression.

4. Write a subjective description of a place in which you report your emotion (fear, joy, boredom) in the place, making each detail contribute to that emotion.

5. Describe yourself in a situation with another person in which you attempt to make clear the complexity and irony of the situation and the relationship, as Baldwin did with his father and Orwell did in "Shooting an Elephant."

6. Write an analysis of the style, tone, and organization of one of the essays in this section.

PART THREE

Argument and Persuasion

Language and Correctness

Issues, assumptions, and methods of refutation

Issues

Before one can argue he must make the question clear. The question, called in debate the proposition, must not only be a single question but usually state or imply a judgment. Propositions of fact, which are common in the realm of law, history, and medicine, are rare in everyday student and nonprofessional life. One does not argue about easily verifiable facts, even though whether or not Mr. X was at his home on the night of January 26th may require complex argument in a courtroom. Argument usually focuses on which of two courses of action to take, or on whether a certain action or decision was good or bad. Intelligent people do not argue about how much aid the United States provided to South America last year. A little research uncovers the answer. But whether we should provide more or less aid this year, or whether we provided too little or too much last year, are questions for argument. Of central importance in that argument will be the establishment of criteria for judging what was enough aid, and it is on this question of establishing values that the two sides take their stand.

The article by Wilson Follett and the typical answer to his position made by Bergen Evans are both arguments insofar as they are concerned with establishing values upon which a dictionary can be judged. Both are concerned, as are the essays following, with the proposition that *Webster's Third International Dictionary* is or is not a good dictionary, that it is or is not what a new dictionary should be. Wilson Follett's article, however, is a review and is not formally organized even though the argument, and the assumptions on which it is based, are implied. The dictionary is not what it should be for a reason; and this reason, since it is common to most of the particular cases cited, is crucial. The dictionary is not what it should be, according to Follett, because the lexicographers have abrogated their authority to judge language usage. This, then, is the crucial issue: in selecting words and putting labels on them, must dictionary makers record what usages they find to be prevalent without passing judgment on them?

Other issues are raised in this argument by the opposition, for example, problems of capitalization, the omission of many proper names from literature and mythology, and the failure to include other information that may very well more properly be found in an encyclopedia; but all participants admit these issues to be of distinctly secondary importance.

A secondary issue of this kind should be distinguished from an admitted issue. An issue granted by a writer as a valid objection to his case is referred to as an admitted issue. One might, for example, admit that he disapproves of the politics of a certain nation and yet argue in favor of granting U.S. aid to that nation. Such an admission would not only clarify the argument but also strengthen it; for readers would then not be alienated by inferring that tacit approval of the nation's politics entered the argument to grant aid to that nation.

Assumptions

Notice that the above example operates upon an assumption: that we can afford to provide economic aid to other nations. Wilson Follett in the essay that follows bases his case against *Webster's Third International Dictionary* upon assumptions. Aside from the assumption, implied by the crucial issue, that certain standards of usage should have been indicated either by selection or by labels, Follett bases his case upon others. First, he assumes that there is "a standard, staple, traditional language of general reading." Secondly, he assumes that readers will accept as standard anything included in a dictionary. Such assumptions, whether they are valid, invalid, or partially one or the other, are obviously an important part of an argument: an opponent who is unwilling to accept them can undercut a whole case. Defenders of the dictionary attack these very assumptions on the part of Follett. They say that a standard English does not exist and that readers need not assume a word to be correct for all occasions simply because they find it in a dictionary.

A student should thus clarify his argument in terms of its issues, its values, and its assumptions. What issue is crucial, what is secondary, and what is to be admitted—without loss and with possible gain—to the other side? What am I assuming that the other side may not grant to be the common ground of the discussion?

An argument must be defensive. Not only in answering a case already stated but in presenting your own, you should consider the other side, construct the issues of the case against you, and either admit or refute those issues.

Methods of refutation

Denial is a matter of counter-assertion; one counters an assertion with its opposite. One must then correct the opponent's facts, deny the relevance of his proof, or deny that what he presents as proof, though relevant, is sufficient.

Distinction may involve discrimination in the use of a word or reinterpretation of a motive or an action. In regard to the principles of liberty and equality, for example, one might attempt to distinguish precisely where the rights of an individual end and those of society begin. Here in the opening pieces on *Webster's Third* Follet summarizes his charges by calling the dictionary a "fighting document." Evans, on the other hand, writing under "sound and fury" from Follett and others, attempts to distinguish the principles behind the making of the dictionary by examining the achievements of "the science of descriptive linguistics."

Retort is the twisting of an opponent's statement or his evidence so that it cuts against his own position. The announcement of a price for a public project may be evidence of frugality to one political party, and to the other evidence of wild extravagance.

Identification of a fallacy in an opponent's reasoning may be a fourth method of refutation or a supplement to denial, distinction, and retort. (*See* Robert Gorham Davis, "Logic and Logical Fallacies.")

Challenging an opponent's authority to discuss a subject may, in some instances, be a fair method of refutation. James Sledd, for example, challenges the preparation of some critics of the dictionary. He assumes that a knowledge of language, dictionaries, and current controversy is a prerequisite for good reviewing. We would expect historians to present evidence on historical questions and doctors to give medical evidence. The distinction should be observed, however, between challenging the authority of an opponent to speak on a particular question and challenging his authority on questions where no specific knowledge or experience is required. Obviously open or covert attacks upon the character of an opponent are entirely out of order.

41 WILSON FOLLETT

Sabotage in Springfield

1   Of dictionaries, as of newspapers, it might be said that the bad ones are too bad to exist, the good ones too good not to be better. No dictionary of a living language is perfect or ever can be, if only because the time required for compilation, editing, and issuance is so great that shadows of obsolescence are falling on parts of any such work before it ever gets into the hands of a user. Preparation of *Webster's Third New International Dictionary of the English Language* began intensively in the Springfield establishment of G. & C. Merriam Company in 1936, but the century was nine months into its seventh decade before any outsider could have his first look at what had been accomplished. His first look is, of course, incompetent to acquaint him with the merits of the new work; these no one can fully discover without months or years of everyday use. On the other hand, it costs only minutes to find out that what will rank as the great event of American linguistic history in this decade, and perhaps in this quarter century, is in many crucial particulars a very great calamity.

2   Why should the probable and possible superiorities of the Third New International be so difficult to assess, the shortcomings so easy? Because the superiorities are special, departmental, and recondite, the shortcomings general and within the common grasp. The new dictionary comes to us with a claim of 100,000 new words or new definitions. These run almost overwhelmingly to scientific and technological terms or meanings that have come into existence since 1934, and especially to words classified as ISV (belonging to the international scientific vocabulary). No one person can possibly use or even comprehend all of them; the coverage in this domain, certainly impressive to the nonspecialist, may or may not command the admiration of specialists. It is said that historians of the graphic arts and of architecture were displeased with the 1934 Webster, both for its omissions and for some definitions of what it included in their fields. Its 1961 successor may have disarmed their reservations; only they can pronounce.

3   But all of us may without brashness form summary judgments about the treatment of what belongs to all of us—the standard, staple, traditional language of general reading and speaking, the ordinary vocabulary and idioms of novelist, essayist, letter writer, reporter, editorial writer, teacher,

From *The Atlantic Monthly* (January, 1962). Reprinted by permission of Mrs. Wilson Follett.

student, advertiser; in short, fundamental English. And it is precisely in this province that Webster III has thrust upon us a dismaying assortment of the questionable, the perverse, the unworthy, and the downright outrageous.

4　Furthermore, what was left out is as legitimate a grievance to the ordinary reader as anything that has been put in. Think—if you can—of an unabridged dictionary from which you cannot learn who Mark Twain was (though *mark twain* is entered as a leadsman's cry), or what were the names of the apostles, or that the Virgin was Mary the mother of Jesus of Nazareth, or what and where the District of Columbia is!

5　The disappointment and the shock are intensified, of course, because of the unchallenged position earned by the really unabridged immediate predecessor of this strange work. *Webster's New International Dictionary,* Second Edition (1934), consummated under the editorship of William Allan Neilson, at once became the most important reference book in the world to American writers, editors, teachers, students, and general readers —everyone to whom American English was a matter of serious interest. What better could the next revision do than extend the Second Edition in the direction of itself, bring it up to date, and correct its scattering of oversights and errata?

6　The 1934 dictionary had been, heaven knows, no citadel of conservatism, no last bastion of puristical bigotry. But it had made shrewd reports on the status of individual words; it had taken its clear, beautifully written definitions from fit uses of an enormous vocabulary by judicious users; it had provided accurate, impartial accounts of the endless guerrilla war between grammarian and antigrammarian and so given every consultant the means to work out his own decisions. Who could wish the forthcoming revision any better fortune than a comparable success in applying the same standards to whatever new matter the new age imposed?

7　Instead, we have seen a century and a third of illustrious history largely jettisoned; we have seen a novel dictionary formula improvised, in great part out of snap judgments and the sort of theoretical improvement that in practice impairs; and we have seen the gates propped wide open in enthusiastic hospitality to miscellaneous confusions and corruptions. In fine, the anxiously awaited work that was to have crowned cisatlantic linguistic scholarship with a particular glory turns out to be a scandal and a disaster. Worse yet, it plumes itself on its faults and parades assiduously cultivated sins as virtues without precedent.

8　Examination cannot proceed far without revealing that Webster III, behind its front of passionless objectivity, is in truth a fighting document. And the enemy it is out to destroy is every obstinate vestige of linguistic punctilio, every surviving influence that makes for the upholding of standards, every criterion for distinguishing between better usages and worse. In other words, it has gone over bodily to the school that construes traditions as enslaving, the rudimentary principles of syntax as crippling, and taste as irrelevant. This revolution leaves it in the anomalous position of loudly glorifying its own ancestry—which is indeed glorious—while tacitly sabotaging the principles and ideals that brought the preceding Merriam-Webster to its unchallengeable pre-eminence. The Third New International is at once a resounding tribute of lip service to the Second and a wholesale repudiation of it—a sweeping act of apology, contrition, and reform.

9   The right-about-face is, of course, particularly evident in the vocabulary approved. Within a few days of publication the new dictionary was inevitably notorious for its unreserved acceptance as standard of *wise up, get hep* (it uses the second as a definition of the first), *ants in one's pants, one for the book; hugeous, nixie, passel, hepped up* (with *hepcat* and *hepster*), *anyplace, someplace,* and so forth. These and a swarm of their kind it admits to full canonical standing by the suppression of such qualifying status labels as *colloquial, slang, cant, facetious,* and *substandard.* The classification *colloquial* it abolishes outright: "it is impossible to know whether a word out of context is colloquial or not." Of *slang* it makes a chary occasional use despite a similar reservation: "No word is invariably slang, and many standard words can be given slang connotations or used so inappropriately as to become slang." *Cornball* is ranked as slang, *corny* is not.

10   The overall effect signifies a large-scale abrogation of one major responsibility of the lexicographer. He renounces it on the curious ground that helpful discriminations are so far beyond his professional competence that he is obliged to leave them to those who, professing no competence at all, have vainly turned to him for guidance. If some George Ade of the future, aspiring to execute a fable in slang, were to test his attempt by the status labels in Webster III, he would quickly discover with chagrin that he had expressed himself almost without exception in officially applauded English. With but slight exaggeration we can say that if an expression can be shown to have been used in print by some jaded reporter, some candidate for office or his speech writer, some potboiling minor novelist, it is well enough credentialed for the full blessing of the new lexicography.

11   This extreme tolerance of crude neologisms and of shabby diction generally, however, is but one comparatively trifling aspect of the campaign against punctilio. We begin to sound its deeper implications when we plunge into the definitions and the copious examples that illustrate and support them. Under the distributive pronoun *each* we find, side by side: "(each of them is to pay his own fine) (each of them are to pay their own fine)." Where could anyone look for a neater, more succinct way to outlaw the dusty dogma that a pronoun should agree in number with its antecedent? Here is the same maneuver again under another distributive, *everybody:* "usu. referred to by the third person singular (everybody is

bringing his own lunch) but sometimes by a plural personal pronoun (everybody had made up their minds).'' Or try *whom* and *whomever:* ''(a . . . recruit whom he hoped would prove to be a crack salesman) (people . . . whom you never thought would sympathize) . . . (I go out to talk to whomever it is) . . . (he attacked whomever disagreed with him).'' It is, then, all right to put the subject of a finite verb in the accusative case—''esp. after a preposition or a verb of which it might mistakenly be considered the object.''

12   Shall we look into what our dictionary does with a handful of the more common solecisms, such as a publisher might introduce into a cooked-up test for would-be copy editors? Begin with *center around* (or *about*). It seems obvious that expressions derived from Euclidean geometry should make Euclidean sense. A center is a point; it is what things are around, not what is around them; they center *in* or *on* or *at* the point. The Second Edition defined the Great White Way as ''That part of Broadway . . . centering about Times Square''—patently an oversight. Is it the same oversight that produces, in the Third: *''heresy . . . 3:* a group or school of thought centering around a particular heresy''? We look up *center* itself, and, lo: ''(a story to tell, centered around the political development of a great state) . . . (more scholarship than usual was centered around the main problems),'' followed by several equivalent specimens.

13   Here is *due to.* First we come on irreproachable definitions, irreproachably illustrated, of *due* noun and *due* adjective, and we think we are out of the woods. Alas, they are followed by the manufacture of a composite preposition, *due to,* got up solely to extenuate such abominations as ''the event was canceled due to inclement weather.'' An adjective can modify a verb, then. And here is a glance at that peculiarly incriminating redundancy of the slipshod writer, *equally as:* ''equally opposed to Communism as to Fascism.'' The intolerable *hardly than* or *scarcely than* construction is in full favor: ''hardly had the birds dropped than she jumped into the water and retrieved them.'' The sequence *different than* has the double approbation of editorial use and a citation: conjunctive *unlike* means ''in a manner that is different than,'' and a passage under *different* reads ''vastly different in size than it was twenty-five years ago.'' Adjectival *unlike* and conjunctive *unlike* both get illustrations that implicitly commend the unanchored and grammarless modifier: ''so many fine men were outside the charmed circle that, unlike most colleges, there was no disgrace in not being a club man''; ''unlike in the gasoline engine, fuel does not enter the cylinder with air on the intake stroke.''

14   This small scattering should not end without some notice of that darling of the advanced libertarians, *like* as a conjunction, first in the meaning of *as,* secondly (and more horribly) in that of *as if.* Now, it is well known to the linguistic historian that *like* was so used for a long time before and

after Langland. But it is as well known that the language rather completely sloughed off this usage; that it has long been no more than a regional colloquialism, a rarely seen aberration among competent writers, or an artificially cultivated irritant among defiant ones. The *Saturday Evening Post,* in which *like* for *as* is probably more frequent than in any other painstakingly edited magazine, has seldom if ever printed that construction except in reproducing the speech or tracing the thoughts of characters to whom it might be considered natural. The arguments for *like* have been merely defensive and permissive. Not for centuries has there been any real pressure of authority on a writer to use *like* as a conjunction—until our Third New International Dictionary decided to exert its leverage.

15   How it is exerted will appear in the following: "(impromptu programs where they ask questions much like I do on the air) . . . (looks like they can raise better tobacco) (looks like he will get the job) (wore his clothes like he was . . . afraid of getting dirt on them) (was like he'd come back from a long trip) (acted like she felt sick) . . . (sounded like the motor had stopped) . . . (the violin now sounds like an old masterpiece should) (did it like he told me to) . . . (wanted a doll like she saw in the store window) . . . (anomalies like just had occurred)."

16   By the processes represented in the foregoing and countless others for which there is no room here, the latest Webster whittles away at one after another of the traditionary controls until there is little or nothing left of them. The controls, to be sure, have often enough been overvalued and overdone by pedants and purists, by martinets and bigots; but more often, and much more importantly, they have worked as aids toward dignified, workmanlike, and cogent uses of the wonderful language that is out inheritance. To erode and undermine them is to convert the language into a confusion of unchanneled, incalculable williwaws, a capricious wind blowing whithersoever it listeth. And that, if we are to judge by the total effect of the pages under scrutiny—2720 of them and nearly 8000 columns of vocabulary, all compact in Times roman—is exactly what is wanted by the patient and dedicated saboteurs in Springfield. They, if they keep their ears to the ground, will hear many echoes of the despairing cry already wrung from one editorial assistant on a distinguished magazine that still puts its faith in standards: "Why have a Dictionary at all if anything goes?"

17   The definitions are reinforced, it will have been conveyed, with copious citations from printed sources. These citations occupy a great fraction of the total space. They largely account for the reduction in the number of entries (from 600,000 to 450,000) and for the elimination of the Gazetteer, the Biographical Dictionary, and the condensed key to pronunciation and symbols that ran across the bottoms of facing pages—all very material deprivations. Some 14,000 authors, we are told, are repre-

sented in the illustrative quotations—"mostly from the mid-twentieth century."

18   Can some thousands of authors truly worth space in a dictionary ever be found in any one brief period? Such a concentration can hardly fail to be, for the purposes of a dictionary, egregiously overweighted with the contemporary and the transient. Any very short period, such as a generation, is a period of transition in the history of English, and any great mass of examples drawn primarily from it will be disproportionately focused on transitional and ephemeral elements. To say that recording English *as we find it today* is precisely the purpose of a new dictionary is not much of a retort. For the bulk of the language that we use has come down to us with but minor, glacially slow changes from time out of mind, and a worthy record of it must stand on a much broader base than the fashions of yesterday.

19   It is, then, a mercy that among the thousands of scraps from recent authors, many of them still producing, we can also find hundreds from Shakespeare, the English Bible, Fielding, Dickens, Hawthorne, Melville, Henry James, Mark Twain, and so on. But the great preponderance of latter-day prose, little of it worth repeating and a good deal of it hardly worth printing in the first place, is likely to curtail by years the useful life of the Third New International.

20   So much is by the way. When we come to the definitions proper we face something new, startling, and formidable in lexicography. The definitions, all of them conformed to a predetermined rhetorical pattern, may be products of a theory—Gestaltist, perhaps?—of how the receiving mind works. The pattern, in the editor's general preface, is described as follows: "The primary objective of precise, sharp defining has been met through development of a new dictionary style based upon completely analytical one-phrase definitions throughout the book. Since the headword in a definition is intended to be modified only by structural elements restrictive in some degree and essential to each other, the use of commas either to separate or to group has been severely limited, chiefly to elements in apposition or in series. The new defining pattern does not provide for a predication which conveys further expository comment."

21   This doctrine of the strictly unitary definition is of course formulated and applied in the interest of a logical integrity and a simplification never before consistently attained by lexical definitions. What is produces, when applied with the rigor here insisted on, is in the first place some of the oddest prose ever concocted by pundits. A typical specimen, from the definition of the simplest possible term: *"rabbit punch* . . . *:* a short chopping blow delivered to the back of the neck or the base of the skull with the edge of the hand opposite the thumb that is illegal in boxing." When the idea, being not quite so simple, requires the one-phrase state-

ment of several components, the definition usually turns out to be a great unmanageable and unpunctuated blob of words strung out beyond the retentive powers of most minds that would need the definition at all. Both theory and result will emerge clearly enough from a pair of specimens, the first dealing with a familiar everyday noun, the second with a mildly technical one:

groan . . . *1:* a deep usu. inarticulate and involuntary often strangled sound typically abruptly begun and ended and usu. indicitave of pain or grief or tension or desire or sometimes disapproval or annoyance.

kymograph . . . *1:* a recording device including an electric motor or clockwork that drives a usu. slowly revolving drum which carries a roll of plain or smoked paper and also having an arrangement for tracing on the paper by means of a stylus a graphic record of motion or pressure (as of the organs of speech, blood pressure, or respiration) often in relation to particular intervals of time.

22   About these typical definitions as prose, there is much that any good reader might well say. What must be said is that the grim suppression of commas is a mere crotchet. It takes time to read such definitions anyway; commas in the right places would speed rather than slow the reading and would clarify rather than obscure the sense, so that the unitary effect—largely imaginary at best—would be more helped than hurt. In practice, the one-phase design without further expository predication lacks all the asserted advantages over a competently written definition of the free conventional sort; it is merely more difficult to write, often impossible to write well, and tougher to take in. Compare the corresponding definitions from the Second Edition:

groan . . . A low, moaning sound: usually, a deep, mournful sound uttered in pain or great distress; sometimes, an expression of strong disapprobation; as, the remark was received with *groans.*

kymograph . . . *a* An automatic apparatus consisting of a motor revolving a drum covered with smoked paper, on which curves of pressure, etc., may be traced.

Everyone professionally concerned with the details of printed English can be grateful to the new Webster for linking the parts of various expressions that have been either hyphenated compounds or separate words—*highlight, highbrow* and *lowbrow, overall, wisecrack, lowercase and uppercase,* and so on. Some of the unions now recognized were long overdue; many editors have already got them written into codes of house usage. But outside this small province the new work is a copy editor's despair, a propounder of endless riddles.

23   What, for example, are we to make of the common abbreviations *i.e.,* and *e.g.?* The first is entered in the vocabulary as *ie* (no periods, no

space), the second as *e g* (space, no periods). In the preliminary list, "Abbreviations Used in This Dictionary," both are given the customary periods. (Oddly, the list translates its *i.e.* into "that is," but merely expands *e.g.* into "exempli gratia.") Is one to follow the vocabulary or the list? What point has the seeming inconsistency?

24   And what about capitalization? All vocabulary entries are in lowercase except for such abbreviations as ARW (air raid warden), MAB (medical advisory board), and PX (post exchange). Words possibly inviting capitalization are followed by such injunctions as *cap, usu cap, sometimes not cap, usu cap 1st A, usu cap A&B* (One of the small idiosyncrasies is that "usu.," the most frequent abbreviation, is given a period when roman, denied it when italic.) From *america,* adjective—all proper nouns are excluded—to *american yew* there are over 175 consecutive entries that require such injunctions; would it not have been simpler and more economical to capitalize the entries? A flat *"cap,"* of course, means "always capitalized." But how often is "usually," and when is "sometimes"? We get dictionaries expressly that they may settle such problems for us. This dictionary seems to make a virtue of leaving them in flux, with the explanation that many matters are subjective and that the individual must decide them for himself—a curious abrogation of authority in a work extolled as "more useful and authoritative than any previous dictionary."

25   The rock-bottom practical truth is that the lexicographer cannot abrogate his authority if he wants to. He may think of himself as a detached scientist reporting the facts of language, declining to recommend use of anything or abstention from anything; but the myriad consultants of his work are not going to see him so. He helps create, not a book of fads and fancies and private opinions, but a Dictionary of the English Language. It comes to every reader under auspices that say, not "Take it or leave it," but rather something like this: "Here in 8000 columns is a definitive report of what a synod of the most trustworthy American experts consider the English language to be in the seventh decade of the twentieth century. This is your language; take it and use it. And if you use it in conformity with the principles and practices here exemplified, your use will be the most accurate attainable by any American of this era." The fact that the compilers disclaim authority and piously refrain from judgments is meaningless: the work itself, by virtue of its inclusions and exclusions, its mere existence, is a whole universe of judgments, received by millions as the Word from on high.

26   And there we have the reason why it is so important for the dictionary maker to keep his discriminations sharp, why it is so damaging if he lets them get out of working order. Suppose he enters a new definition for no better reason than that some careless, lazy, or uninformed scribbler has jumped to an absurd conclusion about what a word means or has been too harassed to run down the word he really wanted. This new definition

is going to persuade tens of thousands that, say, *cohort,* a word of multitude, means one associate or crony "(he and three alleged housebreaking cohorts were arraigned on attempted burglary charges)" or that the vogue word *ambivalence,* which denotes simultaneous love and hatred of someone or something, means "continual oscillation between one thing and its opposite (novels . . . vitiated by an ambivalence between satire and sentimentalism)." To what is the definer contributing if not to subversion and decay? To the swallower of the definition it never occurs that he can have drunk corruption from a well that he has every reason to trust as the ultimate in purity. Multiply him by the number of people simultaneously influenced, and the resulting figure by the years through which the influence continued, and a great deal of that product by the influences that will be disseminated through speech and writing and teaching, and you begin to apprehend the scope of the really enormous disaster that can and will be wrought by the lexicographer's abandonment of his responsibility.

Questions

1. Upon what assumption concerning the public's attitude toward the concept of a dictionary does Follett's argument finally rest?

2. What function do the first two paragraphs serve in relation to the third paragraph and specifically its last sentence?

3. At what points do you find justification, in terms of Follett's word choice and tone, for his title?

4. Does the issue raised in paragraph 4 seem relevant? Why?

5. Do you, as a member of the dictionary-using public, agree with Follett's position in the issue raised in paragraphs 9 and 10? With the examples in paragraphs 11 through 15? How would Follett most probably answer dissent on your part?

6. What admission does Follett make in paragraph 16? What appeals in the same paragraph?

7. In paragraph 18 Follett raises an issue and presents the reply of his opponents. He calls the reply a retort. Is it a retort? How do the assumptions of the two sides differ here?

8. The final two paragraphs restate the crucial issue. How many parts has it? What defensive elements, if any, can you find in its statement?

9. Follett holds the maintenance of "standards" in high regard. What "standards," if any, does he attribute to the makers of *Webster's Third,* and how does he deal with them in his argument?

10. Analyze Follett's use of the principles of parallelism and balance throughout his essay.

42 BERGEN EVANS

But What's a Dictionary For?

1   The storm of abuse in the popular press that greeted the appearance of *Webster's Third New International Dictionary* is a curious
phenomenon. Never had a scholarly work of this stature been attacked
with such unbridled fury and contempt. An article in the *Atlantic* viewed
it as a "disappointment," a "shock," a "calamity," "a scandal and a
disaster." The New York *Times,* in a special editorial, felt that the work
would "accelerate the deterioration" of the language and sternly accused
the editors of betraying a public trust. The *Journal* of the American Bar
Association saw the publication as "deplorable," "a flagrant example of
lexicographic irresponsibility," "a serious blow to the cause of good English." *Life* called it "a non-word deluge," "monstrous," "abominable," and
"a cause for dismay." They doubted that "Lincoln could have modelled
his Gettysburg Address" on it—a concept of how things get written that
throws very little light on Lincoln but a great deal on *Life*.

2   What underlies all this sound and fury? Is the claim of the G. & C.
Merriam Company, probably the world's greatest dictionary maker, that
the preparation of the work cost $3.5 million, that it required the ef-
forts of three hundred scholars over a period of twenty-seven years, working on the largest collection of citations ever assembled in any language
—is all this a fraud, a hoax?

3   So monstrous a discrepancy in evaluation requires us to examine
basic principles. Just what's a dictionary for? What does it propose to
do? What does the common reader go to a dictionary to find? What has
the purchaser of a dictionary a right to expect for his money?

4   Before we look at basic principles, it is necessary to interpose two
brief statements. The first of these is that a dictionary is concerned with
words. Some dictionaries give various kinds of other useful information.
Some have tables of weights and measures on the flyleaves. Some list
historical events, and some, home remedies. And there's nothing wrong
with their so doing. But the great increase in our vocabulary in the past
three decades compels all dictionaries to make more efficient use of their
space. And if something must be eliminated, it is sensible to throw out
these extraneous things and stick to words.

5   Yet wild wails arose. The *Saturday Review* lamented that one can

From *The Atlantic Monthly* (May, 1962). Reprinted by permission of the author.

no longer find the goddess Astarte under a separate heading—though they point out that a genus of mollusks named after the goddess is included! They seemed to feel that out of sheer perversity the editors of the dictionary stooped to mollusks while ignoring goddesses and that, in some way, this typifies modern lexicography. Mr. Wilson Follett, folletizing (his mental processes demand some special designation) in the *Atlantic,* cried out in horror that one is not even able to learn from the Third International "that the Virgin was Mary the mother of Jesus"!

6   The second brief statement is that there has been even more progress in the making of dictionaries in the past thirty years than there has been in the making of automobiles. The difference, for example, between the much-touted Second International (1934) and the much-clouted Third International (1961) is not like the difference between yearly models but like the difference between the horse and buggy and the automobile. Between the appearance of these two editions a whole new science related to the making of dictionaries, the science of descriptive linguistics, has come into being.

7   Modern linguistics gets its charter from Leonard Bloomfield's *Language* (1933). Bloomfield, for thirteen years professor of Germanic philology at the University of Chicago and for nine years professor of linguistics at Yale, was one of those inseminating scholars who can't be relegated to any department and don't dream of accepting established categories and procedures just because they're established. He was as much an anthropologist as a linguist, and his concepts of language were shaped not by Strunk's *Elements of Style* but by his knowledge of Cree Indian dialects.

8   The broad general findings of the new science are:

1. All languages are systems of human conventions, not systems of natural laws. The first—and essential—step in the study of any language is observing and setting down precisely what happens when native speakers speak it.

2. Each language is unique in its pronunciation, grammar, and vocabulary. It cannot be described in terms of logic or of some theoretical, ideal language. It cannot be described in terms of any other language, or even in terms of its own past.

3. All languages are dynamic rather than static, and hence a "rule" in any language can only be a statement of contemporary practice. Change is constant—and normal.

4. "Correctness" can rest only upon usage, for the simple reason that there is nothing else for it to rest on. And all usage is relative.

9   From these propositions it follows that a dictionary is good only insofar as it is a comprehensive and accurate description of current usage. And to be comprehensive it must include some indication of social and regional associations.

10   New dictionaries are needed because English has changed more in the past two generations than at any other time in its history. It has had to adapt to extraordinary cultural and technological changes, two world wars, unparalleled changes in transportation and communication, and unprecedented movements of populations.

11   More subtly, but pervasively, it has changed under the influence of mass education and the growth of democracy. As written English is used by increasing millions and for more reasons than ever before, the language has become more utilitarian and more informal. Every publication in America today includes pages that would appear, to the purist of forty years ago, unbuttoned gibberish. Not that they are; they simply show that you can't hold the language of one generation up as a model for the next.

12   It's not that you mustn't. You *can't*. For example, in the issue in which *Life* stated editorially that it would follow the Second International, there were over forty words, constructions, and meanings which are in the Third International but not in the Second. The issue of the New York *Times* which hailed the Second International as the authority to which it would adhere and the Third International as a scandal and a betrayal which it would reject used one hundred and fifty-three separate words, phrases, and constructions which are listed in the Third International but not in the Second and nineteen others which are condemned in the Second. Many of them are used many times, more than three hundred such uses in all. The Washington *Post,* in an editorial captioned "Keep Your Old Webster's," says, in the first sentence, "don't throw it away," and in the second, "hang on to it." But the old Webster's labels *don't* "colloquial" and doesn't include "hang on to," in this sense, at all.

13   In short, all of these publications are written in the language that the Third International describes, even the very editorials which scorn it. And this is no coincidence, because the Third International isn't setting up any new standards at all; it is simply describing what *Life,* the Washington *Post,* and the New York *Times* are doing. Much of the dictionary's material comes from these very publications, the *Times,* in particular, furnishing more of its illustrative quotations than any other newspaper.

14   And the papers have no choice. No journal or periodical could sell a single issue today if it restricted itself to the American language of twenty-eight years ago. It couldn't discuss half the things we are interested in, and its style would seem stiff and cumbrous. If the editorials were serious, the public—and the stockholders—have reason to be grateful that the writers on these publications are more literate than the editors.

15   And so back to our questions: what's a dictionary for, and how, in 1962, can it best do what it ought to do? The demands are simple. The common reader turns to a dictionary for information about the spelling, pronunciation, meaning, and proper use of words. He wants to know what

is current and respectable. But he wants—and has a right to—the truth, the full truth. And the full truth about any language, and especially about American English today, is that there are many areas in which certainty is impossible and simplification is misleading.

16   Even in so settled a matter as spelling, a dictionary cannot always be absolute. *Theater* is correct, but so is *theatre*. And so are *traveled* and *travelled, plow* and *plough, catalog* and *catalogue,* and scores of other variants. The reader may want a single certainty. He may have taken an unyielding position in an argument, he may have wagered in support of his conviction and may demand that the dictionary "settle" the matter. But neither his vanity nor his purse is any concern of the dictionary's; it must record the facts. And the fact here is that there are many words in our language which may be spelled, with equal correctness, in either of two ways.

17   So with pronunciation. A citizen listening to his radio might notice that James B. Conant, Bernard Baruch, and Dwight D. Eisenhower pronounce *economics* as ECKuhnomiks, while A. Whitney Griswold, Adlai Stevenson, and Herbert Hoover pronounce it EEKuhnomiks. He turns to the dictionary to see which of the two pronunciations is "right" and finds that they are both acceptable.

18   Has he been betrayed? Has the dictionary abdicated its responsibility? Should it say that one *must* speak like the president of Harvard or like the president of Yale, like the thirty-first President of the United States or like the thirty-fourth? Surely it's none of its business to make a choice. Not because of the distinction of these particular speakers; lexicography, like God, is no respecter of person. But because so widespread and con-spicuous a use of two pronunciations among people of this elevation shows that there *are* two pronunciations. Their speaking establishes the fact which the dictionary must record.

19   Among the "enormities" with which *Life* taxes the Third International is its listing of "the common mispronunciation" *heighth*. That it is labeled a "dialectal variant" seems, somehow, to compound the felony. But one hears the word so pronounced, and if one professes to give a full account of American English in the 1960s, one has to take some cognizance of it. All people do not possess *Life's* intuitive perception that the word is so "monstrous" that even to list it as a dialect variation is to merit scorn. Among these, by the way, was John Milton, who, in one of the greatest passages in all literature, besought the Holy Spirit to raise him to the "highth" of his great argument. And even the *Oxford English Dictionary* is so benighted as to list it, in full boldface, right alongside of *Height* as a variant that has been in the language since at least 1290.

20   Now there are still, apparently, millions of Americans who retain, in this as in much else, some of the speech of Milton. This particular pro-nunciation seems to be receding, but the *American Dialect Dictionary* still

records instances of it from almost every state on the Eastern seaboard and notes that it is heard from older people and "occasionally in educated speech," "common with good speakers," "general," "widespread."

21   Under these circumstances, what is a dictionary to do? Since millions speak the word this way, the pronunciation can't be ignored. Since it has been in use as long as we have any record of English and since it has been used by the greatest writers, it can't be described as substandard or slang. But it is heard now only in certain localities. That makes it a dialectal pronunciation, and an honest dictionary will list it as such. What else can it do? Should it do?

22   The average purchaser of a dictionary uses it most often, probably, to find out what a word "means." As a reader, he wants to know what an author intended to convey. As a speaker or writer, he wants to know what a word will convey to his auditors. And this, too, is complex, subtle, and forever changing.

23   An illustration is furnished by an editorial in the Washington *Post* (January 17, 1962). After a ringing appeal to those who "love truth and accuracy" and the usual bombinations about "abdication of authority" and "barbarism," the editorial charges the Third International with "pretentious and obscure verbosity" and specifically instances its definition of "so simple an object as a door."

24   The definition reads:

a movable piece of firm material or a structure supported usu. along one side and swinging on pivots or hinges, sliding along a groove, rolling up and down, revolving as one of four leaves, or folding like an accordion by means of which an opening may be closed or kept open for passage into or out of a building, room, or other covered enclosure or a car, airplane, elevator, or other vehicle.

Then follows a series of special meanings, each particularly defined and, where necessary, illustrated by a quotation.

25   Since, aside from roaring and admonishing the "gentlemen from Springfield" that "accuracy and brevity are virtues," the *Post's* editorial fails to explain what is wrong with the definition, we can only infer from "so simple" a thing that the writer takes the plain, downright, man-in-the-street attitude that a door is a door and any damn fool knows that.

26   But if so, he has walked into one of lexicography's biggest booby traps: the belief that the obvious is easy to define. Whereas the opposite is true. Anyone can give a fair description of the strange, the new, or the unique. It's the commonplace, the habitual, that challenges definition, for its very commonness compels us to define it in uncommon terms. Dr. Johnson was ridiculed on just this score when his dictionary appeared in 1755. For two hundred years his definition of a network as "any thing reticulated or decussated, at equal distances, with interstices between the intersections" has been good for a laugh. But in the merriment one thing is al-

ways overlooked: no one has yet come up with a better definition! Subsequent dictionaries defined it as a mesh and then defined a mesh as a network That's simple, all right.

27   Anyone who attempts sincerely to state what the word *door* means in the United States of America today can't take refuge in a log cabin. There has been an enormous proliferation of closing and demarking devices and structures in the past twenty years, and anyone who tries to thread his way through the many meanings now included under *door* may have to sacrifice brevity to accuracy and even have to employ words that a limited vocabulary may find obscure.

28   Is the entrance to a tent a door, for instance? And what of the thing that seals the exit of an airplane? Is this a door? Or what of those sheets and jets of air that are now being used, in place of old-fashioned oak and hinges, to screen entrances and exits. Are they doors? And what of those accordion-like things that set off various sections of many modern apartments? The fine print in the lease takes it for granted that they are doors and that spaces demarked by them are rooms—and the rent is computed on the number of rooms.

29   Was I gypped by the landlord when he called the folding contraption that shuts off my kitchen a door? I go to the Second International, which the editor of the *Post* urges me to use in preference to the Third International. Here I find that a door is

The movable frame or barrier of boards, or other material, usually turning on hinges or pivots or sliding, by which an entranceway into a house or apartment is closed and opened; also, a similar part of a piece of furniture, as in a cabinet or bookcase.

This is only forty-six words, but though it includes the cellar door, it excludes the barn door and the accordion-like thing.

30   So I go on to the Third International. I see at once that the new definition is longer. But I'm looking for accuracy, and if I must sacrifice brevity to get it, then I must. And, sure enough, in the definition which raised the *Post's* blood pressure, I find the words "folding like an accordion." The thing *is* a door, and my landlord is using the word in one of its currently accepted meanings.

31   We don't turn to a work of reference merely for confirmation. We all have words in our vocabularies which we have misunderstood, and to come on the true meaning of one of these words is quite a shock. All our complacency and self-esteem rise to oppose the discovery. But eventually we must accept the humiliation and laugh if off as best we can.

32   Some, often those who have set themselves up as authorities, stick to their error and charge the dictionary with being in a conspiracy against them. They are sure that their meaning is the only "right" one. And when the dictionary doesn't bear them out they complain about "permissive" attitudes instead of correcting their mistake.

33   The New York *Times* and the *Saturday Review* both regarded as contemptibly "permissive" the fact that one meaning of one word was illustrated by a quotation from Polly Adler. But a rudimentary knowledge of the development of any language would have told them that the underworld has been a far more active force in shaping and enriching speech than all the synods that have ever convened. Their attitude is like that of the patriot who canceled his subscription to the *Dictionary of American Biography* when he discovered that the very first volume included Benedict Arnold!

34   The ultimate of "permissiveness," singled out by almost every critic for special scorn, was the inclusion in the Third International of *finalize*. It was this, more than any other one thing, that was given as the reason for sticking to the good old Second International—that "peerless authority on American English," as the *Times* called it. But if it was such an authority, why didn't they look into it? They would have found *finalize* if they had.

35   And why shouldn't it be there? It exists. It's been recorded for two generations. Millions employ it every day. Two Presidents of the United States—men of widely differing cultural backgrounds—have used it in formal statements. And so has the Secretary-General of the United Nations, a man of unusual linguistic attainments. It isn't permitting the word but omitting it that would break faith with the reader. Because it is exactly the sort of word we want information about.

36   To list it as substandard would be to imply that it is used solely by the ignorant and the illiterate. But this would be a misrepresentation: President Kennedy and U Thant are highly educated men, and both are articulate and literate. Is isn't even a freak form. On the contrary, it is a classic example of a regular process of development in English, a process which has given us such thoroughly accepted words as *generalize, minimize, formalize,* and *verbalize.* Nor can it be dismissed on logical grounds or on the ground that it is a mere duplication of *complete.* It says something that *complete* doesn't say and says it in a way that is significant in the modern bureaucratic world: one usually *completes* something which he has initiated but *finalizes* the work of others.

37   One is free to dislike the word. I don't like it. But the editor of a dictionary has to examine the evidence for a word's existence and seek it in context to get, as clearly and closely as he can, the exact meaning that it conveys to those who use it. And if it is widely used by well-educated, literate, reputable people, he must list it as a standard word. He is not compiling a volume of his own prejudices.

38   An individual's use of his native tongue is the surest index to his position within his community. And those who turn to a dictionary expect from it some statement of the current status of a word or a grammatical construction. And it is with the failure to assume this function that modern

lexicography has been most fiercely charged. The charge is based on a naïve assumption that simple labels can be attached in all instances. But they can't. Some words are standard in some constructions and not in others. There may be as many shades of status as of meaning, and morning lexicography instead of abdicating this function has fulfilled it to a degree utterly unknown to earlier dictionaries.

39   Consider the word *fetch,* meaning to "go get and bring to." Until recently a standard word of full dignity ("Fetch me, I pray thee, a little water in a vessel"—I Kings 17:10), it has become slightly tainted. Perhaps the command latent in it is resented as undemocratic. Or maybe its use in training dogs to retrieve has made some people feel that it is an undignified word to apply to human beings. But, whatever the reason, there is a growing uncertainty about its status, and hence it is the sort of word that conscientious people look up in a dictionary.

40   Will they find it labeled "good" or "bad"? Neither, of course, because either applied indiscriminately would be untrue. The Third International lists nineteen different meanings of the verb *to fetch.* Of these some are labeled "dialectal," some "chiefly dialectal," some "obsolete," one "chiefly Scottish," and two "not in formal use." The primary meaning —"to go after and bring back"—is not labeled and hence can be accepted as standard, accepted with the more assurance because the many shades of labeling show us that the word's status has been carefully considered.

41   On grammatical questions the Third International tries to be equally exact and thorough. Sometimes a construction is listed without comment, meaning that in the opinion of the editors it is unquestionably respectable. Sometimes a construction carries the comment "used by speakers and writers on all educational levels though disapproved by some grammarians." Or the comment may be "used in substandard speech and formerly also by reputable writers." Or "less often in standard than in substandard speech." Or simply "dial."

42   And this very accurate reporting is based on evidence which is presented for our examination. One may feel that the evidence is inadequate or that the evaluation of it is erroneous. But surely, in the face of classification so much more elaborate and careful than any known heretofore, one cannot fly into a range and insist that the dictionary is "out to destroy . . . every vestige of linguistic punctilio . . . every criterion for distinguishing between better usages and worse."

43   Words, as we have said, are continually shifting their meanings and connotations and hence their status. A word which has dignity, say, in the vocabulary of an older person may go down in other people's estimation. Like *fetch.* The older speaker is not likely to be aware of this and will probably be inclined to ascribe the snickers of the young at his speech to that degeneration of manners which every generation has deplored in its

juniors. But a word which is coming up in the scale—like *jazz,* say, or, more recently, *crap*—will strike his ear at once. We are much more aware of offenses given us than of those we give. And if he turns to a dictionary and finds the offending word listed as standard—or even listed, apparently —his response is likely to be an outburst of indignation.

44   But the dictionary can neither snicker nor fulminate. It records. It will offend many, no doubt, to find the expression *wise up,* meaning to inform or to become informed, listed in the Third International with no restricting label. To my aging ears it still sounds like slang. But the evidence—quotations from the *Kiplinger Washington Letter* and the *Wall Street Journal*—convinces me that it is I who am out of step, lagging behind. If such publications have taken to using *wise up* in serious contexts, with no punctuational indication of irregularity, then it is obviously respectable. And finding it so listed and supported, I can only say that it's nice to be informed and sigh to realize that I am becoming an old fogy. But, of course, I don't have to use it (and I'll be damned if I will! "Let them smile, as I do now, At the old forsaken bough Where I cling").

45   In part, the trouble is due to the fact that there is no standard for standard. Ideas of what is proper to use in serious, dignified speech and writing are changing—and with breathtaking rapidity. This is one of the major facts of contemporary American English. But it is no more the dictionary's business to oppose this process than to speed it up.

46   Even in our standard speech some words are more dignified and some more informal than others, and dictionaries have tried to guide us through these uncertainties by marking certain words and constructions as "colloquial," meaning "inappropriate in a formal situation." But this distinction, in the opinion of most scholars, has done more harm than good. It has created the notion that these particular words are inferior, when actually they might be the best possible words in an informal statement. And so—to the rage of many reviewers—the Third International has dropped this label. Not all labels, as angrily charged, but only this one out of a score. And the doing so may have been an error, but it certainly didn't constitute "betrayal" or "abandoning of all distinctions." It was intended to end a certain confusion.

47   In all the finer shades of meaning, of which the status of a word is only one, the user is on his own, whether he likes it or not. Despite *Life's* artless assumption about the Gettysburg Address, nothing worth writing is written *from* a dictionary. The dictionary, rather, comes along afterwards and describes what *has been* written.

48   Words in themselves are not dignified, or silly, or wise, or malicious. But they can be used in dignified, silly, wise, or malicious ways by dignified, silly, wise, or malicious people. *Egghead,* for example, is a perfectly legitimate word, as legitimate as *highbrow* or *long-haired.* But there is

something very wrong and very undignified, by civilized standards, in a belligerent dislike for intelligence and education. *Yak* is an amusing word for persistent chatter. Anyone could say, "We were just yakking over a cup of coffee," with no harm to his dignity. But to call a Supreme Court decision *yakking* is to be vulgarly insulting and so, undignified. Again, there's nothing wrong with *confab* when it's appropriate. But when the work of a great research project, employing hundreds of distinguished scholars over several decades and involving the honor of one of the greatest publishing houses in the world, is described as *confabbing* (as the New York *Times* editorially described the preparation of the Third International), the use of this particular word asserts that the lexicographers had merely sat around and talked idly. And the statement becomes undignified—if not, indeed, slanderous.

49   The lack of dignity in such statements is not in the words, nor in the dictionaries that list them, but in the hostility that deliberately seeks this tone of expression. And in expressing itself the hostility frequently shows that those who are expressing it don't know how to use a dictionary. Most of the reviewers seem unable to read the Third International and unwilling to read the Second.

50   The *American Bar Association Journal,* for instance, in a typical outburst ("a deplorable abdication of responsibility"), picked out for special scorn the inclusion in the Third International of the word *irregardless.* "As far as the new Webster's is concerned," said the *Journal,* "this meaningless verbal bastard is just as legitimate as any other word in the dictionary." Thirty seconds spent in examining the book they were so roundly condemning would have shown them that in it *irregardless* is labeled "nonstand"—which means "nonstandard," which means "not conforming to the usage generally characteristic of educated native speakers of the language." Is that "just as legitimate as any other word in the dictionary"?

51   The most disturbing fact of all is that the editors of a dozen of the most influential publications in America today are under the impression that *authoritative* must mean *authoritarian.* Even the "permissive" Third International doesn't recognize this identification—editors' attitudes being not yet, fortunately, those of the American people. But the Fourth International may have to.

52   The new dictionary may have many faults. Nothing that tries to meet an ever-changing situation over a terrain as vast as contemporary English can hope to be free of them. And much in it is open to honest, and informed, disagreement. There can be linguistic objection to the eradication of proper names. The removal of guides to pronunciation from the foot of every page may not have been worth the valuable space it saved. The new method of defining words of many meanings has disadvantages as well as advantages. And of the half million or more definitions, hundreds, possibly

thousands, may seem inadequate or imprecise. To some (of whom I am one) the omission of the label "colloquial" will seem meritorious; to others it will seem a loss.

53   But one thing is certain: anyone who solemnly announces in the year year 1962 that he will be guided in matters of English usage by a dictionary published in 1934 is talking ignorant and pretentious nonsense.

Questions

1. Compare and contrast the first three paragraphs of Evans' article with the first three of Follett's from the point of view of method of approach to the subject. Describe the tone achieved by each writer and the expectations he creates in the mind of an attentive reader.

2. What kind of issue is raised in paragraph 4, and how effectively is it dealt with in paragraph 5? What kind of issue is raised in paragraph 6, and how effectively is it dealt with in paragraphs 7 and 8? How does the implied analogy between the passing of time and the making of au'omobiles and of dictionaries help or hinder Evans' argument?

3. How does Evans apply the fourth finding of modern linguistics in defense of the makers of the *Third?* Can you convict or acquit Evans of the charge of an argument *ad hominem* in this defense? How does he apply it in defense of the *Third* itself?

4. Does Evans anywhere face the following argument:
   The linguistic needs of any native speaker of a Cree Indian dialect for an unabridged dictionary of his language are so different in degree from the linguistic needs of any native speaker of contemporary American English for a comparable dictionary of his language that a difference in kind exists. Therefore, whatever may be the validity of Bloomfield's findings about Cree Indian dialects and the generalizations based upon them, they are irrelevant for a maker of an unabridged dictionary of American English for today's native speakers?
   How relevant is this argument against Evans' position?

5. What tactics of argument does Evans use to silence the "sound and fury" by critics of the *Third?* Where, for example, does he demonstrate ignorance on the part of opponents of the *Third?* How persuasive is he in each instance in building his own case?

6. Paragraphs 23 through 30 defend the complex definition of *door* in the *Third.* Which definition, that in the *Second* or that in the *Third,* seems the better to you? Why?

7. Why does Evans confront the usage of one native speaker with that of another in an apparent attempt to discredit distinctions among *standards* of usage? Do his efforts ultimately leave him with any margin for linguistic authority (as distinguished from linguistic authoritarianism) apart from his own conscious or unconscious preferences (see the end of paragraph 44)?

8. In paragraph 45 Evans states "there is no standard for standard," and at the beginning of the next paragraph he says "in our standard speech." Is he contradicting himself? How or how not?

9. Evans derides those who object to Polly Adler's being quoted as a linguistic authority and implies that grounds for this objection are similar to those of the patriot who cancelled his subscription to *The Dictionary of American Biography* when the initial volume arrived with a listing for Benedict Arnold. Is Evans' analogy a true or false one? Why?

10. Granted that change makes language less precise and that an unabridged dictionary of any language is more a stream or current than it is a rule or measuring stick, do you think resistance to linguistic change is desirable? On the part of whom? To what extent? Should such a dictionary as the *Third* aim to oppose or to speed up change? What probable effects follow— and even for the makers themselves of a massive dictionary—if it does in fact succeed in accelerating lexical changes in a language?

43   MARIO PEI

The Dictionary as a Battle Front

1   For some years, there have been more and more insistent rumblings from all sorts of quarters concerning the quality of the English imparted in our schools and colleges. Graduates of our educational institutions, the critics have charged, do not know how to spell, punctuate, or capitalize; to divide a thought concept into phrases, sentences, and paragraphs; or to express themselves, either in speech or writing, in the sort of English that is meaningful and acceptable. As a single sample of the many complaints that have been voiced, I may cite a friend who is a high official in WNBC-TV: "Recently we interviewed over a hundred college graduates to fill a post calling for a knowledge of good English. Not one of them made the grade. None of them knew the rules of good writing, and none of them could express himself or herself in clear, simple, forthright English sentences."

2   The blame for this state of affairs has consistently been put upon two branches of the educational world: the teachers of English and the progressive educationists. Books such as "Why Johnny Can't Read" are indictments of modern educational practice. A cultured lay writer, J. Donald Adams of the New York *Times Book Review,* said in his column of December 20, 1959:

From *The Saturday Review* (July 21, 1962). Reprinted by permission of the author.

If more parents who were themselves the recipients of a decent education could be made aware of the asinine statements about the teaching of the English language which are being spewed forth by today's educational theorists, there would be an armed uprising among the Parent-Teacher Associations all over the United States. It would be an uprising armed by common sense and hot indignation, and it would demand and get the scalps of those so-called educators whose indefensible doctrines are rapidly producing a generation of American illiterates . . . The root responsibility for the decline in standards of English rests, I think, with the teachers of English in our primary and secondary schools, and even more so, with the teachers of education who produced them. . . . There is an organization called the National Council of Teachers of English, whose attitudes and activities constitute one of the chief threats to the cultivation of good English in our schools.

3   What critics of present-day methods of teaching English have in the past failed to realize is that the responsibility for the situation lies deeper than the departments of English and the teachers colleges. The practices of both are merely a reflection of the philosophy and theories of a school of linguistics that is in turn linked with a school of cultural anthropology of the equalitarian persuasion whose views color far more than the teaching of languages in general or English in particular.

4   As far back as 1948, in a New York *Herald Tribune* book review, Bernard De Voto came out with a blast at the cultural anthropologists for assuming that methods that seem to work with the Ubangi and the Trobriand Islanders will produce dependable results when applied to the English or Americans. But his was a voice crying in the wilderness. Few people were sufficiently specialized, or interested, to perceive the link between theories presented in scholarly books on anthropology or linguistics and practices that affect the daily lives of all of us.

5   It was only with the appearance of the new third edition of "Webster's Unabridged International Dictionary" late in 1961 that the issues at stake, at least for what concerns language, became clear to the cultured, educated layman of America. For this there was a deep, underlying reason that reaches down to the grass roots of our mores.

6   The English language, as is well known, has no set standard and no accepted authority, in the sense that countries such as France, Italy, and Spain have language academies that undertake to tell the speakers what is and what is not good standard practice. Since the days of Dr. Johnson, who refused to embalm the language and thereby destroy liberty, English speakers have submitted to the Doctrine of Usage rather than to the Voice of Authority. But usage has its own canons. In Britain, something called the King's (or Queen's) English has been enshrined over and above local dialects that range from London's Cockney to super-cultivated Oxford, and from the harsh speech of the North Country to the mellifluous accents of Kent. In America there is no President's American, but there is the Dic-

tionary. From the time of Noah Webster, Americans have been wont to dip into a dictionary, the more abridged the better, to settle questions of usage and proper practice.

7   It may be stressed at this point that at no time did the compilers of the various editions of the Merriam Webster, the most comprehensive dictionary of America, set themselves up as authorities or arrogate the right to tell the people what was right and what was wrong in the matter of language. All they did was to record prevailing usage among the more educated classes. They listed and described plenty of variant regional pronunciations and words. They recorded, too, speech-forms of the lower classes, carefully labeling them "colloquial," "substandard," "vulgar," or "slang." This was not meant to prescribe or proscribe the use of certain forms, but merely to inform the reader as to the distribution of their occurrence. The attitude of the earlier lexicographers seemed to be: "Go ahead and use this form if you want to; but if you do, don't complain if someone says you are using a slang term."

8   The new 1961 edition of the Merriam-Webster has many features to commend it. Not only does it list the multitude of new terms, technological and otherwise, that have entered the language in recent years; it also has the merit of listing, with full definitions and examples, word combinations that have acquired special connotations not inherent in their component parts. The older Webster's defines both "guilt" and "association"; but the new Webster's also gives you "guilt by association." This means that the new edition is a handier tool than the older.

9   But the new edition makes one startling innovation which has recommended itself to the attention of all reviewers and of the general public as well. It blurs to the point of obliteration the older distinction between standard, substandard, colloquial, vulgar, and slang. "Ain't," it says, is now used by many cultivated speakers; "who" in the accusative function and "me" after a copulative verb are of far more frequent occurrence than "whom" and "I," and, by implication, should be preferred. This viewpoint goes right down the line. It led the editor of the New York *Times* to compose a passage that starts:

A passel of double-domes at the G. & C. Merriam Company joint in Springfield, Mass., have been confabbing and yakking for twenty-seven years— which is not intended to infer that they have not been doing plenty work—and now they have finalized Webster's Third New International Dictionary, Unabridged, a new edition of that swell and esteemed word book.

Those who regard the foregoing paragraphs as acceptable English prose will find that the new Webster's is just the dictionary for them.

10   There is more: the older Webster's, insofar as it gave citations, used only established authors, recognized masters of the language. The new Webster's cites profusely from people who are in the public eye, but who can hardly be said to qualify as shining examples of fine speaking or

writing. This leads another critic to complain that Churchill, Maritain, Oppenheimer, and Schweitzer are ranged as language sources side by side with Billy Rose, Ethel Merman, James Cagney, and Ted Williams; Shakespeare and Milton with Polly Adler and Mickey Mantle.

11   Dr. Gove's defense, fully presented in the pages of the same New York *Times* that had thundered editorially against his product, is both able and forthright: a dictionary's function, he said in substance, is to record the language, not to judge or prescribe it. Language, like practically everything else, is in a state of constant flux. It is not responsible to expect it to remain static, to retain unchanged forms that were current at one period but are no longer current today. We have changed our point of view in many fields; why not in language? His defense is, in a sense, a counterattack against the forces of purism, conservatism, and reaction. Why disguise the true function of a dictionary by turning it into a tool of prescriptivism, a fortress of a language traditionalism that no one today really wants? Language, after all, is what people speak, not what someone, be it even Webster, thinks they ought to speak.

12   This both clarifies and restricts the issue. But an issue still remains. Should a dictionary be merely a record of what goes on in language (all language, both high and low), or should it also be not so much a prescriptive tool as a guide for the layman, to not merely what *is usage*, but what is the *best* usage?

13   A speaking community that has been accustomed for the better part of two centuries to rely upon the dictionary to settle questions of usage balks at finding all usage now set on an identical plane. The contention of the objectors is that there are different, clearly identifiable levels of usage, which it is the duty of the dictionary to define. Without necessarily using the terms "correct" and "incorrect," they still would like to see a distinction made between what is better and what is worse.

14   In opposition to their stand, the new philosophy, linguistic and otherwise, seems to be summed up in this formula: "What is is good, simply because it is." Good and bad, right and wrong, correct and incorrect no longer exist. Any reference to any of these descriptive adjectives is a value judgment, and unworthy of the scientific attitude, which prescribes that we merely observe and catalogue the facts, carefully refraining from expressing either judgment or preference.

15   This relativistic philosophy, fully divorced from both ethics and esthetics, is said to be modern, sophisticated, and scientific. Perhaps it is. Some claim that its fruits are to be seen in present-day moral standards, national, international, and personal, as well as in modern so-called art, music, literature, and permissive education.

16   But we are concerned here only with its reflections on the language. The appearance of the new Webster's International has had several major

effects. It has brought the question of permissiveness in language squarely to the attention of millions of educated laymen, who use the dictionary and refer to it for guidance. Without forcing a renunciation of Anglo-American reliance on usage rather than on the Voice of Authority, it has brought into focus the paramount question: "Whose usage? That of the cultivated speakers, or that of the semiliterates?" Finally, it has for the first time brought forth, into the view of the general public, those who are primarily responsible for the shift in attitude and point of view in matters of language—not the ordinary classroom teachers of English, not the educationists of the teachers colleges, but the followers of the American, anthropological, descriptive, structuralistic school of linguistics, a school which for decades has been preaching that one form of language is as good as another; that there is no such thing as correct or incorrect so far as native speakers of the language are concerned; that at the age of five anyone who is not deaf or idiotic has gained a full mastery of his language; that we must not try to correct or improve language, but must leave it alone; that the only language activity worthy of the name is speech on the colloquial, slangy, even illiterate plane; that writing is a secondary, unimportant activity which cannot be dignified with the name of language; that systems of writing serve only to disguise the true nature of language; and that it would be well if we completely refrained from teaching spelling for a number of years.

17   If these pronouncements come as a novelty to some of my readers, it is the readers themselves who are at fault. The proponents of these language theories certainly have made no mystery about them; they have been openly, even vociferously advancing them for years, and this can easily be documented from their voluminous writings.

18   The real novelty of the situation lies in the fact that, through the publication of the new Webster's—compiled in accordance with these principles—the principles themselves and their original formulators, rather than their effects upon the younger generations, now come to the attention of the general public. Lay reviewers generally display their complete awareness.

19   Dwight MacDonald, reviewing the new Webster extensively in the March 10, 1962 *New Yorker,* after claiming that the "scientific" revolution in linguistics has meshed gears with a trend toward permissiveness, in the name of democracy, that is debasing our language by rendering it less precise and thus less effective as communication, goes on to say:

> Dr. Gove and the other makers of 3 are sympathetic to the school of language study that has become dominant since 1934. It is sometimes called Structural Linguistics and sometimes, rather magnificently, just Modern Linguistic Science. . . . Dr. Gove and his editors are part of the dominant movement in the professional study of language—one that has in the last few years established strong beachheads in the National Council of Teachers of English

and the College English Association. . . . As a scientific discipline, Structural Linguistics can have no truck with values or standards. Its job is to deal only with The Facts.

20   Max S. Marshall, Professor of Microbiology at the University of California, writing in *Science,* March 2, 1962, says in part:

Opposed to [believers in a standard of quality in English] with several ringleaders at the head, is a group which goes back some thirty years, but has been actively proselytizing only in relatively recent years. These are the advocates of 'observing precisely what happens when native speakers speak.' These are the self-styled structural linguists, presenting language in a way so foreign that it might be imposed before users of the language discover its existence. . . . Gove declares himself flatly on the side of the structural linguists, calmly assuming, as do their ringleaders, that they are about to take over.

21   The principles of the American school of linguistics described above may come as a shock to some, but there is no need to be shocked. They are based upon definitely observable historical facts. Language invariably changes. Within our own personal experience we have noticed certain forms and expressions once considered slangy turning into regularly accepted parts of the standard language.

22   All that the American school of linguistics advocates is that we accept the process of change in language and submit gracefully to its inevitability. If we persist in hanging on to language forms and concepts that are antiquated and superceded, then we are merely subscribing to what they call "the superstitions of the past." We should be forward-looking, and progressive-minded. We renounce imperialism and colonialism in international relations, and admit nations like Ghana and the Congo to full equality with the established countries of Europe; by the same token, we should view the languages of the Arapahoes and the Zulus as being of equal importance with Latin and French. We believe in democracy and majority rule in political elections. Then, if a majority of the speakers of American English use "ain't," "knowed," "I'll learn you," "I laid on the bed," "who did you see," "between you and I," "like a cigarette should," these forms are by definition standard usage, and the corresponding minority forms, though sanctioned by traditional grammars, are, if not incorrect, at least obsolescent.

23   It may be argued, as does our Professor of Microbiology in *Science,* that "weighing the speech of casual speakers with no pretense of expertness on the same IBM card as usages of topnotch writers of past and present is an example of what the modern linguist calls 'science.' Tabulation is not science. Public opinion polls do not settle questions of science, or even of right and wrong. . . . If the guttersnipes of language do more talking than professors of English they get proportionally more votes."

24   But the structuralistic linguists can easily reply that language is a

matter of habit and convention, not of dogma or esthetics, and that if the basic purpose of semantic communication is achieved, it matters little what linguistic form is used. In engineering, calculations as to stresses and structures must be precise and correct, under penalty of seeing the bridge collapse. In medicine, correct dosage is essential, under penalty of seeing your patient die. But in language, the use of a substandard for a standard form seldom leads to irreparable consequences; at the most, as picturesquely stated by a leader of the school, you may not be invited to tea again.

25   On the other hand, members of the American school of linguistics are not always consistent in the application of their democratic and equalitarian principles. In reply to his critics, Dr. Gove remarked that while comments in lay newspapers and magazines had generally been unfavorable, the learned journals had not yet reviewed the new edition. The implication seemed to be that favorable reviews from a few members of his own clique, read and approved by a small circle of professional structuralistic linguists, would more than offset the generally unfavorable reaction of newspapers like the New York *Times* and magazines like the *New Yorker,* which appeal to large audiences of cultivated laymen. This not only puts the process of democracy into reverse; it comes close to setting up a hierarchy of professional linguists acting as the Voice of Authority for a recalcitrant majority of educated people.

26   There is no doubt in my mind that widespread localisms, slang, vulgarisms, colloquialisms, even obscenities and improprieties, should be duly noted in a comprehensive dictionary, whose first duty is to record what goes on in the field of language. Should such forms be labeled and described for what they are, not in a spirit of condemnation, but merely for the guidance of the reader? That, too, seems reasonable. If this procedure helps to slow up the inevitable process of language change by encouraging the speakers to use what the older dictionaries call standard forms, and discouraging them from using substandard forms, this impresses me as a distinct advantage. Too rapid and too widespread language change is a hindrance to communications. It lends itself to confusion and misunderstanding. The use of a more or less uniform standard by all members of the speaking community is desirable in the interests of efficiency rather than of esthetics. There is no question that within the next 500 years the English language, along with all other languages spoken today, will be so changed as to be practically unrecognizable. This will happen whether we like it or not. But need we deliberately hasten and amplify the process? Between sudden revolution and stolid reaction there is a middle ground of sound conservatism and orderly change.

27   Also, without being puristic to the point of ejecting "ain't" and kindred forms from a dictionary of recorded usage, it might be worth while to recognize the existence of a standard language, neither literary nor

slangy, which has acceptance and is understood practically everywhere in the country, even if everybody does not use it. Such phrases as "Them dogs is us'uns" and "I'll call you up without I can't," which an American structural linguist claims are good, meaningful language to him, merely because they are uttered by some native American speakers, definitely do not form part of that standard language. By all means let us record them for our own information and amusement, but let us not try to palm them off on the public on the general ground that the native speaker can do no wrong, and that "correct" and "incorrect" are terms that can be legitimately applied only to the speech of foreigners attempting to use English.

28   Language is something more than a heritage of sentimental value. It is an indispensable tool of communication and exchange of ideas. The more standardized and universal it is, the more effective it is. The more it is allowed to degenerate into local and class forms, the less effective it becomes. It may be perfectly true that in the past language has been allowed to run its own sweet, unbridled course, with the chips falling where they might. We are now in an age where we no longer believe in letting diseases and epidemics run their natural course, but take active, artificial means to control them. In fact, we endeavor to control natural, physical, and sociological phenomena of all descriptions, from floods to business cycles, from weather to diet, from the monetary system to racial relations. Is it unreasonable for us, far from leaving our language alone, as advocated by the American school of linguistics, to wish to channel it in the directions where it will prove of maximum efficiency for its avowed function, which is that of semantic transfer?

29   For the concern of that other burning question, standards of writing, as apart from standards of speech, ought we not to recognize that until such a time as tapes, recordings, dictaphones and spoken films altogether replace our system of written communications, the latter should be viewed and treated with respect? Again, we need not let ourselves be led too far afield by purely literary or esthetic considerations. The written language, in a modern civilization, is practically on a par with speech as a communications tool. It is incongruous to see our American structuralistic linguists devote so much painstaking attention to phonetic phenomena like pitch, stress, intonation, and juncture, to the fine distinctions between "a light housekeeper" and "a lighthouse keeper," "an iceman" and "a nice man," and yet shrug their shoulders at correct spelling, punctuation, and capitalization. More misunderstandings have occurred over misplaced commas than over misplaced junctures and, a wrong spelling can be just as fatal as a wrong intonation.

30   Perhaps the time has come, in language as in other fields, for the return of reason, and its ascendancy over dogma, whether the latter be of the puristic or of the structuralistic variety.

31   Above all, there is need for sound, scientific consideration of *all* the facts of language, not merely that portion which happens to suit the tastes and inclinations of a small group. Language is more than a set of phonemes, morphemes, junctures, and stresses. It also happens to be our most important instrument of semantic transfer, and the common possession of all of us. If democracy means anything, we, the speakers, have the right to have our say as to how it shall be viewed and used, and not to be forced to subscribe to the prescriptive excesses of what the European professor of linguistics describes as "the God's Truth School."

Questions

1. How does Pei enlarge the context of the argument over the *Third* in his opening paragraphs? To what extent does this enlargement enable him to establish values for judging the dictionary not touched upon by Follett and by Evans?

2. What assumption made by Evans about previous editions of the Merriam Webster is refuted in paragraph 7?

3. What admission is made in paragraph 8? What devices does he use to indicate that the point is merely an admission?

4. What is accomplished by paragraphs 9 and 10? Why does paragraph 11 seem appropriately placed?

5. How is Pei in his statement of the critical issue in paragraph 12 less restrictive than we might expect a critic to be? How is Pei's case strengthened thereby?

6. Paragraphs 14 and 15 state the defender's case. Does Pei's statement of that case seem fair? Is his inclusion of relativism in ethics, art, and philosophy relevant?

7. Paragraph 16 presents Pei's summary of the views of the American structuralist school of linguistics. Compare this summary with that made by Bergen Evans. To what extent is the difference a matter of language and tone?

8. To what extent does Evans focus on stating the principles of the American school of linguistics while Pei discusses the implications and the results of the practice of these principles? What answer does Evans provide to the charges implied by Mario Pei in paragraph 16?

9. What function do paragraphs 18 through 20 serve?

10. Is Pei's charge in paragraph 22 that the structural linguists would have us view the languages of the Arapahoes and the Zulus as being of equal importance with French and Latin relevant? (See Evans, paragraph 7.)

11. Are the analogies in paragraphs 24 and 28 valid?

The Lexicographer's Uneasy Chair

. . . this latest dictionary to bear the Merriam-Webster label is an intellectual achievement of the very highest order.

—SUMNER IVES in *Word Study*

. . . the anxiously awaited work that was to have crowned cisatlantic linguistic scholarship with a particular glory turns out to be a scandal and a disaster.

—WILSON FOLLETT in the *Atlantic*

Somebody had goofed.

—ETHEL MERMAN in *Webster's Third New International Dictionary*

1   But who? Is the goof trademarked, a Merriam-Webster, or is scholarship in Springfield trans-*Atlantic?* The experts will have to answer that question, and thoughtful laymen after using the new dictionary for a long time. This review has more modest aims. Mainly it examines a few issues which less inhibited critics have already raised, suggests some possible limitations of their criticisms, and urges that the serious work of serious scholars must be seriously judged.

2   Everyone knows that the *Third International* is an entirely new dictionary for use today. In this eighth member of a series which began in 1828, the Merriam Company has invested over $3,500,000, almost three times the cost of the 1934 *New International,* so that the statements in *Webster's Third* are backed by over a century of experience, by the evidence of more than 10,000,000 citations, and by the knowledge and skill of a large permanent staff and more than 200 special consultants. To a reviewer, those facts should be rather sobering.

3   Some editors, however, and some reviewers have not been restrained from prompt attacks. They have criticized the *Third International* for its failure to include expected encyclopedic matter, for its technique of definition, and especially for its treatment of what is called usage; and they have charged Dr. Gove and his associates with unwise innovations motivated by the desire to destroy all standards of better and worse in the use of English. While insisting upon the responsibility of lexicographers,

From *College English* (May, 1962). Reprinted with the permission of the National Council of Teachers of English and James Sledd.

some of the attackers have not been equally alert to the responsibility of critics.

4   The question of motives can be dismissed at once. The lexicographers at the Merriam Company, it may safely be assumed, have just one motive: to make the best possible dictionaries. They may have failed, in one respect or another; but such innovations as they actually have made have not been made without the most serious and responsible consideration.

5   The charge of unwise innovation has two parts: first, that an innovation has been made; and second, that it is unwise. Some of the critics have assumed that the editors of the *Third International* have departed from established lexicographical custom by assuming the role of historians, not lawgivers. One reviewer, indeed, to prove his accusation that the lexicographers had abandoned authority for permissiveness, quoted a part of their statement that "the standard of English pronunciation . . . is the usage that now prevails among the educated and cultured people to whom the language is vernacular." He had not bothered to read precisely the same statement in the 1934 *New International*.

6   More generally, too many of the unfavorable critics have ignored the whole history of English lexicography since Samuel Johnson: they have hurried to denounce an innovation as unwise before establishing the fact of innovation. Already in the eighteenth century, the ideal of the standard and standardizing dictionary had been sharply questioned. The encyclopedist Ephraim Chambers declared his view that "the Dictionary-Writer is not supposed to have any hand in the things he relates; he is no more concerned to make the improvements, or establish the significations, than the historian" to fight the battles he describes. Even Johnson said of himself that he did not "form, but register the language," that he did not "teach men how they should think, but relate how they have hitherto expressed their thoughts"; and when Englishmen a century later set out to make the great *Oxford Dictionary,* they assumed from the beginning that the lexicographer is "an historian" of the language, "not a critic." It may be that professional lexicographers have been on the wrong track for two centuries and that in two hours an amateur can set them straight; but in that event the amateur and not the lexicographer would be the innovator. He would do well, before attempting to put his lawgiving theory into practice, to face Johnson's doubts in that magnificent "Preface" and to ask himself the unanswerable question how rational choice among the resources of a language is possible for the man who does not know what those resources are.

7   The relation between a dictionary and an encyclopedia is another problem whose history should have been better known to some reviewers. Few lexicographers are likely to solve it either to their own full satisfaction or to the satisfaction of all their readers. From the *Third Interna-*

tional, the objectors miss the gazetteer and the biographical dictionary of the 1934 volume, and they dislike the new decision to restrict the word-list "to generic words . . . as distinguished from proper names that are not generic." Other readers might just as well make opposite complaints. The hairy-nosed wombat and the hickory shuckworm do not greatly interest the average American, who has equally little need to know the incubation period of the ostrich or the gestation period of the elephant, to contemplate the drawing of a milestone marked "Boston 20 miles," or to examine a colorplate of fishes which is a slander to the catfish and the brook trout; and the occasional philologist might hope for a dictionary which explains words and leaves to the encyclopedia, as Murray said, the description of things. But who can say that he knows infallibly how such decisions should be made? Murray did not claim infallibility but admitted inconsistency in his omission of *African* and inclusion of *Amercan.* Since man and the universe cannot be put between two covers, some things must be omitted; "selection is guided by usefulness"; and usefulness can be guessed at but not measured. Readers who can get the use of a Webster's unabridged will have access to an encyclopedia. They should consult it it when they need to know about people and places. Meanwhile they may be grateful that the *Third International* has made space for as many quotations as it now includes. A dictionary without quotations is like a table of contents without a book.

8   There remain, of the critics' favorite subjects, the technique of definition and the matter of usage. The technique of definition is briefly explained in the editor's preface:

The primary objective of precise, sharp defining has been met through development of a new dictionary style based upon completely analytical one-phrase definitions throughout the book. Since the headword in the definition is intended to be modified only by structural elements restrictive in some degree and essential to each other, the use of commas either to separate or to group has been severely limited, chiefly to units in apposition or in series. The new defining pattern does not provide for a predication which conveys further expository comment. . . . Defining by synonym is carefully avoided by putting all unqualified or undifferentiated terms in small capital letters. Such a term in small capitals should not be considered a definition but a cross-reference to a definition of equivalent meaning that can be substituted for the small capitals.

A large number of verbal illustrations mostly from the mid-twentieth century has been woven into the defining pattern with a view of contributing considerably to the user's interest and understanding by showing a word used in context.

9   If it is not naively optimistic to expect most critics of a dictionary to agree on anything, general approval may be expected for careful synonymies and for the distinction between a synonym and a definition; and

the value of illustrative quotations has been demonstrated by centuries of English lexicography. The objection that not many mid-century authors deserve quotation has already been answered, for it is only another form of the notion that the lexicographer should be a lawgiver and not a historian. It would, moreover, be rash to suggest either that many of the quotations are not particularly informative or that identification by the mere names of the authors makes it impossible to check the quotations or to examine them in their contexts: with 10,000,000 quotations to choose from, the editors must know the possibilities of choice more fully than any critic, and precise references would take up much valuable space.

10　　The definitions themselves are another matter. Without advancing any claim to special competence, an ordinary reader may fairly report that he finds some of the definitions extraordinarily clumsy and hard to follow and that as an English teacher he would not encourage his students to follow the new Merriam-Webster model. The one-phrase definitions of nouns in particular may become confusing because in English it is hard to keep track of the relations among a long series of prepositional phrases, participial phrases, and relative clauses; the reader may simply forget what goes with what, if indeed he ever can find out. A less serious criticism is that the new typeface and the long entries unbroken by indentation are bad for middle-aged eyes. Real mistakes, of course, are extremely rare, but a fisherman may be pardoned an objection to the fourth numbered definition of the noun *keeper* as "a fish large enough to be legally caught." The crime is not catching but keeping an undersized or oversized fish.

11　　Perhaps such a quibble is itself no keeper, and some criticism of the dictionary's treatment of usage has been equally frivolous. An excellent bad example appeared in *Life,* whose editors compressed a remarkable amount of confusion into a single sentence when they attacked "Editor Gove" for "saying that if a word is misused often enough, it becomes acceptable." Though one can argue how much use and by what speakers is enough, consistency would force *Life's* editors into silence. Their sacred kye are scrawnier than Pharaoh's seven kine, and it is shocking that the influence of such a magazine should force learning to debate with ignorance.

12　　Yet so loud a stridulation of critics cannot simply be ignored. There is a real question whether the *Third International,* though justly called "the most comprehensive guide to usage currently available," has recorded usage as precisely as it might have done. Were the editors right to abandon "the status label *colloquial*"? Have they adequately reported not only what people say and write but also those opinions concerning speech and writing which properly enter into their own definitions of *standard* and of *Standard English?* Those are legitimate questions to ask of a dictionary "prepared with a constant regard for the needs of the high school and college student" and of the general reader. However diffidently and respectfully, a reviewer must give the best answers that he can.

13   Several reasons have been offered, by various authorities, for the abandonment of the label *colloquial*. Those reasons are not all alike. It is one thing to say that we cannot know "whether a word out of context is colloquial or not" (Gove), that lexicographers cannot distinguish the "many different degrees of standard usage" by status labels but can only suggest them by quotations (Gove), or that "the bases for discrimination are often too subtle for exact and understandable verbal statement" (Ives); it is quite another thing to argue against marking words *colloquial* because many readers have wrongly concluded that a word so marked is somehow bad (Ives). In a matter to which the editors must have given their best thought, the variety itself of these justifications and the failure to order them in any coherent and inclusive statement is somewhat puzzling; and the impertinent might be tempted to inquire how 200,000 quotations will enable the inexpert reader to do what 10,000,000 quotations did not make possible for the expert lexicographer or how a dictionary can be made at all if nothing can go into it which the ignorant might misinterpret. One reason for the widespread misinterpretation of the policy adopted is surely that the underlying theory has not been clearly explained.

14   And that is not all. The very defenses of the new policy appear sometimes to refute the contention that finer discriminations are not possible than those in *Webster's Third*. When the newspapers attack the dictionary for listing words like *double-dome* and *finalize* as standard, defenders reply by citing other slangy or colloquial or much reprobated terms from the columns of those same newspapers. What is the force of the attack or the defense unless the intelligent layman can draw precisely that distinction between "the formal and informal speech and writing of the educated" which the *Third International* refuses to draw for him? If he lacked that ability, both attackers and defenders would be wasting their citations.

15   Much can be said, of course, about the confusion of styles in modern writing. Perhaps distinctions among styles are now indeed less clear and stable than they were in a less troubled age; perhaps the clumsier writers do ignore the existing distinctions while the sophisticated use them to play sophisticated tunes; perhaps the scrupulously objective lexicographer cannot establish those distinctions from his quotation slips alone. For all that, distinctions do exist. They exist in good writing, and they exist in the linguistic consciousness of the educated. Dr. Gove's definers prove they exist when they give *egghead* as a synonym for *doubledome* but then define *egghead* in impeccably formal terms as "one with intellectual interests or pretensions" or as "a highly educated person." Such opposition between theory and practice strikes even a timid and generally admiring reviewer as rather odd, as though some notion of scientific objectivity should require the scientist to deny that he knows what he knows because he may not know how he knows it.

16   In the absence, then, of convincing argument to the contrary, a simple

reader is left with the uneasy feeling that the abandonment of *"Colloq."* was a mistake which the introduction of more quotations does not quite rectify and that as a teacher he must now provide foreigners and inexperienced students both with some general principles of linguistic choice and with specific instruction in instances where the new dictionary does not discriminate finely enough among stylistic variants. The dictionary leaves unlabeled many expressions which this teacher would not allow a beginning writer to use in serious exposition or argument except for clearly intended and rather special effects: (*to be caught*) *with one's pants down, dollarwise, stylewise* (*s.v. -wise*), (*to give one*) *the bird, dog* "something inferior of its kind," *to enthuse, to level* "deal frankly," *schmaltz, chintzy, the catbird seat, to roll* "rob," *to send* "delight," *shindig, shook-up, square* "an unsophisticated person," *squirrelly, to goof,* and the like. Enforcing such modest niceties will now be more difficult; for classroom lawyers and irate parents will be able to cite the dictionary which the teacher has taught Johnny how to read but which has collapsed the distinction between formal and informal Standard English. Similar difficulties could occur with various mild obscenities, such as *pissed off* and *pisspoor,* which should be marked not only as slang but with some one of the warning labels that the dictionary attaches to the almost quite adequately recorded four-letter words; and the label *slang* itself might well be more freely used with the various synonyms for *drunk—stewed, stinko, stoned, tight, tanked, sozzled, potted, pie-eyed, feeling no pain, blind, looped, squiffed, boiled, fried, high,* etc. Odzooks!

17   The convenience of a classroom teacher, however, is a rather petty criterion by which to judge a great dictionary, and the tiny handful of evidence here alleged must not be taken as justifying the shrill lament that *Webster's Third* is "a scandal and a disaster." The wake has been distinctly premature. Both the dictionary and the language it records are likely to survive the keening critics, whose exaggerations are something of a stumbling block themselves. The mere extent of the information in a dictionary unabridged should fix in a reviewer's mind the salutary knowledge that as no one man can make such a book, so no one man can judge it; but the popular reviews of the *Third International* have merely skimmed its surface and have said little of its technical features or substantial accomplishments. The present discussion will conclude with a few slight remarks on some such matters and with the renewed insistence that longer use and more expert study will be necessary before the dictionary can be definitely judged.

18   Teachers of elementary composition may be especially interested in the dictionary's three well-filled pages on English punctuation. As several recent grammarians have done, the editors attempt to establish definite relations between pointing and intonation, and they pursue that end with some care and vigor: the theory that punctuation may in part be

taught by relating it to pitch-contours and to pauses here receives a better-than-average statement.

19   Yet the composition teacher may still be sceptical. For one thing, no account of English intonation has deserved or won universal acceptance. The editors themselves thus seem to postulate more than the three "pauses" allowed in the Trager-Smith phonology, which their description directly or indirectly follows. What is worse is the failure of the proposed relationships between speech and pointing as one moves from dialect to dialect: rules that may hold in one region do not hold in another. For much Southern American speech and for much Southern British, it is simply not the case that "the rising pause . . . is usually indicated in writing by a comma"; for many speakers and writers in many areas, an exclamation point may correspond to a *low*-pitched "terminal stress" as well as to a high one; and a colon may be used in writing not just for "a fading or sustained pause in speech" but for a "rising pause" or for no pause at all. The editors have weakened their case by stating it too simply and too strongly.

20   For the linguistically inclined, Mr. Edwin Artin's extensive "Guide to Pronunciation" will have a particular attraction. The "Guide" is just that—a guide; "not a treatise on phonetics" or a structural dialectologist's systematic account of American pronunciation, but an explanation of the way the editors have used their new alphabet in their transcriptions. Though the forgetful will regret that the key is no longer before them at each opening, and though a stern phonemicist might call the whole system sloppy, the new alphabet is an arguable solution to an extremely complex theoretical and practical problem and a definite improvement over the more complicated yet less accurate and more misleading diacritical key in the *Webster's* of 1934. The objective in devising the alphabet "was a set of symbols which would represent each speech sound which distinguishes one word from another and each difference in sound which is associated with some large region of the country" (Ives), so that the editors might record both the formal and the informal pronunciations actually heard in cultivated conversation from speakers of the standard dialects in the various regions. The *Third International* can thus do fuller justice than its predecessor did to regional variation and to modes of speech less artificial than the "formal platform speech" of the earlier work.

21   Like every competent writer on American pronunciation, Mr. Artin will be criticized as well as praised. He writes, indeed, at a particularly difficult time, when phonological theory is so unsettled that rival groups among the linguists can scarcely communicate with one another. Since pleasing one group of theorists means displeasing its opponents, since it is easily possible to please neither or none, and since Mr. Artin does not include in his "Guide" the sort of general and historical information which could be found in the corresponding section of the 1934 dictionary, per-

haps he will not have so large an audience as Kenyon reached. His readers will be the kind who will argue the results of equating the medial consonants of *tidal* and *title* because in some dialects they are phonetically identical or of distinguishing them because the preceding diphthongs may be of different lengths and because the consonants of *tide* and *titular* clearly differ. Other readers, if they find the "Guide" hard going, will not risk too much confusion by limiting their study to the table of symbols and to the short section on pronunciation in the "Explanatory Notes."

22   Within the dictionary proper, the word-list first invites examination. Like the addenda to the later editions of the *Second,* the vexing miscellaneous entries at the bottoms of the pages are now gone from *Webster's Third,* either dropped or worked into the main alphabet; numerous obsolete words have disappeared, since the cut-off date has been advanced from 1500 to 1755; and further space for additions has been found by rejecting many no longer useful terms from the rapidly changing and never generally current technical vocabulary with which both the *Second* and the *Third International* are stuffed. This plethora of scientific and technical terms, carefully gathered in an elaborate reading program, is of course no plethora at all but only a comfortable supply for the scientist and technologist, who seem pleased with the dictionary's coverage of their fields; and a general dictionary must make room as well for some regionalisms, for a certain amount of recent slang, and for the new words in general use which so eloquently damn our culture. When all this has been done, it would be unfair to complain that perhaps not enough attention has been paid to the distinctive vocabularies of English-speaking nations other than Britain and the United States.

23   Beyond the word-list, neither space nor the reviewer's competence will allow him to go. He has few complaints about spelling, the only loud one being against *alright;* as far as a layman's knowledge goes, the etymologies are accurate, and beyond that point they remain clear and comprehensible; the discrimination and the arrangement of senses impose silence on the reader who has not studied them with the same care that went into their making; and the synonymies have already proved their practical value. A sweeping conclusion will not be expected of a review whose thesis is that the prematurity of sweeping conclusions has already been sufficiently exemplified, but a moderately serious examination has made a few things perfectly plain about the *Third International.* As a completely new, independent, responsibly edited, unabridged dictionary, no other work can rival it on precisely its own ground. Its merits are infinitely greater than those of the reviews which have lightly questioned them. Time and the experts will ultimately decide its just rank in the world of English lexicography, whether above, below, or alongside its predecessor; but meanwhile it can usefully fill a place in the libraries of a generation.

Questions

1. What issues in the argument over the *Third* does Sledd set aside as secondary and for what reasons?
2. What issues does he single out as primary or crucial? How do they compare and contrast with those distinguished by the previous writers in this section?
3. Although Sledd admits some of the definitions are faulty and the omission of labels of usage is unwise and confusing to the layman, how does he temper the force of his admissions?
4. Granted that Sledd is partially serious when he casually asserts "the convenience of the classroom teacher, however, is a rather petty criterion by which to judge a great dictionary," what criterion is in Sledd's view major and significant in judging a work such as the *Third?*
5. Show at what points Sledd's discussion is the least emotional and the most heavily qualified of these four discussions of *Webster's Third International.* Is a tempered, balanced view always (or ever) the truest view of any controversy or subject?
6. How does Sledd make the theory upon which the *Third* is based clearer than does Follett, Evans, or Pei? Where does he find gaps or weaknesses in the theory?
7. How does Sledd by means of word choice and tone establish a friendly but tentative attitude toward the *Third* and its makers and a reproving but explanatory attitude toward their detractors?
8. Paragraph 6 enlists Samuel Johnson on the side of the defenders. After studying the following section from Johnson's *Preface* to his own dictionary, point out how Sledd has reported Johnson's views correctly or incorrectly.

45   SAMUEL JOHNSON

Preface to:
A Dictionary of the English Language

1   It is the fate of those who toil at the lower employments of life, to be rather driven by the fear of evil, than attracted by the prospect of good; to be exposed to censure, without hope of praise; to be disgraced by miscarriage, or punished for neglect, where success would have been without applause, and diligence without reward.

2   Among these unhappy mortals is the writer of dictionaries; whom mankind have considered, not as the pupil, but the slave of science, the

pionier of literature, doomed only to remove rubbish and clear obstructions from the paths through which Learning and Genius press forward to conquest and glory, without bestowing a smile on the humble drudge that facilitates their progress. Every other authour may aspire to praise; the lexicographer can only hope to escape reproach, and even this negative recompense has been yet granted to very few.

3   I have, notwithstanding this discouragement, attempted a dictionary of the *English* language, which, while it was employed in the cultivation of every species of literature, has itself been hitherto neglected; suffered to spread, under the direction of chance, into wild exuberance; resigned to the tyranny of time and fashion; and exposed to the corruptions of ignorance, and caprices of innovation.

4   When I took the first survey of my undertaking, I found our speech copious without order, and energetick without rules: wherever I turned my view, there was perplexity to be disentangled, and confusion to be regulated; choice was to be made out of boundless variety, without any established principle of selection; adulterations were to be detected, without a settled test of purity; and modes of expression to be rejected or received, without the suffrages of any writers of classical reputation or acknowledged authority.

5   Having therefore no assistance but from general grammar, I applied myself to the perusal of our writers; and noting whatever might be of use to ascertain or illustrate any word or phrase, accumulated in time the materials of a dictionary, which, by degrees, I reduced to method, establishing to myself, in the progress of the work, such rules as experience and analogy suggested to me; experience, which practice and observation were continually increasing; and analogy, which, though in some words obscure, was evident in others.

6   In adjusting the ORTHOGRAPHY, which has been to this time unsettled and fortuitous, I found it necessary to distinguish those irregularities that are inherent in our tongue, and perhaps coeval with it, from others which the ignorance or negligence of later writers has produced. Every language has its anomalies, which, though inconvenient, and in themselves once unnecessary, must be tolerated among the imperfections of human things, and which require only to be registered, that they may not be increased, and ascertained, that they may not be confounded: but every language has likewise its improprieties and absurdities, which it is the duty of the lexicographer to correct or proscribe.

7   As language was at its beginning merely oral, all words of necessary or common use were spoken before they were written; and while they were unfixed by any visible signs, must have been spoken with great diversity, as we now observe those who cannot read catch sounds imperfectly, and utter them negligently. When this wild and barbarous jargon was first reduced to an alphabet, every penman endeavoured to express,

as he could, the sounds which he was accustomed to pronounce or to receive, and vitiated in writing such words as were already vitiated in speech.
The powers of the letters, when they were applied to a new language, must
have been vague and unsettled, and therefore different hands would exhibit
the same sound by different combinations. . . .

8   In this part of the work, where caprice has long wantoned without
controul, and vanity sought praise by petty reformation, I have endeavoured to proceed with a scholar's reverence for antiquity, and a grammarian's regard to the genius of our tongue. I have attempted few alterations,
and among those few, perhaps the greater part is from the modern
to the ancient practice; and I hope I may be allowed to recommend to
those, whose thoughts have been perhaps employed too anxiously on
verbal singularities, not to disturb, upon narrow views, or for minute
propriety, the orthography of their fathers. It has been asserted, that for
the law to be *known,* is of more importance than to be *right.* Change, says
Hooker, is not made without inconvenience, even from worse to better.
There is in constancy and stability a general and lasting advantage, which
will always overbalance the slow improvements of gradual correction.
Much less ought our written language to comply with the corruptions of
oral utterance, or copy that which every variation of time or place makes
different from itself, and imitate those changes, which will again be
changed, while imitation is employed in observing them.

9   This recommendation of steadiness and uniformity does not proceed
from an opinion, that particular combinations of letters have much influence on human happiness; or that truth may not be successfully taught
by modes of spelling fanciful and erroneous: I am not yet so lost in lexicography, as to forget that *words are the daughters of earth, and that things
are the sons of heaven.* Language is only the instrument of science, and
words are but the signs of ideas: I wish, however, that the instrument
might be less apt to decay, and that signs might be permanent, like the
things which they denote. . . .

10   That part of my work on which I expect malignity most frequently
to fasten, is the *Explanation;* in which I cannot hope to satisfy those, who
are perhaps not inclined to be pleased, since I have not always been able
to satisfy myself. To interpret a language by itself is very difficult; many
words cannot be explained by synonimes, because the idea signified by
them has not more than one appellation; nor by paraphrase, because simple ideas cannot be described. When the nature of things is unknown, or
the notion unsettled and indefinite, and various in various minds, the
words by which such notions are conveyed, or such things denoted, will be
ambiguous and perplexed. And such is the fate of hapless lexicography,
that not only darkness, but light, impedes and distresses it; things may be
not only too little, but too much known, to be happily illustrated. To explain, requires the use of terms less abstruse than that which is to be ex-

plained, and such terms cannot always be found; for as nothing can be proved but by supposing something intuitively known, and evident without proof, so nothing can be defined but by the use of words too plain to admit a definition. . . .

11   In every word of extensive use, it was requisite to mark the progress of its meaning, and show by what gradations of intermediate sense it has passed from its primitive to its remote and accidental signification; so that every foregoing explanation should tend to that which follows, and the series be regularly concatenated from the first notion to the last. . . .

12   When first I collected these authorities, I was desirous that every quotation should be useful to some other end than the illustration of a word; I therefore extracted from philosophers principles of science; from historians remarkable facts; from chymists complete processes; from divines striking exhortations; and from poets beautiful descriptions. Such is design, while it is yet at a distance from execution. When the time called upon me to range this accumulation of elegance and wisdom into an alphabetical series, I soon discovered that the bulk of my volumes would fright away the student, and was forced to depart from my scheme of including all that was pleasing or useful in *English* literature, and reduce my transcripts very often to clusters of words, in which scarcely any meaning is retained; thus to the weariness of copying, I was condemned to add the vexation of expunging. Some passages I have yet spared, which may relieve the labour of verbal searches, and intersperse with verdure and flowers the dusty desarts of barren philology. . . .

13   My purpose was to admit no testimony of living authours, that I might not be misled by partiality, and that none of my contemporaries might have reason to complain; nor have I departed from this resolution, but when some performance of uncommon excellence excited my veneration, when my memory supplied me, from late books, with an example that was wanting, or when my heart, in the tenderness of friendship, solicited admission for a favourite name.

14   So far have I been from any care to grace my pages with modern decorations, that I have studiously endeavoured to collect examples and authorities from the writers before the restoration, whose works I regard as *the wells of English undefiled,* as the pure sources of genuine diction. Our language, for almost a century, has, by the concurrence of many causes, been gradually departing from its original *Teutonick* character, and deviating towards a *Gallick* structure and phraseology, from which it ought to be our endeavour to recal it, by making our ancient volumes the ground-work of stile, admitting among the additions of later times, only such as may supply real deficiencies, such as are readily adopted by the genius of our tongue, and incorporate easily with our native idioms.

15   But as every language has a time of rudeness antecedent to perfection, as well as of false refinement and declension, I have been cautious lest

my zeal for antiquity might drive me into times too remote, and croud my book with words now no longer understood. I have fixed *Sidney's* work for the boundary, beyond which I make few excursions. From the authours which rose in the time of *Elizabeth,* a speech might be formed adequate to all the purposes of use and elegance. If the language of theology were extracted from *Hooker* and the translation of the Bible; the terms of natural knowledge from *Bacon;* the phrases of policy, war, and navigation from *Raleigh;* the dialect of poetry and fiction from *Spenser* and *Sidney;* and the diction of common life from *Shakespeare,* few ideas would be lost to mankind, for want of *English* words, in which they might be expressed. . . .

16   Thus have I laboured by settling the orthography, displaying the analogy, regulating the structures, and ascertaining the signification of *English* words, to perform all the parts of a faithful lexicographer: but I have not always executed my own scheme, or satisfied my own expectations. The work, whatever proofs of diligence and attention it may exhibit, is yet capable of many improvements: the orthography which I recommend is still controvertible, the etymology which I adopt is uncertain, and perhaps frequently erroneous; the explanations are sometimes too much contracted, and sometimes too much diffused, the significations are distinguished rather with subtilty than skill, and the attention is harassed with unnecessary minuteness. . . .

17   Yet these failures, however frequent, may admit extenuation and apology. To have attempted much is always laudable, even when the enterprize is above the strength that undertakes it: To rest below his own aim is incident to every one whose fancy is active, and whose views are comprehensive; nor is any man satisfied with himself because he has done much, but because he can conceive little. When first I engaged in this work, I resolved to leave neither words nor things unexamined, and pleased myself with a prospect of the hours which I should revel away in feasts of literature, with the obscure recesses of northern learning, which I should enter and ransack; the treasures with which I expected every search into those neglected mines to reward my labour, and the triumph with which I should display my acquisitions to mankind. When I had thus enquired into the original of words, I resolved to show likewise my attention to things; to pierce deep into every science, to enquire the nature of every substance of which I inserted the name, to limit every idea by a definition strictly logical, and exhibit every production of art or nature in an accurate description, that my book might be in place of all other dictionaries whether appellative or technical. But these were the dreams of a poet doomed at last to wake a lexicographer. I soon found that it is too late to look for instruments, when the work calls for execution, and that whatever abilities I had brought to my task, with those I must finally perform it. To deliberate whenever I doubted, to enquire whenever I was ignorant, would

have protracted the undertaking without end, and, perhaps, without much improvement; for I did not find by my first experiments, that what I had not of my own was easily to be obtained: I saw that one enquiry only gave occasion to another, that book referred to book, that to search was not always to find, and to find was not always to be informed; and that thus to persue perfection, was, like the first inhabitants of Arcadia, to chace the sun, which, when they had reached the hill where he seemed to rest, was still beheld at the same distance from them.

18   I then contracted my design, determining to confide in myself, and no longer to solicit auxiliaries, which produced more incumbrance than assistance: by this I obtained at least one advantage, that I set limits to my work, which would in time be ended, though not completed. . . .

19   Of the event of this work, for which, having laboured it with so much application, I cannot but have some degree of parental fondness, it is natural to form conjectures. Those who have been persuaded to think well of my design, will require that it should fix our language, and put a stop to those alterations which time and chance have hitherto been suffered to make in it without opposition. With this consequence I will confess that I flattered myself for a while; but now begin to fear that I have indulged expectation which neither reason nor experience can justify. When we see men grow old and die at a certain time one after another, from century to century, we laugh at the elixir that promises to prolong life to a thousand years; and with equal justice may the lexicographer be derided, who being able to produce no example of a nation that has preserved their words and phrases from mutability, shall imagine that his dictionary can embalm his language, and secure it from corruption and decay, that it is in his power to change sublunary nature, and clear the world at once from folly, vanity, and affectation.

20   With this hope, however, academies have been instituted, to guard the avenues of their languages, to retain fugitives, and repulse intruders; but their vigilance and activity have hitherto been vain; sounds are too volatile and subtile for legal restraints; to enchain syllables, and to lash the wind, are equally the undertakings of pride, unwilling to measure its desires by its strength. The *French* language has visibly changed under the inspection of the academy; the stile of *Amelot's* translation of Father *Paul* is observed by *Le Courayer* to be *un peu passé;* and no *Italian* will maintain that the diction of any modern writer is not perceptibly different from that of *Boccace, Machiavel,* or *Caro.*

21   Total and sudden transformations of a language seldom happen; conquests and migrations are now very rare: but there are other causes of change, which, though slow in their operation, and invisible in their progress, are perhaps as much superiour to human resistance, as the revolutions of the sky, or intumescence of the tide. Commerce, however

necessary, however lucrative, as it depraves the manners, corrupts the language; they that have frequent intercourse with strangers, to whom they endeavour to accommodate themselves, must in time learn a mingled dialect, like the jargon which serves the traffickers on the *Mediterranean* and *Indian* coasts. This will not always be confined to the exchange, the warehouse, or the port, but will be communicated by degress to other ranks of the people, and be at last incorporated with the current speech.

22   There are likewise internal causes equally forcible. The language most likely to continue long without alteration, would be that of a nation raised a little, and but a little above barbarity, secluded from strangers, and totally employed in procuring the conveniences of life; either without books, or, like some of the *Mahometan* countries, with very few: men thus busied and unlearned, having only such words as common use requires, would perhaps long continue to express the same notions by the same signs. But no such constancy can be expected in a people polished by arts, and classed by subordination, where one part of the community is sustained and accommodated by the labour of the other. Those who have much leisure to think, will always be enlarging the stock of ideas, and every increase of knowledge, whether real or fancied, will produce new words, or combinations of words. When the mind is unchained from necessity, it will range after convenience; when it is left at large in the fields of speculation, it will shift opinions; as any custom is disused, the words that expressed it must perish with it; as any opinion grows popular, it will innovate speech in the same proportion as it alters practice.

23   As by the cultivation of various sciences, a language is amplified, it will be more furnished with words deflected from original sense; the geometrician will talk of a courtier's zenith, or the excentrick virtue of a wild hero, and the physician of sanguine expectations and phlegmatick delays. Copiousness of speech will give opportunities to capricious choice, by which some words will be preferred, and others degraded; vicissitudes of fashion will enforce the use of new, or extend the signification of known terms. The tropes of poetry will make hourly encroachments, and the metaphorical will become the current sense: pronunciation will be varied by levity or ignorance, and the pen must at length comply with the tongue; illiterate writers will at one time or other, by publick infatuation, rise into renown, who, not knowing the original import of words, will use them with colloquial licentiousness, confound distinction, and forget propriety. As politeness increases, some expressions will be considered as too gross and vulgar for the delicate, others as too formal and ceremonious for the gay and airy; new phrases are therefore adopted, which must, for the same reasons, be in time dismissed. *Swift,* in his petty treatise on the *English* language, allows that new words must sometimes be introduced, but proposes that none should be suffered to become obsolete. But what makes

a word obsolete, more than general agreement to forbear it? and how shall it be continued, when it conveys an offensive idea, or recalled again into the mouths of mankind, when it has once become unfamiliar by disuse, and unpleasing by unfamiliarity?

24   There is another cause of alteration more prevalent than any other, which yet in the present state of the world cannot be obviated. A mixture of two languages will produce a third distinct from both, and they will always be mixed, where the chief part of education, and the most conspicuous accomplishment, is skill in ancient or in foreign tongues. He that has long cultivated another language, will find its words and combinations croud upon his memory; and haste and negligence, refinement and affectation, will obtrude borrowed terms and exotick expressions.

25   The great pest of speech is frequency of translation. No book was ever turned from one language into another, without imparting something of its native idiom; this is the most mischievous and comprehensive innovation; single words may enter by thousands, and the fabrick of the tongue continue the same, but new phraseology changes much at once; it alters not the single stones of the building, but the order of the columns. If an academy should be established for the cultivation of our stile, which I, who can never wish to see dependance multiplied, hope the spirit of *English* liberty will hinder or destroy, let them, instead of compiling grammars and dictionaries, endeavour, with all their influence, to stop the licence of translatours, whose idleness and ignorance, if it be suffered to proceed, will reduce us to babble a dialect of *France*.

26   If the changes that we fear be thus irresistible, what remains but to acquiesce with silence, as in the other insurmountable distresses of humanity? It remains that we retard what we cannot repel, that we palliate what we cannot cure. Life may be lengthened by care, though death cannot be ultimately defeated: tongues, like governments, have a natural tendency to degeneration; we have long preserved our constitution, let us make some struggles for our language.

27   In hope of giving longevity to that which its own nature forbids to be immortal, I have devoted this book, the labour of years, to the honour of my country, that we may no longer yield the palm of philology, without a contest, to the nations of the continent. The chief glory of every people arises from its authours: whether I shall add any thing by my own writings to the reputation of *English* literature, must be left to time: much of my life has been lost under the pressures of disease; much has been trifled away; and much has always been spent in provision for the day that was passing over me; but I shall not think my employment useless or ignoble, if by my assistance foreign nations, and distant ages, gain access to the propagators of knowledge, and understand the teachers of truth; if my labours afford light to the repositories of science, and add celebrity to *Bacon,* to *Hooker,* to *Milton,* and to *Boyle.*

28   When I am animated by this wish, I look with pleasure on my book, however defective, and deliver it to the world with the spirit of a man that has endeavoured well. That it will immediately become popular I have not promised to myself: a few wild blunders, and risible absurdities, from which no work of such multiplicity was ever free, may for a time furnish folly with laughter, and harden ignorance in contempt; but useful diligence will at last prevail, and there never can be wanting some who distinguish desert; who will consider that no dictionary of a living tongue ever can be perfect, since while it is hastening to publication, some words are budding, and some falling away; that a whole life cannot be spent upon syntax and etymology, and that even a whole life would not be sufficient; that he, whose design includes whatever language can express, must often speak of what he does not understand; that a writer will sometimes be hurried by eagerness to the end, and sometimes faint with weariness under a task, which *Scaliger* compares to the labours of the anvil and the mine; that what is obvious is not always known, and what is known is not always present; that sudden fits of inadvertency will surprize vigilance, slight avocations will seduce attention, and casual eclipses of the mind will darken learning; and that the writer shall often in vain trace his memory at the moment of need, for that which yesterday he knew with intuitive readiness, and which will come uncalled into his thoughts tomorrow.

29   In this work, when it shall be found that much is omitted, let it not be forgotten that much likewise is performed; and though no book was ever spared out of tenderness to the authour, and the world is little solicitous to know whence proceeded the faults of that which it condemns; yet it may gratify curiosity to inform it, that the *English Dictionary* was written with little assistance of the learned, and without any patronage of the great; not in the soft obscurities of retirement, or under the shelter of academick bowers, but amidst inconvenience and distraction, in sickness and in sorrow. It may repress the triumph of malignant criticism to observe, that if our language is not here fully displayed, I have only failed in an attempt which no human powers have hitherto completed. If the lexicons of ancient tongues, now immutably fixed, and comprised in a few volumes, be yet, after the toil of successive ages, inadequate and delusive; if the aggregated knowledge, and co-operating diligence of the *Italian* academicians, did not secure them from the censure of *Beni;* if the embodied criticks of *France,* when fifty years had been spent upon their work, were obliged to change its oeconomy, and give their second edition another form, I may surely be contented without the praise of perfection, which, if I could obtain, in this gloom of solitude, what would it avail me? I have protracted my work till most of those whom I wished to please have sunk into the grave, and success and miscarriage are empty sounds: I therefore dismiss it with frigid tranquillity, having little to fear or hope from censure or from praise.

Questions

1. What irony is there in paragraph 1?
2. What stylistic devices can you identify in paragraph 3?
3. Name some of the irregularities inherent in our tongue that Johnson discusses in paragraph 6.
4. Does the spelling and capitalization of Jonathan Swift's "A Modest Proposal" give any insight into what Johnson discusses in paragraphs 6 through 9?
5. In paragraph 8, is Johnson's general approach that of the permissive scholar or the prescriptive? Explain. Would he agree with Evans? Follett? Pei? Sledd?
6. How does the phrase in paragraph 9 "words are the daughters of earth, and that things are the sons of heaven" explain Johnson's position? Does he temper his statement?
7. Why did Johnson not use living authors as sources?
8. What period did Johnson set for his earliest limit and why?
9. Would the editors of the *Third* be able to use paragraphs 19 and 20 as testimony in their defense?
10. Would Evans agree with paragraph 26?
11. Why does Johnson conclude the preface to his monumental dictionary with these words: "I therefore dismiss it with frigid tranquillity, having little to fear or hope from censure or from praise"?
12. In paragraph 28, when Johnson is considering his final attitude toward the dictionary, there is an extremely long sentence which begins: "That it will immediately become popular. . . ." The sentence continues to the end of the paragraph. What stylistic devices does Johnson employ to hold the sentence together, to keep it from becoming unwieldy?
13. In paragraph 29, Johnson contrasts his working conditions with those of others who have written. Name some of the balanced contrasts he presents and comment on their effectiveness.

Theme topics

1. Write an essay in which you refute the position taken by one of the critics of Webster's *Third* by using evidence from the others.
2. Isolate a single issue of the controversy over Webster's *Third* and argue your position.
3. Write a statement of the entire controversy over Webster's *Third* to be read by the general reader who knows nothing of either the controversy or the dictionary.
4. Write a *slanted* statement of the entire controversy which pretends to be a simple report of the situation but which actually attempts to sway your innocent reader's response.

5. Write a short satire of either the dictionary, the entire controversy or the critics of the dictionary. You might, for example, write a letter to the editors from a confused man looking for an answer, from an English teacher of the dogmatic school, or from a misguided champion of liberty congratulating the editors. You might write a dialogue in which one person tries to explain the controversy to another. You might write a piece of prose for some specific occasion using the new permissiveness—a speech introducing a guest speaker, a letter to an editor, etc.

Education

Values, absolutes, and focus for argument

Arguments are essentially of two kinds: those for or against a certain course of action and those for or against a certain judgment. What one favors as a course of future action as well as what one approves of the past are both decided on the basis of one's values. The question of values would itself be a simple one if our culture passed on to us a set of absolutes, standards by which we might make judgments. Such, unfortunately, is not the case, as the essays of C. S. Lewis and Philip Wheelwright in this volume illustrate. As C. S. Lewis demonstrates, however, we do believe in right and wrong. For example, in a certain instance we might advocate mercy killing and long before we encountered someone who directed our attention to the absolute "Thou shalt not kill," we would have encountered it in our own sense of guilt. We are then in the grips of an ethical dilemma. On the one hand we feel that in this instance the value above all others is to relieve another of pain in a situation where his agony is acute and his imminent death certain. We argue that "Thou shalt not kill" is no absolute anyway since war and self-defense have already made its application relative to circumstances. On the other hand, we know that the standards by which ordinary men in Western society live, backed by their church, do not admit this to be a circumstance where an exception can be made. There may be exceptions to the absolute of "Thou shalt not kill," but they do not reduce the force of the absolute in this instance. In this argument, then, it is possible to take an absolute position since a fairly clear ethical absolute is relevant. Another instance where it is possible to take an absolute stand, as most college professors do, is in questions of changing college grades. A student gets the grade he earned even though that grade may not represent his superior ability or may prevent a senior from graduating. But most questions are more complex than a simple choice between whether to take the absolute position or make an exception in a particular instance.

There are really four positions possible in certain arguments. These are possible when there are absolute positions both for and against the proposition as well as relative or practical positions on both sides. Arguments of policy are really questions of whether to leave things as they are (maintain the *status quo*) or change them, and sometimes absolutes can be discerned for both positions. One might favor lowering the legal age for drinking on the basis that any restrictions of individual freedom (drinking being an activity that affects the individual alone) are wrong; and one might oppose the change, arguing to keep the present law, on the basis that drinking is wrong and any restrictions on it, therefore, are right. But other positions are also possible and they are not absolute positions. We might argue that nineteen-year-olds drink anyway; and, while admitting that they should not, we might advocate lowering the legal age for the practical, amoral reason that the law should harmonize with practice that cannot be altered without enormous social cost and stress. Notice that this position does not treat the ethical absolute as a crucial issue but as an admitted or secondary one. On the other side, one might argue that lowering the legal age for drinking will increase the amount of drinking and that the change in the law is therefore wrong. This issue might be countered with the position that it is not the amount of drinking but the amount of *bad* drinking that matters and that lowering the legal age would greatly reduce not just illegal drinking but drinking in cars and secret places. Legalizing drinking would reduce the challenge alcohol presents not just to the worst elements of American teen-age society but to all. The last two positions represent relative or practical positions, one for and one against, the proposition that the legal drinking age should be lowered.

The point of the above example is to illustrate that arguments must be given some focus. Decisions must be made about what issue or issues you will treat as crucial and what answer you will give to the positions of all possible opponents. It is possible to focus on either of the absolute positions on drinking and the law, to admit both and focus elsewhere, or to deny either or both of them. It is also possible to focus on a practical issue and use an absolute as a supporting or secondary issue, to argue that the reductions of *bad* drinking is the crucial point and add that individual morality cannot be legislated anyway. It cannot, as the amount of illegal drinking proves; and it should not since it is an infringement of personal rights.

Language, to be sure, is persuasive by its very nature and never purely objective and denotative. The piling up of words on one side of an issue, however, never produces assent and acceptance in the minds of an audience that is either indifferent or hostile at the start. Writers (and speakers), if they are to persuade their readers (and listeners) to their position and are to win minds unequivocally, must keep the issue clear, examine the alternative solutions and so construct counter-arguments that only the one solution they propose seems both plausible and true for their audience. Readers and listeners must not only be led to accept a point of view, or a course of action, as the best in light of all the relevant circumstances but also brought to a reasoned rejection of alternate solutions that have any shred of plausibility or truth. For quite opposite reasons, a judicious and impartial examination of all sides of a question, along with the evidence in support of each, does not produce conviction and is also unsatisfactory for an audience.

Between unreasoned partiality and reasoning impartiality are several middle grounds. A common form of some of the best modern argumentative writing is to leave much of the total argument implied so that the focus can fall upon a persuasive development of an admittedly crucial issue. Many essays in the remainder of this book illustrate various forms of this strategy.

46   KENNETH MOTT

Grouping the Gifted: Pro

1   I regard gifted children as those who possess some quality or innate ability which has been recognized and identified by any number of testing and observation devices and who manifest interest and success in either physical, intellectual, or artistic pursuits.

2   These might be children who are gifted athletes but who have real trouble mastering academic subject matter, or students who are poor athletes but are highly intellectual "quiz kids" who knock the top off all measuring devices. "Gifted" may describe pupils of average intelligence who have exceptional ability in art or music, or it may refer to the child with an IQ of 135 who excels in everything.

3   How can we deal with these gifted? I firmly believe that we should group them as nearly as possible according to interest and ability (giftedness) and challenge them with a type of program that will help them to grow to the fullest extent of their abilities and capacities.

4   This grouping could take the form of special subject arrangements in the elementary grades, a situation in which a class is heterogeneously grouped most of the day but is divided at times into special interest or

From "Grouping the Gifted Is the Best Way," *NEA Journal,* 54 (March, 1965), pp. 10–11. Reprinted by permission of the *NEA Journal* and Kenneth Mott.

ability class groups for special instruction. In high school, it may take the form of grouping students in regular classes according to any number of criteria but basically those of interest and proficiency (or lack of proficiency) in various subject areas.

5   One of the basic arguments against grouping the gifted is the fear of creating a caste of intellectual snobs. Similarly, some educators fear that the average and slow students would come to regard themselves as inferior.

6   If my definition of the gifted is accepted, then these fears are groundless. After all, the schools have grouped gifted athletes for years. Yet how many athletes regard themselves as part of an elite? Do varsity athletes look down upon other pupils as inferior? The vast majority apparently do not.

7   Consider also the amount of "gifted grouping" in speech, music, art, and journalism. Schools have readily grouped the gifted in these areas without any apparent ill effect. To the extent of my observation, encouraging gifted debaters, musicians, artists, and writers to develop their special talents does not create envy or feelings of inferiority among less talented students.

8   If educators sincerely desire to promote individual growth and self-respect, they have no grounds, as far as I can see, to fear any kind of grouping. The teacher, not the manner in which a class is organized, determines students' attitudes toward individual differences. Before he can hope to instill the proper attitude, however, the teacher needs to make a critical analysis of his own attitudes toward such differences.

9   If a group of gifted or nongifted students form the wrong concept about themselves, the fault probably lies with the teachers, parents, or administrators. I have confidence that if teachers accept and respect individual worth, that if they challenge and spark interests in young people, the individual student will mature and grow successfully along the lines of his interests and abilities. I say, let those with similar "gifts" associate, plan, and enjoy being together.

10   Many educators disagree with the idea of gifted grouping because they believe that it does not affect achievement significantly. They cite pilot studies which indicate that no significant change in achievement results when children are separated into slow and accelerated classes.

11   The fact is, however, that in a vast majority of pilot studies the children have been grouped only according to IQ scores, which are far from reliable, and the conclusions have been based on achievement scores which measure only mastery of factual detail.

12   Unfortunately, there are no reliable devices for measuring growth in such areas as creativity, attitudes, personal adjustment, latent interest and talent, and innate capacity.

13   My opinion, which is based on more than a decade in the classroom, is that learning skyrockets when individuals are grouped according to interest and ability and are motivated, challenged, and inspired by a type of schoolwork that will yield some measure of success to them.

14   Heterogeneous classrooms frequently produce frustration in children who are persistently unable to do the same work that most of the other children do. Frustration is also produced when bright children are not properly challenged by their school work, as is too often the case in heterogeneous classrooms.

15   I have little fear of gifted students' being pushed beyond their endurance, for I have faith in the ability of most teachers to recognize the limits to which any student should be pushed. On the other hand, I don't believe giftedness should be wasted away simply because a bright or talented student is content to proceed at what is—for him—a snail's pace or to stand at the top of a class of students with less ability.

16   Several schools with which I am familiar have experimented with grouping the gifted in a reading program. (Their regular procedure had been to have three or four reading groups in one classroom under one teacher. The teacher's time was divided among several small groups.)

17   The experiment involved putting slow readers from different classrooms in one classroom, average readers from different classrooms in another class, and fast readers in still another class. Each classroom still had one teacher, but he no longer had to divide his time among several different groups. The control group consisted of a class organized and taught under the regular procedure mentioned above.

18   After two years, the researchers found greater overall progress at all reading levels in the experimental group. In fact, some slow readers joined the average ones and some average ones moved up to the fast group. In this case, special ability grouping paid dividends all around.

19   I believe the same results could have been achieved in science, social studies, mathematics, or English. By decreasing the range of interest and/or ability levels, the teacher is able to do more toward helping individual growth.

20   While I do not believe that children should be regarded as resources to be molded to the needs of society, I do believe that as individuals they are endowed with certain characteristics and attributes—"gifts" of nature —which represent their potential success in life. Where children have certain "gifts" in common, they should be allowed to work and study together.

47 BRUNO BETTELHEIM
Grouping the Gifted: Con

1   An argument often advanced on behalf of special classes for gifted children is that in regular classrooms these children are held back and possibly thwarted in their intellectual growth by learning situations that are designed for the average child. There can be little doubt that special classes for the gifted can help them to graduate earlier and take their place in life sooner. On the other hand, to take these students out of the regular classroom may create serious problems for them and for society.

2   For example, in regular classrooms, we are told, the gifted child becomes bored and loses interest in learning. This complaint, incidentally, is heard more often from adults, parents, or educators than from students. Nevertheless, on the strength of these complaints, some parents and educators conclude that special classes should be set up for the gifted.

3   Although some children at the top of their class do complain of being bored in school, the issue of why they are bored goes far beyond the work they have in school. If the findings of psychoanalytic investigation of feelings have any validity, feelings of boredom arise as a defense against deep feelings of anxiety. To be bored, therefore, is to be anxious.

4   The student who is bored by his studies is the student who can take few constructive measures of his own to manage his anxieties. Consequently, he represses or denies them; he must ask others, specifically his teachers, to keep him frantically busy, studying and competing intellectually so that he will not feel anxiety.

5   The gifted child who is bored is an anxious child. To feed his neurotic defense mechanisms may serve some needs of society, but to nourish his neurosis certainly does not help him as a human being.

6   Psychology, like nature, does not permit a vacuum. If study material does not hold the student's attention because of his easy mastery of it, the result is not necessarily boredom. Other intellectual interests can fill the unscheduled time. Is it reasonable to assume that gifted children learn only when pressed by the curriculum?

7   Several years ago I observed what happened to a number of gifted children who were taken out of a highly accelerated, highly competitive, private school and placed in a public high school of good academic standing where, by comparison, the work was so easy as to be "boring."

From "Grouping the Gifted," *NEA Journal,* 54 (March, 1965), pp. 8–10. Reprinted by permission of the *NEA Journal* and Bruno Bettelheim.

8   Close inspection revealed an interesting and worthwhile development in most of the transplanted youngsters. In the special school for the gifted, these children had shown little ability to use their own critical judgment. Instead, they had relied heavily on their teachers' direction. In the slower-paced school, no longer having to worry about keeping up, these students began to reflect spontaneously on many problems, some of which were not in the school program.

9   The students acquired on their own a much deeper appreciation of life, art, literature, and other human beings. No longer exhausted by meeting assigned learning tasks, these youngsters had energy to branch out, broaden their interests, and understand far more deeply.

10   Prolonged, rarely assailed security may be the best preparation for tackling difficult intellectual problems. Because the gifted child learns easily, he acquires a feeling of security in a regular class. On the other hand, if such a child is put into a special class where learning is not easy for him, where he is only average among a group of extremely gifted youngsters, he may, as often happens, come to feel that he has only average abilities which are not up to coping with difficult challenges.

11   Another argument advanced for special classes for the gifted is that removing highly capable students from the regular classroom lessens anxiety among the slower learners. Possibly so. But how do anxieties become manageable except through a friendly working relationship with someone felt to be superior—in this case, the faster learners in the classroom?

12   In many of our big cities today, the students left behind in the non-collegiate programs are marked as a lower breed. Indeed, most of them come from poor, lower-class homes. Surrounded by students who have little interest in acquiring an education, lacking companionship with students who want to learn, and receiving no encouragement at home, these children apply themselves even less than they would if there were good students in class with whom to identify.

13   In order to achieve educationally, many children from economically impoverished homes need to be challenged and motivated by example. Grouping deprives these children of such stimulation. They are left behind as second-class students, a situation which is more likely to create hopelessness than to lessen anxiety. Should some of them display outstanding leadership or ability, they are sent away to join their intellectual peers, leaving the nongifted group even more impoverished.

14   Grouping children intelligently has much in common with mountain climbing. In mountain climbing, the guides usually distribute themselves ahead of and behind beginners or less skilled climbers. Placed in the center of the group with people who have learned both the skill and the teamwork required in mountain climbing, the beginner is likely to learn quickly and well.

15   If, however, all of the good climbers are put into one party, and all of the poor ones in another, the second group is likely to fail miserably or perish altogether.

16   When the debate over what is the "best" education for the child reaches an impasse, the argument is frequently switched to what is best for society. Today we are told that we need more scientists and more engineers to "survive." Therefore, we must speed the growth of young people who have the necessary talent.

17   Does anyone really know what the needs of society will be thirty years hence? Can science guarantee survival? Might society not have a greater need for fresh, imaginative ideas on how to organize a worldwide society? Might we not have a greater need for men of broad social vision than for scientists? And since ideas mature slowly, maybe what we need is not a speeding up but a slowing down of our all-too-fast pace.

18   I am not suggesting that we dismiss our concern for the gifted, that we leave well enough alone. On the contrary, our schools can and must be improved. I am simply saying that arguments for the special education of gifted children do not yet rest on scientifically solid ground. What we need now is not quick remedies but carefully balanced and controlled experiments, based on hard thinking and planning.

Questions

1. Both Mott's and Bettelheim's arguments rest upon crucial issues. What are they and how many are there in each case? What does each assume to be the crucial issue of his opposition?
2. Both Mott and Bettelheim use a variety of methods of refutation. What are they? How many different methods does Bettelheim use in paragraph 16 and 17 above?
3. Whose analogy is better Bettelheim's to mountain climbing or Mott's to comparing grouping to the grouping of football players and artists?
4. Find the admitted issues in each essay and explain how they strengthen the case.
5. What assumptions are implied in each position?

Theme topics

1. Since neither Mott nor Bettelheim answers the essential case of the other, write a paper in which you refute one of the positions and argue for your own.
2. Write a paper in which you explain, then criticize or recommend, the program for the gifted in your high school.

48   HUGH KENNER

Don't Send Johnny to College

1   Johnny goes by the official title of "student." Yet Johnny's is the face every professor would prefer to see anywhere but in his classroom, where it blocks with its dreary smile, or its stoical yawn, the educational process on which we are proud to spend annually billions of dollars. By his sheer inert numbers he is making the common pursuit of professors and students—real students—impossible.

2   No one, least of all his professor, wills Johnny an injustice. Even the dean of students, whose lot he renders abysmal, finds it impossible not to like him, though some miraculous multiplication of loafers and fish sends Johnnies in an endless column trooping past the dean's receptionist, to stammer out their tale of dragging grades and just not digging the stuff.

3   Johnnies by the thousand, by the hundred thousand, clutter up every college in the land, where they long ago acquired a numerical majority. If you have a teenager in your home, thinking of college, the chances are you have Johnny. On behalf of my 400,000 colleagues in the academic profession, I'd be grateful if you'd keep him home.

4   Though Johnny is by definition multitudinous and anonymous, bits of Johnnyism stick in every teacher's mind. I remember the set neon smile that greeted me class after class for three whole weeks from a front-row seat just next to the door. The smile's owner and operator—let's call her Jonnie—never said a word, never took a note, never turned a page in her copy of *Gulliver's Travels*. Then, the day after I assigned a paper, the smile was gone, and so was she, apparently for good.

5   A month later, having heard that I would welcome some explanation, Jonnie turned up in my office, smiling. No, she couldn't do papers at all, not at all. Then what, pray, had brought her to a university, where, as everyone knows, one does papers? Well, she had enrolled on the advice of her psychiatrist. He had said the College Experience would be good therapy. Unwilling to monkey with therapy, I referred her, smile and all, to the dean. I've forgotten what he decided. There are so many Johnnies and Jonnies.

6   And there is no end to what their mentors and counselors, not to say psychiatrists, expect a university to do. Teach Johnny to behave like a gentleman. Prevent his simultaneous presence with Jonnie in parked cars

From *Saturday Evening Post*, 237 (November 14, 1964), 12, 16. Copyright © 1964 by Hugh Kenner. Reprinted by permission of The Sterling Lord Agency.

after 10 P.M. Help him (her) get to know girls (boys). Improve his work habits. Open his mind (he has nothing but prejudices). Shut his mouth (he does nothing but talk). Tighten his morals. Loosen his imagination. Spread beneath his slack chin the incredible banquet of Western Civilization. And discharge him fit to earn a better living, make a better marriage and digest (Lord help him) *The New York Times.*

7   The parents and mentors who expect all this expect it not of the college but of the College Experience, which is turning, accordingly, into the experience of living in a whole cityful of Johnnies. (I've just been told by a Sunday supplement that within 35 years many colleges with enrollments of 100,000 to 200,000 will have become cities in their own right.)

8   Johnny (Jonnie) expects none of the wonders of the College Experience, except *in re* girls (boys). Johnny is amiably devoid of expectations. One might say that he goes where he's shoved. One might affirm with more tact that he lends himself amiably to the College Experience, having no better plans. That is what marks him as Johnny, not as a student. A student has a vocation for study. But there's really nothing that Johnny comes to campus burning to learn about.

9   "Real education," wrote Ezra Pound 30 years ago, "must ultimately be limited to men who INSIST on knowing; the rest is mere sheepherding."

10   The mind that insists on knowing is (alas) not to be identified by tests, which explains why, despite the well-publicized vigilance of admissions officers, the number of campus Johnnies keeps rising. A mind that insists on knowing has begun to focus its energies by the time it has been in the world 16 years. By 17 or 18—the age of a college freshman—it has learned the taste of knowledge and the sensation of reaching for more. It may spell erratically, if it is served (like Yeats) by a deficient visual memory. It may calculate imperfectly, if it is (like Einstein) more at home with concepts than with operations. There may be strange gaps in its information, since a young mind cannot be everywhere at once.

11   But what it does not know it will encounter with pleasure. And it *must* learn, as a cat must eat. It may not yet know where its need for knowledge is meant to be satisfied. It may tack about, sails taut, without regard for curricular symmetry, changing majors perhaps more than once. But its tireless curiosity is unmistakable. In time, if all goes well, it will accept training, and the lifelong responsibilities of keeping itself trained.

12   But Johnny has no such appetite, no such momentum. When Johnny applies his brand-new ball-point to his first blue book, each sentence comes out smudged with his unmistakable pawprint. "Newspaper comics are good because they put a rosy glow on the grayish realities of the mind": There you have Johnny ingenuously expressing the state of *his* mind—a gray place which Pogo can occasionally animate, and a place of Good Things and Bad Things where Pogo is a Good Thing.

13   "The three main groups of people are the well-educated, semi-educated and semiuneducated." There is all mankind characterized (a feat that taxed Aristotle), complete with a category for Johnny himself; he never forgets himself.

14   I am not inventing these examples. A colleague of mine gleaned a dozen like them in a single afternoon, from freshman themes at a university that accepts only the top one-eighth of the high-school crop. What they illustrate isn't primarily the "inability to express oneself," i.e., technical difficulties with the English language. What they illustrate is something deeper, probably irremediable; a happy willingness to emulate the motions of thought, since a teacher is standing there expecting such motions, along with a nearly total want of experience of what the process of thinking feels like.

15   "And this is why we should have no prejudice against Negroes and other lower races." That mind, we may say with some confidence, doesn't insist upon knowing. It doesn't know even its own most blatant contradictions. "To analyze this theory, it can be broken down into two parts: men and women." That's what men and women are, for the nonce—they are the parts of Johnny's theory. "The result is a ridiculous fiasco under which the roof falls in." It is indeed, and one does not know whether to marvel more at the oppressive weight of that fiasco, crashing through the roof like a half-ton bear, or at the innocent ease with which Johnny, supposing ideas to be weightless, pats them to and fro like bubbles.

16   But examples don't define a problem which by its very nature arises out of sheer multitudinousness. The amiable dumbbell has for decades been a part of campus folklore, like the absentminded professor. It is when you multiply him by a million that he grows ominous, swamping the campus as with creeping molasses. His uncle of 40 years ago, Joe College, had no more interest in learning than Johnny has, but none of Johnny's baleful power. With a certain talent for grotesque stylization, he conducted his entertaining ballet of raccoon coats, hip flasks, and whiffenpoofery, while the business of the academy, a considerably more modest business than today, went on.

17   What has created the Johnny problem isn't some freakish metamorphosis of Joe College into numberless protozoa, but rather the nearly universal conviction that everybody ought to spend four years at college if it can possibly be managed.

18   Johnny's parents, needless to say, believe this. His state legislator, despite the fantastic costs, tries to believe it, since his constituents seem to. The prospective employer believes it: let Johnny check "none" where the personnel blank inquires after "college record," and Johnny will be lucky to be issued a pick and shovel, let alone a sample kit. Even the college, caught in competitions for funds (which tend to hinge on enrollments), has come to believe it believes it.

19   Meanwhile B.A.'s grow so common that employers who once demanded them now demand M.A.'s, and the Master's requirement in some
fields (not just the academic) has been upgraded to the Ph.D. In the
years since Robert M. Hutchins sardonically proposed that we achieve our
desires with less trouble by granting every American citizen a B.A. at birth,
we have moved closer and closer to a utopia in which everyone receives it
at 21, in return for doing classroom time. One already hears talk of
attendance being compulsory through age 20. In California, where problems tend to surface before New England need worry about them, the state
population rose 50 percent in one decade, and the college population 82
percent. It grows easy to forsee the day when 50 percent of the population
of California (and, after a suitable time lag, of Massachusetts, of New
York, of Illinois and, yes of Montana) will be employed at teaching the
other 50 percent, perhaps changing ends at the half.

20   Clearly something has got to bust, and no one doubts what: the idea
of a university. As an institution for (in Thomas Jefferson's words) "the
instruction of those who will come after us," it's already being trampled
out of recognizable existence by hordes of Johnnies.

21   The real student, struggling against suffocation of the soul, draws
back, or beefs about how "the class" is holding things up, or starts feeling
superior (and energy expended in nourishing a feeling of superiority is
wholly lost). At worst, from being eager he turns merely "sensitive," and
allows his zeal to be leached away. He is deprived, and can rightfully
resent being deprived, of the kind of company he deserves to expect
at a place where, often at considerable sacrifice, he has elected to invest
four years of his life.

22   The professors suffer too. For one thing, they are coming off the
production line too rapidly (though the harried trustees, looking wildly
around at teaching machines and television hookups say "Not rapidly
enough!"). Since there's no way of growing scholars at a pace keyed to
the amoebalike increase of Johnnies, substitutes have begun to be manufactured. As real students are swamped by Johnnies, real professors must
coexist with a swarm of Johnny-professors.

23   And like the real students, the real professors grow obsessed with
futility, and unless they succeed, as some do, in isolating themselves with
advanced students, fall victim to the real occupational hazard of the profession: an inability to believe that anybody can be taught anything. I
once heard of a man who was so startled by the discovery of a real student
that, lest she slip over his horizon, he divorced his wife and married her. I
don't believe that story, but it's indicative; the professor who told it to me
found it believable.

24   There's no doubt that as a nation we settle for only the side effects
and the fringe benefits of what we invest in universities: the products of
physics labs and research stations, and the economic advantages, to which

our economy has been attuned ever since the G. I. Bill, of keeping several million young people off the labor market as long as possible. We are getting even this, though, at the price of a colossal wastage of time and spirit—the time and spirit of the real students on whose behalf the system is allegedly being run. If by the year 2000, as President Clark Kerr of California expects, educational institutions will be the largest single force in the economy, and if attendance to the age of 20 is compulsory, as Dr. Dwayne Orton of I.B.M. expects, why then the economy will in the life-time of most of us have begun devoting its principal energies to the maintenance of huge concentration camps for keeping Johnnies by the multimillion agreeably idle.

25   So do we kick out Johnny? Alas, things will never be that simple again. Our social and economic system has come to depend on Johnny, B.A., in ways that can probably never be unstitched. Moreover, the College Experience probably *is* the most important event in the lives of most of the people who undergo it, even of the hundreds of thousands who learn very little. It is their time of access to the intellectual traffic patterns that define the quality of American life. A Kansan and a Georgian who have both been to college—merely been there—will have more to say to one another than a Vermonter who has and a Vermonter who hasn't. The College Experience is our folk ritual for inducting our adolescents into the 20th century. As part of our established religion, it must be treated as immune from curtailment.

26   Very well, then: the College Experience for Johnny, in his Johnny-classrooms. But let us, in the name of sanity, allow the real students to have *their* version of the College Experience. That means either separate-but-equal facilities, or (better, I think), some college equivalent of the two-track high schools that already exist.

27   One way of arranging a two-track college with minimum disruption is to permit only the real students to pursue majors. The University of Toronto has been doing that for more than half a century. Two decades ago I was one of a group of 40 freshman English majors there. In the soph-omore year there were 20 of us, in the junior year 10; there the ruthless cutting stopped. But the missing 30 were not slung out of school. All but a few hopeless cases were "permitted," as the official formula had it, "to transfer to the pass course," which meant that, if they wanted to stay on at college, they abandoned the major and enrolled in "pass arts."

28   Pass arts was a three-year humanities mixture, leading to the degree of B.A. And it wasn't a ghetto for dropouts; many students enrolled in it to start with. Its degree satisfied employers, parents and the Ontario College of Education. It satisfied Johnny just fine. It gave the university all the advantages of bigness, as the quality of the library testified. It wasn't conducive to snobbery or segregation; every honor student took a couple of pass courses a year, in subjects peripheral to his major.

29   It was, in short, a two-track system, with the tracks parallel, and with means for switching laggards onto the slow track.

30   Everyone, we agree, should have access to all the education he can absorb. Everyone who can absorb education deserves, I would add, a chance to absorb it, free from the distracting tramp of the million-footed Johnny. As colleges now operate, the idea that everybody should be sent to them is nonsense. The only hope is to start operating them differently, detached from the dogma that Johnny is by birthright a student. He needs, in fact, explicit treatment as a nonstudent. There's no inherent reason why the nation's universities shouldn't make special curricular arrangements for several million nonstudents, and more than there's an inherent reason why one of the nation's universities shouldn't be the world's largest purveyor of white mice. (One of them is.)

49   ROBERT M. HUTCHINS
The University and the Multiversity

1   In the next 75 years, or shall we say 25, education may at last come into its own and the ideal university may at last arise. These things could happen because the field will be open for them to happen. The ramshackle structures that now clutter the academic landscape will collapse. It will be seen that they are nothing but Potemkin villages or Hollywood movie sets. It will be evident that whatever their purpose has been they could not accomplish it and that in any event it is time for other purposes.

2   Before the last war education and research were matters of little general interest or public importance. Education was a kind of puberty rite, and research the esoteric indulgence of a few harmless eccentrics. When during the war the scientists showed they could blow up the world, and when it became clear that science and technology were the foundations of industrial expansion, then, to the martial music of the cold war, education and scholarship suddenly became the road to prosperity and power. Governments became embarrassingly affectionate; foundations emptied their cornucopias; politicians dedicated themselves to educational statesmanship; corporations, discovering, as someone has said, that there might be as much money in education as in poverty, threw themselves into

From *The New Republic*, 156 (April 1, 1967), pp. 15–17. This was a convocation address given at The University of Chicago on March 17, 1967. Reprinted by permission of Robert M. Hutchins.

the priest-like task of setting the American people on the path to prosperity and power.

3   But the demands upon the educational system and the expectations of it are built on false premises, sustained by flatulent representations, directed to ignoble ends, which, fortunately, no educational system can achieve. In far less than 75 years it will become clear that the system cannot deliver the goods expected of it. As a certain disillusionment about power sets in, it extends to those institutions which are the servants of power. As we are putting our higher and higher technical proficiency to baser and baser uses, some distrust of technical proficiency as the end of education is bound to appear. As nothing is more certain than that the Americans of the future must be citizens of the world and that the great universities of the future must be world universities, chauvinism in the schools and the enslavement of the universities to the military, to the CIA, to "mission-oriented" governmental agencies, or to any nationalistic programs whatever must begin to seem distasteful even to ordinary readers of ordinary newspapers. The concentration of education on meeting the immediate needs of society, as the most powerful pressure groups interpret them by the methods that appeal to those pressure groups, namely, training, information and service, is obviously the direct opposite of what the times require and will shortly be seen to be so.

4   As the machines take over, as the world becomes computerized and automatic, as the hours, days, and years of labor decline, as free time increases, as a guaranteed annual income supplies every family's basic requirements, what are we going to do with ourselves? On this question an educational system dedicated to training, information and service can shed no light and give no help.

Flattering the spirit of the age

5   The multiversity, which will do for the society anything the society will pay for, exists to flatter the spirit of the age. One trouble with flattering the spirit of the age is that all of a sudden it may turn and bite you. Something of the sort appears to be happening in California. The popular desire, which was formerly, for reasons never made clear, to have a famous multiversity, is now the desire, for reasons equally obscure, to have a cheap one, with clean-shaven students, and relatively few of them. What are you to say to people whose immediate needs you are striving to meet, and even to anticipate, when they tell you they've changed their minds and do not need you any more?

6   If it is said that we shall always want to be prosperous and powerful and that the educational system can always help us to these ends, the

answer is that no causal connection has been established between education and prosperity or power. Nobody knows whether America is prosperous and powerful because of its educational system or in spite of it. Nor do we know whether prosperity and power are legitimate ends for a human society, and under present conditions we have no way of finding out. When all the social institutions that might sit in judgment on the spirit of the age, the church, the press and the university are outshouting one another in the flattering chorus, what chance have we of learning what the spirit ought to be?

7   The reason we are headed for the everlasting bonfire is that we have no critical apparatus that can be continuously brought to bear upon the aims and conduct of our society. To confuse education with training and the transmission of information, and to conceive of the university as the instrument by which we become prosperous and powerful is to guarantee, insofar as an educational system can affect the outcome, the collapse of a civilization.

8   As long as there are jobs, people will have to be trained for them. In view of the rate of technical change, they may have to be trained and re-trained many times during their lives, and almost necessarily on the job. And those training them will have to recognize the ambiguity inherent in any training program: even in such a program you want something more than mere technical proficiency, and the question is how to get it and technical proficiency at the same time. A French scholar, Jean-Claude Passeron, has pointed out that in classical China generals chosen by means of literary competitions lost no more battles than those who were products of military schools. He might have added that the most successful Chinese general of modern times was trained as a librarian. A training program may fail in its own terms by turning out generals well prepared for the last war, but unprepared for the next, and still less for a world in which any major war is unthinkable. In any event, the argument I am making is not that there should be no places in which technical proficiency is the aim, but that the university cannot be one of them.

9   In the same way, people are going to have to try to meet the needs of the society as the society sees them. They are going to have to get things done, solve practical problems, conduct short-run investigations, collect data, dig up facts, count them, and distribute them. All this has to be done. What I am saying is that the university is not a good place to do it. Everybody should learn to read and write, but it does not follow that the university should teach remedial reading and remedial writing.

10   When you try to meet miscellaneous, immediate, low-level needs in a university, you get the multiversity, because these things require little intellectual effort and give your constituency the illusion that you are grappling with "real" problems. The ease and popularity of these activities mean they will overwhelm the essential purpose of the university, which is

the search for understanding, an undertaking neither easy nor popular. The multiversity is not merely a non-university, a pseudo-university; it is an anti-university.

11   The heart of the multiversity is the department. In the nature of the case, the multiversity department, however brilliant its short run results in training and research, cannot understand anything. It exists, like every other subhuman organism, for the survival, reproduction, and expansion of itself. It has no knowledge of the rest of the multiversity, and cannot acquire any. Other departments are its natural enemies, because they are after the students, grants, contracts and appropriations the department wants for itself. A multiversity is, therefore, in a constant state of virtual civil war. It is held together by compromise and log-rolling, that is by Band-aids and Scotch tape. When it is under severe pressure, as in California, the most skillful mediator in the world cannot keep it from falling apart. Nothing can make the multiversity what the university has to be, an intellectual community.

The circle of knowledge

12   A university has to be an intellectual community because nothing can be understood in isolation. The university's aim is to draw the circle of knowledge. Its great role is to tame the excesses of the experts by forcing them to consider their disciplines in the light of the others. The lawyer, historian, scientist or whatever, who aims at technical proficiency, is necessarily isolated from everybody outside his own field because nobody outside his own field can—or should—have any possible interest in what he is doing. Interdisciplinary studies in a multiversity are a sham: the aim is not to draw the circle of knowledge, but to increase the supply of helpful hints available to the technician by bringing in some from other disciplines.

13   Since the multiversity is a conglomerate merger, the form of the business corporation is appropriate to it, with directors, executives, employees, a product, a balance sheet, and "growth." But an intellectual community must be small, and, if it is small enough, its senior members can know all about it. They can take their turns in administration, and the class of professional administrators, to which I have belonged all my life, can be abolished. Boards of trustees and regents can become boards of visitors, criticizing, interpreting, assisting, but not controlling the work of the community, the direction of which must be in the hands of its members.

14   The essential elements of liberal education are the liberal arts, which are language and mathematics. They are the indispensable basis of understanding. Everybody can learn them, and everybody should. The elimination of triviality from the elementary and secondary schools and concentration on giving everybody a liberal education should make it

possible to bring everybody to that pitch of liberal education which would enable him to function as a citizen and a man. It should also fit him for that type of independent study to which the university should be confined. This could be accomplished through a six-year elementary school, a three-year high school, and a three-year college, graduation from which could take place at approximately the age of 18. Those college graduates interested in and qualified for independent study, and only those, should be admitted to the university.

15   The multiversity can do something for graduate and professional students. It can, at least, teach them the tricks of their trade. It can do very little for juniors and seniors, and nothing for freshmen and sophomores. It does no good to exhort multiversity professors to take an interest in undergraduates and at the same time make it clear that appointments and promotions and increases in salary depend on the prosecution and publication of research in which undergraduates take no part. In many multiversity departments an interest in undergraduates is a positively harmful eccentricity, which may be fatal to the prospects of one afflicted with it. For the same reasons liberal education has no chance in the multiversity.

16   The university must assume that the period of instruction, of schooling, is past, that the student is prepared for independent study, that he has the ability and willingness to think, and think for himself. Since I propose liberal education for all, I propose the college for all. I propose the university only for those who have the interest and capacity to join in its work. The aims of the two institutions are different, and it will cause nothing but confusion to make one part of the other.

17   We have more information and less understanding than at any time in history. What power can accomplish, the United States can do. What prosperity can give, the United States can enjoy. Power and prosperity are good things to have if you know what to do with them. At the moment, the United States is the most powerful, the most prosperous, and the most dangerous country in the world.

18   Meanwhile, the civil rights movement is dying, and there are more children in segregated schools than when *Brown* v *Board of Education* was decided. The war on poverty has been lost in the jungles of Southeast Asia. As the rich countries are getting richer, the poor are sinking deeper into destitution, and this, the most explosive situation in the world, will revenge itself upon us in far less than 75 years. We at length appear to be emerging from our fatuous preoccupation with the cold war, but only to fight one of the most miserable and degrading hot wars of modern times.

19   Yet surely the mission of the United States is to help make the world a decent habitation for mankind. For this we need that understanding which leads to wisdom. If education can come into its own, if the ideal university, the incandescent center of independent thought, can arise, we

may have the intellectual means for the effective discharge of our responsibility. The material means are at our disposal.

Questions

1. What is the function of the opening paragraph?
2. In paragraphs 6 and 7 Hutchins refutes what he sees as the crucial issue of his opposition. What is that issue?
3. Discuss the validity of the reasoning in paragraph 9.
4. Upon what absolute position is Hutchins' argument based?
5. To what extent does the article by Hugh Kenner assume the same criticism of the American college and university that Hutchins makes? In what way is Kenner's proposal more tolerant of existing faults?
6. The revolutionary proposal of paragraph 14 appeared in a variant form in an earlier essay ("Colleges are Obsolete," *Saturday Evening Post,* September, 1965). There Hutchins suggested that, since the last two years of high school are college preparatory and since the last two of college are pre-professional, the four years from the eleventh grade through the second year of college be used for four years of liberal education, professional training to follow. Thus students would be required to attend ten grades of schooling and enter a college open to all but not compulsory for four more years. Which is the better proposal?
7. In *The Learning Society* (New York: Frederick Praeger, 1968) Hutchins recommends that all students be educated at public expense and progress according to their ability as far as possible. What effect would a college education at public expense have on his proposal here and on the colleges as they now exist? Is the tracking proposal of Hugh Kenner consistent with Hutchins' proposals?
8. Hutchins has argued in other places that the faults of American values are reflected in American schools. How is that position assumed in this essay? What faults of the schools result from American values?

Theme topics

1. Develop a proposal of your own explaining how high schools and colleges can encourage better students and more students to enter and remain enrolled? Distinguish between what they presently do toward this end, but do poorly, and what they do not now do but ought to do.
2. Write a theme that enumerates the difficulties of putting Hutchins' proposal into practice and suggests methods for dealing with those difficulties.
3. Develop an alternative to or a modification of Hutchins' proposal.
4. Defend Hutchins' proposal against the obvious objection that the educa-

tional system must serve the ends of United States power and prosperity by arguing that those ends will be served anyway but more wisely.

5. Develop a theme from Hutchins' statement in paragraph 14 concerning the liberal arts: "Everyone can learn them and everyone should."

50 CHRISTOPHER JENCKS
An Anti-Academic Proposal

1   According to the conventional wisdom, higher education works best when there is least "outside intervention." "Academic freedom" is thought to be synonymous with virtue, and "the self-regulating community of scholars" is seen as a pedagogic ideal. But is nonintervention by laymen as healthy as everyone claims? One way to answer the question is to compare the research record of American universities with their teaching record, for in research there has been a great deal of outside intervention and very little collective faculty responsibility, while in teaching the faculty has pretty much set its own rules and priorities.

2   Before 1939 the only principle governing research in the better universities was academic freedom. Each faculty member could theoretically investigate whatever he wanted, at whatever pace and in whatever way he wanted, publishing whatever results he judged valuable. In practice, however, most universities gave their professors comparatively little time or money for such work. After World War II the government and the big foundations became increasingly convinced that the universities should be doing more research in a variety of fields, especially the natural sciences and the "hard" social sciences. To achieve this expansion and redirection of effort they offered large grants and contracts to professors who would undertake certain kinds of research. Little effort was made to channel this money through university administrations or to give faculties a collective voice in deciding what kinds of research would be undertaken on "their" campuses. Instead, the principle of individual professorial autonomy was preserved. Each man was left fairly free to make his own bargains and run his own shop.

3   A very different tradition has dominated teaching. Whereas a university research program is supposed to be the cumulative result of hundreds of professors' individual choices, the curriculum is supposed to reflect a

From *Educational Record* 47 (Summer, 1966), pp. 320–326, slightly revised from its original publication: "A New Breed of B.A.'s," *New Republic* 153 (October 23, 1965), pp. 17–22. Reprinted by permission of *The New Republic,* © 1963, Harrison-Blaine of New Jersey, Inc., and by the American Council of Education.

certain measure of central direction and collective control. In principle— and usually in practice—the basic pattern of undergraduate education is set by the faculty as a whole, and every professor is expected to fit into this pattern. The faculty can collectively do away with grades, substitute papers for examinations, substitute tutorials or small seminars for lectures, or reorganize the course system so that students study subjects sequentially rather than simultaneously. But an individual professor who wants to make such changes in his teaching can do so only with the greatest difficulty, after months or years of politicking and endless committee meetings. Even within this framework, a professor has limited freedom in deciding what he will teach. If he is young, he may simply be assigned a course which his department thinks ought to be covered. Whatever his rank, he is likely to encounter difficulties if he wants to offer a course which transcends the usual boundaries of his discipline. There is, in short, no pedagogic counterpart to the research freedom of the professor. There is no presumption that if a man has been made a professor he should be free to teach whatever he wants, to whomever he wants, in whatever way he wants, subject only to the necessity of finding interested students.

4   Teaching has also been subject to less lay intervention and guidance than research. Outside agencies have been far less concerned with getting particular courses taught than with having particular pieces of research done, and they put up far less money for such purposes. Even when the money is available, it is not always taken. Faculty committees which would never think of telling a professor he couldn't take a Federal research contract (even from CIA) will turn down his proposal for a new course or new instructional program.

5   If the conventional wisdom about nonintervention is correct, the American university should have compiled a distinguished record on the teaching side and a rather mediocre record in research. In point of fact, this has not happened. The combination of external financing and individual initiative has encouraged a certain amount of charlatanism and quite a lot of nonsense on the research side, but there has also been an extraordinary amount of brilliant work, a readiness to move into new fields, try new ideas, and respond to real problems. In teaching, on the other hand, collective responsibility and the comparative absence of external financial pressures, far from ensuring a generally high quality of classroom performance, have led to stagnation.

6   The basic pattern of undergraduate instruction has not changed at most universities since the turn of the century. At that time the departmental divisions of knowledge were established, a system of credit hours, lectures, and examinations was worked out, and a pattern of "distribution" and "concentration" requirements was created. All of these endure to this day. The "system" was briefly leavened with general education, but this fashion is now being supplanted by independent study. Some institu-

tions have seasoned the soggy mass with tutorial and seminar programs. These innovations have, however, done little to alter the basic style of undergraduate instruction.

7   The causes of this do not lie, as some claim, in the power or rigidity of administrators. Most administrators are extremely sympathetic to curricular innovation. Control over the curriculum, however, is in the hands of the faculty.

8   Again contrary to popular opinion, the desuetude of the curriculum is not attributable to universal faculty indifference. It is not true, for example, that most faculty members spend most of their time on research or consulting. As a matter of observable fact, most faculty members at most colleges spend most of their time in class, getting ready for class, seeing students, and so forth. Even at the most research-oriented universities, and among the most publication-minded faculty members, teaching usually consumes a considerable amount of time—at least during those semesters when the professor is on campus. The trouble is that these faculty members rarely show anything like as much imagination and daring in their teaching as in their research.

9   This derives, I think, less from the growth of bureaucracy, the seductive charm of military-industrial contracts, or the lure of Washington consulting than from the extraordinary difficulty of getting permission from one's colleagues to try anything new and exciting. On virtually every major university campus in America there are professors who want to develop an interdisciplinary science program for nonscientists, start a small residential college where undergraduates will have a common curriculum and a chance to get to know a small group of faculty, or whatever. These ideas rarely get off the ground. Often they are vetoed by the rest of the faculty, or by one or another faculty committee. Even if an idea is accepted in principle, departments are not willing to release "their" members from conventional teaching duties to try something different. So the only way to break the lockstep is to get outside money to "pay off" the departments and allow them to hire temporary substitutes for those who are doing the unorthodox. Such money is extremely hard to get, especially when the majority of the faculty is unenthusiastic.

10   The inadequacies of the curriculum are, I think, a direct reflection of this paralysis of faculty government. At most universities the faculty is too big to do anything efficiently and too conservative to let individual faculty members decide things for themselves. The Byzantine irrelevance of faculty politics cannot help but be mirrored in the curriculum. Men cling to lectures, examinations, credit hours, prerequisites, and the like not because they are good for the students but because they provide an excellent framework for adjudicating the competing interests of individual professors and departments. What passes for curriculum "reform" often serves a political rather than a pedagogic purpose.

11   Like Congress, university faculties cannot be reformed from within. But their power can be supplanted, as has happened in the research realm. For research purposes the university has been turned into a federation of independent entrepreneurs regulated by panels of academicians who meet regularly in Washington to give out money. My judgment is that the same thing ought to be done in teaching. In other words, professors ought to be given the same freedom to plan and execute a program of instruction that they now have in research.

12   When I have proposed this to professors, I have always been told that it would lead to chaos. Nobody would want to teach freshman English. Everybody would wind up offering courses is esoteric specialties. Some people might stop grading their courses, or might offer only tutorial instruction, or might stop teaching altogether. Crackpots would give courses on civil disobedience and LSD. "Standards" would be lowered. "The meaning of the B.A." would be diluted.

13   These prophecies do not alarm me. If nobody now on the faculty wants to teach illiterate freshmen, new kinds of faculty members should be hired who do. If the existing professors want to teach graduate students rather than undergraduates, that should be their privilege—so long as there are enough interested graduate students to justify keeping them on the payroll. If some students cannot, under this system, find anybody who will teach what they want to learn, they should be helped to transfer. If the graduate schools find it difficult to handle student transcripts which merely record the results of highly diverse encounters between the applicant and various professors, so much the worse for the graduate schools. Undergraduate education has more important functions than the sorting and screening of potential Ph.D.'s.

14   What undergraduate education needs today is not a return to the good old days of "community" and "shared objectives," but an advance toward pluralism and creative anarchy. Such a revolution is not going to come spontaneously from within the universities. No major change ever has. The history of academic innovation is one of dissident minorities within the university winning outside financial support for their ideas and then using the money to enhance their position. In today's curriculum impasse the dissident minority already exists; the missing ingredient is external support. The closest thing to it now is a National Science Foundation grant for curriculum revision. These grants have, however, been restricted to projects which have not just local but national relevance. NSF has been trying to promote curriculum reform at the college level in the same economical way as it did at the elementary and secondary level: by supporting a small group of super-teachers who develop new materials and methods, and then encouraging a much larger group of classroom teachers to adopt them. This is almost certainly not workable at the college level, where everyone wants to "do it himself." Nevertheless, an applicant

for NSF funds who wants to do something only for his own students is not likely to get help under the present rules.

15 If the rules were changed, and appropriations increased, so that college professors in all disciplines could get NSF support for new departures in undergraduate education, both faculty politics and the curriculum might be transformed. To begin with, a local innovator who failed to get support from his department or his faculty could look to Washington for support. If he got help there, this would strengthen his hand back home. (An externally funded proposal always has a better chance of approval than an internally funded one.) In addition, such a program would enhance the status of the able professor who wants to give his best efforts to teaching. He would get full-time secretaries, full summer salary, and other perquisites now reserved to researchers with outside support. More important, his ability to get Federal money would make him an asset to his institution and would make other institutions eager to hire him. As a result, he would no longer have to worry so much about tenure or regular salary increases. If his university wouldn't let him do the kind of teaching he wanted to do, he would be in a strong bargaining position when looking elsewhere. That, in turn, would make his departmental colleagues more conciliatory.

16 A program of this kind should extend not only to small-scale curriculum revision of the traditional sort, but to large-scale experiments which involve setting up new kinds of departments and new kinds of colleges, either within existing universities or independently. The program should not only launch new ventures but should keep them going as long as they continue to do something exciting. It could begin on a fairly small scale —say \$50 million in the first year. But the long-term aim should be to provide a major new source of funds for higher education, having at least as much impact on the *status quo* as research grants have. This implies that Federal grants to teachers should ultimately constitute at least 20 or 30 percent of the nation's overall expenditure for college instruction. This would have meant giving away at least \$500 million last year, and more that \$1 billion in 1970.

17 In principle, such a program should be run by the U.S. Office of Education. On the basis of performance to date, however, and of the general quality of personnel in USOE, it might be better to leave it to the National Science Foundation for the present.

18 Would all of this have any significant effect on the unrest which now troubles many campuses? I doubt it. The kind of reform which most faculty now envisage, and which Washington officials seem ready to sponsor, consists at bottom of improving communication between professors and their potential apprentices. Tactically, this means eliminating lectures, textbooks, memorization, departmental myopia, and other impediments to curiosity, while promoting seminars, tutorials, independent study, inter-

disciplinary courses, and the like. More fundamentally, it means making the undergraduate more of an apprentice-colleague, less of a ward inmate. All that is fine; there are hundreds of thousands of students who would seize such opportunities eagerly. But they are not, by and large, the same students who are now leading protest movements.

19   Because every young American now knows that he has to have a B.A. to become a full citizen, the campuses are crowded with students who have no desire to apprentice themselves to an academic discipline. Traditionally, such students have been herded through a mixture of professional and service courses, injected with a dose of mild liberal arts vaccine, and sent on their way. Now, however, many able but anti-academic students are no longer willing to get C's and keep quiet. If the idiocies were eliminated from the curriculum and the most exciting side of scholarship made immediately accessible, some of these dissidents might become interested in getting A's and becoming scholars. But not many. Difficult as it is for many professors to believe, there are students who are not stupid, hedonistic, or philistine but who nevertheless find the delights of academic analysis, categorization, and discovery rather pale. Such students come to college with hopes that are unrealistic yet legitimate. They want to know something at once novel and old-fashioned: how to lead a good life. They find, however, that the so-called best colleges are not interested in this question. Despite rhetoric about training leaders, the better colleges are organized on the assumption that the good life is in fact the academic life. They offer a few experiences outside the classroom, no future except graduate school, and no adult models except scholars.

20   The quest for other kinds of experience leads these students in many directions: to living among the poor in a slum, to manning a picket line, to civil disobedience and jail, to drug-taking, and (perhaps most commonly) to bed. Conceivably it could also lead them to the classroom, but not so long as the curriculum remains in the hands of scholars dedicated to "objectivity" and "value-free research." Yet these are ideals which curriculum "reform" as currently envisaged is unlikely to challenge. It is the essence of the academic profession to focus attention on questions which are researchable—and by existing academic methods. For some students this is satisfying, but not for the student whose primary concerns are political and moral. All he sees are literature courses which treat novels in terms of form and style rather than substance; philosophy courses which talk about word games and mathematical puzzles rather than ethics, suffering, and death; political science courses in which social justice is never mentioned; economics courses in which computer analysis has precedence over hunger, poverty, and human irrationality; sociology courses which explain why the world is the way it is but say little or nothing about how it might be changed for the better.

21   Perhaps these students' interests and needs cannot be satisfied by any sort of formal education. But I am not convinced of this. Two innovations

seem to me to deserve a try. First, undergraduates should have more contact with nonscholars—with poets, ministers, journalists, civil rights workers, or anyone else from whom they think they can learn. Second, they should have more opportunities to learn outside the classroom, and especially to learn from participation rather than reading. These two changes go together. On the one hand, students will not learn much from nonscholars if contact is confined to lectures or even seminars; on the other hand, scholars are not likely to create an educational program which emphasizes real-life experience rather than abstractions from and about it.

22   America needs a new kind of college, in which the teachers are not drawn primarily from the academic profession, and the pedagogy does not rely primarily on classrooms. There have already been some tentative efforts in this direction. Franconia College in New Hampshire is trying to integrate two years' service with the Peace Corps into its undergraduate program. Both Miles College in Alabama and Tougaloo College in Mississippi have experimented with letting students work in the civil rights movement and making this experience a central part of their formal studies. Cornell has involved some of its students in a project in Fayette County, Tennessee, though it has not done much to link what students learn in Tennessee to their studies in Ithaca. Antioch College has encouraged students to spend semesters in similar activities. But so far as I know no college or university has recognized that off-campus activities of this or other kinds can be the most important source of learning for many undergraduates, and ought, therefore, to be at the center of the undergraduate program. Back on the campus, academic life goes on unchanged, and students seeking a degree are expected to go through all the traditional (and to them boring) rituals. Similarly, while many professors took part in the Vietnam teach-ins, and in this way established an unprecedented relationship with some of their students, Antioch College is the only institution I know where the faculty has tried to understand the peculiar potency of this invention and make similar experiences part of the regular academic program.

23   The disease which afflicts the American university today is in some respects analogous to the one which gripped colleges in the middle of the nineteenth century. The academy was then dominated by a sterile classicism, which disdained any contact with the workaday world. Reformers had sought to introduce science and the professions, but to no avail. The first (though probably not the most important) change occurred when Congress passed the Morrill Act, offering the states money with which to teach farming and engineering. Some of the classical colleges took the money and diversified. Others spurned it and let the states give the money to new colleges, both public and private. The public was served in either case.

24   The system of education which dominates today's universities, while far less narrow than a century ago, is still largely irrelevant to the interest and needs of many undergraduates. The possibilities of internal reform

are meager. Change, if it is to come at all, will depend on outsiders brandishing checkbooks and working with student and faculty minorities on campus.

25   The time has come for Congress to pass a twentieth-century counterpart to the Morrill Act, providing Federal funds to support a new kind of higher education, which would get students out of the classroom. These funds should be available both to established colleges and universities and to new ones. (Many of the applicants would probably be two-year colleges trying to become four-year ones on the cheap, but that is no argument against the idea.) The aim should not be to supplant the existing system of higher education but to supplement it by creating several dozen reputable and prosperous colleges which emphasize experience beyond the campus rather than experience within it. The nature of these experiences and of the instructors who organize and help students interpret them should be left open. Such a college might hire traditional sociologists and anthropologists to run a program centered on field work among one or another variety of nonstudent instead of having students merely read reports and statistics collected by others. Psychologists and psychiatrists might offer work focused on clinical experience with the mentally ill, instead of making this an incidental footnote to a collection of reading lists. A theater director might build study for a degree around the writing and producing of a play. A group of experienced community organizers could set up a course of study which required students to rally local support for or against the police, and to try to understand this activity from a variety of perspectives. Former missionaries, AID officials, anthropologists, and schoolteachers might recruit students to teach Congolese children to read, making such "Peace Corps" work the basis for a liberal education rather than a postscript to it as at present. The only common denominator should be that in each case the student do something off campus which engages his interest and forces him to take a responsible, adult role with which he is not familiar. The intellectual effort should be to make sense of this experience.

26   Such a college would not suit the great majority of teachers or students. It might, however, appeal to a number of individuals who are unhappy with the present system. By creating a context in which nonacademicians could play a useful role in educating undergraduates, it might do something to assuage the teacher shortage. More important, it would create a new route into middle-class adult life, a route which does not involve the pursuit of grades, credits, and academic skills. Such an alternative would not only speak to the malaise which now grips many campuses, but might in the long run lead to the emergence of a new breed of B.A.'s more willing to learn from experience and more engaged in the world around them.

The American Scene

51 ALEXIS DE TOCQUEVILLE
Social Condition of the Anglo-Americans

1   Social condition is commonly the result of circumstances, sometimes of laws, oftener still of these two causes united; but when once established, it may justly be considered as itself the source of almost all the laws, the usages, and the ideas which regulate the conduct of nations: whatever it does not produce, it modifies.

2   If we would become acquainted with the legislation and the manners of a nation, therefore, we must begin by the study of its social condition.

*The striking characteristics of the social
condition of the Anglo-Americans is its
essential democracy*

3   Many important observations suggest themselves upon the social condition of the Anglo-Americans; but there is one which takes precedence of all the rest. The social condition of the Americans is eminently democratic; this was its character at the foundation of the colonies, and it is still more strongly marked at the present day.

4   I have stated in the preceding chapter that great equality existed among the emigrants who settled on the shores of New England. Even the germs of aristocracy were never planted in that part of the Union. The only influence which obtained there was that of intellect; the people were used to reverence certain names as the emblems of knowledge and virtue. Some of their fellow-citizens acquired a power over the others which might

From *Democracy in America* by Alexis de Tocqueville, translated by Henry Reeve, edited and revised by Francis Bowen (New York, The Century Company, 1898).

truly have been called aristocratic, if it had been capable of transmission from father to son.

5   This was the state of things to the east of the Hudson: to the southwest of that river, and as far as the Floridas, the case was different. In most of the States situated to the southwest of the Hudson some great English proprietors had settled, who had imported with them aristocratic principles and the English law of inheritance. I have explained the reasons why it was impossible ever to establish a powerful aristocracy in America; these reasons existed with less force to the southwest of the Hudson. In the South, one man, aided by slaves, could cultivate a great extent of country; it was therefore common to see rich landed proprietors. But their influence was not altogether aristocratic, as that term is understood in Europe, since they possessed no privileges; and the cultivation of their estates being carried on by slaves, they had no tenants depending on them, and consequently no patronage. Still, the great proprietors south of the Hudson constituted a superior class, having ideas and tastes of its own, and forming the centre of political action. This kind of aristocracy sympathized with the body of the people, whose passions and interests it easily embraced; but it was too weak and too short-lived to excite either love or hatred. This was the class which headed the insurrection in the South, and furnished the best leaders of the American Revolution.

6   At this period, society was shaken to its centre. The people, in whose name the struggle had taken place, conceived the desire of exercising the authority which it had acquired; its democratic tendencies were awakened; and having thrown off the yoke of the mother country, it aspired to independence of every kind. The influence of individuals gradually ceased to be felt, and custom and law united to produce the same result.

7   But the law of inheritance was the last step to equality. I am surprised that ancient and modern jurists have not attributed to this law a greater influence on human affairs.[1] It is true that these laws belong to civil affairs; but they ought, nevertheless, to be placed at the head of all political institutions; for they exercise an incredible influence upon the social state of a people, whilst political laws only show what this state already is. They have, moreover, a sure and uniform manner of operating upon society, affecting, as it were, generations yet unborn. Through their means, man acquires a kind of preternatural power over the future lot of his fellow-creatures. When the legislator has once regulated the law of inheritance, he may rest from his labor. The machine once put in motion

---

[1] I understand by the law of inheritance all those laws whose principal object it is to regulate the distribution of property after the death of its owner. The law of entail is of this number: it certainly prevents the owner from disposing of his possessions before his death; but this is solely with the view of preserving them entire for the heir. The principal object, therefore, of the law of entail, is to regulate the descent of property after the death of its owner: its other provisions are merely means to this end.

will go on for ages, and advance, as if self-guided. towards a point indicated beforehand. When framed in a particular manner, this law unites, draws together, and vests property and power in a few hands; it causes an aristocracy, so to speak, to spring out of the ground. If formed on opposite principles, its action is still more rapid; it divides, distributes, and disperses both property and power. Alarmed by the rapidity of its progress, those who despair of arresting its motion endeavor, at least, to obstruct it by difficulties and impediments. They vainly seek to counteract its effect by contrary efforts; but it shatters and reduces to powder every obstacle, until we can no longer see anything but a moving and impalpable cloud of dust, which signals the coming of the Democracy. When the law of inheritance permits, still more when it decrees, the equal division of a father's property amongst all his children, its effects are of two kinds: it is important to distinguish them from each other, although they tend to the same end.

8   In virtue of the law of partible inheritance, the death of every proprietor brings about a kind of revolution in the property; not only do his possessions change hands, but their very nature is altered, since they are parcelled into shares, which become smaller and smaller at each division. This is the direct, and as it were the physical, effect of the law. It follows, then, that, in countries where equality of inheritance is established by law, property, and especially landed property, must constantly tend to division into smaller and smaller parts. The effects, however, of such legislation would only be perceptible after a lapse of time, if the law were abandoned to its own working; for, supposing the family to consist of only two children, (and, in a country peopled as France is, the average number is not above three,) these children, sharing amongst them the fortune of both parents, would not be poorer than their father or mother.

9   But the law of equal division exercises its influence not merely upon the property itself, but it affects the minds of the heirs, and brings their passions into play. These indirect consequences tend powerfully to the destruction of large fortunes, and especially of large domains.

10   Among nations whose law of descent is founded upon the right of primogeniture, landed estates often pass from generation to generation without undergoing division,—the consequence of which is, that family feeling is to a certain degree incorporated with the estate. The family represents the estate, the estate the family,—whose name, together with its origin, its glory, its power, and its virtues, is thus perpetuated in an imperishable memorial of the past and a sure pledge of the future.

11   When the equal partition of property is established by law, the intimate connection is destroyed between family feeling and the preservation of the paternal estate; the property ceases to represent the family; for, as it must inevitably be divided after one or two generations, it has evidently a constant tendency to diminish, and must in the end be completely

dispersed. The sons of the great landed proprietor, if they are few in number, or if fortune befriends them, may indeed entertain the hope of being as wealthy as their father, but not of possessing the same property that he did; their riches must be composed of other elements than his. Now, as soon as you divest the land-owner of that interest in the preservation of his estate which he derives from association, from tradition, and from family pride, you may be certain that, sooner or later, he will dispose of it; for there is a strong pecuniary interest in favor of selling, as floating capital produces higher interest than real property, and is more readily available to gratify the passions of the moment.

12   Great landed estates which have once been divided never come together again; for the small proprietor draws from his land a better revenue, in proportion, than the large owner does from his; and of course, he sells it at a higher rate.[2] The calculations of gain, therefore, which decide the rich man to sell his domain, will still more powerfully influence him against buying small estates to unite them into a large one.

13   What is called family pride is often founded upon an illusion of self-love. A man wishes to perpetuate and immortalize himself, as it were, in his great-grandchildren. Where family pride ceases to act, individual selfishness comes into play. When the idea of family becomes vague, indeterminate, and uncertain, a man thinks of his present convenience; he provides for the establishment of his next succeeding generation, and no more. Either a man gives up the idea of perpetuating his family, or at any rate, he seeks to accomplish it by other means than by a landed estate.

14   Thus, not only does the law of partible inheritance render it difficult for families to preserve their ancestral domains entire, but it deprives them of the inclination to attempt it, and compels them in some measure to co-operate with the law in their own extinction. The law of equal distribution proceeds by two methods: by acting upon things, it acts upon persons; by influencing persons, it affects things. By both these means, the law succeeds in striking at the root of landed property, and dispersing rapidly both families and fortunes.[3]

[2] I do not mean to say that the small proprietor cultivates his land better, but he cultivates it with more ardor and care: so that he makes up by his labor for his want of skill.

[3] Land being the most stable kind of property, we find, from to time, rich individuals who are disposed to make great sacrifices in order to obtain it, and who willingly forfeit a considerable part of their income to make sure of the rest. But these are accidental cases. The preference for landed property is no longer found habitually in any class but among the poor. The small land-owner, who has less information, less imagination, and fewer passions than the great one, is generally occupied with the desire of increasing his estate: and it often happens that by inheritance, by marriage, or by the chances of trade, he is gradually furnished with the means. Thus, to balance the tendency which leads men to divide their estates, there exists another, which incites them to add to them. This tendency, which is sufficient to prevent estates from being divided *ad infinitum,* is not strong enough to create great territorial possessions, certainly not to keep them up in the same family.

15   Most certainly it is not for us, Frenchmen of the nineteenth century, who daily witness the political and social changes which the law of
partition is bringing to pass, to question its influence. It is perpetually
conspicuous in our country, overthrowing the walls of our dwellings, and
removing the landmarks of our fields. But although it has produced great
effects in France, much still remains for it to do. Our recollections, opinions, and habits present powerful obstacles to its progress.

16   In the United States, it has nearly completed its work of destruction,
and there we can best study its results. The English laws concerning the
transmission of property were abolished in almost all the States at the time
of the Revolution. The law of entail was so modified as not materially to
interrupt the free circulation of property. The first generation having passed
away, estates began to be parcelled out; and the change became more and
more rapid with the progress of time. And now, after a lapse of a little
more than sixty years, the aspect of society is totally altered; the families
of the great landed proprietors are almost all commingled with the general
mass. In the State of New York, which formerly contained many of these,
there are but two who still keep their heads above the stream; and they
must shortly disappear. The sons of these opulent citizens have become
merchants, lawyers, or physicians. Most of them have lapsed into obscur-
ity. The last trace of hereditary ranks and distinctions is destroyed,—the
law of partition has reduced all to one level.

17   I do not mean that there is any lack of wealthy individuals in the
United States; I know of no country, indeed, where the love of money
has taken stronger hold on the affections of men, and where a profounder
contempt is expressed for the theory of the permanent equality of property. But wealth circulates with inconceivable rapidity, and experience
shows that it is rare to find two succeeding generations in the full enjoyment of it.

18   This picture, which may, perhaps, be thought to be overcharged, still
gives a very imperfect idea of what is taking place in the new States of the
West and Southwest. At the end of the last century, a few bold adventurers
began to penetrate into the valley of the Mississippi; and the mass of the
population very soon began to move in that direction: communities un-
heard of till then suddenly appeared in the desert. States whose names were
not in existence a few years before, claimed their place in the American
Union; and in the Western settlements we may behold democracy arrived
at its utmost limits. In these States, founded off-hand, and as it were by
chance, the inhabitants are but of yesterday. Scarcely known to one another, the nearest neighbors are ignorant of each other's history. In this
part of the American continent, therefore, the population has escaped the
influence not only of great names and great wealth, but even of the natural
aristocracy of knowledge and virtue. None are there able to wield that
respectable power which men willingly grant to the remembrance of a life

spent in doing good before their eyes. The new States of the West are already inhabited; but society has no existence among them.

19   It is not only the fortunes of men which are equal in America; even their acquirements partake in some degree of the same uniformity. I do not believe that there is a country in the world where, in proportion to the population, there are so few ignorant, and at the same time so few learned, individuals. Primary instruction is within the reach of everybody; superior instruction is scarcely to be obtained by any.[4] This is not surprising; it is, in fact, the necessary consequence of what we have advanced above. Almost all the Americans are in easy circumstances, and can, therefore, obtain the first elements of human knowledge.

20   In America, there are but few wealthy persons; nearly all Americans have to take a profession. Now, every profession requires an apprenticeship. The Americans can devote to general education only the early years of life. At fifteen, they enter upon their calling, and thus their education generally ends at the age when ours begins.[5] Whatever is done afterwards is with a view to some special and lucrative object; a science is taken up as a matter of business, and the only branch of it which is attended to is such as admits of an immediate practical application.

21   In America, most of the rich men were formerly poor; most of those who now enjoy leisure were absorbed in business during their youth; the consequence of which is that, when they might have had a taste for study, they had no time for it, and when the time is at their disposal, they have no longer the inclination

22   There is no class, then, in America, in which the taste for intellectual pleasures is transmitted with hereditary fortune and leisure, and by which the labors of the intellect are held in honor. Accordingly, there is an equal want of the desire and the power of application to these objects.

23   A middling standard is fixed in America for human knowledge. All approach as near to it as they can; some as they rise, others as they descend. Of course, a multitude of persons are to be found who entertain the

[4] This was an exaggerated statement even when De Tocqueville wrote, thirty years ago. But now, in the Atlantic States, through the influence of the Universities and of scientific and literary associations, there are probably, in proportion to the population, as many scholars, men of science, and highly educated men, as in any country of Europe.—AM. ED.

[5] Members of what are called the learned professions—law, physic, and divinity— do not usually begin practice in America before they are twenty-two or twenty-three years old. The average age of the graduates of American Colleges is over twenty years, and two or three years after graduation must be devoted to professional studies. Boys become apprentices in the mechanic trades, it is true, at fourteen years; but this is the usual age for the beginning of apprenticeship in England and on the continent of Europe. As a general rule, children of the poorest parents are not compelled to begin hard labor at so early an age in the United States as in Great Britain. De Tocqueville's statement is confused, because he does not sufficiently indicate which "professions" or "callings" he is speaking of.—AM. ED.

same number of ideas on religion, history, science, political economy, legislation, and government. The gifts of intellect proceed directly from God, and man cannot prevent their unequal distribution. But it is at least a consequence of what we have just said, that although the capacities of men are different, as the Creator intended they should be, Americans find the means of putting them to use are equal.

24   In America, the aristocratic element has always been feeble from its birth; and if at the present day it is not actually destroyed, it is at any rate so completely disabled, that we can scarcely assign to it any degree of influence on the course of affairs.

25   The democratic principle, on the contrary, has gained so much strength by time, by events, and by legislation, as to have become not only predominant, but all-powerful. There is no family or corporate authority, and it is rare to find even the influence of individual character enjoy any durability.

26   America, then, exhibits in her social state an extraordinary phenomenon. Men are there seen on a greater equality in point of fortune and intellect, or, in other words, more equal in their strength, than in any other country in the world, or in any age of which history has preserved the remembrance.

Political consequences of the social condition of the Anglo-Americans

27   The political consequences of such a social condition as this are easily deducible.

28   It is impossible to believe that equality will not eventually find its way into the political world, as it does everywhere else. To conceive of men remaining forever unequal upon a single point, yet equal on all others, is impossible; they must come in the end to be equal upon all.

29   Now I know of only two methods of establishing equality in the political world; every citizen must be put in possession of his rights, or rights must be granted to no one. For nations which are arrived at the same stage of social existence as the Anglo-Americans, it is, therefore, very difficult to discover a medium between the sovereignty of all and the absolute power of one man: and it would be vain to deny that the social condition which I have been describing is just as liable to one of these consequences as to the other.

30   There is, in fact, a manly and lawful passion for equality which incites men to wish all to be powerful and honored. This passion tends to elevate the humble to the rank of the great; but there exists also in the

human heart a depraved taste for equality, which impels the weak to attempt to lower the powerful to their own level, and reduces men to prefer equality in slavery to inequality with freedom. Not that those nations whose social condition is democratic naturally despise liberty; on the contrary, they have an instinctive love of it. But liberty is not the chief and constant object of their desires; equality is their idol: they make rapid and sudden efforts to obtain liberty, and, if they miss their aim, resign themselves to their disappointment; but nothing can satisfy them without equality, and they would rather perish than lose it.

31   On the other hand, in a state where the citizens are all nearly on an equality, it becomes difficult for them to preserve their independence against the aggressions of power. No one among them being strong enough to engage in the struggle alone with advantage, nothing but a general combination can protect their liberty. Now, such a union is not always possible.

32   From the same social position, then, nations may derive one or the other of two great political results; these results are extremely different from each other, but they both proceed from the same cause.

33   The Anglo-Americans are the first nation who, having been exposed to this formidable alternative, have been happy enough to escape the dominion of absolute power. They have been allowed by their circumstances, their origin, their intelligence, and especially by their morals, to establish and maintain the sovereignty of the people.

Questions

1. What reciprocity between cause and effect does Tocqueville point to in his opening paragraphs?

2. What causes, according to Tocqueville, formed the "social condition" of democracy he observed in mid-nineteenth-century America?

3. What is the full scope of operation of the "law of equal distribution of inheritance"? Does Tocqueville see it as a necessary or a sufficient cause?

4. Sustained enjoyment of wealth by a family is a necessary condition for what effect, in Tocqueville's view?

5. Have we today left behind the social aspects of the "democratic principle" described by Tocqueville? What evidence can you cite from your knowledge of present-day America to confirm or challenge Tocqueville's causal analysis?

6. What alternative social consequences does Tocqueville see between the application of the principle of liberty and that of equality? What evidence do you see today to confirm or deny his prediction of the result of this contest between liberty and equality in the United States?

Theme topics

1. Explain what you see as the contemporary relevance of Tocqueville's remarks on the absence of an aristocratic tradition in America.

2. Write an essay explaining your understanding of Tocqueville as he related cause and effect in the America he knew.

3. Discuss, both in reference to the United States of today and Bettelheim's essay "Adjustment for Survival," the validity of Tocqueville's assertion: "To conceive of men remaining forever unequal upon a single point, yet equal on all others is impossible; they must come in the end to be equal upon all."

52   D. W. BROGAN
The Character of American Culture

1   "Culture" is a highly ambiguous term. However I may limit my definition of it, "culture" remains a wide term demanding for its full definition and illustration a range of knowledge that I do not possess.

2   Culture can have two meanings. There is the meaning given to the word by the anthropologist, in which all social habits, techniques, religious practices, marriage customs, in fact everything—including the kitchen sink—is examined to throw light on how a particular society lives and moves, or just exists. Then there is "culture" in a narrower sense, in which we are concerned not with material techniques, not with the social organization that holds society together, but with the ideas, the aesthetic experiences and achievements, and the philosophical or religious ideas that affect and are affected by the aesthetic experiences and achievements of a given society. A special variant of the last sense of "culture" is the narrow identification of the word with the fine arts and the implicit relegation of the fine arts to the margin of life, to what is done in leisure or for leisure.

3   None of these usages of the word is strictly separable from the others. The first usage obviously includes all the possible variations on the meaning and even the most restricted implies the wider meaning as a background. I shall not try, therefore, to attain a rigorous standard of definition or eschew all overlapping of one definition of culture and another. I shall try to deal with the problem of the level and the tone of American culture

in its second sense, but I shall not try to define that second sense narrowly or regard myself as debarred from using illustrations from American life that a culture snob would think showed a confusion of ideas or a lowering of standards. In my view culture that is merely a set of aesthetic practices, merely exemplified in private or even in public taste, is a theme of importance—to be treated by somebody else. What I am concerned with is the problem of cultural standards and achievements in an advanced democratic society, specifically the United States. And that cultural achievement cannot be separated from religion, education, the character of the state, the general aims and ambitions of American society.

4   To fall back on one of my devices already used, what is the cultural "mark" of American society? It is the absence of a strong, received aristocratic tradition, on the one side, and, on the other, the presence of a number of what can loosely, in a social if not a purely political sense, be called "democratic" biases and practices. The fine arts, literature, music, the content of the higher education have from the beginning been affected by the general egalitarian, progressive, optimistic, factual, future-discounting tone of American life. As I shall have occasion to note later, this bias of American life has often produced a powerful reaction and some of the classics of American literature are in the nature of minority protests against just those marks of American society that I have stressed. Nevertheless, American culture, in its widest sense, has these marks and American culture in its narrower sense has them too, even if to many the marks appear as scars.

5   What in the beginning marked off the nascent American culture from that of Europe? One thing I would suggest was poverty, poverty in a society already more egalitarian than that of Europe. People came to America to get rich (among other reasons); they did not arrive rich. Establishing their culture beachheads on the eastern coast, they had not the resources of time or of energy for the reproduction on the American shore of the elaborate cultural life that some of them had shared and all of them had heard of in Europe. There was no demand for a Vandyke, an Inigo Jones, a Milton in seventeenth-century America; no means of producing or sustaining such artists.

6   The contrast with Spanish America is striking in at least one field, that of architecture. The Spanish colonists had two resources that the English colonists lacked: a docile and utilizable Indian population and "treasure," gold and silver. There was from the first in Spanish America a surplus for the fine arts. There was more. There was a government and a church that both aimed at splendor and had the political resources to use the surplus to produce it. It was not only that in English America there were no easily exploitable human and material resources to permit the creation of a materially splendid society. There were no institutions to insist that such splendor should be provided. The royal government, the

churches could not, even if they had wished, force the colonists to produce art works on the scale of the Cathedral of Mexico.

7   Dwelling houses, churches and public buildings were necessarily simple, utilitarian. They could be and sometimes were aesthetically satisfactory as well, but the aim was not splendor. It was utility. Simplicity often is a form of beauty and elegance, but I think that some harm is done to the modern American sense of the beautiful by too much insistence on the triumphs of a simplicity that was imposed by need rather than by choice. From the beginning beauty was associated in American experience with functional fitness. It is an admirable association and, if one has to choose, it is better to have functional fitness than irrelevant ornament, but a certain Puritanical indifference or hostility to mere beauty, mere ornament is or was part of the American inheritance.

8   "Puritanical." I am aware that the word is ambiguous and I have no intention of using it as a term of abuse. But it did matter that the predominant religious tradition of early English America was one that left little place for the "luxe pour Dieu" that produced the great cathedrals and abbeys of Europe. I am aware that English (and American) Puritans had a high and competent sense of the place of music in divine worship. Nevertheless, the new environment was not that provided by Rome for Palestrina or by Leipzig for Bach. Milton was a musically minded Puritan poet, but he would not have found much to gratify his tastes had he emigrated to New England or to Virginia.

9   And if the material and ideological obstacles to the transfer of the more lavish, extravagant and nonutilitarian forms of the arts to America did not work so effectually in the case of literature, the transfer had some special difficulties all the same. One was material; there was, again, no means of accumulating an economic surplus to support the career of letters. It was possible to export the old classical learning and equally important the old and new biblical learning and, what was more important, the Bible itself. And no people that had the Bible made available and treasured by the established order was cut off from the highest literary excellence. Yet again the colonies—with no theaters, no court, no court patronage. as yet no equivalent of the new academies like the Royal Society of London, with the new life constantly calling for new effort, with no leisure class—could not be expected to and did not produce a variegated, nonutilitarian, original culture in the arts or, indeed, in the sciences, in what was then called natural philosophy. It would be absurd to make this a matter of reproach. It was part of the price paid for the establishment of the peculiar and successful Anglo-American society out of which the United States and its present culture have come. All I should like to suggest is that there was a necessary price; it was paid.

10   I am now coming to a more controversial part of my subject, the character of this necessarily democratic culture. That the American cul-

ture, on its aesthetic and intellectual side, is democratic I shall try to show
later. What I want to do at the moment is to stress its early nonaristocratic
character. The European culture from which it stemmed had its democratic elements: its folk ballads dealing with the woes and happiness of
the "lower orders," the "short and simple annals of the poor." It had in its
material works of art plenty of scenes from vulgar life, on the porches of
great cathedrals, or the illuminations of the *Hours* of the Duc de Berry.
But the more splendid forms of artistic achievement in the Middle Ages,
as in the Renaissance, were aristocratic. The great popular legends were
of kings and queens, of princes and princesses, of knights, of crusades and
battles, feuds in castles, not of their less interesting equivalents in cottages.
No doubt there are signs of a protest against this concentration on the
great. The Robin Hood legend is an example. But most people accepted
the distinction. Poor French peasants passed on, with faith and admiration,
the legend of the Four Sons of Aymon and even now it is legends of the
higher feudalism that Sicilian peasants paint on their carts. They would
have agreed with Calpurnia:

> When beggars die, there are no comets seen;
> The heavens themselves blaze forth the death of princes.

11   Now, the settlers brought out from Europe, more specifically from
the British Isles, this aristocratic culture. (The Bible, after all, is full of
kings and nobles; sinners most of them, but interesting sinners. The metaphorical language of the Bible is royal, not democratic.) But in the American environment the aristocratic culture, accepted and admired by the
people, began to wither. The old ballads were brought over but were
transformed, given an American, frontier-bred, forest-bred character. The
legends of kings and princes became legends of men of the people winning the endless war against the wilderness and the Indian. Robin Hood
was a hero that could be transported to the frontier; Richard Coeur de
Lion was not.

12   I attach great importance to the creation of this frontier folk epic, not
only because it tells us of the formation of the modern American culture but because it is the greatest American cultural export. It should be
remembered that it is English America that has produced the only universally accepted new epic theme. The "matter of America" is in the true
succession from the "matter of France" (Roland and the Paladins) and
the "matter of Britain" (King Arthur and the Knights of the Round
Table).

13   It is a matter not of kings and great nobles but of the self-made men
of the forest and later of the prairie; it is a democratic epic theme. As
far as there is a genuine American national tradition of legend, this is it.
I am not altogether convinced that scholars, as well as hard-pressed men

of letters, have not invented some of the prestige of the frontier heroes. I know how the Buffalo Bill legend was created; I have suspicions about Paul Bunyan and Mike Fink; but even if the legend has undergone the shaping hand of the poet or the poetaster or the scholar, that is how great legends are given their final and effective traditional form. And the legend of the West is still living in America—and still exportable to Europe. The conquest of the TV screen by the West in conclusive proof of the power of the legend that for a time represented a fact and for longer met a need of the new American social culture, a need for heroes and heroic deeds in an American and egalitarian context. I should not assert that as an art form the way in which this legend has been given to the American public is one of the greatest human achievements. I doubt if even Fenimore Cooper as a writer is in the class of his model, Scott. But the legend he launched on the world was unlike the legend Scott exported to Europe and America, a modern living legend with a future. It was a legend of heroes chosen not by birth but by themselves.

14   As far as American literary culture has been the embodiment of this heroic legend it has been one of the makers and the marks of the American national ethic. And I, for one, am not disposed to look this gift horse too closely in the mouth or to assess this national asset in a purely literary crucible. If (as I think is true) the American national hero who is most effectively cast in the epic mold and most excites the national curiosity, as well as admiration, is Lincoln, the lesson is reinforced, for here is the folk hero, coming from the folk, embodying in the highest power their possibilities of promotion and achievement. That is one way in which American culture is democratic.

15   There is another, one that is perhaps less edifying, less a pure acquisition. In a famous passage in his book on Hawthorne, Henry James stresses and laments the poverty of resources available to the American man of letters. Compared to his European brother, how little he has to use, how simple the social structure in which he is to set the characters! There is something comic in this long list of things that America has not got. It is, oddly enough, the converse of what Goethe had to say: he congratulated America on its escape from the feudal past that James coveted. And obviously James exemplified in his own work the possibilities of the new American theme contrasted with the old, traditional European themes. But there was something in the Jamesian lament, if not quite what James thought it was. For in the more sophisticated forms of literary art, the egalitarian bias of American life worked against the reception of the more subtle forms of art by the great American public—and there was no substitute for the great American public. There was no center of patronage, of support, of protection for the artist.

16   It is not necessary to swallow all the criticisms of American society fashionable with writers for over a hundred years—criticisms of the aridity

of American culture, of the dry, inhospitable air in which the artist found it difficult to breathe—to recognize that, for some types of artist at any rate, nineteenth-century America—busy building itself up, completing the conquest of the frontier, assimilating the vast immigrant floods—could not be, or at any rate was not, very hospitable to the arts.

17   It was perhaps not accidental that the "golden day" of New England marked not the first efflorescence of a culture but the sunset of the old, learned, theocratic New England way of life, the marriage of the old Puritan conscience with the optimism of the Enlightenment. Emerson, Hawthorne, and the lesser men, Holmes, Lowell and the rest, were fruits of a society declining and which owed its charm and some of its force to its nearly twilight character. There is something paradoxical in this situation and it is a paradox that many Americans refuse to face, but there it is. The New England culture, the best integrated, the most internally harmonious regional culture that America has known, knew its golden day only when its decline was imminent. "Minerva's owl flies only in the dusk," said Hegel, and this deep saying applies to Boston, Concord, Salem. And— a banality that I am almost ashamed to utter—the great figures of American literary culture have been on the whole hostile to or at any rate highly critical of American life. Emerson had his repeated bursts of optimism but the world in which he spent the second half of his life was a world that listened not at all to his deepest message. It is hardly necessary to stress the pessimism of Hawthorne or the ostentatious disillusionment of Henry Adams.

18   And it was not only the New Englanders who were disillusioned, cut off. Whitman alone kept his spirits up and it is to be doubted if his best poetry is really to be found in those paeans to the spirit of democracy, those laudations of "Pioneers, O Pioneers." For Mark Twain the human situation was incurably tragic and for Melville the human illusion inevitably led to a dead end. "Round the world! There is much in that sound to inspire proud feelings, but whereto does all that circumnavigation conduct? Only through numberless perils to the very point whence we started, whence those we left behind secure, were all the time before us." Could there be a more un-American attitude than Melville's (and there are other lessons to the same effect)?

19   Classical American literature is not notably "useful" in the narrow nationalist sense. It is useful in a deeper sense, as is any penetrating, truthful, moving insight into the human situation. But the average American— optimistic, energetic, convinced, despite Melville, that circumnavigation does conduct us somewhere and somewhere worth arriving at—was and is naturally put off by the insistence on the darker side of the American situation. He has too often despised and distrusted the artist who has reciprocated the attitude. Exiled even if he did not leave the territorial bounds of the United States, the artist, the philosopher, the pure scientist

were both cut off and cut themselves off from the main, cheerful stream of national tradition.

20   Of course, the alienation of the artist was not purely an American problem. War on the bourgeoisie, on bourgeois ideals and practices, was one of the common slogans of European life, especially in France. But Dickens and Hugo, social critics as they were, were not cut off from the life of their age as were their American opposite numbers and they were and have remained effective national heroes as no American author, not even as Mark Twain, has been.

21   The consequence has been a separation of what I am prepared to call the higher culture and the less original, more perishable, more optimistic, more American (in the patriotic sense) culture that has unfortunate results even today—or especially today.

22   Here it is necessary to say something of the picture of the American cultural past that American academics have been presenting not so much to the public as to the captive audiences of the colleges. Nothing could be more admirable from a moral as well as an intellectual point of view than the industry and the acuteness and probity with which American scholars have examined all the American past, the works of the great, the near great, and the merely "interesting." But here I take my life in my hands and, as a foreigner, I should like to suggest that in their desire to assess accurately the American cultural past they have tended to stress its utility for the American student to an excessive degree. The ordinary, intelligent, interested but not totally fascinated young man or woman who is introduced to the idea of literature as more than a mere diversion, as an illumination of life and not as a mere distraction from it, may find the great American classics depressing and the lesser lights, so laboriously resurrected or at any rate exhumed, both mediocre and boring. American literary culture is not varied enough (is especially not rich enough in first-class poetry) to provide adequate nutriment for the young.

23   In a legitimate attempt to prove the original value of the American contribution American critics and scholars, it seems to me, have tended to put blinkers round their charges, who might otherwise look out at the great world and discover there much that is profound, illuminating, and nourishing, even for Americans, but which has the handicap of having been written not by Americans nor for Americans but by human beings for human beings. It was the advantage of the old classical curriculum on which the New England masters were brought up that it enforced knowledge of nonnational, of remote types of human achievement, that it insinuated the idea of a common human experience that Homer and Vergil threw light on. Today only the Bible (as far as it is still read apart from being bought) performs that function.

24   Something of the same limitation arises in the study of other aspects of American culture. It was a misfortune that the great expansion of the

United States, in area, in wealth, in ambition, came at a time when in all countries of the new machine world taste was at its lowest, most timid, least connected with the forces of real creation. It is not only in the United States that money was squandered in atrocious imitations of the "Gothic," in inappropriate revivals of the classical, in ingenious and learned but not very relevant exercises in the Romanesque. To repeat, the United States was not the only sufferer. Is there any worse piece of church building erected regardless of cost anywhere in the United States than the Sacré-Coeur in Montmartre? Germany, France, and England are full of railway stations, government buildings, town halls that cannot be exceeded for unbeautiful ingenuity in any American city. (And I have some peculiarly unlucky America cities in mind.) Yet in the European cities, as a rule, the past has left achievements that ought to have put the modern architects and patrons to shame.

25   In many American cities there was nothing to offset the extravagantly outrageous taste of the gilded age—or later. Of course, there were pioneers like Louis Sullivan and many American cities have buildings of the late nineteenth and the early twentieth century that architects from Europe go on pilgrimage to. But visually the United States boomed at a bad time. And we have here, I think, another cause of alienation between the American and the higher culture of his country and age.

26   What of it? Is his situation any worse than that of the representative Englishman or Frenchman? Do they admire and use the products of the highest culture in their age and country? Of course not. But the American is in a special position. He is in Henry James's America, where the background to the arts has to be created and assimilated, where democratic judgment is part of the national ethos, where reverence is a quality reserved for a few sacred political slogans and institutions, where the not totally harmful snob values of an aristocratic culture are absent. The American is left to himself, not only because he does not accept leaders but because many leaders will not lead. For that reason, and possibly for others, the American cultural scene is peculiarly divided, the national unity, so remarkable at other levels, is here almost totally missing.

27   On the one hand, the American willingness to try anything once aids the arts, aids the preacher of new aesthetic or social doctrine. Just as American law tolerates, to a degree that surprises the European visitor, unorthodox systems of medicine, just as every known form of religious belief gets a welcome, so every new form of the arts, every new theory, every new form of practice finds buyers, in both a financial and a psychological sense. If from one point of view America suffers by having no accepted standards of excellence, she gains in another by not being hidebound by accepted standards of excellence. The very absence of what I may call "normative" institutions is a blessing. At any rate, it may seem so when the role of the French Academy in one field and the English Royal Academy in another is contemplated.

28   Probably at no time in history has the seller of cultural goods had it so good, in the sense that buyers will not be choked off by a mere inability to understand what it is all about. In face of the claims of the new art forms, in literature, in music, in painting, in sculpture, even in architecture, millions of Americans act like so many Texans afraid not to buy a potential oil well. What is offered may be unintelligible and unattractive, but it may conceal a gusher all the same. (I hasten to say that I am not describing buyers who are looking for a cash capital gain, but buyers in the widest sense of the term, who do not want to miss what may be the great cultural revelation of the age.)

29   This hospitality applies not only to the arts but to other aspects of culture, and notably to religion and what may be called philosophy. The American who seeks deliverance in analysis or in some new psychological school, who wants to master Zen Buddhism in ten easy lessons in a direct descendant of the seekers after knowledge whom Emerson made fun of more than a century ago—but who provided Emerson with a great part of his audiences and readers. It is not the searching after new things that is new, it is the evaporation, in the century since the decline of the Transcendentalists, of the old orthodoxy against which Emerson and his brethren reacted.

30   Here, again, the American situation is not unique. All over the Western world the seekers are as numerous as in St. Paul's Athens and the doctrines offered are much more varied. I am reduced to uttering a platitude when I stress the speed and diversity of change in our contemporary world. Our picture of it is changing so fast that it is vain to look for a central core of doctrine round which we can arrange our cultural life. If the modern world has such a core, a central and triumphant discipline, it is in physics, and who that is not quite a respectable mathematician can even begin to grasp what the physicists are doing? We can grasp in general what their allies and pupils, the engineers, are doing. Each new satellite, each new threat of more murderous rocketry, keeps them in our mind and we know that they can provide the means for destroying us. We are all in the Western world in the same cultural boat, in a world we never made where old patterns are dissolving and changing too fast for us to adjust easily or comfortably or even to decide what we should adjust to.

31   But what is different in the American situation is first of all the democratic tradition of culture which I have briefly described. The old traditional order of a "higher" culture handed down from above—representing overtly aristocratic values or, at any rate, being based on the premise that some forms of culture are superior to others and that superiority is not simply an aspect of their popularity—is probably dying in Europe. But it is not yet dead. It visibly survives in the curriculum of the schools, in the prestige still attached to traditional hierarchical values, and (this is a matter where nothing but intuition can be relied on) in a genuine humility

before the claims of the traditional culture that produces a willingness to learn that in turn results, in a good many cases, in a genuine conversion to the standards of a higher culture and a genuine appreciation of its products.

32   It is true that this acceptance of the traditional culture, this docile readiness to be initiated into it as far as natural talents and acquired knowledge make it possible, is not quite that immersion in the highest things that the preachers of culture, Matthew Arnold and T. S. Eliot, have meant. Nevertheless, the attitude preserves the older culture long enough for it to be possible to hope that a new culture, fusing the best of old and new, may arrive before general barbarism does.

33   The 800,000 copies of a translation of the *Odyssey* sold in England may not represent a genuine readiness to put oneself in the way of understanding of a remote way of life or a willingness to see and feel the human situation in another form from that to which we are habituated. But they do represent something that, faced with the products of the lower culture, with rock 'n' roll and the comics, we may be inclined to forget does exist.

34   If (as I think is the case) much of the pessimism of the "intellectuals" in America, in Britain, in Europe, arises from the collapse of the hopes based on the democratization of society, the end of the belief that the only things needed to win the masses to the higher culture were leisure, abundance, more "education," cheap books as well as the novel possibilities of radio and TV, then it is worth while to remind ourselves that not all those hopes were vain.

35   It is even more dangerous to blind ourselves to the facts of our situation (here I include both Britain and the United States in a common dilemma). We can do this in a new way as well as in the old way that asserted that we all must needs love the better when we see it. We can persuade ourselves that the new popular art forms are the natural successors of the old art forms, that they represent an inevitable adjustment to a new form of society. Thus rock 'n' roll is a necessary reflection of contemporary malaise; Li'l Abner, the equivalent of the great popular authors of the past, of Mark Twain and Dickens. If the boys and girls who pour out from high schools don't want to read, in a sense can't read, the reflection is on the absurd prestige we attach to reading or on the absurd and irrelevant reading matter issued to the aspiring young and their turning to other art forms than literature.

36   There is some plausibility in all these defenses of abdication in favor of popular adolescent taste. I think it likely that the literary arts may be giving way in prestige, perhaps in cultural utility, to other arts, to the plastic arts and, above all, to music. Music, I think, has become the refuge of the intelligent man and woman today and that not because hi-fi has enabled him to gratify his tastes but because those tastes have produced the market for hi-fi. I think that a timid reverence for "classics" may mean that school reading programs have a diseducative effect, since serious

reading becomes associated with boredom. And in any group of intelligent boys and girls there are sure to be young men and young women of whom some have no more an eye for reading than others have an ear for music, or others the ability to do simple sums.

37   But the present cultural crisis is not concerned with these cases. It is right to discriminate among comics, to point out the superiority of "Li'l Abner" over records of violence, empty of ideas, for example. It is right to insist on the technical superiority of a great jazz performer like Louis Armstrong over the current wailers and moaners. These last may enable a great many of the young to express themselves vicariously, but it is a dangerous extension of democratic prejudice to assert that all forms of self-expression are commendable or equally admirable and promising. It is wrong and a "treason of the learned" to exalt the art forms that are most popular today simply because they are popular in merely numerical terms. "Dare to be a Daniel" was the message of a popular hymn. "Dare to be a square" is a motto I should like to see adopted by more academics and other ex officio molders of the public mind.

38   The reasons why this motto is not adopted are various. One is the division, at any rate in the literary field, between the temper of the greatest American artists and the national temper. The national temper is optimistic, still deeply impressed by the belief in progress and still prone to believe that somewhere a solution can be found, if we try hard enough, for the temporarily distressing human condition. Yet this was not and is not the temper of the most critically esteemed American writers and to be a devoted admirer of Mr. Faulkner, for example, is to be in that degree unAmerican.

39   Then there is a division between the more sophisticated artists and the aspiring public that I believe to be greater than in any historical period known to me. Again, this division is not confined to the United States; it is a chasm in all the Western countries. Literature, the visual arts, music, philosophy are all practiced at a high degree of sophistication by highly trained specialists. They are also studied and appreciated by highly sophisticated devotees. But much of the production of the modern artist (using the term in its widest connotation) makes small or no appeal to the average man, not even to the intelligent average man who is conscious that his life would be fuller and better if the arts spoke more loudly to him than they do.

40   I have said that this division is new. I do not believe that in the thirteenth and fourteenth centuries all the good Catholic worshipers appreciated the scholastic philosophers or fully understood the achievement of Chartres. *The Divine Comedy* and the *Summa* were not popular works or within the reach of everybody. Nor do I believe that all Athenians knew by what divine skill the Parthenon got its proportions or appreciated all that Sophocles meant or were fit to be admitted to the Academy. I could multiply the examples.

41   But I think the modern situation is different. What a very modern musician means by music or a very modern nonrepresentational artist means by painting or many modern writers mean by literature has only a remote and often invisible connection with what the average sensual man means by these arts. I am aware that public taste has to be educated, that there were people who thought Mozart hard to follow and definitely discordant, that there were people who thought the Impressionists were simply incompetent. Maybe it is going to be like that for all the arts now in such confusion, now cut off, as so often they are, from what used to be their normal audience.

42   Even if we are all going to make the grade we haven't made it yet, and the average man is tempted, not unreasonably, to throw his hand in. He may exalt the claims of various jazz schools to be art forms as rich as classical music and its heirs or he may deny that classical music has any legitimate heirs. He may see or profess to see in fine camera work the true succession to the great painters, in the engineers the fit heirs of the architects. He may abandon pure literature altogether as a means of spiritual refreshment and turn to history, geography, travel, "know-how" books for more information. If he does so he will be in grave danger of reinforcing in himself the innate American belief that George Santayana commented on, the confidence in quantity, the preference for things that can be measured, the emphasis on more rather than on better, the identification of more *with* better. In our world emphasis on number, on measurable magnitudes, is one of the necessities of life, a necessity that presses ever more hardly on us.

43   But a life based on a belief that all that should be valued can be measured is like a life based on the belief that all that has to be learned can be taught. It is doomed to emotional sterility and to a sense of deception. Life is not like that and it is painful to find this out too late. What is missing in that life is what I have already alluded to in my remarks on education—the sense of excellence.

44   The danger to the notion of excellence does not lie only in the irrelevant emphasis on measurable quantity. It can and often does lie in the attribution to mediocrity of the power and prestige of excellence. Here, again at the risk of uttering platitudes, I have to join in the attack on the mass media. For it is possible to argue that they do less harm in their exaltation of the palpably trivial and transitory than in the excessive seriousness with which minor triumphs in the lively arts are greeted. That these lively arts can be diverting I do not deny. So can detective stories, so can much light and some low literature. I do not shudder at a *Saturday Evening Post* cover or wince when I hear of the prices paid for tickets to a fashionable musical.

45   But a lot of harm is done when a great popular success like *South Pacific* or *My Fair Lady* is puffed up until the distinction between talent

and genius is lost sight of, between the work to which one may give the adjective "immortal" with no pedantic scruple and commercial productions of high amusement value that are extremely unlikely to survive the generation that welcomed them. It is not a question of commercial motive. Shakespeare and Molière were both highly commercial men of the theater. It is a question of not giving the rank of a masterpiece to what is simply agreeable, for if you do that you cannot savor the real masterpieces—which is a great loss to the individual and in the aggregate to the national culture. *My Fair Lady* is not *The Marriage of Figaro; By Love Possessed* is not *War and Peace* or *The Ambassadors.*

46   What I am pleading for is the presentation to the young of the concept that there is such a thing as excellence, that the unexamined life, the emotionally banal life, the life animated by a religion of mere good works and with no philosophy behind it, is inferior to the fuller life of the artist, the philosopher, the saint. And since most of us cannot be any of these things, the next best thing for us is the humble, industrious, and informed admiration for these great achievements of the human spirit.

47   This is, above all, the function of the universities. To them come a high proportion of the young people who are capable of this initiation. It is against these young people that so much in the modern world—not only in the American modern world but especially in the American modern world—conspires. They need fortification; they need knowledge imparted without pedantry but also without any easy submission to the taste of the hour or the natural laziness of the human mind. The United States has probably never known a period in which its cultural prestige was greater, in literature, in painting, in music, but the achievements that win the respectful interest of the outside world are not those that the mass of the American people (including congressmen in that mass) understand or are likely to understand.

48   A society that in addition to its immense economic and technical prestige has the prestige of being hospitable to the new, the original, the fruitful in the arts, that welcomes new ideas as well as new gimmicks, has an immense advantage in the contest for men's minds. It is not the novelty of the offerings so much as the possibility of novelty that wins the doubtful faced as an alternative with dogmatism, irrelevant domination of the arts by politics, the regular search for a safe common denominator. There is no such common denominator that is compatible with excellence. The notion of excellence is in this sense undemocratic, but it is not unAmerican. It was certainly an idea dear to Jefferson and to Lincoln. It will suffice if American public opinion and its official organs remember that "every man hath business and desire such as it is."

49   American life will be richer and more seductive if it permits and encourages the really exceptional, the really original man to pursue his bent, of course allowing for the fact that there will be phonies and flops at least

as often as men of genius or even of remarkable talent. But this waste is one of the luxuries that the United States can now afford. And it must afford it if its way of life is to compete at all levels with that of its rival. It can compete on the technical level (if the United States goes all out). It can compete hands down at the level of popular diversion for, as we know, the iron curtain can hardly keep out American popular music and I suspect that the comics would please millions behind the curtain. But it is not merely as an instrument in the cold war that I urge a bold and possibly offensive insistence on excellence. It is because the great success story of the American people deserves excellence in every human activity. It would be unworthy of the people who have wrought the American miracle in so many fields to settle for less.

50   A great triumph of the American spirit would be the fostering of a literary and artistic culture that freely took in all the contributions of its ancestral cultures, confident that to be American is to be not exclusive but welcoming and that Shakespeare and the Bible play a greater part in the making of American culture than Melville, than even Mark Twain. It will be most American when it is most universal.

Questions

1. At what points in his essay does Brogan call attention to a subject only to divide it into two portions and then balance one against the other?
2. Examine again Whyte's essay on the casual style. What devices that he enumerates there does Brogan use? Would you call Brogan a "casual stylist"? Why?
3. Compare and contrast Tocqueville's discussion of the United States and its absence of a strong aristocratic tradition with Brogan's.
4. Distinguish the various senses in which Brogan uses the word "culture."
5. What conditions does Brogan see as unique in American cultural history? What conditions are shared in common with other cultures?
6. Has Brogan himself "dared to be a square" in discussing America and its culture? Has he elicited your consent to most of his hopes and prescriptions for the present and future of American cultural life? Why?
7. What does Brogan mean at the end, after having stressed the uniqueness of American culture, when he says America will be "most American when it is most universal"?

Theme topics

1. Write a definition of American culture using elements from your own observation and others from Brogan, Trilling, Tocqueville, and McGinley.

2. Write a defense of American culture which answers Brogan's charges. Make certain that you admit some issues and provide concrete evidence from your own observation for your refutation.

3. Write a defense of American culture that focuses upon Brogan's charge that America lacks the higher culture of Europe with which to counter forces of the Atomic Age.

53   KENNETH KENISTON

Youth, Change and Violence

1   We often feel that today's youth are somehow "different." There is something about today's world that seems to give the young a special restlessness, an increased impatience with the "hypocrisies" of the past, and yet an open gentleness and a searching honesty more intense than that of youth in the past. Much of what we see in today's students and nonstudents is of course familiar: to be young is in one sense always the same. But it is also new and different, as each generation confronts its unique historical position and role.

2   Yet we find it hard to define the difference. Partly the difficulty derives from the elusive nature of youth itself. Still this generation seems even more elusive than most—and that, too, may be one of the differences. Partly the problem stems from the sheer variety and number of "youth" in a society where youth is often protracted into the mid-twenties. No one characterization can be adequate to the drop-outs and stay-ins, hawks and doves, up-tights and cools, radicals and conservatives, heads and seekers that constitute American youth. But although we understand that the young are as various as the old in our complex society, the sense that they are different persists.

3   In giving today's American youth this special quality and mood, two movements have played a major role: the New Left and the hippies. Both groups are spontaneous creations of the young; both are in strong reaction to what Paul Goodman calls the Organized System; both seek alternatives to the institutions of middle-class life. Radicals and hippies are also different from each other in numerous ways, from psychodynamics to ideology. The hippie has dropped out of a society he considers irredeemable:

From *The American Scholar,* 37 (Spring, 1968), 227–245. Included in expanded form in *Young Radicals* (New York: Harcourt, Brace & World, 1968). © 1968 by Kenneth Keniston. Reprinted by permission of Harcourt, Brace & World, Inc., and the author.

his attention is riveted on interior change and the expansion of personal consciousness. The radical has not given up on this society: his efforts are aimed at changing and redeeming it. Furthermore, both "movements" together comprise but a few percent of their contemporaries. But, although neither hippies nor New Leftists are "representative" of their generation, together they are helping to give this generation its distinctive mood. By examining the style of these young men and women, we come closer to understanding what makes their generation "different."

The style of post-modern youth

4   Today's youth is the first generation to grow up with "modern" parents; it is the first "post-modern" generation. This fact alone distinguishes it from previous generations and helps create a mood born out of modernity, affluence, rapid social change and violence. Despite the many pitfalls in the way of any effort to delineate a post-modern style, the effort seems worth making. For not only in America but in other nations, new styles of dissent and unrest have begun to appear, suggesting the slow emergence of youthful style that is a reflection of and reaction to the history of the past two decades.*

5   In emphasizing "style" rather than ideology, program or characteristics, I mean to suggest that the communalities in post-modern youth groups are to be found in the *way* they approach the world, rather than in their actual behavior, ideologies or goals. Indeed, the focus on process rather than program is itself a prime characteristic of the post-modern style, reflecting a world where flux is more obvious than fixed purpose. Post-modern youth, at least in America, is very much in process, unfinished in its development, psychologically open to a historically unpredictable future. In such a world, where ideologies come and go, and where revolutionary change is the rule, a style, a *way* of doing things, is more possible to identify than any fixed goals or constancies of behavior.

Fluidity, flux, movement

6   Post-modern youth display a special personal and psychological openness, flexibility and unfinishedness. Although many of today's youth have achieved a sense of inner identity, the term "identity" suggests a fixity, stability and "closure" that many of them are not willing to accept: with these young men and women, it is not always possible to speak of the "normal resolution" of identity issues. Our earlier fear of the ominous

---

* In the effort to delineate this style, I have been helped and influenced by Robert J. Lifton's concept of Protean Man. For a summary of his views, see *Partisan Review*, Winter 1968.

psychiatric implications of "prolonged adolescence" must now be qualified by an awareness that in post-modern youth many adolescent concerns and qualities persist long past the time when (according to the standards in earlier eras) they should have ended. Increasingly, post-modern youth are tied to social and historical changes that have not occurred, and that may never occur. Thus, psychological "closure," shutting doors and burning bridges, becomes impossible. The concepts of the personal future and the "life work" are ever more hazily defined; the effort to change oneself, redefine oneself or reform oneself does not cease with the arrival of adulthood.

7   This fluidity and openness extends through all areas of life. Both hippie and New Left movements are nondogmatic, nonideological, and to a large extent hostile to doctrine and formula. In the New Left, the focus is on "tactics"; amongst hippies, on simple direct acts of love and communication. In neither group does one find clear-cut long-range plans, life patterns laid out in advance. The vision of the personal and collective future is blurred and vague: later adulthood is left deliberately open. In neither group is psychological development considered complete; in both groups, identity, like history, is fluid and indeterminate. In one sense, of course, identity development takes place; but, in another sense, identity is always undergoing transformations that parallel the transformations of the historical world.

Generational identification

8   Post-modern youth views itself primarily as a part of a generation rather than an organization; they identify with their contemporaries as a group, rather than with elders; and they do not have clearly defined leaders and heroes. Their deepest collective identification is to their own group or "Movement"—a term that in its ambiguous meanings points not only to the fluidity and openness of post-modern youth, but to its physical mobility, and the absence of traditional patterns of leadership and emulation. Among young radicals, for example, the absence of heroes or older leaders is impressive: even those five years older are sometimes viewed with mild amusement or suspicion. And although post-modern youth is often widely read in the "literature" of the New Left or that of consciousness-expansion, no one person or set of people is central to their intellectual beliefs. Although they live together in groups, these groups are without clear leaders.

9   Identification with a generational movement, rather than a cross-generational organization or a nongenerational ideology, distinguishes post-modern youth from its parents and from the "previous" generation. In addition, it also creates "generational" distinctions involving five years and less. Within the New Left, clear lines are drawn between the "old New

Left" (approximate age, thirty), the New Left (between twenty-two and twenty-eight) and the "new New Left" or "young kids" (under twenty-two). Generations, then, are separated by a very brief span; and the individual's own phase of youthful usefulness—for example, as an organizer—is limited to a relatively few years. Generations come and go quickly; whatever is to be accomplished must therefore be done soon.

10   Generational consciousness also entails a feeling of psychological disconnection from previous generations, their life situations and their ideologies. Among young radicals, there is a strong feeling that the older ideologies are exhausted or irrelevant, expressed in detached amusement at the doctrinaire disputes of the "old Left" and impatience with "old liberals." Among hippies, the irrelevance of the parental past is even greater: if there is any source of insight, it is the timeless tradition of the East, not the values of the previous generation in American society. But in both groups, the central values are those created in the present by the "Movement" itself.

Personalism

11   Both groups are highly personalistic in their styles of relationship. Among hippies, personalism usually entails privatism, a withdrawal from efforts to be involved in or to change the wider social world; among young radicals, personalism is joined with efforts to change the world. But despite this difference, both groups care most deeply about the creation of intimate, loving, open and trusting relationships between small groups of people. Writers who condemn the depersonalization of the modern world, who insist on "I-thou" relationships, or who expose the elements of anger, control and sadism in nonreciprocal relationships, find a ready audience in post-modern youth. The ultimate measure of man's life is the quality of his personal relationships; the greatest sin is to be unable to relate to others in a direct, face-to-face, one-to-one relationship.

12   The obverse of personalism is the discomfort created by any nonpersonal, "objectified," professionalized and, above all, exploitative relationship. Manipulation, power relationships, superordination, control and domination are at violent odds with the I-thou mystique. Failure to treat others as fully human, inability to enter into personal relationships with them, is viewed with dismay in others and with guilt in oneself. Even with opponents the goal is to establish intimate confrontations in which the issues can be discussed openly. When opponents refuse to "meet with" young radicals, this produces anger and frequently demonstrations. The reaction of the Harvard Students for a Democratic Society when Secretary McNamara did not meet with them to discuss American foreign policies is a case in point. Equally important, perhaps the most profound source of personal guilt among post-modern youth is the "hangups" that make intimacy and love difficult.

Nonasceticism

13   Post-modern youth is nonascetic, expressive and sexually free. The sexual openness of the hippie world has been much discussed and criticized in the mass media. One finds a similar sexual and expressive freedom among many young radicals, although it is less provocatively demonstrative. It is of continuing importance to these young men and women to overcome and move beyond inhibition and puritanism to a greater physical expressiveness, sexual freedom, capacity for intimacy, and ability to enjoy life.

14   In the era of the Pill, then, responsible sexual expression becomes increasingly possible outside of marriage, at the same time that sexuality becomes less laden with guilt, fear and prohibition. As asceticism disappears, so does promiscuity: the personalism of post-modern youth requires that sexual expression must occur in the context of "meaningful" human relationships, of intimacy and mutuality. Marriage is increasingly seen as an institution for having children, but sexual relationships are viewed as the natural concomitant of close relationships between the sexes. What is important is not sexual activity itself, but the context in which it occurs. Sex is right and natural between people who are "good to each other," but sexual exploitation—failure to treat one's partner as a person—is strongly disapproved.

Inclusiveness

15   The search for personal and organizational inclusiveness is still another characteristic of post-modern youth. These young men and women attempt to include both within their personalities and within their movements every opposite, every possibility and every person, no matter how apparently alien. Psychologically, inclusiveness involves an effort to be open to every aspect of one's feelings, impulses and fantasies, to synthesize and integrate rather than repress and dissociate, not to reject or exclude any part of one's personality or potential. Interpersonally, inclusiveness means a capacity for involvement with, identification with and collaboration with those who are superficially alien: the peasant in Vietnam, the poor in America, the nonwhite, the deprived and deformed. Indeed, so great is the pressure to include the alien, especially among hippies, that the apparently alien is often treated more favorably than the superficially similar: thus, the respect afforded to people and ideas that are distant and strange is sometimes not equally afforded those who are similar, be they one's parents or their middle-class values. One way of explaining the reaction of post-modern youth to the war in Vietnam is via the concept of inclusiveness: these young men and women react to events in Southeast Asia much as if they occurred in Newton, Massachusetts, Evanston,

Illinois, Harlem, or Berkeley, California: they make little distinction in their reactions to their fellow Americans and those overseas.

16   One corollary of inclusiveness is intense internationalism. What matters to hippies or young radicals is not where a person comes from, but what kind of relationship is possible with him. The nationality of ideas matters little: Zen Buddhism, American pragmatism, French existentialism, Indian mysticism or Yugoslav communism are accorded equal hearings. Interracialism is another corollary of inclusiveness: racial barriers are minimized or nonexistent, and the ultimate expressions of unity between the races, sexual relationships and marriage, are considered basically natural and normal, whatever the social problems they currently entail. In post-modern youth, then, identity and ideology are no longer parochial or national; increasingly, the reference group is the world, and the artificial subspeciation of the human species is broken down.

Antitechnologism

17   Post-modern youth has grave reservations about many of the technological aspects of the contemporary world. The depersonalization of life, commercialism, careerism and familism, the bureaucratization and complex organization of advanced nations—all seem intolerable to these young men and women, who seek to create new forms of association and action to oppose the technologism of our day. Bigness, impersonality, stratification and hierarchy are rejected, as is any involvement with the furtherance of technological values. In reaction to these values, post-modern youth seeks simplicity, naturalness, personhood and even voluntary poverty.

18   But a revolt against technologism is only possible, of course, in a technological society; and to be effective, it must inevitably exploit technology to overcome technologism. Thus in post-modern youth, the fruits of technology—synthetic hallucinogens in the hippie subculture, modern technology of communication among young radicals—and the affluence made possible by technological society are a precondition for a post-modern style. The demonstrative poverty of the hippie would be meaningless in a society where poverty is routine; for the radical to work for subsistence wages as a matter of choice is to *have* a choice not available in most parts of the world. Furthermore, to "organize" against the pernicious aspects of the technological era requires high skill in the use of modern technologies of organization: the long-distance telephone, the use of the mass media, high-speed travel, the mimeograph machine and so on. In the end, then, it is not the material but the spiritual consequences of technology that postmodern youth opposes: indeed, in the developing nations, those who exhibit a post-modern style may be in the vanguard of movements toward modernization. What *is* adamantly rejected is the contamination of life and the values of technological organization and production.

It seems probable that a comparable rejection of the psychological consequences of current technology, coupled with the simultaneous ability to exploit that technology, characterizes all dissenting groups in all epochs.

Participation

19   Post-modern youth is committed to a search for new forms of groups, of organizations and of action where decisionmaking is collective, arguments are resolved by "talking them out," self-examination, interpersonal criticism and group decision-making are fused. The objective is to create new styles of life and new types of organization that humanize rather than dehumanize, that activate and strengthen the participants rather than undermining or weakening them. And the primary vehicle for such participation is the small, face-to-face primary group of peers,

20   The search for new participatory forms of organization and action can hardly be deemed successful as yet, especially in the New Left, where effectiveness in the wider social and political scene remains to be demonstrated. There are inherent differences between the often task-less, face-to-face group that is the basic form of organization for both hippies and radicals and the task-oriented organization—differences that make it difficult to achieve social effectiveness based solely on small primary groups. But there may yet evolve from the hippie "tribes," small Digger communities, and primary groups of the New Left, new forms of association in which self-criticism, awareness of group interaction, and the accomplishment of social and political goals go hand in hand. The effort to create groups in which individuals grow from their participation in the group extends far beyond the New Left and the hippie world; the same search is seen in the widespread enthusiasm for "sensitivity training" groups and even in the increasing use of groups as a therapeutic instrument. Nor is this solely an American search: one sees a similar focus, for example, in the Communist nations, with their emphasis on small groups that engage in the "struggle" of mutual criticism and self-criticism.

21   The search for effectiveness combined with participation has also led to the evolution of "new" styles of social and political action. The newness of such forms of political action as parades and demonstrations is open to some question; perhaps what is most new is the *style* in which old forms of social action are carried out. The most consistent effort is to force one's opponent into a personal confrontation with one's own point of view. Sit-ins, freedom rides, insistence upon discussions, silent and nonviolent demonstrations—all have a prime objective to "get through to" the other side, to force reflection, to bear witness to one's own principles, and to impress upon others the validity of these same principles. There is much that is old and familiar about this, although few of today's young radicals or hippies are ideologically committed to

Gandhian views of nonviolence. Yet the underlying purpose of many of the emerging forms of social and political action, whether they be "human be-ins," "love-ins," peace marches or "teach-ins," has a new motive—hope that by expressing one's own principles, by "demonstrating" one's convictions, one can through sheer moral force win over one's opponents and lure them as well into participating with one's own values.

Antiacademicism

22   Among post-modern youth, one finds a virtually unanimous rejection of the "merely academic." This rejection is one manifestation of a wider insistence on the relevance, applicability and personal meaningfulness of knowledge. It would be wrong simply to label this trend "anti-intellectual," for many new radicals and not a few hippies are themselves highly intellectual people. What is demanded is that intelligence be engaged with the world, just as action should be informed by knowledge. In the New Left, at least amongst leaders, there is enormous respect for knowledge and information, and great impatience with those who act without understanding. Even amongst hippies, where the importance of knowledge and information is less stressed, it would be wrong simply to identify the rejection of the academic world and its values with a total rejection of intellect, knowledge and wisdom.

23   To post-modern youth, then, most of what is taught in schools, colleges and universities is largely irrelevant to living life in the last third of the twentieth century. Many academics are seen as direct or accidental apologists for the Organized System in the United States. Much of what they teach is considered simply unconnected to the experience of post-modern youth. New ways of learning are sought: ways that combine action with reflection upon action, ways that fuse engagement in the world with understanding of it. In an era of rapid change, the accrued wisdom of the past is cast into question, and youth seeks not only new knowledge, but new ways of learning and knowing.

Nonviolence

24   Finally, post-modern youth of all persuasions meets on the ground of nonviolence. For hippies, the avoidance of and calming of violence is a central objective, symbolized by gifts of flowers to policemen and the slogan, "Make love, not war." And although nonviolence as a philosophical principle has lost most of its power in the New Left, nonviolence as a psychological orientation is a crucial—perhaps *the* crucial—issue. The nonviolence of post-modern youth should not be confused with pacificism: these are not necessarily young men and women who believe in turning the other cheek or who are systematically opposed to fighting for

what they believe in. But the basic style of both radicals and hippies is profoundly opposed to warfare, destruction and exploitation of man by man, and to violence whether on an interpersonal or an international scale. Even among those who do not consider nonviolence a good in itself, a psychological inoculation against violence, even a fear of it, is a unifying theme.

The credibility gap: principle and practice

25   In creating the style of today's youth, the massive and violent social changes of the past two decades have played a central role. Such social changes are not only distantly perceived by those who are growing up, but are immediately interwoven into the texture of their daily lives as they develop. The social changes of the postwar era affect the young in a variety of ways: in particular, they contribute to a special sensitivity to the discrepancy between principle and practice. For during this era of rapid social change the values most deeply embedded in the parental generation and expressed in their behavior in time of crisis are frequently very different from the more "modern" principles, ideals and values that this generation has professed and attempted to practice in bringing up its children. Filial perception of the discrepancy between practice and principle may help explain the very widespread sensitivity amongst postmodern youth to the "hypocrisy" of the previous generation.

26   The grandparents of today's twenty-year-olds were generally born at the end of the nineteenth century, and brought up during the pre-World War I years. Heirs of a Victorian tradition as yet unaffected by the value revolutions of the twentieth century, they reared their own children, the parents of today's youth, in families that emphasized respect, the control of impulse, obedience to authority, and the traditional "inner-directed" values of hard work, deferred gratification and self-restraint. Their children, born around the time of the First World War, were thus socialized in families that remained largely Victorian in outlook.

27   During their lifetimes, however, these parents (and in particular the most intelligent and advantaged among them) were exposed to a great variety of new values that often changed their nominal faiths. During their youths in the 1920's and 1930's, major changes in American behavior and American values took place. For example, the "emancipation of women" in the 1920's, marked by the achievement of suffrage for women, coincided with the last major change in actual sexual behavior in America: during this period, women began to become the equal partners of men, who no longer sought premarital sexual experience solely with women of a lower class. More important, the 1920's and the 1930's were an era when

older Victorian values were challenged, attacked and all but discredited, especially in educated middle-class families. Young men and women who went to college during this period (as did most of the parents of those who can be termed "post-modern" today) were influenced outside their families by a variety of "progressive," "liberal," and even psychoanalytic ideas that contrasted sharply with the values of their childhood families. Moreover, during the 1930's, many of the parents of today's upper middle-class youth were exposed to or involved with the ideals of the New Deal, and sometimes to more radical interpretations of man, society and history. Finally, in the 1940's and 1950's, when it came time to rear their own children, the parents of today's elite youth were strongly influenced by "permissive" views of child-rearing that again contrasted sharply with the techniques by which they themselves had been raised. Thus, many middle-class parents moved during their lifetime from the Victorian ethos in which they had been socialized to the less moralistic, more humanitarian, and more "expressive" values of their own adulthoods.

28   But major changes in values, when they occur in adult life, are likely to be far from complete. To have grown up in a family where unquestioning obedience to parents was expected, but to rear one's own children in an atmosphere of "democratic" permissiveness and self-determination—and never to revert to the practices of one's own childhood—requires a change of values more total and comprehensive than most adults can achieve. Furthermore, behavior that springs from values acquired in adulthood often appears somewhat forced, artificial or insincere to the sensitive observer. Children, clearly the most sensitive observers of their own parents, are likely to sense a discrepancy between their parents' avowed and consciously-held values and their "basic instincts" with regard to child-rearing. Furthermore, the parental tendency to "revert to form" is greatest in times of family crisis, which are of course the times that have the greatest effect upon children. No matter how "genuinely" parents held their "new" values, many of them inevitably found themselves falling back on the lessons of their own childhoods when the chips were down.

29   In a time of rapid social change, then, a special *credibility gap* is likely to open between the generations. Children are likely to perceive a considerable discrepancy between what their parents avow as their values and the actual assumptions from which parental behavior springs. In many middle-class teen-agers today, for example, the focal issue of adolescent rebellion against parents often seems to be just this discrepancy: the children arguing that their parents' endorsement of independence and self-determination for their children is "hypocritical" in that it does not correspond with the real behavior of the parents when their children actually seek independence. Similar perceptions of parental "hypocrisy" occur around racial matters: for example, there are many parents who in principle support racial and religious equality, but become violently upset

when their children date someone from another race or religion. Around political activity similar issues arise. For example, many of the parents of today's youth espouse in principle the cause of political freedom, but are not involved themselves in politics and oppose their children's involvement lest they "jeopardize their record" or "ruin their later career."

30   Of course, no society ever fully lives up to its own professed ideals. In every society there is a gap between creedal values and actual practices, and in every society, the recognition of this gap constitutes a powerful motor for social change. But in most societies, especially when social change is slow and institutions are powerful and unchanging, there occurs what can be termed *institutionalization of hypocrisy*. Children and adolescents routinely learn when it is "reasonable" to expect that the values people profess will be implemented in their behavior, and when it is not reasonable. There develops an elaborate system of exegesis and commentary upon the society's creedal values, excluding certain people or situations from the full weight of these values, or "demonstrating" that apparent inconsistencies are not really inconsistencies at all. Thus, in almost all societies, a "sincere" man who "honestly" believes one set of values is frequently allowed to ignore them completely, for example, in the practice of his business, in his interpersonal relationships, in dealings with foreigners, in relationships to his children, and so on—all because these areas have been officially defined as exempt from the application of his creedal values.

31   In a time of rapid social change and value change, however, the institutionalization of hypocrisy seems to break down. "New" values have been in existence for so brief a period that the exemptions to them have not yet been defined, the situations to be excluded have not yet been determined, and the universal gap between principle and practice appears in all of its nakedness. Thus, the mere fact of a discrepancy between creedal values and practice is not at all unusual. But what is special about the present situation of rapid value change is, first, that parents themselves tend to have two conflicting sets of values, one related to the experience of their early childhood, the other to the ideologies and principles acquired in adulthood; and second, that no stable institutions or rules for defining hypocrisy out of existence have yet been fully evolved. In such a situation, children see the Emperor's nakedness with unusual clarity, recognizing the value conflict within their parents and perceiving clearly the hypocritical gap between creed and behavior.

32   This argument suggests that the post-modern youth may not be confronted with an "objective" gap between parental preaching and practice any greater than that of most generations. But they are confronted with an unusual internal ambivalance within the parental generation over the values that parents successfully inculcated in their children, and they are "deprived" of a system of social interpretation that rationalizes the dis-

crepancy between creed and deed. It seems likely, then, that today's youth may simply be able to perceive the universal gulf between principle and practice more clearly than previous generations have done.

33   This points to one of the central characteristics of post-modern youth: they insist on taking seriously a great variety of political, personal and social principles that "no one in his right mind" ever before thought of attempting to extend to such situations as dealings with strangers, relations between the races, or international politics. For example, peaceable openness has long been a creedal virtue in our society, but it has never been extended to foreigners, particularly with dark skins. Similarly, equality has long been preached, but the "American dilemma" has been resolved by a series of institutionalized hypocrisies that exempted Negroes from the application of this principle. Love has always been a central value in Christian society, but really to love one's enemies—to be generous to policemen, customers, criminals, servants and foreigners—has been considered folly.

34   These speculations on the credibility gap between the generations in a time of rapid change may help explain two crucial facts about post-modern youth: first, they frequently come from highly principled families with whose principles they continue to agree; second, that they have the outrageous temerity to insist that individuals and societies live by the values they preach. And these speculations may also explain the frequent feeling of those who have worked intensively with student radicals or hippies that, apart from the "impracticality" of some of their views, these sometimes seem to be the only clear-eyed and sane people in a society and a world where most of us are still systematically blind to the traditional gap between personal principle and practice, national creed and policy, a gap that we may no longer be able to afford.

Violence: sadism and cataclysm

35   Those who are today in their early twenties were born near the end of World War II, the most violent and barbarous war in world history. The lasting imprint of that war can be summarized in the names of three towns: Auschwitz, Hiroshima and Nuremberg. *Auschwitz* points to the possibility of a "civilized" nation embarking on a systematized, well-organized and scientific plan of exterminating an entire people. *Hiroshima* demonstrated how "clean," easy and impersonal cataclysm could be to those who perpetrate it, and how demonic, sadistic and brutal to those who experience it. And *Nuremberg* summarizes the principle that men have an accountability above obedience to national policy, a responsibility to conscience more primary even than fidelity to national law. These three lessons are the matrix for the growth of post-modern youth.

36   The terror of violence that has hung over all men and women since the Second World War has especially shaped the outlooks of today's youth. In the first memories of a group of young radicals, for example, one finds the following recollections: a dim recall of the end of World War II; childhood terror of the atomic bomb; witnessing the aftermath of a violent riot in the United States; being frightened by a picture of a tank riding over rubble; being violently jealous at the birth of a younger brother; taking part in "gruesome" fights in the school yard. Such memories mean many things, but in them, violence-in-the-world finds echo and counterpart in the violence of inner feelings. The term "violence" suggests both of these possibilities: the *psychological* violence of sadism, exploitation and aggression, and the *historical* violence of war, cataclysm and holocaust. In the lives of most of this generation, the threats of inner and outer violence are fused, each activating, exciting and potentiating the other. To summarize a complex thesis into a few words: *the issue of violence is to this generation what the issue of sex was to the Victorian world.*

37   Stated differently, what is most deeply repressed, rejected, feared, controlled and projected onto others by the post-modern generation is no longer their own sexuality. Sex, for most of this generation, is much freer, more open, less guilt- and anxiety-ridden. But violence, whether in one's self or in others, has assumed new prominence as the prime source of inner and outer terror. That this should be so in the modern world is readily understandable. Over all of us hangs the continual threat of a technological violence more meaningless, absurd, total and unpremeditated than any ever imagined before. Individual life always resonates with historical change; history is not merely the backdrop for development, but its ground. To be grounded in the history of the past two decades is to have stood upon, to have experienced both directly and vicariously, violent upheaval, violent worldwide revolution, and the unrelenting possibility of worldwide destruction. To have been alive and aware in America during the past decade has been to be exposed to the assassination of a President and the televised murder of his murderer, to the well-publicized slaughter of Americans by their fellow countrymen, and to the recent violence in our cities. To have been a middle-class child in the past two decades is to have watched daily the violence of television, both as it reports the bloodshed and turmoil of the American and non-American world, and as it skillfully elaborates and externalizes in repetitive dramas the potential for violence within each of us.

38   It therefore requires no assumption of an increase in biological aggression to account for the salience of the issue of violence for post-modern youth. The capacity for rage, spite and aggression is part of our endowment as human beings: it is a constant potential of human nature. But during the past two decades—indeed, starting before the Second World War—we have witnessed violence and imagined violence on a scale more

frightening than ever before. Like the angry child who fears that his rage
will itself destroy those around him, we have become vastly more sensitive
to and fearful of our inner angers, for we live in a world where even the
mildest irritation, multiplied a billionfold by modern technology, might
destroy all civilization. The fact of violent upheaval and the possibility of
cataclysm has been literally brought into our living rooms during the
past twenty years: it has been interwoven with the development of a whole
generation.

39   It should not surprise us, then, that the issue of violence is a focal
concern for those of contemporary youth with the greatest historical consciousness. The hippie slogan "Make love, not war" expresses their sentiment, albeit in a form that the "realist" of previous generations might deem
sentimental or romantic. Although few young radicals would agree with the
wording of this statement, the underlying sentiment corresponds to their
basic psychological orientation. For them, as for many others of their
generation, the primary task is to develop new psychological, political
and international controls on violence. Indeed, many of the dilemmas of
today's young radicals seem related to their extraordinarily zealous efforts
to avoid any action or relationship in which inner or outer violence might
be evoked. Distaste for violence animates the profound revulsion many of
today's youth feel toward the war in Southeast Asia, just as it underlies a
similar revulsion against the exploitation or control of man by man. The
same psychological nonviolence is related to young radicals' avoidance of
traditional leadership lest it lead to domination, to their emphasis on
person-to-person participation and "confrontation," and even to their un-
willingness to "play the media" in an attempt to gain political effectiveness. Even the search for forms of mass political action that avoid physical
violence—a preference severely tested and somewhat undermined by the
events of recent months—points to a considerable distaste for the direct expression of aggression.

40   I do not mean to suggest that post-modern youth contains a dis-
proportionate number of tight-lipped pacifists or rage-filled deniers of their
own inner angers. On the contrary, among today's youth, exuberance,
passionateness and zest are the rule rather than the exception. Nor are
hippies and young radicals incapable of anger, rage and resentment—
especially when their principles are violated. But for many of these young
men and women, the experiences of early life and the experience of the
postwar world are joined in a special sensitivity to the issue of violence,
whether in themselves or in others. This confluence of psychological and
historical forces helps explain the intensity of their search for new forms
of social organization and political action that avoid manipulation, domination and control, just as it contributes to their widespread opposition to
warfare of all kinds.

41   Yet the position of psychologically nonviolent youth in a violent world
is difficult and paradoxical. On the one hand, he seeks to minimize vio-

lence, but on the other, his efforts often elicit violence from others. At the same time that he attempts to work to actualize his vision of a peaceful world, he must confront more directly and continually than do his peers the fact that the world is neither peaceful nor just. The frustration and discouragement of his work repetitively reawaken his anger, which must forever be rechanneled into peaceful paths. Since he continually confronts destructiveness and exploitation in the world, his own inevitable potential for destructiveness and exploitiveness inevitably arouses in him great guilt. The young men and women who make up the New Left in America, like other post-modern youth, have far less difficulty in living with their sexual natures than did their parents; but what they continue to find difficult to live with, what they still repress, avoid and counteract is their own potential for violence. It remains to be seen whether, in the movement toward "resistance" and disruption of today's young radicals, their psychological nonviolence will continue to be reflected in their actions.

42   In pointing to the psychological dimension of the issue of violence, I do not mean to attribute causal primacy either to the experiences of early life or to their residues in adulthood. My thesis is rather that for those of this generation with the greatest historical awareness, the psychological and historical possibility of violence have come to potentiate each other. To repeat: witnessing the acting out of violence on a scale more gigantic than ever before, or imaginatively participating in the possibility of world-wide holocaust activates the fear of one's own violence; heightened awareness of one's inner potential for rage, anger or destructiveness increases sensitivity to the possibility of violence in the world.

43   This same process of historical potentiation of inner violence has occurred, I believe, throughout the modern world, and brings with it not only the intensified efforts to curb violence we see in this small segment of post-modern youth, but other more frightening possibilities. Post-modern youth, to an unusual degree, remain open to and aware of their own angers and aggressions, and their awareness creates in them a sufficient understanding of inner violence to enable them to control it in themselves and oppose it in others. Most men and women, young or old, possess less insight: their inner sadism is projected onto others whom they thereafter loathe or abjectly serve; or, more disastrously, historically-heightened inner violence is translated into outer aggression and murderousness, sanctioned by self-righteousness.

44   Thus, if the issue of violence plagues post-modern youth, it is not because these young men and women are more deeply rage-filled than most. On the contrary, it is because such young men and women have confronted this issue more squarely in themselves and in the world than have any but a handful of their fellows. If they have not yet found solutions, they have at least faced an issue so dangerous that most of us find it too painful even to acknowledge, and they have done so, most remarkably, without identifying with what they oppose. Their still-incomplete lives pose

for us all the question on which our survival as individuals and as a world depends: Can we create formulations and forms to control historical and psychological violence before their fusion destroys us all?

Questions

1. What techniques of definition does Kenneth Keniston use to discuss today's youth?
2. What other methods of exposition does he use?
3. Although the essay takes the form of exposition rather than argument, what Keniston says is arguable, a personal interpretation. In the first five paragraphs, what does he say to guard his thesis against possible opposition? What admission does he make?
4. Show how Keniston takes special care to keep the opposition against his thesis in mind as he argues that the credibility gap (paragraphs 25–34) between parents and youth of this generation is definitively different from the one that has always existed between generations.
5. Show how in each paragraph Keniston uses illustration to support his generalizations.

Theme topics

1. Write a theme refuting, qualifying or supporting the thesis of "Youth, Change and Violence," or refute, qualify, or support some part of the analysis of youth that it presents.
2. Write a narrative incident that might be used as illustration supporting or refuting some point made by Kenneth Keniston.

54   PHYLLIS McGINLEY

Suburbia: Of Thee I Sing

1   Twenty miles east of New York City as the New Haven Railroad flies sits a village I shall call Spruce Manor. The Boston Post Road, there, for the length of two blocks, becomes Main Street, and on one side

of that thundering thoroughfare are the grocery stores and the drug stores and the Village Spa where teen-agers gather of an afternoon to drink their cokes and speak their curious confidences. There one finds the shoe repairers and the dry cleaners and the second-hand stores which sell "antiques" and the stationery stores which dispense comic books to ten-year-olds and greeting cards and lending library masterpieces to their mothers. On the opposite side stand the bank, the fire house, the public library. The rest of this town of perhaps four or five thousand people lies to the south and is bounded largely by Long Island Sound, curving protectively on three borders. The movie theater (dedicated to the showing of second-run, single-feature pictures) and the grade schools lie north, beyond the Post Road, and that is a source of worry to Spruce Manorites. They are always a little uneasy about the children, crossing, perhaps, before the lights are safely green. However, two excellent policemen—Mr. Crowley and Mr. Lang—station themselves at the intersections four times a day, and so far there have been no accidents.

2   Spruce Manor in the spring and summer and fall is a pretty town, full of gardens and old elms. (There are few spruces, but the village Council is considering planting a few on the station plaza, out of sheer patriotism.) In the winter, the houses reveal themselves as comfortable, well-kept, architecturally insignificant. Then one can see the town for what it is and has been since it left off being farm and woodland some sixty years ago—the epitome of Suburbia, not the country and certainly not the city. It is a commuter's town, the living center of a web which unrolls each morning as the men swing abroad the locals, and contracts again in the evening when they return. By day, with even the children pent in schools, it is a village of women. They trundle mobile baskets at the A&P, they sit under driers at the hairdressers, they sweep their porches and set out bulbs and stitch up slip covers. Only on weekends does it become heterogeneous and lively, the parking places difficult to find.

3   Spruce Manor has no country club of its own, though devoted golfers have their choice of two or three not far away. It does have a small yacht club and a beach which can be used by anyone who rents or owns a house here. The village supports a little park with playground equipment and a counselor, where children, unattended by parents, can spend summer days if they have no more pressing engagements.

4   It is a town not wholly without traditions. Residents will point out the two-hundred-year-old manor house, now a minor museum; and in the autumn they line the streets on a scheduled evening to watch the Volunteer Firemen parade. That is a fine occasion, with so many heads of households marching in their red blouses and white gloves, some with flaming helmets, some swinging lanterns, most of them genially out of step. There is a bigger parade on Memorial Day with more marchers than watchers and with the Catholic priest, the rabbi, and the Protestant ministers each

delivering a short prayer when the paraders gather near the War Memorial. On the whole, however, outside of contributing generously to the Community Chest, Manorites are not addicted to municipal get-togethers.

5   No one is very poor here and not many families rich enough to be awesome. In fact, there is not much to distinguish Spruce Manor from any other of a thousand suburbs outside of New York City or San Francisco or Detroit or Chicago or even Stockholm, for that matter. Except for one thing. For some reason, Spruce Manor has become a sort of symbol to writers and reporters familiar only with its name or trival aspects. It has become a symbol of all that is middle-class in the worst sense, of settled-downness or rootlessness, according to what the writer is trying to prove; of smug and prosperous mediocrity—or even, in more lurid novels, of lechery at the country club and Sunday morning hangovers.

6   To condemn Suburbia has long been a literary cliché, anyhow. I have yet to read a book in which the suburban life was pictured as the good life or the commuter as a sympathetic figure. He is nearly as much a stock character as the old stage Irishman: the man who "spends his life riding to and from his wife," the eternal Babbitt who knows all about Buicks and nothing about Picasso, whose sanctuary is the club locker room, whose ideas spring ready-made from the illiberal newspapers. His wife plays politics at the P.T.A. and keeps up with the Joneses. Or—if the scene is more gilded and less respectable—the commuter is the high-powered advertising executive with a station wagon and an eye for the ladies, his wife a restless baggage given to too many cocktails in the afternoon.

7   These clichés I challenge. I have lived in the country, I have lived in the city. I have lived in an average Middle Western small town. But for the best eleven years of my life I have lived in Suburbia and I like it.

8   "Compromise!" cried our friends when we came here from an expensive, inconvenient, moderately fashionable tenement in Manhattan. It was the period in our lives when everyone was moving somewhere. Farther uptown, farther downtown, across town to Sutton Place, to a half-dozen rural acres in Connecticut or New Jersey or even Vermont. But no one in our rather rarefied little group was thinking of moving to the suburbs except us. They were aghast that we could find anything appealing in the thought of a middle-class house on a middle-class street in a middle-class village full of middle-class people. That we were tired of town and hoped for children, that we couldn't afford both a city apartment and a farm, they put down as feeble excuses. To this day they cannot understand us. You see, they read the books. They even write them.

9   Compromise? Of course we compromise. But compromise, if not the spice of life, is its solidity. It is what makes nations great and marriages happy and Spruce Manor the pleasant place it is. As for its being middle-class, what is wrong with acknowledging one's roots? And how free we are! Free of the city's noise, of its ubiquitous doormen, of the soot on the

windowsill and the radio in the next apartment. We have released ourselves from the seasonal hegira to the mountains or the seashore. We have only one address, one house to keep supplied with paring knives and blankets. We are free from the snows that block the countryman's roads in winter and his electricity which always goes off in a thunderstorm. I do not insist that we are typical. There is nothing really typical about any of our friends and neighbors here, and therein lies my point. The true suburbanite needs to conform less than anyone else; much less than the gentleman farmer with his remodeled salt-box or than the determined cliff dweller with his necessity for living at the right address. In Spruce Manor all addresses are right. And since we are fairly numerous here, we need not fall back on the people nearest us for total companionship. There is not here, as in a small city away from truly urban centers, some particular family whose codes must be ours. And we could not keep up with the Joneses even if we wanted to, for we know many Joneses and they are all quite different people leading the most various lives.

10   The Albert Joneses spend their weekends sailing, the Bertram Joneses cultivate their delphinium, the Clarence Joneses—Clarence being a handy man with a cello—are enthusiastic about amateur chamber music. The David Joneses dote on bridge, but neither of the Ernest Joneses understands it, and they prefer staying home of an evening so that Ernest Jones can carve his witty caricatures out of pieces of old fruit wood. We admire each other's gardens, applaud each other's sailing records; we are too busy to compete. So long as our clapboards are painted and our hedges decently trimmed, we have fulfilled our community obligations. We can live as anonymously as in a city or we can call half the village by their first names.

11   On our half-acre or three-quarters, we can raise enough tomatoes for our salads and assassinate enough beetles to satisfy the gardening urge. Or we can buy our vegetables at the store and put the whole place to lawn without feeling that we are neglecting our property. We can have privacy and shade and the changing of the seasons and also the Joneses next door from whom to borrow a cup of sugar or a stepladder. Despite the novelists, the shadow of the country club rests lightly on us. Half of us wouldn't be found dead with a golf stick in our hands, and loathe Saturday dances. Few of us expect to be deliriously wealthy or world-famous or divorced. What we do expect is to pay off the mortgage and send our healthy children to good colleges.

12   For when I refer to life here, I think, of course, of living with children. Spruce Manor without children would be a paradox. The summer waters are full of them, gamboling like dolphins. The lanes are alive with them, the yards overflow with them, they possess the tennis courts and the skating pond and the vacant lots. Their roller skates wear down the asphalt, and their bicycles make necessary the twenty-five-mile speed limit. They converse interminably on the telephones and make rich the

dentist and the pediatrician. Who claims that a child and a half is the American middle-class average? A nice medium Spruce Manor family runs to four or five, and we count proudly, but not with amazement, the many solid households running to six, seven, eight, nine, even up to twelve. Our houses here are big and not new, most of them, and there is a temptation to fill them up, let the décor fall where it may.

13   Besides, Spruce Manor seems designed by providence and town planning for the happiness of children. Better designed than the city; better, I say defiantly, than the country. Country mothers must be constantly arranging and contriving for their children's leisure time. There is no neighbor child next door for playmate, no school within walking distance. The ponds are dangerous to young swimmers, the woods full of poison ivy, the romantic dirt roads unsuitable for bicycles. An extra acre or two gives a fine sense of possession to an adult; it does not compensate children for the give-and-take of our village, where there is always a contemporary to help swing the skipping rope or put on the catcher's mitt. Where in the country is the Friday evening dancing class or the Saturday morning movie (approved by the P.T.A.)? It is the greatest fallacy of all time that children love the country as a year-around plan. Children would take a dusty corner of Washington Square or a city sidewalk, even, in preference to the lonely sermons in stones and books in running brooks which their contemporaries cannot share.

14   As for the horrors of bringing up progeny in the city, for all its museums and other cultural advantages (so perfectly within reach of suburban families if they feel strongly about it), they were summed up for me one day last winter. The harried mother of one, speaking to me on the telephone just after Christmas, sighed and said, "It's been a really wonderful time for me, as vacations go. Barbara has had an engagement with a child in our apartment house every afternoon this week. I have had to take her almost nowhere." Barbara is eleven. For six of those eleven years, I realized, her mother must have dreaded Christmas vacation, not to mentoin spring, as a time when Barbara had to be entertained. I thought thankfully of my own daughters whom I had scarcely seen since school closed, out with their skis and their sleds and their friends, sliding down the roped-off hill half a block away, coming in hungrily for lunch and disappearing again, hearty, amused, and safe—at least as safe as any sled-borne child can be.

15   Spruce Manor is not Eden, of course. Our taxes are higher than we like, and there is always that eight-eleven in the morning to be caught and we sometimes resent the necessity of rushing from a theater to a train on a weekday evening. But the taxes pay for our really excellent schools and for our garbage collections (so that the pails of orange peels need not stand in the halls overnight as ours did in the city) and for our water supply which does not give out every dry summer as it frequently does in

the country. As for the theaters—they are twenty miles away and we don't get to them more than twice a month. But neither, I think, do many of our friends in town. The eight-eleven is rather a pleasant train, too, say the husbands; it gets them to work in thirty-four minutes and they read the papers restfully on the way.

16   "But the suburban mind!" cry our die-hard friends in Manhattan and Connecticut. "The suburban conversation! The monotony!" They imply that they and I must scintillate or we perish. Let me anatomize Spruce Manor, for them and for the others who envision Suburbia as a congregation of mindless housewives and amoral go-getters.

17   From my window, now, on a June morning, I have a view. It contains neither solitary hills or dramatic skyscrapers. But I can see my roses in bloom, and my foxglove, and an arch of trees over the lane. I think comfortably of my friends whose houses line this and other streets rather like it. Not one of them is, so far as I know, doing any of the things that suburban ladies are popularly supposed to be doing. One of them, I happen to know, has gone bowling for her health and figure, but she has already tidied up her house and arranged to be home before the boys return from school. Some, undoubtedly, are ferociously busy in the garden. One lady is on her way to Ellis Island, bearing comfort and gifts to a Polish boy—a seventeen-year-old stowaway who did slave labor in Germany and was liberated by a cousin of hers during the war—who is being held for attempting to attain the land of which her cousin told him. The boy has been on the Island for three months. Twice a week she takes this tedious journey, meanwhile besieging courts and immigration authorities on his behalf. This lady has a large house, a part-time maid, and five children.

18   My friend around the corner is finishing her third novel. She writes daily from nine-thirty until two. After that her son comes back from school and she plunges into maternity; at six, she combs her pretty hair, refreshes her lipstick, and is charming to her doctor husband. The village dancing school is run by another neighbor, as it has been for twenty years. She has sent a number of ballerinas on to the theatrical world as well as having shepherded for many a successful season the white-gloved little boys and full-skirted little girls through their first social tasks.

19   Some of the ladies are no doubt painting their kitchens or a nursery; one of them is painting the portrait, on assignment, of a very distinguished personage. Some of them are nurses' aides and Red Cross workers and supporters of good causes. But all find time to be friends with their families and to meet the 5:32 five nights a week. They read something besides the newest historical novel, Braque is not unidentifiable to most of them, and their conversation is for the most part as agreeable as the tables they set. The tireless bridge players, the gossips, the women bored by their husbands live perhaps in our suburb, too. Let them. Our orbits need not cross.

20   And what of the husbands, industriously selling bonds or practicing law or editing magazines or looking through microscopes or managing offices in the city? Do they spend their evenings and their weekends in the gaudy bars of Fifty-second Street? Or are they the perennial house-holders, their lives a dreary round of taking down screens and mending drains? Well, screens they have always with them, and a man who is good around the house can spend happy hours with the plumbing even on a South Sea island. Some of them cut their own lawns and some of them try to break par and some of them sail their little boats all summer with their families for crew. Some of them are village trustees for nothing a year and some listen to symphonies and some think Milton Berle ought to be President. There is a scientist who plays wonderful bebop, and an insurance salesman who has bought a big old house nearby and with his own hands is gradually tearing it apart and reshaping it nearer to his heart's desire. Some of them are passionate hedge-clippers and some read Plutarch for fun. But I do not know many—though there may be such— who either kiss their neighbor's wives behind doors or whose idea of sprightly talk is to tell you the plot of an old movie.

21   It is June, now, as I have said. This afternoon my daughters will come home from school with a crowd of their peers at their heels. They will eat up the cookies and drink up the ginger ale and go down for a swim at the beach if the water is warm enough, that beach which is only three blocks away and open to all Spruce Manor. They will go unattended by me, since they have been swimming since they were four, and besides there are lifeguards and no big waves. (Even our piece of ocean is a com-promise.) Presently it will be time for us to climb into our very old Studebaker—we are not car-proud in Spruce Manor—and meet the 5:32. That evening expedition is not vitally necessary, for a bus runs straight down our principal avenue from the station to the shore, and it meets all trains. But it is an event we enjoy. There is something delightfully ritual-istic about the moment when the train pulls in and the men swing off, with the less sophisticated children running squealing to meet them. The women move over from the driver's seat, surrender the keys, and receive an absentminded kiss. It is the sort of picture that wakes John Marquand screaming from his sleep. But, deluded people that we are, we do not realize how mediocre it all seems. We will eat our undistinguished meal, probably without even a cocktail to enliven it. We will drink our coffee at the table, not carry it into the living room; if a husband changes for dinner here it is into old and spotty trousers and more comfortable shoes. The children will then go through the regular childhood routine—complain about their homework, grumble about going to bed, and finally accom-plish both ordeals. Perhaps later the Gerald Joneses will drop in. We will talk a great deal of unimportant chatter and compare notes on food prices; we will also discuss the headlines and disagree. (Some of us in the Manor

are Republicans, some are Democrats, a few lean plainly leftward. There are probably anti-Semites and anti-Catholics and even anti-Americans. Most of us are merely anti-antis.) We will all have one highball, and the Joneses will leave early. Tomorrow and tomorrow and tomorrow the pattern will be repeated. This is Suburbia.

22   But I think that some day people will look back on our little interval here, on our Spruce Manor way of life, as we now look back on the Currier and Ives kind of living, with nostalgia and respect. In a world of terrible extremes, it will stand out as the safe, important medium.

23   Suburbia, of thee I sing!

Questions

1. In singing the praises of life in suburbia, Miss McGinley is careful to raise and refute point by point the case stated by others against it. What issues does she raise on behalf of her opponents and then discount?

2. What methods of refutation does she employ against her opponents and how successfully does she use them?

3. Are there any issues that she ignores, that is, fails to raise and answer? If so, what are they?

4. What aspects of suburban life does she personally seem to prize most highly?

5. What is the function of the following word choices in the first two paragraphs: thundering thoroughfare, curious confidences, lending library masterpieces, curving protectively, trundle mobile baskets? Why has she chosen these and other details for the opening paragraphs? Name choices from her essay that would, if listed initially, destroy the dominant impression she creates there.

6. Compromise is the charge she says her friends make against her. She retorts that compromise is life's solidity. "It is what makes nations great and marriages happy." How true or false is this analogy when applied to suburban life?

7. In paragraph 9 she says that the true suburbanite needs to conform less than anyone else. What evidence does she give and how persuasive is it?

Theme topics

1. Write a description of some suburban community which makes the opposite impression of that made by Phyllis McGinley's opening paragraphs.

2. Write the argument against suburbia that Phyllis McGinley has refuted in her essay.

3. Write an argument against Phyllis McGinley's in which you refute her refutation.

55 VINCENT HARDING

Black Power and the American Christ

1   The mood among many social-action-oriented Christians today suggests that it is only a line thin as a razor blade that divides sentimental yearning over the civil rights activities of the past from present bitter recrimination against "Black Power." As is so often the case with reminiscences, the nostalgia may grow more out of a sense of frustration and powerlessness than out of any true appreciation of the meaning of the past. This at least is the impression one gets from those seemingly endless gatherings of old "true believers" which usually produce both the nostalgia and the recriminations. Generally the cast of characters at such meetings consists of well-dressed, well-fed Negroes and whites whose accents almost blend into a single voice as they recall the days "when we were all together, fighting for the same cause." The stories evoke again the heady atmosphere, mixed of smugness and self-sacrifice, that surrounded us in those heroic times when nonviolence was our watchword and integration our heavenly city. One can almost hear the strains of "our song" as men and women remember how they solemnly swayed in the aisles or around the charred remains of a church or in the dirty southern jails. Those were the days when Martin Luther King was the true prophet and when we were certain that the civil rights movement was God's message to the churches— and part of our smugness grew out of the fact that *we* knew it while all the rest of God's frozen people were asleep.

A veil between then and now

2   But as the reminiscences continue a veil seems to descend between then and now. The tellers of the old tales label the veil Black Power, and pronounce ritual curses on Stokely Carmichael and Floyd McKissick and their followers.

3   The trouble with these meetings is that they are indeed becoming ritual, cultic acts of memory that blind us to creative possibilities. Because that "veil" may be a wall, not primarily for separating but for writing

From *The Christian Century* (January 4, 1967), pp. 10–13. Copyright 1967 Christian Century Foundation. Reprinted by permission from the January 4, 1967 issue of *The Christian Century* and the author.

on—both sides of it. Or it may be a great sheet "let down from heaven"; or a curtain before the next act can begin. Most of us appear totally incapable of realizing that there may be more light in blackness than we have yet begun to glimpse.

4   Such possibilities should be pondered especially by those of us who combine the terrible privileges of blackness and Christian commitment within a single life. We are driven to see not only what was happening in our warm, genteel days of common black-white struggle, but to grasp clearly what is happening now. We have no choice but to hold Black Power in our black arms and examine it, convinced that Christ is Lord of this too. Anyone who is black and claims to be a part of the company of Christ's people would be derelict if he failed to make such an examination and to proclaim with fear and trembling and intimations of great joy what he has discovered.

5   Perhaps the first and central discovery is also the most obvious: there is a strong and causative link between Black Power and American Christianity. Indeed one may say with confidence that whatever its other sources, the ideology of blackness surely grows out of the deep ambivalence of American Negroes to the Christ we have encountered here. This ambivalence is not new. It was ours from the beginning. For we first met the American Christ on slave ships. We heard his name sung in hymns of praise while we died in our thousands, chained in stinking holds beneath the decks, locked in with terror and disease and sad memories of our families and homes. When we leaped from the decks to be seized by sharks we saw his name carved on the ship's solid sides. When our women were raped in the cabins they must have noticed the great and holy books on the shelves. Our introduction to this Christ was not propitious. And the horrors continued on America's soil. So all through the nation's history many black men have rejected this Christ—indeed the miracle is that so many accepted him. In past times our disdain often had to be stifled and sullen, our anger silent and self-destructive. But now we speak out. Our anger is no longer silent; it has leaped onto the public stage, and demands to be seen and dealt with—a far more healthy state of affairs for all concerned.

6   If the American Christ and his followers have indeed helped to mold the Black Power movement, then might it not be that the God whom many of us insist on keeping alive is not only alive but just? May he not be attempting to break through to us with at least as much urgency as we once sensed at the height of the good old "We Shall Overcome" days? Perhaps he is writing on the wall, saying that we Christians, black and white, must choose between death with the American Christ and life with the Suffering Servant of God. Who dares deny that God may have chosen once again the black sufferers for a new assault on the hard shell of indifference and fear that encases so many Americans?

7   If these things are difficult to believe perhaps we need to look more closely both at the American Christ and the black movement he has helped to create. From the outset, almost everywhere we blacks have met him in this land, this Christ was painted white and pink, blond and blue-eyed—and not only in white churches but in black churches as well. Millions of black children had the picture of this pseudo-Nazarene burned into their memory. The books, the windows, the paintings, the film-strips all affirmed the same message—a message of shame. This Christ shamed us by his pigmentation, so obviously not our own. He condemned us for our blackness, for our flat noses, for our kinky hair, for our power, our strange power of expressing emotion in singing and shouting and dancing. He was sedate, so genteel, so white. And as soon as we were able, many of us tried to be like him.

Glad to be black

8   For a growing edge of bold young black people all that is past. They fling out their declaration: "No white Christ shall shame us again. We are glad to be black. We rejoice in the darkness of our skin, we celebrate the natural texture of our hair, we extol the rhythm and vigor of our songs and shouts and dances. And if your American Christ doesn't like that, you know what you can do with him." That is Black Power: a repudiation of the American culture-religion that helped to create it and a quest for a religious reality more faithful to our own experience.

9   These young people say to America: "We know your Christ and his attitude toward Africa. We remember how his white missionaries warned against Africa's darkness and heathenism, its savagery and naked jungle heart. We are tired of all that. This Africa that you love and hate, but mostly fear—this is our homeland. We saw you exchange your Bibles for our land. We watched you pass out tracts and take in gold. We heard you teach hymns to get our diamonds, and you control them still. If this is what your Christ taught you, he is sharp, baby, he is shrewd; but he's no savior of ours. We affirm our homeland and its great black past, a past that was filled with wonder before your white scourge came. You can keep your Christ. We'll take our home." That is Black Power: a search for roots in a land that has denied us both a past and a future. And the American Christ who has blessed the denial earns nothing but scorn.

10   The advocates of Black Power know this Christ well. They see his people running breathlessly, cursing silently, exiting double-time from the cities with all their suffering people. They see this white throng fleeing before the strangled movement of the blacks out of the ghettos, leaving their stained-glass mausoleums behind them. This very exodus of the

Christians from the places where the weak and powerless live has been one of the primary motivating forces of Black Power.

11   The seekers of Black Power, seeing their poorest, most miserable people deserted by the white American Christians, have come to stand with the forlorn in these very places of abandonment. Now they speak of Black Unity, and the old Christian buildings are filled with Negroes young and old studying African history. The new leaders in the ghettos tell them: "Whites now talk about joining forces, but who has ever wanted to join forces with you? They only want to use you—especially those white American Christian liars. They love you in theory only. They love only your middle-class incarnations. But they are afraid of you—you who are black and poor and filled with rage and despair. They talk about 'progress' for the Negro, but they don't mean *you*."

12   These young people whose names we old "true believers" intone in our nightly litanies of frustrated wrath have listened with the perception born of alienation to white Christians speaking to Negroes of "our people and your people, our churches and your churches, our community and your community, our schools and your schools." And they hear this hypocrisy crowned with the next words from bleeding Christian hearts: "Of course some of your most spiritual (and quiet) people may come to our churches, and your wealthiest (and cleanest) people may move into our communities, and your brightest children may come to our schools. But never forget: we expect regular hymns of gratitude for our condescension. Always remember that they are still ours and not yours—people and communities and schools and churches." And as an afterthought: "But of course we all love the same Christ."

Sensitized by apprehension

13   To this the angry children of Malcolm X shout fiercely: "To hell with you and your Christ! If you cannot live where we live, if your children cannot grow where we grow, if you cannot suffer what we suffer, if you cannot learn what we learn, we have no use for you or your cringing Christ. If we must come to where you are to find quality and life, then this nation is no good and integration is irrelevant."

14   Then Black Power leaders turn to the people of the ghettos. "Let us use the separateness that the white Christians have imposed upon us," they say to the black brothers. "Let us together find our own dignity and our own power, so that one day we may stand and face even those who have rejected us, no longer begging to be accepted into their dying world, but showing them a world transformed, a world where we have shaped our own destiny. We shall build communities of our own, where men are truly

brothers and goods are really shared. The American Christ is a Christ of separation and selfishness and relentless competition for an empty hole. We want no part of him."

15   Let there be no mistake. These evangels of a new movement are not deaf. They hear all the American words. They listen when good Christians ask: "Why should we pay our taxes to support those lazy deadbeats, those winos, those A.D.C. whores? Our money doesn't belong to them. Our money . . . our money . . ." Sensitized by long years of apprehension, the blacks need only look into the mirror to know who those "deadbeats" and "winos" are and what the "A.D.C. whores" look like. At the same time they wonder why the same white Christians sing no sad songs about tax rebates for General Motors' investments in South Africa's apartheid, and why they raise no complaints about the tax money given to farmers for planting nothing.

16   They open that American family magazine the *Saturday Evening Post* and find an enlightened northern editor saying to rebellious blacks that all whites are Mississippians at heart. He adds: "We will do our best, in a half-hearted way, to correct old wrongs. [Our] hand may be extended grudgingly and patronizingly, but anyone who rejects that hand rejects his own best interests." To those who live in the realm of Black Consciousness this snarling voice is the voice of the people of the American Christ. Out of their anguished indignation the black rebels reply: "We reject your limp, bloodied hand and your half-hearted help. We shall use our own black hands and lives to build power. We shall love our own people. We shall lead them to a new justice, based on the kind of power that America respects—not nonviolence and forgiveness, but votes and money and violent retaliation. We shall beg no more. You shall define our best interests no longer. Take your Mississippi hand and your Cicero Christ and may both of them be damned." That is Black Power.

17   As black men they have long seen into the heart of American darkness. They have no patriotic illusions about this nation's benevolent intentions toward the oppressed nonwhite people of the world, no matter how often the name and compassion of divinity are invoked. With eyes cleared by pain they discern the arrogance beneath the pious protestations. The American Christ leads the Hiroshima-bound bomber, blesses the Marines on their way to another in the long series of Latin American invasions, and blasphemously calls it peace when America destroys an entire Asian peninsula. And as black men they know from their own hard experience that these things can happen because this nation, led by an elder of the church, is determined to have its way in the world at any cost—to others. How often have the white-robed elders led the mob thirsting for the black man's blood!

18   Black people are not fooled by the churchly vestments of humility. They hear arrogant white pastors loudly counting dollars and members, and

committees smugly announcing the cost of their new modern churches—
hollow tombs for Christ. They hear the voices: "Negroes, oh Negroes, you
must be humble, like Christ. You must be patient and long-suffering.
Negroes, don't push so hard. Look at all we've given you so far." And the
voices trail off: "Negroes, dear Negroes, remember our Lord taught how
good it is to be meek and lowly." And then a whisper: "'Cause if you
don't, niggers, if you don't, we'll crush you."

So the Black Power advocates sanely shout, "Go to hell, you whited
sepulchers, hypocrites. All you want is to cripple our will and prolong our
agony, and you use your white Christ to do it." To the black people they
say: "Don't grovel, don't scrape. Whether you are 1 per cent or 50 per
cent or 100 per cent black, you are men, and you must affirm this in the
face of all the pious threats. You must proclaim your manhood just as the
white Christians do—in arrogance, in strength and in power. But the arrogance must be black, and the strength must be black, and black must
be the color of our power."

Christian blasphemers

20   Then comes the sharpest of all moments of truth, when Christian voices are raised in hostility and fear, directing their missionary chorus
to the young men drained of hope by the ghetto. "Black boys," they say,
"rampaging, screaming, laughing black boys, you must love—like Christ
and Doctor King. Black boys, please drop your firebombs. Violence never
solved anything. You must love your enemies—if they're white and American and represent law and order. You must love them for your rotting
houses and for your warped education. You must love them for your non-
existent jobs. Above all, you must love them for their riot guns, their billy
clubs, their hatred and their white, white skin."

21   It would be terrifying enough if the voices stopped on that emasculat-
ing note. But they go on: "Just the same, black boys, if the enemies have
been properly certified as such by our Christian leaders, and if they're poor
and brown and 10,000 miles away, you must hate them. You must scream
and rampage and kill them, black boys. Pick up the firebombs and char
them good. We have no civilian jobs for you, of course, but we have guns
and medals, and you must kill those gooks—even if some of them do
resemble the image reflected in the night-black pool of your tears."

22   What can a nation expect in response to such vicious words? It gets
the truth—far more than it deserves. For the black men reply: "Hypocrites, white hypocrites, you only want to save your skin and your piled-up
treasure from the just envy-anger of your former slaves, your present serfs
and your future victims. In the name of this Christ you deny our past,

demean our present and promise us no future save that of black merce-
naries in your assaults upon the world's dark and desperate poor."

23   Their rage cries out: "Give us no pink, two-faced Jesus who counsels
love for you and flaming death for the children of Vietnam. Give us no
blood-sucking savior who condemns brick-throwing rioters and praises
dive-bombing killers. That Christ stinks. We want no black men to follow
in *his* steps. Stop forcing our poor black boys into your legions of shame.
We will not go."

24   "If we must fight," they say, "let it be on the streets where we have
been humiliated. If we must burn down houses, let them be the homes
and stores of our exploiters. If we must kill, let it be the fat, pious white
Christians who guard their lawns and their daughters while engineering
slow death for us. If we must die, let it be for a real cause, the cause of
black men's freedom as black men define it. And may all the white elders
die well in the causes they defend." This is Black Power—the response to
the American Christ.

25   Unbelievable words? If any Christian dare call them blasphemous,
let him remember that the speakers make no claims about Christ or God.
Only we Christians—black and white—do that. If the just creator-father
God is indeed alive, and if Jesus of Nazareth was his Christ, then we
Christians are blasphemers. We are the ones who take his name in vain.
We are the ones who follow the phony American Christ and in our every
act declare our betrayal of the resurrected Lord.

26   If judgment stands sure it is not for Stokely Carmichael alone but
for all of us. It is we Christians who made the universal Christ into an
American mascot, a puppet blessing every mad American act, from the
extermination of the original possessors of this land to the massacre of
the Vietnamese on their own soil—even, perhaps, to the bombing of the
Chinese mainland in the name of peace.

27   If judgment stands sure it is not primarily upon SNCC that it will
fall, but upon those who have kidnaped the compassionate Jesus—the
Jesus who shared all he had, even his life, with the poor—and made him
into a profit-oriented, individualistic, pietistic cat who belongs to his own
narrowly-defined kind and begrudges the poor their humiliating subsistence budgets. These Christians are the ones who have taken away our
Lord and buried him in a place unknown.

28   We shall not escape by way of nostalgia or recrimination. For if he
whom we call the Christ is indeed the Suffering Servant of God and man,
what excuse can there be for those who have turned him into a crossless
puppet, running away from suffering with his flaxen locks flapping in the
wind?

29   If God is yet alive we cannot afford time to reminisce about the good
old days of the civil rights movement when everybody knew the words of
the songs. The time of singing may be past. It may be that America must

now stand under profound and damning judgment for having turned the redeeming lover of all men into a white, middle-class burner of children and destroyer of the revolutions of the oppressed.

Chance for redemption

30   This may be God's message for the church—through Black Power. It is a message for all who claim to love the Lord of the church. If this reading is accurate, our tears over the demise of the civil rights movement may really be tears over the smashing of an image we created or the withdrawal of a sign we were no longer heeding. Therefore if we weep, let it not be for the sins of SNCC and CORE but for our own unfaithfulness and for our country's blasphemy. And let us begin to pray that time may be granted us to turn from blond dolls to the living, revolutionary Lord who proclaimed that the first shall be last and the last, first.

31   If this message can break the grip of self-pity and nostalgia on us, the power of blackness may yet become the power of light and resurrection for us all. Has it not been said that God moves in mysterious ways his wonders to perform? I can conceive of nothing more wonderful and mysterious than that the blackness of my captive people should become a gift of light for this undeserving nation—even a source of hope for a world that lives daily under the threat of white America's arrogant and bloody power. Is that too much to hope for? Or is the time for hoping now past? We may soon discover whether we have been watching a wall or a curtain—or both.

Questions

1. Enumerate the ways in which Harding sees the American Christ as a cause of the Black Power movement.
2. Is this essay a well-constructed persuasive argument or simply an explanation of how a group of people feel about a set of historical facts? Regardless of how you decide, what are the crucial issues of Harding's position?
3. Harding fails to make certain admissions even though they would make his case more acceptable to a wider audience of white people. What are these admissions, and what does he gain by not including them? Distinguish between those that are implied and those he would not make.
4. Since Harding's purpose in this essay discussing the sources of its power does not include a discussion of the specific aims of the Black Power movement, we must infer what he sees them to be. Some help may be gained

from Stokely Carmichael: ("Power and Racism," *New York Review of Books,* September 22, 1966):

> Black people do not want to "take over" this country. They don't want to "get Whitey". . . . The white man is irrelevant to blacks, except as an oppressive force. Blacks want to be in his place, yes, but not in order to terrorize and lynch and starve him. They want to be in his place because that is where a decent life can be had.

What does Stokely Carmichael mean by "oppressive force"? How does Harding imply that the oppressive force may be made a constructive force?

5. What does Harding mean in paragraph 28: "We shall not escape by way of nostalgia or recrimination"?

Theme topics

1. Construct a more tightly argued, less passionate and persuasive, essay than Harding's to make the same point.
2. Write an analysis of the style of this essay.
3. Construct an argument in which you answer Harding's question in the next to last sentence: "Or is the time for hope now past?"
4. Write an argument refuting the following statement by an avowed American Christian: "A liberal is a man who wants to spend my money."

56   JOHN SIMON
The Boo Taboo

1   And the voice of the booer shall be heard in the land! What our theatres, opera houses and concert halls need is the introduction of the two-party system; as of now, all they have got is a dictatorship. It is the dictatorship of the assenters over the voices of dissent, of the applauders and cheerers over the booers and hissers, and its effect on our performing arts is to encourage the status quo, however mediocre or lamentable it may be. There is an urgent or, if I may say so, crying need for the voices of protest to be given equal rights and equal time.

2   In a pioneer essay on the subject, the famous English drama critic, James Agate, wrote: "It seems to me to be unfair to allow the happy fellow to blow off steam by means of applause, and to deny the miserable man

From *New York Magazine* I (June 24, 1968), pp. 46–48. Reprinted by permission of *New York Magazine* and John Simon.

that small amount of hissing and booing which presumably are his safety-valve." But although Agate's 1926 essay comes out in defense of booing, it does not pursue its subject beyond a few light-hearted remarks and droll suggestions. Let us examine more closely what makes an American audience in 1968 only applaud.

3   There are, obviously, those who applaud because they genuinely liked the play, opera, concert, recital or ballet. Their judgment may be questioned, but their motives can not. But what about the others, the fellow-grovelers? There are those who appplaud because it is the thing to do. There are those who believe, without any real feelings or opinions about what they have just witnessed, that applause shows discernment, connoisseurship, culture. There are others (and I proceed in an ascending order of sinisterness) who clap to show off: as if the loudness of their palms equaled the weightiness of their opinions. This group excels not only at the manual thunderclap but also at vocal bombardment. They erupt into promiscuous roars of *Bravo,* and even *Bravi* and *Brava,* to display either their knowledge of Italian, or their deftness in distinguishing the number and sex of the performers. At ballets, they applaud every last *entrechat,* drowning out the music and interrupting the flow of the work; at plays, they applaud every witticism, obliterating words and whole lines, and destroying the continuum of a scene. At the opera, they start their din in time to cut off the singer's last notes and the concluding orchestral accompaniment; at concerts, unfamiliar with the music, they applaud at the wrong places, and incite loud shushing. They want to get there with their noise first, loudest, and longest, their motto being, apparently, "I am heard, therefore I exist."

4   No better, however, are those who applaud because others are doing it, or because they have read favorable reviews, or because they firmly believe that whatever is put on at the Met, Philharmonic or Carnegie Hall, or at a large Broadway theatre is guaranteed to be good. Things do not change much; back in 1885 Shaw observed: "In every average audience there is a certain proportion of persons who make a point of getting as much as possible for their money—who will *encore,* if possible, until they have had a ballad for every penny in their shilling . . . There is also a proportion —a large one—of silly and unaccustomed persons who, excited by the novelty of being at a concert, and dazzled by the glitter and glory of the Bow-street temple of Art, madly applaud whenever anyone sets the example. Then there are good-natured people who lend a hand to encourage the singer. The honest and sensible members of the audience, even when they are a majority, are powerless against this combination of thoughtless good-nature, folly, and greed."

5   Needless to say, I am for applause and even for cheering, however magnanimous or misguided the motive. Though I understand the 1609 preface to *Troilus and Cressida,* which recommends the play as one "never clapper-clawed with the palms of the vulgar," I am more in agreement with

the imposing rages Paul Henry Lang, then music critic of *The Herald Tribune,* used to fly into every Eastertime when productions of *Parsifal* at the Met were greeted by the audience with reverential silence as though they were attending church services. But audience demonstrations should not interfere with what is happening on stage—does the entrance of a well-known actor have to be heralded by a clash of cymbal-like palms from the fans?—and, above all, they should not be the sole licensed spectator behavior, to the exclusion of counterdemonstrations. The boo and the hiss must also be franchised, as long as they do not obscure the actual sounds of performance.

6   I have used some political terminology deliberately. The American public must be awakened to the dignity and importance of art by education, criticism, and also—yes—by the lowly boo. Art matters fully as much as politics, the public must be told; for it is the politics of the spirit, while politics proper are the politics of the body. All that good government can give us is material well-being, the political and economic order and plenty enabling us to cultivate our minds and spirits. This cultivation, however, is the function of several disciplines—science, social science, philosophy, religion, etc.—not the least important, and possibly the most penetrating, of which is art. Thus what happens in the realm of the arts—which help us to see, feel, think and understand—is as significant as what happens in politics. Should then, I repeat, the politics of the mind and spirit be reduced to a one-party system?

7   The problem with the American audience is that it does not truly apprehend art. It is either in awe of it, or indifferent to it, or regards it as a commodity to be bought from time to time, like chutney or a new doormat. The first attitude stems from the Puritan origins of this country: the stage has taken over from the pulpit—which is quite an irony, considering how the Puritans loathed the theatre. The second attitude derives from general lack of culture: it takes, regrettably, centuries to acquire the kind of culture Europe, India, China and Japan can boast of (and relatively little time to lose it—but that is another story). The third attitude results from the materialism of this society. But the healthy attitude toward art is a spontaneous give-and-take between stage and auditorium, a frank expression of approval or dispraise.

8   In a diary entry for April 19, 1897, Gerhart Hauptmann wrote, "The playwright does not write for the stage but for the souls of men. The stage is a mediator between him and these souls." In a 1946 article, Jean Cocteau spoke of "the bouncing back and forth of balls between the audience and the playwright." Whether you think of the relationship as communion or contest, there has to be an easeful exchange between platform and pit. European audiences have not been afraid to boo or hiss (or, according to the local equivalent, whistle) plays, operas, performances, whatever displeased them. The tradition is an ancient one. It is said that

Euripides, approaching eighty, was driven from Athens by the jeers of his fellow-citizens. Far from cramping his style, this critical exile elicited from him *The Bacchae,* very possibly his most important play.

9   In our time, booing or its equivalent flourishes in many European countries. It reaches its acme at the Opera House in Parma, where the din of protesting audiences is sometimes considerably worse than what is being protested. But even this, for all its excess, strikes me as a sounder attitude than supine reverence without discrimination. For one thing, that audience really knows and cares about *bel canto,* and will not accept treasonable facsimiles. The singer may feel hurt, but if he is an artist sure of his ability, he will fight back and live to sing unhampered and applauded another day. As for the author, let me quote again from Agate's little essay: " 'A certain number of fleas is good for a dog,' once said an American humorist, 'it prevents him from brooding upon being a dog.' A certain amount of booing is good for a playwright; at any rate, it prevents him from brooding about being a successful one and thus growing intolerably vain."

10   Reminiscing about a director whom he admired, Brecht remarked in a 1939 lecture, "On Experimental Theatre," "Piscator's stage was not indifferent to applause, but it preferred a discussion." A discussion is all very well, of course, but hard to come by in a theatre or concert hall; the dialogue of applause and booing will, to some extent, take its place. Probably the most famous such contest occurred at the premiere of Victor Hugo's *Hernani,* of which I quote a brief account from *The Oxford Companion to French Literature:* "The first two performances of *Hernani* [at the Comédie Française, 25 and 27 Feb. 1830] count among the great battles of the Romantics. News had spread that the piece was in every way—subject, treatment, and versification—a break with the dramatic conventions, and the theatre was packed with partisans. Below, in the expensive seats, were the traditionalists, determined to crush the play and with it the dangerous innovations of the new School. Above were the hordes of Hugo's admirers—young writers, artists, and musicians—led by Théophile Gautier (wearing a cherry-coloured satin doublet which became legendary) and Petrus Borel, and all equally determined to win the day. At both performances they outclapped, outshouted, and generally outdid the occupants of the stalls and boxes, with such effect that the success of the play—and of the Romantic Movement—was thenceforth assured." The "Battle of *Hernani*" had actually begun in the street hours before curtain time, while Hugo supporters waited for the doors to open; one of them, Balzac, was hit in the face by a cabbage stalk a jeerer had plucked from the gutter.

11   But *Hernani* and Hugo prevailed, as Euripides had, as every important author, composer, performer has prevailed against unwarranted booing—and there is hardly an illustrious name in the verbal or musical theatre that escaped without some hisses and catcalls. But catcalls are cat-

nip to genius, and even to talent. On the other hand, I am persuaded that many an unworthy work or artist was hastened to oblivion by well-placed hisses and boos; unfortunately for the documentation of my case, histories of past fakes and no-talents do not get written. As for today's impostors, they are still very much with us—perhaps from a lack of vociferous opposition.

12   It is not that booing does not occur in New York; but it is usually isolated and ineffectual. One of the rare exceptions took place at Carnegie Hall when the superb Russian cellist, Mstislav Rostropovich, saw fit to compound his error of commissioning a work for cello and orchestra from Lukas Foss by actually performing that work. It was an aleatoric mess, its garishness heightened by having some of the instruments, including the soloist's cello, electronically amplified, and the thing was conducted by the cockily histrionic composer in a manner that was almost more offensive than the piece itself. The battle of jeers and cheers was truly invigorating to experience—I joined in heartily with the former—and the victory, I think, was ours. At any rate, the work (whose pretentious title I have happily forgotten) has not, to my knowledge, shown up in concert since.

13   As a critic of drama and film I, of course, do not boo plays and movies (it does little good to boo celluloid, in any case); I review them instead. But at other events, where I am a paying customer and not a critic, I feel free to boo. When the Hamburg State Opera brought to New York its production of Gunther Schuller's derivative, pretentious, and vacuous *The Visitation* (an inept transposition of Kafka's *The Trial* into a simplistic American South), there was, I gather, quite some booing at its first performance at the Met. I attended the second, at which, for whatever reason, there were no boos, except for mine at the final curtain. A man came up to me and congratulated me on my good sense and courage. This was typical: the average American theatregoer, even when he realizes that he is being abused, wants someone else to do his protesting for him.

14   Another good time to protest is when the theatre provides a largely homosexual audience with Instant Camp. I remember, for example, a Poulenc memorial concert in Carnegie Hall, shortly after the composer's death. Among other events, Jennie Tourel performed some Poulenc songs, accompanied by Leonard Bernstein. There was Miss Tourel, the vocal and visual wreck of a once passable singer: splintered voice, wizened and overmade-up face, decrepit figure stuffed into a militantly Shirley Temple-ish outfit. At the piano, Bernstein was at his ham-actorish best. The two, when they were not loving up the audience, flirted with each other, throwing lateral kisses, courtseys, and lovelorn *oeillades* across the stage. When they did get around to Poulenc, Miss Tourel not only made the songs crack in more directions than her made-up, she even burdened the lovely French words with something like a full-blown Bronx accent. Meanwhile, inverting

the usual procedure, the ivories seemed to be tickling Leonard Bernstein, who was carrying on like a cockatoo in orgasm. When this appalling Lenny and Jennie act was over, I naturally booed it. A Frenchwoman, in the intermission, came up to shake my hand; several of my acquaintances in that generally orgiastic audience carefully cut me dead.

15   The most illuminating occurrence for me was a recent Saturday matinee at the Met. It was Barrault's wretched staging of *Carmen,* with Richard Tucker as Don José. Now Tucker had once been in possession of a good, strong voice; but he had never been a genuine artist with a sensé of shading, expressive range, a feeling for the emotional depth of the part or the language in which he was singing. By this time, with even his basic organ gone, Tucker is long overdue for retirement. In this Don José, Tucker's voice was as off as it had been for years, his phrasing as unlovely as it had always been. Visually, he was a geriatric travesty; histrionically, even by the shockingly low standards of operatic acting, a farce. Even his French was, let us say, hyper-Tourelian. After he got through mangling the Flower Song, and after the orchestra was through as well, I added to the general applause three loud *phooeys*—a *phooey* cuts through applause better than a boo or hiss.

16   The reaction was instantaneous. From several boxes around the one I sat in came frantic retaliation—mostly of the "Shut up!" or "How dare you?" or "Go home!" variety, though one middle-aged woman intoned lachrymosely, "He has given you *years* of beauty!" When the lights went on, Rudolf Bing, who was sitting a couple of boxes away, had already dispatched his Pinkerton men after me, right into the box; but I walked out ignoring their reprimands. In the corridor, I was set upon by a mob of some 20 or 30 people berating me and following me almost to the bar with their objurgations and insults. The gist of it was that this sort of thing wasn't tolerated here, and if I was a foreign guest, I should behave or get the hell back wherever I came from. And that if I did not like it, I could not applaud or just leave. I countered that it did not seem to me fair and democratic to allow musical illiterates to clap and bellow their approval to their hearts' content, while someone who recognized the desecration of art was condemned to polite silence. In the following intermission (there had been no further incident during the next act), one of Bing's hugest goons, scowling ferociously, was back in the box once more, this time accompanied by a polite and human-sized person who introduced himself courteously as James Heffernan, house manager.

17   To summarize the ensuing battle of wits—if that is the term for it— Mr. Heffernan's point was that in Italy, where such a tradition exists, booing was fine, but that in "this house" it just wasn't done. My point was that if there was no such tradition here, it was high time to instigate one for the need was dire. Heffernan put forward that such booing might discourage the singer, to which I replied that that *was* the general idea. He

then said that other people enjoying the performance were disturbed. I indicated that my boos did not come during the performing, which is more than could be said for some of the bravos and applause, and that if the audience had so little confidence in its own enthusiasm that one booer could make them doubt it, maybe doubt was called for. I added that if he wanted to exercise his authority usefully, he might go after the ignorant parvenus who talk through performances when they are not rattling their candy wrappers or jangling their vulgar bracelets. He admitted that this was a nuisance, but that, still and all, if I wished to protest, which he generously granted me the right to do, I should send a letter to Mr. Bing or Mr. Tucker. I told him that I would gladly write both of them my request that they retire, but that I doubted they would get my message. (The eminent poet and librettist, W. H. Auden, has remarked that he will not set foot in the Met while Bing is running it.) So, with a mixture of pleading and threatening looks, Heffernan and his sidekick left. I suspect that had my date and I been less well dressed, and had our seats been less expensive, the treatment accorded us would have been rather less ceremonious.

18   One understands, without condoning, the management's attitude— particularly when a boo is heard, thanks to Texaco, across the U.S. and Canada. But the fury of the audience needs analyzing. It is caused, in part, by the middle-class American's confusion of critical indignation with bad manners, his incomprehension that at a theatre or opera house more is at stake than in your or the Jones's parlor. But, more importantly, it is the anger of the insecure *nouveau riche* who has paid a dozen Dollars for his seat, and who, for that much money, wants to be sure he is getting grade-A, U.S.-certified culture. He himself hasn't the foggiest notion what that might be; so if a boo implies that he might be gettting damaged goods and, worse yet, be duped by them, his defensive dander is up.

19   As for the performer's attitude, it is useful to consult the epilogue of William Redfield's *Letters from an Actor* to find out how Richard Burton responded to one solitary booer of his Hamlet: in boundless fury at his wife's refusing to commiserate with him, he kicked in a television screen with his bare foot, damaging his toes as well. And it is even more enlightening to see how Redfield, who acted in that *Hamlet,* interprets the incident: "Now a booer, rare though he be, can be evaluated in a number of ways: (1) He is probably drunk, (2) if he isn't drunk, he is likely a frustrated actor, (3) if he is neither, he is certainly a minority, for booing is not a custom among American audiences, (4) he may very well be wrong." To which I should like to add (5), which hardly occurs to Redfield, that he may very well be right.

20   It is quite true in this country that the moment someone boos, the majority of the audience, including formerly passive elements, consider it their sacred duty to bravo and applaud for dear life, and prove thereby their dissociation from and superiority to the infamous booer. So booers

will not have an easy time of it, either inside the hall or in the corridors outside. Sometimes, as in the case of *Hernani* (a poor play, by the way), history itself will prove them wrong. Yet in a day when the theatre is in sad shape, sinking ever deeper into public apathy, audience participation, sometimes of the most desperate kind, is universally viewed as the salvation. Booing, as long as it does not drown out the actual performance, seems to me a valid form of audience participation, one that would convince the lethargic of how vitally concerned some people are with the theatre. The effect on the authors and performers would be to keep them more in trim. And indignation, unhealthily stifled, would not force many out of the theatres altogether. We must stop being a nation of sheep-like theatregoers who wouldn't say boo to a goose—or turkey.

Society and the Individual

57   PLATO
Crito

SOCRATES. Why have you come at this hour, Crito? It must be quite early?

CRITO. Yes, certainly.

SOCRATES. What is the exact time?

CRITO. The dawn is breaking.

SOCRATES. I wonder that the keeper of the prison would let you in.

CRITO. He knows me, because I often come, Socrates; moreover I have done
him a kindness.

SOCRATES. And are you only just come?

CRITO. No, I came some time ago.

SOCRATES. Then why did you sit and say nothing, instead of awakening me   10
at once?

CRITO. Why, indeed, Socrates, I myself would rather not have all this sleep-
lessness and sorrow. But I have been wondering at your peaceful slum-
bers, and that was the reason why I did not awaken you, because I
wanted you to be out of pain. I have always thought you happy in the
calmness of your temperament; but never did I see the like of the easy,
cheerful way in which you bear this calamity.

SOCRATES. Why, Crito, when a man has reached my age he ought not to be
repining at the prospect of death.

CRITO. And yet other old men find themselves in similar misfortunes, and   20
age does not prevent them from repining.

From *The Works of Plato,* translated by Benjamin Jowett. Published by The Claren-
don Press, Oxford.
    Socrates, in Plato's *Apology,* states the charge against him: "Socrates is an evil-
doer, and a curious person, who searches into things under the earth and in heaven,
and he makes the worse appear the better cause; and he teaches the aforesaid doctrines to others." The word *evildoer* in the above quotation is defined by the remainder of the quotation. There is no other action than that of free inquiry of which
Socrates was guilty.

SOCRATES. That may be. But you have not told me why you come at this early hour.

CRITO. I come to bring you a message which is sad and painful; not, as I believe, to yourself, but to all of us who are your friends, and saddest of all to me.

SOCRATES. What! I suppose that the ship has come from Delos, on the arrival of which I am to die?

CRITO. No, the ship has not actually arrived, but she will probably be here to-day, as persons who have come from Sunium tell me that they left her there; and therefore to-morrow, Socrates, will be the last day of 10 your life.

SOCRATES. Very well, Crito; such is the will of God, I am willing; but my belief is that there will be a delay of a day.

CRITO. Why do you say this?

SOCRATES. I will tell you. I am to die on the day after the arrival of the ship?

CRITO. Yes; that is what the authorities say.

SOCRATES. But I do not think that the ship will be here until to-morrow; this I gather from a vision which I had last night, or rather only just now, when you fortunately allowed me to sleep.

CRITO. And what was the nature of the vision? 20

SOCRATES. There came to me the likeness of a woman, fair and comely, clothed in white raiment, who called to me and said: "O Socrates, the third day hence to Phthia shalt thou go."

CRITO. What a singular dream, Socrates!

SOCRATES. There can be no doubt about the meaning, Crito, I think.

CRITO. Yes; the meaning is only too clear. But, Oh! my beloved Socrates, let me entreat you once more to take my advice and escape. For if you die I shall not only lose a friend who can never be replaced, but there is another evil: people who do not know you and me will believe that I might have saved you if I had been willing to give money, but that I 30 did not care. Now, can there be a worse disgrace than this—that I should be thought to value money more than the life of a friend? For the many will not be persuaded that I wanted you to escape, and that you refused.

SOCRATES. But why, my dear Crito, should we care about the opinion of the many? Good men, and they are the only persons who are worth considering, will think of these things truly as they happened.

CRITO. But do you see, Socrates, that the opinion of the many must be regarded, as is evident in your own case, because they can do the very greatest evil to any one who has lost their good opinion. 40

SOCRATES. I only wish, Crito, that they could; for then they could also do the greatest good, and that would be well. But the truth is, that they can do neither good nor evil: they can not make a man wise or make him foolish; and whatever they do is the result of chance.

CRITO. Well, I will not dispute about that; but please to tell me, Socrates,
whether you are not acting out of regard to me and your other friends:
are you not afraid that if you escape hence we may get into trouble
with the informers for having stolen you away, and lose either the
whole or a great part of our property; or that even a worse evil may
happen to us? Now, if this is your fear, be at ease; for in order to save
you we ought surely to run this, or even a greater risk; be persuaded,
then, and do as I say.

SOCRATES. Yes. Crito, that is one fear which you mention, but by no means
the only one.

CRITO. Fear not. There are persons who at no great cost are willing to save
you and bring you out of prison; and as for the informers, you may
observe that they are far from being exorbitant in their demands; a little money will satisfy them. My means, which, as I am sure, are ample,
are at your service, and if you have a scruple about spending all mine,
here are strangers who will give you the use of theirs; and one of them,
Simmias the Theban, has brought a sum of money for this very purpose; and Cebes and many others are willing to spend their money too.
I say therefore, do not on that account hesitate about making your
escape, and do not say, as you did in the court, that you will have a
difficulty in knowing what to do with yourself if you escape. For men
will love you in other places to which you may go, and not in Athens
only; there are friends of mine in Thessaly, if you like to go to them,
who will value and protect you, and no Thessalian will give you any
trouble. Nor can I think that you are justified, Socrates, in betraying
your own life when you might be saved; this is playing into the hands
of your enemies and destroyers; and moreover I should say that you
were betraying your children; for you might bring them up and educate
them; instead of which you go away and leave them, and they will have
to take their chance; and if they do not meet with the usual fate of
orphans, there will be small thanks to you. No man should bring children into the world who is unwilling to persevere to the end in their
nurture and education. But you are choosing the easier part, as I think,
not the better and manlier, which would rather have become one who
professes virtue in all his actions, like yourself. And indeed, I am
ashamed not only of you, but of us who are your friends, when I reflect
that this entire business of yours will be attributed to our want of
courage. The trial need never have come on, or might have been
brought to another issue; and the end of all, which is the crowning
absurdity, will seem to have been permitted by us, through cowardice
and baseness, who might have saved you, as you might have saved
yourself, if we had been good for anything (for there was no difficulty
in escaping); and we did not see how disgraceful, Socrates, and also

miserable all this will be to us as well as to you. Make your mind up then, or rather have your mind already made up, for the time of deliberation is over, and there is only one thing to be done, which must be done, if at all, this very night, and which any delay will render all but impossible; I beseech you therefore, Socrates, to be persuaded by me, and to do as I say.

SOCRATES. Dear Crito, your zeal is invaluable, if a right one; but if wrong, the greater the zeal the greater the evil; and therefore we ought to consider whether these things shall be done or not. For I am and always have been one of those natures who must be guided by reason, whatever the reason may be which upon reflection appears to me to be the best; and now that this fortune has come upon me, I can not put away the reasons which I have before given: the principles which I have hitherto honored and revered I still honor, and unless we can find other and better principles on the instant, I am certain not to agree with you; no, not even if the power of the multitude could inflict many more imprisonments, confiscations, deaths, frightening us like children with hobgoblin terrors. But what will be the fairest way of considering the question? Shall I return to your old argument about the opinions of men? some of which are to be regarded, and others, as we were saying, are not to be regarded. Now were we right in maintaining this before I was condemned? And has the argument which was once good now proved to be talk for the sake of talking;—in fact an amusement only, and altogether vanity? That is what I want to consider with your help, Crito:—whether, under my present circumstances, the argument appears to be in any way different or not; and is to be allowed by me or disallowed. That argument, which, as I believe, is maintained by many who assume to be authorities, was to the effect, as I was saying, that the opinions of some men are to be regarded, and of other men not to be regarded. Now you, Crito, are a disinterested person who are not going to die tomorrow—at least, there is no human probability of this, and you are therefore not liable to be deceived by the circumstances in which you are placed. Tell me then, whether I am right in saying that some opinions, and the opinions of some men only, are to be valued, and other opinions, and the opinions of other men, are not to be valued. I ask you whether I was right in maintaining this?

CRITO. Certainly.

SOCRATES. The good are to be regarded, and not the bad?

CRITO. Yes.

SOCRATES. And the opinions of the wise are good, and the opinions of the unwise are evil?

CRITO. Certainly.

SOCRATES. And what was said about another matter? Was the disciple in gymnastics supposed to attend to the praise and blame and opinion of every man, or of one man only—his physician or trainer, whoever that was?

CRITO. Of one man only.

SOCRATES. And he ought to fear the censure and welcome the praise of that one only, and not of the many?

CRITO. That is clear.

SOCRATES. And he ought to live and train, and eat and drink in the way which seems good to his single master who has understanding, rather than according to the opinion of all other men put together?   10

CRITO. True.

SOCRATES. And if he disobeys and disregards the opinion and approval of the one, and regards the opinion of the many who have no understanding, will he not suffer evil?

CRITO. Certainly he will.

SOCRATES. And what will the evil be, whither tending and what affecting, in the disobedient person?

CRITO. Clearly, affecting the body; that is what is destroyed by the evil.

SOCRATES. Very good; and is not this true, Crito, of other things which we need not separately enumerate? In the matter of just and unjust, fair   20 and foul, good and evil, which are the subjects of our present consultation, ought we to follow the opinion of the many and to fear them; or the opinion of the one man who has understanding, and whom we ought to fear and reverence more than all the rest of the world: and whom deserting we shall destroy and injure that principle in us which may be assumed to be improved by justice and deteriorated by injustice;—is there not such a principle?

CRITO. Certainly there is, Socrates.

SOCRATES. Takes a parallel instance:—if, acting under the advice of men who have no understanding, we destroy that which is improvable by   30 health and deteriorated by disease—when that has been destroyed, I say, would life be worth having? And that is—the body?

CRITO. Yes.

SOCRATES. Could we live, having an evil and corrupted body?

CRITO. Certainly not.

SOCRATES. And will life be worth having, if that higher part of man be depraved, which is improved by justice and deteriorated by injustice? Do we suppose that principle, whatever it may be in man, which has to do with justice and injustice, to be inferior to the body?

CRITO. Certainly not.   40

SOCRATES. More honored, then?

CRITO. Far more honored.

SOCRATES. Then, my friend, we must not regard what the many say of us: but what he, the one man who has understanding of just and unjust,

will say, and what the truth will say. And therefore you begin in error
when you suggest that we should regard the opinion of the many about
just and unjust, good and evil, honorable and dishonorable.—Well,
some one will say, "but the many can kill us."

CRITO. Yes, Socrates; that will clearly be the answer.

SOCRATES. That is true: but still I find with surprise that the old argument
is, as I conceive, unshaken as ever. And I should like to know whether
I may say the same of another proposition—that not life, but a good
life, is to be chiefly valued?

CRITO. Yes, that also remains.   10

SOCRATES. And a good life is equivalent to a just and honorable one—that
holds also?

CRITO. Yes, that holds.

SOCRATES. From these premises I proceed to argue the question whether I
ought or ought not to try and escape without the consent of the Athenians: and if I am clearly right in escaping, then I will make the
attempt; but if not, I will abstain. The other considerations which you
mention, of money and loss of character and the duty of educating children, are, as I fear, only the doctrines of the multitude, who would be
as ready to call people to life, if they were able, as they are to put them   20
to death—and with as little reason. But now, since the argument has
thus far prevailed, the only question which remains to be considered is,
whether we shall do rightly either in escaping or in suffering others to
aid in our escape and paying them in money and thanks, or whether
we shall not do rightly; and if the latter, then death or any other calamity which may ensue on my remaining here must not be allowed to
enter into the calculation.

CRITO. I think that you are right, Socrates; how then shall we proceed?

SOCRATES. Let us consider the matter together, and do you either refute
me if you can, and I will be convinced, or else cease, my dear friend,   30
from repeating to me that I ought to escape against the wishes of the
Athenians: for I am extremely desirous to be persuaded by you, but
not against my own better judgment. And now please to consider my
first position, and do your best to answer me.

CRITO. I will do my best.

SOCRATES. Are we to say that we are never intentionally to do wrong, or
that in one way we ought and in another way we ought not to do wrong,
or is doing wrong always evil and dishonorable, as I was just now saying, and as has been already acknowledged by us? Are all of our former
admissions which were made within a few days to be thrown away?   40
And have we, at our age, been earnestly discoursing with one another
all our life long only to discover that we are no better than children?
Or are we to rest assured, in spite of the opinion of the many, and in
spite of consequences whether better or worse, of the truth of what

was then said, that injustice is always an evil and dishonor to him who acts unjustly? Shall we affirm that?

CRITO. Yes.

SOCRATES. Then we must do no wrong?

CRITO. Certainly not.

SOCRATES. Nor when injured injure in return, as the many imagine; for we must injure no one at all?

CRITO. Clearly not.

SOCRATES. Again, Crito, may we do evil?

CRITO. Surely not, Socrates.

SOCRATES. And what of doing evil in return for evil, which is the morality of the many—is that just or not?

CRITO. Not just.

SOCRATES. For doing evil to another is the same as injuring him?

CRITO. Very true.

SOCRATES. Then we ought not to retaliate or render evil for evil to anyone, whatever evil we may have suffered from him. But I would have you consider, Crito, whether you really mean what you are saying. For this opinion has never been held, and never will be held, by any considerable number of persons; and those who are agreed and those who are not agreed upon this point have no common ground, and can only despise one another when they see how widely they differ. Tell me, then, whether you agree with and assent to my first principle, that neither injury nor retaliation nor warding off evil by evil is ever right. And shall that be the premise of our argument? Or do you decline and dissent from this? For this has been of old and is still my opinion; but, if you are of another opinion, let me hear what you have to say. If, however, you remain of the same mind as formerly, I will proceed to the next step.

CRITO. You may proceed, for I have not changed my mind.

SOCRATES. Then I will proceed to the next step, which may be put in the form of a question:—Ought a man to do what he admits to be right, or ought he to betray the right?

CRITO. He ought to do what he thinks right.

SOCRATES. But if this is true, what is the application? In leaving the prison against the will of the Athenians, do I wrong any? or rather do I not wrong those whom I ought least to wrong? Do I not desert the principles which were acknowledged by us to be just? What do you say?

CRITO. I can not tell, Socrates; for I do not know.

SOCRATES. Then consider the matter in this way:—Imagine that I am about to play truant (you may call the proceeding by any name which you like), and the laws and the government come and interrogate me: "Tell us, Socrates," they say; "what are you about? are you going by an act of yours to overturn us—the laws and the whole state, as far as in you lies? Do you imagine that a state can subsist and not be overthrown, in which the decisions of law have no power, but are set aside and overthrown by individuals?" What will be our answer, Crito, to these and the like words? Anyone, and especially a clever rhetorician, will have a good deal to urge about the evil of setting aside the law which requires a sentence to be carried out; and we might reply, "Yes; but the state has injured us and given an unjust sentence." Suppose I say that?

CRITO. Very good, Socrates.

SOCRATES. "And was that our agreement with you?" the law would say; "or were you to abide by the sentence of the state?" And if I were to express astonishment at their saying this, the law would probably add: "Answer, Socrates, instead of opening your eyes: you are in the habit of asking and answering questions. Tell us what complaint you have to make against us which justifies you in attempting to destroy us and the state? In the first place did we not bring you into existence? Your father married your mother by our aid and begat you. Say whether you have any objection to urge against those of us who regulate marriage?" None, I should reply. "Or against those of us who regulate the system of nurture and education of children in which you were trained? Were not the laws, who have the charge of this, right in commanding your father to train you in music and gymnastic?" Right, I should reply. "Well then, since you were brought into the world and nurtured and educated by us, can you deny in the first place that you are our child and slave, as your fathers were before you? And if this is true you are not on equal terms with us; nor can you think that you have a right to do to us what we are doing to you. Would you have any right to strike or revile or do any other evil to a father or to your master, if you had one, when you have been struck or reviled by him, or received some other evil at his hands?—you would not say this? And because we think right to destroy you, do you think that you have any right to destroy us in return, and your country as far as in you lies? And will you, O professor of true virtue, say that you are justified in this? Has a philosopher like you failed to discover that our country is more to be valued and higher and holier far than mother or father or any ancestor, and more to be regarded in the eyes of the gods and of men of understanding? also to be soothed, and gently and reverently entreated when angry, even more than a father, and if not persuaded, obeyed? And when we are punished by her, whether with imprisonment or stripes, the punishment is to be endured in silence; and if she lead us to wounds or death in battle, thither we follow as is right; neither may any one yield or retreat or leave his rank, but whether in battle or in a court of law, or in any other place, he must do what his city and his country order him; or he must change their view of what is just: and if he may do no violence to his father or mother, much less may he do violence to his country." What answer shall we make to this, Crito? Do the laws speak truly, or do they not?

CRITO. I think that they do.

SOCRATES. Then the laws will say: "Consider, Socrates, if this is true, that in your present attempt you are going to do us wrong. For, after having brought you into the world, and nurtured and educated you, and given you and every other citizen a share in every good that we had to give, we further proclaim and give the right to every Athenian, that if he does not like us when he has come of age and has seen the ways of the city, and made our acquaintance, he may go where he pleases and take his goods with him; and none of us laws will forbid him or interfere with him. Any of you who does not like us and the city, and who wants to go to a colony or to any other city, may go where he likes, and take his goods with him. But he who has experience of the manner in which we order justice and administer the state, and still remains, has entered into an implied contract that he will do as we command him. And he who disobeys us is, as we maintain, thrice wrong; first, because in disobeying us he is disobeying his parents; secondly, because we are the authors of his education; thirdly, because he has made an agreement with us that he will duly obey our commands; and he neither obeys them nor con- vinces us that our commands are wrong; and we do not rudely impose them, but give them the alternative of obeying or convincing us;—that is what we offer, and he does neither. These are the sort of accusations to which, as we were saying, you, Socrates, will be exposed if you ac- complish your intentions; you, above all other Athenians." Suppose I ask, why is this? they will justly retort upon me that I above all other men have acknowledged the agreement. "There is clear proof," they will say, "Socrates, that we and the city were not displeasing to you. Of all Athenians you have been the most constant resident in the city, which, as you never leave, you may be supposed to love. For you never went out of the city either to see the games, except once when you went to the Isthmus, or to any other place unless when you were on military service; nor did you travel as other men do. Nor had you any curiosity to know other states or their laws: your affections did not go beyond us and our state; we were your special favorites, and you acquiesced in our government of you; and this is the state in which you begat your children, which is proof of your satisfaction. Moreover, you might, if you had liked, have fixed the penalty at banishment in the course of the trial—the state which refuses to let you go now would have let you go then. But you pretended that you preferred death to exile, and that you were not grieved at death. And now you have forgotten these fine sen- timents, and pay no respect to us the laws, of whom you are the de- stroyer; and are doing what only a miserable slave would do, running away and turning your back upon the compacts and agreements which you made as a citizen. And first of all answer this very question: Are we right in saying that you agreed to be governed according to us in deed, and not in word only? Is that true or not?" How shall we answer that, Crito? Must we not agree?

CRITO. There is no help, Socrates.

SOCRATES. Then will they not say: "You, Socrates, are breaking the covenants and agreements which you made with us at your leisure, not in any haste or under any compulsion or deception, but having had seventy years to think of them, during which time you were at liberty to leave the city, if we were not to your mind, or if our covenants appeared   10 to you to be unfair. You had your choice, and might have gone either to Lacedaemon or Crete, which you often praise for their good government, or to some other Hellenic or foreign state. Whereas you, above all other Athenians, seemed to be so fond of the state, or, in other words, for us her laws (for who would like a state that has no laws), that you never stirred out of her; the halt, the blind, the maimed were not more stationary in her than you were. And now you run away and forsake your agreements. Not so, Socrates, if you will take our advice; do not make yourself ridiculous by escaping out of the city.

"For just consider, if you transgress and err in this sort of way,   20 what good will you do either to yourself or to your friends? That your friends will be driven into exile and deprived of citizenship, or will lose their property, is tolerably certain; and you yourself, if you fly to one of the neighboring cities, as, for example, Thebes or Megara, both of which are well-governed cities, will come to them as an enemy, Socrates, and their government will be against you, and all patriotic citizens will cast an evil eye upon you as a subverter of the laws, and you will confirm in the minds of the judges the justice of their own condemnation of you. For he who is a corrupter of the laws is more than likely to be corrupter of the young and foolish portion of mankind. Will you then   30 flee from well-ordered cities and virtuous men? and is existence worth having on these terms? Or will you go to them without shame, and talk to them, Socrates? And what will you say to them? What you say here about virtue and justice and institutions and laws being the best things among men. Would that be decent of you? Surely not. But if you go away from well-governed states to Crito's friends in Thessaly, where there is a great disorder and license, they will be charmed to have the tale of your escape from prison, set off with ludicrous particulars of the manner in which you were wrapped in a goatskin or some other disguise, and metamorphosed as the fashion of runaways is—that is very   40 likely; but will there be no one to remind you that in your old age you violated the most sacred laws from a miserable desire of a little more life. Perhaps not, if you keep them in a good temper; but if they are out of temper you will hear many degrading things; *you will live, but how?*

—as the flatterer of all men, and the servant of all men; and doing what?—eating and drinking in Thessaly, having gone abroad in order that you may get a dinner. And where will be your fine sentiments about justice and virtue then? Say that you wish to live for the sake of your *children,* that you may bring them up and educate them—will you take them into Thessaly and deprive them of Athenian citizenship? Is that the benefit which you would confer upon them? Or are you under the impression that they will be better cared for and educated here if you are still alive, although absent from them; or that your friends will take care of them? Do you fancy that if you are an inhabi- 10
tant of Thessaly they will take care of them, and if you are an inhabitant of the other world they will not take care of them? Nay; but if they who call themselves friends are truly friends, they surely will.

"Listen, then, Socrates, to us who have brought you up. Think not of life and children first, and of justice afterwards, but of justice first, that you may be justified before the princes of the world below. For neither will you or any that belong to you be happier or holier or juster in this life, or happier in another, if you do as Crito bids. Now you depart in innocence, a sufferer and not a doer of evil; a victim, not of the laws, but of men. But if you go forth, returning evil for evil, and 20
injury for injury, breaking the covenants and agreements which you have made with us, and wronging those whom you ought least to wrong, that is to say, yourself, your friends, your country, and us, we shall be angry with you while you live, and our brethren, the laws in the world below, will receive you as an enemy; for they will know that you have done your best to destroy us. Listen, then, to us and not to Crito."

This is the voice which I seem to hear murmuring in my ears, like the sound of the flute in the ears of the mystic; that voice, I say, is humming in my ears, and prevents me from hearing any other. And I 30
know that anything more which you may say will be vain. Yet speak, if you have anything to say.

CRITO. I have nothing to say, Socrates.

SOCRATES. Then let me follow the intimations of the will of God.

Questions

1. When Socrates says that the many can make a man neither wise nor foolish and that what they do is the result of chance, what does he mean?

2. If the opinion of the many can result in the death of Socrates, why does he rebuke Crito for saying that the many can do the greatest evil to one who has lost their good opinion?

3. Show how Socrates' position in the argument with Crito—and presumably

his entire life and thought—is based on the following premise (or absolute):
"Not life, but a good life is to be chiefly valued."

4. What for Socrates is the good life and what is its relation to his distinction between "the one and the many?" If the one is to be valued over the many, why, as Socrates presumably reports on the voices humming in his ear, are the many (i.e. the laws) so decisive in the argument?

5. How will Socrates harm the state by escaping?

6. What absolute (or premise) underlies Crito's arguments for urging Socrates to escape? How could you argue more persuasively from this same absolute?

7. What relationship exists between Socrates' absolute and the last line of the dialogue: "Then let me follow the intimations of the will of God"?

8. If the opinion of the good—who are few in number—should be regarded only, how shall we recognize them when they speak?

9. How is the basic relation between the state and its citizens in the United States today different from or similar to that of the state and its citizens in ancient Athens?

Theme topics

1. Write a summary of Socrates' reasoning and his decision.

2. Write an essay showing the contemporary importance of Socrates' view of the opinion of the many.

3. Write a dialogue, as realistic as possible, to illustrate the irrationality of most people's thinking in certain areas; one party should attempt either to persuade the other to or dissuade him from a certain decision and course of action.

58   JONATHAN SWIFT

A Modest Proposal

for preventing the Children of poor People in Ireland, *from being a Burden to their Parents or Country; and for making them beneficial to the Publick.* (Written in the Year 1729)

1   IT is a melancholly Object to those, who walk through this great Town, or travel in the Country; when they see the *Streets,* the *Roads,* and *Cabbin-doors* crowded with *Beggars* of the Female Sex, followed by three, four, or six Children, *all in Rags,* and importuning every Passenger for an

Alms.   These *Mothers,* instead of being able to work for their honest Livelyhood, are forced to employ all their Time in stroling to beg Sustenance for their *helpless Infants;* who, as they grow up, either turn *Thieves* for want of Work; or leave their *dear Native Country, to fight for the Pretender in* Spain, or sell themselves to the *Barbadoes.*

2   I THINK it is agreed by all Parties, that this prodigious Number of Children in the Arms, or on the Backs, or at the *Heels* of their *Mothers,* and frequently of their *Fathers,* is *in the present deplorable State of the Kingdom,* a very great additional Grievance; and therefore, whoever could find out a fair, cheap, and easy Method of making these Children sound and useful Members of the Commonwealth, would deserve so well of the Publick, as to have his Statue set up for a Preserver of the Nation.

3   BUT my Intention is very far from being confined to provide only for the Children of *professed Beggars*: It is of a much greater Extent, and shall take in the whole Number of Infants at a certain Age, who are born of Parents, in effect as little able to support them, as those who demand our Charity in the Streets.

4   AS to my own Part, having turned my Thoughts for many Years, upon this important Subject, and maturely weighed the several *Schemes of other Projectors,* I have always found them grosly mistaken in their Computation. It is true a Child, *just dropt from its Dam,* may be supported by her Milk, for a Solar Year with little other Nourishment; at most not above the Value of two Shillings; which the Mother may certainly get, or the Value in *Scraps,* by her lawful Occupation of *Begging*: And, it is exactly at one Year old, that I propose to provide for them in such a Manner, as, instead of being a Charge upon their *Parents,* or the *Parish,* or *wanting Food and Raiment* for the rest of their Lives; they shall, on the contrary, contribute to the Feeding, and partly to the Cloathing, of many Thousands.

5   THERE is likewise another great Advantage in my *Scheme,* that it will prevent those *voluntary Abortions,* and that horrid Practice of *Women murdering their Bastard Children*; alas! too frequent among us; sacrificing the *poor innocent Babes,* I doubt, more to avoid the Expence than the Shame; which would move Tears and Pity in the most Savage and inhuman Breast.

6   THE Number of Souls in *Ireland* being usually reckoned one Million and a half; of these I calculate there may be about Two hundred Thousand Couple whose Wives are Breeders; from which Number I subtract thirty thousand Couples, who are able to maintain their own Children; although I apprehend there cannot be so many, under *the present Distresses of the Kingdom*; but this being granted, there will remain an Hundred and Seventy Thousand Breeders. I again subtract Fifty Thousand, for those Women who miscarry, or whose Children die by Accident, or Disease, within the Year. There only remain an Hundred and Twenty Thousand Children of poor Parents, annually born: The Question therefore is, How

this Number shall be reared, and provided for? Which, as I have already said, under the present Situation of Affairs, is utterly impossible, by all the Methods hitherto proposed: For we can *neither employ them in Handicraft* or *Agriculture*; we neither build Houses, (I mean in the Country) nor cultivate Land: They can very seldom pick up a Livelyhood *by Stealing* until they arrive at six Years old; except where they are of towardly Parts; although, I confess, they learn the Rudiments much earlier; during which Time, they can, however, be properly looked upon only as *Probationers*; as I have been informed by a principal Gentleman in the County of *Cavan,* who protested to me, that he never knew above one or two Instances under the Age of six, even in a Part of the Kingdom *so renowned for the quickest Proficiency in that Art.*

7   I AM assured by our Merchants, that a Boy or a Girl before twelve Years old, is no saleable Commodity; and even when they come to this Age, they will not yield above Three Pounds, or Three Pounds and half a Crown at most, on the Exchange; which cannot turn to Account either to the Parents or the Kingdom; the Charge of Nutriment and Rags, having been at least four Times that Value.

8   I SHALL now therefore humbly propose my own Thoughts; which I hope will not be liable to the least Objection.

9   I HAVE been assured by a very knowing *American* of my Acquaintance in *London*; that a young healthy Child, well nursed, is, at a Year old, a most delicious, nourishing, and wholesome Food; whether *Stewed, Roasted, Baked, or Boiled*; and, I make no doubt, that it will equally serve in a *Fricasie,* or *Ragoust.*

10   I DO therefore humbly offer it to *publick Consideration,* that of the Hundred and Twenty Thousand Children, already computed, Twenty thousand may be reserved for Breed; whereof only one Fourth Part to be Males; which is more than we allow to *Sheep, black Cattle,* or *Swine*; and my Reason is, that these Children are seldom the Fruits of Marriage, *a Circumstance not much regarded by our Savages*; therefore, *one Male* will be sufficient to serve *four Females.* That the remaining Hundred thousand, may, at a Year old, be offered in Sale to the *Persons of Quality* and *Fortune,* through the Kingdom; always advising the Mother to let them suck plentifully in the last Month, so as to render them plump, and fat for a good Table. A Child will make two Dishes at an Entertainment for Friends; and when the Family dines alone, the fore or hind Quarter will make a reasonable Dish; and seasoned with a little Pepper or Salt, will be very good Boiled on the fourth Day, especially in *Winter.*

11   I HAVE reckoned upon a Medium, that a Child just born will weigh Twelve Pounds; and in a solar Year, if tolerably nursed, encreaseth to twenty eight Pounds.

12   I GRANT this Food will be somewhat dear, and therefore very *proper for Landlords*; who, as they have already devoured most of the Parents, seem to have the best Title to the Children.

13   INFANTS Flesh will be in Season throughout the Year; but more plentiful in *March,* and a little before and after: For we are told by a grave * Author, an eminent *French* Physician, that *Fish being a prolifick Dyet,* there are more Children born in *Roman Catholick Countries* about Nine Months after *Lent,* than at any other Season: Therefore reckoning a Year after *Lent,* the Markets will be more glutted than usual; because the Number of *Popish Infants,* is, at least, three to one in this Kingdom; and therefore it will have one other Collateral Advantage, by lessening the Number of *Papists* among us.

14   I HAVE already computed the Charge of nursing a Beggar's Child (in which List I reckon all *Cottagers, Labourers,* and Four fifths of the *Farmers*) to be about two Shillings *per Annum,* Rags included; and I believe, no Gentleman would repine to give Ten Shillings for the *Carcase of a good fat Child;* which, as I have said, will make four Dishes of excellent nutritive Meat, when he hath only some particular Friend, or his own Family, to dine with him.   Thus the Squire will learn to be a good Landlord, and grow popular among his Tenants; the Mother will have Eight Shillings net Profit, and be fit for Work until she produceth another Child.

15   THOSE who are more thrifty (*as I must confess the Times require*) may flay the Carcase; the Skin of which, artificially dressed, will make admirable *Gloves for Ladies,* and *Summer Boots for fine Gentlemen.*

16   AS to our City of *Dublin;* Shambles may be appointed for this Purpose, in the most convenient Parts of it; and Butchers we may be assured will not be wanting; although I rather recommend buying the Children alive, and dressing them hot from the Knife, as we do *roasting Pigs.*

17   A VERY worthy Person, *a true Lover of his Country,* and whose Virtues I highly esteem, was lately pleased, in discoursing on this Matter, to offer a Refinement upon my Scheme.   He said, that many Gentlemen of this Kingdom, having of late destroyed their Deer; he conceived, that the Want of Venison might be well supplied by the Bodies of young Lads and Maidens, not exceeding Fourteen Years of Age, nor under twelve; so great a Number of both Sexes in every County being now ready to starve, for Want of Work and Service: And these to be disposed of by their Parents, if alive, or otherwise by their nearest Relations.   But with due Deference to so excellent a Friend, and so deserving a Patriot, I cannot be altogether in his Sentiments.   For as to the Males, my *American* Acquaintance assured me from frequent Experience, that their Flesh was generally tough and lean, like that of our School-boys, by continual Exercise, and their Taste disagreeable; and to fatten them would not answer the Charge. Then, as to the Females, it would, I think, with humble Submission, *be a Loss to the Publick,* because they soon would become Breeders themselves: And besides it is not improbable, that some scrupulous People might be

* Rabelais.

apt to censure such a Practice (although indeed very unjustly) as a little bordering upon Cruelty; which, I confess, hath always been with me the strongest Objection against any Project, how well soever intended.

18   B U T in order to justify my Friend; he confessed, that this Expedient was put into his Head by the famous *Salmanaazor*, a Native of the Island *Formosa*, who came from thence to *London*, about twenty Years ago, and in Conversation told my Friend, that in his Country, when any young Person happened to be put to Death, the Executioner sold the Carcase to *Persons of Quality,* as a prime Dainty; and that, in his Time, the Body of a plump Girl of fifteen, who was crucified for an Attempt to poison the Emperor, was sold to his Imperial *Majesty's prime Minister of State*, and other great *Mandarins* of the Court, *in Joints from the Gibbet*, at Four hundred Crowns. Neither indeed can I deny, that if the same Use were made of several plump young girls in this Town, who, without one single Groat to their Fortunes, cannot stir Abroad without a Chair, and appear at the *Play-house*, and *Assemblies* in foreign Fineries, which they never will pay for; the Kingdom would not be the worse.

19   S O M E Persons of a desponding Spirit are in great Concern about that vast Number of poor People, who are Aged, Diseased, or Maimed; and I have been desired to employ my Thoughts what Course may be taken, to ease the Nation of so grievous an Incumbrance. But I am not in the least Pain upon that Matter; because it is very well known, that they are every Day *dying*, and *rotting*, by *Cold* and *Famine*, and *Filth*, and *Vermin*, as fast as can be reasonably expected. And as to the younger Labourers, they are now in almost as hopeful a Condition: They cannot get Work, and consequently pine away for Want of Nourishment, to a Degree, that if at any Time they are accidentally hired to common Labour, they have not Strength to perform it; and thus the Country, and themselves, are in a fair Way of being soon delivered from the Evils to come.

20   I H A V E too long digressed; and therefore shall return to my Subject. I think the Advantages by the Proposal which I have made, are obvious, and many, as well as of the highest Importance.

21   F OR, *First,* as I have already observed, it would greatly lessen the *Number of Papists*, with whom we are yearly overrun; being the principal Breeders of the Nation, as well as our most dangerous Enemies; and who stay at home on Purpose, with a Design to *deliver the Kingdom to the Pretender*; hoping to take their Advantage by the Absence *of so many good Protestants*, who have chosen rather to leave their Country, than stay at home, and pay Tithes against their Conscience, to an idolatrous *Episcopal Curate.*

22   S E C O N D L Y, The poorer Tenants will have something valuable of their own, which, by Law, may be made liable to Distress, and help to pay their Landlord's Rent; their Corn and Cattle being already seized, and *Money a Thing unknown.*

23   THIRDLY, Whereas the Maintenance of an Hundred Thousand Children, from two Years old, and upwards, cannot be computed at less than ten Shillings a Piece *per Annum*, the Nation's Stock will be thereby encreased Fifty Thousand Pounds *per Annum*; besides the Profit of a new Dish, introduced to the Tables of all *Gentlemen of Fortune* in the Kingdom, who have any Refinement in Taste; and the Money will circulate among ourselves, the Goods being entirely of our own Growth and Manufacture.

24   FOURTHLY, The constant Breeders, besides the Gain of Eight Shillings *Sterling per Annum,* by the Sale of their Children, will be rid of the Charge of maintaining them after the first Year.

25   FIFTHLY, This Food would likewise bring great *Custom to Taverns,* where the Vintners will certainly be so prudent, as to procure the best Receipts for dressing it to Perfection; and consequently, have their Houses frequented by all the *fine Gentlemen*, who justly value themselves upon their Knowledge in good Eating; and a skilful Cook, who understands how to oblige his Guests, will contrive to make it as expensive as they please.

26   SIXTHLY, This would be a great Inducement to Marriage, which all wise Nations have either encouraged by Rewards, or enforced by Laws and Penalties. It would encrease the Care and Tenderness of Mothers towards their Children, when they were sure of a Settlement for Life, to the poor Babes, provided in some Sort by the Publick, to their annual Profit instead of Expence. We should soon see an honest Emulation among the married Women, *which of them could bring the fattest Child to the Market.* Men would become as *fond* of their Wives, during the Time of their Pregnancy, as they are now of their *Mares* in Foal, their *Cows* in Calf, or *Sows* when they are ready to farrow; nor offer to beat or kick them, (as it is too *frequent* a Practice) for fear of a Miscarriage.

27   MANY other Advantages might be enumerated. For instance, the Addition of some Thousand Carcasses in our Exportation of barrelled Beef: The Propagation of *Swines Flesh*, and Improvement in the Art of making good *Bacon*; so much wanted among us by the great Destruction of *Pigs*, too frequent at our Tables, and are no way comparable in Taste, or Magnificence, to a well-grown fat yearling Child; which, roasted whole, will make a considerable Figure at a *Lord Mayor's Feast*, or any other publick Entertainment. But this, and many others, I omit; being studious of Brevity.

28   SUPPOSING that one Thousand Families in this City, would be constant Customers for Infants Flesh; besides others who might have it at *merry Meetings*, particularly *Weddings* and *Christenings*; I compute that *Dublin* would take off, annually, about Twenty Thousand Carcasses; and the rest of the Kingdom (where probably they will be sold somewhat cheaper) the remaining Eighty Thousand.

29   I CAN think of no one Objection, that will possibly be raised against this Proposal; unless it should be urged, that the Number of People will be thereby much lessened in the Kingdom. This I freely own; and it was indeed one principal Design in offering it to the World. I desire the Reader will observe, that I calculate my Remedy *for this one individual Kingdom of* IRELAND, *and for no other that ever was, is, or I think ever can be upon Earth.* Therefore, let no man talk to me of other Expedients: *Of taxing our Absentees at five Shillings a Pound: Of using neither Cloaths, nor Houshold Furniture except what is of our own Growth and Manufacture: Of utterly rejecting the Materials and Instruments that promote foreign Luxury: Of curing the Expensiveness of Pride, Vanity, Idleness, and Gaming in our Women: Of introducing a Vein of Parsimony, Prudence and Temperance: Of learning to love our Country, wherein we differ even from* LAPLANDERS, *and the Inhabitants of* TOPINAMBOO: *Of quitting our Amimosities, and Factions*; *nor act any longer like the* Jews, *who were murdering one another at the very Moment their City was taken: Of being a little cautious not to sell our Country and Consciences for nothing: Of teaching Landlords to have, at least, one Degree of Mercy towards their Tenants.* Lastly, *Of putting a Spirit of Honesty, Industry, and Skill into our Shop-keepers; who, if a Resolution could now be taken to buy only our native Goods, would immediately unite to cheat and exact upon us in the Price, the Measure, and the Goodness; nor could ever yet be brought to make one fair Proposal of just Dealing, though often and earnestly invited to it.*

30   THEREFORE I repeat, let no Man talk to me of these and the like Expedients; till he hath, at least, a Glimpse of Hope, that there will ever be some hearty and sincere Attempt to put *them in Practice.*

31   BUT, as to my self; having been wearied out for many Years with offering vain, idle, visionary Thoughts; and at length utterly despairing of Success, I fortunately fell upon this Proposal; which, as it is wholly new, so it hath something *solid* and *real*, of no Expence, and little Trouble, full in our own Power; and whereby we can incur no Danger in *disobliging* ENGLAND: For, this Kind of Commodity will not bear Exportation; the Flesh being of too tender a Consistence, to admit a long Continuance in Salt; *although, perhaps, I could name a Country, which would be glad to eat up our whole Nation without it.*

32   AFTER all, I am not so violently bent upon my own Opinion, as to reject any Offer proposed by wise Men, which shall be found equally innocent, cheap, easy, and effectual. But before something of that Kind shall be advanced, in Contradiction to my Scheme, and offering a better; I desire the Author, or Authors, will be pleased maturely to consider two Points. *First,* As Things now stand, how they will be able to find Food and Raiment, for a Hundred Thousand useless Mouths and Backs? And

secondly, There being a round Million of Creatures in human Figure, throughout this Kingdom; whose whole Subsistence, put into a common Stock, would leave them in Debt two Millions of Pounds *Sterling*; adding those, who are Beggars by Profession, to the Bulk of Farmers, Cottagers, and Labourers, with their Wives and Children, who are Beggars in Effect; I desire those Politicians, who dislike my Overture, and may perhaps be so bold to attempt an Answer, that they will first ask the Parents of these Mortals, Whether they would not, at this Day, think it a great Happiness to have been sold for Food at a Year old, in the Manner I prescribe; and thereby have avoided such a perpetual Scene of Misfortunes, as they have since gone through; by the *Oppression of Landlords*; the Impossibility of paying Rent, without Money or Trade; the Want of common Sustenance, with neither House nor Cloaths, to cover them from the Inclemencies of Weather; and the most inevitable Prospect of intailing the like, or greater Miseries upon their Breed for ever.

33   I PROFESS, in the Sincerity of my Heart, that I have not the least personal Interest, in endeavouring to promote this necessary Work; having no other Motive than the *publick Good of my Country, by advancing our Trade, providing for Infants, relieving the Poor, and giving some Pleasure to the Rich.* I have no Children, by which I can propose to get a single Penny; the youngest being nine Years old, and my Wife past Child-bearing.

Questions

1. The terms "projector" and "proposal" had a distinctly pejorative tone in the early eighteenth century. The "projector" was generally one who put forth some hare-brained economic scheme in order to attract investors. These "proposals" were rife in Swift's time—the "South Seas Bubble" might be regarded as a prototype, and a fantastically successful one. In light of these facts, what sort of person is the narrator? Why is he appropriate to the ironic tone of the whole argument?

2. Examine all the images, and their contexts, of animals and of eating.

3. What rhetorical devices does the projector use to disarm possible opposition to his scheme?

4. What functions do asides and digressions, self-confessed or otherwise, play in this essay?

5. At what points, if any, in the proposal does the mask of the projector wear thin and the real attitudes of Swift show through?

6. At what points is the projector most rigorously practical? At what points does the projector, if taken literally, most outrage your own sense of humanity? Why?

7. Ireland in Swift's time was in desperate straits economically. It was plagued by absentee landlords and lack of native products whose sale would directly

benefit Ireland. On the basis of evidence in his essay, describe the audience Swift was attempting to reach. What is he, as opposed to the projector, trying to persuade his readers to do?

Theme topics

1. Write a satire of your own in which you establish the character of the speaker through his own language. Use any political or social type of person you wish, but work in detail as Swift does.
2. Write a modern adaptation of Swift's proposal in which the subject is some poverty group of the present (ADC mothers, Hippies, college students, dropouts, addicts, draft dodgers, winos, etc.)

59   HENRY DAVID THOREAU
Civil Disobedience

1   I heartily accept the motto, "That government is best which governs least"; [1] and I should like to see it acted up to more rapidly and systematically. Carried out, it finally amounts to this, which also I believe —"That government is best which governs not at all"; and when men are prepared for it, that will be the kind of government which they will have. Government is at best but an expedient; but most governments are usually, and all governments are sometimes, inexpedient. The objections which have been brought against a standing army, and they are many and weighty, and deserve to prevail, may also at last be brought against a standing government. The standing army is only an arm of the standing government. The government itself, which is only the mode which the people have chosen to execute their will, is equally liable to be abused and perverted before the people can act through it. Witness the present Mexican war, the work of comparatively a few individuals using the standing government as their tool; for, in the outset, the people would not have consented to this measure. [2]

2   This American government—what is it but a tradition, though a recent one, endeavoring to transmit itself unimpaired to posterity, but each instant losing some of its integrity? It has not the vitality and force of a

[1] See Jefferson's *First Inaugural* (1801) for the genesis of this idea.
[2] In New England a highly unpopular war, looked upon as a device to increase slave territory.

single living man; for a single man can bend it to his will. It is a sort of wooden gun to the people themselves. But it is not the less necessary for this; for the people must have some complicated machinery or other, and hear its din, to satisfy that idea of government which they have. Governments show thus how successfully men can be imposed on, even impose on themselves, for their own advantage. It is excellent, we must all allow. Yet this government never of itself furthered any enterprise, but by the alacrity with which it got out of its way. *It* does not keep the country free. *It* does not settle the West. *It* does not educate. The character inherent in the American people has done all that has been accomplished; and it would have done somewhat more, if the government had not sometimes got in its way. For government is an expedient by which men would fain succeed in letting one another alone; and, as has been said, when it is most expedient, the governed are most let alone by it. Trade and commerce, if they were not made of india-rubber, would never manage to bounce over the obstacles which legislators are continually putting in their way; and, if one were to judge these men wholly by the effects of their actions and not partly by their intentions, they would deserve to be classed and punished with those mischievous persons who put obstructions on the railroads.

3   But, to speak practically and as a citizen, unlike those who call themselves no-government men, I ask for, not at once no government, but *at once* a better government. Let every man make known what kind of government would command his respect, and that will be one step toward obtaining it.

4   After all, the practical reason why, when the power is once in the hands of the people, a majority are permitted, and for a long period continue, to rule is not because they are most likely to be in the right, nor because this seems fairest to the minority, but because they are physically the strongest. But a government in which the majority rule in all cases cannot be based on justice, even as far as men understand it. Can there not be a government in which majorities do not virtually decide right and wrong, but conscience?—in which majorities decide only those questions to which the rule of expediency is applicable? Must the citizen ever for a moment, or in the least degree, resign his conscience to the legislator? Why has every man a conscience, then? [3] I think that we should be men first, and subjects afterward. It is not desirable to cultivate a respect for the law, so much as for the right. The only obligation which I have a right to assume is to do at any time what I think right. It is truly enough said that a corporation has no conscience; but a corporation of conscientious men is a corporation *with* a conscience. Law never made men a whit more just; and, by means of their respect for it, even the well-disposed are daily

[3] Echoes a controversy in the Constitutional Convention. The Jeffersonians, favoring majority rule, overcame Hamilton and Adams, who represented the conservative minority.

made the agents of injustice. A common and natural result of an undue respect for law is, that you may see a file of soldiers, colonel, captain, corporal, privates, powder-monkeys, and all, marching in admirable order over hill and dale to the wars, against their wills, ay, against their common sense and consciences, which makes it very steep marching indeed, and produces a palpitation of the heart. They have no doubt that it is a damnable business in which they are concerned; they are all peaceably inclined. Now, what are they? Men at all? or small movable forts and magazines, at the service of some unscrupulous man in power? Visit the Navy Yard, and behold a marine, such a man as an American government can make, or such as it can make a man with its black arts—a mere shadow and reminiscence of humanity, a man laid out alive and standing, and already, as one may say, buried under arms with funeral accompaniments, though it may be,

> "Not a drum was heard, not a funeral note,
>   As his corse to the rampart we hurried;
> Not a soldier discharged his farewell shot
>   O'er the grave where our hero we buried." [4]

5   The mass of men serve the state thus, not as men mainly, but as machines, with their bodies. They are the standing army, and the militia, jailers, constables, *posse comitatus,* etc. In most cases there is no free exercise whatever of the judgment or of the moral sense; but they put themselves on a level with wood and earth and stones; and wooden men can perhaps be manufactured that will serve the purpose as well. Such command no more respect than men of straw or a lump of dirt. They have the same sort of worth only as horses and dogs. Yet such as these even are commonly esteemed good citizens. Others—as most legislators, politicians, lawyers, ministers, and office-holders—serve the state chiefly with their heads; and, as they rarely make any moral distinctions, they are as likely to serve the devil, without *intending* it, as God. A very few—as heroes, patriots, martyrs, reformers in the great sense, and *men*—serve the state with their consciences also, and so necessarily resist it for the most part; and they are commonly treated as enemies by it. A wise man will only be useful as a man, and will not submit to be "clay," and "stop a hole to keep the wind away," but leave that office to his dust at least:

> "I am too high-born to be propertied,
>   To be a secondary at control,
>   Or useful serving-man and instrument
> To any sovereign state throughout the world." [5]

6   He who gives himself entirely to his fellow men appears to them useless and selfish; but he who gives himself partially to them is pronounced a benefactor and philanthropist.

[4] From Charles Wolfe's "The Burial of Sir John Moore" (1817).
[5] Shakespeare's *King John,* Act V, Sc. ii, 11. 79–82.

7   How does it become a man to behave toward this American government today? I answer, that he cannot without disgrace be associated with it. I cannot for an instant recognize that political organization as *my* government which is the *slave's* government also.

8   All men recognize the right of revolution; that is, the right to refuse allegiance to, and to resist, the government, when its tyranny or its inefficiency are great and unendurable. But almost all say that such is not the case now. But such was the case, they think, in the Revolution of '75. If one were to tell me that this was a bad government because it taxed certain foreign commodities brought to its ports, it is most probable that I should not make an ado about it, for I can do without them. All machines have their friction; and possibly this does enough good to counterbalance the evil. At any rate, it is a great evil to make a stir about it. But when the friction comes to have its machine, and oppression and robbery are organized, I say, let us not have such a machine any longer. In other words, when a sixth of the population of a nation which has undertaken to be the refuge of liberty are slaves, and a whole country is unjustly overrun and conquered by a foreign army, and subjected to military law, I think that it is not too soon for honest men to rebel and revolutionize. What makes this duty the more urgent is the fact that the country so overrun is not our own, but ours is the invading army.

9   Paley, a common authority with many on moral questions, in his chapter on the "Duty of Submission to Civil Government," resolves all civil obligation into expediency; and he proceeds to say that "so long as the interest of the whole society requires it, that is, so long as the established government cannot be resisted or changed without public inconveniency, it is the will of God . . . that the established government be obeyed—and no longer. This principle being admitted, the justice of every particular case of resistance is reduced to a computation of the quantity of the danger and grievance on the one side, and of the probability and expense of redressing it on the other." [6] Of this, he says, every man shall judge for himself. But Paley appears never to have contemplated those cases to which the rule of expediency does not apply, in which a people, as well as an individual, must do justice, cost what it may. If I have unjustly wrested a plank from a drowning man, I must restore it to him though I drown myself. This, according to Paley, would be inconvenient. But he that would save his life, in such a case, shall lose it. This people must cease to hold slaves, and to make war on Mexico, though it cost them their existence as a people.

10   In their practice, nations agree with Paley; but does anyone think that Massachusetts does exactly what is right at the present crisis?

> "A drab of state, a cloth-o'-silver slut,
>   To have her train borne up, and her soul trail in the dirt."

[6] From William Paley's *Principles of Moral and Political Philosophy* (1785).

Practically speaking, the opponents to a reform in Massachusetts are not a hundred thousand politicians at the South, but a hundred thousand merchants and farmers here, who are more interested in commerce and agriculture than they are in humanity, and are not prepared to do justice to the slave and to Mexico, *cost what it may*. I quarrel not with far-off foes, but with those who, near at home, co-operate with, and do the bidding of, those far away, and without whom the latter would be harmless. We are accustomed to say, that the mass of men are unprepared; but improvement is slow, because the few are not materially wiser or better than the many. It is not so important that many should be as good as you, as that there be some absolute goodness somewhere; for that will leaven the whole lump. There are thousands who are *in opinion* opposed to slavery and to the war, who yet in effect do nothing to put an end to them; who, esteeming themselves children of Washington and Franklin, sit down with their hands in their pockets, and say that they know not what to do, and do nothing; who even postpone the question of freedom to the question of free trade, and quietly read the prices-current along with the latest advices from Mexico, after dinner, and, it may be, fall asleep over them both. What is the price-current of an honest man and patriot today? They hesitate, and they regret, and sometimes they petition; but they do nothing in earnest and with effect. They will wait, well disposed, for others to remedy the evil, that they may no longer have it to regret. At most, they give only a cheap vote, and a feeble countenance and Godspeed, to the right, as it goes by them. There are nine hundred and ninety-nine patrons of virtue to one virtuous man. But it is easier to deal with the real possessor of a thing than with the temporary guardian of it.

11 All voting is a sort of gaming, like checkers or backgammon, with a slight moral tinge to it, a playing with right and wrong, with moral questions; and betting naturally accompanies it. The character of the voters is not staked. I cast my vote, perchance, as I think right; but I am not vitally concerned that that right should prevail. I am willing to leave it to the majority. Its obligation, therefore, never exceeds that of expediency. Even voting *for the right* is *doing* nothing for it. It is only expressing to men feebly your desire that it should prevail. A wise man will not leave the right to the mercy of chance, nor wish it to prevail through the power of the majority. There is but little virtue in the action of masses of men. When the majority shall at length vote for the abolition of slavery, it will be because they are indifferent to slavery, or because there is but little slavery left to be abolished by their vote. *They* will then be the only slaves. Only *his* vote can hasten the abolition of slavery who asserts his own freedom by his vote.

12 I hear of a convention to be held at Baltimore, or elsewhere, for the selection of a candidate for the Presidency, made up chiefly of editors, and men who are politicians by profession; but I think, what is it to any in-

dependent, intelligent, and respectable man what decision they may come to? Shall we not have the advantage of his wisdom and honesty, nevertheless? Can we not count upon some independent votes? Are there not many individuals in the country who do not attend conventions? But no: I find that the respectable man, so called, has immediately drifted from his position, and despairs of his country, when his country has more reason to despair of him. He forthwith adopts one of the candidates thus selected as the only *available* one, thus proving that he is himself *available* for any purposes of the demagogue. His vote is of no more worth than that of any unprincipled foreigner or hireling native, who may have been bought. O for a man who is a *man,* and, as my neighbor says, has a bone in his back which you cannot pass your hand through! Our statistics are at fault: the population has been returned too large. How many *men* are there to a square thousand miles in this country? Hardly one. Does not America offer any inducement for men to settle here? The American has dwindled into an Odd Fellow—one who may be known by the development of his organ of gregariousness, and a manifest lack of intellect and cheerful self-reliance; whose first and chief concern, on coming into the world, is to see that the almshouses are in good repair; and, before yet he has lawfully donned the virile garb,[7] to collect a fund for the support of the widows and orphans that may be; who, in short, ventures to live only by the aid of the Mutual Insurance company, which has promised to bury him decently.

13   It is not a man's duty, as a matter of course, to devote himself to the eradication of any, even the most enormous, wrong; he may still properly have other concerns to engage him; but it is his duty, at least, to wash his hands of it, and, if he gives it no thought longer, not to give it practically his support. If I devote myself to other pursuits and contemplations, I must first see, at least, that I do not pursue them sitting upon another man's shoulders. I must get off him first, that he may pursue his contemplations too. See what gross inconsistency is tolerated. I have heard some of my townsmen say, "I should like to have them order me out to help put down an insurrection of the slaves, or to march to Mexico—see if I would go"; and yet these very men have each, directly by their allegiance, and so indirectly, at least, by their money, furnished a substitute. The soldier is applauded who refuses to serve in an unjust war by those who do not refuse to sustain the unjust government which makes the war; is applauded by those whose own act and authority he disregards and sets at naught; as if the state were penitent to that degree that it hired one to scourge it while it sinned, but not to that degree that it left off sinning for a moment. Thus, under the name of Order and Civil Government, we are all made at last to pay homage to and support our own meanness. After the first blush of sin comes its indifference; and from immoral it

[7] Roman boys put on the *toga virilis* at the end of their fourteenth year.

becomes, as it were, *un*moral, and not quite unnecessary to that life which we have made.

14   The broadest and most prevalent error requires the most disinterested virtue to sustain it. The slight reproach to which the virtue of patriotism is commonly liable, the noble are most likely to incur. Those who, while they disapprove of the character and measures of a government, yield to it their allegiance and support are undoubtedly its most conscientious supporters, and so frequently the most serious obstacles to reform. Some are petitioning the State to dissolve the Union, to disregard the requisitions of the President.[8] Why do they not dissolve it themselves—the union between themselves and the State—and refuse to pay their quota into its treasury? Do not they stand in the same relation to the State that the State does to the Union? And have not the same reasons prevented the State from resisting the Union which have prevented them from resisting the State?

15   How can a man be satisfied to entertain an opinion merely, and enjoy *it?* Is there any enjoyment in it, if his opinion is that he is aggrieved? If you are cheated out of a single dollar by your neighbor, you do not rest satisfied with knowing that you are cheated, or with saying that you are cheated, or even with petitioning him to pay you your due; but you take effectual steps at once to obtain the full amount, and see that you are never cheated again. Action from principle, the perception and the performance of right, changes things and relations; it is essentially revolutionary, and does not consist wholly with anything which was. It not only divides States and churches, it divides families; ay, it divides the *individual,* separating the diabolical in him from the divine.

16   Unjust laws exist: shall we be content to obey them, or shall we endeavor to amend them, and obey them until we have succeeded, or shall we transgress them at once? Men generally, under such a government as this, think that they ought to wait until they have persuaded the majority to alter them. They think that, if they should resist, the remedy would be worse than the evil. But it is the fault of the government itself that the remedy *is* worse than the evil. *It* makes it worse. Why is it not more apt to anticipate and provide for reform? Why does it not cherish its wise minority? Why does it cry and resist before it is hurt? Why does it not encourage its citizens to be on the alert to point out its faults, and *do* better than it would have them? Why does it always crucify Christ, and excommunicate Copernicus and Luther, and pronounce Washington and Franklin rebels?

17   One would think, that a deliberate and practical denial of its authority was the only offence never contemplated by government; else, why has it not assigned its definite, its suitable and proportionate, penalty? If a man who has no property refuses but once to earn nine shillings for the State,

[8] Polk's call for volunteers for the war against Mexico.

he is put in prison for a period unlimited by any law that I know, and determined only by the discretion of those who placed him there; but if he should steal ninety times nine shillings from the State, he is soon permitted to go at large again.

18   If the injustice is part of the necessary friction of the machine of government, let it go, let it go: perchance it will wear smooth—certainly the machine will wear out. If the injustice has a spring, or a pulley, or a rope, or a crank, exclusively for itself, then perhaps you may consider whether the remedy will not be worse than the evil; but if it is of such a nature that it requires you to be the agent of injustice to another, then, I say, break the law. Let your life be a counter-friction to stop the machine. What I have to do is to see, at any rate, that I do not lend myself to the wrong which I condemn.

19   As for adopting the ways which the State has provided for remedying the evil, I know not of such ways. They take too much time, and a man's life will be gone. I have other affairs to attend to. I came into this world, not chiefly to make this a good place to live in, but to live in it, be it good or bad. A man has not everything to do, but something; and because he cannot do *everything*, it is not necessary that he should do *something* wrong. It is not my business to be petitioning the Governor or the Legislature any more than it is theirs to petition me; and if they should not hear my petition, what should I do then? But in this case the State has provided no way: its very Constitution is the evil. This may seem to be harsh and stubborn and unconciliatory; but it is to treat with the utmost kindness and consideration the only spirit that can appreciate or deserves it. So is all change for the better, like birth and death, which convulse the body.

20   I do not hesitate to say, that those who call themselves Abolitionists should at once effectually withdraw their support, both in person and property, from the government of Massachusetts, and not wait till they constitute a majority of one, before they suffer the right to prevail through them. I think that it is enough if they have God on their side, without waiting for that other one. Moreover, any man more right than his neighbors constitutes a majority of one already.

21   I meet this American government, or its representative, the State government, directly, and face to face, once a year—no more—in the person of its tax-gatherer; this is the only mode in which a man situated as I am necessarily meets it; and it then says distinctly, Recognize me; and the simplest, the most effectual, and, in the present posture of affairs, the indispensablest mode of treating with it on this head, of expressing your little satisfaction with and love for it, is to deny it then. My civil neighbor, the tax-gatherer, is the very man I have to deal with—for it is, after all, with men and not with parchment that I quarrel—and he has voluntarily chosen to be an agent of the government. How shall he ever know well what he is and does as an officer of the government, or as a man, until

he is obliged to consider whether he shall treat me, his neighbor, for whom he has respect, as a neighbor and well-disposed man, or as a maniac and disturber of the peace, and see if he can get over this obstruction to his neighborliness without a ruder and more impetuous thought or speech corresponding with his action. I know this well, that if one thousand, if one hundred, if ten men whom I could name—if ten *honest* men only —ay, if *one* HONEST man, in this State of Massachusetts, *ceasing to hold slaves,* were actually to withdraw from this copartnership, and be locked up in the county jail therefor, it would be the abolition of slavery in Amer-ica. For it matters not how small the beginning may seem to be: what is once well done is done forever. But we love better to talk about it: that we say is our mission. Reform keeps many scores of newspapers in its service, but not one man. If my esteemed neighbor, the State's ambassador, who will devote his days to the settlement of the question of human rights in the Council Chamber, instead of being threatened with the prisons of Carolina,[9] were to sit down the prisoner of Massachusetts, that State which is so anxious to foist the sin of slavery upon her sister—though at present she can discover only an act of inhospitality to be the ground of a quarrel with her—the Legislature would not wholly waive the subject the follow-ing winter.

22   Under a government which imprisons any unjustly, the true place for a just man is also a prison. The proper place today, the only place which Massachusetts has provided for her freer and less desponding spirits, is in her prisons, to be put out and locked out of the State by her own act, as they have already put themselves out by their principles. It is there that the fugitive slave, and the Mexican prisoner on parole, and the Indian come to plead the wrongs of his race should find them; on that separate, but more free and honorable, ground, where the State places those who are not *with* her, but *against* her—the only house in a slave State in which a free man can abide with honor. If any think that their influence would be lost there, and their voices no longer afflict the ear of the State, that they would not be as an enemy within its walls, they do not know by how much truth is stronger than error, nor how much more eloquently and effectively he can combat injustice who has experienced a little in his own person. Cast your whole vote, not a strip of paper merely, but your whole influence. A minority is powerless while it conforms to the majority; it is not even a minority then; but it is irresistible when it clogs by its whole weight. If the alternative is to keep all just men in prison, or give up war and slavery, the State will not hesitate which to choose. If a thousand men were not to pay their tax-bills this year, that would not be a violent and bloody measure, as it would be to pay them, and enable the State to com-

---

[9] Thoreau refers to Samuel Hoar of Concord who, in 1844, was sent to Charles-ton, South Carolina, to protest against the seizure of Negro seamen from Massachu-setts. He was rather unceremoniously ejected from the city.

mit violence and shed innocent blood. This is, in fact, the definition of a peaceable revolution, if any such is possible. If the tax-gatherer, or any other public officer, asks me, as one has done, "But what shall I do?" my answer is, "If you really wish to do anything, resign your office." When the subject has refused allegiance, and the officer has resigned his office, then the revolution is accomplished. But even suppose blood should flow. Is there not a sort of blood shed when the conscience is wounded? Through this wound a man's real manhood and immortality flow out, and he bleeds to an everlasting death. I see this blood flowing now.

23   I have contemplated the imprisonment of the offender, rather than the seizure of his goods—though both will serve the same purpose—because they who assert the purest right, and consequently are most dangerous to a corrupt State, commonly have not spent much time in accumulating property. To such the State renders comparatively small service, and a slight tax is wont to appear exorbitant, particularly if they are obliged to earn it by special labor with their hands. If there were one who lived wholly without the use of money, the State itself would hesitate to demand it of him. But the rich man—not to make any invidious comparison—is always sold to the institution which makes him rich. Absolutely speaking, the more money, the less virtue; for money comes between a man and his objects, and obtains them for him; and it was certainly no great virtue to obtain it. It puts to rest many questions which he would otherwise be taxed to answer; while the only new question which it puts is the hard but superfluous one, how to spend it. Thus his moral ground is taken from under his feet. The opportunities of living are diminished in proportion as what are called the "means" are increased. The best thing a man can do for his culture when he is rich is to endeavor to carry out those schemes which he entertained when he was poor. Christ answered the Herodians according to their condition. "Show me the tribute-money," said he—and one took a penny out of his pocket—if you use money which has the image of Caesar on it, and which he has made current and valuable, that is, *if you are men of the State,* and gladly enjoy the advantages of Caesar's government, then pay him back some of his own when he demands it. "Render therefore to Caesar that which is Caesar's, and to God those things which are God's"—leaving them no wiser than before as to which was which; for they did not wish to know.

24   When I converse with the freest of my neighbors, I perceive that, whatever they may say about the magnitude and seriousness of the question, and their regard for the public tranquillity, the long and the short of the matter is, that they cannot spare the protection of the existing government, and they dread the consequences to their property and families of disobedience to it. For my own part, I should not like to think that I ever rely on the protection of the State. But, if I deny the authority of the State when it presents its tax bill, it will soon take and waste all my property, and so harass me and my children without end. This is hard. This

makes it impossible for a man to live honestly, and at the same time comfortably, in outward respects. It will not be worth the while to accumulate property; that would be sure to go again. You must hire or squat somewhere, and raise but a small crop, and eat that soon. You must live within yourself, and depend upon yourself always tucked up and ready for a start, and not have many affairs. A man may grow rich in Turkey even, if he will be in all respects a good subject of the Turkish government. Confucius said: "If a state is governed by the principles of reason, poverty and misery are subjects of shame; if a state is not governed by the principles of reason, riches and honors are the subjects of shame." No: until I want the protection of Massachusetts to be extended to me in some distant Southern port, where my liberty is endangered, or until I am bent solely on building up an estate at home by peaceful enterprise, I can afford to refuse allegiance to Massachusetts, and her right to my property and life. It costs me less in every sense to incur the penalty of disobedience to the State than it would to obey. I should feel as if I were worth less in that case.

25   Some years ago, the State met me in behalf of the Church, and commanded me to pay a certain sum toward the support of a clergyman whose preaching my father attended, but never I myself. "Pay," it said, "or be locked up in the jail." I declined to pay. But, unfortunately, another man saw fit to pay it. I did not see why the schoolmaster should be taxed to support the priest, and not the priest the schoolmaster; for I was not the State's schoolmaster, but I supported myself by voluntary subscription. I did not see why the lyceum should not present its tax bill, and have the State to back its demand, as well as the Church. However, at the request of the selectmen, I condescended to make some such statement as this in writing: "Know all men by these present, that I, Henry Thoreau, do not wish to be regarded as a member of any incorporated society which I have not joined." This I gave to the town clerk; and he has it. The State, having thus learned that I did not wish to be regarded as a member of that church, has never made a like demand on me since; though it said that it must adhere to its original presumption that time. If I had known how to name them, I should then have signed off in detail from all the societies which I never signed on to; but I did not know where to find a complete list.

26   I have paid no poll-tax for six years. I was put into a jail once on this account, for one night; and, as I stood considering the walls of solid stone, two or three feet thick, the door of wood and iron, a foot thick, and the iron grating which strained the light, I could not help being struck with the foolishness of that institution which treated me as if I were mere flesh and blood and bones, to be locked up.[10] I wondered that it should have concluded at length that this was the best use it could put me to, and had never thought to avail itself of my services in some way. I saw

[10] Henry Seidel Canby thinks that this famous night occurred on the 23rd or 24th of July, 1846.

that, if there was a wall of stone between me and my townsmen, there was a still more difficult one to climb or break through before they could get to be as free as I was. I did not for a moment feel confined, and the walls seemed a great waste of stone and mortar. I felt as if I alone of all my townsmen had paid my tax. They plainly did not know how to treat me, but behaved like persons who are underbred. In every threat and in every compliment there was a blunder; for they thought that my chief desire was to stand the other side of that stone wall. I could not but smile to see how industriously they locked the door on my meditations, which followed them out again without let or hindrance, and *they* were really all that was dangerous. As they could not reach me, they had resolved to punish my body; just as boys, if they cannot come at some person against whom they have a spite, will abuse his dog. I saw that the State was half-witted, that it was timid as a lone woman with her silver spoons, and that it did not know its friends from its foes, and I lost all my remaining respect for it, and pitied it.

27   Thus the State never intentionally confronts a man's sense, intellectual or moral, but only his body, his senses. It is not armed with superior wit or honesty, but with superior physical strength. I was not born to be forced. I will breathe after my own fashion. Let us see who is the strongest. What force has a multitude? They only can force me who obey a higher law than I. They force me to become like themselves. I do not hear of *men* being *forced* to live this way or that by masses of men. What sort of life were that to live? When I meet a government which says to me, "Your money or your life," why should I be in haste to give it my money? It may be in a great strait, and not know what to do: I cannot help that. It must help itself; do as I do. It is not worth the while to snivel about it. I am not responsible for the successful working of the machinery of society. I am not the son of the engineer. I perceive that, when an acorn and a chestnut fall side by side, the one does not remain inert to make way for the other, but both obey their own laws, and spring and grow and flourish as best they can, till one, perchance, overshadows and destroys the other. If a plant cannot live according to its nature, it dies; and so a man. . . .

Questions

1. Show how each of the following quotations reveals Thoreau's fundamental assumptions concerning the nature of man and the state:

   All voting is a sort of gaming, like checkers or backgammon, with a slight moral tinge to it, a playing with right and wrong, with moral questions; and betting naturally accompanies it. (Paragraph 11)

Action from principle, the perception and the performance of right, changes things and relations; it is essentially revolutionary, and does not consist wholly with anything which was. (Paragraph 15)

. . . any man more right than his neighbors constitutes a majority of one already. (Paragraph 20)

Under a government which imprisons any unjustly, the true place for a just man is also a prison. (Paragraph 22)

2. Show how Thoreau develops his thesis—"that government is best which governs least"—by negative arguments in paragraph 2. How effective are these arguments?

3. Compare Thoreau's view of the citizen in paragraph 3 with Plato's. In what essential matters do they disagree? In paragraph 16 Thoreau comments on the persecution of the "wise minority." Again compare with Plato.

4. Show how the first 6 paragraphs lead up to the transitional first sentence in paragraph 7. Why does Thoreau use a rhetorical question here? How effective is it?

5. What is implied by Thoreau's final analogy of man to the oak and the chestnut?

6. Examine the images Thoreau uses to describe conditions or institutions he approves of, he disapproves of. What does his imagery reveal of his taste and temperament?

Theme topics

1. Rather than work logically to set forth his position, Thoreau uses a number of epigrams, anecdotes and quotations that reflect a central position comprised of attitudes and assumptions. Write a theme in which you clarify Thoreau's attitudes and assumptions and show how they work in forming his opinions on war, majority rule, taxation, established religion and urban life.

2. After clearly formulating an answer to question 6 above, write your own essay on civil disobedience within the frame of Thoreau's taste and temperament but addressed to the political and social realities of our own day.

3. Write an essay in which you compare and contrast Thoreau's view of man's place in the state with that of Plato.

60 CLINTON ROSSITER
Conservatism

1   *Conservatism* is one of the most confusing words in the glossary of political thought and oratory. Indeed, it could well have been "conservatism" that Justice Holmes had in mind when he wrote, with characteristic felicity, "A word is not a crystal, transparent and unchanged; it is the skin of a living thought and may vary greatly in color and content according to the circumstances and time in which it is used." One need not spend more than an hour with the literature of the revival to realize that few words are quite so variable in color and content. The failure of Americans to agree on the meaning of "conservatism" has distorted opinion and cramped discussion of some of the most pressing issues of our time. Small wonder that several leading political theorists have proposed that *conservatism,* along with its partner-in-confusion *liberalism,* be sold for scrap.

2   Words, however, are not easily scrapped; and even if these wise men could agree upon or coin an acceptable substitute—an unlikely prospect— the rest of us would doubtless go right on using a word that is, after all, an extremely useful tool when properly handled. I have lived too long with "conservatism" and have heard too many thoughtful men wrangle over its meaning to launch this study without stating my own definitions and begging the reader to agree with them . . . .

3   Before I state them, we should perhaps take notice of—and thus put safely out of the way—some of the popular uses of "conservatism," which has become in modern America, as it was in Macaulay's England, "the new cant word." Words like "cautious," "prudent," "stodgy," and "old-fashioned" have gone out of favor in our daily speech. Everything and everybody is "conservative" these days: the football team that stays on the ground, the investor who prefers General Motors to Wildcat Oil, the skipper who takes a reef in a twenty-knot breeze, the young man who wears white button-down shirts instead of Harry Truman Specials, the publisher who never takes a flier without balancing it with two solid textbooks, the collector who prefers Wyeth to Kuniyoshi or even Klee to Pollock. While no one can object to these popular uses, which doubtless bring comfort to the users, they must not be permitted to obscure the really

From *Conservatism in America,* by Clinton Rossiter. 2nd Edition, New York: Vintage 1962, pp. 5–10. © 1955, 1962 by Clinton Rossiter. Reprinted by permission of Alfred A. Knopf, Inc.

important connotations of "conservatism" in the language of politics and culture. There are, I believe, four connotations with which students of American conservatism must be fully conversant.

4   The first denotes a certain temperament or psychological stance. *Temperamental conservatism* is simply a man's "natural" disposition to oppose any substantial change in his manner of life, work, and enjoyment. Psychologists agree generally that all human beings exhibit conservative traits to some degree at some time in their lives, and in most men these appear to be dominant. The important traits in the conservative temperament, all of them largely non-rational in character, would seem to be habit, inertia, fear, and emulation.

5   Habit is the disposition to do the same things in the same way, especially if one has learned to do them skillfully by constant repetition. Habit among humans is largely but not completely a product of culture, a sign that the individual has worked out an adjustment with his environment. William James considered it "the enormous flywheel of society, its most precious conservative agent. It alone is what keeps us all within the bounds of ordinance."

6   Human beings, like matter, prefer to retain their "state of rest of uniform rectilinear motion so long as . . . not acted upon by an external force." Inertia calls for no exertion, while innovation, as Thorstein Veblen wrote in his *Theory of the Leisure Class,* "involves a degree of mental effort—a more or less protracted and laborious effort to find and keep one's bearings under the altered circumstances." Veblen, characteristically, went on to explain the "conservatism of the poor" in these terms, asserting that "progress is hindered by underfeeding and excessive physical hardship." There is little reason to argue with this distressing observation, but we may find inertia in the reluctance of men in all classes and situations— and even more obviously women—to expend extra effort to meet the problems of change. One important element in the intensified conservatism of old age is the progressive reduction of energy and growth of inertia. The "conservatism of ignorance," the bane of social reformers through all the ages, can also be explained in terms of inertia.

7   Fear is both an instinctive and culture-determined element in the psychology of conservatism; as such it takes the shape of anxiety, guilt, or shame. Fear of the unknown and unexpected, fear of the unconventional and irregular, fear of the group's disapproval and one's own weaknesses —these and a thousand other fears persuade a man to be conservative. The most important fear of all in shaping the conservative temperament is the fear of change, which dislocates, discomforts, and worst of all, dispossesses.

8   Emulation is a product of both a fear of alienation from the group and a craving for its approval. Appearing in developed societies as the desire for respectability, it leads men to acquiesce in the status quo and conform

to the standards of their group. "To uphold the old," wrote A. B. Wolfe, "to abide by the established, to refrain from much criticism of things as they are, to think none but conventional thoughts—these are the avenues to day-by-day respectability," and thus, it should be added, to peace and security.

9   The social importance of the conservative temperament needs no demonstration. When men gather into groups, as they have no choice but to do, this temperament becomes essential to both survival and progress. Without it men cannot hope to solve such ever-present problems as procurement of food and shelter, division of labor, maintenance of law and order, education, and procreation. Without it they cannot find the release from tension and insecurity that permits them to engage in creative thought and adventurous activity. Individual men and entire societies both rely heavily on the conservative temperament, the "natural" desire for security, safety, and peace.

10   The "conservatism of possession" is what many men seem to have in mind when they describe a person or argument or course of action as conservative. *Possessive conservatism* is the attitude of the man who has something substantial to defend against the erosion of change, whether it be his status, reputation, power, or, most commonly property—and it need not appear "substantial" to anyone but him. This is not a posture struck only by the well-placed and well-to-do. The even or at least endurable tenor of the possessive conservative's existence depends largely on what he has and holds; threats to his property or status are threats to his interests, routine, and comfort. Like temperamental conservatism, the conservatism of possession is a self-centered, non-speculative frame of mind opposed to change of any type and from any direction. It is only incidentally an attitude toward social and political reform. The possessive conservative looks on new trends and tastes and on proposals of reform as threats not to the community, but to his place in it. It is conceivable, if not very probably, for him to be a man with an essentially radical temperament. In most conservatives possession and temperament fuse into a formidable bias against irregularity and dislocation.

11   The third and most common use of this word is to describe what I must call, for want of a handier phrase, *practical conservatism*. This is the conservatism of temperament and possession operating in a new dimension, the community, but not on the higher plane of speculative thought. It is the attitude of the man who has looked beyond his own comings and goings and has recognized, however fuzzily, that he is a member of a society worth defending against reform and revolution. He recognizes further that such defense calls for something more than holding his own place and property. He has pushed beyond the first two conservatisms and is prepared to oppose disruptive change in the legal, political, economic, social, religious, or cultural order. The practical conservative has managed

to rise some distance above his own interests to sublimate the meaner urges into devotion to his community.

12   The complexity of traits that shapes this attitude includes habit, inertia, fear, emulation, and the urge for security and secure possession, but two things have been added in sufficient measure to transform it into a high order of conservatism: the sense of membership in a community and a dislike or fear of political and social radicalism. What has not been added is the urge to reflect. The practical conservative's devotion to his community, it should be noted, is neither a cause nor an effect of considered thought. Practical conservatism is just that: a sense of satisfaction and identity with the status quo that may be classed only by extreme courtesy as a philosophy or tradition or faith. Most men adopt simple, non-speculative attitudes toward society and its problems, and most conservatives are therefore practical conservatives. Many such men are hardly conscious of their conservative bent; many, especially in America deny that they are conservatives at all. Yet all are firmly in the ranks of those who are satisfied with things as they are and distrust the proponents of sweeping change.

13   The last and highest kind is *philosophical conservatism*. The philosophical conservative subscribes consciously to principles designed to justify the established order and guard it against careless tinkering and determined reform. His conservatism is explained in intellectual as well as psychological, social, and economic terms. Nurture has joined with nature to make him the man he is. He is conscious of the history, structure, ideals, and traditions of his society, of the real tendencies and implications of proposals of reform, and of the importance of conservatism in maintaining a stable social order. He is aware that he is a conservative, and that he must therefore practice a conservative politics. This awareness of his nature and mission is to a substantial degree the result of hard thinking under radical pressure; he has examined his principles, candidly if not always enthusiastically, and found them good. His loyalty to country projects into the past, and his sense of history leads him to appreciate the long and painful process through which it developed into something worth defending. Moreover, his loyalty is so profound that he is ready to transcend the conservatism of possession by suffering privation and deprivation, and a large dose of unpopularity, in defense of cherished institutions and values. Awareness, reflection, traditionalism, and at least some degree of disinterestedness—these are the qualities that distinguish the genuine conservative from all others who bear this label. He is a rare bird in any country, an even rarer one in this; and as he is rare, so is he precious—no less precious, I would insist, than that other rare bird, the genuine liberal. His leadership, both active and intellectual, can alone transform a confused mass of practical conservatives into a purposeful conservative movement. . . .

61 LEARNED HAND

Freedom of Dissent

1   What do we mean by "principles of civil liberties and human rights"? We cannot go far in that inquiry until we have achieved some notion of what we mean by Liberty; and that has always proved a hard concept to define. The natural, though naïve, opinion is that it means no more than that each individual shall be allowed to pursue his own desires without let or hindrance; and that, although it is true that this is practically impossible, still it does remain the goal, approach to which measures our success. Why, then, is not a beehive or an anthill a perfect example of a free society? Surely you have been a curious and amused watcher beside one of these.

2   In and out of their crowded pueblo the denizens pass in great number, each bent upon his own urgent mission, quite oblivious of all the rest except as he must bend his path to avoid them. It is a scene of strenuous, purposeful endeavor in which each appears to be, and no doubt in fact is, accomplishing his own purpose; and yet he is at the same time accomplishing the purpose of the group as a whole. As I have gazed at it, the sentence from the Collect of the Episcopal prayer-book has come to me: "Whose service is perfect freedom."

3   Why is it, then, that we so positively rebel against the hive and the hill as a specimen of a free society? Why is it that such prototypes of totalitarianisms arouse our deepest hostility? Unhappily it is not because they cannot be realized, or at least because they cannot be approached, for a substantial period. Who can be sure that such appalling forecasts as Aldous Huxley's *Brave New World* or Orwell's *1984* are not prophetic? Indeed, there have often been near approaches to such an order.

4   Germany at the end of 1940 was probably not far removed from one, and who of us knows that there are not countless persons today living within the boundaries of Russia and perhaps of China who are not willing partners, accepting as their personal aspirations the official definitions of the good, the true and the beautiful? Indeed, there have been, and still are, in our own United States large and powerful groups who, if we are to judge their purposes by their conduct, see treason in all dissidence and would welcome an era in which all of us should think, feel and live in consonance with duly prescribed patterns.

From *New York Times Magazine* (February 6, 1955). Reprinted as "A Fanfare for Prometheus," *The Spirit of Liberty* (New York: Knopf Vintage, 1959) pp. 221–228. © 1955 by The New York Times Company. Reprinted by permission of The New York Times Company and Alfred A. Knopf, Inc.

5   Human nature is malleable, especially if you can indoctrinate the disciple with indefectible principles before anyone else reaches him. (I fancy that the Janissaries were as fervent Mohammedans as the authentic Turks.) Indeed, we hear from those who are entitled to an opinion that at times the abject confessions made in Russia by victims who know that they are already marked for slaughter are not wrung from them by torture or threats against their families. Rather, they come from partisans, so obsessed with the faith that when they are told that the occasion calls for scapegoats and that they have been selected, recognize and assent to the propriety of the demand and cooperate in its satisfaction. It is as though when the right time comes, the drones agreed to their extinction in the interest of the hive.

6   Nor need we be surprised that men so often embrace almost any doctrines, if they are proclaimed with a voice of absolute assurance. In a universe that we do not understand, but with which we must in one way or another somehow manage to deal, and aware of the conflicting desires that clamorously beset us, between which we must choose and which we must therefore manage to weigh, we turn in our bewilderment to those who tell us that they have found a path out of the thickets and possess the scales by which to appraise our needs.

7   Over and over again such prophets succeed in converting us to unquestioning acceptance; there is scarcely a monstrous belief that has not had its day and its passionate adherents, so eager are we for safe footholds in our dubious course. How certain is any one of us that he, too, might not be content to follow any fantastic creed, if he was satisfied that nothing would ever wake him from the dream? And, indeed, if there were nothing to wake him, how should he distinguish its articles from the authentic dictates of verity?

8   Remember, too, that it is by no means clear that we are happier in the faith we do profess than we should be under the spell of an orthodoxy that was safe against all heresy. Cruel and savage as orthodoxies have always proved to be, the faithful seem able to convince themselves that the heretics, as they continue to crop up, get nothing worse than their due, and to rest with an easy conscience.

9   In any event, my thesis is that the best answer to such systems is not so much in their immoral quality—immoral though they be—as in the fact that they are inherently unstable, because they are at war with our only trustworthy way of living in accord with the facts. For I submit that it is only by trial and error, by insistent scrutiny and by readiness to re-examine presently accredited conclusions that we have risen, so far as in fact we have risen, from our brutish ancestors, and I believe that in our loyalty to these habits lies our only chance, not merely of progress, but even of survival.

10   They were not indeed a part of our aboriginal endowment: Man, as he emerged, was not prodigally equipped to master the infinite diversity of

his environment. Obviously, enough of us did manage to get through; but it has been a statistical survival, for the individual's native powers of adjustment are by no means enough for his personal safety any more than are those of other creatures. The precipitate of our experience is far from absolute verity, and our exasperated resentment at all dissent is a sure index of our doubts. Take, for instance, our constant recourse to the word, "subversive," as a touchstone of impermissible deviation from accepted canons.

11   All discussions, all debate, all dissidence tends to question and in consequence to upset existing convictions: that is precisely its purpose and its justification. He is, indeed, a "subversive" who disputes those precepts that I most treasure and seeks to persuade me to substitute his own. He may have no shadow of desire to resort to anything but persuasion; he may be of those to whom any forcible sanction of conformity is anathema; yet it remains true that he is trying to bring about my apostasy, and I hate him just in proportion as I fear his success.

12   Contrast this protective resentment with the assumption that lies at the base of our whole system that the best chance for truth to emerge is a fair field for all ideas. Nothing, I submit, more completely betrays our latent disloyalty to this premise to all that we pretend to believe than the increasingly common resort to this and other question-begging words. Their imprecision comforts us by enabling us to suppress arguments that disturb our complacency and yet to continue to congratulate ourselves on keeping the faith as we have received it from the Founding Fathers.

13   Heretics have been hateful from the beginning of recorded time; they have been ostracized, exiled, tortured, maimed and butchered; but it has generally proved impossible to smother them, and when it has not, the society that has succeeded has always declined. Facades of authority, however imposing, do not survive after it has appeared that they rest upon the sands of human conjecture and compromise.

14   And so, if I am to say what are "the principles of civil liberties and human rights," I answer that they lie in habits, customs—conventions, if you will—that tolerate dissent and can live without irrefragable certainties; that are already to overhaul existing assumptions; that recognize that we never see save through a glass, darkly, and that at long last we shall succeed only so far as we continue to undertake "the intolerable labor of thought"—that most distasteful of all our activities.

15   If such a habit and such a temper pervade a society, it will not need institutions to protect its "civil liberties and human rights"; so far as they do not, I venture to doubt how far anything else can protect them: whether it be Bills of Rights, or courts that must in the name of interpretation read their meaning into them.

16   This may seem to you a bleak and cheerless conclusion, too alien to our nature to be practical. "We must live from day to day"—you will say—

"to live is to act, and to act is to choose and decide. How can we carry on at all without some principles, some patterns to meet the conflicts in which each day involves us?" Indeed, we cannot, nor am I suggesting that we should try; but I *am* suggesting that it makes a vital difference—*the* vital difference—whether we deem our principles and our patterns to be eternal verities, rather than the best postulates so far attainable.

17   Was it not Holmes who said: "The highest courage is to stake everything on a premise that you know tomorrow's evidence may disprove"? "Ah"—you will reply—"there's the rub. That may be the highest courage, but how many have it? You are hopelessly wrong if you assume the general prevalence of such a virtue; ordinary men must be given more than conjectures if they are to face grave dangers."

18   But do you really believe that? Do you not see about you every day and everywhere the precise opposite? Not alone on the battlefield but in the forest, the desert and the plain; in the mountains, at sea, on the playing field, even in the laboratory and the factory—yes (do not laugh), at the card table and the racetrack—men are forever putting it "upon the touch to win or lose it all." Without some smack of uncertainty and danger, to most of us the world would be a tepid, pallid show.

19   Surely, like me, you have all felt something of this when you have looked on those pathetic attempts to depict in paint or stone the delights of Paradise. I own that the torments of hell never fail to horrify me; not even the glee of the demons in charge is an adequate relief, though the artist has generally been successful in giving a veracious impression of the gusto with which they discharge their duties.

20   But when I turn to the Congregation of the Blessed, I cannot avoid a sense of anti-climax; strive as I may, the social atmosphere seems a bit forced; and I recall those very irreverent verses of Lowes Dickinson:

> Burning at first no doubt would be worse,
> But time the impression would soften,
> While those who are bored with praising the Lord,
> Would be more bored with praising him often.

21   By some happy fortuity man is a projector, a designer, a builder, a craftsman; it is among his most dependable joys to impose upon the flux that passes before him some mark of himself, aware though he always must be of the odds against him. His reward is not so much in the work as in its making; not so much in the prize as in the race. We may win when we lose, if we have done what we can; for by so doing we have made real at least some part of that finished product in whose fabrication we are most concerned—ourselves.

22   And if at the end some friendly critic shall pass by and say, "My friend, how good a job do you really think you have made of it all?" we can answer, "I know as well as you that it is not of high quality, but I did

put into it whatever I had, and that was the game I started out to play."

23   It is still in the lap of the gods whether a society can succeed, based on "civil liberties and human rights," conceived as I have tried to describe them; but of one thing at least we may be sure: the alternatives that have so far appeared have been immeasurably worse, and so, whatever the outcome, I submit to you that we must press along. Borrowing from Epictetus, let us say to ourselves: "Since we are men we will play the part of a Man," and how can I better end than by recalling to you the concluding passage of "Prometheus Unbound"?

> To suffer woes which Hope thinks infinite;
> To forgive wrongs darker than death or night;
> To defy Power, which seems omnipotent
> To love, and bear; to hope till Hope creates
> From its own wreck the thing it contemplates;
> Neither to change, nor falter, nor repent;
> This, like thy glory, Titan, is to be
> Good, great and joyous, beautiful and free;
> This is alone Life, Joy, Empire and Victory.

Questions

1. In paragraph 1, Justice Hand suggests a simplistic definition of liberty and then uses a beehive or anthill as an example. Why? What initial point is he trying to make?
2. How is this initial point developed in paragraphs 2 and 3?
3. In paragraph 11, is Justice Hand describing Socrates, as Socrates sees himself in *Crito*? Would Hand and Socrates agree, basically? Would they agree about the nature of dissent?
4. Consider Hand's comment on heretics in Paragraph 13. What relevance has this to Thoreau's position?
5. Examine Hand and Socrates in light of Rossiter's categories. Is there some way in which they are all conservatives?

Theme topics

1. Write an essay in which you note the importance of dissent in some particular area and attempt to define its limits.
2. Dissent is heresay/Dissent is freedom. Choose one or the other or both and write an essay illustrating your thesis, being sure to focus on a specific issue.

62 LOREN EISELEY

The Uncompleted Man

1   The nature into which Shakespeare's Macbeth dabbles so unsuc-
cessfully with the aid of witchcraft, in the famous scene on the heath, is
unforgettable in literature. We watch in horrified fascination the malevolent
change in the character of Macbeth as he gains a dubious insight into the
unfolding future—a future which we know to be self-created. This scene,
fearsome enough at all times, is today almost unbearable to the discerning
observer. Its power lies in its symbolic delineation of the relationship of
Macbeth's midnight world to the realm of modern science—a relationship
grasped by few.

2   The good general, Banquo, who, unlike Macbeth, is wary of such
glimpses into the future as the witches have allowed the two companions,
seeks to restrain his impetuous comrade. " 'Tis strange," Banquo says,

> And oftentimes, to win us to our harm
> The instruments of darkness tell us truths,
> Win us with honest trifles, to betray's
> In deepest consequence.

Macbeth who, in contrast to Banquo, has immediately seized upon the self-
imposed reality induced by the witches' prophecies, stumbles out of their
toils at the last, only to protest in his dying hour:

> And be these juggling fiends no more believ'd . . .
> That keep the word of promise to our ear
> And break it to our hope!

3   Who, we may now inquire, are these strange beings who waylaid
Macbeth, and why do I, who have spent a lifetime in the domain of science,
make the audacious claim that this old murderous tale of the scientific
twilight extends its shadow across the doorway of our modern laboratories?
These bearded, sexless creatures who possess the faculty of vanishing into
air or who reappear in some ultimate flame-wreathed landscape only to
mock our folly, are an exteriorized portion of ourselves. They are projections from our own psyche, smoking wisps of mental vapor that proclaim
our subconscious intentions and bolster them with Delphic utterances—
half-truths which we consciously accept, and which then take power over
us. Under the spell of such oracles we create, not a necessary or real future,

From *Harper's Magazine* 228 (March, 1964), pp. 51–54. Copyright © 1964, by
Harper's Magazine. Reprinted by permission of Loren Eiseley.

but a counterfeit drawn from within ourselves, which we then superimpose, through purely human power, upon reality. Indeed one could say that these phantoms create a world which is at the same time spurious and genuine, so complex is our human destiny.

4   Every age has its style in these necromantic projections. The corpse-lifting divinations of the Elizabethan sorcerers have given way, in our time, to other and, at first sight, more scientific interpretations of the future. Today we know more about man, where he has come from, and what we may expect of him—or so we think. But there is one thing, in my belief, which identifies Macbeth's "juggling fiends" in any age, whether these uncanny phantoms appear as witches, star readers, or today's technologists. This quality is their claim to omniscience—an omniscience only half-stated on the basis of the past or specious present, and always lacking in genuine knowledge of the future. The leading characteristic of the future they present is its fixed, static, inflexible quality.

5   Such a future is fated beyond human will to change, just as Macbeth's demons, by prophecy, worked in him a transformation of character which then created inevitable tragedy. Until the appearance of the witches on the heath gave it shape, that tragedy existed only as a latent possibility in Macbeth's subconscious. Similarly, in this age, one could quote those who seek control of man's destiny by the evocation of his past. Their wizardry is deceptive because their spells are woven out of a genuine portion of reality—which, however, has taken on this always identifiable quality of fixity in an unfixed universe. The ape is always in our hearts, we are made to say, although each time a child is born something totally and genetically unique enters the universe, just as it did long ago when the great ethical leaders—Christ, the Buddha, Confucius—spoke to their followers.

6   Man escapes definition even as the modern phantoms in militarist garb proclaim—as I have heard them do—that man will fight from one side of the solar system to the other, and beyond. The danger, of course, is truly there, but it is a danger which, while it lies partially in what man is, lies much closer to what he chooses to believe about himself. Man's whole history is one of transcendence and of self-examination, which have led him to angelic heights of sacrifice as well as into the bleakest regions of despair. The future is not truly fixed but the world arena is smoking with the caldrons of those who would create tomorrow by evoking, rather than exorcising, the stalking ghosts of the past.

7   Even this past, however, has been far deeper and more pregnant with novelty than the short-time realist can envisage. As an evolutionist I never cease to be astounded by the past. It is replete with more features than one world can realize. Perhaps it was this that led the philosopher Santayana to speak of men's true natures as not adequately manifested in their condition at any given moment, or even in their usual habits. "Their real

nature," he contended, "is what they would discover themselves to be if they possessed self-knowledge, or as the Indian scripture has it, if they became what they are." I should like to approach this mystery of the self, which so intrigued the great philosopher, from a mundane path strewn with the sticks and stones through which the archaeologist must pick his way.

8   Let me illustrate what I mean by a very heavy and peculiar stone which I keep upon my desk. It has been split across; carbon black, imprinted in the gray shale, is the outline of a fish. The chemicals that composed the fish—most of them at least—are still there in the stone. They are, in a sense, imperishable. They may come and go, pass in and out of living things, trickle away in the long erosion of time. They are inanimate, yet at one time they constituted a living creature.

9   Often at my desk, now, I sit contemplating the fish. It does not have to be a fish. It could be the long-horned Alaskan bison on my wall. For the point is, you see, that the fish is extinct and gone, just as those great heavy-headed beasts are gone, just as our massive-faced and shambling forebears of the Ice Age have vanished. The chemicals still about us here took a shape that will never be seen again so long as grass grows or the sun shines. Just once out of all time there was a pattern that we call *Bison regius,* a fish-like amphibian called *Ichthyostega,* and, at this present moment, a primate who knows, or thinks he knows, the entire score. In the past there has been armor; there have been bellowings out of throats like iron furnaces; there have been phantom lights in the dark forest, and toothed reptiles winging through the air. It has all been carbon and its compounds, the black stain running perpetually across the stone.

10   But though the elements are known, nothing in all those shapes is now returnable. No living chemist can shape a dinosaur, no living hand can start the dreaming tentacular extensions that characterize the life of the simplest ameboid cell. Finally, as the greatest mystery of all, I who write these words on paper, cannot establish my own reality. I am, by any reasonable and considered logic, dead. This may be a matter of concern to you reading these words; but if it is any consolation, I can assure you that you are as dead as I. For, on my office desk, to prove my words is the fossil out of the stone, and there is the carbon of life stained black on the ancient rock.

11   There is no life in the fossil. There is no life in the carbon in my body. As the idea strikes me—and believe me it comes as a profound shock—I run down the list of elements. There is no life in the iron, there is no life in the phosphorus, the nitrogen does not contain me, the water that soaks my tissues is not I. What am I then? I pinch my body in a kind of sudden desperation. My heart knocks, my fingers close around the pen. There is, it seems, a semblance of life here.

12   But the minute I start breaking this strange body down into its constituents, it is dead. It does not know me. Carbon does not speak, calcium does not remember, iron does not weep. Even if I hastily reconstitute their combinations in my mind, rebuild my arteries, and let oxygen in the grip of hemoglobin go hurrying through a thousand conduits, I have a kind of machine, but where in all this array of pipes and hurried flotsam is the dweller?

13   From whence, out of what steaming pools or boiling cloudbursts did he first arise? What forces can we find which brought him up the shore, scaled his body into an antique, reptilian shape and then cracked it like an egg to let a soft-furred animal with a warmer heart emerge? And we? Would it not be a good thing if man were tapped gently like a fertile egg to see what might creep out? I sometimes think of this as I handle the thick-walled skulls of the animal men who preceded us, or ponder over those remote splay-footed creatures whose bones lie deep in the world's wastelands at the very bottom of time.

14   With the glooms and night terrors of those vast cemeteries I have been long familiar. A precisely similar gloom enwraps the individual life of each of us. There are moments in my bed at midnight, or watching the play of moonlight on the ceiling, when this ghostliness of myself comes home to me with appalling force, when I lie tense, listening as if removed, far off, to the footfalls of my own heart, or seeing my own head on the pillow turning restlessly with the round staring eyes of a gigantic owl. I whisper "Who?" to no one but myself in the silent, sleeping house—the living house gone back to sleep with the sleeping stones, the eternally sleeping chair, the picture that sleeps forever on the bureau, the dead, also sleeping, though they walk in my dreams. In the midst of all this dark, this void, this emptiness, I, more ghostly than a ghost, cry "Who? Who?" to no answer, aware only of other smaller ghosts like the bat sweeping by the window or the dog who, in repeating a bit of his own lost history, turns restlessly among nonexistent grasses before he subsides again upon the floor.

15   "Trust the divine animal who carries us through the world," writes Emerson. Like the horse who finds the way by instinct when the traveler is lost in the forest, so the divine within us, he contends, may find new passages opening into nature; human metamorphosis may be possible. Emerson wrote at a time when man still lived intimately with animals and pursued wild, dangerous ways through primeval forests and prairies. Emerson and Thoreau lived close enough to nature to know something still of animal intuition and wisdom. They had not reached that point of utter cynicism—that distrust of self and of the human past which leads finally to total entrapment in that past, "man crystallized," as Emerson again was shrewd enough to observe.

16   This entrapment is all too evident in the writings of many concerned with the evolutionary story of man. Their gaze is fixed solely upon a past into which, one begins to suspect, has been poured a certain amount of today's frustration, venom, and despair. Like the witches in *Macbeth,* these men are tempting us with seeming realities about ourselves until these realities take shape in our minds and become the future. It is not necessary to break the code of DNA in order to control human destiny. The tragedy is that men are already controlling it even while they juggle retorts and shake vials in search of a physical means to enrich their personalities. We would like to contain the uncontainable future in a glass, have it crystallized out before us as a powder to swallow. All then, we imagine, would be well.

17   As our knowledge of the genetic mechanism increases, both scientists and journalists bombard our ears with ingenious accounts of how we are to control, henceforth, our own evolution. We who have recourse only to a past which we misread and which has made us cynics would now venture to produce our own future out of this past alone. Again I judge this self-esteem as a symptom of our time, our powerful, misused technology, our desire not to seek the good life but to produce a painless mechanical version of it—our willingness to be good if goodness can, in short, be swallowed in a pill.

18   Once more we are on the heath of the witches, or, to come closer to our own time, we are in the London laboratory where the good Doctor Jekyll produced a potion and reft out of his own body the monster Hyde.

19   Nature, as I have tried to intimate in this little dissection, is never quite where we see it. It is a becoming as well as a passing, but the becoming is both within and without our power. It is this lesson, with all our hard-gained knowledge, that is so difficult to comprehend. All along the evolutionary road it could have been said, "This is man," if there had then been such a magical self-delineating and mind-freezing word. It could have immobilized us at any step of our journey. It could have held us hanging to the bough from which we actually dropped; it could have kept us cowering, small-brained and helpless, whenever the great cats came through the reeds. It could have stricken us with terror before the fire that was later to be our warmth and weapon against Ice Age cold. At any step of the way, the word *man,* in retrospect, could be said to have encompassed just such final limits.

20   Each time the barrier has been surmounted. Man is not man. He is elsewhere. There is within us only that dark, divine animal engaged in a strange journey—that creature who, at midnight, knows its own ghostliness and senses its far road. "Man's unhappiness," brooded Carlyle, "comes of his Greatness; it is because there is an Infinite in him, which with all his cunning he cannot quite bring under the Finite." This is why hydrogen,

which has become the demon element of our time, should be seen as the intangible dagger which hung before Macbeth's vision, but which had no power except what was lent to it by his own mind.

21   The terror that confronts our age is our own conception of ourselves. Above all else this is the potion which the modern Dr. Jekylls have concocted. As Shakespeare foresaw:

> It hath been taught us from the primal state
> That he which is was wished until he were.

This is not the voice of the witches. It is the clear voice of a great poet almost four centuries gone, who saw at the dawn of the scientific age what was to be the darkest problem of man: his conception of himself. The words are quiet, almost cryptic; they do not foretell. They imply a problem in free will. Shakespeare, in this passage, says nothing of starry influences, machinery, beakers, or potions. He says, in essence, one thing only: that what we wish will come.

22   I submit to you that this is the deadliest message man will ever encounter in all literature. It thrusts upon him inescapable choices. Shakespeare's is the eternal, the true voice of the divine animal, piercing, as it has always pierced, the complacency of little centuries in which, encamped as in hidden thickets, men have sought to evade self-knowledge by describing themselves as men.

63   RICHARD E. SULLIVAN
The End of the "Long Run"

1   If, a thousand years from now, there still remains a civilized society interested in its past, the historians of that distant era will undoubtedly seek some explanation of the role and significance of the 20th century in the total stream of human history. Their evaluations of this troubled era will probably be numerous. Already the analysts of human behavior have begun to diverge in their generalizations concerning the fundamental nature of the 20th century. They speak in terms of the ethic of the "organization man," of the victory of "the rebel," of the plight of "the lonely crowd," and of "the revolt of the masses." Their estimates of the trends of this century suggest strongly that there is emerging a radical change in human outlook, capable of causing those looking back from the

From *The Centennial Review of Arts & Sciences, 4,* No. 3 (Summer, 1960), pp. 391–408. Reprinted by permission of the author and the publisher.

vantage point of a thousand years hence to conclude that the 20th century was the point of departure for a fundamental adjustment of human values.

2   However, after all manner of historians of the year 3000 A.D. have picked over the bones of the 20th century and pronounced their judgment of its place in the historical continuum, the consummate historian and artist—the Toynbee of the 31st century—will have his say. I suspect that he will disregard most of the trends that seem so world-shaking to us in the 1960's in favor of a very simple characterization of our century. He will say that this was the first century in world history when man ceased believing that time was working in favor of his deliverance. He will point out that during the 20th century all men were faced with the possibility that one twist of fate, one gesture, one ill-chosen word, one ill-conceived act could result in the annihilation of civilization and humanity. Once that fact had sunk into the mass consciousness, our 31st century Toynbee will say, then man could no longer explain his disposition to suffer evils on the ground that developments "in the long run" would remove them. Humanity could no longer depend on its ancient and respectable rationale for delaying the solution of problems, for condoning wickedness, for suffering tyranny, and for fending off danger—dependence on "the long run" developments which would remove the present source of discomfort.

3   Perhaps as an historian I am too sensitive about the phrase "the long run." I have heard my fellow historians use it to explain nearly everything across the whole spectrum of history. I have read repeatedly the works of scholars who went to the utmost pains to describe a problem that bedeviled a past generation and who then proceeded to say that "in the long run" this difficulty resolved itself because of the emergence of new factors and forces. One cannot be subjected to this experience hundreds of times without being seduced into the assumption that "the long run" is some kind of fourth dimensional force which intervenes in human affairs to resolve all problems automatically and painlessly, irrespective of how wisely or foolishly men may act at any given moment. Probably one could best define the historian as a disciple of the gospel of "the long run," meaning that his function is and has always been to assure people that time works in favor of the welfare of men. However, if the historian is the high priest of this cult, around him are legions of worshippers whose acts prove that they are true believers. They go penniless to buy a car or a house with complete trust that in the long run they will find the wherewithal to pay for it. They sire children with genuine faith that the long run course of development will provide happiness for their offspring. They pour their best energies into the creation of some seemingly fantastic machine or organization that promises in the long run to benefit someone. With charming innocence they console the heartbroken with the advice that time has a way of solving everything. They even sacrifice their lives for a cause on the completely unprovable assumption that their immolation will benefit the future. Faith

in the magic of "the long run" is seemingly as much a part of the human make-up as the brain or the liver.

4   So it has been since the beginning of human endeavor. A history of the world could be written around the theme of human reliance on the long run solution. It would leave little unaccounted for. Men have always been more content to wait for things to develop than to grapple with issues actively and immediately. They have been satisfied to suffer unspeakable indignities in the simple faith that eventually, "in the long run," their situation would be alleviated. The revolutionist, intent on acting *immediately* to relieve human misery, is actually a rare figure in human history, although in the past he sometimes has been presented as the prime mover in the historical process. He attracts so much attention, I believe, simply because he represents such a unique specimen in the totality of mankind, such an unusual departure from the norm. The real moving force in human history has been the trusting, essentially lazy, somewhat frightened, yet always optimistic man who was sure that, if he waited, cosmic justice would be done in his favor. So numerous has been his breed that "waiting for the long run developments" has always been a decisive factor in shaping human affairs.

II

5   Skimming back across the ages will supply numerous examples to demonstrate the antiquity of the "long run" interpretation of the working of destiny. Although he left posterity poorly informed about his mental processes, the most primitive Old Stone Age hunter probably found his greatest consolation during the lean season in the conviction that by waiting he would take his game; indeed the very method of his hunting emphasized the wisdom of waiting for nature to thrust her fruits on him in the form of an unsuspecting animal that wandered across his path by accident. Certainly by the time the great civilizations of the ancient Near East had emerged, men had surrendered to the long run point of view. Both Egyptian and Babylonian religious literature is replete with the spirit of calm resignation to the fact that the divinely ordained and controlled universe contained a safe refuge for puny man. No matter how the raging gods might shake the universal fundaments, still the outcome would be happy. The Nile might not flood for years, bringing desperate famine to Egypt, but the evil days would pass and those who waited would be rewarded. Here is the Egyptian way of expressing this conviction of the inevitable beneficence of the universe, as contained in a hymn to the god of the Nile: "If he is sluggish, then nostrils are stopped up, and everybody is *poor*. If there be a cutting down in the food-offerings of the gods, then a

million men perish among mortals, covetousness is practised, the entire land is in fury, and great and small are on the execution block. But people are different when he approaches. . . . When he rises then the land is in jubilation, then every belly is in joy, every backbone takes on laughter, and every tooth is exposed." Or, as related in Babylonian mythology, a devastating flood loosed by a vengeful god might destroy all things; yet, some other god was always considerate enough to provide for the protection of man, assuring that he would again flourish. In the long run the Egyptians and the Babylonians, plus the many later Near Eastern people who adopted their basic outlooks, felt that they had nothing to fear. The universal order assured them a place and a portion of happiness. What could be fitter symbols of the faith that time worked for man than the pyramids, dedicated to the preservation of a dead body until such time as its immortality was provided for, even if that process required ages?

6   Much more explicit were the Hebrew exponents of the idea that "in the fulness of time"—*i.e.,* in the long run—all things would evolve toward perfection. The idea saturates the prophetic writings of the Old Testament. These writings were produced at a period in Hebrew history when, judged by the expectation of the chosen children of Yahweh, the future looked hopeless. The Hebrews had suffered division of their hard-won national kingdom, conquest at the hands of the vicious Assyrians and sinful Chaldeans, and mass deportation from their native soil and sacred temple to whorish Babylon. These tragedies were accompanied by a paralyzing religious confusion which took the form of extensive apostasy from Yahweh-worship. Yet listen to what the prophets cried in the midst of misery: "Come, my people, enter thou into thy chambers, and shut thy doors about thee: hide thyself as it were for a little moment, until the indignation is overpast." (Isaiah 26:20). How must the "little moment" be spent? "And the people shall be oppressed, everyone by another, and everyone by his neighbor: the child shall behave himself proudly against the ancient, and the base against the honourable." (Isaiah 3:5). "And they shall look unto the earth; and behold trouble and darkness, dimness of anguish; and they shall be driven to darkness." (Isaiah 8:22). But all that would pass. "Behold, the Lord God will come with strong hand. . . . He shall feed his flock like a shepherd." (Isaiah 40:10-11). "The ransomed of the Lord shall return, and come to Zion with songs and everlasting joy upon their heads: they shall obtain joy and gladness, and sorrow and sighing shall flee away." (Isaiah 35:10). How long Zion must wait and suffer the prophets never say. Yet waiting is the solution to the problem. In the fulness of time today's ills will be resolved by a cosmic force beyond man's control, yet working for his ultimate deliverance.

7   Greek thought reflected a similar easy confidence that things would unfold themselves for the good, no matter how dreadful the present might be. Who can forget the patiently waiting Penelope engaged in her senseless

spinning amidst her greedy, too anxious suitors? Why did she not act to resolve her quandary? Because the operation of the universal order would bring back Ulysses. Homer the artist would have outraged man's moral sense by requiring so good a woman to bustle about trying to solve her own problems; time would resolve the issue. Greek drama in general breathes the wisdom of accepting the present with the assurance that the future will remove the evil and the pain at hand. Inexorably, without overt human action, the house of Agamemnon is brought to justice for its transgressions, and the world is set aright. In the *Oresteia,* Aeschylus provides the theme of most Greek tragedies when he has Clytemnestra greet the returning Agamemnon with these words, "Maid-servants, why do you delay? Straightway spread the purple tapestry, that Justice may guide his steps to a home he little hoped to see." Orestes sums up what wisdom lay at the other end of that carpet when in the *Eumenides* he says: "Time, that smooths all things, hath smoothed the front of my offence." In the long run all is made right with gods and men; that is a law of the universe. Let none think that in Greece this philosophy was confined to the unenlightened believers in hoary myths. In his *Republic,* the rationalistic Plato reflects a comparable trust that the passage of time would resolve even the greatest difficulties. After wrestling with a definition of the philosopher king and repeatedly demonstrating how remote the perfect political order is from the existent world, Socrates and his companions conclude that no philosopher king or perfect state ever existed. Yet this is no cause for despair. They agree that in the course of ages a philosopher king *might* be born and that his virtue *might* be recognized so that "he might bring into existence the ideal polity about which the world is so incredulous." (*Republic,* VI, 502). Socrates concludes on what is almost a triumphant note: "But we have sufficiently shown, in what has preceded, that all this, if only possible, is assuredly for the best." (*Republic,* VI, 502).

8   Christian thinkers caught up these many threads out of the ancient past to reassert a philosophy of history that assured all believers of the inevitable working out of things for the salvation of humanity. Their confident affirmations, made amid the disheartening spectacle of the collapse of the Roman Empire, the degeneration of Graeco-Roman moral values, and the onslaught of the barbarians, were unquestionably of major significance in unloosing the energy needed to establish a Christian civilization over much of Europe, western Asia, and northern Africa. St. Paul catalogued enough evidence of human iniquity to force a man with any sense of justice to the conclusion that humanity was damned. Yet he did not reach that conclusion. "For I reckon that the sufferings of this present time are not worthy to be compared to the glory which shall be revealed in us." (Romans 8:18). "For we know that the whole creation groaneth and travaileth in pain together until now. . . . We are saved by hope: but hope that is seen is not hope; for what a man seeth, why doth he yet hope for?"

(Romans 8:23-24). "Therefore, my beloved brethren, be ye stedfast, unmoveable, always abounding in the work of the Lord, forasmuch as ye know that your labour is not in vain in the Lord." (I Corinthians 15:58). In the "fulness of time" (Ephesians 1:10) all would be made right; every Christian could build his life around that precept. St. Augustine made it unnecessary for the Christian to trust in hope unseen by constructing a compelling philosophy of history embracing the past in its entirety to prove that God's will would be done. By his reckoning, abundant evidence existed outside Scripture to prove that there was a purpose in history and that that purpose operated to exalt the good over the evil, to alleviate the tainted past and present by providing a perfect city of God in the future, to exalt Jerusalem over Babylon. The Christian, according to Augustine, need not despair, for God "orders all events in His providence until the beauty of the completed course of time, of which the component parts are the dispensations adapted to each successive age, shall be finished, like the grand melody of some ineffably wise master of song." Dante's *Divine Comedy* supplied the most adroit artistic expression of the Christian conviction that a beneficial order assures human well-being. The poet's long trek from earth to the bottom of hell and thence into the presence of God serves as a symbolical representation of humanity's passage through time to ultimate fulfillment. Few pieces of art surpass the *Divine Comedy* as a statement of hope in ultimate perfection of mankind.

III

9   The passage of centuries and the flow of intellectual pursuits into new channels gradually eroded the basis of the old faith that in the long run all things work out for the best. Most of the hope of the ancients rested in their conviction that superhuman powers had ordained the ultimate perfection of man and the world. This premise eventually came under attack. The humanists of the Renaissance period doubted that man needed to depend on divinity for anything. Rationalists concluded to their own satisfaction that man possessed in his intellect a tool capable of elevating him to divine heights. Scientists discovered a method by which rational powers could be harnessed to the performance of feats surpassing the deeds of the gods. Slowly the proponents of these new schools of thought hacked to pieces the foundations of the old cosmic optimism upon which men found assurance that an almighty power would save everything if one would wait for that power to unfold its plans through time.

10   However, the revolt against God which, during the last four or five centuries, has rocked the foundations of the value system of western society has hardly disturbed the superstructure, man's happy confidence that

things will work out for the best. If anything, faith in "the long run" grew as faith in the Almighty declined. New reasons have been discovered to assure men that *time* would advance all things toward perfection and resolve all the evils that press in upon humanity. God can now be neutral or even non-existent. For the rationalists of the Enlightenment, the key to perfection was education, that is, the process of unshackling man's innate rational powers. Education was a process requiring time, a leading out that occurred step by step. John Locke and his disciples assured the world that the ideal polity could be created by reasonable men entering a compact for that purpose; they need only discover the right moment "in the course of human events" to end forever the tyranny that had plagued unenlightened men. It remained for the scientists of the 19th century with their theory of evolution to formulate a surer guarantee of ultimate perfection than did all the powers of Osiris, Yahweh, or Zeus. Evolutionism was the doctrine of "the long run" *par excellence*. It applied not only to flowers, bugs, planets, and man the physical being; evolutionism became the basic premise for a whole new science: social science. Herbert Spencer defined the new creed in these words: "Whether it be in the development of the Earth, in the development of Life upon its surface, in the development of Society, of Government, of Manufactures, of Commerce, of Language, Literature, Science, Art, this same evolution of the simple into the complex, through successive differentiations, holds throughout. . . . Progress is not an accident but a necessity. What we call evil and immorality must disappear. It is certain that man must become perfect." The prophets of ancient Israel could not have done better in assuring all that the millenium would arrive in spite of anything. Even the most radical revolutionary movements of the last century were in a sense softened by the universal faith in the inevitability of progress. Marx could thunder in one breath that the workers of the world must arise violently to put off their chains; yet in the next he assured his audience that the downfall of the existing order and the coming of Utopia were inevitable. Thus the smashing of the old icons that has made the centuries since the Renaissance so lively has not in the least threatened one of man's greatest refuges, namely, the idea that in "the long run" nothing but good can befall man. Even with God banished, men found powerful reasons to live with "every tooth exposed," sure that all would be well with them.

11   These scraps of evidence selected from out of man's past estimates of ultimate lot offer only vague hints of the powerful grip of what has unquestionably been an eternal mooring for human life. Through the ages, in a multitude of ways, individuals and societies have lived and died happy in the thought that ultimately things would be perfect. Again and again the realities staring men in the face have been distorted to fit that frame of reference. Again and again action has been delayed because of a conviction that the passage of time would resolve what was currently evil and

inhuman. It has become second nature for men to smile in the face of adversity, to bear all indignities with good cheer, and to move slowly but assuredly toward a happy future.

12   And why should not man in the past have felt this trust in "the long run?" His own abilities and his environment have always, at least on the surface, combined to demonstrate empirically that such a faith was infinitely wise. Nature has always seemed an unassailable bastion assuring men that nothing cataclysmic will happen. The processes of reproduction evidenced in nature seemed to bespeak eternity. For all his demonstrated genius for evil, man seemed powerless to effect any fundamental change in nature. He could do no more than scratch the surface of the earth, clear away isolated patches of foliage, block up a few of the myriad streams that ribboned the continents, or kill a handful of his fellows. Who could think that such puny efforts had a chance to alter the fundamental process of nature—storm, earthquake, flood, and reproduction of the species? Neither had man's past efforts to affect changes in his own society been spectacular. Lacking instruments of mass communication and rapid transportation, his evil schemes and good intentions came to fruition slowly and imperfectly in any society and in any age. His days on earth were pitifully limited, making it almost a certainty that he would die, a martyr as it were, before his cause bore fruit. Well might he echo the reproof of Ozymandias: "Look on my works, Ye Mighty, and despair!" It was senseless to joust violently with destiny. The good things came slowly, as many wise men discerned in looking back across the past. Vergil reflected this sense of the necessity of growth in time when he argued in the *Aeneid* that all the centuries between Aeneas' flight from Troy and Augustus' victory at Actium were necessary to bring forth Roman greatness. Medieval chroniclers demonstrated the same concept when they began their histories of local monasteries by starting with Adam. The slowness of change was not, however, cause for despair. Things did improve—in the long run. Herodotus knew of the great antiquity of the Egyptians, but he did not doubt the superiority of the Greeks. Thus, like two great beacons, nature's order and man's own demonstrated capabilities have always taught to past generations a single piece of wisdom: man should live with an eye toward the long run, doing nothing rash to relieve the troubles of the present but continuing down existent paths with assurance that all would be well.

IV

13   Now, at mid-20th century, we are face to face with an awesome fact. We no longer have the least assurance that the passage of time will resolve our difficulties, that either the plans of benign gods or the inexora-

ble processes of nature or the wisdom of man are working for the perfection of the unwise and the imperfect. Anyone viewing the present objectively must conclude that man's ancient consoling faith in "the long run" is only an opiate, suspending its users in a fantastic world. Already some have put aside the pipe and, after the initial shock of abstinence, are beginning to discern the realities of the moment. The dimensions of the real situation are indeed monstrous and terrifying. For it is clear that nothing assures that civilization or even life itself will exist a millennium or a year or a minute hence. No one can live as if some force beyond human control assures a happy future unless he is willing to live in a dream world. All must eliminate any considerations of "the long run" from their calculations. For the first time in history, men must face the implications of living within a framework in which the future is a dubious quantity.

14   It requires no great wisdom to discern why "the long run" can no longer figure very seriously in human calculations. Man has succeeded in wrecking the pillars upon which he had previously constructed his faith that the cosmic order moved toward perfection. The gods, of course, have long since been made to yield their control of destiny. Nature's processes have been made to surrender to human intervention, so that man has acquired extensive powers of manipulation over nature. So successful has been his assault on nature that it is now conceivable that the course of nature could be changed radically at any moment. The neutralization of gravity, the explosion of planets, the leveling of mountains, the manipulation of the weather, the creation of new forms of life, the transmutation of existent species—these are but a few of the feats that man now has it within his power to perform. Such power signifies that the future order of nature will be what man chooses it to be. Certainly no one can believe any longer that nature is an impersonal force nudging humanity toward a golden age and preventing man from destroying himself. Yet within the memory of living men that assumption was made without question.

15   With the gods and nature deposed as protective forces, can man still rely on his own power to save himself and to assure his own inevitable progress? Alas, even man's self-deification has been destroyed by his advancing self-knowledge. His vaunted reason has been demonstrated to be but a thin veneer hiding elemental forces of irrationality, his mind a shapeless lump capable of being twisted into a myriad of transitory forms. His body might well become the plaything of some demon who would choose to endow him with two heads or an aluminum heart or might suffer grotesque mutations resulting from irradiated genes. For human flesh itself is part of the natural order over which man has seized power. Man's senses can be tricked and his cognitive powers blurred by a variety of psychological devices, many of which are already in use to convince him that he needs hundreds of things to make his life more comfortable, happier, safer, and less demanding. Indeed, it is no feat at all at present to empty a man's head of one set of values and pump in another; the job requires not

much more effort than changing a tire, or at most, rewiring an electronic computer. On the basis of present knowledge, only the hopelessly naive would place much trust in man's innate trustworthiness to work out—in the long, short, or any length of run—sensible solutions to human problems.

V

16   With God, nature, and man all dethroned as positive forces assuring the ultimate salvation of the universe, it is indeed a strange new world we face. Never in the history of man has life seemed so meaningless, as a legion of modern poets, artists, and philosophers have attested, sometimes too vehemently to suit those who still live in the comfortable old world where one could trust "the long run" to remove all that was unpleasant, ugly, and evil.

17   What are the implications of this new world? What is in store for anyone facing reality?

18   It is possible that the startling discovery that the world has no built-in mechanism guaranteeing its ultimate perfection will be the most salutary revelation in human history. Man may finally cease squatting on his intellectual and spiritual haunches awaiting the inevitable alleviation of his current misery in "the long run." He might stay his hand at some contemplated evil out of the realization that his power to manipulate nature and other men is so great that an ill-considered act could unloose a cosmic hecatomb. This alone would mark a spectacular improvement in human conduct. More important, man might be spurred to creativity by the realization that only positive, constructive action could affect any improvement in human affairs.

19   However, to hold up such a rosy prospect of the new world is to prophesy against all the omens. The end of "the long run" seems rather to presage a troubled future spun out by several truly lost generations. Already men are demonstrating that something precious has been removed from their midst and that they are panic-stricken by the prospect of a future that could bring their destruction as easily as their perfection. Probably no one knows yet how severe will be the trauma caused by the breaking of the idol of "the long run," but at least some portents have emerged to indicate that mankind may be entering an age of fantastic disturbances, all springing from his lost hope that everything will be well in the fulness of time. Disturbing as it may be, let us list a few of these signs, admitting that the list might be lengthened considerably.

20   First, men in ever increasing numbers will abandon all interest in the past. Ever since the cave dwellers sat around their fires trying to remember what custom said about the problem of the moment, men have al-

ways looked to the past to discern a pattern that would supply them wisdom to meet the present. They did so on the assumption that vast movements developing in time characterized the drama of life and that man must ride along with these movements. This is an almost impossible belief now, since nature and men can be manipulated quickly to achieve prodigious alterations of the course of affairs. The past suddenly becomes irrelevant. Why look back for wisdom when the wisdom gained may be negated by a madman with a hydrogen bomb? Thus a generation with no roots in the past is coming into existence; this is a kind of rootlessness with which the world has not previously had to deal. An historian shudders at the implications.

21   Deprived of hope for the future and trust in the past, men will snatch ever more greedily for the security of the present moment. It will not take them long to decide that the only security of the present lies in pleasure. Only those things and those actions which bring contentment and comfort at this instant offer an intelligent safeguard against believing in false gods in this insecure world where universal destruction is as likely as salvation. Universal Epicureanism may be bearable, but let no one forget Burn's thought: "Pleasures are like poppies spread,/You seize the flower, its bloom is shed."

22   It seems clear that men will become increasingly reluctant to work for the rewards of a tenuous future. Not to sacrifice one's mite of time and pleasure in order to labor for a future that may not emerge is logical to the thoughtful, soothing to the slothful. Yet a world lacking men who are willing to work or even reluctant to work will be an impossible world. Work in some form is a *sine qua non* for a civilization; its absence in any society threatens the vitality of that society.

23   Most men, doubtful of the future, will hardly find it sensible to serve a cause. For causes are goals that their adherents trust and believe will be fulfilled in "the long run." No historian can evade the conclusions that through the past ages human striving to hasten the inevitable has been a decisive force in shaping human destiny. To serve a cause demands that one assume that there will be a future in which the cause can come true. Put the future in doubt or admit that its shape may be inconceivably different from the present and a great cause makes little sense. The ordinary mortal will be compelled to decide that nothing can be gained from sincere devotion to a cause whose achievement is extremely dubious. He might better live unencumbered by commitments to the future. Needless to say, it will be a strange world when one can find no crusaders; yet that world is being born and may soon be heavily populated.

24   All signs clearly suggest that we are approaching an age that will be marked by a frenzied, hysterical approach to its own current problems. This is to be expected in a world where mere indecision may unloose forces capable of destroying everything. Take away the old assurance that

whatever the decision, it cannot be fatal because time operates to solve all things, and individuals and societies can no longer approach the issue with calm and deliberation. Decisions must now be leaped at lest delay spell catastrophe. Petty problems create major dilemmas because of the immense power that man can now unloose with little effort; thus we must expect to live constantly in a state of hysteria-breeding fear. Under the impact of repeated, soul-wringing crises, men's thresholds of response may rise, necessitating the application of ever stronger stimuli to evoke reaction. This situation, calling into play all the tricks of mass communication, must necessarily increase the cacophony assaulting human sanity. This can hardly be the old world, where the burden of decision could occasionally be put aside for a few moments of rest and blessed silence, a retreat made possible by the conviction that in the long run all would be well, whatever the decision of the moment might be.

25   Finally, and most terrifying of all, is the possibility that we stand at the beginning of an age of complete amorality. For is not any code of morals fundamentally a set of rules for behavior built on the predication that there is a certain unalterable order in the universe? Remove the unalterable and you negate the morality. At the moment it seems obvious that necessity of all kinds has been abolished. God, nature, and humanity are either discredited or malleable, depending on what man chooses to do with his knowledge and skill. It is inconceivable that any code of morals could have sanction or relevance in this situation. Man is finally free to do what he pleases, which is the exact opposite of living in a moral situation.

26   Has the picture been painted too darkly? Is what has been said nothing but an historian's naive lament over the passing of a bygone age? Perhaps. The picture is far from clear at the moment. However, there is every indication that a revolutionary change in our system of values is under way as a consequence of the advances made in human knowledge and skill over the last few decades. What has happened is nothing less than the establishment of man's control over his own destiny. In essence, man has finally become free, no longer restricted by jealous gods, plodding nature, or halting humanity. His knowledge has brought him the power to bend the course of events out of what previously seemed a predetermined trajectory. However, this freedom has required the giving of an earnest which most men are surrendering reluctantly and with grave reservations. Once having gained the power and the freedom to make the world and mankind what he wants, then man can no longer rest assured that impersonal forces, beyond human control, work to improve and eventually perfect humanity. There is no "long run" in which trust can be placed while men indulge in irrationality, meanness, or whatever foible strikes their fancy. A cynic might protest that in reality there never was a "long run" in which men could trust; those things in which men in the past trusted—God, nature, human intelligence—were as much chimeras

a thousand years ago as now. This protestation, however true it may be, really is not very impressive. The real significance of the moment, the fundamental condition that will make the historians of the year 3000 A.D. —if such there be—look back on the 20th century as a turning point in human history, lies in the fact that recent developments have demonstrated dramatically, obviously, and beyond doubt that man is on his own and cannot trust in "the long run." Never has humanity had to face this fact; therefore, there has never been a moment comparable to the present.

Questions

1. Identify the analysts of the twentieth century from the phrases Sullivan quotes in paragraph 1. What argumentative value does he extract from the Toynbee analogy in paragraph 2? How does he anticipate and discount in advance any reservation in the reader's mind that he, as an historian, is discussing events that are remote and esoteric from the point of view of the experience of the average man today?

2. Sullivan divides his essay into five numbered parts. What does each contribute to his overall argument? What devices of transition does he use to link them together (paragraphs 4 and 5, 8 and 9, 12 and 13, 15 and 16)?

3. How does Sullivan use questions to organize his material? Examine his use of quotations. Does he ever make a major generalization without employing a direct quotation to illustrate his point? If so, in which cases might direct quotation strengthen his overall argument?

4. Sullivan cites evidence to prove God, nature, and man have failed in the consciousness of contemporary man as "long-run" hopes for the universe's salvation. Does he prove his case to your satisfaction? How would you challenge his "skimming back across the ages"? What corroborative items, which he has failed to cite, would you add to his "scraps of evidence"?

5. What in the past has deterred the "long-run" harmful effects of irrationality and deliberate evil? Why or why not is all hope of deterrence now gone in Sullivan's view? Granted the validity of his thesis, what probable consequences does he foresee? What other probable consequences, if any, would you predict from the same evidence, and how would they contradict or corroborate Sullivan's?

Theme topics

1. Write a paper in which you examine the concepts of "freedom" and "rationality" in the context of points of view expressed or assumed in Hand's, Plato's, and Sullivan's essays. Choose your illustrations from sources other than these three pieces.

2. Write an essay in which your thesis is either "mankind controls events" or, conversely, "events control mankind." Use points of view and illustrations, quoted directly or indirectly, from essays throughout this section and from any other pertinent selection in this anthology or elsewhere. Strive to achieve logical transitions between paragraphs and to integrate illustrative material smoothly with general statements.

Biographical Notes

RICHARD D. ALTICK (1915—), professor of English at Ohio State University, is best known for his work in the general field of literary scholarship as seen in *The Scholar Adventurers* (1950) and in *The Art of Literary Research* (1963).

WYSTAN HUGH AUDEN (1907—), British-born poet and essayist, is perhaps best known for his *Selected Poems* (1940).

JAMES BALDWIN (1924—), American essayist and novelist, has been an eloquent spokesman for American Negroes. Among his works are *Another Country* (1961), *Nobody Knows My Name* (1961), *The Fire Next Time* (1963), and *Tell Me How Long the Train's Been Gone* (1968).

JACQUES BARZUN (1907—), Professor of History and Dean of the Graduate Faculty at Columbia University, has published frequently on history and literature. A few of his works are *Darwin, Marx, Wagner* (1941), *Teacher in America* (1944), and *Berlioz and the Romantic Century* (1950).

ERIC BERNE (1910—), a psychiatrist, has lectured at Yale and is now in private practice in California. He has written *The Mind in Action* (1947) and *Games People Play* (1964).

BRUNO BETTELHEIM (1903—), born and educated in Vienna, is a professor of psychiatry, psychology, and education at the University of Chicago. His latest work is *The Empty Fortress* (1967).

WILLIAM BLAKE (1757–1827), British poet, artist, and mystic, is most famous for works such as *Songs of Innocence* (1789), *Songs of Experience* (1794), *The Book of Thel* (1789), and *Jerusalem* (1804).

WAYNE C. BOOTH (1921—), Dean of the College of the University of Chicago, is the author of *The Rhetoric of Fiction* (1961).

SIR DENIS W. BROGAN (1900—), professor of political science at Cambridge, England, is a well-known writer on the Americas. Some of his better-known works are *The American Character* (1944), *The English People* (1948), *Politics in America* (1954), *America in the Modern World* (1960), and *Worlds in Conflict* (1967).

JOHN CIARDI (1916—), poet and essayist, has taught at the University of Kansas City, Harvard, and Rutgers and is poetry editor of the *Saturday Review*. Among his poetic works are *Homeward to America* (1940) and the first two volumes of his translation of Dante's *Divine Comedy* (1954, 1961).

ELEANOR CLARK (1913—), married to Robert Penn Warren, is a writer and critic, author of *Rome and a Villa* (1952) and *The Oysters of Locmariaquer*, winner of a 1965 National Book Award.

ALISTAIR COOKE (1908—), British-born newspaper correspondent and television commentator, has written *One Man's America* (1952).

DAVID DAICHES (1912—), has taught at the Universities of Edinburgh, Oxford, Chicago, Cornell, Indiana, and Sussex. He is the author of *The Novel and the Modern World* (1939), *Virginia Woolf* (1942), *A Study of Literature* (1948) and *Critical Approaches to Literature* (1956).

ROBERT GORHAM DAVIS (1908—), professor of English at Columbia University, has written *C. P. Snow* (1955) and edited *Ten Modern Masters* (1959).

LOREN C. EISELEY (1907—), professor of anthropology at the University of Pennsylvania, is the author of *Darwin's Century* (1958), *The Firmament of Time* (1960), and *The Mind as Nature* (1962).

BERGEN EVANS (1904—), essayist, television personality, and a professor of English at Northwestern University, is the author of such lively works as *The Natural History of Nonsense* (1946), *The Spoor of Spooks* (1954), and *The Dictionary of Contemporary American Usage* (1957).

WILSON FOLLETT (1887–1963) was the author of *The Modern Novel* (1923) and *Modern American Usage: a Guide,* completed by Jacques Barzun and others (1966).

ERICH FROMM (1900—), German-born social critic and psychoanalyst, has taught at Yale and Harvard. His publications include *Escape from Freedom* (1941), *The Sane Society* (1955), *The Art of Loving* (1956), and *The Heart of Man* (1964).

DONALD B. GIBSON (1933—), associate professor of English at the University of Connecticut, is author of *The Fiction of Stephen Crane* to be published in 1969.

LEARNED HAND (1872–1961) received his law degree from Harvard. Appointed Federal District Judge of the Southern District of New York in 1909, he was Judge of the U.S. District Court, Second Circuit from 1924 to 1951. Many of his papers and addresses are collected in *The Spirit of Liberty* (1959).

VINCENT HARDING (1931—), head of the Department of History and Social Science at Spelman College in Atlanta, holds a Ph.D. from the University of Chicago. He is currently working on a book entitled *Black Radicalism in America.*

S. I. HAYAKAWA (1906—), professor of language arts at San Francisco State College, is the author of *Language in Thought and Action* (rev. ed., 1963), perhaps the most widely read book in the field of semantics.

GERARD MANLEY HOPKINS, S.J. (1844–1888), English poet and religious, was a stylistic innovator whose poetry was published posthumously in 1918. His poetry was collected by Robert Bridges in *Poems* (1918).

ROBERT HUFF (1924—), who teaches English at Western Washington State College, has written two collections of poems, *Col. Johnson's Ride* (1959) and *The Course* (1966).

ROBERT M. HUTCHINS (1899—), former president and chancellor of the University of Chicago and president of the Fund for the Republic, is now head of the Center for the Study of Democratic Institutions, Santa Barbara, California. Best known among his books are *The Higher Learning in America* (1936),

Some Observations on American Education (1956), and *The Learning Society* (1968).

CHRISTOPHER JENCKS (1936—), resident fellow of the Institute of Policy Studies in Washington, D.C., is visiting lecturer at the Harvard Graduate School of Education. He is the author with David Riesman of *The Academic Revolution* (1968).

SAMUEL JOHNSON (1709–1784), poet, essayist, and lexicographer, wrote *The Vanity of Human Wishes* (1749), *The Rambler* (1750–1752), *The Idler* (1758–1760), and *The Lives of the Poets* (1779–1781). The *Preface* printed here is from his famous *Dictionary* (1755).

ALFRED KAZIN (1915—) is an eminent American critic and essayist. Among his works are *A Walker in the City* (1951) and *Starting Out in the Thirties* (1965).

HUGH KENNER (1923—), professor of English at the University of California, Santa Barbara, has published numerous critical works, among them: *Dublin's Joyce* (1956), *Gnomon* (1958), and *Samuel Beckett* (1961).

JOHN FITZGERALD KENNEDY (1917–1963), 35th President of the United States, was the author of *Why England Slept* (1940), *Profiles in Courage* (1955), and *A Nation of Immigrants* (1964).

KENNETH KENISTON (1930—), who teaches in the department of psychiatry at the Yale University School of Medicine, is the author of *The Uncommitted: Alienated Youth in American Society* (1965) and *Young Radicals: Notes on Committed Youth* (1968).

PHILIP LARKIN (1922—), British poet and novelist, librarian of the University of Hull, wrote *The North Ship* (1945), *Girl in Winter* (1963), *Jill* (1964) and *The Whitsun Weddings* (1964).

ALEXANDER LEIGHTON (1908—), psychiatrist and head of the Department of Behavioral Sciences of the Harvard School of Public Health, is the author of *Human Relations in a Changing World* (1949) and *The Character of Danger* (1963).

C. S. LEWIS (1898–1963), professor of medieval and renaissance literature at Cambridge University, is the author of *Allegory of Love* (1936), *The Screwtape Letters* (1942, 1946), and *Studies in Words* (1967). He tells the story of his conversion to Christianity in *Surprised by Joy* (1956).

PHYLLIS MCGINLEY (1905—), known for her light verse, was awarded the Pulitzer Prize for Poetry in 1961. She has published many collections of verse, among them: *The Love Letters of Phyllis McGinley* (1954), *Wonderful Time* (1966) and *A Wreath of Christmas Legends* (1967).

ANDREW MARVELL (1621–1678), British statesman and poet, though a Puritan Member of Parliament is best known for his Miscellaneous Poems and especially for his distinctly un-Puritan "To His Coy Mistress."

KENNETH MOTT (1927—), formerly Supervisor of Social Studies, State of Louisiana, Department of Education, is currently an executive of the Stanley Projection Company, Alexandria, Louisiana.

FLANNERY O'CONNOR (1925–1964), an outstanding Southern novelist and short story writer, is best remembered for *A Good Man Is Hard to Find* (1955),

The Violent Bear It Away (1960), and *Everything That Rises Must Converge* (1965).

GEORGE ORWELL (1903–1950), journalist and social commentator born in India, spent five years in Burma in police work after graduating from Eton. His later work includes such classics as *Animal Farm* (1946) and *Nineteen Eighty-Four* (1949). Many essays are collected in *The Orwell Reader* (1956).

MARIO PEI (1901—), educator and linguist, is professor of romance philology at Columbia University. Among his works are *The Story of Language* (1949) and *Language Today* (1967).

SYLVIA PLATH (1932–1963), brilliant young poetess, wrote two volumes of verse, *The Colossus* (1960) and *Ariel* (1965).

PLATO (c. 427–347 B.C.), pupil of Socrates and teacher of Aristotle, was one of the greatest figures in all philosophy. His most notable productions were *The Republic* and *The Dialogues*.

CLINTON ROSSITER (1917—), who received his doctorate from Princeton, joined the Department of Government at Cornell in 1946. Among his works are *Conservatism in America* (2nd ed., 1962) and *The American Presidency* (1960).

JEAN-PAUL SARTRE (1905—), French philosopher, man of letters, and spokesman with Albert Camus for the post-war existentialists, has been published widely in translation. Some of these translations are *Baudelaire* (1950), *No Exit and Three Other Plays* (1946), *Literature and Existentialism* (1949), *Existential Psychoanalysis* (1953), *Being and Nothingness* (1956), and *The Age of Reason* (1960).

WILLIAM SHAKESPEARE (1564–1616), poet and playwright, is acknowledged to be first among English writers. The poem printed here is from *Sonnets* (1609).

JOHN SIMON (1925—) is drama critic of *Hudson Review* and other periodicals. There are two collections of his reviews, *The Acid Test* (1963) on the theater and *Private Screenings* (1967) on the movies.

JAMES SLEDD (1914—), philologist and professor of English at the University of Texas, edited *Dr. Johnson's Dictionary* (1955) with Gwin Kolb and *Dictionaries and THAT Dictionary* (1962) with Wilma Ebbitt.

W. D. SNODGRASS (1926—), who has taught at Cornell, the University of Rochester, and Wayne State University, was awarded the Pulitzer Prize in 1960 for his first book of poetry, *Heart's Needle* (1959).

RICHARD SULLIVAN (1908—), novelist and professor of English at Notre Dame University, has published, among other works, *The Dark Continent* (1943) and *The Fresh and Open Sky* (1950).

JONATHAN SWIFT (1667–1745), Irish-born cleric, satirist, and poet, was the author of *Gulliver's Travels* (1726), *The Battle of the Books* (1704), *The Tale of a Tub* (1704), and many other essays such as *The Modest Proposal* (1729).

HENRY DAVID THOREAU (1817–1862) was a naturalist and philosopher whose devotion to freedom and nonconformity is best expressed in *Walden or Life in the Woods* (1854) and in the essay reprinted here, *On the Duty of Civil Disobedience* (1849).

JAMES THURBER (1894–1961), one of America's greatest humorists, published such collections of his prose pieces as *The Middle-Aged Man on the Flying Trapeze* (1935), *My World—and Welcome to It* (1942), *The Beast in Me* (1948), and *Lanterns and Lances* (1961).

ALEXIS DE TOCQUEVILLE (1805–1859) was a famous French statesman and author, best known for his penetrating analysis of early America in *Democracy in America* (1835).

JOHN UPDIKE (1932—) received the National Book Award in 1964 for *The Centaur* (1963). Some earlier works include *The Poorhouse Fair* (1959) and *Rabbit, Run* (1960).

EUDORA WELTY (1909—), Southern novelist and short story writer, is known for such works as *Bride of Innisfallen and Other Stories* (1955), *Delta Wedding* (1946), and *The Shoe Bird* (1964).

PHILIP WHEELWRIGHT (1901—), a professor of philosophy at the University of California at Riverside, has taught at many universities. He has published *The Way of Philosophy* (1954), *The Burning Fountain* (1954), and *A Critical Introduction to Ethics* (3rd ed., 1959).

WILLIAM H. WHYTE, JR. (1917—) has been assistant managing editor of *Fortune*. He has written *Is Anybody Listening?* (1952) and *The Organization Man* (1956).

SAMUEL T. WILLIAMSON (1891–1962) has written *Frank Gannett: A Biography* (1940) and, with Herbert Harris, *Trends in Collective Bargaining* (1945).